THIS
SACRED
EARTH

THIS
SACRED
EARTH

Religion, Nature, Environment

EDITED BY

ROGER S. GOTTLIEB

Routledge

New York and London

Published in 1996 by
Routledge
29 West 35th Street
New York, NY 10001

Published in Great Britain by
Routledge
11 New Fetter Lane
London EC4P 4EE

Library of Congress Cataloging-in-Publication Data

This sacred earth : religion, nature, environment / edited by Roger S. Gottlieb.
       p.   cm.
   Includes bibliographical references.
   ISBN 0-415-91232-6 (hb). — ISBN 0-415-91233-4 (pbk.)
    1. Human ecology—Religious aspects.   2. Philosophy of nature.   3. Ecofeminism.
4. Deep ecology—Religious aspects.   I. Gottlieb, Roger S.
   GF80.T49   1995
   291.1'78362—dc20   95-11986
                                                      CIP

For all beings who have suffered needlessly because of human folly and injustice:
May we remember their pain and change our ways.

CONTENTS

PREFACE AND ACKNOWLEDGMENTS   xi

INTRODUCTION   *Religion in an Age of Environmental Crisis*   1

PART I   *The Moment of Seeing*
Selections from Nature Writers Linking Nature and Spirit   15

Henry David Thoreau	from "Walking"	18
Barry Lopez	from *Arctic Dreams: Imagination and Desire in a Northern Landscape*	21
Rachel Carson	from *The Sense of Wonder*	23
Ralph Waldo Emerson	"Nature"	25
John Muir	from *Thousand-Mile Walk to the Gulf*	27
Aldo Leopold	from *A Sand County Almanac*	29
Annie Dillard	"Teaching a Stone to Talk"	32
Linda Hogan	"The Kill Hole"	37
Stephanie Kaza	"House of Wood"	41

PART II   *How Have Traditional Religions Viewed Nature?*   45

Fanetorens (Ray Fadden)	"The Creation"	50
Joseph L. Henderson and Maud Oakes	"Death and Rebirth of the Universe" (Hindu)	55
	"The Parade of Ants" (Hindu)	56
	"The Five Suns" (Aztec)	59
	"Persephone" (Greek)	60
Robert Pogue Harrison	from *Forests: The Shadow of Civilization*	63
Lao Tzu	from the *Tao Te Ching*	67
Hebrew Bible	Selections	71
Louis Ginzberg	from *Legends of the Bible*	84
Daniel Swartz	"Jews, Jewish Texts, and Nature: A Brief History"	87
David Kinsley	"Christianity as Ecologically Harmful"	104
	"Christianity as Ecologically Responsible"	116
Michael Kioni Dudley	"Traditional Native Hawaiian Environmental Philosophy"	125

J. Donald Hughes	from *American Indian Ecology*	131
Chatsumarn Kabilisingh	"Early Buddhist Views on Nature"	147
O. P. Dwivedi`	"*Satyagraha* for Conservation: Awakening the Spirit of Hinduism"	151
Mawil Y. Izzi Deen (Samarrai)	"Islamic Environmental Ethics: Law and Society"	164
John S. Mbiti	"African Views of the Universe"	174

PART III *Ecotheology in an Age of Environmental Crisis*
Transforming Tradition

		181
Lynn White	"The Historical Roots of Our Ecologic Crisis"	184
Roderick Nash	"The Greening of Religion"	194
Pope John Paul II	"The Ecological Crisis: A Common Responsibility"	230
American Baptist Churches, USA	"Creation and the Covenant of Caring"	238
Evangelical Lutheran Church in America	"Basis for Our Caring,"	243
Liberating Life	"A Report to the World Council of Churches"	251
John F. Haught	"Christianity and Ecology"	270
Sallie McFague	"The Scope of the Body: The Cosmic Christ"	286
Arthur Waskow	"What is Eco-Kosher?"	297
Arthur Green	"Vegetarianism: A *Kashrut* for our Age"	301
Ken Jones	"Getting Out of Our Own Light"	303
Theodore Walker, Jr.	"African-American Resources for a More Inclusive Liberation Theology"	309

PART IV *Ecotheology in an Age of Environmental Crisis*
Ecofeminist Spirituality

		317
Rosemary Radford Ruether	"Ecofeminism: Symbolic and Social Connections of the Oppression of Women and the Domination of Nature"	322
Anne Primavesi	"Ecofeminism and Canon"	334
Shamara Shantu Riley	"Ecology Is a Sistah's Issue Too: The Politics of Emergent Afrocentric Ecowomanism"	346
Susan Griffin	from *Woman and Nature: The Roaring Inside Her*	361
Paula Gunn Allen	"The Woman I Love is a Planet; The Planet I Love is a Tree"	364
Riane Eisler	"Messages from the Past: The World of the Goddess"	369

Vandana Shiva	from *Staying Alive*	382
Brooke Medicine Eagle	"The Rainbow Bridge"	386
Terry Tempest Williams	"The Clan of One-Breasted Women"	390
Carol Adams	"Destabilizing Patriarchal Consumption"	397

PART V   *Ecotheology in an Age of Environmental Crisis*
                    Spiritual Deep Ecology   403

Edna St. Vincent Millay	"The Fawn"	407
Albert Schweitzer	"Man and Creature"	408
Thomas Berry	"Into the Future"	410
Joanna Macy	"Faith, Power, and Ecology"	415
Brian Walsh, Marianne B. Karsh, and Nik Ansell	"Trees, Forestry, and the Responsiveness of Creation"	423
Warwick Fox	"Transpersonal Ecology and the Varieties of Identification"	436

PART VI   *Religious Practice for a Sacred Earth*   445

Thich Nhat Hanh	"Earth Gathas"	449
Ellen Bernstein and Dan Fink	"Blessings and Praise"	451
	"*Bal Tashchit*"	459
Black Elk	"*Wiwanyag Wachipi:* The Sun Dance"	470
National Council of Churches of Christ	"A Service of Worship: The Earth is the Lord's— A Liturgy of Celebration, Confession, Thanksgiving, and Commitment"	480
Kenneth Kraft	"The Greening of Buddhist Practice"	484
John Seed	"Invocation"	499
John Seed and Joanna Macy	"Gaia Meditations"	501
John Seed and Pat Fleming	"Evolutionary Remembering"	503
Marina Lachecki	"The Blessing of the Water"	507

PART VII   *Ecology, Religion, and Society*   511

Roger S. Gottlieb	"Spiritual Deep Ecology and the Left: An Attempt at Reconciliation"	516
Charlene Spretnak	"Beyond Humanism, Modernity, and Patriarchy"	532
	"Ten Key Values of the American Green Movement"	534

Max Oelschlaeger	from *Caring for Creation*	537
Bron Taylor	"Earth First!: From Primal Spirituality to Ecological Resistance"	545
B. D. Sharma	"On Sustainability"	558
Bruce M. Sullivan	"Paradise Polluted: Religious Dimensions of the *Vrindāvana* Ecology Movement"	565
M. L. Daneel	"African Independent Churches Face the Challenge of Environmental Ethics"	572
Catherine Ingram	"Interview with Cesar Chavez"	586
Judith N. Scoville	"Valuing the Land: Ecological Theology in the Context of Agriculture"	596
Paul Gorman	"New Story/Old Story: Citizenship in Earth"	604
Melody Ermachild Chavis	"Street Trees"	607
David Spangler	"Imagination, Gaia, and the Sacredness of the Earth"	611
Dieter T. Hessel	"Now that Animals Can Be Genetically Engineered: Biotechnology in Theological-Ethical Perspective"	620
The First National People of Color Environmental Leadership Summit	"Principles of Environmental Justice"	634
Religious Leaders at the Summit on Environment	"Statement by Religious Leaders at the Summit on the Environment"	636
Joint Appeal by Religion and Science for the Environment	"Declaration of the 'Mission to Washington'"	640
United States Catholic Conference	"Catholic Social Teaching and Environmental Ethics"	643
	"Recommendations for Moving Environmental Concerns into Parish Life"	650

SUGGESTIONS FOR FURTHER READING   655

SOME ORGANIZATIONS TO CONTACT   661

ABOUT THE CONTRIBUTORS   669

PREFACE AND ACKNOWLEDGMENTS

This book surveys traditional religious perspectives on nature, and shows how contemporary theologians, spiritual teachers, and religious institutions are responding to humanity's devastation of the environment.

I have chosen particular selections for a number of reasons, including historical importance, depth of insight, and quality of writing or representation of a particular tradition. And I have tried to enable the reader of *This Sacred Earth* to gain both a comprehensive overview of the field and some quiet moments of spiritual illumination. While I am happy with what is here, I also regret that many fine authors were omitted.

There is clearly a disproportionate amount of space given here to Judaism and Christianity relative to other religions. My reasoning is that these are the dominant traditions of the overwhelming majority of the people who will read this book; and that the close relationship between the dominant Western traditions and the environmental effects of European industrialism and imperialism make it critically important for us to assess quite carefully the content and meaning of those traditions. There are also, however, extensive selections from non-Western religions, indigenous teachings, and nondenominational spiritual thinkers.

This book is organized into seven parts, each with a particular focus. This focus is outlined in the general introduction and in introductions to each part. Nevertheless, a number of pieces are hard to categorize, and some overlap exists. For instance, Kenneth Kraft's essay on the environmental orientation of new, Buddhist, meditation practices, is placed in Part VI, "Religious Practice for a Sacred Earth." But since the essay also presents material concerning Buddhist environmental social action, it is also relevant to Part VII, "Ecology, Religion, Society." Clearly, some of the analyses of past views in Part II contain material relevant to contemporary ecotheology, in Part III.

One cannot help approaching the task of anthologizing such a vast range of material with a certain amount of fear and trembling—and, perhaps, a little *chutzpah* as well. Perhaps I would not have been so bold if I did not think that this book was needed; or if I were not confident, as I indeed am, that other books in this area will compensate for whatever deficiencies exist here.

As the preparation of a manuscript draws to a close, there is nothing more pleasurable than giving thanks to the many people who helped along the way.

To begin with, I am deeply indebted to Joanna Macy, Miriam Greenspan, and Bill McKibben; all three helped open my mind and heart to the spiritual dimensions of the environmental crisis.

Bettina Bergo and Miriam Greenspan provided extremely useful responses to my own contributions to this book.

Many colleagues took time from their own busy lives to give me very helpful feedback on proposed contents and to suggest resources: Carol Adams, William Beers, Ellen Bernstein, Eugene Bianchi, Marcia Falk, Ethan Fladd, Tamara Frankiel, Beverly Harrison, Stephanie Kaza, Belden Lane, Catherine Mchale, John Mabry, Wes Mott, Linda Nef, Kodzo Tita Pongo, Judith Scoville, Bron Taylor, Arthur Waskow, and Susan Zakin.

My very special appreciation goes to staff at Worcester Polytechnic Institute: Penny Rock from the Humanities Department and the Interlibrary Loan Services of Gordon Library.

Routledge has been a pleasure to work with in this process. Maura Burnett helped organize a response session at the American Academy of Religion. Maura and Mary Carol De Zuetter put in a great deal of work dealing with a seemingly endless list of permissions. Andrew Rubin has been close at hand for promotions and marketing.

Marlie Wasserman, my editor at Routledge, deserves a separate appreciation. Working with me from the beginning, she provided enthusiastic support and intelligent feedback, was always there to answer my anxious phone calls, and made a challenging project much easier.

Most importantly, this book is only possible because of the open-hearted and clear-minded writings of dozens of theologians, scholars and spiritual seekers.

Together with grassroots activists, environmental organizations, passionate neighborhood committees, international coalitions and lovers of life everywhere—and with the help of God, Goddess, and the Spirit of Trees, Rocks, and Water—may we find a way to rediscover the sacredness of the earth.

RELIGION IN AN AGE OF ENVIRONMENTAL CRISIS

If we were not so single-minded
about keeping our lives moving,
and for once could do nothing,
perhaps a huge silence
might interrupt this sadness
of never understanding ourselves
and of threatening ourselves with
death.

—Pablo Neruda

The best remedy, for those who are afraid, lonely, or unhappy is to go outside, somewhere where they can be quite alone with the heavens, nature, and God. Because only then does one feel that all is as it should be and that God wishes to see people happy, amidst the simple beauty of nature. As long as this exists, and it certainly always will, I know that then there will always be comfort for every sorrow. . . .

—Anne Frank

If a person kills a tree before its time, it is like having murdered a soul.

—Rebbe Nachman of Bratslav,
eighteenth century

RELIGION IN AN AGE OF ENVIRONMENTAL CRISIS

THE PROBLEM BEFORE THE PROBLEM

The problem is humanity's devastation of the natural world. The problem before the problem is that it is very difficult to face this devastation. Threats to the environment are so often threats to our own lives and the people—or parts of nature—that we love, threats about which we can often do virtually nothing. And the hazards involved are so enormous, so potentially irreversible, that it may seem easier to hide from the information than to take it in. As Joanna Macy observes, ". . . we are barraged by data that render questionable the survival of our culture, our species, and even our planet as a viable home for conscious life. Despair, in this context . . . is the loss of the assumption that the species will inevitably pull through."[1] Not surprisingly many of us skip over the environmental articles in the newspaper, pass up the magazines focusing on ecological issues, and do our best to ignore the lurking feelings of doom. Wouldn't we prefer to continue with "business as usual"?

On the first day of my environmental philosophy course I tell students of my own fear, grief, and anger about the ecological crisis. I then ask them to speak in turn about what they feel. They respond hesitantly, emboldened by my example but still unsure that a university classroom is the proper place for emotions. As the hour progresses, however, their statements become increasingly more revealing.

"I'm terribly angry," one will say, "because the field where I used to hunt for grasshoppers was turned into a parking lot for a mall; and they hardly even use it. What a waste."

"I'm scared," a young woman admits. "Every time I go out in the sun in the summer I think about skin cancer. My aunt died from it."

Several young men tell me they don't see much use in thinking about all these problems. I ask one: "What would happen if you *did* think about it?" "I don't know," he replies, "I'm not sure I could go on with what I'm supposed to do in this life. If I started to cry, I might never stop."

It helps to begin not with a long list of environmental problems, but with the acknowledgment that our anguish over the fate of the earth is a real element in our everyday emotional lives. Bury these emotions as we may, they surface whenever we hear of another oil spill, another summer day in the city with "unhealthy air," another childhood forest or meadow turned into a parking lot. Before we can take in or effectively act in response to the environmental crisis we must admit just how deeply we feel for the earth. This admission helps us emerge from hidden despair, psychic numbing and the frantic attempts to fill our time with a "busyness" which distracts us from the problem. The alternative is to continue to mask the truth—or to pretend we feel nothing about it. This strategy takes a significant psychic toll. If we deny what we feel when we read of a species made extinct, or a leaking toxic dump, we may start to deaden ourselves, and come to suffer what Kierkegaard called "a disorder of feelings, the disorder consisting in not having any."

There is nothing shameful or "weak" in the pain we feel about the environment. Grief and fear are rational responses to our losses and perils. And sorrow over what we have done is a hopeful sign that despite everything we can still love and mourn.

THE PROBLEM

Pesticides are used in agriculture in all parts of the world. While most cases of acute, high-exposure poisoning are related to occupational exposure (there are more than 200,000 deaths world-wide each year, mainly in this population, from acute pesticide poisoning), significant exposure can occur through ingestion of treated food.... With respect to low-level exposure to humans, the toxic outcomes of greatest concern are cancer, immunotoxicity, and the reproductive effects....[2]

Weedkiller found in high levels in US tap water.

—*Boston Globe,* October 19, 1994

In our conversations with Filipinos about their dreams and hopes and their children's prospects, they often raise on their own the topic that we have come to study: the future of the country's natural resources.

"What will your children be when they grow up?" we ask a poor fisherman in Bataan. He sighs. "My father was a fisherman and so I too am a fisherman. I was born a fisherman. But the fish are dying. So there will be no fish for my son to catch.... A peasant woman whose family grows rice on a small plot of land ... gives a strikingly similar answer: "The forests are disappearing, and so the soil of our rice field is being washed to the sea. There will be no soil left by the time our children are grown.... How will they grow rice?"[3]

[In Central America] the widespread destruction of forests for cattle ranching is . . . resulting in regional climatic changes. A pristine rainforest canopy acts as a protective umbrella, breaking the force of torrential downpours and recycling the moisture throughout the ecosystem. But with the clearing of the forest, water-recycling systems are destroyed. Daytime temperatures rise on the converted savannas, decreasing relative humidity and precipitation levels while increasing the rate of transpiration. As a result the grasslands and surrounding forests suffer from increased drought stress. . . . When it does rain, the water rushes off the barren slopes to cause downstream flooding, soil erosion, and siltation of waterways.[4]

The U.S. government estimates that over sixteen thousand active landfills have been sopped with industrial and agricultural hazardous wastes. Most are located near small towns and farming communities—and the contents of all of them, according to the Environmental Protection Agency, will eventually breach their linings and penetrate the soil, as many already have done. Underground chemical and petroleum storage tanks scattered throughout cities, suburbs, and rural American number between three and five million; 30 percent already leak. . . . According to industry's own reports, 22 billion pounds of toxic chemicals are spewed into the air, water, and soil each year. . . . The Congressional Office of Technology Assessment estimates the real figure to be vastly higher.[5]

Con Ed Admits to Conspiracy to Cover Up Asbestos in Blast.

—*New York Times*, November 1, 1994

Which of the following animals is extinct; and which is endangered?

—Quiz on the back of a breakfast cereal box

Daddy, could a time come when there are no more trees?

—Anna Gottlieb, age 7

The above passages reveal some of the critical features of the environmental crisis. First, there is its sheer magnitude: the staggering amount of toxic chemicals in the U.S. alone; the fact that pesticides are used in "every part of the world." Second, the range of areas represented even in these few quotations reminds us that the environmental crisis is a global event.

Third, however, no matter how immense this crisis, its impact is immediate, personal, direct. The disappearance of fish from *this* river, the high incidence of leukemia on *this* street, *this* particular childhood Eden lost to a mall. Facile generalizations about "tree-huggers" or "environmental extremists" make little sense when we find out, for instance, that the Canadian Dermatological Society has advised that because of UV radiation coming through a weakened Ozone layer school playgrounds must be built in shaded areas and that recess should never be between 10 AM and 2 PM; or that due to environmental pollution average male sperm counts have dropped 50 percent over the last 50 years and testicular cancer has risen 300 to 400 percent.

❧

A brief overview of the environmental crisis provides us with at least the following eight areas of acute concern:

1. *Global climate/atmospheric change.* Burning fossil fuels, releasing methane into the atmosphere, and destroying the rainforest threaten us with an unprecedentedly fast global warming. This climate change will alter the living conditions for the entire planet and lead to what Bill McKibben calls the "end of nature." That is, an earth in which *everything* bears the stamp of human acts, because *everything* is affected by the human-altered climate. Global warming will cause unforeseen damage to agriculture, wild lands, and animals; and the rise of the oceans from melting polar icecaps will submerge coastlines and threaten the lives of island peoples.

The reduction in the ozone layer, which shields the earth from UV rays, poses an immediate danger to human health because these rays damage the immune system, increase skin cancer and cataracts, and threaten the DNA molecules of all living things. Also vulnerable are the phytoplankten, the foundation of the oceanic food chain, which are weakened by UV exposure.[6]

2. *Toxic wastes.* Chemical, heavy metal, biological, and nuclear wastes have accumulated in staggering quantities. Concentrated in dumps and distributed throughout the atmosphere, water system, and land, they are found in every region, no matter how remote. The result is a plague of environmentally caused diseases; most obviously the dramatic increase in cancer, both in general and especially in areas closest to sources of toxic materials.

3. *Loss of land.* From overuse of chemical agriculture and the destruction of forests, the loss of land threatens the production of food throughout the developing nations and leads to erosion and desertification. Massive erosion can also destroy ecosystem balance in rivers and coastal fishing areas.

4. *Loss of species.* This has become what some call a "crisis of biodiversity." With the decimation of a variety of habitats, as well as the killing of animals for sport, use, or food, current rates of extinction are reducing the number of species to the lowest since the end of the age of dinosaurs, 65 million years ago. The result is incalculable *human* loss. Potential medicines vanish, ecosystems are destabilized, and irreplaceable natural beauties are lost forever. There is also damage to our ethical faith in humanity's own worth. Those who believe that nature has its own value apart from people's interests see these mass, human-caused extinctions as a kind of mass murder.

5. *Loss of wilderness.* Ecosystems free to develop without human interference or intrusion have become increasingly rare. Besides the loss of biodiversity this entails, human beings face a strange and paradoxical loneliness. People are everywhere; yet we are haunted by the loss of that natural Other which has been our long-time companion for biological ages. As Edward Abbey observes, "We need wilderness, because we are wild animals."[7]

6. *Devastation of indigenous peoples.* These are the last examples of human communities integrated into nonhuman nature. As their environments are poisoned, native peoples lose their land and culture, and too often their lives.

> The discovery of anything which can be exploited is tantamount to the crack of doom for the Indians, who are pressured to abandon their lands or be slaughtered on them. And economic discoveries do not have to be exceptional for the Indians to be plundered.[8]

7. *Human patterns and quantities of consumption.* These patterns are unsustainable. The developed world's insatiable consumerism depletes natural resources and contributes to global warming and the accumulation of waste. In the underdeveloped world overpopulation relative to existing technological resources and political organization decimates the landscape. In particular, a widespread culture of meat-eating undermines ecosystem integrity through the overutilization of water, grazing land, chemicalized pesticides, and food additives; and constitutes a horribly inefficient drain on resources of vegetable food that might alleviate world hunger.

8. *Genetic engineering.* Such engineering seems to promise miracle cures for everything from food shortages to inherited diseases. Yet it also menaces us with the dismal prospects of engineered life forms and the potentially catastrophic invention of insufficiently tested organisms. Just as the nuclear industry developed before adequate thought was given to the disposal of nuclear wastes or the global effects of nuclear fallout, so genetic engineering has come into existence before we have, as a world society, given adequate consideration to what this magnitude of human control over evolution could possibly mean. Given our track record with pesticides and toxic chemicals, and the level of maturity of our political and economic elites, it seems highly doubtful that we are ready to create new life forms.

And so we have an "environmental crisis." And this has created, in turn, an emotional crisis of despair over our planet's future, and a crisis of confidence in humanity's right to further develop industrial civilization. Past certitudes about humanity's special place in the world seem absurd when our species is poisoning that world.

In fact, *the environmental crisis is a crisis of our entire civilization.* It casts doubt on our political, economic, and technological systems, on theoretical science and Western philosophy, on how we consume or eat. Corporate greed, nationalistic aggression, obsessions with technological "development," philosophical attitudes privileging "man's" reason above the natural world, addictive consumerism . . . all these collaborate in the emerging ruin of the earth.

Yet from the early conservation efforts of the late nineteenth century to the wide range of organizations throughout the world today, a global environmental movement has resisted this ruin. Environmentalists recognize that despite the enormous accomplishments of our technological civilization, we have begun a process of environmental degradation not unlike a slow collective suicide. Accordingly, there are now a plethora of political, social, intellectual, and spiritual responses to the environmental crisis, responses which seek to keep people from further devastating humanity's own natural setting.

RELIGION IN AN AGE OF ENVIRONMENTAL CRISIS

By "religion" I mean those systems of belief, ritual, institutional life, spiritual aspiration, and ethical orientation which are premised on an understanding of human beings as *other* or *more than simply* their purely social or physical identities. Teachings can be marked as "religious" in the way they assert (as in Judaism, Christianity, and Islam) that people are essentially connected to a Supreme Being whose authority is distinct from worldly powers; or by the Buddhist belief that we can achieve a state of consciousness which transcends the attachments and passions of our ordinary social egos; or in the Wiccan celebration of human sexuality as an embodiment of the life-giving force of the Goddess rather than as the source of purely individual gratification. Religious attitudes thus turn on a sense of what theologian Paul Tillich called "ultimate significance." They seek to orient us to that which is of compelling importance beyond or within our day-to-day concerns.

At the same time, religions provide norms of conduct for the familiar interpersonal settings of family, community, and world. Religious moral teachings presuppose a spiritual foundation and are meant to root our everyday behavior in a spiritual truth about who we really are.

Finally, religions provide rituals—acts of prayer, meditation, collective contrition, or celebration—to awaken and reinforce a personal and communal sense of our connections to the Ultimate Truth(s). These practices aim to cultivate an impassioned clarity of vision in which the world and the self are, as Miriam Greenspan put it, "charged with the sacred."

This understanding of "religion" allows us to include here paradigm religions of both West and East, suppressed native traditions, and prepatriarchal goddess worship; as well as more individual, idiosyncratic, and eclectic spiritual visions. All such voices will be heard in this volume.

ॐ

How has religion shaped our understanding of and our conduct towards nature? And how has the environmental crisis challenged and transformed modern theology and spiritual practice? As key components of every human civilization, religions are necessarily critical elements of the environmental crisis. Yet in recent years religious institutions have also tried to alter our current destructive patterns. In short, religions have been neither simple agents of environmental domination nor unmixed repositories of ecological wisdom. In complex and variable ways, they have been both.

Historically, religions have taught us to perceive and to act on nonhuman nature in terms of particular *human* interests, beliefs, and social structures. Through religious myths and laws we have socialized nature, framing it in human terms. And to a great extent we have done so to satisfy *our* needs, abilities and power relations. Yet at the same time *religion has also represented the voice of nature to humanity.* Spiritual teachings have celebrated and consecrated our ties to the nonhuman world, reminding us of our delicate and inescapable partnership with air, land, water, and fellow living beings. To assess religion's view of nature—and to see how contemporary theology deals with the environmental crisis—we must therefore attend with care to the full range of writings and practices which religious traditions offer.

Consider, for instance, that many writers have found in biblical writings about "man's" right to "master the earth" *(Genesis* 1:28) an essential source for the havoc wreaked by Western societies upon the earth. Other religious environmentalists have discovered environmentally positive passages in classic texts, and claim that Judaism and Christianity are "really" more environmentally minded than they seemed at first glance. Yet whatever marginalized ecological voices or texts may be found now, it is also true that the Judeo-Christian tradition was taken by its leading authorities to have a predominant meaning over the centuries, and especially during the modern age. And this meaning was typically concerned (at best) with the "wise use" of the earth and its creatures, and not with any notion of their inherent value.[9]

> The social and moral traditions that have been dominant in the West ... have not involved the idea that animals, trees, or the land in their own right, as distinct from their owners or their Creator, have moral standing. Only a few saints and reformers have taught that people have direct moral responsibilities to nonhuman creatures.[10]

In support of this observation, we need only reflect on how few and far between were the religious voices opposing the last century's juggernaut of technological development and environmental degradation.

In any case, the full answer to our dilemmas will not be found in identifying past views. The environmental agenda of religions is continually set and reset by their adherents, as they engage in the complex and controversial process of reinventing traditions to meet contemporary concerns.

Further, whatever of environmental value we may find in particular Biblical passages (e.g., the injunction to be kind to your enemy's animals) or writings of particular saints (e.g., the nature poetry of 12th-century Catholic Julian of Norwich) it is too much to expect ancient traditions to be fully adequate to the crisis of today. Despite the brilliance or revelatory quality of the founding teachings, or the way those teachings have been elaborated over the centuries, we now live in a very different world.

To begin with, ancient traditions could not have foreseen the scope of modern technological power. No past empire was able to threaten the earth's climate or so pollute the air and water that mother's breast milk may not be fit for their babies to drink. Also, the spread of democracy and the critical intellectual tendencies embedded in Enlightenment philosophy and modern science cast heavy doubt on any particular religion's claims to absolute truth. This doubt leads some people to a complete rejection of religion. For many others, abandoning the claim to literal veracity of a particular theology allows adherents of very different traditions to recognize common ground and celebrate each other's spiritual gifts. This ecumenism is, I believe, quite beyond the imagination of earlier religious thinkers.[11]

Similarly, the recent feminist critique of religion has identified patriarchal biases in virtually all established traditions. Modern spiritual life therefore has the historically unprecedented task of respecting women as individuals and recognizing the social contributions and spiritual gifts entailed by women's experience.

❦

This book—and the enormous literature from which it has been taken—demonstrates that there has already been an extensive range of religious responses to environmental problems. Within this range we can identify four general approaches, more than one of which may be found in any given writer.

Ecotheologians have sought to *reinterpret* old traditions: finding and stressing passages in classic texts that help us face the current crisis. Thus we are reminded that the *Talmud* instructs us not to live in a city without trees; or that St. Francis's love of animals makes him a kind of early, Christian, Deep Ecologist. Thinkers have also tried to *extend* more familiar religious beliefs, especially ethical ones concerning love and respect for other people, to nonhuman nature. Nature becomes the Body of God, or the "neighbor" whom we must treat as we would like to be treated. Creative ecotheologians *synthesize* elements of different traditions.[12] As part of the ecumenical tendency of contemporary spiritual life described above, we see some Christian thinkers unhesitatingly using Taoist images of humanity's integration into a natural setting, or Jews quoting Buddhist nature poetry. In particular, ideas from indigenous, or native peoples—communities whose relations to nature originated before the current mode of the domination of the earth—have been studied. Finally spiritual thinkers are *creating* new ideas, practices, and organizations.

Contemporary ecotheology voices the sorrow of a broken-hearted earth and expresses our despair over the past and fear for the future. Simultaneously, theoreticians of religion and the environment alike question whether and in what ways religious energies can be connected to secular environmental philosophy and ecological activism.

Yet why do we need religion at all? Why can't governments, corporations, and individuals just stop polluting and eliminating species—and let religion be an essentially private matter of personal faith?

The first answer is that for many people religious beliefs provide primary values concerning our place in the universe, our obligations to other people and other life forms, and what makes up a truly "good" life. All these are part of the religious world-view and part of what must be scrutinized and altered if we are to pull through. Further, we have historical examples, from the U.S. civil rights movement to the nonviolent campaigns of Indian independence from the British, of creative and successful mergings of religion and social action.

In fact, the significance of religion is heightened because several of the guiding lights of modernity have become increasingly suspect. Faith in science and materialist/liberal democracies has been undermined by the political violence, technological disasters and cultural bankruptcy of the late 20th century. Purely secular radical politics have been rendered doubtful by the economic failures and totalitarian political excesses of communism. Hence spiritual perspectives can be a source of social direction as well as personal inspiration. From Buddhist teachings about compassion for animals to Christian creation theology, from Native American images of the "sacred hoop" of life to indigenous people's political resistance to the environmental desecration of their sacred lands, religious teachings and practices are bound up in humanity's ongoing struggles to live in harmony with an increasingly threatened earth.

I want also to stress that the pain we feel over the environmental crisis is *not* solely a self-interested desire to lower cancer rates or retain some wilderness in which to hike. Our response is, in the broadest sense of the term, a *spiritual* one; that is, it involves our deepest concerns about what is truly of lasting importance in our lives. I remember reading McKibben's *The End of Nature*—with its thesis that human global climate alteration spells the "end of nature" as an autonomous presence—and feeling a deep sense of desolation. I also felt that an enormous and unrectifiable sacrilege had been committed, a sacrilege of which I, as a beneficiary of modern technological society, was partly guilty. My feelings were not simply a fear for my own health or recreational possibilities, but a concern for what I would like to call my soul.

Finally, spiritual resources can help us face the truth of the present without giving way to despair. Environmentally oriented prayer, meditation, celebration, and confession all seem particularly appropriate to our current plight.

ABOUT THE BOOK

This Sacred Earth provides representative historical and contemporary selections from traditional religions and contemporary ecotheology. Original sources, documents, and the writings of modern theologians and social activists are joined by scholarly reflections on theology, religious history, and religion's social role.

We begin with reflections by a variety of naturalist writers. Here we find that a spiritual encounter with nature may arise in the most casual and unexpected of ways; and that a brief moment of grace on this sacred earth may forever alter how we think and feel about our one and only home.

Part II surveys the views of traditional religions on nature. This survey will give the reader a sense of both the historic roots and the heterogeneity of religious attitudes in this area. By "nature" I mean that commonsense construct in which we view the universe, the geological earth and its life forms as a prehuman unity, separate and independent from humanity. We will see that religions provided the normative basis for respectful as well as domineering views of nature, for ecological sanity as well as unrestrained domination. It is this broad scope which allows some contemporary ecotheologians to recommend a "return to the sources" while others council a rejection of tradition altogether.

Parts III through V investigate "Ecotheology in an Age of Environmental Crisis." Here we realize that the concept of the "environment" has emerged alongside that of "nature" to express our awareness of how human society threatens the very conditions which make our lives possible. The "environment" we might say, is nonhuman nature considered as an object of human practice; especially, it is nonhuman nature considered as the victim of our cancerous models of economic growth, commodity worship, militarism, scientism, and patriarchal ideologies of domination. While past religious traditions focused their major attention on "nature" and paid little if any attention to "the environment," contemporary theology is now facing a natural world threatened by humanity.

Throughout Parts III, IV, and V there are contrasts between "liberal" or "conservationist" outlooks, which seek to preserve "nature" because of human needs; and a more "deep ecological" approach which sees nature as having value in its own right. Similarly, some viewpoints tend to focus solely on the natural world; while others see integral connections between the domination of nature and the oppression of social groups.

Part III contains writings clearly identifiable by religious tradition; for example, new environmental theologies by self-identified Jews, Christians, and Buddhists. Part IV focuses on ecofeminist spirituality, which is based in the realization that patriarchal society dominates women and nature with parallel ideologies and practices. Spiritual deep ecology—which offers an ecological rethinking of human identity—is explored in Part V.

In Part VI, "Religious Practice for a Sacred Earth," we encounter a variety of religious observances devised in response to the environment in general and the ecological crisis in particular.

Part VII explores the complex relations between religions, society, and politics. There now exists a spiritually based sense that modern industrial practices are not just "polluting the environment," but are actually desecrating the earth. This sensibility has been embodied in political movements resisting the forces of ecological degradation; and joined that resistance to concerns structured around class, race, gender, or ethnic differences. This Part also explores some of the familiar but confusing aspects of trying to live a spiritual life while remaining closely in touch with one's social surroundings.

⁊⦿

Simultaneously the voice of God and the product of human insight, folly, and hope, religious teachings are part of social struggles. Our study of religion and the environment, therefore, raises many questions. I will explore some of these in Introductions to each Part, but some deserve brief mention here.

Who has the right to appropriate—to write about, teach, and profit from—the environmental practices and ideas of the indigenous or native peoples who have been the victims of cultural and physical genocide?

When we talk of what "people" have done to the earth, will we recognize the ways in which the environmental crisis was created not just by a generalized "humanity" but by social structures determining decisive differences in power and wealth, differences mapped along lines of race and gender as well as class?

If we seek a truly "sustainable" social order who or what will we be sustaining? and whose voices will determine what is truly of value and what is unnecessary or oppressive?

How much of our environmental concern stems from our own desires for health or pleasure—and how much from a love of nature for its own integrity and value?

Can we harmonize our love of God's creation with our concern for social justice? Can either be truly fulfilled without the other?

⁊⦿

The task before us is very great and the outcome deeply uncertain. Yet if we devote ourselves to it, we will at least have the satisfaction of knowing that what we are doing with our lives is important. I hope that this text may fuel our awareness of what needs to be done—even as it also helps remind us of our simple joy in the divinity of the earth.

NOTES

1. Joanna Macy, *World as Lover, World as Self* (Berkeley, CA: Parallax Press, 1991), pp. 16–7.

2. Elizabeth Bowen, and Howard Hu, "Food Contamination due to Environmental Pollution," in *Critical Condition: Human Health and the Environment,* eds. Eric Chivian, Michael McCally, Howard Hu and Andrew Haines (Cambridge: MIT Press, 1993), pp. 50–52.

3. Robin Broad, *Plundering Paradise: The Struggle for the Environment in the Philippines* (Berkeley: University of California Press, 1993), p. 17.

4. Daniel Faber, *Environment Under Fire: Imperialism and theEcological Crisis in Central America* (New York: Monthly Review Press, 1993), p. 144.

5. Fred Setterberg and Lonny Shavelson, *Toxic Nation: The Fight to Save Our Communities from Chemical Contamination* (New York: John Wiley & Sons, 1993), p. 4.

6. Some scientists believe that the recent dramatic reduction in frog populations stems from exposure of their eggs to increased UV radiation.

7. Edward Abbey, *The Journey Home* (New York: Penguin, 1977), p. 229.

8. Darcy Ribeiro, Brazilian anthropologist, quoted in Al Gedicks, *The New Resource Wars* (Boston: South End Press, 1992), p. 13.

9. The complexity of the issues is revealed in the considerable debate over the precise meaning of this (and other) Biblical passages. Some commentators see the "mastery" as understood within a master/servant model which presumes reciprocal responsibility and care. By contrast, the critically important 11th-century Talmudic scholar Moses Nachmanides (the Ramban) states that "mastery" means God "gave them power and dominion over the earth to do as they wish with the cattle, the reptiles, and all that crawl in the dust, and to build ... and from its hills to dig copper, and other similar things." (Ramban, *Commentary on the Torah, Genesis* (New York: Shilo Publishing House, 1971) p. 55). A modern interpretation of *Genesis* claims:

> In a sense, the universe is like a machine that was built for a specific purpose. Every part of its design was dictated by a particular need, and the machine is maintained only so long as its purpose remains valid.... The universe was brought into existence as the means by which to carry out the Torah. Remove the Torah and there is no need for the universe.

> —*The Family Chumash: Bereishis,* Overviews by Rabbi Nosson Scherman (New York: Mesorah Publications, 1989), p. ix.

Yet the contrary view is expressed by Maimonides, perhaps the most influential medieval rabbinical authority:

> It should not be believed that all the beings exist for the sake of the existence of humanity. On the contrary, all the other beings too have been intended for their own sakes, and not for the sake of something else....

> —*Guide to the Perplexed,* Part III, Chapter 13, quoted in *Judaism and Ecology,* a Hadassah Study Guide (New York: Hadassah, 1993), p. 110.

The most complete study of *Genesis* 1:28 is Jeremy Cohen, *Be Fertile and Increase, Fill the Earth and Master It: The Ancient and Medieval Career of a Biblical Text* (Ithaca and London: Cornell University Press, 1989).

10. Steven C. Rockefeller, "Faith and Community in an Ecological Age," in Steven C. Rockefeller and John C. Elder, eds. *Spirit and Nature: Why the Environment is a Religious Issue* (Boston: Beacon Press, 1992), p. 142.

11. For a development of this theme see Roger S. Gottlieb, ed. *A New Creation: America's Contemporary Spiritual Voices* (New York: Crossroad, 1990).

12. Some thinkers believe that only by uniting insights from virtually all established traditions can we possibly develop a theology adequate to the demands of our age. See Charlene Spretnak, *States of Grace* (San Francisco: HarperSanFrancisco, 1992).

PART I

THE
MOMENT
OF SEEING

Selections from
Nature Writers
Linking Nature and Spirit

this earth is in our hands
let it fly, a bird of earth and light
All that moves will rejoice. . . .

—Meridel Le Sueuer

&

The indescribable innocence and beneficence of Nature—of sun and wind and rain, of summer and winter—such health, such cheer, they afford forever! . . . Shall I not have intelligence with the earth? Am I not partly leaves and vegetable mold myself?

—Henry David Thoreau

&

The plants give off the fragrance of their flowers. The precious stones reflect their brilliance to others. Every creature yearns for a loving embrace. The whole of nature serves humanity, and in this service offers all her bounty.

—Hildegard of Bingen

&

No more cars in national parks. Let the people walk. Or ride horses, bicycles, mules, wild pigs—anything—but keep the automobiles and the motorcycles and all their motorized relatives out. We have agreed not to drive our automobiles into cathedrals, concert halls, art museums, legislative assemblies, private bedrooms and the other sanctums of our culture; and we should treat our national parks with the same deference, for they, too, are holy places. An increasingly pagan and hedonistic people (thank God!) we are learning that the forests and mountains and desert canyons are holier than our churches. Therefore let us behave accordingly.

—Edward Abbey

The worship of God, Gods, or Goddesses, prayers for forgiveness or bounty, ethical imperatives to love our neighbors—or at least have compassion on them—all these are familiar and essential elements of religious life. Perhaps less familiar, but certainly as essential, is that "moment of seeing" which occurs when some perfectly magical—and perhaps also perfectly ordinary—experience of nature awakens our spirits.

This awakening can take many forms. We may find ourselves, as Thoreau understands it, discovering our true nature in wildness—a wildness of place matched, he believes, by our own potential wildness of spirit. Barry Lopez, John Muir, Rachel Carson and Ralph Waldo Emerson find a divine presence of awe, delight and magic in the natural world.

This presence may affect some of our basic values. In a modern age of "human rights," obligations to social groups and struggles of oppressed peoples, we may also ask: Of what value is nature? Can we speak of love or mutual respect for a particular tree, an endangered species, or an ecosystem? When Aldo Leopold describes humanity as simply a "plain citizen" of a complex natural setting, or John Muir challenges our presumption that the earth is made only for us, they are responding to the sacred quality of the earth and revisioning the place of humanity on that earth.

Annie Dillard, by contrast, finds herself desolate and lonely in a world in which nature no longer "talks" to her. This moment of seeing shows that our religious sensibility may be awakened as much by grief as by bounty.

Finally, Linda Hogan and Stephanie Kaza weave together reflections on the love of nature and ethical concern for the human community.

from "WALKING"

Henry David Thoreau

I wish to speak a word for Nature, for absolute freedom and wildness, as contrasted with a freedom and culture merely civil—to regard man as an inhabitant, or a part and parcel of Nature, rather than a member of society. I wish to make an extreme statement, if so I may make an emphatic one, for there are enough champions of civilization: the minister and the school committee and every one of you will take care of that. . . .

The West of which I speak is but another name for the Wild; and what I have been preparing to say is, that in Wildness is the preservation of the World. Every tree sends its fibers forth in search of the Wild. The cities import it at any price. Men plow and sail for it. From the forest and wilderness come the tonics and barks which brace mankind. Our ancestors were savages. The story of Romulus and Remus being suckled by a wolf is not a meaningless fable. The founders of every state which has risen to eminence have drawn their nourishment and vigor from a similar wild source. It was because the children of the Empire were not suckled by the wolf that they were conquered and displaced by the children of the northern forests who were.

I believe in the forest, and in the meadow, and in the night in which the corn grows. We require an infusion of hemlock, spruce or arbor vitae in our tea. There is a difference between eating and drinking for strength and from mere gluttony. The Hottentots eagerly devour the marrow of the koodoo and other antelopes raw, as a matter of course. Some of our northern Indians eat raw the marrow of the Arctic reindeer, as well as various other parts, including the summits of the antlers, as long as they are soft. And herein, perchance, they have stolen a march on the cooks of Paris. They get what usually goes to feed the fire. This is probably better than stall-fed beef and slaughterhouse pork to make a man of. Give me a wildness whose glance no civilization can endure—as if we lived on the marrow of koodoos devoured raw. . . .

Life consists with wildness. The most alive is the wildest. Not yet subdued to man, its presence refreshes him. One who pressed forward incessantly and never rested from his labors, who grew fast and made infinite demands on life, would always find himself in a new country or wilderness, and surrounded by the raw material of life. He would be climbing over the prostrate stems of primitive forest-trees.

Hope and the future for me are not in lawns and cultivated fields, not in towns and cities, but in the impervious and quaking swamps. When, formerly, I have analyzed my partiality for some farm which I had contemplated purchasing, I have frequently found that I was attracted solely by a few square rods of impermeable and unfathomable bog—a natural sink in one corner of it. That was the jewel which dazzled me. I derive more of my subsistence from the swamps which surround my native town than from the cultivated gardens in the village. . . .

In literature it is only the wild that attracts us. Dullness is but another name for tameness. It is the uncivilized free and wild thinking in Hamlet and the Iliad, in all the scriptures and mythologies, not learned in the schools, that delights us. As the wild duck is more swift and beautiful than the tame, so is the wild—the mallard—thought, which 'mid falling dews wings its way above the fens. A truly good book is something as natural, and as unexpectedly and unaccountably fair and perfect, as a wild-flower discovered on the prairies of the West or in the jungles of the East. Genius is a light which makes the darkness visible, like the lightning's flash, which perchance shatters the temple of knowledge itself—and not a taper lighted at the hearthstone of the race, which pales before the light of common day. . . .

In short, all good things are wild and free. There is something in a strain of music, whether produced by an instrument or by the human voice—take the sound of a bugle in a summer night, for instance—which by its wildness, to speak without satire, reminds me of the cries emitted by wild beasts in their native forests. It is so much of their wildness as I can understand. Give me for my friends and neighbors wild men, not tame ones. The wildness of the savage is but a faint symbol of the awful ferity with which good men and lovers meet.

I love even to see the domestic animals reassert their native rights—any evidence that they have not wholly lost their original wild habits and vigor; as when my neighbor's cow breaks out of her pasture early in the spring and boldly swims the river, a cold, gray tide, twenty-five or thirty rods wide, swollen by the melted snow. It is the buffalo crossing the Mississippi. This exploit confers some dignity on the herd in my eyes—already dignified. The seeds of instinct are preserved under the thick hides of cattle and horses, like seeds in the bowels of the earth, an indefinite period. . . .

I rejoice that horses and steers have to be broken before they can be made the slaves of men, and that men themselves have some wild oats still left to sow before they become submissive members of society. Undoubtedly, all men are not equally fit subjects for civilization; and because the majority, like dogs and sheep, are tame by inherited disposition, this is no reason why the others should have their natures broken that they may be reduced to the same level. Men are in the main alike, but they were made several in order that they might be various. If a low use is to be served, one man will do nearly or quite as well as another; if a high one, individual excellence is to be regarded. Any man can stop a hole to keep the wind away, but no other man could serve so rare a use as the author of this illustration did. Confucius says, "The skins of the tiger and the leopard, when they are tanned, are as the skins of the dog and the sheep tanned." But it is not the part of a true culture to tame tigers, any more than it is to make sheep ferocious; and tanning their skins for shoes is not the best use to which they can be put. . . .

Here is this vast, savage, howling mother of ours, Nature, lying all around, with such beauty, and such affection for her children, as the leopard; and yet we are so early weaned from her breast to society, to that culture which is exclusively an interaction of man on man—a sort of breeding in and in, which produces at most a merely English nobility, a civilization destined to have a speedy limit. . . .

I would not have every man nor every part of a man cultivated, any more than I would have every acre of earth cultivated: part will be tillage, but the greater part will be meadow and forest, not only serving an immediate use, but preparing a mould against a distant future, by the annual decay of the vegetation which it supports. . . .

We had a remarkable sunset one day last November. I was walking in a meadow, the source of a small brook, when the sun at last, just before setting, after a cold, gray day, reached a clear stratum in the horizon, and the softest, brightest morning sunlight fell on the dry grass and on the stems of the trees in the opposite horizon and on the leaves of the shrub oaks on the hillside, while our shadows stretched long over the meadow east ward, as if we were the only motes in its beams. It was such a light as we could not have imagined a moment before, and the air also was so warm and serene that nothing was wanting to make a paradise of that meadow. When we reflected that this was not a solitary phenomenon, never to happen again, but that it would happen forever and ever, an infinite number of evenings, and cheer and reassure the latest child that walked there, it was more glorious still.

The sun sets on some retired meadow, where no house is visible, with all the glory and splendor that it lavishes on cities, and perchance as it has never set before—where there is but a solitary marsh hawk to have his wings gilded by it, or only a musquash looks out from his cabin, and there is some little black-veined brook in the midst of the marsh, just beginning to meander, winding slowly round a decaying stump. We walked in so pure and bright a light, gilding the withered grass and leaves, so softly and serenely bright, I thought I had never bathed in such a golden flood, without a ripple or a murmur to it. The west side of every wood and rising ground gleamed like the boundary of Elysium, and the sun on our backs seemed like a gentle herdsman driving us home at evening.

So we saunter toward the Holy Land, till one day the sun shall shine more brightly than ever he has done, shall perchance shine into our minds and hearts, and light up our whole lives with a great awakening light, as warm and serene and golden as on a bankside in autumn.

Henry David Thoreau

from *ARCTIC DREAMS: IMAGINATION AND DESIRE IN A NORTHERN LANDSCAPE*

Barry Lopez

One summer evening I was camped in the western Brooks Range of Alaska with a friend. From the ridge where we had pitched our tent we looked out over tens of square miles of rolling tundra along the southern edge of the calving grounds of the Western Arctic caribou herd. During those days we observed not only caribou and wolves, which we'd come to study, but wolverine and red fox, ground squirrels, delicate-legged whimbrels and aggressive jaegers, all in the unfoldings of their obscure lives. One night we watched in awe as a young grizzly bear tried repeatedly to force its way past a yearling wolf standing guard alone before a den of young pups. The bear eventually gave up and went on its way. We watched snowy owls and rough-legged hawks hunt and caribou drift like smoke through the valley.

On the evening I am thinking about—it was breezy there on Ilingnorak Ridge, and cold; but the late-night sun, small as a kite in the northern sky, poured forth an energy that burned against my cheekbones—it was on that evening that I went on a walk for the first time among the tundra birds. They all build their nests on the ground, so their vulnerability is extreme. I gazed down at a single horned lark no bigger than my fist. She stared back resolute as iron. As I approached, golden plovers abandoned their nests in hysterical ploys, artfully feigning a broken wing to distract me from the woven grass cups that couched their pale, darkly speckled eggs. Their eggs glowed with a soft, pure light, like the window light in a Vermeer painting. I marveled at this intense and concentrated beauty on the vast table of the plain. I walked on to find Lapland longspurs as still on their nests as stones, their dark eyes gleaming. At the nest of two snowy owls I stopped. These are more formidable animals than plovers. I stood motionless. The wild glare in their eyes receded. One owl settled back slowly over its three eggs, with an aura of primitive alertness. The other watched me, and immediately sought a bond with my eyes if I started to move.

I took to bowing on these evening walks. I would bow slightly with my hands in my pockets, toward the birds and the evidence of life in their nests—because of their fecundity, unexpected in this remote region, and because of the serene arctic light that came down over the land like breath, like breathing.

I remember the wild, dedicated lives of the birds that night and also the abandon with which a small herd of caribou crossed the Kokolik River to the northwest, the incident of only a few moments. They pranced through like wild mares, kicking up sheets of water across the evening sun and shaking it off on the far side like huge dogs, a bloom of spray that glittered in the air around them like grains of mica.

I remember the press of light against my face. The explosive skitter of calves among grazing caribou. And the warm intensity of the eggs beneath these resolute birds. Until then, perhaps because the sun was shining in the very middle of the night, so out of tune with my own customary perception, I had never known how benign sunlight could be. How forgiving. How run through with compassion in a land that bore so eloquently the evidence of centuries of winter. . . .

Whatever evaluation we finally make of a stretch of land, however, no matter how profound or accurate, we will find it inadequate. The land retains an identity of its own, still deeper and more subtle than we can know. Our obligation toward it then becomes simple: to approach with an uncalculating mind, with an attitude of regard. To try to sense the range and variety of its expression—its weather and colors and animals. To intend from the beginning to preserve some of the mystery within it as a kind of wisdom to be experienced, not questioned. And to be alert for its openings, for that moment when something sacred reveals itself within the mundane, and you know the land knows you are there. . . .

In the face of a rational, scientific approach to the land, which is more widely sanctioned, esoteric insights and speculations are frequently overshadowed, and what is lost is profound. The land is like poetry: it is inexplicably coherent, it is transcendent in its meaning, and it has the power to elevate a consideration of human life.

from THE SENSE OF WONDER

Rachel Carson

One stormy autumn night when my nephew Roger was about twenty months old I wrapped him in a blanket and carried him down to the beach in the rainy darkness. Out there, just at the edge of where-we-couldn't-see, big waves were thundering in, dimly seen white shapes that boomed and shouted and threw great handfuls of froth at us. Together we laughed for pure joy—he a baby meeting for the first time the wild tumult of Oceanus, I with the salt of half a lifetime of sea love in me. But I think we felt the same spine-tingling response to the vast, roaring ocean and the wild night around us.

A night or two later the storm had blown itself out and I took Roger again to the beach, this time to carry him along the water's edge, piercing the darkness with the yellow cone of our flashlight. Although there was no rain the night was again noisy with breaking waves and the insistent wind. It was clearly a time and place where great and elemental things prevailed.

Our adventure on this particular night had to do with life, for we were searching for ghost crabs, those sand-colored, fleet-legged beings which Roger had sometimes glimpsed briefly on the beaches in daytime. But the crabs are chiefly nocturnal, and when not roaming the night beaches they dig little pits near the surf line where they hide, seemingly watching and waiting for what the sea may bring them. For me the sight of these small living creatures, solitary and fragile against the brute force of the sea, had moving philosophic overtones, and I do not pretend that Roger and I reacted with similar emotions. But it was good to see his infant acceptance of a world of elemental things, fearing neither the song of the wind nor the darkness nor the roaring surf, entering with baby excitement into the search for a "ghos."

It was hardly a conventional way to entertain one so young, I suppose, but now, with Roger a little past his fourth birthday, we are continuing that sharing of adventures in the world of nature that we began in his babyhood, and I think the results are good. The sharing includes nature in storm as well as calm, by night as well as day, and is based on having fun together rather than on teaching.

A child's world is fresh and new and beautiful, full of wonder and excitement. It is our misfortune that for most of us that clear-eyed vision, that true instinct for what is beautiful and awe-inspiring, is dimmed and even lost before we reach adulthood. If I had influence

Pages 8–10 and 88–89 from *The Sense of Wonder* by Rachel Carson. Photographs by Charles Pratt. Copyright © 1956 by Rachel L. Carson. Copyright © renewed 1984 by Roger Christie. Reprinted by permission of HarperCollins Publishers, Inc. and Frances Collin.

with the good fairy who is supposed to preside over the christening of all children I should ask that her gift to each child in the world be a sense of wonder so indestructible that it would last throughout life, as an unfailing antidote against the boredom and disenchantments of later years, the sterile preoccupation with things that are artificial, the alienation from the sources of our strength.

What is the value of preserving and strengthening this sense of awe and wonder, this recognition of something beyond the boundaries of human existence? Is the exploration of the natural world just a pleasant way to pass the golden hours of childhood or is there something deeper?

I am sure there is something much deeper, something lasting and significant. Those who dwell, as scientists or laymen, among the beauties and mysteries of the earth are never alone or weary of life. Whatever the vexations or concerns of their personal lives, their thoughts can find paths that lead to inner contentment and to renewed excitement in living. Those who contemplate the beauty of the earth find reserves of strength that will endure as long as life lasts. There is symbolic as well as actual beauty in the migration of the birds, the ebb and flow of the tides, the folded bud ready for the spring. There is something infinitely healing in the repeated refrains of nature—the assurance that dawn comes after night, and spring after the winter.

I like to remember the distinguished Swedish oceanographer, Otto Pettersson, who died a few years ago at the age of ninety-three, in full possession of his keen mental powers. His son, also world-famous in oceanography, has related in a recent book how intensely his father enjoyed every new experience, every new discovery concerning the world about him.

"He was an incurable romantic," the son wrote, "intensely in love with life and with the mysteries of the cosmos." When he realized he had not much longer to enjoy the earthly scene, Otto Pettersson said to his son: "What will sustain me in my last moments is an infinite curiosity as to what is to follow."

"NATURE"

Ralph Waldo Emerson

To go into solitude, a man needs to retire as much from his chamber as from society. I am not solitary whilst I read and write, though nobody is with me. But if a man would be alone, let him look at the stars. The rays that come from those heavenly worlds, will separate between him and what he touches. One might think the atmosphere was made transparent with this design, to give man, in the heavenly bodies, the perpetual presence of the sublime. Seen in the streets of cities, how great they are! If the stars should appear one night in a thousand years, how would men believe and adore; and preserve for many generations the remembrance of the city of God which had been shown! But every night come out these envoys of beauty, and light the universe with their admonishing smile.

The stars awaken a certain reverence, because though always present, they are inaccessible; but all natural objects make a kindred impression, when the mind is open to their influence. Nature never wears a mean appearance. Neither does the wisest man extort her secret, and lose his curiosity by finding out all her perfection. Nature never became a toy to a wise spirit. The flowers, the animals, the mountains, reflected the wisdom of his best hour, as much as they had delighted the simplicity of his childhood.

When we speak of nature in this manner, we have a distinct but most poetical sense in the mind. We mean the integrity of impression made by manifold natural objects. It is this which distinguishes the stick of timber of the wood-cutter, from the tree of the poet. The charming landscape which I saw this morning, is indubitably made up of some twenty or thirty farms. Miller owns this field, Locke that, and Manning the woodland beyond. But none of them owns the landscape. There is a property in the horizon which no man has but he whose eye can integrate all the parts, that is, the poet. This is the best part of these men's farms, yet to this their warranty-deeds give no title.

To speak truly, few adult persons can see nature. Most persons do not see the sun. At least they have a very superficial seeing. The sun illuminates only the eye of the man, but shines into the eye and the heart of the child. The lover of nature is he whose inward and outward senses are still truly adjusted to each other; who has retained the spirit of infancy even into the era of manhood. His intercourse with heaven and earth, becomes part of his daily food. In the presence of nature, a wild delight runs through the man, in spite of real sorrows. Nature says,—he is my creature, and maugre all his impertinent griefs, he shall be glad with

From *Nature: Addresses and Lectures*, published in 1849.

me. Not the sun or the summer alone, but every hour and season yields its tribute of delight; for every hour and change corresponds to and authorizes a different state of the mind, from breathless noon to grimmest midnight. Nature is a setting that fits equally well a comic or a mourning piece. In good health, the air is a cordial of incredible virtue. Crossing a bare common, in snow puddles, at twilight, under a clouded sky, without having in my thoughts any occurrence of special good fortune, I have enjoyed a perfect exhilaration. I am glad to the brink of fear. In the woods too, a man casts off his years, as the snake his slough, and at what period soever of life, is always a child. In the woods, is perpetual youth. Within these plantations of God, a decorum and sanctity reign, a perennial festival is dressed, and the guest sees not how he should tire of them in a thousand years. In the woods, we return to reason and faith. There I feel that nothing can befall me in life,—no disgrace, no calamity, (leaving me my eyes,) which nature cannot repair. Standing on the bare ground,—my head bathed by the blithe air, and uplifted into infinite space,—all mean egotism vanishes. I become a transparent eye-ball; I am nothing; I see all; the currents of the Universal Being circulate through me; I am part or particle of God. The name of the nearest friend sounds then foreign and accidental: to be brothers, to be acquaintances,—master or servant, is then a trifle and a disturbance. I am the lover of uncontained and immortal beauty. In the wilderness, I find something more dear and connate than in streets or villages. In the tranquil landscape, and especially in the distant line of the horizon, man beholds somewhat as beautiful as his own nature.

The greatest delight which the fields and woods minister, is the suggestion of an occult relation between man and the vegetable. I am not alone and unacknowledged. They nod to me, and I to them. The waving of the boughs in the storm, is new to me and old. It takes me by surprise, and yet is not unknown. Its effect is like that of a higher thought or a better emotion coming over me, when I deemed I was thinking justly or doing right.

Yet it is certain that the power to produce this delight, does not reside in nature, but in man, or in a harmony of both. It is necessary to use these pleasures with great temperance. For, nature is not always tricked in holiday attire, but the same scene which yesterday breathed perfume and glittered as for the frolic of the nymphs, is overspread with melancholy today. Nature always wears the colors of the spirit. To a man laboring under calamity, the heat of his own fire hath sadness in it. Then, there is a kind of contempt of the landscape felt by him who has just lost by death a dear friend. The sky is less grand as it shuts down over less worth in the population.

Ralph Waldo Emerson

from *THOUSAND-MILE WALK TO THE GULF*

John Muir

A THOUSAND-MILE WALK

The world, we are told, was made especially for man—a presumption not supported by all the facts. A numerous class of men are painfully astonished whenever they find anything, living or dead, in all God's universe, which they cannot eat or render in some way what they call useful to themselves. They have precise dogmatic insight of the intentions of the Creator, and it is hardly possible to be guilty of irreverence in speaking of *their* God any more than of heathen idols. He is regarded as a civilized, law-abiding gentleman in favor either of a republican form of government or of a limited monarchy; believes in the literature and language of England; is a warm supporter of the English constitution and Sunday schools and missionary societies; and is as purely a manufactured article as any puppet of a half-penny theater.

With such views of the Creator it is, of course, not surprising that erroneous views should be entertained of the creation. To such properly trimmed people, the sheep, for example, is an easy problem—food and clothing "for us," eating grass and daisies white by divine appointment for this predestined purpose, on perceiving the demand for wool that would be occasioned by the eating of the apple in the Garden of Eden.

In the same pleasant plan, whales are storehouses of oil for us, to help out the stars in lighting our dark ways until the discovery of the Pennsylvania oil wells. Among plants, hemp, to say nothing of the cereals, is a case of evident destination for ships' rigging, wrapping packages, and hanging the wicked. Cotton is another plain case of clothing. Iron was made for hammers and ploughs, and lead for bullets; all intended for us. And so of other small handfuls of insignificant things.

But if we should ask these profound expositors of God's intentions, How about those man-eating animals—lions, tigers, alligators—which smack their lips over raw man? Or about those myriads of noxious insects that destroy labor and drink his blood? Doubtless man was intended for food and drink for all these? Oh, no! Not at all! These are unresolvable difficulties connected with Eden's apple and the Devil. Why does water drown its lord? Why do so many minerals poison him? Why are so many plants and fishes deadly enemies? Why is

Reprinted from *Thousand Mile Walk to the Gulf* by John Muir, 1916.

the lord of creation subjected to the same laws of life as his subjects? Oh, all these things are satanic, or in some way connected with the first garden.

Now, it never seems to occur to these farseeing teachers that Nature's object in making animals and plants might possibly be first of all the happiness of each one of them, not the creation of all for the happiness of one. Why should man value himself as more than a small part of the one great unit of creation? And what creature of all that the Lord has taken the pains to make is not essential to the completeness of that unit—the cosmos? The universe would be incomplete without man; but it would also be incomplete without the smallest transmicroscopic creature that dwells beyond our conceitful eyes and knowledge.

from *A SAND COUNTY ALMANAC*

Aldo Leopold

WILDERNESS

Wilderness is the raw material out of which man has hammered the artifact called civilization.

Wilderness was never a homogeneous raw material. It was very diverse, and the resulting artifacts are very diverse. These differences in the end-product are known as cultures. The rich diversity of the world's cultures reflects a corresponding diversity in the wilds that gave them birth.

For the first time in the history of the human species, two changes are now impending. One is the exhaustion of wilderness in the more habitable portions of the globe. The other is the world-wide hybridization of cultures through modern transport and industrialization. Neither can be prevented, and perhaps should not be, but the question arises whether, by some slight amelioration of the impending changes, certain values can be preserved that would otherwise be lost.

To the laborer in the sweat of his labor, the raw stuff on his anvil is an adversary to be conquered. So was wilderness an adversary to the pioneer.

But to the laborer in repose, able for the moment to cast a philosophical eye on his world, that same raw stuff is something to be loved and cherished, because it gives definition and meaning to his life. This is a plea for the preservation of some tag-ends of wilderness, as museum pieces, for the edification of those who may one day wish to see, feel, or study the origins of their cultural inheritance.

THE ETHICAL SEQUENCE

This extension of ethics, so far studied only by philosophers, is actually a process in ecological evolution. Its sequences may be described in ecological as well as in philosophical terms. An ethic, ecologically, is a limitation on freedom of action in the struggle for existence. An ethic, philosophically, is a differentiation of social from anti-social conduct. These are two definitions of one thing. The thing has its origin in the tendency of interdependent individuals or groups to evolve modes of co-operation. The ecologist calls these symbioses. Politics and economics are advanced symbioses in which the original free-for-all competition has been replaced, in part, by co-operative mechanisms with an ethical content.

The complexity of co-operative mechanisms has increased with population density, and with the efficiency of tools. It was simpler, for example, to define the anti-social uses of sticks and stones in the days of the mastodons than of bullets and billboards in the age of motors.

The first ethics dealt with the relation between individuals; the Mosaic Decalogue is an example. Later accretions dealt with the relation between the individual and society. The Golden Rule tries to integrate the individual to society; democracy to integrate social organization to the individual.

There is as yet no ethic dealing with man's relation to land and to the animals and plants which grow upon it. Land, like Odysseus' slave-girls, is still property. The land-relation is still strictly economic, entailing privileges but not obligations.

The extension of ethics to this third element in human environment is, if I read the evidence correctly, an evolutionary possibility and an ecological necessity. It is the third step in a sequence. The first two have already been taken. Individual thinkers since the days of Ezekiel and Isaiah have asserted that the despoliation of land is not only inexpedient but wrong. Society, however, has not yet affirmed their belief. I regard the present conservation movement as the embryo of such an affirmation.

An ethic may be regarded as a mode of guidance for meeting ecological situations so new or intricate, or involving such deferred reactions, that the path of social expediency is not discernible to the average individual. Animal instincts are modes of guidance for the individual in meeting such situations. Ethics are possibly a kind of community instinct in-the-making.

THE COMMUNITY CONCEPT

All ethics so far evolved rest upon a single premise: that the individual is a member of a community of interdependent parts. His instincts prompt him to compete for his place in that community, but his ethics prompt him also to co-operate (perhaps in order that there may be a place to compete for).

The land ethic simply enlarges the boundaries of the community to include soils, waters, plants, and animals, or collectively: the land.

This sounds simple: do we not already sing our love for and obligation to the land of the free and the home of the brave? Yes, but just what and whom do we love? Certainly not the soil, which we are sending helter-skelter downriver. Certainly not the waters, which we assume have no function except to turn turbines, float barges, and carry off sewage. Certainly not the plants, of which we exterminate whole communities without batting an eye. Certainly not the animals, of which we have already extirpated many of the largest and most beautiful species. A land ethic of course cannot prevent the alteration, management, and use of these 'resources,' but it does affirm their right to continued existence, and, at least in spots, their continued existence in a natural state.

In short, a land ethic changes the role of *Homo sapiens* from conqueror of the land-community to plain member and citizen of it. It implies respect for his fellow-members, and also respect for the community as such.

In human history, we have learned (I hope) that the conqueror role is eventually self-defeating. Why? Because it is implicit in such a role that the conqueror knows, *ex cathedra,* just what makes the community clock tick, and just what and who is valuable, and what and who is worthless, in community life. It always turns out that he knows neither, and this is why his conquests eventually defeat themselves.

In the biotic community, a parallel situation exists. Abraham knew exactly what the land was for: it was to drip milk and honey into Abraham's mouth. At the present moment, the assurance with which we regard this assumption is inverse to the degree of our education.

The ordinary citizen today assumes that science knows what makes the community clock tick; the scientist is equally sure that he does not. He knows that the biotic mechanism is so complex that its workings may never be fully understood.

"TEACHING A STONE TO TALK"

Annie Dillard

I

The island where I live is peopled with cranks like myself. In a cedar-shake shack on a cliff—but we all live like this—is a man in his thirties who lives alone with a stone he is trying to teach to talk.

Wisecracks on this topic abound, as you might expect, but they are made as it were perfunctorily, and mostly by the young. For in fact, almost everyone here respects what Larry is doing, as do I, which is why I am protecting his (or her) privacy, and confusing for you the details. It could be, for instance, a pinch of sand he is teaching to talk, or a prolonged northerly, or any one of a number of waves. But it is, in fact, I assure you, a stone. It is—for I have seen it—a palm-sized oval beach cobble whose dark gray is cut by a band of white which runs around and, presumably, through it; such stones we call "wishing stones," for reasons obscure but not, I think, unimaginable.

He keeps it on a shelf. Usually the stone lies protected by a square of untanned leather, like a canary asleep under its cloth. Larry removes the cover for the stone's lessons, or more accurately, I should say, for the ritual or rituals which they perform together several times a day.

No one knows what goes on at these sessions, least of all myself, for I know Larry but slightly, and that owing only to a mix-up in our mail. I assume that like any other meaningful effort, the ritual involves sacrifice, the suppression of self-consciousness, and a certain precise tilt of the will, so that the will becomes transparent and hollow, a channel for the work. I wish him well. It is a noble work, and beats, from any angle, selling shoes.

Reports differ on precisely what he expects or wants the stone to say. I do not think he expects the stone to speak as we do, and describe for us its long life and many, or few, sensations. I think instead that he is trying to teach it to say a single word, such as "cup," or "uncle." For this purpose he has not, as some have seriously suggested, carved the stone a little mouth, or furnished it in any way with a pocket of air which it might then expel. Rather—and I think he is wise in this—he plans to initiate his son, who is now an infant living with Larry's estranged wife, into the work, so that it may continue and bear fruit after his death.

II

Nature's silence is its one remark, and every flake of world is a chip off that old mute and immutable block. The Chinese say that we live in the world of the ten thousand things. Each of the ten thousand things cries out to us precisely nothing.

God used to rage at the Israelites for frequenting sacred groves. I wish I could find one. Martin Buber says: "The crisis of all primitive mankind comes with the discovery of that which is fundamentally not-holy, the a-sacramental, which withstands the methods, and which has no 'hour,' a province which steadily enlarges itself." Now we are no longer primitive; now the whole world seems not-holy. We have drained the light from the boughs in the sacred grove and snuffed it in the high places and along the banks of sacred streams. We as a people have moved from pantheism to pan-atheism. Silence is not our heritage but our destiny; we live where we want to live.

The soul may ask God for anything, and never fail. You may ask God for his presence, or for wisdom, and receive each at his hands. Or you may ask God, in the words of the shop-keeper's little gag sign, that he not go away mad, but just go away. Once, in Israel, an extended family of nomads did just that. They heard God's speech and found it too loud. The wilderness generation was at Sinai; it witnessed there the thick darkness where God was: "and all the people saw the thunderings, and the lightnings, and the noise of the trumpet, and the mountain smoking." It scared them witless. Then they asked Moses to beg God, please, never speak to them directly again. "Let not God speak with us, lest we die." Moses took the message. And God, pitying their self-consciousness, agreed. He agreed not to speak to the people anymore. And he added to Moses, "Go say to them, Get into your tents again."

III

It is difficult to undo our own damage, and to recall to our presence that which we have asked to leave. It is hard to desecrate a grove and change your mind. The very holy mountains are keeping mum. We doused the burning bush and cannot rekindle it; we are lighting matches in vain under every green tree. Did the wind use to cry, and the hills shout forth praise? Now speech has perished from among the lifeless things of earth, and living things say very little to very few. Birds may crank out sweet gibberish and monkeys howl; horses neigh and pigs say, as you recall, oink oink. But so do cobbles rumble when a wave recedes, and thunders break the air in lightning storms. I call these noises silence. It could be that wherever there is motion there is noise, as when a whale breaches and smacks the water—and wherever there is stillness there is the still small voice, God's speaking from the whirlwind, nature's old song and dance, the show we drove from town. At any rate, now it is all we can do, and among our best efforts, to try to teach a given human language, English, to chimpanzees.

In the forties an American psychologist and his wife tried to teach a chimp actually to speak. At the end of three years the creature could pronounce, in a hoarse whisper, the words "mama," "papa," and "cup." After another three years of training she could whisper, with difficulty, still only "mama," "papa," and "cup." The more recent successes at teaching chimpanzees American Sign Language are well known. Just the other day a chimp told us, if we can believe that we truly share a vocabulary, that she had been sad in the morning. I'm sorry we asked.

What have we been doing all these centuries but trying to call God back to the mountain, or, failing that, raise a peep out of anything that isn't us? What is the difference between a cathedral and a physics lab? Are not they both saying: Hello? We spy on whales and on interstellar radio objects; we starve ourselves and pray till we're blue.

IV

I have been reading comparative cosmology. At this time most cosmologists favor the picture of the evolving universe described by Lemaître and Gamow. But I prefer a suggestion made years ago by Valéry—Paul Valéry. He set forth the notion that the universe might be "head-shaped."

The mountains are great stone bells; they clang together like nuns. Who shushed the stars? There are a thousand million galaxies easily seen in the Palomar reflector; collisions between and among them do, of course, occur. But these collisions are very long and silent slides. Billions of stars sift among each other untouched, too distant even to be moved, heedless as always, hushed. The sea pronounces something, over and over, in a hoarse whisper; I cannot quite make it out. But God knows I have tried.

At a certain point you say to the woods, to the sea, to the mountains, the world, Now I am ready. Now I will stop and be wholly attentive. You empty yourself and wait, listening. After a time you hear it: there is nothing there. There is nothing but those things only, those created objects, discrete, growing or holding, or swaying, being rained on or raining, held, flooding or ebbing, standing, or spread. You feel the world's word as a tension, a hum, a single chorused note everywhere the same. This is it: this hum is the silence. Nature does utter a peep—just this one. The birds and insects, the meadows and swamps and rivers and stones and mountains and clouds: they all do it; they all don't do it. There is a vibrancy to the silence, a suppression, as if someone were gagging the world. But you wait, you give your life's length to listening, and nothing happens. The ice rolls up, the ice rolls back, and still that single note obtains. The tension, or lack of it, is intolerable. The silence is not actually suppression; instead, it is all there is.

V

We are here to witness. There is nothing else to do with those mute materials we do not need. Until Larry teaches his stone to talk, until God changes his mind, or until the pagan gods slip back to their hilltop groves, all we can do with the whole inhuman array is watch it. We can

Annie Dillard

stage our own act on the planet—build our cities on its plains, dam its rivers, plant its top-soils—but our meaningful activity scarcely covers the terrain. We do not use the songbirds, for instance. We do not eat many of them; we cannot befriend them; we cannot persuade them to eat more mosquitoes or plant fewer weed seeds. We can only witness them—whoever they are. If we were not here, they would be songbirds falling in the forest. If we were not here, material events like the passage of seasons would lack even the meager meanings we are able to muster for them. The show would play to an empty house, as do all those falling stars which fall in the daytime. That is why I take walks: to keep an eye on things. And that is why I went to the Galápagos islands.

All this becomes especially clear on the Galápagos islands. The Galápagos islands are just plain here—and little else. They blew up out of the ocean, some plants blew in on them, some animals drifted aboard and evolved weird forms—and there they all are, whoever they are, in full swing. You can go there and watch it happen, and try to figure it out. The Galápagos are a kind of metaphysics laboratory, almost wholly uncluttered by human culture or history. Whatever happens on those bare volcanic rocks happens in full view, whether anyone is watching or not.

What happens there is this, and precious little it is: clouds come and go, and the round of similar seasons; a pig eats a tortoise or doesn't eat a tortoise; Pacific waves fall up and slide back; a lichen expands; night follows day; an albatross dies and dries on a cliff; a cool current upwells from the ocean floor; fishes multiply, flies swarm, stars rise and fall, and diving birds dive. The news, in other words, breaks on the beaches. And taking it all in are the trees. The *palo santo* trees crowd the hillsides like any outdoor audience; they face the lagoons, the lava lowlands, and the shores.

I have some experience of these *palo santo* trees. They interest me as emblems of the muteness of the human stance in relation to all that is not human. I see us all as *palo santo* trees, holy sticks, together watching all that we watch, and growing in silence.

In the Galápagos, it took me a long time to notice the *palo santo* trees. Like everyone else, I specialized in sea lions. My shipmates and I liked the sea lions, and envied their lives. Their joy seemed conscious. They were engaged in full-time play. They were all either fat or dead; there was no halfway. By day they played in the shallows, alone or together, greeting each other and us with great noises of joy, or they took a turn offshore and body-surfed in the breakers, exultant. By night on the sand they lay in each other's flippers and slept. Everyone joked, often, that when he "came back," he would just as soon do it all over again as a sea lion. I concurred. The sea lion game looked unbeatable.

But a year and a half later, I returned to those unpeopled islands. In the interval my attachment to them had shifted, and my memories of them had altered, the way memories do, like particolored pebbles rolled back and forth over a grating, so that after a time those hard bright ones, the ones you thought you would never lose, have vanished, passed through the grating, and only a few big, unexpected ones remain, no longer unnoticed but now selected out for some meaning, large and unknown.

Such were the *palo santo* trees. Before, I had never given them a thought. They were just miles of half-dead trees on the red lava sea cliffs of some deserted islands. They were only a name in a notebook: "*Palo santo*—those strange white trees." Look at the sea lions! Look at the flightless cormorants, the penguins, the iguanas, the sunset! But after eighteen months the wonderful cormorants, penguins, iguanas, sunsets, and even the sea lions, had dropped from my holey heart. I returned to the Galápagos to see the *palo santo* trees.

They are thin, pale, wispy trees. You walk among them on the lowland deserts, where they grow beside the prickly pear. You see them from the water on the steeps that face the sea, hundreds together, small and thin and spread, and so much more pale than their red soils that any black-and-white photograph of them looks like a negative. Their stands look like blasted orchards. At every season they all look newly dead, pale and bare as birches drowned in a beaver pond—for at every season they look leafless, paralyzed, and mute. But in fact, if you look closely, you can see during the rainy months a few meager deciduous leaves here and there on their brittle twigs. And hundreds of lichens always grow on their bark in mute, overlapping explosions which barely enlarge in the course of the decade, lichens pink and orange, lavender, yellow, and green. The *palo santo* trees bear the lichens effortlessly, unconsciously, the way they bear everything. Their multitudes, transparent as line drawings, crowd the cliffsides like whirling dancers, like empty groves, and look out over cliff-wrecked breakers toward more unpeopled islands, with their freakish lizards and birds, toward the grieving lagoons and the bays where the sea lions wander, and beyond to the clamoring seas.

Now I no longer concurred with my shipmates' joke; I no longer wanted to "come back" as a sea lion. For I thought, and I still think, that if I came back to life in the sunlight where everything changes, I would like to come back as a *palo santo* tree, one of thousands on a cliffside on those godforsaken islands, where a million events occur among the witless, where a splash of rain may drop on a yellow iguana the size of a dachshund, and ten minutes later the iguana may blink. I would like to come back as a *palo santo* tree on the weather side of an island, so that I could be, myself, a perfect witness, and look, mute, and wave my arms.

VI

The silence is all there is. It is the alpha and the omega. It is God's brooding over the face of the waters; it is the blended note of the ten thousand things, the whine of wings. You take a step in the right direction to pray to this silence, and even to address the prayer to "World." Distinctions blur. Quit your tents. Pray without ceasing.

"THE KILL HOLE"

Linda Hogan

In New Mexico there were an ancient people called the Mimbres. They were skilled potters. What they made was far superior to the work of later potters in the Southwest. The Mimbres formed bowls out of rich, red clay that held generations of life, and they painted that shaped clay with animals, people, plants, and even the dusty wind that still inhabits the dry New Mexico land.

Like the Anasazi and other ancient nations, these were people of the mystery, having abandoned their place and vanished into a dimension that has remained unknown to those of us who have come later. But before they disappeared into the secret, the Mimbres "killed" their pots by breaking a hole in the center of each one. It is thought that the hole served to release the spirit of the pot from the clay, allowing it to travel with them over land and to join them in their burial grounds. It is called a "kill hole."

At the third death I attended, I thought of these earlier people, and wondered about the kill hole, how life escapes the broken clay of ourselves, travels away from the center of our living. It's said that at death, the fontanelle in the top of the skull opens, the way it is open when we are born into the world. Before her spirit escaped through the crown, I wanted to ask that dying woman what she could tell me about life. But dying is hard work and it leaves little time for questions. That afternoon, there was time only for human comfort as the woman balanced those last hours between the worlds of life and raspy death.

That woman died in California, not far from the place where Ishi, the last Yana Indian, was found in 1911. Ishi came from a small group of Indians who lived undiscovered for over fifty years in the Mill Creek area, concealed by forest. They knew the secret of invisibility. Not even a cloud of smoke had revealed their whereabouts. But as the settling of the continent expanded to the West, and as the logging of the forests continued, Ishi was found, finally, by surveyors who must have believed he was not a man in the way they were men, for they carried away his few possessions as souvenirs for their families.

For the next four years Ishi lived in a museum as a living exhibit. He offered scholars his tools, his crafts, and his language. His was a tremendous gift to the people who were near him, but during that time he was transformed from a healthy man into a wasted skeleton. He died from tuberculosis, one of the diseases of civilization. But sometimes death has such a

Reprinted with permission of the author. This essay appeared in *Parabola: The Magazine of Myth and Tradition,* Volume 13:2, May 1988, pp. 50 -53.

strange way of turning things inside out, so that what is gone becomes as important as what remains. Such an absence defines our world as surely as a Mimbres pot contains a bowl of air, or as a woman's dying body holds a memory and history of life. This is especially true in the case of Ishi; his story illuminates the world of civilization and its flaws. It tells us what kind of people we are, with our double natures. It speaks of loss and of emptiness that will never again be filled, of whole cultures disappeared, of species made extinct, all of these losses falling as if through a hole, like a spirit leaving earth's broken clay.

In our own time, there have been events as striking as the discovery of Ishi, events that, in their passing, not only raise the question of what kind of people we are, but give us reason to ask what is our rightful place within the circle of life, we beautiful ones who are as adept at creation as we are at destruction?

One of these events, one that haunts us like a shadow from the dark periphery of our lives, is the recent research where apes were taught American sign language. Through that language of the hands, a dialogue began between signing chimpanzees and human beings, a dialogue that bridged the species barrier for perhaps the first time. Within a relatively short time, the chimps learned to communicate with humans and with one another. They asked questions, expressed abstract thought, and combined signs and symbols to create new words they had not been taught by their human teachers. With their hands, they spoke a world of emotion, of feelings similar to our own. One angry chimp called his handler, "dirty." Another one, Ally, developed hysterical paralysis when separated from his mother. Later, one of the subjects had to be tranquilized as he was taken away, distraught and protesting, and sold into scientific research.

From these studies, we learned that primates have a capacity for love and resistance, that they not only have a rich emotional life, but that they are able to express their pain and anguish. This is an event whose repercussions astonish us with their meaning, whose presence throws us into an identity crisis equal to that in Galileo's time when the fabric of belief was split wide open to reveal that earth was not the center of the universe. This event bespeaks our responsibility to treat with care and tenderness all the other lives who share our small world. Yet the significance of this research has gone largely unheeded. Many members of the scientific community played down the similarities between apes and humans, ignoring the comfort of such connections. They searched instead for new definitions of language and intelligence, ones that would exclude apes from our own ways of speaking and thinking. They searched for a new division, another wall between life and life. In itself, this search sheds light on us, and in that light, we seem to have had a failure of heart.

But perhaps this armor of defense comes from another failure, from the downfall of our beliefs about who and what we are as human beings. One by one, in our lifetimes, our convictions about ourselves and our place within the world have been overturned. Once the use of tools was considered to be strictly a human ability. Then it was found that primates and other species make use of tools. Then altruism was said to be what distinguished us from other species, until it was learned that elephants try to help their sick, staying the long hours beside their own dying ones, caressing and comforting them. And we can't even say that art is an activity that sets us apart, since those same compassionate elephants also make art. In fact, when the artist de Kooning was shown anonymous paintings by elephants, he thought the artist to be a most talented individual, one who knew how to "finish" and compose a drawing. On hearing that the artist was an elephant, he said, "That's a damned talented elephant." Jane Goodall, also on the subject of art, says that not only do chimpanzees make and name paintings, but that when shown their artwork as much as a year later, they remember the title they originally gave it.

Even humor is not entirely limited to humans. Recently Jane Goodall also related an exchange between the signing gorilla Koko and trainer Penny Patterson. A researcher was visiting them, and Penny wanted Koko to exhibit her intelligence.

Penny held up a piece of white cloth.

"Koko, what color is this?"

Koko signed, "Red."

Because the gorilla made an error, the woman asked again. "Koko, what color is this?"

Koko again replied, "Red."

Exasperated, the trainer said, "Koko, if you want to eat supper, you'd better answer the question. What color is this?"

Koko leaned forward and picked a tiny piece of red lint off the white cloth, looked her caretaker in the eye, showed her the lint, and laughed. "Red, Red, red, red!"

Still wanting a place of our own, a place set aside from the rest of the creation, now it is being ventured that maybe our ability to make fire separates us, or perhaps the desire to seek revenge. But no matter what direction the quest for separation might take, there has been a narrowing down of the difference between species, and we are forced to ask ourselves once again: what is our rightful place in the world, our responsibility to the other lives on the planet? It's a question of crucial importance as we live in this strange and confusing time, when so many of our scientists prefer to meddle with the creation of new life forms rather than to maintain and care for those, even human lives, who are already in our presence. Oren Lyons, Iroquois traditionalist, has said, "We forget and we consider ourselves superior, but we are after all a mere part of this creation. And we must consider to understand where we are. And we stand somewhere between the mountain and the ant, somewhere and only there as part and parcel of the creation ."

We are of the animal world. We are part of the cycles of growth and decay. Even having tried so hard to see ourselves apart, and so often without a love for even our own biology, we are in relationship with the rest of the planet, and that connectedness tells us we must reconsider the way we see ourselves and the rest of nature.

A change is required of us, a healing of the betrayed trust between humans and earth. Caretaking is the utmost spiritual and physical responsibility of our time, and perhaps that stewardship is finally our place in the web of life, our work, the solution to the mystery of what we are. There are already so many holes in the universe that will never again be filled, and each of them forces us to question why we permitted such loss, such tearing away at the fabric of life, and how we will live with our planet in the future.

Ishi is just one of those losses. Ishi was what he called himself, and the word meant only "man." Ishi kept his real name to himself. It was his only possession, all that remained for him of a lost way of life. He was the last of a kind of human being. His absence left us wondering about these lives of ours that unfold in the center of a tragic technology. When we wake up in the night, full of fear, we know the hole is all around us, pulling at even our dreams. We learn from what has fallen through before us. It's why we study history. It's why I wished a dying woman would balance between the worlds a moment, teetering there, and gaze backward in time to tell me any wise secret of survival. The kill hole where everything falls out is not just found in earth's or the body's clay. It is a dusky space between us and others, the place where our compassion has fallen away, our capacity for love failed. It is the time between times, a breached realm where apes inform us of a truth we fear to face. It is a broken mirror that reveals to us our own shady and dualistic natures and lays bare our human history of cruelty as well as love. What we are lives in that abyss. But we have also to ask if this research is not a great step in creating a bridge across that broken world, if these first explorations between humans and apes are not hands held out in welcome. Some of us have reached out across the solitude of our lives with care and mercy, have touched away the space between us all.

There is a Mandan story that tells how the killed buffalo left through a hole in the sky. From that hole, it's said, the grandmother still looks down at earth, watching over her children.

Today in San Diego, a young California condor is breaking a hole in an egg, pecking its way through to life. There are only twenty-eight California condors left in the world, all of them in captivity. They've been dwelling on the brink of extinction. But how amazing it is, this time a new life coming in, turning another way through that hole. A mending is taking place, a life emerging like the thread out of the labyrinth, the thread leading out of a Navajo rug's pattern of loss. The old woman in the sky is looking down on us, keeping watch.

"HOUSE OF WOOD"

Stephanie Kaza

I have woken up at the end of a long week of tiredness. I am too tired to go anywhere. Too tired to seek out a tree for comfort. Too tired to walk in the forest on the mountain. Too full of the sadness and tenderness that speaks through me as I teach about how we are living with the environment, how we are dying with the environment. It is difficult work to be present with the state of the world. The more I pay attention to the economic and political forces driving environmental deterioration, the less certain I am that anything I do will stop it. My heart aches for the thoughtless deaths of so many trees. Sometimes I long for a break from the destruction and grief.

Here in my home I find some comfort in the beauty and simplicity of this house. I am grateful to be surrounded by wood and by the memory of trees. Wood walls and ceiling, a beautiful oak floor, paned glass and wood windows, kitchen cupboards crafted of wood. From all sides I am embraced by wood. The presence of trees soothes my eyes and soul. The natural warm brown color is restful. It is just what it is, nothing extra. No decorations, no wallpaper, no paint, no layers of anything masking the wood. The simplicity is refreshing. I appreciate the unevenness and random variation of the wood.

All these trees—the oaks in the floor, the firs and redwoods in the walls, the cedar in the yarn chest—are trees of the Pacific forest, trees of my homeland. But here in the house they are quiet and alone, no longer dancing in the wind or singing with the birds. It feels a bit like a tree cemetery—in elegant form, of course. It is hard to think of the wood as dead. It doesn't feel like I live in a house of death. The grain of the wood is too alive. Its memory is too vivid, etched from the experience of lifetimes. I feel the histories of individual trees; they resonate in each beam and board.

One thing is wrong though—the straightness. All of the wood has been cut into straight forms. Trees, however, are not entirely straight, especially the hardwoods. It is convenient to live in this straightness. It makes walking and organizing things easier. It works well with gravity and the desire of the inner ear for balance. But I miss the graceful curves of the living tree. I miss the tangle of branches, the intimate spaces between the twigs and fingers of each limb. Planed surfaces in a house have all the intimacy ironed out of them. They have been flattened, standardized, regulated, cut to conform to human design. In the process the trees' own naturally beautiful shapes have been altered beyond recognition.

So this is the pain of it: in leaving its life-form behind, the wood has become an object for human use. Object—where is the heart in that? An object is something to carry around, to count, to purchase, to collect. It is something separate. The process of objectification begins with the first cut toward straightness. After the trees are felled, the conspiracy of object continues in the timber sales reports, lumberyard accounts, and architectural plans. The carpenters perhaps cradled the wood in their hands as they built this house, but did they remember the once-living trees? I wonder who among the many people who deal with wood as product have walked in the forests of these trees and listened to their voices. When the memory of tree has vanished and the connection is broken, the wood becomes corpse, or not even corpse, but something that appears to have never been alive.

The wood ceiling here is supported by two big crossbeams and pillars. I look up at these beams often because the shape and design are compelling. They form a cross. I look at this cross of wood and imagine a person suspended, connected to the wood. The image of Jesus with downcast head and pierced hands and feet evokes a powerful response of compassion. I can't help but identify with the human agony of his experience.

But what about the wood of the cross? I wonder if Jesus was embraced by the spirit of tree in his painful death. He did not die alone. Even in his last moments he was supported by life. The cross served as a connecting link to the ground, touching the common soil of our lives. Jesus on high hung part way between grounded reality and the mysterious unknown. Many have focused on the transcendent theme of his story, but what about his fundamental connection to the earth through the cross? Is this not an equally valid route to spiritual awakening?

But the cross was only a piece of a tree. Why didn't they nail him to a living tree? Perhaps that would have offered too much life force and spiritual strength. But also the tree represents intimacy; a cross speaks of exposure. This central religious story is about crucifixion of tree as much as crucifixion of person. The curving intimacy of the tree was symbolically replaced by the linear abstraction of the cross. This is the loss I feel—the living tree reduced to objectified pieces, the loss of life as it really is—vivid and unsimplifiable.

In the midst of his own tragic story, I wonder if Jesus noticed the loss of tree life. As a great teacher of compassion and a carpenter himself, I want to believe that Jesus had some care and concern for trees. It seems to me that his gospel of love applies to relationships with trees as well as people. In the story of the crucifixion, the tree did not have any choice in the decision to end its life and to be disfigured in death. The tree did not ask to be sacrificed any more than Jesus did. And the tree could not cry out to others, "My God, my God, why hast Thou forsaken me?" The recorders of history passed on the story of the great wrongdoing to Jesus, but they overlooked the story of the cross.

Gazing at the crossbeams of my house, I am caught by this double crucifixion, and with my culture I still carry the pain and woundedness of both deaths. In studying the story of

Jesus, people ask themselves over and over, what does it mean? Theologians, ministers, ordinary people want to know how this suffering speaks to their lives. It encourages the practice of compassion, forgiveness, and the development of spiritual strength. The story is passed on to others, and the search for meaning stays alive.

The story of the tree is another matter. The loss has barely been noticed. The drama of tree death is repeated over and over again, day after day, decade after decade, century after century. As if in a daze, people permit the continuous execution of millions of tree martyrs, whose crosses become chopsticks, tables, paper, and buildings. I am as much a part of this web of sacrifice as anyone, and that is painful. I cannot find an easy way to live with integrity in the midst of this confusion. I am weary with wondering how much will be destroyed before we find the tree behind Jesus.

PART II

HOW HAVE TRADITIONAL RELIGIONS VIEWED NATURE?

I, the fiery life of divine essence, am aflame beyond the beauty of the meadows, I gleam in the waters, and I burn in the sun, moon, and stars . . . I awaken everything to life.

—Hildegard of Bingen

Pleasant it looked,
this newly created world.
Along the entire length and breadth
of the earth, our grandmother,
extended the green reflection
of her covering and the escaping odors
were pleasant to inhale.

—Winnebago/Native American

Apprehend God in all things,
for God is in all things.
Every single creature is full of God
and is a book about God.
Every creature is a word of God.
If I spent enough time with the tiniest creature—
even a caterpillar—
I would never have to prepare a sermon. So full of God
is every creature.

—Meister Eckhart

Assuredly the creation
of the heavens
And the earth
Is greater
Than the creation of humankind;
Yet most people understand not.

—*Koran*

We sit in the lap of our Mother ... We shall soon pass, but the place where we now rest will last forever.

—Lakota saying

Of all that the Holy One created in His world, He did not create a single thing that is useless.

—Talmud

When a tree that bears fruit is cut down, its moan goes from one end of the world to the other, yet no sound is heard.

—Midrash

Religions help situate human beings in both the natural and the social worlds. The latter function is served by their moral teachings, the former by a combination of creation myths, narrative accounts of the origin of particular phenomenon (for example, death), and norms governing our relation with our natural surroundings. To find out how "traditional" (that is, predating the modern age) religions viewed nature, we must consult a broad range of stories, philosophical accounts and moral teachings. What follows in Part II is a representative sampling from that range, one that supports three tentative generalizations.

First, we see that human beings have taken nature to be something which requires an explanation. The Bible's account of creation, no less than Greek mythology's story of how the change of the seasons began, shows that people have wanted to put the multiplicity, variability and sheer scope of their natural surrounding into a humanly comprehensible framework.

Second, we see that these accounts, for all their diversity, share a common bond: nature is to be made sense of in a way that directly connects it to the fundamental values of human existence. The contrast between the religious view of nature and that of modern (post-sixteenth century) science is thus revealed. For science, the natural world serves as a neutral backdrop to human activities, to be studied, manipulated and mastered at will. It is, as Albert Camus put it, a setting of "benign indifference." To the religious sensibility, the universe is "enchanted": the gift of a loving God, a land destined for a holy people, the cosmic analog of our own mothers, a setting filled with spirit forces who are to be our guardians, or, perhaps, even a temptation to be overcome.

Yet, third, traditional religions represent nature in very different ways. These differences hold within as well as between religions, hardly surprising when we remember for how long and in how many different settings some of these traditions have existed. The notion that people are to "master the earth" (Genesis 1:28), even if interpreted as defining a relation which includes responsibility and care, is different from a view that sees nature as a model for human virtue (as it is at times portrayed in Taoism); or in which animals or parts of the landscape can serve as guides of spiritual development (as in Australian Aboriginal or certain Native American traditions). When in the ancient Sumerian epic, *Gilgamesh,* the hero seeks immortality by destroying the forest (see Harrison's retelling below), we see a bitter anticipation of the contemporary devastation of the rain forest. The teachings of Native Hawaiian religion, by contrast, contain values which may help us achieve a more sane and modest relation to nature.

Selections from original texts and commentary by scholars in Part II reflect the central point that we now read religious traditions in a fundamentally new way: we need to know in what ways they support or obstruct our desperate task of recovering some ecological sanity. The complex nature of our traditions leads to considerable controversy here. Thus some people claim that the view of nature in the Hebrew Bible is supportive of unrestrained domination of nature. Others argue that the Talmudic tradition of Rabbinical Judaism is actually conducive to a restrained and nature-respecting (if not worshipping) form of life. Daniel Swartz's reading of the full historic range of Jewish teachings, and Ginzburg's brief selection from Jewish poetic textual interpretation and biblical retelling (Midrash) reveal a rich and multifaceted tradition—one not easily summarized as having any single attitude toward nature.

A number of critics have suggested that the environmental destruction flowing from European science, industrial capitalism and colonialism is particularly compatible with Europe's dominant religion. And some writers have suggested that there is a more nature-respecting view in Chinese, Indian, African or indigenous religions. In David Kinsley's selection, however, we see that Christianity—like Judaism—shows a variety of faces towards nature.

Assessing the environmental viability of different religious traditions is a central task of this book. In this section, alongside the examination of Judaism and Christianity, there are writings from or discussions of Native American, Hindu, African, Islamic, Buddhist, Hawaiian, and Chinese ways of imagining and understanding the natural world.

To make matters more complicated still: the enormous variability of religious attitudes towards nature may lead us to wonder if the conduct of religious institutions about the environment at any particular time is as much a product of the general culture, politics and economic structure of the wider society as it is of the religions themselves.

"THE CREATION"

Fanetorens (Ray Fadden)

 Many Winters in the past (arrow going backward)

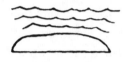 the Earth was entirely covered by a great blanket of water. There was no sun, moon, or stars and so there was no light. All was darkness.

 At that time, the only living creatures of the world were water animals such as the beaver, muskrat, duck and loon.

 Far above earth was the Land of Happy Spirits where lived Rawennio, the Great Ruler. In the center of this upper world was a giant tree.

 This great tree was an apple tree whose roots sank deep into the ground.

 One day, Rawennio pulled this giant tree up by its roots.

 The Great Spirit called his daughter who lived in the Upper World and commanded her to look into the pit caused by the uprooted tree.

Reprinted with permission from *Akwesasne Notes* (1972 and 1992).

This woman, who was to be the mother of the Good and Evil Spirits, came and looked into the hole by the uprooted tree.

She saw far below her the Lower World covered with water and surrounded by heavy clouds.

"You are to go to this world of darkness," said the Great Spirit. Gently lifting her, he dropped her into the hole.

She floated downward.

Far below on the dark water floated the water animals. Looking upward, they saw a great light, which was the Sky Woman, slowly falling toward them.

Because her body shone as a great light they were at first frightened.

Fear filled their hearts and they dove beneath the deep waters.

But upon coming to the surface again, they lost their fear. They began to plan what they would do for the woman when she reached the water.

"We must find a dry place for her to rest on," said the beaver, and he plunged beneath the water in search of some earth. After a long time, the beaver's dead body floated to the top of the water.

The loon tried next, but his body never came to the surface of the water. Many of the other water creatures dived, but all failed to secure any earth.

Finally, the muskrat went below and after a long time, his dead body floated to the surface of the water. His little claws were closed tight. Upon opening them, a little earth was found.

Fanetorens (Ray Fadden)   51

The water creatures took this earth, and calling a great turtle, they patted the earth firmly on her broad back. Immediately, the turtle started to grow larger. The earth also increased.

This earth became North America, a great island. Sometimes the earth cracks and shakes, and waves beat hard against the seashore. White people say, "Earthquake." The Mohawk say, "Turtle is stretching."

The Sky Woman had now almost reached the earth. "We must fly up and let her rest upon our backs so as to make her landing easy," said the chief of the white swans. Flying upward, a great flock of white swans allowed the Sky Woman to rest upon their backs. Gently, they bore her to earth.

After a time, the Sky Woman gave birth to twins. One who became the Good Spirit was born first. The other, the Evil Spirit, while being born, caused his mother so much pain that she died during his birth.

The Good Spirit immediately took his mother's head and hung it in the sky. It became the sun. The Good Spirit, from his mother's body, fashioned the moon and stars and placed them in the sky.

The rest of his mother's body he buried under the earth. That is why living things find nourishment from the soil. They spring from Mother Earth.

The Evil Spirit put darkness in the west sky to drive the sun before it.

The Good Spirit created many things which he placed upon the earth. The Evil Spirit tried to undo the work of his brother by creating evil. The Good Spirit made tall and beautiful trees such as the pine and hemlock.

Fanetorens (Ray Fadden)

The Evil Spirit stunted some trees. In others, he put knots and gnarls. He covered some with thorns, and placed poison fruit on them.

The Good Spirit made animals such as the deer and the bear.

The Evil Spirit made poisonous animals, lizards, and serpents to destroy the animals of the Good Spirit's creation.

The Good Spirit made springs and streams of good, pure water.

The Evil Spirit breathed poison into many of the springs. He put snakes into others.

The Good Spirit made beautiful rivers protected by high hills.

The Evil Spirit pushed rocks and dirt into the rivers causing the current to become swift and dangerous. Everything that the Good Spirit made, his wicked brother tried to destroy.

Finally, when the earth was completed, the Good Spirit fashioned man out of some red clay. He placed man upon the earth, and told him how he should live. The Evil Spirit, not to be outdone, fashioned a creature out of the white foam of the sea. What he made was the monkey.

After mankind and the other creatures of the world were created, the Good Spirit bestowed a protecting spirit upon each of his creations.

Fanetorens (Ray Fadden)   53

He then called the Evil Spirit, and told him that he must cease making trouble upon the earth. This the Evil Spirit refused to do. The Good Spirit became very angry with his wicked brother. He challenged his brother to combat, the victor to become ruler of the earth. They used the thorns of a giant apple tree as weapons.

They fought for many suns (days).

Finally, the Evil Spirit was overcome.

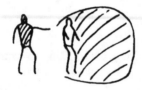

The Good Spirit now became ruler over the earth. He banished his wicked brother to a dark cave under the earth. There he must always remain.

But the Evil Spirit has wicked servants who roam the earth. These wicked spirits can take the shape of any creature that the Evil Spirit desires them to take. They are constantly influencing the minds of men, thus causing men to do evil things.

That is why every person has both a bad heart and a good heart. No matter how good a man seems, he has some evil. No matter how bad a man seems, there is some good about him. No man is perfect.

The Good Spirit continues to create and protect mankind. He controls the spirits of good men after death. The Evil Spirit takes charge of the souls of wicked men after death.

"DEATH AND REBIRTH OF THE UNIVERSE" *(Hindu)*;

"THE PARADE OF ANTS" *(Hindu)*;

"THE FIVE SUNS" *(Aztec)*;

"PERSEPHONE" *(Greek)*

Joseph L. Henderson and Maud Oakes

DEATH AND REBIRTH OF THE UNIVERSE (HINDU)[1]

The cosmic unit of time, according to Hindu mythical astronomy, is the Kalpa, or a day of Brahma the creator. Brahma creates in the morning, and at night the three worlds, ... Earth, Heaven and Hell, are reduced to chaos, every being that has not obtained liberation retaining its essence which takes form according to its Karma, when Brahma wakes up in the morning. Thus the eventful days and nights pass on, till Brahma reaches the hundredth year of his life when "not only the three worlds but all planes and all beings, Brahma himself, Devas, Rishis, Asuras, men, creatures and matter" are all resolved into Mahapralaya (the great cataclysm). After a hundred years of chaos, another Brahma is born.... A Kalpa or day of Brahma is equivalent to 4,320,000,000 earth years....

The manner of destruction of the world at the end of the Kaliyuga[2] is differently described in the Puranas. In one account it is related that Vishnu will appear as Kalki, "an armed warrior, mounted on a white horse, furnished with wings and adorned with jewels, waving over his head with one hand the sword of destruction and holding in the other a disc.

The horse is represented as holding up the right fore-leg; and when he stamps on the earth with that, the tortoise supporting the serpent Shesha on whose hood the world rests, shall fall into the deep, and so rid himself of the load; and by that means all the wicked inhabitants of the world will be destroyed."

In the Bhagbata we are told that the "age of destruction is so horrible that during it the clouds never fall on the earth as drops of rain for one hundred years. The people then find no food to eat . . . and are compelled to eat one another. Being thus overpowered by what is wrought by time, the men gradually lead themselves to utter destruction."

Elsewhere the universal cataclysm is predicted in vivid detail. "After a drought lasting many years, seven blazing suns will appear in the firmament; they will drink up all the waters. Then the wind-driven fire will sweep over the earth, consuming all things; penetrating to the netherworld it will destroy what is there in a moment; it will burn up the universe. Afterwards many coloured and brilliant clouds will collect in the sky looking like herds of elephants decked with wreaths of lightning. Suddenly they will burst asunder, and rain will fall incessantly for twelve years until the whole world . . . is covered with water. The clouds will vanish. Then the self-created lord, the first cause of everything, will absorb the winds and go to sleep. The universe will become one dread expanse of water."

"THE PARADE OF ANTS" (HINDU) [3]

During the period of the supremacy of the dragon, the majestic mansions of the lofty city of the gods had cracked and crumbled. The first act of Indra was to rebuild them. All the divinities of the heavens were acclaiming him their savior. Greatly elated in his triumph [over the dragon] and in the knowledge of his strength, he summoned Vishvakarman, the god of arts and crafts, and commanded him to erect such a palace as should befit the unequaled splendor of the king of the gods.

The miraculous genius, Vishvakarman, succeeded in constructing in a single year a shining residence, marvelous with palaces and gardens, lakes and towers. But as the work progressed, the demands of Indra became even more exacting and his unfolding visions vaster. He required additional terraces and pavilions, more ponds, groves, and pleasure grounds. Whenever Indra arrived to appraise the work, he developed vision beyond vision of marvels remaining to be contrived. Presently the divine craftsman, brought to despair, decided to seek succor from above. He would turn to the demiurgic creator, Brahma, the pristine embodiment of the Universal Spirit, who abides far above the troubled Olympian sphere of ambition, strife, and glory.

When Vishvakarman secretly resorted to the higher throne and presented his case, Brahma comforted the petitioner. "You will soon be relieved of your burden," he said. "Go home in peace." Then, while Vishvakarman was hurrying down again to the city of Indra, Brahma himself ascended to a still higher sphere. He came before Vishnu, the Supreme Being,

Joseph L. Henderson and Maud Oakes

of whom he himself, the Creator, was but an agent. In beatific silence Vishnu gave ear, and by a mere nod of the head let it be known that the request of Vishvakarman would be fulfilled.

Early next morning a brahmin boy, carrying the staff of a pilgrim, made his appearance at the gate of Indra, bidding the porter announce his visit to the king. The gate-man hurried to the master, and the master hastened to the entrance to welcome in person the auspicious guest. The boy was slender, some ten years old, radiant with the luster of wisdom. Indra discovered him amidst a cluster of enraptured, staring children. The boy greeted the host with a gentle glance of his dark and brilliant eyes. The king bowed to the holy child and the boy cheerfully gave his blessing. The two retired to the hall of Indra, where the god ceremoniously proffered welcome to his guest with oblations of honey, milk, and fruits, then said: "O Venerable Boy, tell me of the purpose of your coming."

The beautiful child replied with a voice that was as deep and soft as the slow thundering of auspicious rain clouds. "O King of Gods, I have heard of the mighty palace you are building, and have come to refer to you the questions in my mind. How many years will it require to complete this rich and extensive residence? What further feats of engineering will Vishvakarman be expected to accomplish? O Highest of Gods,"—the boy's luminous features moved with a gentle, scarcely perceptible smile—"no Indra before you has ever succeeded in completing such a palace as yours is to be."

Full of the wine of triumph, the king of the gods was entertained by this mere boy's pretension to a knowledge of Indras earlier than himself. With a fatherly smile he put the question: "Tell me, Child! Are they then so very many, the Indras and Vishvakarmans whom you have seen—or at least whom you have heard of?"

The wonderful guest calmly nodded. "Yes, indeed, many have I seen." The voice was as warm and sweet as milk fresh from the cow, but the words sent a slow chill through Indra's veins. "My dear child," the boy continued, "I knew your father, Kashyapa, the Old Tortoise Man, lord and progenitor of all the creatures of the earth. And I knew your grandfather, Marichi, Beam of Celestial Light, who was the son of Brahma. Marichi was begotten of the god Brahma's pure spirit; his only wealth and glory were his sanctity and devotion. Also, I know Brahma, brought forth by Vishnu from the lotus calix growing from Vishnu's navel. And Vishnu himself—the Supreme Being, supporting Brahma in his creative endeavor—him too I know."

"O King of Gods, I have known the dreadful dissolution of the universe. I have seen all perish, again and again, at the end of every cycle. At that terrible time, every single atom dissolves into the primal, pure waters of eternity, whence originally all arose. Everything then goes back into the fathomless, wild infinity of the ocean, which is covered with utter darkness and is empty of every sign of animate being. Ah, who will count the universes that have passed away, or the creations that have risen afresh, again and again, from the formless abyss of the vast waters? Who will number the passing ages of the world, as they follow each other endlessly? And who will search through the wide infinities of space to count the universes side by side, each containing its Brahma, its Vishnu, and its Shiva? Who will count the Indras in them all—those Indras side by side, who reign at once in all the innumerable worlds; those others who passed away before them; or even the Indras who succeed each other in any given line, ascending to godly kingship, one by one, and, one by one, passing away? King of Gods, there are among your servants certain who maintain that it may be possible to number the grains of sand on earth and the drops of rain that fall from the sky, but no one will ever number all those Indras. This is what the Knowers know.

"The life and kingship of an Indra endure seventy-one eons, and when twenty-eight Indras have expired, one Day and Night of Brahma has elapsed. But the existence of one Brahma, measured in such Brahma Days and Nights, is only one hundred and eight years. Brahma follows Brahma; one sinks, the next arises; the endless series cannot be told. There is no end to the number of those Brahmas—to say nothing of Indras.

"But the universes side by side at any given moment, each harboring a Brahma and an Indra: who will estimate the number of these? Beyond the farthest vision, crowding outer space, the universes come and go, an innumerable host. Like delicate boats they float on the fathomless, pure waters that form the body of Vishnu. Out of every hair-pore of that body a universe bubbles and breaks. Will you presume to count them? Will you number the gods in all those worlds—the worlds present and the worlds past?"

A procession of ants had made its appearance in the hall during the discourse of the boy. In military array, in a column four yards wide, the tribe paraded across the floor. The boy noted them, paused, and stared, then suddenly laughed with an astonishing peal, but immediately subsided into a profoundly indrawn and thoughtful silence.

"Why do you laugh?" stammered Indra. "Who are you, mysterious being, under this deceiving guise of a boy?" The proud king's throat and lips had gone dry, and his voice continually broke. "Who are you, Ocean of Virtues, enshrouded in deluding mist?"

The magnificent boy resumed: "I laughed because of the ants. The reason is not to be told. Do not ask me to disclose it. The seed of woe and the fruit of wisdom are enclosed within this secret. It is the secret that smites with an ax the tree of worldly vanity, hews away its roots, and scatters its crown. This secret is a lamp to those groping in ignorance. This secret lies buried in the wisdom of the ages, and is rarely revealed even to saints. This secret is the living air of those ascetics who renounce and transcend mortal existence; but worldlings, deluded by desire and pride, it destroys."

The boy smiled and sank into silence. Indra regarded him, unable to move. "O Son of a brahmin," the king pleaded presently, with a new and visible humility, "I do not know who you are. You would seem to be Wisdom Incarnate. Reveal to me this secret of the ages, this light that dispels the dark."

Thus requested to teach, the boy opened to the god the hidden wisdom. "I saw the ants, O Indra, filing in long parade. Each was once an Indra. Like you, each by virtue of pious deeds once ascended to the rank of a king of gods. But now, through many rebirths, each has become again an ant. This army is an army of former Indras."

"Piety and high deeds elevate the inhabitants of the world to the glorious realm of the celestial mansions, or to the higher domains of Brahma and Shiva and to the highest sphere of Vishnu; but wicked acts sink them into the worlds beneath, into pits of pain and sorrow, involving reincarnation among birds and vermin, or out of the wombs of pigs and animals of the wild, or among trees, or among insects. It is by deeds that one merits happiness or anguish, and becomes a master or a serf. It is by deeds that one attains to the rank of a king or brahmin, or of some god, or of an Indra or a Brahma. And through deeds again, one contracts disease, acquires beauty and deformity, or is reborn in the condition of a monster.

"This is the whole substance of the secret. This wisdom is the ferry to beatitude across the ocean of hell.

"Life in the cycle of the countless rebirths is like a vision in a dream. The gods on high, the mute trees and the stones, are alike apparitions in this phantasy. But Death administers the law of time. Ordained by time, Death is the master of all. Perishable as bubbles are the good and evil of the beings of the dream. In unending cycles the good and evil alternate. Hence, the wise are attached to neither, neither the evil nor the good. The wise are not attached to anything at all."

The boy concluded the appalling lesson and quietly regarded his host. The king of gods, for all his celestial splendor, had been reduced in his own regard to insignificance.... [Then] the brahmin boy, who had been Vishnu, disappeared.... The king was alone, baffled and amazed.

"THE FIVE SUNS" (AZTEC)[4]

The Aztec gods were givers of the laws of nature. In this tale, their struggles give rise to the death and rebirth of the universe. The well-known Aztec Calendar Stone called "Eagle Bowl" is an image of a cosmic cycle (Plate 3). On it are carved the symbols of the five suns.

The nocturnal Tezcatlipoca,[5] whose *nahual* or disguise is the jaguar, its spotted skin resembling the heavens with their myriad stars, was the first to become a sun, and with him began the first era of the world. The first men created by the gods were giants; they neither sowed grain nor tilled the soil, but lived by eating acorns and other fruits and wild roots. Tezcatlipoca was also the constellation of Ursa Major, whom the Aztecs pictured as a jaguar. While he was ruling the world as the sun, his enemy, Quetzalcoatl, struck him a blow with his staff. Tezcatlipoca fell into the water, changing into a jaguar. He devoured the giants, and the earth was depopulated and the universe was without a sun. This occurred on the day called "Jaguar."

Then Quetzalcoatl became the sun, until the jaguar struck him down with a blow of his paw. Then a great wind arose, and all the trees were uprooted, and the greater part of mankind perished. Those men who survived were transformed into monkeys, that is, into subhuman creatures. This took place on the day "Wind." Men at that time ate only pine nuts or *acocentli*. The creator gods then chose Tlaloc, the god of rain and celestial fire, as the sun, but Quetzalcoatl made the fire rain down, and men either perished or were changed into birds. This happened on the day "4 Rain." The sustenance of men during this age was a seed called *acecentli*, or "water corn."

Then Quetzacoatl selected Tlaloc's sister as the sun. She was the goddess Chalchiuhtlicue, "the lady of the jade skirts," goddess of water. But no doubt it was Tezcatlipoca who caused it to rain so hard that the earth was flooded and men either perished or were transformed into fish. This occurred on the day called "4 Water." During this age men ate . . . *teocentli,* the ancestor of corn.[6]

Laurette Sejourne believes that there were five suns. The face in the centre of the Calendar Stone is the face of Quetzalcoatl, our present sun.

That is why the Fifth Sun (five is the number of the centre), is the Sun of Movement [earthquake], . . . "The name of this Sun is Naollin (Four Movements), now is ours, by which today we live. . . . It was also the Sun of Quetzalcoatl. . . ."

This sun, whose emblem is a human face, not only represents the central region, but also what is above and what is below, that is, heaven and earth. The symbol of the world is thus brought together in a cross.

"PERSEPHONE" (GREEK)[7]

Persephone, . . . was in the Nysian plain with the Ocean nymphs gathering flowers. She plucked the rose, the violet, . . . when she beheld a narcissus of surprising size and beauty, an object of amazement . . . for one hundred flowers grew from one root; unconscious of danger the maiden stretched forth her hand to seize the wondrous flower, when suddenly the wide earth gaped, Hades in his gold chariot rose, and catching the terrified goddess carried her off in it shrieking to her father for aid, unheard and unseen by gods or mortals, save only Hecate, . . . who heard her as she sat in her cave, and by king Helios, whose eye nothing on earth escapes.

So long as the goddess beheld the earth and starry heavens, the fishy sea and the beams of the sun, so long she hoped to see her mother and the tribes of the gods; and the tops of the mountains and the depth of the sea resounded with her divine voice. At length her mother heard: she tore her head-attire with grief, cast a dark robe around her, and like a bird hurried "over moist and dry." Of all she inquired tidings of her lost daughter, but neither gods nor men nor birds could give her intelligence. Nine days she wandered over the earth, with flaming torches in her hands; she tasted not of nectar or ambrosia, and never once entered the bath. On the tenth morning Hecate met her.... Together they proceed to Helios:... and Demeter entreats that he will say who the ravisher is. The god of the sun,... tells her that it was Hades, who by permission of her sire had carried her [Persephone] away to be his queen;...

... the goddess, incensed at the conduct of Zeus, abandoned the society of the gods, and came down among men. But now she was heedless of her person, and no one recognized her. Under the disguise of an old woman,... she came to Eleusis, and sat ... by a well, beneath the shade of an olive tree....

The Princess Kallidike [who had come to the well to draw water] tells the goddess ... to wait till she had consulted her mother, Metaneira, who had a young son in the cradle, of whom, if the stranger could obtain the nursing her fortune would be made; ... [Metaneira] agreed to hire the nurse at large wages; ... As she entered the house a divine splendor shone all around.... She undertook the rearing of the babe,... beneath her care "he throve like a god." ...

It was the design of Demeter to make him immortal, but the curiosity and folly of Metaneira deprived him of the intended gift.... Demeter tells who she is, and directs that the people of Eleusis should raise an altar and temple to her ... and the temple was speedily raised. The mourning goddess took up her abode in it, but a dismal year came upon mankind; the earth yielded no produce, ... in vain was the seed of barley cast into the ground; "well-garlanded Demeter" would suffer no increase. The whole race of man ran risk of perishing, the dwellers of Olympos of losing gifts and sacrifices, had not Zeus discerned the danger and thought on a remedy. He ... invites Demeter back to Olympos, but the disconsolate goddess will not comply with the call.... she will not ascend to Olympos, or suffer the earth to bring forth, till she has seen her daughter. (*Plate* 14.)

... Zeus sends ... [Hermes] to Erebos, to endeavor to prevail on Hades to suffer Persephone to return to the light.... he [Hermes] quickly reached the "secret places of earth," and found the king at home ... with his wife, who was mourning for her mother. On making known to Hades the wish of Zeus, "the king of the Subterraneans smiled with his brows" and yielded compliances. He kindly addressed Persephone, granting her permission to return to her mother. The goddess instantly sprang up with joy, and heedlessly swallowed a grain of pomegranate which he presented to her.

Hermes conducted his fair charge safe to Eleusis ... and Persephone sprang from the car to meet and embrace her mother....

Demeter anxiously inquired if her daughter had tasted anything while below; . . . if but one morsel had passed her lips, nothing could save her from spending one-third of the year with her husband; she should however pass the other two with her and the gods.

Persephone ingenuously confesses the swallowing of the grain of pomegranate, and then relates to her mother the whole story. . . . Zeus sends Rhea to invite them back to heaven. Demeter now complies.

NOTES

1. P. Thomas, *Epics, Myths and Legends of India* (8th ed.; Bombay: D. B. Taraporevala Sons & Co., Ltd., n.d.). p. 4-6.

2. The day of Brahma is divided into 1,000 Mahayugas (great ages) of equal length, each consisting of four Yugas; namely, Krita, Threta, Dwapara, and Kali. Kaliyuga is the present age of degeneration (and consists of 432,000 years).

3. Heinrich Zimmer, *Myths and Symbols in Indian Art and Civilization,* (Princeton: Princeton University Press, 1971), pp. 3-10.

4. Alfonso Caso, *The Aztecs,* tr. Lowell Dunham (Norman, Oklahoma: University of Oklahoma Press, 1958), pp. 14-15.

5. Tezcatlipoca . . . signified the noctural cycle and was connected with the moon and all stellar gods, hence he brought misfortune, death, and destruction, and war associated with witchcraft.

6. Another legend reverses the order of the suns.

7. L. Schmitz, *Keightley's Classical Mythology* (London: G. Bell & Sons, 1896), pp. 152–56.

from FORESTS: THE SHADOW OF CIVILIZATION

Robert Pogue Harrison

Gilgamesh was the legendary but real king of Uruk, a Sumerian city born under the auspices of Anu—god of the sky. He lived during the Early Dynastic II period, around 2700 B.C., some six hundred years before the composition of the first Sumerian epics that commemorate him. In the Sumerian and Babylonian literature Gilgamesh is commonly referred to as the "builder of the walls of Uruk." The epitaph effectively summarizes his civic heroism. Walls, no less than writing, define civilization. They are monuments of resistance against time, like writing itself, and Gilgamesh is remembered by them. Walls protect, divide, distinguish; above all, they *abstract*. The basic activities that sustain life—agriculture and stock breeding, for instance—take place beyond the walls. Within the walls one is within an emporium; one is within the jurisdiction of a bureaucracy; one is within the abstract identity of race, city, and institutionalized religion; in short, one is within the lonely enclosure of history. Gilgamesh is the builder of such walls that divide history from prehistory, culture from nature, sky from earth, life from death, memory from oblivion.

But the same walls that individuate the city, as well its hero, are precisely what oppress Gilgamesh, at least insofar as the epic cycle portrays him. Within his walls Gilgamesh finds himself exposed to insidious reminders of the fatality of personal death—the linear finality of human existence. It is in direct response to his aggravated sense of transience that Gilgamesh decides to undertake his forest journey. In the following passage from Samuel Noah Kramer's translation of "Gilgamesh and the Land of the Living," we hear Gilgamesh declaring to his friend Enkidu that he would perform some glorious deed by which he may inscribe himself within the annals of historical memory:

> O Enkidu, not (yet) have brick and stamp brought forth the fated end,
> I would enter the "land," I would set up my name,
> In its places where the names have been raised up, I would raise up my name,
> In its places where the names have not been raised up, I would raise up the names of the gods.
> (4–7)

The "land" where Gilgamesh would go and set up his name is the forested Cedar Mountain. Because he has not yet achieved a lasting fame, because he has not yet *stamped his name in brick* (or in the tablets of the scribes), Gilgamesh must go to the "land" and slay the forest demon, Huwawa. This is the deed that will monumentalize him in stone or brick—preserve his memory after death.

But again, why precisely a forest journey? Before we can answer the question we should listen to Gilgamesh's plea to Utu, the Sumerian Sun god. Utu is the god who must grant Gilgamesh the permission to undertake the journey, for the land is in Utu's charge. The god does not understand Gilgamesh's irrational desire to go to the land, nor does he initially approve of the idea. Huwawa, whom Gilgamesh would slay, is after all a sacred forest demon. Utu does not understand why Gilgamesh wishes to challenge the demon. To convince the god of his desperate need to undertake the journey, Gilgamesh offers a pathetic confession:

> "O Utu, I would enter the 'land,' be thou my ally,
> I would enter the land *of the cut-down* cedar, be thou my ally."
> Utu of heaven answers him:
> "... verily thou art, but what art thou to the 'land'?"
> "O Utu, a word I would speak to thee, to my word thy ear,
> *I would have it reach thee,* give ear to it.
> In my city man dies, oppressed is the heart,
> Man perishes, heavy is the heart,
> I *peered over* the wall,
> Saw the dead bodies ... *floating on* the river;
> As for me, I too will be served thus; verily 'tis so.
> Man, the tallest, cannot stretch to heaven,
> Man the widest, cannot *cover* the earth.
> Not (*yet*) *have brick and stamp* brought forth *the fated end,*
> I would enter the 'land,' I would set up my name." (17–31)

In ancient Sumerian funeral rites, the bodies of the dead were floated down the river in ceremonious processions. Gilgamesh has peered over the walls of his city and has seen the bodies floating on the river. In other words he has seen beyond life to the inanimate corpse—the mere object drifting toward decomposition and reintegration with the earth. He has peered over the wall of history and seen the remorseless transcendence of nature. With despair in his heart he has looked at the outlying earth: dumb, inert, insurmountable, revolving her relentless cycles, turning kings into cadavers, waiting impassively to draw all things into her oblivion. Is this not intolerable for someone who is a builder of walls, someone who is devoted to the memorial transcendence of history? Must Gilgamesh not react to the scene of dead bodies floating on the river by challenging such oblivion with the might of memory?

We come closer to accounting psychologically for Gilgamesh's desire to undertake the forest journey. He wants the glory of his deed to spare him from such oblivion. But what glory is there in slaying the forest demon? When Gilgamesh obtains the necessary permission from Utu for his journey, he arrives at the sacred cedar forests and engages Huwawa in battle, cutting off the demon's head. The cutting off of Huwawa's head represents, in its poetic image, the cutting down of the cedar forest. The "glory" of this exploit can be understood only against the historical background. We know from the written records that certain Sumerian individuals actually achieved considerable fame by undertaking expeditions to the cedar forests and seizing huge quantities of timber. Timber was a precious commodity for the Sumerians, since the alluvial plains of Mesopotamia were by that time devoid of forests. In the Early Dynastic periods the Sumerians apparently got their timber from the east, in nearby Elam, but after the deforestation of these regions they had to travel much further to the Amanus mountains in the north. To obtain wood they had to undertake dangerous expeditions to the mountains, cut down the cedars and pines, and ferry the logs back to the cities down the rivers. Such exploits were fraught with peril, especially since the forests were often defended by fierce forest tribes, but a leader could derive considerable fame from a successful expedition.

We can understand, therefore, why Gilgamesh's desire for monumental fame might lead him to conceive of a forest expedition. But the epic probes the hero's psychological motivations much deeper than this. There is more to Gilgamesh's inspiration than mere childish heroism and desire for fame through adventure. If Gilgamesh resolves to kill the forest demon, or to deforest the Cedar Mountain, it is because forests represent the quintessence of what lies beyond the walls of the city, namely the earth in its enduring transcendence. Forests embody another, more ancient law than the law of civilization. When Gilgamesh declares to Utu, "Man, the tallest, cannot stretch to heaven," he avows that human beings, however great, cannot become gods, or attain immortality. And when he declares: "Man the widest, cannot *cover* the earth," he avows that neither can they be like forests, which cover the earth and endure through the millennia according to their own self-regenerating cycles. Gilgamesh, in other words, is trapped within walls that close him off from two dimensions of transcendence, the one vertical and the other horizontal.

Gilgamesh journeys toward the forest as toward the veritable frontier of civilization. The forest is the counterpart of his city. He imagines perhaps that he could transcend the walls that enclose him through an act of massive deforestation. But to understand the hero's deeper psychological motivations we must try to imagine what really goes on in his mind when he peers over the walls of Uruk.

Gilgamesh peers over the walls and sees human bodies floating down the river in funeral processions. The sight of these bodies inspires in him the idea of a forest expedition. It is a visionary moment for Gilgamesh. In revolt against the scene of finitude, Gilgamesh has a vision: he will go to the forests, cut down the trees, and send the logs down the river to the city. In other words, he will make the trees share the fate of those who live within the walls. *Logs will become the cadavers.* The hero who dies within the city will project his own personal fate onto the forests. This is no doubt what Gilgamesh means when he says that he would enter the land and raise up his name. For if he is not wide enough to "cover the earth," yet may he still uncover it.

It is a sorry fact of history that human beings have never ceased reenacting the gesture of Gilgamesh. The destructive impulse with respect to nature all too often has psychological causes that go beyond the greed for material resource or the need to domesticate an environment. There is too often a deliberate rage and vengefulness at work in the assault on nature and its species, as if one would project onto the natural world the intolerable anxieties of finitude which hold humanity hostage to death. There is a kind of childish furor that needs to create victims without in order to exorcise the pathos of victimage within. The epic of *Gilgamesh* tells the story of such furor; but while Gilgamesh ends up as the ultimate victim of his own despair, the logs meanwhile float down the river like bodies of the dead.

From the epic cycle as a whole in its Sumerian and Akkadian versions, we gather that Gilgamesh's expedition to the Cedar Mountain was in fact a vain attempt to overcome the source of his afflictions. To begin with, the slaying of Huwawa angers the gods. It was a sacrilege, for Huwawa had the dignity of a sacred being. In some versions of the story, Gilgamesh's beloved friend, Enkidu, must pay for the crime of killing Huwawa with his own life. Upon the death of his friend Gilgamesh falls into an exacerbated state of melancholy, consuming himself with thoughts about death. Fame and the monuments of memory no longer console him for the fact of dying. That is why Gilgamesh sets out on another journey, this time in search of everlasting life. Yet the long and desperate quest for personal immortality only leads him to the knowledge that death is the ineluctable and nonnegotiable condition of life—that the cadaverous logs he sent down to the city from the Cedar Mountain cannot spare him his last journey of all down the very same river. And this, at the dawn of civilization, is called "wisdom."

from THE *TAO TE CHING*

Lao Tzu

ONE

Tao, the path of subtle truth,
cannot be conveyed with words.
That which can be conveyed with words
is merely a relative conception.
Although names have been applied to it,
the subtle truth is indescribable.
One may designate Nothingness as the origin of the universe,
And Beingness as the mother of the myriad things.
From the perspective of Nothingness,
one may perceive the gentle operation of the universe.
From the perspective of Beingness,
one may distinguish individual things.
Although differently named,
Nothingness and Beingness are one indivisible whole.
The truth is so subtle.
As the ultimate subtlety, it is the Gate of All Wonders.

FOUR

The gentle Way of the universe appears to be empty,
yet its usefulness is inexhaustible.
Fathomless, it could be the origin of all things.
It has no sharpness,
yet it rounds off all sharp edges.
It has no form,
yet it unties all tangles.
It has no glare,

Reprinted from *The Complete Works of Lao Tzu: Tao Te Ching and Hua Hu Ching* translated by Hua-Ching Ni, 1979, with permission of Seven Star Communications.

yet it merges all lights.
It harmonizes all things
and unites them as one integral whole.
It seems so obscure,
yet it is the Ultimate Clarity.
Whose offspring it is can never be known.
It is that which existed before any divinity.

FIVE

The virtue of the universe is wholeness.
It regards all things as equal.
The virtue of the sage is wholeness.
He too regards all things as equal.
The universe may be compared to a bellows.
It is empty,
yet it never fails to generate.
The more it moves,
the more it brings forth.
Many words lead one nowhere.
Many pursuits in different directions
only bring about exhaustion.
Rather, embrace the profound emptiness
and silence within.

SIX

The subtle essence of the universe is eternal.
It is like an unfailing fountain of life which
flows forever in a vast and profound valley.
It is called the Primal Female, the Mysterious Origin.
The operation of the opening and closing
of the subtle Gate of the Origin performs
the Mystical Intercourse of the universe.
The Mystical Intercourse brings forth all things
from the unseen sphere into the realm of the manifest.
The Mystical Intercourse of yin and yang
is the root of universal life.
Its creativity and effectiveness are boundless.

TEN

Can you always embrace Oneness
without the slightest separation of body and mind?
Can you maintain undivided concentration
until your vital force is as supple as a newborn baby's?
Can you clarify your inner vision to be flawless?
Can you love your people and serve your state
with no self-exaltation?
As Life's Gate opens and closes
in the performance of birth and death,
Can you maintain the receptive, feminine principle?
After achieving the crystal clear mind,
can you remain detached and innocent?
Give birth to and nourish all things
without desiring to possess them.
Give of yourself,
without expecting something in return.
Assist people, but do not attempt to control them.
This is to realize the integral virtue of the universe.

ELEVEN

Thirty spokes together make a wheel for a cart.
It is the empty space in the center
of the wheel which enables it to be used.
Mold clay into a vessel;
it is the emptiness within
that creates the usefulness of the vessel.
Cut out doors and windows in a house;
it is the empty space inside
that creates the usefulness of the house.
Thus, what we have may be something substantial,
But its usefulness lies in the unoccupied, empty space.
The substance of your body is enlivened
by maintaining the part of you that is unoccupied.

THIRTY-FOUR

Tao, the subtle energy of the universe,
is omnipresent.
It may go to the left or the right.
All things derive their life from it,
and it holds nothing back from them,
Yet it takes possession of nothing.
It accomplishes its purpose,
but it claims no merit.
It clothes and feeds all,
but has no ambition to be master over anyone.
Thus it may be regarded as 'the Small.'
All things return to it, and it contains them,
Yet it claims no authority over them.
Thus it may be recognized as 'the Great.'
The wise one who never attempts
to be emotionally great
And who accomplishes each small task with full devotion,
as if it were the greatest of tasks
Is naturally recognized as great.

SEVENTY-TWO

When people lack a sense of pure spiritual piety
toward natural life,
then awful things happen in their life.
Therefore, respect where you dwell.
Love your life and livelihood.
Because you do not disparage
your life and livelihood,
You will never become tired of life.
Thus, one of whole virtue respects his own life,
But is not egotistical.
He loves his life, but does not exalt himself.
He holds a sense of spiritual serenity for all things,
and disparages nothing.
Hence, he does what is right
and gives up what is not right.

from THE HEBREW BIBLE

GENESIS

1 When God began to create heaven and earth—[2]the earth being unformed and void, with darkness over the surface of the deep and a wind from God sweeping over the water—[3] God said, "Let there be light"; and there was light. [4]God saw that the light was good, and God separated the light from the darkness. [5]God called the light Day, and the darkness He called Night. And there was evening and there was morning, a first day.

[6]God said, "Let there be an expanse in the midst of the water, that it may separate water from water." [7]God made the expanse, and it separated the water which was below the expanse from the water which was above the expanse. And it was so. [8]God called the expanse Sky. And there was evening and there was morning, a second day.

[9]God said, "Let the water below the sky be gathered into one area, that the dry land may appear." And it was so. [10]God called the dry land Earth, and the gathering of waters He called Seas. And God saw that this was good. [11]And God said, "Let the earth sprout vegetation: seed-bearing plants, fruit trees of every kind on earth that bear fruit with the seed in it." And it was so. [12]The earth brought forth vegetation: seed-bearing plants of every kind, and trees of every kind bearing fruit with the seed in it. And God saw that this was good. [13]And there was evening and there was morning, a third day.

[14]God said, "Let there be lights in the expanse of the sky to separate day from night; they shall serve as signs for the set times—the days and the years; [15]and they shall serve as lights in the expanse of the sky to shine upon the earth." And it was so. [16]God made the two great lights, the greater light to dominate the day and the lesser light to dominate the night, and the stars. [17]And God set them in the expanse of the sky to shine upon the earth, [18]to dominate the day and the night, and to separate light from darkness. And God saw that this was good. [19]And there was evening and there was morning, a fourth day.

[20]God said, "Let the waters bring forth swarms of living creatures, and birds that fly above the earth across the expanse of the sky." [21]God created the great sea monsters, and all the living creatures of every kind that creep, which the waters brought forth in swarms, and all the winged birds of every kind. And God saw that this was good. [22]God blessed them, saying, "Be fertile and increase, fill the waters in the seas, and let the birds increase on the earth." [23]And there was evening and there was morning, a fifth day.

[24]God said, "Let the earth bring forth every kind of living creature: cattle, creeping things,

From *The TANAKH: The New JPS Translation According to the Traditional Hebrew Text.* Copyright 1985 by the Jewish Publication Society. Used by permission.

and wild beasts of every kind." And it was so. ²⁵God made wild beasts of every kind and cattle of every kind, and all kinds of creeping things of the earth. And God saw that this was good. ²⁶And God said, "Let us make man in our image, after our likeness. They shall rule the fish of the sea, the birds of the sky, the cattle, the whole earth, and all the creeping things that creep on earth." ²⁷And God created man in His image, in the image of God He created him; male and female He created them. ²⁸God blessed them and God said to them, "Be fertile and increase, fill the earth and master it; and rule the fish of the sea, the birds of the sky, and all the living things that creep on earth."

²⁹God said, "See, I give you every seed-bearing plant that is upon all the earth, and every tree that has seed-bearing fruit; they shall be yours for food. ³⁰And to all the animals on land, to all the birds of the sky, and to everything that creeps on earth, in which there is the breath of life, [I give] all the green plants for food." And it was so. ³¹And God saw all that He had made, and found it very good. And there was evening and there was morning, the sixth day.

2 The heaven and the earth were finished, and all their array. ²On the seventh day God finished the work that He had been doing, and He ceased on the seventh day from all the work that He had done. ³And God blessed the seventh day and declared it holy, because on it God ceased from all the work of creation that He had done. ⁴Such is the story of heaven and earth when they were created.

When the LORD God made earth and heaven—⁵when no shrub of the field was yet on earth and no grasses of the field had yet sprouted, because the LORD God had not sent rain upon the earth and there was no man to till the soil, ⁶but a flow would well up from the ground and water the whole surface of the earth—⁷the LORD God formed man from the dust of the earth. He blew into his nostrils the breath of life, and man became a living being.

⁸The LORD God planted a garden in Eden, in the east, and placed there the man whom He had formed. ⁹And from the ground the LORD God caused to grow every tree that was pleasing to the sight and good for food, with the tree of life in the middle of the garden, and the tree of knowledge of good and bad.

¹⁵The LORD God took the man and placed him in the garden of Eden, to till it and tend it. ¹⁶And the LORD God commanded the man, saying, "Of every tree of the garden you are free to eat; ¹⁷but as for the tree of knowledge of good and bad, you must not eat of it; for as soon as you eat of it, you shall die."

¹⁸The LORD God said, "It is not good for man to be alone; I will make a fitting helper for him." ¹⁹And the LORD God formed out of the earth all the wild beasts and all the birds of the sky, and brought them to the man to see what he would call them; and whatever the man called each living creature, that would be its name. ²⁰And the man gave names to all the cattle and to the birds of the sky and to all the wild beasts; but for Adam no fitting helper was found. ²¹So the LORD God cast a deep sleep upon the man; and, while he slept, He took one of his ribs and closed up the flesh at that spot. ²²And the LORD God fashioned the rib that He

had taken from the man into a woman; and He brought her to the man. ²³Then the man said,

> "This one at last
> Is bone of my bones
> And flesh of my flesh.
> This one shall be called Woman,
> For from man was she taken."

²⁴Hence a man leaves his father and mother and clings to his wife, so that they become one flesh.

²⁵The two of them were naked, the man and his wife, yet they felt no shame.

3 ¹Now the serpent was the shrewdest of all the wild beasts that the LORD God had made. He said to the woman, "Did God really say: You shall not eat of any tree of the garden?" ²The Woman replied to the serpent, "We may eat of the fruit of the other trees of the garden. ³It is only about fruit of the tree in the middle of the garden that God said: 'You shall not eat of it or touch it, lest you die.'" ⁴And the serpent said to the woman, "You are not going to die, ⁵but God knows that as soon as you eat of it your eyes will be opened and you will be like divine beings who know good and bad." ⁶When the woman saw that the tree was good for eating and a delight to the eyes, and that the tree was desirable as a source of wisdom, she took of its fruit and ate. She also gave some to her husband, and he ate. ⁷Then the eyes of both of them were opened and they perceived that they were naked; and they sewed together fig leaves and made themselves loincloths.

⁸They heard the sound of the LORD God moving about in the garden at the breezy time of day; and the man and his wife hid from the LORD God among the trees of the garden. ⁹The LORD God called out to the man and said to him, "Where are you?" ¹⁰He replied, "I heard the sound of You in the garden, and I was afraid because I was naked, so I hid." ¹¹Then He asked, "Who told you that you were naked? Did you eat of the tree from which I had forbidden you to eat?" ¹²The man said, "The woman You put at my side—she gave me of the tree, and I ate." ¹³And the LORD God said to the woman, "What is this you have done!" The woman replied, "The serpent duped me, and I ate." ¹⁴Then the LORD God said to the serpent,

> "Because you did this,
> More cursed shall you be
> Than all cattle
> And all the wild beasts:
> On your belly shall you crawl
> And dirt shall you eat
> All the days of your life.
> ¹⁵I will put enmity
> Between you and the woman,

And between your offspring and hers;
They shall strike at your head,
And you shall strike at their heel."

¹⁶And to the woman He said,

"I will make most severe
Your pangs in childbearing;
In pain shall you bear children.
Yet your urge shall be for your husband,
And he shall rule over you."

¹⁷To Adam He said, "Because you did as your wife said and ate of the tree about which I commanded you, 'You shall not eat of it,'

Cursed be the ground because of you;
By toil shall you eat of it
All the days of your life:
¹⁸Thorns and thistles shall it sprout for you.
But your food shall be the grasses of the field;
¹⁹By the sweat of your brow
Shall you get bread to eat,
Until you return to the ground—
For from it you were taken.
For dust you are,
And to dust you shall return."

²⁰The man named his wife Eve, because she was the mother of all the living. ²¹And the LORD God made garments of skins for Adam and his wife, and clothed them.

²²And the LORD God said, "Now that the man has become like one of us, knowing good and bad, what if he should stretch out his hand and take also from the tree of life and eat, and live forever!" ²³So the LORD God banished him from the garden of Eden, to till the soil from which he was taken. ²⁴He drove the man out, and stationed east of the garden of Eden the cherubim and the fiery ever-turning sword, to guard the way to the tree of life.

8 ¹⁵God spoke to Noah, saying, ¹⁶"Come out of the ark, together with your wife, your sons, and your sons' wives. ¹⁷Bring out with you every living thing of all flesh that is with you: birds, animals, and everything that creeps on earth; and let them swarm on the earth and be fertile and increase on earth." ¹⁸So Noah came out, together with his sons, his wife, and his sons' wives. ¹⁹Every animal, every creeping thing, and every bird, everything that stirs on earth came out of the ark by families.

²⁰Then Noah built an altar to the LORD and, taking of every clean animal and of every

clean bird, he offered burnt offerings on the altar. ²¹The LORD smelled the pleasing odor, and the LORD said to Himself: "Never again will I doom the earth because of man, since the devisings of man's mind are evil from his youth; nor will I ever again destroy every living being, as I have done.

²²So long as the earth endures,
Seedtime and harvest,
Cold and heat,
Summer and winter,
Day and night,
Shall not cease."

9 God blessed Noah and his sons, and said to them, "Be fertile and increase, and fill the earth. ²The fear and the dread of you shall be upon all the beasts of the earth and upon all the birds of the sky—everything with which the earth is astir—and upon all the fish of the sea; they are given into your hand. ³Every creature that lives shall be yours to eat; as with the green grasses, I give you all these. ⁴You must not, however, eat flesh with its life-blood in it. ⁵But for your own life-blood I will require a reckoning: I will require it of every beast; of man, too, will I require a reckoning for human life, of every man for that of his fellow man!

⁶Whoever sheds the blood of man,
By man shall his blood be shed;
For in His image
Did God make man.

⁷Be fertile, then, and increase; abound on the earth and increase on it."

⁸And God said to Noah and to his sons with him, ⁹"I now establish My covenant with you and your offspring to come, ¹⁰and with every living thing that is with you—birds, cattle, and every wild beast as well—all that have come out of the ark, every living thing on earth. ¹¹I will maintain My covenant with you: never again shall all flesh be cut off by the waters of a flood, and never again shall there be a flood to destroy the earth."

¹²God further said, "This is the sign that I set for the covenant between Me and you, and every living creature with you, for all ages to come. ¹³I have set My bow in the clouds, and it shall serve as a sign of the covenant between Me and the earth. ¹⁴When I bring clouds over the earth, and the bow appears in the clouds, ¹⁵I will remember My covenant between Me and you and every living creature among all flesh, so that the waters shall never again become a flood to destroy all flesh. ¹⁶When the bow is in the clouds, I will see it and remember the everlasting covenant between God and all living creatures, all flesh that is on earth. ¹⁷That," God said to Noah, "shall be the sign of the covenant that I have established between Me and all flesh that is on earth."

EXODUS

23 [5]When you see the ass of your enemy lying under its burden and would refrain from raising[b] it, you must nevertheless raise it with him.

[10]Six years you shall sow your land and gather in its yield; [11]but in the seventh you shall let it rest and lie fallow. Let the needy among your people eat of it, and what they leave let the wild beasts eat. You shall do the same with your vineyards and your olive groves.

[12]Six days you shall do your work, but on the seventh day you shall cease from labor, in order that your ox and your ass may rest, and that your bondman and the stranger may be refreshed.

LEVITICUS

19 [9]When you reap the harvest of your land, you shall not reap all the way to the edges of your field, or gather the gleanings of your harvest. [10]You shall not pick your vineyard bare, or gather the fallen fruit of your vineyard; you shall leave them for the poor and the stranger: I the LORD am your God.

22 [26]The LORD spoke to Moses, saying: [27]When an ox or a sheep or a goat is born, it shall stay seven days with its mother, and from the eighth day on it shall be acceptable as an offering by fire to the LORD. [28]However, no animal from the herd or from the flock shall be slaughtered on the same day with its young.

25 The LORD spoke to Moses on Mount Sinai: [2]Speak to the Israelite people and say to them:

When you enter the land that I assign to you, the land shall observe a sabbath of the LORD. [3]Six years you may sow your field and six years you may prune your vineyard and gather in the yield. [4]But in the seventh year the land shall have a sabbath of complete rest, a sabbath of the LORD: you shall not sow your field or prune your vineyard. [5]You shall not reap the aftergrowth of your harvest or gather the grapes of your untrimmed vines; it shall be a year of complete rest for the land. [6]But you may eat whatever the land during its sabbath will produce—you, your male and female slaves, the hired and bound laborers who live with you, [7]and your cattle and the beasts in your land may eat all its yield.

26 [3]If you follow My laws and faithfully observe My commandments, [4]I will grant your rains in their season, so that the earth shall yield its produce and the trees of the field their fruit. [5]Your threshing shall overtake the vintage, and your vintage shall overtake the sowing; you shall eat your fill of bread and dwell securely in your land.

DEUTERONOMY

20 ¹⁹When in your war against a city you have to besiege it a long time in order to capture it, you must not destroy its trees, wielding the ax against them. You may eat of them, but you must not cut them down. Are trees of the field human to withdraw before you into the besieged city? ²⁰Only trees that you know do not yield food may be destroyed; you may cut them down for constructing siegeworks against the city that is waging war on you, until it has been reduced.

22 ⁶If, along the road, you chance upon a bird's nest, in any tree or on the ground, with fledglings or eggs and the mother sitting over the fledglings or on the eggs, do not take the mother together with her young. ⁷Let the mother go, and take only the young, in order that you may fare well and have a long life.

25 ⁴You shall not muzzle an ox while it is threshing.

ISIAH

24 ⁴The earth is withered, sear;
The world languishes, it is sear;
The most exalted people of the earth languish.
⁵For the earth was defiled
Under its inhabitants;
Because they transgressed teachings,
Violated laws,
Broke the ancient covenant.

PSALMS

65 ¹⁰You take care of the earth and irrigate it;
    You enrich it greatly,
    with the channel of God full of water;
    You provide grain for men;
    for so do You prepare it.
¹¹Saturating its furrows,
    leveling its ridges,

    You soften it with showers,
    You bless its growth.
¹²You crown the year with Your bounty;
    fatness is distilled in Your paths;

¹³the pasturelands distill it;

    the hills are girded with joy.

¹⁴The meadows are clothed with flocks,

    the valleys mantled with grain;

    they raise a shout, they break into song.

    slow to anger, abounding in steadfast love.

104 Bless the Lord, O my soul;

    O Lord, my God, You are very great;

    You are clothed in glory and majesty,

    ²wrapped in a robe of light;

    You spread the heavens like a tent cloth.

³He sets the rafters of His lofts in the waters,

    makes the clouds His chariot,

    moves on the wings of the wind.

⁴He makes the winds His messengers,

    fiery flames His servants.

⁵He established the earth on its foundations,

    so that it shall never totter.

⁶You made the deep cover it as a garment;

    the waters stood above the mountains.

⁷They fled at Your blast,

    rushed away at the sound of Your thunder,

    ⁸—mountains rising, valleys sinking—

    to the place You established for them.

⁹You set bounds they must not pass

    so that they never again cover the earth.

¹⁰You make springs gush forth in torrents;

    they make their way between the hills,

    ¹¹giving drink to all the wild beasts;

    the wild asses slake their thirst.

¹²The birds of the sky dwell beside them

    and sing among the foliage.

¹³You water the mountains from Your[a] lofts;

    the earth is sated from the fruit of Your work.

¹⁴You make the grass grow for the cattle,

    and herbage for man's labor

    that he may get food out of the earth—

    ¹⁵wine that cheers the hearts of men

    oil that makes the face shine,

    and bread that sustains man's life.

¹⁶The trees of the Lord drink their fill,
>   the cedars of Lebanon, His own planting,
¹⁷where birds make their nests;
>   the stork has her home in the junipers.
¹⁸The high mountains are for wild goats;
>   the crags are a refuge for rock-badgers.
¹⁹He made the moon to mark the seasons;
>   the sun knows when to set.
²⁰You bring on darkness and it is night,
>   when all the beasts of the forests stir.
²¹The lions roar for prey,
>   seeking their food from God.
²²When the sun rises, they come home
>   and couch in their dens.
²³Man then goes out to his work,
>   to his labor until the evening.
²⁴How many are the things You have made, O Lord;
>   You have made them all with wisdom;
>   the earth is full of Your creations.
²⁵There is the sea, vast and wide,
>   with its creatures beyond number,
>   living things, small and great.
²⁶There go the ships,
>   and Leviathan that You formed to sport with.
²⁷All of them look to You
>   to give them their food when it is due.
²⁸Give it to them, they gather it up;
>   open Your hand, they are well satisfied;
>   ²⁹hide Your face, they are terrified;
>   take away their breath, they perish
>   and turn again into dust;
>   ³⁰send back Your breath, they are created,
>   and You renew the face of the earth.
³¹May the glory of the Lord endure forever;
>   may the Lord rejoice in His works!
³²He looks at the earth and it trembles;
>   He touches the mountains and they smoke.
³³I will sing to the Lord as long as I live;
>   all my life I will chant hymns to my God.
³⁴May my prayer be pleasing to Him;

I will rejoice in the LORD.
³⁵May sinners disappear from the earth,

and the wicked be no more.

Bless the LORD, O my soul.

Hallelujah.

JOB

12 ⁷But ask the beasts, and they will teach you;

The birds of the sky, they will tell you,

⁸Or speak to the earth, it will teach you;

The fish of the sea, they will inform you.

⁹Who among all these does not know

That the hand of the LORD has done this?

¹⁰In His hand is every living soul

And the breath of all mankind.

¹⁷He makes counselors go about naked[b]

And causes judges to go mad.

¹⁸He undoes the belts of kings,

And fastens loincloths on them.

¹⁹He makes priests go about naked,

And leads temple-servants astray.

38 Then the LORD replied to Job out of the tempest and said:

²Who is this who darkens counsel,

Speaking without knowledge?

³Gird your loins like a man;

I will ask and you will inform Me.

⁴Where were you when I laid the earth's foundations?

Speak if you have understanding.

⁵Do you know who fixed its dimensions

Or who measured it with a line?

⁶Onto what were its bases sunk?

Who set its cornerstone

⁷When the morning stars sang together

And all the divine beings shouted for joy?

⁸Who closed the sea behind doors

When it gushed forth out of the womb,

⁹When I clothed it in clouds,

Swaddled it in dense clouds,

¹⁰When I made breakers My limit for it,

And set up its bar and doors,

¹¹And said, "You may come so far and no farther;
Here your surging waves will stop"?
¹²Have you ever commanded the day to break,
Assigned the dawn its place,
¹³So that it seizes the corners of the earth
And shakes the wicked out of it?
¹⁴It changes like clay under the seal
Till [its hues] are fixed like those of a garment.
¹⁵Their light is withheld from the wicked,
And the upraised arm is broken.
¹⁶Have you penetrated to the sources of the sea,
Or walked in the recesses of the deep?
¹⁷Have the gates of death been disclosed to you?
Have you seen the gates of deep darkness?
¹⁸Have you surveyed the expanses or the earth?
If you know of these—tell Me.
¹⁹Which path leads to where light dwells,
And where is the place of darkness,
²⁰That you may take it to its domain
And know the way to its home?
²¹Surely you know, for you were born then,
And the number of your years is many!
²²Have you penetrated the vaults of snow,
Seen the vaults of hail,
²³Which I have put aside for a time of adversity,
For a day of war and battle?
²⁴By what path is the west wind dispersed,
The east wind scattered over the earth?
²⁵Who cut a channel for the torrents
And a path for the thunderstorms,
²⁶To rain down on uninhabited land,
On the wilderness where no man is,
²⁷To saturate the desolate wasteland,
And make the crop of grass sprout forth?
²⁸Does the rain have a father?
Who begot the dewdrops?
²⁹From whose belly came forth the ice?
Who gave birth to the frost of heaven?
³⁰Water congeals like stone,
And the surface of the deep compacts.
³¹Can you tie cords to Pleiades

Or undo the reins of Orion?
³²Can you lead out Mazzaroth in its season,
Conduct the Bear with her sons?
³³Do you know the laws of heaven
Or impose its authority on earth?
³⁴Can you send up an order to the clouds
For an abundance of water to cover you?
³⁵Can you dispatch the lightning on a mission
And have it answer you, "I am ready"?
³⁶Who put wisdom in the hidden parts?
Who gave understanding to the mind?
³⁷Who is wise enough to give an account of the heavens?
Who can tilt the bottles of the sky,
³⁸Whereupon the earth melts into a mass,
And its clods stick together.
³⁹Can you hunt prey for the lion,
And satisfy the appetite of the king of beasts?
Go follow the tracks of the sheep,
And graze your kids^f
By the tents of the shepherds.

SONG OF SONGS

2 I am a rose of Sharon,
A lily of the valleys.
²Like a lily among thorns,
So is my darling among the maidens.
³Like an apple tree among trees of the forest,
So is my beloved among the youths.
I delight to sit in his shade,
And his fruit is sweet to my mouth.
⁴He brought me to the banquet room
And his banner of love was over me.
⁵"Sustain me with raisin cakes,
Refresh me with apples,
For I am faint with love."
⁶His left hand was under my head,
His right arm embraced me.
⁷I adjure you, O maidens of Jerusalem,
By gazelles or by hinds of the field:

Do not wake or rouse
Love until it please!
[8]Hark! My beloved!
There he comes,
Leaping over mountains,
Bounding over hills.
[9]My beloved is like a gazelle
Or like a young stag.
There he stands behind our wall,
Gazing through the window,
Peering through the lattice.
[10]My beloved spoke thus to me,
"Arise, my darling;
My fair one, come away!

from LEGENDS OF THE BIBLE

Louis Ginzberg

ALL THINGS PRAISE THE LORD

"Whatever God created has value." Even the animals and the insects that seem useless and noxious at first sight have a vocation to fulfill. The snail trailing a moist streak after it as it crawls, and so using up its vitality, serves as a remedy for boils. The sting of a hornet is healed by the house-fly crushed and applied to the wound. The gnat, feeble creature, taking in food but never secreting it, is a specific against the poison of a viper, and this venomous reptile itself cures eruptions, while the lizard is the antidote to the scorpion.

Not only do all creatures serve man, and contribute to his comfort, but also God "teacheth us through the beasts of the earth, and maketh us wise through the fowls of heaven." He endowed many animals with admirable moral qualities as a pattern for man. If the Torah had not been revealed to us, we might have learnt regard for the decencies of life from the cat, who covers her excrement with earth; regard for the property of others from the ants, who never encroach upon one another's stores; and regard for decorous conduct from the cock, who, when he desires to unite with the hen, promises to buy her a cloak long enough to reach to the ground, and when the hen reminds him of his promise, he shakes his comb and says, "May I be deprived of my comb, if I do not buy it when I have the means." The grasshopper also has a lesson to teach a man. All the summer through it sings, until its belly burst, and death claims it. Though it knows the fate that awaits it, yet it sings on. So man should do his duty toward God, no matter what the consequences. The stork should be taken as a model in two respects. He guards the purity of his family life zealously, and toward his fellows he is compassionate and merciful. Even the frog can be the teacher of man. By the side of the water there lives a species of animals which subsist off aquatic creatures alone. When the frog notices that one of them is hungry, he goes to it of his own accord, and offers himself as food, thus fulfilling the injunction, "If thine enemy be hungry, give him bread to eat; and if he be thirsty, give him water to drink."

The whole of creation was called into existence by God unto His glory, and each creature has its own hymn of praise wherewith to extol the Creator. Heaven and earth, Paradise and hell, desert and field, rivers and seas—all have their own way of paying homage to God. The hymn of the earth is, "From the uttermost part of the earth have we heard songs, glory to the

---

Ginzberg, Louis; *Legends of the Bible*, 1956. Reprinted with permission of the Jewish Publication Society.

Righteous." The sea exclaims, "Above the voices of many waters, the mighty breakers of the sea, the Lord on high is mighty."

Also the celestial bodies and the elements proclaim the praise of their Creator—the sun, moon, and stars, the cloud and the winds, lightning and dew. The sun says, "The sun and moon stood still in their habitation, at the light of Thine arrows as they went, at the shining of Thy glittering spear"; and the stars sing, "Thou art the Lord, even Thou alone; Thou hast made heaven, the heaven of heavens, with all their host, the earth and all things that are thereon, the seas and all that is in them, and Thou preservest them all; and the host of heaven worshippeth Thee."

Every plant, furthermore, has a song of praise. The fruitful tree sings, "Then shall all the trees of the wood sing for joy, before the Lord, for He cometh; for He cometh to judge the earth"; and the ears of grain on the field sing, "The pastures are covered with flocks; the valleys also are covered over with corn; they shout for joy, they also sing."

Great among singers of praise are the birds, and greatest among them is the cock. When God at midnight goes to the pious in Paradise, all the trees therein break out into adoration, and their songs awaken the cock, who begins in turn to praise God. Seven times he crows, each time reciting a verse. The first verse is: "Lift up your heads, O ye gates; and be ye lift up, ye everlasting doors, and the King of glory shall come in. Who is the King of glory? The Lord strong and mighty, the Lord mighty in battle." The second verse: "Lift up your heads, O ye gates; yea, lift them up, ye everlasting doors and the King of glory shall come in. Who is this King of glory? The Lord of hosts, He is the King of glory." The third: "Arise, ye righteous, and occupy yourselves with the Torah, that your reward may be abundant in the world hereafter." The fourth: "I have waited for Thy salvation, O Lord!" The fifth: "How long wilt thou sleep, O sluggard? When wilt thou arise out of thy sleep?" The sixth: "Love not sleep, lest thou come to poverty; open thine eyes, and thou shalt be satisfied with bread." And the seventh verse sung by the cock runs: "It is time to work for the Lord, for they have made void Thy law."

The song of the vulture is: "I will hiss for them, and gather them; for I have redeemed them, and they shall increase as they have increased"—the same verse with which the bird will in time to come announce the advent of the Messiah, the only difference being, that when he heralds the Messiah he will sit upon the ground and sing his verse, while at all other times he is seated elsewhere when he sings it.

Nor do the other animals praise God less than the birds. Even the beasts of prey give forth adoration. The lion says: "The Lord shall go forth as a mighty man; He shall stir up jealousy like a man of war; He shall cry, yea, He shall shout aloud; He shall do mightily against his enemies." And the fox exhorts unto justice with the words: "Woe unto him that buildeth his house by unrighteousness, and his chambers by injustice; that useth his neighbor's service without wages, and giveth him not his hire."

Louis Ginzberg

Yea, the dumb fishes know how to proclaim the praise of their Lord. "The voice of the Lord is upon the waters," they say, "the God of glory thundereth, even the Lord upon many waters"; while the frog exclaims, "Blessed be the name of the glory of His kingdom forever and ever!"

Contemptible though they are, even the reptiles give praise unto their Creator. The mouse extols God with the words: "Howbeit Thou art just in all that is come upon me; for Thou hast dealt truly, but I have done wickedly." And the cat sings: "Let everything that hath breath praise the Lord. Praise ye the Lord."

"JEWS, JEWISH TEXTS, AND NATURE: A BRIEF HISTORY"

Daniel Swartz

Once upon a time—but this is neither a fairy tale nor a bedtime story—we knew less about the natural world than we do today. Much less. But we understood that world better, much better, for we lived ever so much closer to its rhythms.

Most of us have wandered far from our earlier understanding, from our long-ago intimacy. We take for granted what our ancestors could not, dared not, take for granted; we have set ourselves apart from the world of the seasons, the world of floods and rainbows and new moons. Nor, acknowledging our loss, can we simply reverse course, pretend to innocence in order to rediscover intimacy. Too much has intervened.

But we can explore the ways we once were, the times when we lived off the land, when we lived in the Land.

Our purpose in so doing is not to shake our heads in disbelief, whether at the naivete of old or the alienation of our own time. We do it in order to assess the ingredients of our loss, as also of our gain, to inquire whether here and there, perhaps even more than merely here and there, our modern sophistication can be married to the ancient intimacy, whether we can move from our discord with nature to an informed harmony with this, God's universe.

Accordingly, this is not about the good old days. It is about us, and about how we came to where we are. It is about our people and its relationship to the natural world.

Not all of us, throughout all our history, lived intimately with nature, but some of us did most of the time and most of us did some of the time.

Which of us? When? What is, in fact, the story of our shifting relationship with the natural environment? And where does that story, along with our own, point us now?

THE BIBLICAL PERIOD

Among its many facets, the Bible is the story of people who cared about and knew intimately the land around them. That knowledge is richly, even lavishly, reflected in the language of the prophets and psalmists, in the poetry of the Song of Songs and Job. Indeed, the extravagant

This essay appeared in *To Till and To Tend: A Guide to Jewish Environmental Study and Action*, published by The Coalition on the Environment and Jewish Life.

use of natural metaphor suggests that a vocabulary drawn from the world of nature was accessible to all.

Today, when we encounter God as a *nesher*, a griffin vulture (as we do in Deuteronomy 32:11), we must pause to examine just what is intended by the term. But we may surmise that then, when people first encountered that way of depicting God, they knew that the reference was to God as a fiercely protective parent, one who carries its young on its back to help them learn how to fly. Similarly, when Isaiah compares Israel to a terebinth oak in the fall (6:11–13), his listeners could appreciate immediately the two-edged nature of his metaphor. The terebinth is most glorious just before all its leaves drop—but it is also among the hardiest of trees, even sprouting again from a cut-off stump.

No modern audience can appreciate as intuitively as the listeners of old the Song of Song's lyrical description of spring flowers reappearing on the Earth or of a lily among the thorns. So, too, the psalmists' hymns to all of creation, joining with the song of heaven's birds and young lions at their hunt (see, e.g., Psalms 104 and 148). And consider the difference between a modern dweller in cities and the ancients in comprehending the sheer power of God's promise to Abraham that he would have descendants like the stars in the sky: in the one case, the stars are perceived only through a haze of light and soot; in the other, the night sky dense with brilliant stars was part of the common experience.

The language of nature came to the people naturally, as it were, for their lives were bound up with the richness of the land, with the pastoral and agricultural economy of the time. That is why they tended the land so lovingly, that is why the cycles of their celebrations followed the seasons of the land (see, e.g. Leviticus 23). And though their efforts to tame the land, to make it more productive and more dependable, were often marvels of ingenuity, they understood, as well, the limits to their mastery—for they knew God as Sovereign of the Land, and, through such institutions as the Sabbatical year and the Jubilee (Leviticus 25), they acknowledged God's ownership.

It followed that they had to treat the land well—not only to give it rest, but to respect and plant trees, keep water sources clean, create parks near urban areas, regulate sewage disposal, avoid causing pain to animals. And they understood intuitively as well the connection between their responsibility to care for the environment and justice: Since the land was God's, not only should it be protected, but its rich produce should be shared with the poorest of God's children (Leviticus 19).

In a world where warfare typically included efforts by the victor to degrade drastically the environment of the vanquished—cutting down trees, fouling waters, and salting the Earth—our forebears behaved exceptionally, in all senses of the word. They developed the principle of *bal tash-chit,* do not destroy (Deuteronomy 20:19). Do not cut down trees even to prevent ambush or to build siege engines; do not foul waters or burn crops even to cause an enemy's submission. And if, even in extremis, one is to avoid causing needless harm to

Daniel Swartz

the environment, *al akhat kama v'khama*—how much the more so—during the ordinary course of life.

We speak, then, of a time when people were possessed of an ideal vision of harmony, of *shlemut,* wholeness and peace. No, it was not an idyllic time, for they could not fully translate their vision into reality. No Eden, not any longer: the promised abundance had to be teased and more often wrested from the Earth by the sweat of the brow, and the seasons had a way of being fickle, not bestowing their appointed blessings. Hence work, hence prayer, hence, too, Shabbat, a time to rest from work, a time to remind themselves of God's endless beneficence, a time to dream of a time yet to come, when the world will be entirely Shabbat. And in that final and endless time, the wolf will lie down with the lamb, and humankind will be at peace with all of nature (See, e.g., Isaiah 65:21–25; Joel 2:21–24.).

In short, our ancient ancestors knew the wonderful reciprocity of Creation: Creation's sheer magnificence turns the heart towards its Creator (see, e.g., Isaiah 40), and the heart that has turned to God opens, inevitably, towards Creation, towards the awesome integrity of the natural universe that is God's gift.

ADDITIONAL QUOTES

When you reap the harvest of your land, you shall not reap all the way to the edges of your field, or gather the gleanings of your harvest . . . but you shall leave them for the poor and the stranger: I the Eternal am your God (Leviticus 19:9–20).

A time is coming . . . when the mountains shall drip with wine and all the hills shall wave with grain. I will restore My people Israel, I will plant them upon their soil (Amos 9:13–15).

Let the heavens rejoice and the earth exult! Let the sea and all within it thunder, the fields and everything in them exult! Then shall all the forest trees shout for joy, at the presence of the Eternal One, who is coming to rule the Earth; God will rule the world justly and its people in faithfulness (Psalm 96:11–13).

But ask the beasts, and they will teach you; the birds of the sky, and they will tell you; or speak to the earth and it will teach you; the fish of the sea, they will inform you. Who among all these does not know that the hand of the Eternal has done this? (Job 12:7–9)

For now the winter is past, the rains are over and gone. The blossoms have appeared in the land. The time of the song-bird has come; the song of the turtledove is heard in our land. The green figs form on the fig tree, the blossoming vines give off fragrance (Song of Songs 2:11–13).

THE ERA OF THE MISHNAH AND THE TALMUD

During the period when the Mishnah and Talmud were developed, although many of us became dwellers in cities, our urbanization was far from complete. Farming, perhaps because a large percentage of Mishnaic sages were farmers, was considered the normative way of life. We read, for example, in *Avot d'Rabbi Nathan* (30:6) that "one who purchases grain in the market is like an infant whose mother is dry [and so needs to be taken to a wet nurse], while one who eats from what one has grown is like an infant raised at its mother's breast."

The mystics of this period wrote *bekhalot* hymns, which visionary poets recited during their attempts to ascend through the "heavenly palaces." These hymns evoked the majesty of God by reference to the wonders of the Earth, as did the prayers of the early *paytanim* (such as Yose ben Yose). Even into the late Talmudic era of the fifth and sixth centuries, our sages remained knowledgeable about the natural environment, and they wrote with great concern about it.

One testament to their concern is the panoply of blessings they developed. Through these, the experience of the natural world, as well as interactions between people and nature, became sanctified. Not only the tasting of foods, but the fragrance of blossoms, the sight of mountains, the sound of thunder were to be blessed. Talmudic sages added such rituals of blessing as the *Kiddush Levanah*, a blessing for the renewal of the moon (which was later revived by medieval mystics and still later adopted by the Hasidim of the 18th century). Such blessings showed that God was author of the wonders of nature. And as to the work of human hands, such as the baking of bread, the rabbis understood that even such work was bound up in a sacred partnership of God and humanity, as given form in the bowels of nature.

Most of all, the myriad blessings reflected and reminded those who recited them of the foundational belief: God owns everything in the world; we are but tenants in the garden, meant to till and to tend, to serve and to guard.

The premise that "you and what you possess are God's" (*Avot* 3:7) underlies most of Talmudic thinking, both about the environment and about the nature of *mitzvot* in general. The doing of *mitzvot* acknowledges that we live in a God-centered and not a human-centered universe, that because of God's ownership, we have a variety of obligations to the Divine will. The rabbis further believed that many *mitzvot*, such as the Sabbatical year, had as their *central* purpose the reaffirmation of God's ownership of the land (*Sanhedrin* 39a). Philo, writing at the same time as the Mishnaic sages, devoted a whole treatise, *De Cherubim*, to the notion that humans cannot truly own anything, for all is God's. As was true with their biblical ancestors, this understanding of ownership strengthened for them the link between treating the environment justly and justly sharing with all of God's children the products of creation.

The particular and compelling gift of these sages is that they made their concerns concrete, translated ethical principles into codes of action. While *Genesis Rabbah* and *Leviticus Rabbah*, written at roughly the same time, express general concerns about the preservation of species and the sacredness of planting trees, the Mishnah and Gemarra set definite limits on the use of any one species and regulate in detail the planting of trees in urban areas. The Talmudic sages translated the general principle of *Bal Tashchit* into a series of specific prohibitions against wasteful actions. Similarly, they developed extensive regulations on the dispos-

Daniel Swartz

al of hazardous waste, and they curtailed industries that might cause air pollution (See, e.g. *Bava Batra* 25a.). Nor did they consider these matters to be secondary or delegate these concerns to others; the heads of the *Bet Din* themselves were to inspect wells (*Tosefta Shekalim* 1:2). Only through concrete acts such as these could the vision of the age of redemption become a reality.

ADDITIONAL QUOTES

Rabbi Shimon Bar Yochai said, three things are of equal importance, earth, humans, and rain. Rabbi Levi ben Hiyyata said: . . . to teach that without earth, there is no rain, and without rain, the earth cannot endure, and without either, humans cannot exist (*Genesis Rabbah*, 13:3).

Rabbi Yohanan ben Zakkai . . . used to say: if you have a sapling in your hand, and someone should say to you that the Messiah has come, stay and complete the planting, and then go to greet the Messiah (*Avot de Rabbi Nathan*, 31b).

How can a person of flesh and blood follow God? . . . God, from the very beginning of creation, was occupied before all else with planting, as it is written, "And first of all [*mikedem,* usually translated as "in the East"], the Eternal God planted a Garden in Eden [Genesis 2:8] Therefore . . . occupy yourselves first and foremost with planting (*Leviticus Rabbah* 25:3).

MEDIEVAL AND RENAISSANCE TIMES

The urbanization of Jews continued throughout the Middle Ages. In some cases, our land was seized, or we were forbidden to own land, or we were in other ways forced off the land; in others, economic pressures, ranging from prohibitive taxes to business restrictions, as well as shifting economic opportunities, led us toward the cities.

But not all Jews became urban. In Europe, through the 1400s, many Jews cultivated vineyards. In the Islamic world, Jews played a vital role in agricultural life, first throughout the region, then, as we were displaced from the land, along its periphery.

From the beginning of this period, a number of important Jewish texts with environmental sensitivities, such as the late collections of *midrash*, Ecclesiastes *Rabbah, Midrash Tankhuma,* and *Midrash Tehillim,* were composed. Joseph Kimkhi, in his commentary on Genesis, wrote that the "us" in God's "Let *us* make humans" refers to God working together with nature and the Earth. And the expansion of Jewish mysticism and poetry also created an abundance of works concerned with the environment.

This concern was both practical and theological. Maimonides as a physician saw the ill effects environmental degradation could have on the health, and he proposed regulations to counter them (See, e.g. his *Treatise on Asthma*). Joseph Caro wrote about the responsibility of communities to plant trees (*Tur, Hoshen Mishpat* #175), while various responsa of Rabbi Yitzhak ben Sheshet (Ribash), of the early 14th century, deal with urban pollution issues, including noise pollution, and their effects on urban dwellers (See, e.g. *Responsa* 196).

But many of the sages of this period also viewed the beauty of the created world in a broader sense, as a path towards the love and contemplation of God. Both Maimonides and his son, Abraham, wrote that one could come to love God by contemplating God's great works in nature, and that such contemplation was in fact essential to spiritual development (*Sefer HaMada*, 2.2; *Ha-Mispil La-Avodat Ha-Shem*). The Jewish philosopher, Bakhya ibn Pekuda, wrote that Jews should engage in "meditation upon creation" in order to sense God's majesty (*Duties of the Heart*, 137). *Sefer Ha-Hinukh*, a compilation by medieval pietists, claimed that those who truly love God cannot bear to waste even a grain of mustard (#529).

The vast number of Kabbalistic works developed during this time took contemplation of nature a step further, for, according to the *Zohar*, nature itself is a garment of the *Shekhina*. "*Perek Shira*," a mystical poem from circa 900, has verses from all types of creatures singing God's praise. Abraham Abulafia began a tradition of Jewish mysticism that included outdoor meditation. And the mystics of Safed developed intricate *Tu B'shvat* Seders, to celebrate the presence of God in nature.

But mystics though they were, they did not restrict their relationship with nature to contemplation. Rather, they treated nature with great respect in deed as well as thought. As Moses Cordovero, author of one of these *Tu B'shvat Haggadot*, wrote in a tract about the sorts of ethical behavior in which mystics should engage, that "the principle of wisdom is to extend acts of love toward everything, including plants and animals" (*Tomer Devorah*, #3).

The particularly intense concern for and involvement with nature we find among the mystics might suggest that nature was somehow outside "mainstream" concerns. That was not the case. On the contrary, we find an abiding involvement with and appreciation of nature among some of the most "mainstream" rabbis and poets. Some of the greatest Sephardic sages, for example, were also talented nature poets. So, Moses ibn Ezra, in his poem "The Rose," wrote: "The garden put on a coat of many colors, and its grass garments were like the robes of a brocade . . . at their head advanced the rose; he came out from among the guard of leaves and cast aside his prison-clothes."

Judah Ha-Levi, perhaps the greatest poet of his age, in "A Letter to his Friend Isaac," wrote:

"And now the Spring is here with yearning eyes; midst shimmering golden flowerbeds, on meadows carpeted with varied hues, in richest raiment clad she treads. She weaves a tapestry of blooms over all."

Nahum, a 13th century Sephardic *paytan,* wrote:

"Winter is gone, gone is my sorrow. The fruit tree is in flower, and my heart flowers with joy. O hunted gazelle, [a reference to the *Shekhina*] who escaped far from my hut, come back. Trees of delight sway among the shadows."

And Abraham ibn Ezra, one of the great Torah commentators, wrote in his poem, "God Everywhere,"

> "Wherever I turn my eyes, around on Earth or to the heavens/I see you in the field of stars/I see You in the yield of the land/in every breath and sound, a blade of grass, a simple flower, an echo of Your holy Name."

All these poets saw nature as beautiful and worthy in and of itself—and also as a path toward the most beautiful and worthy of all, God.

Another lasting contribution to an environmental ethic by these medieval sages is in the elaboration of the Mishnaic principle of "moderation." They elucidated a principle of moderation opposed to both a hedonism that requires ever-increasing consumption in futile attempts to satisfy ever-expanding appetites, and to an asceticism that devalues the natural world, for, as Judah Ha-Levi wrote, "the holy law imposes no asceticism, but demands rather that we grant each physical faculty . . . its due" (*Kuzari*, 2:5). Of all the medieval sages, Maimonides was the foremost exponent of moderation, writing that "good deeds are ones that are equibalanced between too much and too little" (*Eight Chapters*, 54), and that "the right way is the mean in each group of dispositions common to humanity. One should only desire that which the body needs and cannot do without. One should eat only when hungry and not gorge oneself, but leave the table before the appetite is fully satisfied. . . . This is the way of the wise" (*Hilchot Deot*, 1). Nor was Maimonides the only sage promoting the "golden mean." Ibn Gabirol wrote, "abandon both extremes and set about the right mean" (*Ethics*, 145).

ADDITIONAL QUOTES

Rabbi Shimon said, "the shade spread over us by these trees is so pleasant! We must crown this place with words of Torah" (*Zohar*, 2:127a).

When Noah came out of the ark, he opened his eyes and saw the whole world completely destroyed. He began crying for the world and said, God, how could you have done this? . . . God replied, Oh Noah, how different you are from the way Abraham . . . will be. He will argue with me on behalf of Sodom and Gomorrah when I tell him that I plan their destruction. . . . But you, Noah, when I told you I would destroy the entire world, I lingered and delayed, so that you would speak on behalf of the world. But when you knew you would be safe in the ark, the evil of the world did not touch you. You thought of no one but your family. And now you complain? Then Noah knew that he had sinned (*Midrash Tankhuma, Parashat Noach*).

It should not be believed that all the beings exist for the sake of the existence of humanity. On the contrary, all the other beings too have been intended for their own sakes, and not for the sake of something else (Maimonides, *Guide for the Perplexed*, 456).

FROM THE RISE OF MODERNITY TO TODAY

On the eve of the modern period came the rise of Hasidism. In villages throughout Eastern Europe, beginning in the 18th century and continuing through the 19th, the rebbes of this movement spoke, often ecstatically, about the importance of a close relationship with the natural environment. The Baal Shem Tov, the founder of Hasidism, said that a man should consider himself as a worm, and all other small animals as his companions in the world, for all of them are created (*Tzava'at ha-Rivash*). Rabbi Schneur Zalman, the founder of the Chabad branch of Hasidism, taught that God is in all nature, a view he based on the fact that, in *gematria,* the name of God—*Elokim*—is equivalent to *ha-teva,* nature. Rabbi Zev Wolf taught that the wonders of the soil and of growing are to be contemplated before blessing food; the Medibozer Rebbe said that "God placed sparks of holiness within everything in nature" (*Butzina DeNehorah,* 22); Rabbi Nachman of Bratzlav, the great-grandson of the Baal Shem Tov and the Hasidic rebbe most closely attuned to nature, wrote that if we quest for God, we can find God revealed in all of creation (*Likkute Mohoran,* II, #12). Nachman prescribed to his followers daily prayer in fields, teaching that their prayers would be strengthened by those of every blade of grass (*Sichot Ha-Ran,* 227).

Even the erstwhile opponents of the Hasidim, such as some of the rabbis who started the *Musar* movement, joined with them in appreciation of nature. Rabbi Joseph Leib Bloch wrote that a good Jew "will be filled with wonder and excitement at the sight of the glories of nature ... and will know how to use these feelings for the sublime purpose of recognizing the Creator" (*Sha'arey Da'at,* I, 194).

With the dawn of the 19th century, a radical transformation of the Jewish circumstance commenced. It is doubtful whether, short of wartime, so much change in social circumstance was ever compressed in so short a period as the change we experienced in the 19th century. At the dawn of the century, Europe was home to 1.5 million of the world's then 2.5 million Jews. In the course of that century, Europe was utterly transformed, and we along with it. Old social, political, and economic structures crumbled; new possibilities emerged, enticed. Educational and economic opportunities, new places and new ideologies beckoned. And people moved: In 1813, there were some 8,000 Jews in Warsaw; by 1900, there were 219,128. In 1789, there were 114 Jews in Budapest; by 1900, there were 166,198; in 1816, there were 3,373 Jews in Berlin; by 1900, there were 92,206.

But even during this explosive time, significant rural populations remained. Thus, at the beginning of the 20th century, over 14 percent of Galician Jews were still engaged in agriculture. Many Jews emigrating to both North and South America (including, for example, the family of Rabbi Alexander Schindler) farmed during their first generation in the New World. And, perhaps more significantly, this period saw the rise of the first movements within Judaism advocating a return to the land, a reconnection with nature.

In Europe, the *Haskalah,* the "enlightenment," encouraged the establishment of thousands of farms during the 19th century in central and southern Russia. The *Haskalah* sought to reinvigorate the Jewish spirit—and many of its writers believed that there was no better way to do so than through renewed contact with nature. A number of Chaim Nachman Bialik's poems reflect this contact, such as his "At Twilight:" "They [our fantasies] will soar to the heights rustling like doves, and sail along into the distance and vanish. There, upon the purple mountain ridges, the roseate islands of splendor, they will silently flutter to rest."

But the *Haskalah* poet most committed to a return to nature was Saul Tchernikovsky:

"And if you ask me of God, my God/'Where is God that in joy we may worship?'/Here on Earth too God lives, not in heaven alone/A striking fir, a rich furrow, in them you will find God's likeness. Divine image incarnate in every high mountain. Wherever the breath of life flows, you will find God embodied./And God's household? All being: the gazelle, the turtle, the shrub, the cloud pregnant with thunder/ . . . God-in-Creation is God's eternal name."

Numerous Yiddish poets, both in Europe and America, wrote nature poems, some of which were influenced by Walt Whitman, such as "A Song," by Yehoash:

"A song of grass, a song of Earth, a song of gold ore in the womb of rock, a song of tin-white brook that bathes the body of the moon, a song of famished wolves that howl upon their snow-capped steppes."

Malka Heifetz Tussman's poems show a particular sensitivity to, perhaps even identification with, nature, as in her poem, "Songs of the Priestess:"

"Gather me up like wheat. Cut quickly/ and bind me/before autumn's whirlwind sweeps me away./ Hurry/I am fully ripe."

Numerous Yiddish prose authors, such as Mendele Mokher Seforim in his *Of Bygone Days* and Joseph Opatoshu in his *Romance of a Horsethief,* show a great affinity for the beauties of the natural world.

But it was in the Zionist movement, particularly in elements of the *kibbutz* movement, that the return to nature found its strongest supporters. A.D. Gordon, the best-known of such advocates, wrote "And when you, O human, will return to Nature, that day your eyes will open, you will stare straight into the eyes of Nature and in its mirror you will see your image. You will know .. that when you hid from Nature, you hid from yourself. . . . We who have been turned away from Nature—if we desire life, we must establish a new relationship with Nature" (*Mivhar Ketavim,* 57–58).

For his part, Rabbi Abraham Isaac Kook saw the return to nature as part of the sacred task of the Jew in Israel, necessary to create "strong and holy flesh" (*Orot,* 171). Some of the Zionist poets directly tied their love of nature to the return to the Land; here, religion per se was abandoned, but the secularized product was infused with spirituality. So Rachel (Rachel Blustein) wrote, in one of her most famous poems,

> "Land of mine, I have never sung to you nor glorified your name with heroic deeds/or the spoils of battle/all I have done is plant a tree/on the silent shores of the Jordan."

Others, such as Leah Goldberg, in her "Songs of the River," wrote of the beauty of nature in and of itself, apart from any Zionist aspirations:

> "My brother the river, eternally wandering/ Renewed day by day, and changing, and one/ My brother the flow, between your banks/ Which flows like myself between spring and fall."

There was an ideological point to such expression, for the early Zionist pioneers were taken (not to say obsessed) with the idea that the health of the Jewish people depended on its reconnection with nature, from which it had been so radically cut off in Europe. From A.D. Gordon's "Religion of Labor," his desire to "strike our roots deep into its [the land's] life-giving substance, and stretch out our branches into sustaining and creating air and sunlight," up until the extraordinary passion of contemporary Israelis to know the contours of their land, endlessly hiking through it and learning its ways, we may discern the echoes of an ancient tradition.

ADDITIONAL QUOTES

Nature is of the very essence of Deity (Israel Baal Shem Tov, *Shivkhe Ha-Besht*, 329).

Master of the Universe, grant me the ability to be alone; may it be my custom to go outdoors each day among the trees and grass and all growing things, and there may I be alone, and enter into prayer (Nachman of Bratzlav, *Maggid Sichot*, 48).

On Tu B'shvat/when spring comes/An angel descends/ledger in hand/and enters each bud, each twig, each tree, and all our garden flowers./From town to town, from village to village/the angel makes a winged way/searching the valleys, inspecting the hills/flying over the desert/and returns to heaven./And when the ledger will be full/of trees and blossoms and shrubs/when the desert is turned into a meadow/and all our land a watered garden/the Messiah will appear (Shin Shalom, modern Israeli poet).

I can contemplate a tree. I can accept it as a picture. . . . I can feel it as a movement. . . . I can assign it to a species and observe it as an instance. . . . I can overcome its uniqueness and form so rigorously that I can recognize it only as an expression of law. . . . I can dissolve it into a number, into a pure relation between numbers, and externalize it. Throughout all of this the tree, the tree remains my object and has its time span, its kind and condition. But it can also happen, if will and grace are joined, that as I contemplate the tree I am drawn into a relation, and the tree ceases to be an It (Martin Buber, *I and Thou*, 57–58).

GUIDING PRINCIPLES
FOR THE PRESENT AND FUTURE

Comes the question: What relevance has that tradition today? Or, more broadly: As important as is our past relationship with the environment, as a source of both counsel and inspiration, how are we today to develop guiding principles for our present relationship to the environment?

The effort to develop such principles, tied whenever possible to our tradition—tradition here understood as an amalgam of our texts and our experiences—is open-ended. Here, we offer seven principles, asking that they be understood as we understand the Four Questions of the Passover *Haggadah,* not as an authoritative or exhaustive list but as an effort to move us forward on our journey.

IDEALS AND ACTION, *HALACHA* AND FATE

One of the most basic of Jewish principles is that we are required to find ways to translate our ideals into a concrete course of action. Judaism has never been satisfied with rhetorical commitments; the *halacha* comes to give concrete shape to our most valued principles. Such concretization is not without its difficulties and controversies. We may, for example, become so overwhelmed at the complexity of the analysis and the actions it calls forth that we do nothing. How can one person help solve a global crisis?

But, as Rabbi Tarfon reminds us (*Pirke Avot,* 2:21), "We are not obligated to complete the task; neither are we free to abstain from it."

And then there is the problem of translation itself. Take even the most consensual ideal, one from which virtually no one would think to dissent, translate it into an action program, and suddenly there is debate, bickering, sometimes crippling dissensus. That is the real world.

Still, it is in the work of translation that we transform ourselves from *luftmentshen* to *mentshen.* And as difficult as the process is, it also reminds us of one of the central freedoms our faith proclaims: freedom from fate. Through our actions, we can choose life and blessing. It is up to us, even if it is not always or entirely clear which paths lead where. To succumb to inaction because the problems we face are complex, because our ideals are challenging, because there is pain along the way, is to abrogate our partnership with God in creating a better world, to abandon our stewardship along with our ideals, along, finally, with our humanity.

Knowing how arduous the process, how do we muster the courage and energy to begin the translation process? One helpful metaphor might be the image Maimonides discusses in *Hilchot Teshuvah,* in the context of a discussion of preparation for the High Holidays. As one approaches the Days of Awe, he writes, one should consider the entire world as if it were exactly balanced between acts of righteousness and of evil. The very next action you take, therefore, can save or condemn the world.

Imagine, then, if we were to set aside one day a year, perhaps *Tu B'shvat* or a new Jewish holiday created around Earth Day, as an environmental holiday of reflection. In preparation for that day, we would undertake a *heshbon*, a searching account, of the environmental consequences of our actions—as individuals, as a community, as a nation. We would imagine the world's ecosystem balanced on a scale, would think of our next action in terms of how it might save or condemn. After this time of reflection, we could return, reinvigorated and renewed, to the task of the reformation of behavior—and we could plan the changes in our educational efforts, in our life-styles, and in our advocacy work that such reformation requires of us. No more than a beginning, but at least a beginning, renewed each year just as we renew ourselves, our relationships, our devotion, each year. Nor need we wait for unanimity in the Jewish community before we take action—one city's Jewish population, or one synagogue, or even one family could begin the task.

God's Ownership and the Terms of Our Lease

How do we root our action plan in our Judaic tradition? First of all, by implementing our belief that this is God's world, not ours. To take seriously the notion that we are but leasing the planet from God is to provide ourselves with specific behavioral guidelines. One who leases is called, in general, a *shomer*, usually translated as a guardian. The specific type of lease we have on the Earth is that of a *sho'el*, a borrower. Borrowers may use any part of what they borrow—but they must ensure that, at the end of the term of the lease, and at any given moment during the lease, the property is at least as valuable as it was at the beginning of the lease (See, e.g. *Shulkhan Arukh, Hoshen Mishpat* 291, 292). This is similar to the principle of *tzon barzel*, an arrangement whereby a husband may use some of his wife's property—but only on the condition that it is never lowered in value.

Harvest a tree? Not without planting another. Farm the land? Not without allowing it periodic rest and rejuvenation. See to it that any degradation of the environment is accompanied by an equivalent restoration. Evaluate land use on the basis of how it improves or degrades the environment, so that, for example, agricultural practices that prevent soil erosion, crops that are easier on the land, requiring less irrigation and pesticides, and harvesting methods that preserve the integrity of the ecosystem are given strong preference. Attempt in each of our own lives to strike such a balance, conserving energy, supporting environmental causes, planting trees, as a path toward restoration of what we have used or abused.

While such efforts at balance are not required by present *halacha*, we should remember that the *Shulkhan Arukh* acknowledges this standard in regulating leases. (See, e.g. *Hoshen Mishpat* 308, 324).

THE UNITY OF CREATION—
INESCAPABLE CONSEQUENCES AND FUTURE GENERATIONS

Through our acceptance of the one Creator, we come to realize the unity of all creation. But if we truly believe in the unity and integrity of the universe, especially of the part of creation we know as the Earth, we must begin carefully to consider the consequences of our actions on that world. We need to realize that just as there is no action that is not recorded by *Shomer Yisrael,* the Guardian of Israel, so too is there no action without consequence to God's creation, the biosphere, no "elsewhere" to dump our garbage that will not, eventually, come floating back to haunt us.

Environmental costs were once labelled "externalities" by economists, for a laissez-faire doctrine does not weigh them in its working. But we have come to realize that these costs are not "external" at all, that they affect all of us. Since all aspects of our biosphere are woven together, any tearing of the fabric of life, the *Zohar's* "garment of the *Shekhina,*" is likely eventually to begin unravelling humanity's own threads.

In essence, we need to start conducting "environmental impact statements" on our daily lives. What happens when we waste water or energy? How does that affect the biosphere as a whole? Our local ecosystem? Our own health and well-being?

But what if we cannot be certain of those consequences? Is the fact that our behavior *may* be hazardous to the planet's health sufficient to make change in that behavior a moral imperative?

Rabbi Jacob Ettinger (*Responsa Binyan Zion,* 137) proposes that in such circumstances, we ask three questions: First, how "unreasonable" is the hazard, with "unreasonableness" defined in this context as a hazard that any "a well-informed individual would willingly spend money to eliminate." Second, how reversible are the damages if they do occur? And last, how likely is it, in the view of the best experts, that this potential hazard will come to pass?

The question that Rabbi Ettinger does *not* include in this calculus may be even more telling than the three questions he does. He does not propose that we ask anything about the timetable of hazard, about *when* the feared consequence may unfold. That omission is conscious and fully in keeping with our tradition. Our sages, when regulating potential dangers in the public domain, or even in areas that might in the future become part of the public domain, always viewed the fate of future generations with utmost concern, always sought to avoid endangering future generations with the same zeal with which they sought to protect their own. For our covenant is not just "with those standing here with us this day," but also "with those who are not here with us this day," (Deuteronomy 29:13–14), that is, with *all* the future generations.

Our actions should also be guided by a desire for seamless justice. The rabbis interpreted the repetition of the word *tzedek*, justice, in Deuteronomy's command "justice, justice shall you pursue" (16:20), as indicating that we must seek justice in both our means and our ends, both when it is to our advantage and when it is not (See, e.g., the commentary of Bakhya Ben Asher on this verse). Ends: No individual, group, or nation, should suffer disproportionately from environmental health hazards or ecosystem degradation. Means: As we work toward repairing ecosystems, solving environment problems, we need to ensure an equitable distribution of the costs of these solutions.

But does not a heightened concern for the health of the environment impose undue burdens on the poorer nations? In conscience, how can we, whose stunning economic development took place during a time of indifference to its environmental consequences, now turn to the poorer nations, seeking so desperately to escape their grinding poverty, and insist that they incorporate into their development plans a sensitivity to the environmental impact of those plans? Can we address the human needs of poorer countries even as we work toward the solution of global environmental problems?

First, we need to realize that long-term solutions to the latter problem often help solve the former. When the environment in third world countries is degraded, no one suffers more immediately or more severely than the poor. Conversely, when the environment is protected in a thoughtful manner, it often provides health and economic benefits to these same poor communities.

Furthermore, one can infer from Jewish sources that wealthier countries should subsidize environmental protection in poorer ones. The *Shulkhan Arukh* discusses the collections of taxes from a town in order to build a wall that benefits everyone in the town. If economic factors are equal, those close to the wall, who derive more protection from it, pay more—but if economic factors are not equal, those who can afford to pay more do so, for the whole town benefits (*Hoshen Mishpat*, 163:3). By analogy, this entire globe is our "town"; the whole global community benefits when any country protects its environment—and some countries are much more able to afford such protection than others. The same concern for seamless justice should guide our environmental work in the United States as well. We should pay particular attention to communities that have been disproportionately burdened by environmental health hazards and make sure that they have the necessary resources to turn their environment from a hazard to a source of health and joy.

Stewardship—A Covenental Trust

Lately, certain followers of "deep ecology" have subjected the notion of stewardship to harsh criticism. They ask, isn't it inherently and arrogantly hierarchical, placing humanity at the center of the universe? Doesn't it assume that the world cannot function without us, when evidence suggests, in fact, that ecosystems frequently work better without human interference? In the end, doesn't stewardship serve as a justification for domination and exploitation?

Understood in context, however, the Jewish notion of stewardship is a moral category, one that speaks of responsibility rather than of unlimited privilege, of a theocentric rather than anthropocentric universe. In Genesis 2:15, the first humans are commanded "to till and to tend" the Earth. This formulation hints at a kinship with the rest of creation that becomes even clearer when we look at the Hebrew more closely. *Avad* means not only to till, or even to work in a more general sense; it means also, and more powerfully, to serve or to participate in worship of the Divine. Thus, our "tilling" is more properly understood as service to God's Earth, a service that is not only a profound responsibility but a direct and critical part of our connection with and worship of God as well. And *shamar,* or "tend," means not only to tend, but more commonly, to guard or to watch over. What these meanings have in common is that the *shomrim* guard property that does not *belong* to them, but that is *entrusted* to them.

Good *shomrim* fulfill that trust, tending to the needs of that which they steward before tending to their own (see *Berakhot* 40a for examples). And all humans can indeed live in such a harmony with that which we serve and tend. But we also have the capacity—some might say the tendency—to destroy, merely by stepping outside the ordained relationship that assigns us a covenental trusteeship rather than raw domination.

The urge to such domination, however, not only violates the insights and commands of our tradition, a tradition that goes so far as to interpret the very words "rule" and "subdue," in Genesis 1:26 and 1:28, as signifying limited stewardship (see, e.g., *Yevamot* 65b, Genesis *Rabbah* 8:12 and the commentaries of Rashi and Sforno on these verses). It is also, in a word, stupid. For it is that urge, unencumbered by religious sensibility, unencumbered by responsibility for future generations, unencumbered by concern for our neighbors, that hastens the destruction of the very world we seek to master.

COMMUNAL RESPONSIBILITIES VS. INDIVIDUAL RIGHTS

The Jewish tradition has a strong communal orientation, one that has limited individual rights by placing them within the context of and subordinating them to communal responsibilities. For the good of the community, even "private property" could be taken, under the principle of *hefker bet din hefker,* literally, "what the court declares ownerless is ownerless," the Mishnaic version of "eminent domain." More generally, a community could both coerce its residents to take positive actions for the good of the community and prohibit them from actions held to be deleterious to the community. This prohibition went so far, for example, as to enable residents of a courtyard or sealed alley generally to prohibit any profession (excluding the teaching of Torah) from being performed in that area if it threatened, because of noise or noxious odors, to reduce the quality of life for the residents (See *Shulkhan Arukh,* Hoshen Mishpat 231:20, 161, 162, and 156 for a series of such regulations).

Such restrictions were even more stringent if a health hazard was suspected. In such cases, even if it could be demonstrated that a person's very livelihood might be lost, that bankruptcy might ensure, the practice of the endangering profession could nonetheless be prohibited. The general rule, set down by the Ribash, is that "a person is not permitted to save himself from injury by causing injury to his neighbor" (*Responsa:* 196).

What moral lessons can be inferred from these situations and applied to our contemporary global crisis? If we view the whole globe as a large community, whose citizens are as bound together through the connections of the biosphere as are residents of a courtyard, and if we factor in the undeniable health hazards of pollution, it can be argued that the community has the right, perhaps even the duty, to prohibit actions that degrade the environment—even when such prohibition imposes significant costs on the actors.

What, then, are our communal responsibilities to the environment? In general, even when human activity requires some use of, and consequent damage to, natural resources, decisions should be made in favor of the least destructive method feasible (See, e.g., *Bava Kamma* 91b). A minority opinion in *Shabbat* 140b goes even further. According to this minority view, when an individual chooses one type of food over another merely because of preference and not out of need, and when the "preferred" food is more costly to the environment, that individual is "wasting," and thus violating *bal tashchit* (the prohibition against waste), a violation that the community is entitled to prohibit. Perhaps it has come time to follow this minority opinion, to prohibit, for example, environmentally costly packaging that serves no purpose other than "convenience," or to limit consumption deemed extravagant by the community.

Many recent writers have begun to elaborate this into a principle they call "eco-kashrut," a set of guidelines for personal consumption. These guidelines ask questions such as: are fur coats "kosher?" What about styrofoam, or gas-guzzling autos?

Societal Goals—Sabbath Peace

Our final guiding principle speaks in the broadest terms, as a reminder that all the while we are engaged in detailed policy debates and behavioral adjustments, we ought not, dare not, lose sight of our ultimate goal. How may that goal be defined? At the risk of intimidating the reader, is it really not time for us to speak candidly of the tension between our lives as consumers and our lives as fully human beings—a little lower than the angels, if you will? And is it not time for us to seek, perhaps through our concern for the environment, a redirection of our own purposes and perceptions? Yes, the environment is at stake; so, also, are we.

One may prefer this economic theory or that, one may take what view one wishes of the question of "small is good" vs. "bigger is better." On virtually any reading, we in the industrialized world have allowed our appetites to outrun both our resources and our humanity (see *Pirke Avot* 2:7, 4:1, 4:21 and Maimonides' frequent teachings on the "golden mean," especially his *Eight Chapters,* for some of the many examples of calls for moderation in our tradition.). The acquisition of things becomes the measure of all value, and we are thereby diminished. More: In worshiping the idol of consumption, we do damage to the environment. More still: We do damage to our souls, to a society that might know *shalom,* might know contentment. And we have been given the first step to that *shalom* through Shabbat itself. With the pause of Shabbat, we become, as we read in Exodus (31:17), "re-ensouled" (*va-yinafash*). For the institution of Shabbat, of sacred self-imposed limits, of not working to create but of enjoying creation just as it is, helps bring us closer to peace and contentment.

Say "contentment," and some will think the very word subversive, for it suggests an end to acquisition. But this is neither an argument for asceticism nor even a deprecation of material goods. Our sages did not condemn materialism. Indeed, they wrote that without bread, there can be no Torah (*Pirke Avot* 3:21). But they were acutely aware, at the same time, of the need for balance, a balance we scarcely any longer recognize. Humankind does not, after all, live by bread alone.

ADDITIONAL RESOURCES

Cohen, Jeremy. *"Be Fertile and Increase—Fill the Earth and Master It": The Ancient and Midrashic Career of a Biblical Text* (Ithaca: Cornell University Press, 1989). An in-depth examination of the controversial Genesis 1:28 passage.

Farb, Peter, and Harry McNaught. *The Land, Wildlife, and People of the Bible.* (New York: Harper and Row, 1967). A natural history of the land of Israel, with an examination of ecological conditions in the Middle East over the past 3,000 years.

Hareuveni, Nogah. *Ecology in the Bible.* (Kiryat Ono, Israel: Neot Kedumim, 1974); *Nature in Our Biblical Heritage* (1980); *Trees and Shrubs in Our Biblical Heritage* (1984). This trio of books examines how an understanding of biblical and early rabbinic attitudes toward nature can illuminate both environmental issues and the Jewish tradition.

Rabinowitz, Louis I. *Torah and Flora.* Sanhedrin Press, 1979. A guide, arranged by Torah portion, to the significance and symbolism of plants in the Torah.

Shochet, Elijah J. *Animal Life in Jewish Tradition: Attitudes and Relationships* (New York: KTAV, 1984). Provides history, from biblical times to modernity, of Jewish attitudes toward legal traditions about the animal kingdom.

Stein, David E., ed. *A Garden of Choice Fruits.* (Philadelphia: Shomrei Adamah, 1991). A collection (without commentary) of some 200 short quotes from Jewish texts about environmental attitudes and issues.

"CHRISTIANITY AS ECOLOGICALLY HARMFUL"

and

"CHRISTIANITY AS ECOLOGICALLY RESPONSIBLE"

David Kinsley

"CHRISTIANITY AS ECOLOGICALLY HARMFUL"

DOMINATION OF NATURE AND ANTHROPOCENTRISM IN CHRISTIANITY AND THE BIBLE

The critique of the Bible and Christianity as constituting primarily negative influences in the advent and development of contemporary ecological crises usually makes three general arguments to support its point of view. First, in the Bible and Christianity nature is stripped of its gods, goddesses, and spirits and ceases to be regarded as divine. Second, the Bible and Christianity are strongly anthropocentric and teach that human beings are divinely ordained to rule over and dominate all other species and nature generally. Third, many Christian writings, and much Christian theology, relegate nature and matter generally to a low status relative to the divine, which is equated with spirit alone.

DESACRALIZATION OF NATURE

Those who indict the Bible and Christianity as encouraging ecological exploitation say that the Bible and Christianity reject the pagan worldview in which nature is permeated by spirits that are associated with, or inhabit, natural objects such as trees, animals, rivers, mountains, and the planets. In the words of Lynn White, Jr.: "Popular religion in antiquity was animistic.

Kinsley, David, *Ecology and Religion*, © 1994, pp. 103–114, 115–123, 2 chapters. Reprinted by permission of Prentice-Hall Inc., Englewood Cliffs, NJ.

Every stream, every tree, every mountain contained a guardian spirit who had to be carefully propitiated before one put a mill in a stream, or cut the tree, or mined the mountain."[1] Christianity, White argues, in opposing and destroying pagan animism, "made it possible to exploit nature in a mood of indifference to the feelings of natural objects."[2] In this view, Christianity replaced all of the old gods, many of whom were nature deities. To a great extent, due to this biblical/Christian revolution, nature was demystified; this formed the theoretical basis for the later scientific worldview, which sees nature as completely nonsacred and passive, fit to be controlled and manipulated by human beings. Arnold Toynbee says:

> Man was divorced from his natural environment, which was divested of its former aura of divinity. Man was licensed to exploit an environment that was no longer sacrosanct. The salutary respect and awe with which man had originally regarded his environment was thus dispelled by Judaic monotheism in the versions of its Israelite originators and of Christians and Muslims.[3]

Lynn White, again, puts the matter in no uncertain terms:

> To a Christian a tree can be no more than a physical fact. The whole concept of the sacred grove is alien to Christianity and to the ethos of the West. For nearly two millennia Christian missionaries have been chopping down sacred groves which are idolatrous because they assume spirit in nature.[4]

In short, according to this view, the Bible and the religions based upon it adopted an anti-nature view of the world, a view of the world that postulates a transcendent deity who creates the world but does not invest himself in it in such a way to make it holy or sacred. Critics see the Old Testament opposition to the worship of Baal as opposition to nature worship by followers of the new biblical deity, who transcends nature and is not to be confused with it. Because of this Old Testament bias against nature, critics say, Christianity was predisposed to a desacralized view of nature that laid the foundation for scientific and technological manipulation of nature.

DOMINATION OF NATURE

Those who indict the Bible and Christianity as contributing to ecological exploitation also emphasize the theme of human domination of nature and the strong tendency to anthropocentrism, which they say pervades both the Bible and the religions it inspired. According to this view, the Bible sets human beings against nature, makes human beings superior to, and in control of, nature. The Buddhist scholar D. T. Suzuki says:

> The Nature-Man dichotomy issues, as I think, from the Biblical account in which the creator is said to have given mankind the power to dominate over all creation. It is fundamentally due

to this story that the Western people talk so much about conquering Nature. When they invent a flying machine, they say they have conquered the air; when they climb up to the top of Mt. Everest, they make the loud announcement that they have succeeded in conquering the mountain.[5]

Lynn White, again in forceful language, makes a similar point:

> Especially in its Western form, Christianity is the most anthropocentric religion the world has seen. . . . Man shares, in great measure, God's transcendence of nature. Christianity, in absolute contrast to ancient paganism and Asia's religions . . . not only established a dualism of man and nature but also insisted that it is God's will that man exploit nature for his proper ends.[6]

Three passages from the Bible[7] are most frequently cited to substantiate this interpretation:

> Then God said, "Let us make man in our image, after our likeness; and let them have dominion over the fish of the sea, and over the birds of the air, and over the cattle, and over all the earth, and over every creeping thing that creeps upon the earth." So God created man in his own image, in the image of God he created him; male and female he created them. And God blessed them, and God said to them, "Be fruitful and multiply, and fill the earth and subdue it; and have dominion over the fish of the sea and over the birds of the air and over every living thing that moves upon the earth." And God said, "Behold, I have given you every plant yielding seed which is upon the face of all the earth, and every tree with seed in its fruit; you shall have them for food."
> (Gen. 1:26–29)

> And God blessed Noah and his sons, and said to them, "Be fruitful and multiply, and fill the earth. The fear of you and the dread of you shall be upon every beast of the earth, and upon every bird of the air, upon everything that creeps on the ground and all the fish of the sea; into your hand they are delivered. Every moving thing that lives shall be food for you; and as I gave you the green plants, I give you everything."
> (Gen. 9:1–3)

> Yet thou hast made him little less than God,
>   and dost crown him with glory and honor.
> Thou hast given him dominion over the works of thy hands;
>   thou hast put all things under his feet;
> all sheep and oxen,
>   and also the beasts of the field,
> the birds of the air, and the fish of the sea,
>   whatever passes along the paths of the sea.
>   (Ps. 8:5–8)

These passages, say ecology critics of the Bible, depict the world as created primarily, if not exclusively, for humankind.[8] They betray a strongly anthropocentric view of reality in which God is primarily interested in human beings and delegates to them mastery over his creation. These passages, they say, can lead to human arrogance vis-à-vis the natural world. In the view of Ian McHarg, a famous landscape architect, the Western, biblically based religious traditions reduce nature to inconsequence in the process of glorifying human beings. "Judaism and Christianity have long been concerned with justice and compassion for the acts of man to man, but they have traditionally assumed nature to be a mere backdrop for the human play."[9]

The Bible itself, in the view of its ecologically minded critics, is primarily a story that features the drama of human salvation. In this drama, human ethics and morality are central, as are certain historical events, such as the exodus from Egypt, the migration to the promised land, the building of the temple, and the coming of Jesus as the messiah. In this story, the relationship between human beings and nature is not important or of interest to the biblical writers. Offensive human action is almost invariably understood in the context of human-to-human or human-to-divine affairs.

The biblical attitude toward the Baal cult, the indigenous religion of Canaan, is interpreted by ecology-minded critics as a criticism of a religious view that emphasized rapport with, reverence for, and propitiation of the powers latent in the land—in short, a criticism of nature religion. In the Bible, these critics say, human spiritual fulfillment involves orienting oneself to the transcendent presence of God and not to the mysterious powers of the earth. Harmony is defined in terms of proper relations with God, not with proper attitudes toward the land or toward the spirits who dwell in the land. The land, or nature, is only sacred indirectly, as having been created by God. It is not intrinsically sacred, worthy of respect and reverence in itself, and to revere the land in itself is considered idolatry in the Bible and Christianity, according to these critics.

DEGRADATION OF NATURE AND MATTER

The third major criticism ecologically minded critics have of Christianity is its tendency to degrade nature and matter generally. This denigration of nature is associated with the tendency in Christianity, these critics say, to elevate the spiritual. Christianity in particular, and the Bible to a lesser extent, thinks of spiritual fulfillment or salvation in terms of spiritual ascent in which one's spiritual identity or soul escapes from or transcends earthly identity and material limitations. A human being's spiritual home, in this view, is in heaven and not on earth. A person's spiritual destiny is aimed at a heavenly realm or dimension that is fundamentally different from, if not opposed to, the earthly realm. In this view, as articulated by certain Christian thinkers, a person's earthly life is primarily understood as a temporary sojourn during which one is bound, restricted, or otherwise limited. In essence, one's life on earth is understood to be a sojourn in a foreign land. In this view, the primary theological concerns have to do with God and the salvation of the soul. The world, the earth, nonhuman forms of life, and nature generally are subsidiary concerns, at the least, and are denigrated at worst.

Opposed to what we might call this spiritual motif, which is dominated by the image of an ascent to heaven or God, is what we might call the ecological motif, according to which the human spirit is understood to be rooted in the biophysical order.[10] God's presence in the physical world is celebrated. In this view, the interrelations between God, man, and nature are carefully affirmed. To the ecologically minded critics of Christianity, the Christian tradition almost entirely lacks the ecological motif and is dominated by the spiritual motif.

The alienation from nature and denigration of the material world that developed in early Christian theology might be traced to the Bible. In the case of many early Christian theologians, though, it was Neoplatonism with its idea of the Great Chain of Being, rather than the Bible, that formed the philosophical basis of their thought. According to the philosopher Plotinus (205–70 C.E.), reality is hierarchical in nature. God, who is pure spirit, is at the apex of this hierarchy, while nonspiritual beings, which include plants, animals, and inanimate objects, are at its bottom. The hierarchy is graded according to the extent of the spiritual nature of beings; those beings who are most spiritual are near the top of the hierarchy, and those who are least spiritual and more material are at the bottom. Humans, as embodied spirits who are characterized by both spirit and matter, are below God and the angels but above all other living beings.[11]

In this hierarchy of being, the most important division is not between the creator and his or her creatures (as it is in the Bible, for example) but between spiritual and nonspiritual beings. Among the spiritual beings, besides God, are the angels and human beings. All other creatures below the human in the hierarchy are nonspiritual beings. Although sensible and sentient, they are simply material beings having no souls or spirits. Human beings are unique. They are spiritual beings, but they are enfleshed in material bodies. So they share a spiritual identity with higher creatures in the chain, but they also share an identity with the lower creatures.

THE THEOLOGY OF ORIGEN (185–254 C.E.)

The earliest and probably best example of a Christian theologian who proceeded according to Neoplatonic principles, and in the process tended to degrade nature and matter, was Origen (185–254). According to Origen, God creates the world after and because of a spiritual rebellion in heaven in which certain rational spirits turn away from God (this is the Fall, according to Origen). God creates the world as a gracious act in order to prevent human beings, who are rational spirits, from falling completely into the realm of nonbeing. The fallen spirits, instead of going completely out of existence, become enmeshed in the material world that God has created for them. Having become enmeshed or encased in matter, these fallen spirits then long for release and return to heaven and proximity to God. The material world, according to Origen, is created primarily by God as a kind of purgatory where fallen human beings are educated through trials and tribulations to return to the realm of pure spirit from which they have fallen.[12]

Origen has a low opinion of the material world, especially the human body, toward which he adopted a radically ascetic attitude. "The world of flesh is the world of demons. Gross matter . . . is the domain of Satan."[13] Creatures that inhabit the hierarchy of being below humans—the beasts, plants, and the rest of nature—are not considered fallen spirits at all but are regarded by Origen as beings whose purpose is to provide a background for the moral education of humans. This world resembles "a pernicious wilderness" for Origen; at one point he likens the creation of humanity to "the birth of a child, and the world of irrational and inanimate things to 'the afterbirth which is created with the child.'"[14] For Origen, then, nonhuman creatures have no other role or value than their relations to human beings. They have no intrinsic spiritual nature or goal and are created entirely for human purposes.

Salvation, then, is the process whereby human beings (and other spiritual beings such as the planets) regain their original spiritual state. Salvation was described by Origen in very spiritualistic terms. When this salvation takes place, when all of humanity is saved, the physical world will have no purpose and will return to nothingness. In terms of the resurrected body, a Christian doctrine that gave Origen some difficulty, he spoke of a body that will be like ether, having celestial purity and clearness, in short, a body that is almost entirely spiritual in nature.[15] Salvation for Origen, then, is primarily an ascent from the material to the spiritual, or an ascent during which the dross of matter is gradually shed and the human being is refined. It is absolutely clear in Origen that the material creation is not humankind's home. That home is in heaven, where matter has no place, where only a highly etherealized body can exist, where all lesser creatures in the chain of being have no place at all.

In order to conform his theology to the Bible, Origen usually interprets biblical texts allegorically. For example, he interprets the expulsion of Adam and Eve from the Garden of Eden as the fall of the rebellious angels into the material world. The migration and long journey to the promised land of the Hebrews is interpreted as the human species' gradual ascent to salvation. Egypt is explained as the condition of bondage to the material world, while the exodus is explained as the beginning of the return to heaven.

In the theology of Origen, then, we have a clear and definite degrading or depreciation of nature and matter. Human life on earth is understood to be unnatural to the spiritual nature of human beings and has to be overcome in the spiritual quest.[16] Nature is interpreted solely in terms of its role in educating, refining, and reorienting human beings in their quest for salvation. To a great extent, nature is seen as a cage or prison that restricts and binds the spiritual nature of human beings.

Some of Origen's specific ideas, such as reincarnation and the role of Jesus as a wisdom bearer, were later condemned as heretical by the church. However, the overall logic and structure of his theology and his fairly radical distinction between spirit and matter, between the soul and the body, remained influential in Christian theology.

THE THEOLOGY OF THOMAS AQUINAS

Turning to Thomas Aquinas (1225–74), who lived nearly a thousand years after Origen, we continue to see themes that were central in Origen's thought appearing as important Thomistic emphases. According to Aquinas, the creation of the world is intended to mirror God's goodness. Creation is the overflowing of divine goodness. In his view of creation, each kind of being has an integrity of its own and is meant, in its own way, to suggest the nature of God. An essential characteristic of the creation, however, is its hierarchical nature. Among all creatures living in the world, a human being is the most spiritual and rational and so is seen by Aquinas as the most sublime. The lower and less-spiritual creatures, according to Aquinas, mirror the divine by serving higher creatures. They do not share in divine goodness to the extent that humans do and because of this are subordinate to humans. Indeed, their natures are defined in terms of their subservience to human beings. In the words of Aquinas: "As we observe . . . imperfect beings serve the needs of more noble beings; plants draw their nutriment from the earth, animals feed on plants, and these in turn serve man's use. We conclude, then, that lifeless beings exist for living beings, plants for animals, and the latter for man. . . . The whole of material nature exists for man, inasmuch as he is a rational animal."[17]

All creatures serve the good of the whole in this theology by serving human purposes and needs. "Nature is seen more as an object for human use, which satisfies biological needs and serves spiritual knowledge, than as a subject in its own right."[18] Again, in the words of Aquinas himself: "We believe all corporeal things to have been made for man's sake, wherefore all things are stated to be subject to him. Now they serve man in two ways, first as sustenance of his bodily life, secondly, as helping him to know God, inasmuch as man sees the invisible things of God by the things that are made."[19]

In Aquinas's thinking about salvation, the lesser beings and the physical world are clearly subordinated to the destiny of the human race. The human race will be perfected by means of salvation, and this perfection implies a transcendence of the material world. Aquinas used the analogy that the material creation is the dwelling of human beings; dwellings must be suitable for the inhabitants, but the material creation will not be suitable for totally redeemed and renewed human beings. The perfection or renewal of humankind in salvation leaves the less-perfect world of material creation and the lower creatures behind. In short, in Aquinas's view, the lesser animals are not capable of renewal and perfection, as human beings are. They are outside of, and irrelevant to, the ultimate salvific process.

St. Bonaventure (1221–74) and Dante Alighieri (1265–1321)

The works of St. Bonaventure and Dante, two very important medieval thinkers, confirm the themes we have discussed in the works of Aquinas. Like Aquinas, Bonaventure and Dante saw the creation of the world as a good thing. It is the result of the overflowing of God's goodness, and their works affirm the beauty of the creation. The world is not wicked or degraded but, as the creation of God, is good. The world is only relatively good, however, and assumes a subordinate place in the cosmic scheme of things when Bonaventure and Dante speak of the spiritual progress of human beings. In both of their writings, the theme of spiritual ascent is extremely strong and tends to reduce the physical world to secondary status. Although nature is extolled as the work of God, there is no emphasis in either Bonaventure or Dante on establishing rapport with nature, communing with nature, or revering nature as such. Indeed, in the spiritual ascent, nature is increasingly transcended; in both authors it is clear that humankind's spiritual home is in heaven, which is above, beyond, and superior to the material creation. Though both saw the world as charged with divine glory, a person's ultimate destiny is "total release from the biophysical order."[20] In Dante's tour of the three-tiered cosmos, it is clear that a human being's home is not on earth, "surrounded by the birds and snakes and trees and streams. His home is far above in the ethereal regions of absolute, pure, and imageless spiritual transcendence."[21]

The Reformation: Luther and Calvin

In their dissent from much of medieval Christian thought, the reformers Martin Luther (1483–1546) and John Calvin (1509–64) tended to reject the idea of human beings ascending through their own effort to inhabit a heavenly sphere that transcends the earth. In their descriptions of salvation they emphasized, rather, the descent of God to earth. However, in their theology this does not mean that they gave a particularly positive interpretation to nature. On the contrary, as we shall see, nature is still very much in the background of their theology. God's descent to earth in the person of Jesus is primarily, if not exclusively, related to the salvation of human beings and has little or nothing to do with the status of nature. Nature is not of much interest either in its own right or as a revelation of the nature and glory of God. It is of interest primarily in terms of its relevance to human beings. For Luther, nature is intended by God primarily to be a dwelling for human beings. Luther said, for example, that "night and day alternate for the purpose of refreshing our bodies by rest. The sun shines that work may be done."[22] There was also a tendency in Luther to comment on the negative aspects of nature and to think of nature generally as "standing under the 'left hand of God,' the wrathful, alien hand of God."[23] Luther wrote: "God's wrath also appears on the earth in all creatures. . . . And what of thorns, thistles, water, fire, caterpillars, flies, fleas, and bedbugs? Collectively and individually, are not all of them messengers who preach to us concerning sin and God's wrath?"[24]

For Luther, nature is not something one seeks to commune with. Nor did Luther see in nature evidence of God's glory. For him nature is, at times anyway, a conspiracy of "hostile energies . . . which motivate the despairing soul to seek out and to cling to 'the right hand of God.' . . . Nature has the effect of drawing the despairing soul to seek the humanity of Christ."[25] It repulses more than it attracts.

For Calvin, also, human beings and their relations with God are the central concerns of his writings. Nature is subsidiary, the background for the truly significant drama of human salvation. Calvin tended to view God as characterized primarily by will and power. God's principal relationship to nature is as its governor. God controls and directs nature; as God's agent or special creation, human beings are to imitate this relationship in their dealings with nature. The emphasis in Calvin is not on communing with nature, nor on transcending nature in one's salvific quest. The emphasis is on transforming nature, remolding it to God's glory.

Human Domination of Nature in Early Modern England

The sixteenth to eighteenth centuries in Western Europe saw the end of the medieval period, the end of Christian unity under a strong papacy, the rise of nationalism, the exploration of Africa, Asia, and America by Europeans, the rise of individualism, the rise of mercantilism, the discovery and application of the modern scientific method, the spread of colonialism, and the explosion of industrial technology and the rise of factory production. These centuries saw the birth and early development of the modern period.

Throughout this period, Christianity remained vigorous and dominated the cultural, historical, artistic, and political aspects of life in Western Europe and America. To a great extent, the Bible and Christianity were called upon to support and reinforce aspects of modernism, such as technology, science, and colonialism. Some of the themes we have pointed out as antiecological were drawn upon or underlined, while others were quietly dropped. The ideas that were dropped concerned ascetic aloofness from nature, or withdrawal from nature, and the attempt to ascend above the material world to a sublime, spiritual destiny. Although the spiritual tendencies in Christianity remained, they were not emphasized as theological justifications for most aspects of modernism.

The themes of anthropocentrism, human domination of nature, and the superiority of human beings over all other creatures were the themes that were most popular in justifying many aspects of the modern period. A brief sampling of comments from early modern England will illustrate this. In biblical commentaries of this period, nature is interpreted almost exclusively in anthropocentric terms. The pernicious aspects of nature, for example, were interpreted as the result of the human Fall. That is, as a punishment against Adam and Eve, God made nature turn nasty, whereas before the Fall nature had been benign and friendly to human beings. After the Fall, many commentators said, the earth declined in beauty and richness. Noxious plants, thorns, and thistles appeared to replace vegetation that had been completely agreeable to human beings. The land became less fertile and demanded hard work to cultivate it. Annoying insects appeared, and many animals that had been tame and friendly to human beings became wild and dangerous.[26] Nature is described as flawed, fallen, rebellious, and odious, not in itself but as the result of human moral action. It is a reflection of the human condition. It is understood strictly from an anthropocentric point of view. As one commentator put it: "The creatures were not made for themselves, but for the use and service of man. Whatsoever change for the worse is come upon them is not their punishment, but part of ours."[27]

If an animal seemed by nature inimical to human beings, this was by divine plan as a punishment for the Fall, or perhaps to instruct human beings in some fashion. One commentator on this theme put the matter succinctly: "He made others for man, and man for himself. All things were created principally for the benefit and pleasure of man." Yet another said: "The only purpose of animals is to minister to man, for whose sake all the creatures were made that are made."[28]

> It was with human needs in mind that the animals had been carefully designed and distributed. Camels, observed a preacher in 1696, had been sensibly allotted to Arabia, where there was no water, and savage beasts "sent to deserts, where they may do less harm." It was a sign of God's providence that fierce animals were less prolific than domestic ones and that they lived in dens by day, usually coming out only at night, when men were in bed. Moreover, whereas members of wild species all looked alike, cows, horses and other domestic animals had been conveniently variegated in colour and shape, in order "that mankind may the more readily distinguish and claim their respective property." The physician George Cheyne in 1705 explained that the Creator made the horse's excrement smell sweet, "because he knew that men would often be in its vicinity."[29]

William Byrd wrote that horseflies had been created by God to tests the patience and wits of human beings. George Owen said that the lobster had been created to give human beings food, to provide them with exercise in taking it apart to eat it, and as an example to human beings of the utility of armor. Henry More in 1653 wrote that cattle and sheep had been given life by God simply to keep their meat fresh until human beings were ready to eat them. William Kirby found the louse useful in the overall divine scheme of things because it taught human beings the usefulness of cleanliness.[30]

Vegetables and minerals were regarded in the same way. Henry More thought that their only purpose was to enhance human life. Without wood, men's houses would have been merely a "bigger sort of beehive or bird's nest, made of contemptible sticks and stray and dirty mortar"; and, without metals, men would have been deprived of the "glory and pomp" of war, fought with swords, guns and trumpets; instead there would have been "nothing but howlings and shoutings of poor naked men belabouring one another . . . with sticks or dully falling together by the ears at fisticuffs." Even weeds and poisons had their essential uses, noted a herbalist: for they exercised the "industry of man to weed them out. . . . Had he nothing to struggle with, the fire of his spirit would be half extinguished."[31]

Such views assumed that God had created the world, and every creature in it, for some human purpose. The entire creation was perceived to have been ordered specially for humankind. This anthropocentrism was linked with the conviction that it was a divine mandate that humankind dominate nature. Other creatures had no rights and were primarily in existence to be disposed of in any way human beings found fitting.

Domestication of animals was seen as a perfect example of what God had intended in creating them. Sheep, pigs, and cows were said to be better off under human care than left to be attacked by wild predators; while the slaughter of animals for human consumption might seem cruel, Thomas Robinson in 1709 said that such killing should be understood as a blessing rather than a cruelty because of its efficiency which minimized pain and spared animals from suffering the pains of old age.[32] Human authority over nature was viewed as virtually unlimited; John Day in 1620 said that humankind "might use it as he pleased for his profit or for his pleasure." Plants and animals were said to have no rights at all. Samuel Gott said that "we may put them to any kind of death that the necessity either of our food or physic will require."[33]

During this period in Western Europe, a commonly accepted goal of human endeavor was to triumph over nature, and much Christian theology of the day was happy to provide the moral rationale for it. Most popular and professional theology of the day had no sympathy with veneration for nature, which was seen as a constraint against the human campaign to completely rule over all other creatures. In this period, "human civilization was virtually synonymous with the conquest of nature."[34]

It was in this context that modern Western science began to take shape, and it is clear that the goals of science were seen to be in harmony with the theological emphasis on human domination of nature as a God-given right. Quite often, indeed typically, scientists would phrase their goals and purposes in theological imagery. For Francis Bacon (1561–1626), for example, the aim of science was to provide human beings with the knowledge necessary to restore their dominion over nature which they had lost as a result of the Fall. William Forsyth, in speaking about the importance of studying the behavior of caterpillars, said: "It would be of great service to get acquainted as much as possible with the economy and natural history of all these insects, as we might thereby be enabled to find out the most certain method of destroying them."[35] Botany and zoology were clearly pragmatic in their aims and sought through knowledge of plants and animals to extend human domination over them for human utilization.

The human domination of other species became a central theme during this period of history in European civilization. The evolution and development of human society, culture, and civilization were viewed as the gradual process whereby human beings defended themselves against wild beasts, domesticated certain species, and eventually came to dominate them. The human conquest and possession of the earth was the result, primarily, of human beings outwitting, overpowering, and dominating other species.[36]

Throughout this period, considerable attention was given to the issue of human uniqueness. In discussing this issue, almost all who gave opinions on the subject assumed the superiority of the human species over all the rest. The entire thrust of the discussion was toward emphasizing the radical differences between human beings and other creatures. Human superiority justified the ways in which humans dominated other creatures. The reasons given for human superiority were many, but the most common are familiar to most of us: human beings alone are rational, humans alone are capable of moral action, humans alone have a soul or animating principle.

A particularly important trend in this discussion of human superiority was the increasing tendency to view nature as dead matter and other species as machines. Human beings alone, it was asserted, were endowed with spirit or soul. Animals, although they behaved in ways similar to humans, were actually without spirits or souls and were best understood, it was argued, on the model of machines. For René Descartes (1596–1650), for example, "the human body was also an automaton; after all, it performed many unconscious functions, like that of digestion. But the difference was that within the human machine there was a mind and therefore a separate soul, whereas brutes were automata without minds or souls. Only man combined both matter and intellect."[37]

That the biblical and Christian themes emphasized in the above discussion continue to influence modern attitudes toward nature is readily apparent. The impetus behind technological development and scientific mastery is still understood by many people to be mastery of nature. This is particularly clear in medical science and technology. Although theological or biblical language and imagery are not necessarily employed, the logic of such themes as anthropocentrism, the domination of nature, and the superiority of human beings is typically understood to have a transcendent mandate.

For several centuries the rightness of these views was hardly questioned. Some cranks did object to what they viewed as human arrogance and pride, but for the most part human beings felt quite self-righteous in their quest to tame, civilize, and otherwise dominate nature even if that meant destroying large parts of it. Recently, attitudes have begun to change. Many religiously minded people have tried to find ecologically positive aspects to the biblical and Christian traditions in an attempt to harmonize their reverence for both the Bible and nature.

&

"CHRISTIANITY AS ECOLOGICALLY RESPONSIBLE"

Problems with the Mastery Hypothesis

We have looked at arguments that the Bible and Christianity are responsible for teaching human mastery of the environment, a mastery that has led to exploitation of nature and ecological crises. There are some problems with the mastery hypothesis, however, and in examining these problems we can also consider some positive facets of both the Bible and Christianity as sources for ecological spirituality.

Desacralization of nature

Proponents of the mastery hypothesis argue that the Bible's desacralization of nature led to a lack of reverence for nature. In contrast to the Bible, these people say, was the pagan world represented by contemporary cultures of the ancient Near East and the Mediterranean basin, in which nature was governed and pervaded by spirits, gods, and goddesses. The matter, though, is not this simple, by any means. First, there were many examples in the pagan world of people making use of the natural environment. Agriculture itself is manipulation of the land. Building, logging, canal building—all were widespread in the pagan world and were not hindered because of belief in nature spirits. A more accurate picture of the pagan world probably would emphasize that some groves, mountains, and streams were viewed as especially sacred, while others were not.

Second, the Bible has several passages that suggest that the natural world was respected, if not revered, while, conversely, there are no passages that suggest that nature was viewed as dead matter to be easily manipulated by human beings. Psalm 96:11–13 says, for example:

> *Let the heavens be glad, and let the earth rejoice;*
> > *let the sea roar, and all that fills it;*
> > *let the field exult, and everything in it!*
> *Then shall all the trees of the wood sing for joy*
> > *before the LORD, for he comes,*

David Kinsley

> *for he comes to judge the earth.*
> *He will judge the world with righteousness,*
> *and the peoples with his truth.*

In Psalm 148:1–13, we get another glimpse of a view of the natural world that sees it as alive and responding to God in a moral fashion:

> *Praise the LORD!*
> *Praise the LORD from the heavens,*
> *praise him in the heights!*
> *Praise him, all his angels,*
> *praise him, all his host!*
> *Praise him, sun and moon,*
> *praise him, all you shining stars!*
> *Praise him, you highest heavens,*
> *and you waters above the heavens!*
> *Let them praise the name of the LORD!*
> *For he commanded and they were created.*
> *And he established them for ever and ever;*
> *he fixed their bounds which cannot be passed.*
> *Praise the LORD from the earth,*
> *you sea monsters and all deeps,*
> *fire and hail, snow and frost,*
> *stormy wind fulfilling his command!*
> *Mountains and all hills,*
> *fruit trees and all cedars!*
> *Beasts and all cattle,*
> *creeping things and flying birds!*
> *Kings of the earth and all peoples,*
> *princes and rulers of the earth!*
> *Young men and maidens together,*
> *old men and children!*
> *Let them praise the name of the LORD,*
> *for his name alone is exalted;*
> *his glory is above earth and heaven.*

On the basis of passages such as these, one scholar, commenting on the Old Testament's view of nature, has written:

> For the Bible, the natural world is "alive," or "animate." In numerous . . . passages, the earth as a whole, certain lands in particular, the soil, vegetation, and animal life are depicted as vibrant, sensitive, responsive, and reactive to the good and evil wrought by God and man. They enter

into moral and even legal relations. They can be obedient or disobedient to God. These facts confirm the impression ... that a quasi-human, moral "life" pervades all of nature—earth and seas, mountains and valleys, stars and planets. It is therefore fair to conclude that nature is far from "de-animated" in Biblical thought.[38]

The natural world may not be seen as sacred or divine in the Bible, but it is certainly not dead, lifeless, and outside the divine moral framework. It can be abused, offended, and degraded by human beings and react with repulsion and other sentiments.

Domination of nature

Proponents of the mastery hypothesis also stress the idea of human dominance of nature in the Bible. Again, the situation is similar to the issue of desacralization. Dominance of nature is a theme that can easily be found in pagan religion, and there is much evidence that pagan civilizations practiced a fairly active program of trying to master nature. Critics of the mastery hypothesis argue that it is therefore incorrect to say that this theme is exclusively or even primarily biblical. Also, critics of the mastery hypothesis point out, the Bible puts considerable restrictions on human dominion over nature; it teaches restraint in human domination of the earth. Nowhere does the Bible teach human tyranny over nature, which is what some advocates of the mastery hypothesis say. In many places the Bible makes clear that human beings do not have dominion over the heavens and that they are excluded therefrom; heaven, which includes the celestial bodies, is said to be beyond human dominion. Restrictions are also placed on how humans treat nature, or certain natural beings or objects, in the Mosaic laws. There are restrictions on cutting down fruit trees (Deut. 20:19–20), there is a command to let the land lie fallow every seventh year (Lev. 25:1–7), humans are forbidden to eat certain "unclean" animals, and many laws pertain to dietary restrictions. Another law forbids killing a mother and her offspring, as in the example of the birds' nest (Deut. 22:6–7). Treatment of animals is often mentioned, and the tendency in such cases seems to be in the direction of humane treatment of them, particularly domesticated animals (for example, Deut. 25:4). One scholar concludes, after reflecting on these laws: "In general, man's dominance over the animals in the Bible is limited by the fact that the happiness of animals, like the happiness of men, is an end or purpose of the arrangement of Creation. God cares about the welfare of the animals, not merely to maintain a supply of food and labour for man, but because they are 'good' in themselves."[39]

Degradation of the body and matter

A third argument presenting the negative side of Christian views on nature and the environment concerned the degradation of the body and matter. In fact, this theme does not arise in the Bible. Although the earth suffers negative consequences as a result of the fall of humankind, the bounty of the earth generally is celebrated in the Bible, and the theme of the promised land, a land flowing with milk and honey, is central. The body-soul dichotomy does not occur in the Bible. The view of matter as negative seems to have arisen primarily in pagan Greek thought. Although there are many examples of postbiblical Christian thinkers who view spirit and matter as dichotomous, who view matter and the body as lower manifestations of the divine than spirit, there are Christian writers who celebrate the material creation and who reject the extreme position of Origen in which matter (and the body) are understood to be cages for spirit and souls.

Perhaps the best way to demonstrate the fact that the Christian tradition does not consistently and unanimously adopt a negative attitude toward nature is to give a few examples of thinkers who praise nature as part of God's creation, which is good.

IRENAEUS (CA. 130–200)

Unlike Origen, who lived at about the same time (185–254), Irenaeus had a positive view of the physical body and the material creation. For Irenaeus, the physical world is humanity's specially created home, which is blessed and cared for by God, who takes on human form in order to redeem humankind. For Irenaeus, the divine plan is for creation as a whole to move toward fulfillment. It is God's plan for the creation to be redeemed along with humankind. That is, for Irenaeus, the creation as a whole is part of the divine plan of renewal.[40] God is not aloof from the material creation, as he is for Origen and others, but is invested in it (although not contained by it). Like a father, Irenaeus said, God nourishes and tends his creation.

Unlike many Christian theologians, Irenaeus also minimized the theme of the earth as cursed because of Adam's sin. Irenaeus taught that the majority of creatures after the Fall continue to remain obedient to God's will. Nature, then, retains its goodness. Irenaeus was also positive in his view of the human body, which, he said, manifests the "the skillful touches of God" and shows in many ways the great wisdom of God.[41]

While Irenaeus tended to stress the centrality of human beings in the creation and in the divine plan and tended to interpret the nature of the creation in terms of how it serves humankind, he was positive in his overall assessment of the physical creation and the human body.

AUGUSTINE (354–430)

The most important Christian theologian prior to St. Thomas Aquinas (1225–74) was Augustine. His theology dominated Christian thought for centuries, and he is still important in Christian theology. Sometimes he is typified as a thinker who had a fairly low opinion of the physical creation and the human body. This is primarily because in his early writing he was very much influenced by Neoplatonism and the idea of the Great Chain of Being, which portrays matter as lowly in the divine scheme of things, and because of his self-confessed struggle with his own sexuality, which he considered in rebellion against his spiritual inclinations. In his mature thought, however, he affirmed the beauty and goodness of the creation and the physical body and in this respect offers another example of Christian theologians who resist the tendency to view the physical creation (including the body) as low in a spiritual hierarchy of being.

In his mature thought, Augustine wrote that the ultimate purpose of the whole creation is beauty and that the purpose of creation is to glorify God in all his splendor. The creation, that is, for Augustine, is meant to reflect the wonders, goodness, and glories of God, and as such it is beautiful. Writing against the views of heretics who denigrated the creation, Augustine said: "They do not consider how admirable these things are in their own places, how excellent in their own natures, how beautifully adjusted to the rest of creation, and how much grace they contribute to the universe by their own contributions, as to a commonwealth."[42]

For Augustine, every creature has an "existence fitting it," and although we, from our limited perspective, may not understand the place of a given being, or may even be repelled by it, Augustine was convinced that in its way that being glorifies the creator. And while Augustine sometimes marveled at the utility of the creation for human beings and pointed out the uses of different species for humans, he insisted that each being in its own nature, not in terms of its usefulness to humans, is beautiful and glorifies God.

In speaking of God's relationship to the creation, Augustine referred to God as a shepherd who cares for his creation. He pictured God as brooding over the world like an attentive parent and compared God to a bird protecting and warming her nest.[43] In another image he spoke of God as an artist before a work of art: "As the creative will of a sculptor hovers over a piece of wood, or as the spiritual soul spreads through all the limbs of the body; thus it is with the Holy Ghost; it hovers over all things with a creative and formative power."[44] For Augustine, God is diffused throughout his creation, and to the keen observer the wonder of God's presence in his creation is everywhere to be seen. "For who is there that considers the works of God, whereby this whole world is governed and regulated, who is not overwhelmed with miracles? If he considers the vigorous power of a single grain of any seed whatever, it is a mighty thing, it inspires him with awe."[45]

In agreement with Irenaeus, Augustine said that the Fall only affected human beings, not nature, and that Satan is not in control of the physical creation (which some theologians such as Origen believed). On the contrary, the creation is not fallen but is sublime in its beauty and testifies to its creator, who is beauty itself. In words and images that were taken up hundreds of years later by Francis of Assisi, Augustine said:

> How can I tell you of the rest of creation, with all its beauty and utility, which the divine goodness has given to man to please his eyes and serve his purposes . . .? Shall I speak of the mani-

fold and various loveliness of sky, and earth, and sea; of the plentiful supply and wonderful qualities of the light; of sun, moon, and stars; of the shade of trees; of the colors and perfume of flowers; of the multitude of birds, all differing in plumage and in song; of the variety of animals, of which the smallest in size are often the most wonderful; of the works of ants and bees astonishing us more than the huge bodies of whales? Shall I speak of the sea, which itself is so grand a spectacle, when it arrays itself . . . in vestures of various colors . . . ?[46]

Ask the loveliness of the earth, ask the loveliness of the sea, ask the loveliness of the wide airy spaces, ask the loveliness of the sky, ask the order of the stars, ask the sun, making the daylight with its beams, ask the moon tempering the darkness of the night that follows, ask the living things which move in the waters, which tarry on the land, which fly in the air; ask the souls that are hidden, the bodies that are perceptive; the visible things which must be governed, the invisible things that govern—ask these things, and they will all answer you, Yes, see we are lovely. Their loveliness is their confession. And all these lovely but mutable things, who has made them, but Beauty immutable?[47]

For Augustine, the creation may not be divine in itself, but it testifies to the divine in its every facet and is suffused with the divine in its daily expressions.

FRANCIS OF ASSISI (1182–1226)

It is in the life St. Francis of Assisi that we have the most unambiguous example in medieval Christianity of the affirmation and embrace of nature. St. Francis's love of and solidarity with nature are well-known and celebrated in Christianity, and a great many legends featuring Francis portray him communicating with birds, animals, and plants. Francis's rapport with nature, his interest in and love for it, is often described in terms of its relationship to the religious life, aspects of the life of Jesus, or its utility for human beings. When referring to nature in his preaching, Francis often related it to the spiritual life or to the drama of salvation. For example, Francis said that the lark "is like a good Religious, flying as she praises God most sweetly . . . condemning earthly things, always intent on praising God." And he is said to have liked worms because Jesus was supposed to have said: "I am a worm and no man."[48]

But Francis's embrace of nature is more intense than this kind of example would suggest, and less utilitarian. It is clear in descriptions of his life and from his writings that Francis had affection for nonhuman creatures as brothers and sisters, and in this sense he stands apart from almost all other Christians who came before or after him. Nonhuman creatures may have exemplified or symbolized aspects of the spiritual life and may have had a utilitarian function for Francis, as they did for other Christians, but Francis also, it is clear, saw in them beings who had intrinsic worth, beings for whom he felt love and regard. He valued individual animals and would often go out of his way to protect them from harm.[49]

In Francis, we find a man who achieved rapport with animals and even plants, who communed with them in an intense fashion, and who understood this kinship in Christian theological terms. In an early account of his life by Celano we read:

> When he found an abundance of flowers, he preached to them and invited them to praise the Lord as though they were endowed with reason. In the same way he exhorted with the sincerest purity cornfields and vineyards, stones and forests and all the beautiful things of the fields, fountains of water and the green things of the gardens, earth and fire, air and wind, to love God and serve him willingly. Finally, he called all creatures "brother" and in a most extraordinary manner, a manner never experienced by others, he discerned the secrets of creatures with his sensitive heart.[50]

In many stories about Francis, animals are described as responding gently and affectionately to him in return. When given a rabbit, "he held it affectionately and seemed to pity it like a mother. Then, warning it gently not to let itself be caught again, he allowed it to go free. But every time he put it on the ground to let it off, the hare immediately jumped into his arms, as if in some mysterious way it realized the love he had for it. Eventually Francis had the friars bring it off to a safer place in the woods."[51] In another story of the saint, he is described as singing a duet with a nightingale. It was only due to exhaustion that Francis had to desist, whereupon the bird flew to his hand, where he fed it, praised it, and gave it his blessing.[52]

The best-known work of Francis is his "Canticle of the Sun," in which he praised God for the beauty and usefulness of all aspects of the created world:

> Most High, omnipotent, good Lord,
> All praise, glory, honor, and blessing are yours.
> To you alone, Most High, do they belong,
> And no man is worthy to pronounce your name.
> Be praised, my Lord, with all your creatures,
> Especially Sir Brother Sun,
> Who brings the day, and you give light to us through him.
> How handsome he is, how radiant, with great splendor!
> Of you, Most High, he bears the likeness.
> Be praised, my Lord, for Sister Moon and the Stars.
> In heaven you have formed them, bright, and precious, and beautiful.
> Be praised, my Lord, for Brother Wind,
> And for Air, for Cloud, and Clear, and all weather,
> By which you give your creatures nourishment.
> Be praised, my Lord, for Sister Water,
> She is very useful, and humble, and precious, and pure.
> Be praised, my Lord, for Brother Fire,
> By whom you light up the night.

David Kinsley

How handsome he is, how happy, how powerful and strong!
Be praised, my Lord, for our Sister, Mother Earth.
Who nourishes and governs us,
And produces various fruits with many-colored flowers and herbs.
Praise and bless the Lord,
And give thanks and serve him with great humility.[53]

It is striking in this famous poem of Francis that he praises particularly so many aspects of the inanimate creation. What is viewed ordinarily as inanimate and unconscious matter—sun, moon, wind, water, and fire—is viewed by Francis as very much part of divine cosmic consciousness. For Francis, what we refer to as "dumb nature" is far from dumb; it is eloquent in singing and testifying to the beauty of its creator.

NOTES

1. Lynn White, Jr., "The Historical Roots of Our Ecological Crisis," in Ian Barbour, ed., *Western Man and Environmental Ethics* (Reading, Mass.: Addison-Wesley Publishing Co., 1973), p. 25.

2. Ibid.

3. Arnold Toynbee, *The Toynbee-Ikeda Dialogue* (Tokyo: Kodansha International, 1976), p. 39.

4. White, p. 28.

5. Daisetz T. Suzuki, "The Role of Nature in Zen Buddhism," *Eranos-Jahrbuch*, vol. 22 (1953), p. 292.

6. White, p. 25.

7. All biblical quotations are from *The Holy Bible: Revised Standard Version* containing the Old and New Testaments (New York: Thomas Nelson & Sons, 1952).

8. The complexity of the above passages, and the variety of ways in which such passages have been interpreted over the centuries by Christians and Jews, is discussed in great detail by Jeremy Cohen, "*Be Fruitful and Increase, Fill the Earth and Master It*": *The Ancient and Medieval Career of a Biblical Text* (Ithaca, N.Y.: Cornell University Press, 1989). According to Cohen, interpretations of these passages as containing a license for human beings to develop and exploit nature are quite modern, and certainly no earlier than the eighteenth century.

9. Ian McHarg, "The Place of Nature in the City of Man," in Barbour, ed., p. 175.

10. These terms and images are suggested by H. Paul Santmire, *The Travail of Nature: The Ambiguous Ecological Promise of Christian Theology* (Philadelphia: Fortress Press, 1985), p. 9ff.

11. Ibid., pp. 45–46.

12. Ibid., pp. 49–50.

13. Ibid., p. 50.

14. Ibid.

15. Ibid., p. 51.

16. Ibid., p. 52.

17. Cited in ibid., p. 91.

David Kinsley　　123

18. Ibid., pp. 91–92.

19. Ibid., p. 92.

20. Ibid., p. 105.

21. Ibid.

22. Cited in ibid., p. 124.

23. Ibid., p. 125.

24. Cited in ibid.

25. Ibid.

26. Keith Thomas, *Man and the Natural World* (London: Allen Lane, 1983), pp. 17–18.

27. Ibid., p. 18.

28. Ibid.

29. Ibid., p. 19.

30. Ibid., pp. 19–20.

31. Ibid., pp. 20.

32. Ibid., pp. 20–21.

33. Ibid., p. 21.

34. Ibid., p. 25.

35. Ibid., p. 27.

36. Ibid., p. 28.

37. Ibid., p. 33.

38. Richard Cameron Wybrow, "The Bible, Baconism, and Mastery over Nature: The Old Testament and Its Modern Misreading" (Ph.D. dissertation, McMaster University, Hamilton, Ont., Canada, 1990), p. 206.

39. Ibid., p. 264.

40. H. Paul Santmire, *The Travail of Nature: The Ambiguous Ecological Promise of Christian Theology* (Philadelphia: Fortress Press, 1985), pp. 38–39.

41. Ibid., p. 40.

42. Cited in ibid., pp. 61–62.

43. Ibid., pp. 62–63.

44. Cited in ibid., p. 63.

45. Cited in ibid.

46. Cited in ibid., p. 66.

47. Cited in ibid., pp. 66–67.

48. Cited in ibid., p. 107.

49. Ibid., p. 109.

50. Roger Sorrell, *St. Francis of Assisi and Nature* (Oxford: Oxford University Press, 1988), p. 68.

51. Ibid., p. 133.

52. Santmire, p. 109.

53. Cited in Sorrell, p. 101.

"TRADITIONAL NATIVE HAWAIIAN ENVIRONMENTAL PHILOSOPHY"

Michael Kioni Dudley

A FISH STORY

If one meets a Hawaiian fisherman loading his nets and gear into his truck, he never asks if the man is going fishing.[1] He might ask if the man is going *holoholo* (out for a ride) or he might ask if he is going to the mountains. But if he asks if the man is going fishing, the man will remove his gear out of the truck, and that will be the end of fishing for the day. For the fish will "hear" and know that the fisherman is coming, and they won't be there when he gets to the sea.

One also hears that senior Hawaiians are sometimes observed talking to plants and trees before picking their flowers—asking before taking—and that they often leave offerings when they take something of significance.

Many Hawaiians also believe that they have ancestral spirits (*'aumakua*) who dwell in animal or other nature forms. Among these are the *mo'o* (lizards), various birds and fish, rainbows, various cloud forms, forests, and mountains. Perhaps the best known of the ancestral spirits is Pele, the goddess who dwells in Kilauea volcano. Pele, in her lava form, flows down among the people on occasion. Hawaiians know the nature forms to which their families are related. They think of their ancestral spirits and the nature forms they inhabit as family members. When they encounter their *'aumakua*, they recognize the occurrence as special: a greeting, or possibly a warning, or an affirmation of the correctness of some action.

Actions such as these certainly reflect a different world view. In ancient *Hawai'i*, humans, gods, and nature formed a consciously interacting and interrelating cosmic community. All the species of nature were thought to be sentient—capable of knowing, choosing, and acting. Through evolution, all were related as kin. Hawaiians lived in a community in which humans, gods, and nature cared for one another and watched over and protected one another as fami-

---

Reprinted by permission of the author. This essay originally appeared in *Ethics, Religion, and Biodiversity*, edited by Lawrence S. Hamilton (1993, White Horse Press).

ly. There were rules to be observed in the community with nature—environmental ethics. Humans were expected to do their part, and the gods and nature were expected to respond. A reciprocation from any of the three required its own reciprocation in return.

The world today runs according to the Western person's perspective. That perspective treats nature as a commodity, as scientifically measurable forces, and as resources to be used, rather than as fellow beings in an interrelating world community.

What doesn't correspond with a Western person's world view is seen as of little value and as something that can and probably should be ignored. But an approach to life developed over thousands of years must contain much wisdom. During the two millennia that Hawaiian people lived in these islands, they developed a complete and unique system of thought. This explained their world and how things in it interrelated with one another, and also how people fit into the complete picture. Like the Indians, Chinese, Japanese, American Indians, and others, Hawaiians approached the world from a distinctively non-Western perspective. This Hawaiian perspective or world view formed the basis for a philosophical tradition which, although very different from the modern Western view, does explain the world just as adequately. One can function in today's world while approaching it from the traditional Hawaiian-thought framework just as well as one can by approaching it from the Western-thought framework. Certainly, for island dwellers, there must be special insights and wisdom in the Hawaiian approach.

MATTER AND SPIRIT IN EVOLUTIONARY THEORY

In Hawaiian thought, there are close parallels between humans and nature. Hawaiians traditionally have viewed the entire world as being alive in the same way that humans are alive. They have thought *all* of nature as conscious—able to know and to act—and able to interrelate with humans. The Hawaiians had a quite elaborately worked out theory of evolution: its ascent of species, as told in the famous chant *Kumulipo,* corresponds surprisingly well with Darwinian theory. The *Kumulipo* speaks of spirit as well as matter: in contrast to Judeo-Christian thought, it presents both matter and spirit as existing in the beginning, existing quite separately. In further contrast to Western thought, *both* matter and spirit are seen to be conscious, if we define "conscious" as active, knowledgeable, able to make choices, and able to reduce will to action. As evolution progressed, spirit inhabited the various material species, so that they seem to have both material consciousness and spiritual consciousness. Nature, like humans, then, had the conscious ability to know and to act, to watch over, to protect, and to interrelate with humans. Humans, who stood at the top of the evolutionary ladder, formed a continuum of consciousness with nature beneath them, in sharp contrast with Western thought where humans are the anomaly, the only beings who think.

Michael Kioni Dudley

Hawaiians also viewed the land, the sky, the sea, and all the other species of nature preceding them as family—as conscious ancestral beings who had evolved earlier on the evolutionary ladder, who cared for and protected humans, and who deserved similar treatment (*aloha ʻaina* [love for the land]) in return.

THE ROLE OF THE CHIEF

In Hawaiian evolutionary theory, humans stood at the top of evolved nature. At the pinnacle of human society, and therefore of all else, stood the *aliʻi nui* (high chief or king). The *aliʻi nui* was thought to have a special relationship with nature, a nurturing and sustaining control.

The high chiefs sometimes demonstrated their power over nature in dramatic ways, such as by halting lava flows. King Kamehameha I is said to have saved his fishponds from approaching lava by standing before the flow, making offerings, and appeasing the goddess Pele, who indwelt the flowing lava.

Newspaper accounts and letters of missionaries tell of a similar event witnessed in 1881 when Princess Ruth, who rejected the Christian religion of the *haole* (white person), demonstrated the power of both her station and of the old religion by standing before a lava flow at the outskirts of Hilo, making offerings to that presence of Pele, and stopping the flow.

The Hawaiian word *ea* means "the living breath." Even more specifically, it is the "life-force" which manifests itself as breath in people, and which also exists in everything in the cosmos. For most ancient peoples, the living breath was the sign that the life-force dwelt in a person. When one stopped breathing, the life-force had gone.

The chief's relation with the lands was so intertwined that when he died, the lands also died. The chant "Fallen is the Chief" relates this. At the death of Chief Keoua, the chant says:

Puna is dead! Puna is dead!
The breath of life (*ea*) and the breathing are gone.
The spirit has fled.

The soul of the land, and "its living breath" (*ke ea o ka ʻaina*), left it just as the chief's soul and his living breath (*ea*) left his body.

The presence of the living chief held everything together: the gods, humans, and nature. When the chief died, everything came apart: people's relationship with the lands, people's relationship with the gods, and people's relationship with others—the whole societal structure. People went about nude and engaged in sexual acts in public. They gashed themselves, knocked out their teeth, shaved their heads, and burned marks on their bodies to remember the chief. The *kapu* system (the religious laws or taboos) also fell apart, completing the disorder throughout all of nature: women entered the *heiau*, ate bananas, coconuts, and pork, and climbed over the sacred places. And women and men ate together—all acts punishable by death under the *kapu* system.

It then devolved upon the new *ali'i nui* to renew life to the land and to restore order to nature. After the mourning period, when the new *ali'i nui* was enthroned, the direction and structure of society were restored, reestablishing order among the people by reinstating the *kapu* system. Through presence and prayers, the chief then built a new relationship with the gods and with nature, revivifying nature and setting everything right again. The chant "Fallen is the Chief" tells of a new chief as he takes over the land.

> The island was untamed, that the chief knew well.
> On his becoming guardian it was more and more tamed.
> He fed the small fish,
> > he gathered them together like bonito.
> Streams of country people of the island follow;
> Now the tail of the land wags
> Like that of a well-fed favorite dog.

Once the new chief reestablished the *kapu* system and restored order to society, and once he calmed nature and brought it under his nurturing control, then it once more could be said *Ua mau ke ea o ka 'aina* (The living breath of the land continues on) *i ka pono* (since [the king is in his place of leadership and] everything is ordered correctly again).

This whole belief system is exemplified in a situation that arose in 1843 in which King Kamehameha III was temporarily forced to cede rule of the islands to Britain. He knew when he ceded that his action would cause a rupture in his chiefly, nurturing rapport with the lands. The lands themselves would suffer during this time of cession. But he had hopes that once the lands were returned he could again bring them under his chiefly nurturing power, and they would flourish as they had.

After 5 months of British occupation, on July 31, 1843, the lands were restored to the king by Admiral Thomas. At that time King Kamehameha III came before the people again on the steps of Kawaiaha'o Church and proclaimed, *Ua mau ke ea o ka 'aina i ka pono* (The lands breathe again, nature lives on and prospers, now that the king has been restored to his proper place and has resumed his nurturing relationship with it—now that things are properly ordered again).

THE HAWAIIAN EXPERIENCE OF REALITY

The chants of the Hawaiians told them that they had descended from the cosmos itself and from its many plant and animal species. They felt a kinship with nature not experienced by people who see a break between humankind and the species of nature which have preceded them in the evolutionary advance. In the Western world, where the cleavage is most pronounced, animals are disdained as having senses but no reason; the plant world is recognized as alive, but in no way even aware; and the elements of the cosmos are treated as inert objects that follow mechanical laws. Hawaiians, on the other hand, view all these beings as sentient ancestral forms that interrelate with them as family. Therefore, they experience reality differently because of these views.

The difference in how the Hawaiian and the Westerner experience reality can be illustrated by the reaction of a person in an unfamiliar building who, rushing to a meeting late, opens one door and finds a storeroom filled with canned items, then opens another which is the front door to a lecture in session. Entering the "empty" storeroom elicits a totally different response than entering a lecture room full of people, even though one might not know a single person in the disturbed lecture. Canned items on shelves mean nothing to a person; they lack that which gives them significance: consciousness. The storeroom is "empty." The people in the lecture give meaning to the other encounter. It is their consciousness, their seeing a person blunder which makes the difference. The surprise and embarrassment the person experiences come about because of the people's consciousness, and with it their ability to relate and to help or hurt. These are all perceived immediately and undifferentiated from the appearance of their bodies in a person's total comprehension of the scene. Recognized consciousness makes demands on the perceiver, demands for correct behavior and correct relationship. For the Hawaiians, there are no empty storerooms. Confronting the world about them, they experience conscious beings at every turn, and along with this their interpersonal demands.

Further, there is also a real difference between coming upon someone recognized as a relative and meeting someone who is not. In perceiving one who is kin, a person experiences not only an added awareness of relationship, but also an emotional feeling of belongingness.

As Hawaiians view the world, what they actually *see* is the same as what Westerners see, but what they *perceive as seen* is different. It might be noted that Hawaiians of the past and many Hawaiians today are unaware that others do—or even can—perceive things without perceiving them as conscious and related to them as kin.

It is true that most Hawaiians today do not formally learn the traditional philosophy as it is described in these pages. Yet they approach the world in a Hawaiian way that fits hand-in-glove with the philosophy. Hawaiian philosophy mirrors a centuries-old approach to life which cannot be expunged from the culture. The Hawaiians who ache for the land as they watch Westerners—and now the Asians—buy it up and pave it over may not be able to say *how* they are related to the land, but they know they are in their bones. The Hawaiians who put their lives on the line standing in front of a bulldozer may not know why they must defend the land in that way, but they cannot turn away. With or without the philosophical tradition, Hawaiians know that they form a community with nature around them. Nature constantly and consciously in good faith provides for and protects them, and they are compelled from deep within to protect nature in turn. They do this with the same courage and bravery non-Hawaiians summon to defend *their* family and community from an aggressor. [A complete discussion of this topic can be found in *A Hawaiian Nation I: Man, Gods, and Nature,* by Michael Kioni Dudley, Na Kane O Ka Malo Press, P. O. Box 970, Waipahu, Hawaii 96797.]

from *AMERICAN INDIAN ECOLOGY*

J. Donald Hughes

THE UNSPOILED CONTINENT

Long before the first European ship dropped anchor off the shores of the New World, the western continent was the home of the American Indians. They had lived here for twenty, thirty, forty thousand years. There was not a section of land unknown to some Indian tribe, and there was nowhere, from the slowly shifting arctic ice shelves to the blowing sand dunes of the Colorado Desert, where they did not go. Indians hunted buffalo on the plains and deer in the eastern forests. They planted corn in rich river bottomlands and near springs in the high desert. They caught salmon in the northwestern streams and set their boats on the Pacific waves in search of the great whales. Everywhere they went, they had learned to live with nature; to survive and indeed prosper in each kind of environment the vast land offered in seemingly infinite variety.

And they did all this without destroying, without polluting, without using up the living resources of the natural world. Somehow they had learned a secret that Europe had already lost, and which we seem to have lost now in America—the secret of how to live in harmony with Mother Earth, to use what she offers without hurting her; the secret of receiving gratefully the gifts of the Great Spirit.

When Indians alone cared for the American earth, this continent was clothed in a green robe of forests, unbroken grasslands, and useful desert plants, filled with an abundance of wildlife. Changes have occurred since people with different attitudes have taken over. More than fifty years ago, an Omaha Indian elder expressed it this way:

> When I was a youth the country was very beautiful. Along the rivers were belts of timberland, where grew cottonwoods, maples, elms, ash, hickory and walnut trees, and many other kinds. Also there were various kinds of vines and shrubs. And under these grew many good herbs and beautiful flowering plants. In both the woodland and the prairie I could see the trails of many kinds of animals and hear the cheerful songs of birds of many kinds. When I walked abroad I could see many forms of life, beautiful living creatures of many kinds which Wakanda had placed here; and these were after their manner walking, flying, leaping, running,

Hughes, J. Donald; *American Indian Ecology*, 1983. Reprinted with permission of Texas Western Press.

playing all about. But now the face of all the land is changed and sad. The living creatures are gone. I see the land desolate, and I suffer . . . loneliness.[1]

When the first European explorers coasted the shores, ascended the rivers, and trekked overland, they constantly remarked at the richness and variety of the new land: deep, fertile soil, flourishing woodlands, prairies full of high grass and myriads of flowers, and clear rivers of good water. The land teemed with the wildlife that sometimes did not even flee at the approach of the invaders. The waters had as many fish as the sky had birds, and Europeans had never seen so many birds—nor would they ever again. The marshlands thronged with them and flights of passenger pigeons darkened the sky for hours as they moved overhead like a living wind. The Indians had been hunting, fishing, and gathering in America not for centuries but for millenia, and there were still as many buffalo on the plains and salmon in the rivers as there could be. The land was not untouched, but it was unspoiled.

In fact, it was so unspoiled that the Europeans thought they were finding a "wilderness." Again and again that word appears in the explorers' and settlers' journals, and in all the European languages the word for wilderness means loneliness, a deserted territory, a land without human inhabitants. In English it is "wild-deer-ness," the place of wild beasts, not of men. To those European strangers it was either a threatening, ragged, untrodden tract empty of human life, or a Garden of Eden still as it was when the hand of the Creator rested, a sublime solitude unmarked by the axe, plow, or wheel. This was not the Indian view. Luther Standing Bear, reflecting on the way his people had looked at the world of nature, said:

> We did not think of the great open plains, the beautiful rolling hills, and winding streams with tangled growth, as "wild." Only to the white man was nature a "wilderness" and only to him was the land "infested" with "wild" animals and "savage" people. To us it was tame. Earth was bountiful and we were surrounded with the blessings of the Great Mystery.[2]

Then who were the Indians?—the newcomers asked. That they were all around, no European could deny. Every place the explorers went, they met Indians in hunting parties, farming towns, fishing villages, and further to the south, in cities with multi-storied dwellings and fantastic pyramids. How could a land thronging with inhabitants be a wilderness? Simply because it *looked* like a wilderness to the Europeans. It was unmarred, unexploited, to their eyes. They regarded the Indians as savages, wild denizens of a wild land, like a human species of predator in the forest. Or as the children of nature, living as noble, uncorrupted innocents in a state of grace, or at least ignorance of civilization. In either case, the Indians were thought to be few in number (European diseases, spreading from distant first contacts, often depopulated entire districts before they were entered by the explorers and settlers). And how could people who made so few changes in the land and forests actually be said to "occupy" or "own" the land?[3] Often the Europeans speak as if the new country had been uninhabited before they arrived.

But they were wrong. They could not have been more wrong. The condition of the New World as it met "the eyes of discovery" was a testimonial to the ecological wisdom of the Indians, both their attitudes and their ways of treating the natural environment. Nature flourished in the New World while the Old World was already deteriorating. Why? How was the North American continent preserved ecologically intact while it was in the hands of the Indians? What the Europeans saw before them was not a wilderness, an empty land. It was the artifact of a civilization whose relationship to the living world was perceived by the Indians in terms that Europeans would not grasp at all. If anyone asked Indians what they thought about animals, trees, and mountains, they answered by talking about the powerful spiritual beings that were those things. No European, whether he be Christian, rationalist, Jew, or deist, could possibly believe in ideas like those. They simply dismissed the Indians as believers in superstition, worshippers of devils, or simple people who held naive primitive opinions that Europeans had once held, too, in the distant and unenlightened past. But the Indian attitudes—the Indian philosophy and religion, if those restrictive words can even be used to apply to the wholeness of Indian thought—enabled the Indians to live in and to change the American environment without seriously degrading it. Their very languages, which few Europeans bothered to learn, revealed a view of nature so foreign to that of the Europeans, and in many ways so far beyond it, that we are only beginning to appreciate it today. If all the resources of modern anthropology, psychology, and linguistics are only now piecing together the picture of the ecology and culture of Indians before Columbus, it is not surprising that the Europeans who first arrived did not understand what they were seeing.

It was not a wilderness—it was a community in nature of living beings, among whom the Indians formed a part, but not all. There were also animals, trees, plants, and rivers, and the Indians regarded themselves as relatives of these, not as their superiors. An Indian took pride not in making a mark on the land, but in leaving as few marks as possible: in walking through the forest without breaking branches, in building a fire that made as little smoke as possible, in killing one deer without disturbing the others.

Of course they made changes in their surroundings. All living things do; buffalos make wallows and bees build hives. Everywhere that people live, their activities have an effect on the natural environment. Mankind and human culture are agents of change in nature. Indians were no exception. Skilled, experienced Indian hunters killed moose in the north woods; they did so for thousands of years, long enough to exert a force of hunting selection on the moose population. They killed the slower ones, the less alert ones, more easily. So the moose of North America were different animals—faster, more alert perhaps—than they would have been if Indians had not been hunting them. Similar things happened to many other species in the forest ecosystems. The forest itself reflected the presence and character of its human inhabitants. Their land was not a wilderness, but a woodland park that had known expert hunters for millennia. Corn-growing Indians cleared the land, often by burning, and in some places in the South their planted fields stretched from one village to the next. Where they had established permanent towns, they tended to use up nearby trees for firewood: when Coronado came to Zuñi, he said the people had to go some distance away from the village to find junipers. But almost everything the Indians did kept them in balance with nature.[4]

For the Indians, living in careful balance with the natural environment was necessary to survival, since they lived so close to it and depended on it so completely. If they made serious mistakes in their treatment of nature, they felt the results right away; that is, they got immediate feedback. If they acted in ways that would destroy the balance of the natural communities where they found their food, clothing and shelter, then those communities would not provide for their needs any longer. Indians did not see this relationship as working in purely economic ways. Their actions were guided on every side by their view that nature is composed of a host of spirit persons who can talk to human beings and respond in a number of ways to the treatment they receive. They knew they had to be careful with those beings who shared the world with them because their lives were closely interlocked with them and they had to depend on them. And every part of their lives was involved in the relationship with nature.

For most modern urban people, our philosophy of life or how we think we see the world is one thing, and how we act in daily life is another. But for the Indians, life was all of one piece. How they perceived the natural environment, and how they treated it through the customary activities that were their ways of life, formed a consistent whole for each group.

THE SACRED UNIVERSE

Anyone who looks at American Indian art with a sense of appreciation is impressed by the way in which it incorporates the images of nature. The designs represent clouds, the sun, moon, and stars, mountains, animals, birds, plants, insects, and the spirit beings that walk abroad in the world. Even the simplest decorated basket shows that the artist meant to relate his or her work to the whole universe. And a basket can be a microcosm, a mandala of the spirit life that Indians found both in nature and within themselves. Everything they made, whether it was painted pottery, weaving, embroidery, costumes, sand paintings, or petroglyphs, manifested their feeling for the many forms found in the natural world. A lodge of the Eastern plains, built of the same brown earth on which it stood, was made "round like the day and the sun and the path of the stars."[5] The startling shape and color of a Northwest carver's brilliantly painted eagle arrests us and says, "This man felt power in the eagle. He admired that great bird." Indians loved nature, not in any romantic sentimental way, but with an honest, respectful love born of daily contact. The Indian attitude toward nature was never merely utilitarian. The Pawnees sang of plants this way:

"Spring is opening,
I can smell the different perfumes
of the white weeds used in the dance."[6]

J. Donald Hughes

They lived most of their lives in the out-of-doors, where they could look up to "behold the beauty of yonder moving black sky," to "behold the black clouds rolling through the sky," in the words of an Osage song. To think that they loved the changing moods of nature is not to read our own feelings back into the Indian experience; they themselves tell us how they felt in songs and prayers recorded long ago, such as this one of the Teton Sioux:

> "May the sun rise well
> May the earth appear
> Brightly shone upon
> May the moon rise well
> May the earth appear
> Brightly shone upon."[7]

The unmistakable Indian attitude toward nature is appreciation, varying from calm enjoyment to awestruck wonder. Indian poems, songs and descriptions are full of natural images that reflect a pure interest in environmental beauty. They liked to "listen to the song the needles make when the wind blows," according to Popovi Da, and "count the many shades of blue in the sky."[8]

Their attitude toward the natural world and their place within it was well expressed in the deservedly famous speech of Chief Seattle, of the Duwamish tribe, delivered before the governor of Washington Territory in 1853, at the new town that had been named in the Chief's honor. Seattle was fortunate in having a translator, Dr. Henry Smith, of considerable literary skill. Here is a portion of the speech:

> Our dead never forget the beautiful world that gave them being. They still love its verdant valleys, its murmuring rivers, its magnificent mountains, sequestered vales and verdant lined lakes and bays . . .
>
> Every part of this soil is sacred in the estimation of my people. Every hillside, every valley, every plain and grove, has been hallowed by some sad or happy event in days long vanished. Even the rocks, which seem to be dumb and dead as they swelter in the sun along the silent shore, thrill with memories of stirring events connected with the lives of my people . . .[9]

The images that recur in the words of the great Indian orator are those of nature; "the return of the sun or the seasons," "the stars that never change," the grass, the trees. They recur even more powerfully in the songs and chants used in the sacred ceremonies. In Indian ritual poetry, some natural objects and animals are not named directly, but referred to in short formulas that may remind us of the epithets of Homer by their cameo-like descriptions of natural characteristics. The Papagos, for example, may call the sun "the shining traveler," ground squirrels "stayers in houses," and the coyote "the woolly comrade"; while the Navajos can refer to the latter animal as "howler through the dawn."[10] Here are two lines from an Apache song celebrating a joyful union of the people with the source of all things:

The sunbeams stream forward, dawn boys, with shimmering shoes, . . . On the beautiful mountains above, it is daylight.[11]

Deep appreciation of nature is not limited to a few tribes, nor does any tribe seem to lack it. Here is part of a Papago speech given at the time of purification after a pilgrimage to the sea to obtain salt:

> Then to the east they went, and, looking back,
> They saw the earth lie beautifully moist and finished.
> Then out flew Blue Jay magician;
> Soft feathers he pulled out and let them fall,
> Till earth was blue (with flowers).
> Then out flew Yellow Finch magician;
> Soft feathers he pulled out and let them fall,
> Till earth was yellow (with flowers).
> Thus it was fair, our year.[12]

A Zuñi rain prayer further illustrates the way in which sensitivity to natural beauty pervades ritual poetry:

> Yonder on all sides our fathers,
> Priests of the mossy mountains,
> All those whose sacred places are round about,
> Creatures of the open spaces
> You of the wooded places,
> We have passed you on your roads
>
> . . .
> You of the forest,
> You of the brush,
> All you who in divine wisdom,
> Stand here quietly,
>
> . . .
> You will go before.
>
> . . .
> We have given our plume wands human form,
> With the massed cloud wing
>
> Of the one who is our grandfather,
> The male turkey,
> With eagle's thin cloud wings,
> And with the striped cloud wings
> And massed cloud tails
> Of all the birds of summer.[13]

J. Donald Hughes

Navajo prayers constantly repeat the word *hozho,* which is environmental beauty, the happiness one experiences by being in harmony with nature. As the Navajo put it, "My surroundings everywhere shall be beautiful as I walk about; the Earth is beautiful." This is expressed in what is possibly the best known American Indian ritual poem, a song from the Navajo night chant:

> Oh you who dwell among the cliffs
> In the house made of dawn,
> House made of evening light,
> House made of dark cloud,
> House made of he-rain,
> House made of dark mist,
> House made of she-rain,
> House made of pollen,
> House made of grasshoppers,
> Where the dark mist curtains the doorway,
> The path to which is on the rainbow,
> Where the zigzag lightning stands high on top,
> Where the he-rain stands high on top,
> Oh, male divinity,
> With your moccasins of dark cloud, come to us.
>
> . . .
>
> In beauty I walk.
> With beauty before me, I walk.
> With beauty behind me, I walk.
> With beauty below me, I walk.
> With beauty above me, I walk.
> With beauty all around me, I walk.
> It is finished in beauty.[14]

The beauty referred to is both spiritual beauty and the pervading beauty of the natural world. And appreciation for it is expressed not only in words, but in "walking," that is, a way of living, a way of treating the world. As Black Elk, a Sioux holy man, spoke in words addressed to Mother Earth, "Every step that we take upon You should be done in a sacred manner; each step should be as a prayer." "Because You have made Your will known to us," he continued, "we will walk the path of life in holiness, bearing the love and knowledge of you in our hearts!"[15]

The attitude of Indians toward the natural environment was basically what we would call spiritual or religious, although religion for them was not separated from the rest of life. Their actions in respect to nature were in harmony with their view of the world as a sacred place, so if we wish to understand why they practiced conservation and avoided destructive exploitation, we will find that it is just as important to study their religion as it is to study their economy.

Indian languages had no word for "religion"; they expressed the idea by something like the Isleta Pueblo term "life-way" or 'life-need." To them, everything in their traditional way of life was sacred. For the Hopis, religion was simply "the Hopi way," including everything in life as Hopis saw and lived it. The Hopis spent about a third of their waking lives in ritual dances, prayers, songs, and preparation for ceremonials. But they did not see these activities as different, "Sunday" things. Though Indians would select special days for tribal celebrations, they felt that "Every dawn as it comes is a holy event, and every day is holy."[16]

So the Indians saw all their experiences with nature as having what we would call a spiritual dimension. The ethics that told them how to treat the environment was part of their religious world view. They would explain their attitudes toward nature in religious terms, and their religion was a religion of nature. It was simple in its general outlines and highly complex in its details, especially when tribal differences are taken into account. It had no systematic theology that can be subjected to the kind of rational analysis that the philosophers of non-Indian Western Civilization like to make. It had no "either/or." Some Indian religious ideas may seem to be contradictory at first glance to those educated in the European-American tradition. But if all Indian conceptions of nature are taken together, they will be seen to fit into a single, harmonious world view.

The Indians saw themselves as at one with nature. All their traditions agree on this. Nature is the larger whole of which mankind is only a part. People stand within the natural world, not separate from it; and are dependent on it, not dominant over it. All living things are one, and people are joined with birds and trees, predators and prey, rocks and rain in a vast, powerful, interrelationship. "The whole universe is enhanced with the same breath, rocks, trees, grass, earth, all animals, and men," said Intiwa, a Hopi.[17] "We are in one nest," was a Taos Pueblo saying concerning humans, animals and birds.[18] "That comfortable gap which we have left between ourselves and all other life on the planet, the Apache bridged in a stride."[19]

At the end of the Lakota Sioux cermony of the sacred pipe, all the participants would cry out, "We are related!" Joseph Epes Brown explains that these words do not only acknowledge "the relatedness of the immediate participating group. There is also an affirmation of the mysterious interrelatedness of all that is."[20]

The world, in Indian eyes, exists in intricate balance in all its parts, as male is balanced by female and the cardinal directions are in harmony with one another. Human beings must stay in harmony with it, and constantly strive to maintain the balance. The more powerful beings in the universe are not necessarily friendly or hostile to mankind, but rather indispensable parts of a carefully balanced whole, and therefore tend to sustain and preserve humanity along with everything else as long as the balance is not upset. This perception of nature is not so far from the ecological concept of the "balance of nature."

If people suffer, it is usually because they are out of harmony with nature, and though this is not always the fault of the individual, harmony must be restored. Every action in

J. Donald Hughes

regard to nature must have its reciprocal action. The offerings made in many Indian ceremonies are not so much "sacrifices" as things given in exchange for other things taken or killed, to maintain the balance. A ceremony is one way in which people contribute to maintaining the world as it should be. Since mankind is related to the universe in reciprocity and balance, an act correctly performed should always obtain the appropriate response. A gift given compels a gift in return. A Papago, on offering tobacco or arrows, says "I give you this; now bring me luck."[21] In a Tewa myth, Spider Old Woman replied to a hunter who had given feathers to her, "We have to help you, because you never forget us; because you always take feathers out for us, we help you."[22] So Indians knew that human actions are a response to nature, but also that everything we do affects nature and calls forth a response. And the response is not impersonal.

They saw everything in nature as alive, not just animate, but fully alive in the way people are alive, conscious and sentient. The Zuñis, for example, called everything, whether it be a star, mountain, flower, eagle, or the earth itself, *ho'i,* a "living person." Some American Indians were primarily hunters, gatherers, or fishers, and others were planters. But all of them looked on the natural environment as a world of spiritual reality. That is, the earth and the living creatures in it were not "things" to be used. They were living beings, personalities possessing power. So Indians did not feel themselves to be the only real persons in a world of things; in their experience, all creatures were alive with the same life that was in them, and trees and rivers, snakes, bluejays, and elk, reverberated with power and resonated with spirit.

When this way of looking at the world is explained to modern non-Indians, they often assume that Indian beliefs are an attempt to *explain* nature. Since Indians lacked concepts like atoms, cold fronts, the second law of thermodynamics, and germs, these people think, Indians thought up ideas like spirits, guardians, and the wisdom of animals to supply causes for what they saw happening around them. But this is not true. The Indian view of nature comes from deeper inside the human psyche than mere rational thought or intellectual curiosity, although Indians certainly had these too. But Indians regarded things in nature as spiritual beings, not because they were seeking some explantation for natural phenomena, but because human beings experience a spiritual resonance in nature. Indians feel a bear, a tree, a corn plant, or a mountain as a sentient presence that can hear and understand their words, and respond. A public ceremonial like a Pueblo Indian rain dance can be expected, if done properly, to set up the same kind of resonance with the clouds, so that the people are in harmony with the forces of nature, and receive what they need to live. All this is conceived as a process, not of bending nature to human will, but of subordinating the human will to natural rhythms. Sickness may be understood, for example, as the result of getting out of harmony with nature, and the healing process as one of re-establishing the harmony by removing impediments to it. It is quite understandable, then, that animals, fish, birds, and plants are invoked to aid medicine men and women.

Nature was to them a great, interrelated community including animals, plants, human beings, and some things that Americans of the Western European tradition would call physical objects on the one hand, and purely spirits on the other. No person, tribe, or species within the living unity of nature was seen as self-sufficient, human beings possibly least of all. The Indian did not define himself or herself as primarily an autonomous individual, but as a part of a whole; a member of the tribe, a living being like other living beings, a part of nature. Because of this deep kinship, Indians accorded to every form of life the right to live, perpetuate its species, and follow the way of its own being as a conscious fellow creature. Animals were treated with the same consideration and respect as human beings.

Mankind was not the master of life, but one of its many manifestations, related to all the other creatures. As Black Elk said, "With all beings and all things we shall be as relatives."[23] To Indians, "Man is not lord of the universe. The forests and the fields have not been given him to despoil. He is equal in the world with the rabbit and the deer and the young corn plant."[24] Nature was not some European feudal fief with mankind as steward or subduer, but a primitive democracy in which every creature had its place, with privileges and duties to the others. In fact, the Indian view of the human role in nature is almost the reverse of the Western European understanding of "dominion." Greater power resides in natural forces and spiritual beings than in the hands of mankind. Human beings cannot dominate the natural world, for it is vastly more powerful and enduring than mankind.

> The Cheyenne in no sense believes that he can control nature. Although his environment is hard and life is precarious, he sees it as a good environment. It is one, however, with which he must keep himself in close tune through careful and tight self-control. . . . Man must fit himself to the conditions of environmental organization and functioning.[25]

Animals and plants can be addressed in prayer because, in all of nature, they are powers closest to human beings and may be willing to help them, provided they are approached in the proper manner. They are like human beings—and may even be human beings of another sort, or in disguise, or on another level of existence—but they are more mysterious, more holy, closer to the sources of power. They must be given at least the same respect and reciprocal fairness one would accord to a member of one's own tribe.

So everything in nature was powerful, able to help or harm. Mankind depended on the other beings for life, and they depended on mankind to maintain the proper balance. Living things must not be hurt or killed needlessly. If any species were totally destroyed or driven away from an area, it would leave a terrible gap that could not be filled unless it were to return. Mankind should hold a reciprocating, mutually beneficial relationship with each type of being. And as a result, all Indian groups were very careful about how they treated animals, plants, and every other part of nature. They developed practices, differing in detail from place to place, that tended to conserve living creatures and preserve the balance of nature within their own living space.

American Indian ethics in regard to nature is, therefore, protective and life-preserving. It is a combination of reverence for life and affirmation to life, of which Albert Schweitzer would doubtless have approved. To Indians, the earth was a reality, not illusion, and it was loved, not callously exploited. The Hopis prayed for the welfare of all living things. Nothing could be killed except out of necessity. All tribes had similar ideas, feeling that every creature must be treated with care, never injured. The real "people" living in the world are not humans alone, but all spirit beings.

This viewing of the world in a sacred perspective was therefore, the caring for every aspect of the natural environment: "the wingeds, the two-leggeds, and the four-leggeds, are really the gifts of *Wakan-Tanka*. They are all *wakan* and should be treated as such."[26] This saying of Black Elk's uses two Dakota words for concepts that are fundamental to understanding how Indians related to the environment. The first is *wakan*, "power," the sacred power that permeates all natural forms and movements. The Indian's world was full of power, and of beings who had power, or were power. It would not be wise to attempt to define the exact relationships between these powers, or to make too fine a destinction between personal and impersonal power. The power that animates the universe and gives it regularity was described in one aspect as an impersonal force, or in another aspect as a personal deity, but these ideas were not opposed; they were two ends of a continuum. The Iroquois experienced an invisible force which they call *orenda*; other tribes had other names for a mysterious power that might often manifest itself in natural phenomena. The *wakonda* of Siouan-speaking tribes had its counterpart in *maxpe* of the Crows, the Hidatsa *xupa,* and the Algonquian *manito,* all standing for the power perceived in nature. More personalized was *Tirawa* of the Pawnees, a supreme being who revealed himself through nature, or the "Wise One Above," *Heamma wihio* of the Cheyennes, whose emblems were the sun and the spider that spins from itself.

The second word used by Black Elk is *Wakan-Tanka,* his people's name for the Great Spirit or "Great Mystery." The sense of a "Master of life," one spirit who breathed in everything and included all other spirits, existed in virtually every tribe.[27] Names in the different Indian languages show how they understood the Great Spirit. The Apache supreme being was called Life Giver. The Algonquian *Manitou* and the Cherokee *Esaugetuh Emissee* mean "Giver of Breath." Others, like the Papagos, used a word meaning "Earthmaker"; the Crow word *Ah-badt-dadt-deah* signifies "The One Who Made All Things." There was the concept of a lofty creator being who made everything, like *Alquntam* of the Bella Coola, "from whom come, and to whom belong, all myths,"[28] or the Haidas' *Sins Sganagwai,* "Power of the Shining Heavens," who was believed to give power to all things in nature, and of whom it could be said, "whatever one thinks, he knows."[29] Although some tribes did not necessarily regard the

Great Spirit and the Creator as the same, such an identification was usual. Black Elk gave voice to what was no doubt the feeling of most Indians when he prayed,

> O Father and Grandfather *Wakan-Tanka,* You are the source and end of everything. My Father *Wakan-Tanka,* You are the one who watches over and sustains all life. O my Grandmother, You are the earthly source of all existence.[30]

The world and all the good things in it were seen as the gifts of the Makers, to be received and used with thankfulness and reverent care. In this prayer, as is so often true in Indian expressions, the Great Spirit is addressed with terms of relationship that are both masculine and feminine. Tribes like the Utes and Zuñi used words meaning "The Great He-She." The Tewa creators, the Corn Mothers, were clearly female. The result of all these ideas for Indians was that everything in the natural environment was seen as a gift of the Great Spirit. As Black Hawk said, "I never take a drink of water from a spring without being mindful of His goodness."[31]

But the Great Spirit was not alone in the world. The Indians recognized that nature is complicated, not simple, and there are things that are hard to understand. Why is the land so often steep and rocky along our trail? Why are rivers so crooked? Why do we have to die? Stories are told of a devious counterpart of the Creator, The Trickster, who was responsible for many of the paradoxes in nature. Although he had been the cause of much trouble, he was not really unfriendly or the enemy of mankind. It was just that he had a way of turning things upside down, of being lazy or contrary, of playing jokes on others. Sometimes his tricks were blessings in disguise. He, too, had many names: Warty, Flint, Rabbit, Bluejay, Coyote, etc. According to the Navajo, when the world was created, Coyote was given a blanket full of stars to place in the sky, with instructions to put them carefully in rows, equally spaced. Had he followed the Creator's orders, the sky might now look like a larger version of the blue field of the American flag. But after putting a few stars in place, Coyote decided that the whole job was too much work, so muttering the Navajo equivalent of "the heck with it," he flipped the blanket and sent the stars spinning across the sky into the magnificent disarray we now behold.[32] But who could find a way across the land and sea at night if all the stars looked the same? Coyote's pranks were sometimes good, sometimes bad. The Zuñis said he made maize edible. He was also responsible for the fact that stones will not float in water, and that people die. But if people did not die, the great circle of human life could not be completed, and then how could babies be born? So the Trickster, the dark side of the Creator, is necessary to complete the sacred universe.

Still another great power was Mother Earth herself, or Grandmother Earth, a generous being who supported mankind, providing fruits, roots, fish, and animals. In the important Apache coming of age ceremony, the young woman is seen as becoming one with the fruitful Earth Goddess. Earth is a basic reality. A Mandan song repeats, "earth always endures," and a Teton song might be phrased "Old men, you said earth only endures; you spoke truly, you are right."[33] Such was the death chant of White Antelope at Sand Creek: "Nothing lives long except the earth and the mountains."[34] Mother Earth was respected as the continuing source of life for all living creatures, giving birth and sustenance, as more of Black Elk's words explain:

> We are of earth, and belong to You. O Mother Earth from whom we receive our food, You care for our growth as do our own mothers. Every step that we take upon You should be done in a sacred manner; each step should be as a prayer.[35]

The practical result of this perspective was care for the natural world. Since the earth herself was conceived of as being alive, an aspect of that care was to refrain from harming the earth. For this reason, Indians often objected to frontier miners who dug holes in the ground, or farmers who plowed, thus tearing the breast of Mother Earth. Indian farmers used a digging stick, an implement that symbolized the natural process of fertilization.

They were taught their useful arts by legendary givers of culture, for the spirits were the first farmers, hunters, singers, runners, weavers, and players of games. The Papagos' Elder Brother or Morning Star taught the art of making a wine from the fruit of the saguaro cactus. Some culture heroes were animals; many groups say, for example, the Mockingbird taught languages and songs and Spider Woman taught weaving. Among agricultural people, the giver of maize had a high standing. For the Navajos, it was Talking God who gave maize to Whiteshell Woman and her sister, Turquoise Woman. Other agricultural deities include the Zuñi Corn Maidens; Iyatiku, the Keres creator who is also goddess of maize; Muingwu, the Hopi god of vegetation; and Masau'u, the great god who met the Hopi and showed them his ability to grow crops to maturity in a single day. Poshaiangkia, the Zuñi culture hero sometimes given the inaccurate name "Montezuma," and who had the Beast Gods as his warriors, was traditionally the teacher both of agriculture and of ceremonies.

Great natural phenomena were regarded as particularly powerful spirits. The Sun, a powerful being, was sometimes closely identified with the Master of Breath, and as the evident quickener of life, was an important deity for all tribes. Sunrise was the greatest daily event, and the annual march of the Sun from north to south and back again was seen to control the seasons, the growth of crops and the habits of wild creatures. Prayers were said at dawn and ceremonies performed at the solstices. Children were presented to the Sun, and he was often regarded as the father of heroes.

Other powers of the sky were personified: often Sky himself, the Thunder People, Rainbows, and the Stars. Shotuknangu was the Hopi god of the sky, stars, and lightning. Other superhuman entities were the Moon, the Winds, and Fire. There were countless beings abroad in the world; water monsters, little people, giants; all dwellers of the forest who expected gifts, and who might cause or cure diseases or psychoses. Windigo, the cannibal spirit, was especially feared. The Iroquois false face curing societies attempted to use the power of the forest spirits for the good of tribal members. Masks representing these beings were carved directly in the wood of standing trees, and used in ceremonies.

As we have seen, animals and plants were seen as spirits, too. The eagle soared so high in the sky that he was identified with the sun. Like human beings, the other creatures were believed to worship the mysterious power in which they shared. The leaves of cottonwood trees rustling in the wind were believed to be their voices praying to the Great Spirit who gave them the power to stand upright.

All the outward forms seen by Indians in the natural environment concealed personality and power which might be invoked. So they were constantly speaking to those manifested inner realities in words that, they trusted, were understood. A daily morning prayer was usually addressed to the sun, as in this Kwakiutl example: "Look at me Chief, that nothing evil may happen to me this day, made by you as you please, Great-Walking-To-and-Fro-All-Over-the-World, Chief."[36] As the careful man passed beside a steep mountain, he would speak to it, "Please make yourself firm."[37] Migrating birds were asked to take sickness far away. A Clayoquot Indian sang to a rough sea,

> Breakers, roll more easily.
> Don't break so high
> Become quiet.[38]

There were traditional prayers to use when nearing a waterfall, first seeing a lark, or glimpsing almost any animal of land, sea, or air. Walking about or gliding in his canoe, a traditional Indian would be holding constant conversation with the sacred universe.

Ecologists in recent years have been trying to get people to think of the world in ecological terms: to see everything as connected to everything else, to see ourselves not as the rulers of the earth but as fellow citizens with all other forms of life, and to see the earth as a biosphere in which natural systems operate endlessly to recycle water, oxygen, nutrients and energy among living and non-living parts of the environment. But American Indians would have recognized these ideas as soon as they were explained to them. Their philosophy was already ecological. When they wanted to make a picture of the universe, they drew a great endless circle, perhaps adding the lines of the four directions inside. To them, everything was connected, everything partook of the roundness, everything shared the same life.

NOTES

1. Melvin R. Gilmore, "Indians and Conservation of Native Life," *Torreya* 27 (November–December 1927): 98.

2. Luther Standing Bear, *Land of the Spotted Eagle* (Lincoln: University of Nebraska Press, 1978), p. 38.

3. There is full discussion of the idea that Indians didn't "use" the land in William T. Hagan, "Justifying Dispossession of the Indian: The Land Utilization Argument," in *American Indian Environments: Ecological Issues in Native American History,* ed. Christopher Vecsey and Robert W. Venables (Syracuse, New York: Syracuse University Press, 1980), pp. 65–80.

4. One of the most enlightening examinations of the opinons of both Indians and non-Indians supporting and opposing the idea that Indians were primal environmentalists is by Christopher Vecsey, "American Indian Environmental Religions," in *American Indian Environments,* ed. Vecsey and Venables, pp. 1–37.

5. Hal Borland, *When the Legends Die* (New York: Bantam Books, 1964), p. 18.

6. Frances Densmore, *Pawnee Music.* Burean of American Ethnology, Bulletin No. 93 (Washington: Government Printing Office, 1929), p. 49.

7. Frances Densmore, *Teton Sioux Music.* Burean of American Ethnology, Bulletin No. 61 (Washington: Government Printing Office, 1918), pp. 99–100.

8. Popovi Da, "Indian Values," *The Living Wilderness* 34 (Spring 1970): 26.

9. W. C. Vanderwerth, ed., *Indian Oratory: Famous Speeches by Noted Indian Chieftains* (Norman: University of Oklahoma Press, 1971), pp. 120–21.

10. Ruth Murray Underhill, *Papago Indian Religion* (New York: Columbia University Press, 1946), pp. 33, 98; Willard W. Hill, *The Agricultural and Hunting Methods of the Navajo Indians* (Yale University Publications in Anthropology, No. 18, New Haven, 1938), p. 72.

11. John Collier, *On the Gleaming Way: Navajos, Eastern Pueblos, Zuñis, Hopis, and Their Land: and Their Meanings to the World* (Repring. Denver: Sage Books, 1962), p. 132.

12. Underhill, *Papago Religion,* p. 238. Underhill's translation has "shaman" instead of "magician."

13. Ruth L. Bunzel, "Zuñi Ritual Poetry," *Forty-seventh Annual Report of the Bureau of American Ethnology,* 1929–1930 (Washington: Government Printing Office, 1932), pp. 643–44.

14. Washington Matthews, "Navajo Legends," *American Folklore Society Memoirs* 5(1879): 273–75.

15. Black Elk, *The Sacred Pipe,* ed. Joseph Epes Brown (New York: Penguin Books, 1973), pp. 13–14.

16. Ibid., p. 7.

17. Elsie Clews Parsons, *Pueblo Indian Religion* (Chicago: University of Chicago Press, 1939), p. 198.

18. Elsie Clews Parsons, *Isleta Paintings,* ed. by Esther S. Goldfrank. Bureau of American Ethnology, Bulletin No. 181 (Washington: Government Printing Office, 1962), p. 78.

19. Edward F. Castetter and Morris Edward Opler, *The Ethnobiology of the Chiricahua and Mescalero Apache.* University of New Mexico Bulletin No. 297; Biological Series, vol. 4, no. 5, part 3 (Albuquerque: Univesrity of New Mexico Press, 1936), p. 16.

20. Joseph Epes Brown, "The Roots of Renewal," in *Seeing With a Native Eye: Essays on Native American Religion,* ed. Walter Holden Capps (New York: Harper & Row, 1976), p. 32

21. Underhill, *Papago Religion,* pp. 22–23.

22. Parsons, *Pueblo REligion,* p. 207.

23. Black Elk, *The Sacred Pipe,* p. 105.

24. Ruth L. Bunzel, "Introduction to Zuñi Ceremonialism," *Forty-seventh Annual Report of the Bureau of American Ethnology,* 1929–30 (Washington, Government Printing Office, 1932), p. 488.

25. E. Adamson Hoebel, *The Cheyennes: Indians of the Great Plains* (New York: Holt, Rinehart, and Winston, 1960), pp. 84–875.

26. Black Elk, *Sacred Pipe,* p. xx.

27. Ake Hultkrantz heard the Plains Cree Indian Stand Cuthand say, "The Supreme Being is in everything; he is in all of nature, in man and all the animals." *Belief and Worship in Native North America,* ed. Christopher Vecsey (Syracuse, New York: Syracuse University Press, 1981), p. 126.

28. Thomas F. McIlwraith, *The Bella Coola Indians,* 2 vols. (Toronto: University of Toronto Press, 1948), 1:32, 345.

29. John R. Swanton, *Contributions to the Ethnology of the Haida.* American Museum of Natural History, Memoirs, vol 8, part 1 (New York, 1909), p. 13.

30. Black Elk, *Sacred Pipe,* p. 14.

31. George S. Snyderman, "Concepts of Land Ownership Among the Iroquois and Their Neighbors," in *Symposium on Local Directory in Iroquois Culture,* ed. by William N. Fenton. Smithsonian Institution, Bureau of American Ethnology, Bulletin 149 (1952); 16.

32. Ethelou Yazzie, ed., *Navajo History,* vol. 1 (Many Farms, Arizona: Navajo Community College Press, 1971), pp. 21, 23.

33. Frances Densmore, *Mandan and Hidatsa Music.* Bureau of American Ethnology, Bulletin No. 80 (Washington: Government Printing Office, 1923), p. 50; Densmore, *Teton Sioux Music,* p. 357.

34. George E. Hyde. *Life of George Bent, Written from His Letters* (Norman: University of Oklahoma Press, 1968), p. 155.

35. Black Elk, *Sacred Pipe,* pp. 12–13.

36. Franz Boas, *The Religion of the Kwakiutl Indians,* Part II: Translations (New York: Columbia University Press, 1930), p. 177.

37. McIlwraith, *Bella Coola,* 1:92.

38. Frances Densmore, *Nootka and Quileute Music.* Bureau of American Ethnology, Bulletin No. 124 (Washington: Government Printing Office, 1939), p. 282.

"EARLY BUDDHIST VIEWS ON NATURE"

Chatsumarn Kabilsingh

Buddhism views humanity as an integral part of nature, so that when nature is defiled, people ultimately suffer. Negative consequences arise when cultures alienate themselves from nature, when people feel separate from and become aggressive towards natural systems. When we abuse nature, we abuse ourselves. Buddhist ethics follow from this basic understanding. Only when we agree on this common ground can we save ourselves, let alone the world.

In order to explore the connection between Buddhism and nature, Wildlife Fund Thailand has sponsored a project called Buddhism and Nature Conservation. This project is particularly interested in finding teachings of the Buddha which relate to nature and its conservation. A team of researchers has combed the texts and discovered a surprisingly large store of beautiful and valuable teachings in Buddhism relating to nature and respect for wildlife and natural resources.

The *Jataka,* the richly narrated birth stories of Buddhism, are abundant with poetic appreciations of nature. Passage after passage celebrates forests, waters, and the Earth's wild creatures. Here we find a "Garden of Delight," where grass is ever green, all trees bear fruit good to eat, and streams are sweet and clean, "blue as beryl." Nearby is "a region overrun and beautified with all manner of trees and flowering shrubs and creepers, resounding with the cries of swans, ducks and geese. . . ." Next is reported an area "yielding from its soil all manner of herbs, overspread with many a tangle of flowers," and listing a rich variety of wild animals: antelope, elephant, buffalo, deer, yak, lion, rhinoceros, tiger, panther, bear, hyena, otter, hare, and more.[1]

All Buddhist literature states that the Buddha was born in a grove of sal, lovely straight-backed trees with large leaves. According to legend, when the Buddha was born he took seven steps, and lotus flowers sprang up as he walked. As a youth, he is said to have meditated in the shade of the jambo, one of the 650 species of myrtle.

The Buddha's further study was in the company of a banyan, and his enlightenment was under the spreading branches of a tree recognized for its special place in human faith even in its scientific name, *Ficus religiosa.* Also known as the Bo, Bodhi, or peepul, this tree is sacred in both Buddhism and Hinduism.

Reprinted from *Dharma Gaia: A Harvest of Essays in Buddhism and Ecology* edited by Allan Hunt Badiner (1990) with permission of Parallax Press, Berkeley, CA, USA.

The early Buddhist community lived in the forest under large trees, in caves, and in mountainous areas. Directly dependent on nature, they cultivated great respect for the beauty and diversity of their natural surroundings.

In the *Sutta-Nipata,* one of the earliest texts, the Buddha says:

Know ye the grasses and the trees . . . Then know ye the worms, and the moths, and the different sorts of ants . . . Know ye also the four-footed animals small and great, the serpents, the fish which range in the water, the birds that are borne along on wings and move through the air . . . Know ye the marks that constitute species are theirs, and their species are manifold.[2]

There is a story of a monk who cut down the main branch of a tree: The spirit who resided in that tree came forward and complained to the Buddha that a monk had cut off his child's arm. From then on, monks were forbidden to cut down trees.[3]

The Buddha encouraged acting with compassion and respect for the trees, noting that they provide natural protection for the beings who dwell in the forest. On one occasion, the Buddha admonished some travelers who, after resting under a large banyan tree, proceeded to cut it down. Much like a friend, the tree had given them shade. To harm a friend is indeed an act of ingratitude.[4]

The *Anguttara Nikaya* tells a similar story:

Long ago, Brahmin Dhamika, Rajah Koranya, had a steadfast king banyan tree and the shade of its widespread branches was cool and lovely. Its shelter broadened to twelve leagues. None guarded its fruit, and none hurt another for its fruit.

Now then came a man who ate his fill of fruit, broke a branch, and went his way. Thought the spirit dwelling in that tree: How amazing, how astonishing it is, that a man should be so evil as to break a branch off the tree after eating his fill. Suppose the tree were to bear no more fruit. And the tree bore no more fruit.[5]

What about the treatment of animals? Every healthy forest is home for wildlife, so when a monk accepts the forest as his home, he also respects the animals who live in the forest. Early Buddhists maintained this kind of friendly attitude toward their natural surroundings and opposed the destruction of forests or their wildlife.[6]

The first precept in Buddhism is "Do not kill." This precept is not merely a legalistic prohibition, but a realization of our affinity with all who share the gift of life. A compassionate heart provides a firm ground for this precept.

Those who make their living directly or indirectly from killing animals will experience the karmic consequences. The resultant pain is described in the texts as being "sharp as spears" and as terrifying as being "thrown head-down into a river of fire."[7] A person who tortures or kills animals will always harbor a deep sorrow within:

Chatsumarn Kabilsingh

When, householder, the taker of life, by reason of his taking life, breeds dread and hatred in this world, or when he breeds dread and hatred in the next world, he experiences in the mind pain and grief; but he who abstains from taking life breeds no dread and hatred in this world and in the next world . . . Thus that dread and hatred has ceased for him, who abstained from taking life.[8]

The community of monks are forbidden by the *Vinaya,* the ancient rules of conduct, from eating ten different kinds of meat, mostly animals of the forest.[9] The Buddha taught his disciples to communicate to animals their wishes for peace and happiness. This was only possible when they did not eat the animals' flesh, and harbored no thoughts of harming them. When a monk died from a snakebite, the Buddha advised the community to generate compassion and dedicate the merit to the family of snakes.[10]

When we look at the Buddha's pronouncements on water conservation, it is astonishing to see that he actually set down rules forbidding his disciples to contaminate water resources. For example, monks were dissuaded from throwing their waste or leftover food into rivers and lakes, and they were urged to guard the lives of all living beings abiding there.[11] In the *Vinaya Pitaka* there are detailed descriptions of how to build toilets and water wells.[12] One of the eight good qualities of the ocean is "cleanliness," and another is that it "must be the abode of various kinds of fish." Those who destroy or contaminate water resources do so at great karmic peril.[13] This illustrates early awareness of the need to preserve natural resources.

The early Buddhist community lived comfortably within nature, and the Buddha included many examples and similes from nature in his teachings:

Suppose there is a pool of water, turbid, stirred up and muddied. Just so a turbid mind. Suppose there is a pool of water, pure, tranquil and unstirred, where a man can see oysters and shells, pebbles and gravel, and schools of fish. Just so an untroubled mind.[14]

Buddhism holds a great respect for and gratitude toward nature. Nature is the mother that gives rise to all the joyful things in life. Among the beautiful expressions in Buddhist literature showing mutual relation and interdependence of humankind and wildlife, there was early on a realization that survival of certain species was in danger, and that losing such creatures diminishes the Earth: "Come back, O Tigers! to the woods again, and let it not be leveled with the plain. For without you, the axe will lay it low. You, without it, forever homeless go."[15]

Another well-known and much loved teaching which exemplifies the central core of compassion in Buddhism is the *Metta Sutta:* "Thus, as a mother with her own life guards the life of her own child, let all embracing thoughts for all that lives be thine."[16]

His Holiness the Fourteenth Dalai Lama of Tibet who stands prominently among Buddhist leaders of the world who are farsighted, has repeatedly expressed his concern for environmental protection. "Our ancestors viewed the Earth as rich, bountiful and sustainable," said His Holiness. "We know this is the case, but only if we take care of it." In one of his recent speeches on the subject of ecology, he points out that the most important thing is to have a peaceful heart. Only when we understand the true nature lying within can we live harmoniously with the rest of the natural world.

In this respect, the Buddhist practice of cultivating awareness and calmness through meditation is vital. Buddhism is very much a religion of this world, this life, and the present moment. In the past it has often been misunderstood as otherworldly or life-denying. In fact, Buddhism can be meaningful only when it is relevant to our everyday lives and to our environment. The Buddhist tradition counsels us to treasure and conserve nature, of which human beings are an active part. Each of us must choose the extent to which we will bring to life the teachings of the Buddha. If we cannot hand over a better world to future generations, it is only fair that they have at least as green a world to live in as we do.

NOTES

1. *Jataka Stories*, edited by E.B. Cowell, Vol. IV–V (1957).

2. *Sutta-Nipata*, translated by V. Fausboll (Delhi, India: Motilal Banarsidass, 1968).

3. *Paccittiya, Bhutagama Vagga,* Thai Tripitaka, Vol. 2, p. 347.

4. *Ibid.,* Vol. 27, p. 370.

5. *Anguttara Nikaya, Gradual Sayings,* Vol. 3, p. 262.

6. *Payaka Jataka, op. cit.* Vol. 27:417, p. 107.

7. *Ibid.,* Vol. 28:92, p. 35.

8. *Gradual Sayings,* Vol. 4, p. 273.

9. *Ibid.,* Vol. 4, p. 60–61.

10. *Ibid.,* Vol. 7, p. 9.

11. *Ibid.,* Vol. 25:300, p. 313.

12. *Ibid.,* Vol. 7, p. 48.

13. *Ibid.,* Vol. 26:104, p. 174.

14. *Ibid.,* Vol. 1, p. 6–7.

15. *Khuddakapatha* (London: Pali Text Society, 1960).

16. *Ibid.*

"*SATYAGRAHA* FOR CONSERVATION: AWAKENING THE SPIRIT OF HINDUISM"

O. P. Dwivedi

The World Commission on Environment and Development acknowledged that to reconcile human affairs with natural laws "our cultural and spiritual heritages can reinforce our economic interests and survival imperatives."[1] But until very recently, the role of our cultural and spiritual heritages in environmental protection and sustainable development was ignored by international bodies, national governments, policy planners, and even environmentalists. Many fear that bringing religion into the environmental movement will threaten objectivity, scientific investigation, professionalism, or democratic values. But none of these need be displaced in order to include the spiritual dimension in environmental protection. That dimension, if introduced in the process of environmental policy planning, administration, education, and law, could help create a self-consciously moral society which would put conservation and respect for God's creation first, and relegate individualism, materialism, and our modern desire to dominate nature in a subordinate place. Thus my plea for a definite role of religion in conservation and environmental protection.

From the perspective of many world religions, the abuse and exploitation of nature for immediate gain is unjust, immoral, and unethical. For example, in the ancient past, Hindus and Buddhists were careful to observe moral teachings regarding the treatment of nature. In their cultures, not only the common person but also rulers and kings followed those ethical guidelines and tried to create an example for others. But now in the twentieth century, the materialistic orientation of the West has equally affected the cultures of the East. India, Sri Lanka, Thailand, and Japan have witnessed wanton exploitation of the environment by their own peoples, despite the strictures and injunctions inherent in their religions and cultures. Thus, no culture has remained immune from human irreverence towards nature. How can we change the attitude of human beings towards nature? Are religions the answer?

I believe that religion can evoke a kind of awareness in persons that is different from scientific or technological reasoning. Religion helps make human beings aware that there are limits to

This essay was reprinted from *Ethics of Environment and Development*, edited by J. Ronald Engel and Joan Gibb Engel, Copyright 1990. Reprinted by permission of John Wiley & Sons. Ltd.

their control over the animate and inanimate world and that their arrogance and manipulative power over nature can backfire. Religion instils the recognition that human life cannot be measured by material possessions and that the ends of life go beyond conspicuous consumption.

As a matter of fact, religion can provide at least three fundamental mainstays to help human beings cope in a technological society. First, it defends the individual's existence against the depersonalizing effects of the technoindustrial process. Second, it forces the individual to recognize human fallibility and to combine realism with idealism. Third, while technology gives the individual the physical power to create or to destroy the world, religion gives the moral strength to grow in virtue by nurturing restraint, humility, and liberation from self-centeredness.[2] Directly and indirectly, religion can be a powerful source for environmental conservation and protection. Thus, we need a strategy for conservation that does not ignore the powerful influence of religions, but instead draws from all religious foundations and cultures.

World religions, each in their own way, offer a unique set of moral values and rules to guide human beings in their relationship with the environment. Religions also provide sanctions and offer stiffer penalties, such as fear of hell, for those who do not treat God's creation with respect. Although it is true that, in the recent past, religions have not been in the forefront of protecting the environment from human greed and exploitation, many are now willing to take up the challenge and help protect and conserve the environment. But their offer of help will remain purely rhetorical unless secular institutions, national governments, and international organizations are willing to acknowledge the role of religion in environmental study and education. And I believe that environmental education will remain incomplete until it includes cultural values and religious imperatives. For this, we require an ecumenical approach. While there are metaphysical, ethical, anthropological and social disagreements among world religions, a synthesis of the key concepts and precepts from each of them pertaining to conservation could become a foundation for a global environmental ethic. The world needs such an ethic.

THE RELIGION AND ENVIRONMENT DEBATE

In 1967, the historian, Lynn White, Jr., wrote an article in *Science* on the historical roots of the ecological crisis.[3] According to White, what people do to their environment depends upon how they see themselves in relation to nature. White asserted that the exploitative view that has generated much of the environmental crisis, particularly in Europe and North America, is a result of the teachings of late medieval Latin Christianity, which conceived of humankind as superior to the rest of God's creation and everything else as created for human use and enjoyment. He suggested that the only way to address the ecological crisis was to reject the view that nature has no reason to exist except to serve humanity. White's proposition impelled sci-

O. P. Dwivedi

entists, theologians, and environmentalists to debate the bases of his argument that religion could be blamed for the ecological crisis.

In the course of this debate, examples from other cultures were cited to support the view that, even in countries where there is religious respect for nature, exploitation of the environment has been ruthless. Countries where Hinduism, Buddhism, Taoism and Shintoism have been practised were cited to support the criticism of Thomas Derr, among others, that "We are simply being gullible when we take at face value the advertisement for the ecological harmony of nonwestern cultures." Derr goes on to say:

> even if Christian doctrine had produced technological culture and its environmental troubles, one would be at a loss to understand the absence of the same result in equally Christian Eastern Europe. And conversely, if ecological disaster is a particularly Christian habit, how can one explain the disasters non-Christian cultures have visited upon their environments? Primitive cultures, Oriental cultures, classical cultures—all show examples of human dominance over nature which has led to ecological catastrophe. Overgrazing, deforestation and similar errors of sufficient magnitude to destroy civilizations have been committed by Egyptians, Assyrians, Romans, North Africans, Persians, Indians, Aztecs, and even Buddhists, who are foolishly supposed by some Western admirers to be immune from this sort of thing.[4]

This chapter challenges Derr's assertion with respect to the role of the Hindu religion in the ecological crisis. We need to understand how a Hindu's attitude to nature has been shaped by his religion's view of the cosmos and creation. Such an exposition is necessary to explain the traditional values and beliefs of Hindus and hence what role Hindu religion once played with respect to human treatment of the environment. At the same time, we need to know how it is that this religion, which taught harmony with and respect for nature, and which influenced other religions such as Jainism and Buddhism, has been in recent times unable to sustain a caring attitude towards nature. What are the features of the Hindu religion which strengthen human respect for God's creation, and how were these features repressed by the modern view of the natural environment and its resources?[5]

THE SANCTITY OF LIFE IN HINDUISM

The principle of the sanctity of life is clearly ingrained in the Hindu religion. Only God has absolute sovereignty over all creatures; thus, human beings have no dominion over their own lives or non-human life. Consequently, humanity cannot act as a viceroy of God over the planet, nor assign degrees of relative worth to other species. The idea of the Divine Being as the one underlying power of unity is beautifully expressed in the *Yajurveda*:

> The loving sage beholds that Being, hidden in mystery,
> wherein the universe comes to have one home;

Therein unites and therefrom emanates the whole;

The Omnipresent One pervades souls and matter like warp and woof in created beings.

(*Yajurveda* 32.8)[6]

The sacredness of God's creation means no damage may be inflicted on other species without adequate justification. Therefore, all lives, human and nonhuman, are of equal value and all have the same right to existence. According to the *Atharvaveda,* the Earth is not for human beings alone, but for other creatures as well:

Born of Thee, on Thee move mortal creatures;

Thou bearest them—the biped and the quadruped;

Thine, O Earth, are the five races of men, for whom

Surya (Sun), as he rises spreads with his rays

the light that is immortal. (*Atharvaveda* 12.1–15)[7]

Srsti: God's Creation

Hindus contemplate divinity as the one in many and the many in one. This conceptualization resembles both monotheism and polytheism. Monotheism is the belief in a single divine Person. In monotheistic creeds that Person is God. Polytheism, on the other hand, believes in the many; and the concept of God is not monarchical. The Hindu concept of God resembles monotheism in that it portrays the divinity as one, and polytheism is that it contemplates the divinity as one in many. Although there are many gods, each one is the Supreme Being. This attitude we may call non-dualistic theism.

The earliest Sanskrit texts, the Veda and Upanishads, teach the non-dualism of the supreme power that existed before the creation. God as the efficient cause, and nature, *Prakrti,* as the material cause of the universe, are unconditionally accepted, as is their harmonious relationship. However, while these texts agree on the concept of non-dualistic theism, they differ in their theories regarding the creation of the universe. Why have different theories been elaborated in the Veda and the Upanishads? This is one of the most important and intriguing questions we can ask. A suitable reply is given in the Rigveda:

He is one, but the wise call him by different names; such as Indra, Mitra, Varuna, Agni, Divya—one who pervaded all the luminous bodies, the source of light; Suparna—the protector and preserver of the universe; whose works are perfect; Matriswa—powerful like wind; Garutman—mighty by nature. (*Rigveda* 1.164.46)[8]

The Hindu concept of creation can be presented in four categories. First is the Vedic theory, which is followed by further elaboration in Vedanta and Sankhya philosophies; the second is Upanishadic theory; the third is known as Puranic theory; and the fourth is enunciated in the great Hindu epics *Ramayana* and *Mahabharata*. Although the Puranic theory differs from the other three, a single thought flows between them. This unifying theory is well stated in the Rigveda:

> The *Vedas* and the universal laws of nature which control the universe and govern the cycles of creation and dissolution were made manifest by the All-knowing One. By His great power were produced the clouds and the vapors. After the production of the vapors, there intervened a period of darkness after which the Great Lord and Controller of the universe arranged the motions which produce days, nights, and other durations of time. The Great One then produced the sun, the moon, the earth, and all other regions as He did in previous cycles of creation. (*Rigveda* 10:190.1–3)

All the Hindu scriptures attest to the belief that the creation, maintenance, and annihilation of the cosmos is completely dependent on the Supreme will. In the *Gita*, Lord Krishna says to Arjuna: "Of all that is material and all that is spiritual in this world, know for certain that I am both its origin and dissolution." (*Gita* 7.6).[9] And the Lord says: again "The whole cosmic order is under me. By my will it is manifested again and again and by my will, it is annihilated at the end" (*Gita* 9.8). Thus, for ancient Hindus, both God and *Prakriti* (nature) was to be one and the same. While the *Prajapati* (as mentioned in Regveda) is the creator of sky, the earth, oceans, and all other species, he is also their protector and eventual destroyer. He is the only Lord of creation. Human beings have no special privilege or authority over other creatures; on the other hand, they have more obligations and duties.

Duties to Animals and Birds

The most important aspect of Hindu theology pertaining to treatment of animal life is the belief that the Supreme Being was himself incarnated in the form of various species. The Lord says: "This form is the source and indestructible seed of multifarious incarnations within the universe, and from the particle and portion of this form, different living entities, like demi-gods, animals, human beings and others, are created" (*Srimad-Bhagavata* Book I, Discourse III: 5).[10] Among the various incarnations of God (numbering from ten to twenty-four depending upon the source of the text), He first incarnated Himself in the form of a fish, then a tortoise, a boar, and a dwarf. His fifth incarnation was as a manlion. As Rama he was closely associated with monkeys, and as Krishna he was always surrounded by the cows. Thus, other species are accorded reverence.

Further, the Hindu belief in the cycle of birth and rebirth where a person may come back as an animal or a bird gives these species not only respect, but also reverence. This provides a solid foundation for the doctrine of *ahimsa*—nonviolence against animals and human beings alike. Hindus have a deep faith in the doctrine of non-violence. Almost all the

Hindu scriptures place strong emphasis on the notion that God's grace can be received by not killing his creatures or harming his creation: "God, Kesava, is pleased with a person who does not harm or destroy other non-speaking creatures or animals" (*Visnupurana* 3.8.15). To not eat meat in Hinduism is considered both an appropriate conduct and a duty. Yajnavalkya Smriti warns of hell-fire (*Ghora Naraka*) to those who are the killers of domesticated and protected animals: "The wicked person who kills animals which are protected has to live in hell-fire for the days equal to the number of hairs on the body of that animal" (*Yajnavalkyasmriti, Acaradhyayah,* v. 180). By the end of the Vedic and Upanishadic period, Buddhism and Jainism came into existence, and the protection of animals, birds and vegetation was further strengthened by the various kings practicing these religions. These religions, which arose in part as a protest against the orthodoxy and rituals of Hindu religion, continued its precepts for environmental protection. The Buddhist emperor, Ashoka (273–236 BCE), promoted through public proclamations the planting and preservation of flora and fauna. Pillar Edicts, erected at various public places, expressed his concerns about the welfare of creatures, plants and trees and prescribed various punishments for the killing of animals, including ants, squirrels, and rats.

Flora in Hindu Religion

As early as in the time of *Rigveda,* tree worship was quite popular and universal. The tree symbolized the various attributes of God to the Regvedic seers. Regveda regarded plants as having divine powers, with one entire hymn devoted to their praise, chiefly with reference to their healing properties. (Regveda 10.97) During the period of the great epics and Puranas, the Hindu respect for flora expanded further. Trees were considered as being animate and feeling happiness and sorrow. It is still popularly believed that every tree has a *Vriksa-devata,* or "tree deity," who is worshipped with prayers and offerings of water, flowers, sweets, and encircled by sacred threads. Also, for Hindus, the planting of a tree is still a religious duty. Fifteen hundred years ago, the *Matsya Purana* described the proper ceremony for tree planting:

> Clean the soil first and water it. Decorate trees with garlands, burn the guggula perfume in front of them, and place one pitcher filled with water by the side of each tree. Offer prayer and oblation and then sprinkle holy water on trees. Recite hymns from the Regveda, Yajur and Sama and kindle fire. After such worship the actual plantation should be celebrated. He who plants even one tree, goes directly to Heaven and obtains Moksha. (*Matsya Purana* 59.159)

The cutting of trees and destruction of flora were considered a sinful act. *Kautilya's Arthasastra* prescribed various punishments for destroying trees and plants:

> For cutting off the tender sprouts of fruit trees or shady trees in the parks near a city, a fine of six panas shall be imposed; for cutting of the minor branches of the same trees, twelve panas,

and for cutting off the big branches, twenty four panas shall be levied. Cutting off the trunks of the same, shall be punished with the first amercement; and felling shall be punished with the middlemost amercement. (*Kautilya's Arthasastra* III 19: 197)[11]

The Hindu worship of trees and plants has been based partly on utility, but mostly on religious duty and mythology. Hindu ancestors considered it their duty to save trees; and in order to do that they attached to every tree a religious sanctity.

Pradushana: Pollution and Its Prevention in Hindu Scriptures

Hindu scriptures revealed a clear conception of the ecosystem. On this basis a discipline of environmental ethics developed which formulated codes of conduct (*dharma*) and defined humanity's relationship to nature. An important part of that conduct is maintaining proper sanitation. In the past, this was considered to be the duty of everyone and any default was a punishable offence. Hindu society did not even consider it proper to throw dirt on a public path. Kautilya wrote:

> The punishment of one-eighth of a pana should be awarded to those who throw dirt on the roads. For muddy water one-fourth Pana, if both are thrown the punishment should be double. If latrine is thrown or caused near a temple, well, or pond, sacred place, or government building, then the punishment should increase gradually by one pana in each case. For urine the punishment should be only half. (*Kautilya's Arthasastra* II 36: 145)[12]

Hindus considered cremation of dead bodies and maintaining the sanitation of the human habitat as essential acts. When, in about 200 BCE, Caraka wrote about *Vikrti* (pollution) and diseases, he mentioned air pollution specifically as a cause of many diseases.

> The polluted air is mixed with bad elements. The air is uncharacteristic of the season, full of moisture, stormy, hard to breathe, icy cool, hot and dry, harmful, roaring, coming at the same time from all directions, badsmelling, oily, full of dirt, sand, steam, creating diseases in the body and is considered polluted. (*Caraka Samhita, Vimanastanam* III 6:1)[13]

Similarly, about water pollution, *Caraka Samhita* says:

> Water is considered polluted when it is excessively smelly, unnatural in color, taste and touch, slimy, not frequented by aquatic birds, aquatic life is reduced, and the appearance is unpleasing (*Caraka Samhita, Vimanastanam* III 6:2).[14]

Water is considered by Hindus as a powerful media of purification and also as a source of energy. Sometimes, just by the sprinkling of pure water in religious ceremonies, it is believed purity is achieved. That is why, in Regveda, prayer is offered to the deity of water: "The waters in the sky, the waters of rivers, and water in the well whose source is the ocean, may all these sacred waters protect me" (*Rigveda* 7.49.2). The healing property and medicinal value of water has been universally accepted, provided it is pure and free from all pollution. When polluted water and pure water were the point of discussion among ancient Indian thinkers, they were aware of the reasons for the polluted water. Therefore Manu advised: "One should not cause urine, stool, cough in the water. Anything which is mixed with these unpious objects, blood and poison, should not be thrown into water" (*Manusmrti* IV: 56).[15]

Still today, many rivers are considered sacred. Among these, the river Ganges is considered by Hindus as the most sacred and respectable. Disposal of human waste or other pollutants has been prohibited since time immemorial:

> One should not perform these 14 acts near the holy waters of the river Ganga: i.e., remove excrement, brushing and gargling, removing cerumen from body, throwing hairs, dry garlands, playing in water, taking donations, performing sex, attachment with other sacred places, praising other holy places, washing clothes, throwing dirty clothes, thumping water and swimming. (*Pravascitta Tatva* 1.535)

Persons doing such unsocial activities and engaging in acts polluting the environment were cursed: "A person, who is engaged in killing creatures, polluting wells, and ponds, and tanks and destroying gardens, certainly goes to hell" (*Padmapurana, Bhoomikhanda* 96: 7–8).

EFFECTIVENESS OF HINDUISM IN CONSERVATION

The effectiveness of any religion in protecting the environment depends upon how much faith its believers have in its precepts and injunctions. It also depends upon how those precepts are transmitted and adapted in everyday social interactions. In the case of the Hindu religion, which is practised as *dharma*—way of life—many of its precepts became ingrained in the daily life and social institutions of the people. Three specific examples are given below to illustrate this point.

THE CASTE SYSTEM AND SUSTAINABLE DEVELOPMENT

The Hindu religion is known for its elaborate caste system which divides individuals among four main castes and several hundred sub-castes. Over the centuries, the system degenerated into a very rigid, hereditarily determined, hierarchical, and oppressive social structure, particularly for the untouchables and lower castes. But the amazing phenomenon is that it lasted for so many millennia even with centuries of domination by Islamic and Christian cultures.

One explanation by the ecologist, Madhav Gadgil, and the anthropologist, Kailash Malhotra, is that the caste system, as continued until the early decades of the twentieth century, was actually based on an ancient concept of sustainable development which disciplined the society by partitioning the use of natural resources according to specific occupations (or castes); and "created" the right social milieu in which sustainable patterns of resource use were encouraged to "emerge."[16] The caste system regulated the occupations that individuals could undertake. Thus, an "ecological space" was created in ancient Hindu society which helped to reduce competition among various people for limited natural resources. A system of "resource partitioning" emerged whereby the primary users of natural resources did not worry about encroachment from other castes. At the same time, these users also knew that if they depleted the natural resources in their own space, they would not survive economically or physically because no one would allow them to move on to other occupations. Religious injunctions also created the psychological environment whereby each caste or sub-caste respected the occupational boundaries of the others. In a sense, the Hindu caste system can be seen as a progenitor of the concept of sustainable development.

But the system started malfunctioning during the British Raj when demands for raw materials for their fast-growing industrial economy had to be met by commercial exploitation of India's natural resources. As traditional relationships between various castes started disappearing, competition and tension grew. The trend kept on accelerating in independent India, as each caste (or sub-caste) tried to discard its traditional role and seize eagerly any opportunity to land a job. When this happened, the ancient religious injunction for doing one's prescribed duty within a caste system could no longer be maintained; this caused the disappearance of the concept of "ecological space" among Hindus. There is no doubt that the caste system also degenerated within and became a source of oppression; nevertheless, from an ecological spacing view point, the caste system played a key role in preserving India's natural riches for centuries.

BISHNOIS: DEFENDERS OF THE ENVIRONMENT

The Bishnois are a small community in Rajasthan, India, who practise a religion of environmental conservation. They believe that cutting a tree or killing an animal or bird is blasphemy. Their religion, an offshoot of Hinduism, was founded by Guru Maharaj Jambaji, who was born in 1451 CE in the Marwar area. When he was young he witnessed how, during a severe drought, people cut down trees to feed animals but when the drought continued, nothing was left to feed the animals, so they died. Jambaji thought that if trees are protected, animal life would be sustained, and his community would survive. He gave 29 injunctions and principal among them being a ban on the cutting of any green tree and killing of any animal or bird. About 300 years later, when the King of Jodhpur wanted to build a new palace, he sent his soldiers to the Bishnois area where trees were in abundance. Villagers protested, and when soldiers would not pay any attention to the protest, the Bishnois, led by a woman, hugged the trees to protect them with their bodies. As soldiers kept on killing villagers, more and more of the Bishnois came forward to honour the religious injunction of their Guru Maharaj Jambaji. The massacre continued until 363 persons were killed defending trees. When the king heard about this human sacrifice, he stopped the operation, and gave the Bishnois state protection for their belief.[17]

Today, the Bishnois community continues to protect trees and animals with the same fervour. Their community is the best example of a true Hindu-based ritual defence of the environment in India, and their sacrifices became the inspiration for the Chipko movement of 1973.

THE CHIPKO MOVEMENT

In March 1973, in the town of Gopeshwar in Chamoli district (Uttar Pradesh, India), villagers formed a human chain and hugged the earmarked trees to keep them from being felled for a nearby factory producing sports equipment. The same situation later occurred in another village when forest contractors wanted to cut trees under licence from the Government Department of Forests. Again, in 1974, women from the village of Reni, near Joshimath in the Himalayas, confronted the loggers by hugging trees and forced contractors to leave. Since then, the *Chipko Andolan* (the movement to hug trees) has grown as a grassroots ecodevelopment movement.[18]

The genesis of the Chipko movement is not only in the ecological or economic background, but in religious belief. Villagers have noted how industrial and commercial demands have denuded their forests, how they cannot sustain their livelihood in a deforested area, and how floods continually play havoc with their small agricultural communities. The religious basis of the movement is evident in the fact that it is inspired and guided by women. Women have not only seen how their men would not mind destroying nature in order to get money while they had to walk miles in search of firewood, fodder and other grazing materials, but, being more religious, they also are more sensitive to injunctions such as *ahimsa*. In a sense, the Chipko movement is a kind of feminist movement to protect nature from the greed of men. In the Himalayan areas, the pivot of the family is the woman. It is the woman who worries most about nature and its conservation in order that its resources are available for her family's sustenance. On the other hand, men go away to distant places in search of jobs, leaving women and old people behind. These women also believe that each tree has a *Vriksadevata* (tree god) and that the deity *Van Devi* (the Goddess of forests) will protect their family welfare. They also believe that each green tree is an abode of the Almighty God *Hari*.

The Chipko movement has caught the attention of others in India. For example, in Karnataka state, the Appiko movement began in September 1983, when 163 men, women, and children hugged the trees and forced the lumberjacks to leave. That movement swiftly spread to the adjoining districts. These people are against the kind of commercial felling of

O. P. Dwivedi

trees which clears the vegetation in its entirety. They do recognize the firewood needs of urban people (mostly poor) and therefore do not want a total ban on felling. However, they are against indiscriminate clearing and would like to see a consultative process established so that local people are able to participate in timber management.

These three examples are illustrative of the practical impact of Hinduism on conservation and sustainable development. While the effectiveness of the caste system to act as a resource partitioning system is no longer viable, the examples of Bishnois and Chipko/Appiko are illustrative of the fact that when appeal to secular norms fails, one can draw on the cultural and religious sources for "forest *satyagraha*." ("Satyagraha" means "insistance or persistence in search of truth." In this context, the term "forest satyagraha" means "persistence in search of truth pertaining to the rights of trees.")

LOSS OF RESPECT FOR NATURE

If such has been the tradition, philosophy, and ideology of Hindu religion, what then are the reasons behind the present state of environmental crisis? As we have seen, our ethical beliefs and religious values influence our behavior towards others, including our relationship with all creatures and plant life. If, for some reason, these noble values become displaced by other beliefs which are either thrust upon the society or transplanted from another culture through invasion, then the faith of the masses in the earlier cultural tradition is shaken. As the foreign culture, language and system of administration slowly takes root and penetrates all levels of society, and as appropriate answers and leadership are not forthcoming from the religious leaders and Brahmans, it is only natural for the masses to become more inward-looking and self-centered. Under such circumstances, religious values which acted as sanctions against environmental destruction do not retain a high priority because people have to worry about their very survival and freedom; hence, respect for nature gets displaced by economic factors.

That, it seems, is what happened in India during the 700 years of foreign cultural domination. The ancient educational system which taught respect for nature and reasons for its preservation was no longer available. On the other hand, the imported culture was unable to replace the ancient Hindu religion; consequently, a conflict continued between the two value systems. The situation became more complex when, in addition to the Muslim culture, the British introduced Christianity and Western secular institutions and values. While it is too easy to blame these external forces for the change in attitudes of Hindus towards nature, nevertheless it is a fact that they greatly inhibited the religion from continuing to transmit ancient values which encourage respect and due regard for God's creation.

The Hindu religion teaches a renunciation of worldly goods, and preaches against materialism and consumerism. Such teachings could act as a great source of strength for Hindu societies in their struggle to achieve sustainable development. I detect in countries like India and Nepal a revival of respect for ancient cultural values. Such a revival need not turn into fundamentalism; instead it could be based on the lessons learned from environmental destruction in the West, and on the relevant precepts enshrined in the Hindu scriptures. That should not cause any damage to the secularism now practised in India. As a matter of fact, this could develop into a movement whereby spiritual guidance is made available to the secular system of governance and socioeconomic interaction.

HOPE FOR OUR COMMON FUTURE

Mahatma Gandhi warned that "nature had enough for everybody's need but not for everybody's greed." Gandhi was a great believer in drawing upon the rich variety of spiritual and cultural heritages of India. His *satyagraha* movements were the perfect example of how one could confront an unjust and uncaring though extremely superior power. Similarly, the Bishnois, Chipko, and Appiko people are engaged in a kind of "forest *satyagraha*" today. Their movements could easily be turned into a common front—"satyagraha for the environment"—to be used against the forces of big government and big business. This could include such other movements as *Mitti Bachao Abhiyan* (save the soil movement), *Van Mahotsava* (tree planting ceremony), *Chetna March* (public awareness march), *Kalpavriksha* (voluntary organization in Delhi for environmental conservation), and many others. The Hindu people are accustomed to suffering a great level of personal and physical hardships if such suffering is directed against unjust and uncaring forces. The minds of the Hindu people are slowly being awakened through the Chipko, Appiko, Bishnois, Chetna March, and other movements. *Satyagraha* for conservation could very well be a rallying point for the awakened spirit of Hinduism.

Hindu culture, in ancient and medieval times, provided a system of moral guidelines towards environmental preservation and conservation. Environmental ethics, as propounded by ancient Hindu scriptures and seers, was practised not only by common persons, but even by rulers and kings. They observed these fundamentals sometimes as religious duties, often as rules of administration or obligation for law and order, but either way these principles were properly knitted with the Hindu way of life. In Hindu culture, a human being is authorized to use natural resources, but has no divine power of control and dominion over nature and its elements. Hence, from the perspective of Hindu culture, abuse and exploitation of nature for selfish gain is unjust and sacreligious. Against the continuation of such exploitation, the only viable strategy appears to be *satyagraha* for conservation.

O. P. Dwivedi

NOTES

1. World Commission on Environment and Development, *Our Common Future* (New York: Oxford University Press, 1987), 1.

2. O.P. Dwivedi, "Man and Nature: A Holistic Approach to a Theory of Ecology," *The Environmental Professional* 10 (1987): 8–15.

3. Lynn White, Jr., "The Historical Roots of Our Ecologic Crisis," *Science* 155 (March 1967): 1203–7.

4. Thomas S. Derr, "Religion's Responsibility for the Ecological Crisis: An Argument Run Amok," *World View* 18 (1975): 43.

5. These questions have been examined in detail in O.P. Dwivedi and B.N. Tiwari, *Environmental Crisis and Hindu Religion* (New Delhi: Gitanjali Publishing, 1987).

6. *The Yajurveda,* trans. Devi Chand, (New Delhi: Munsiram Manoharlal Publishers, 1982).

7. *The Atharvaveda,* trans. Devi Chand, (New Delhi: Munsiram Manoharlal Publishers, 1982).

8. *Rigveda,* comp. Mahrishi Dayanand Saraswati, (New Delhi: Sarvadeshik Arya Pratinidhi Sabha, 1974), 12 vols.

9. *The Bhagavad Gita,* commentator Swami Chidbhavananda, (Tirruchirapalli: Sri Ramakrishna Tapovanam, 1974).

10. *Srimad Bhagavata Mahapurana,* trans. C. L. Goswami and M. A. Sastri, (Gorakhpur: Gita Press, 1982), 2 vols.

11. R. Shamasastry, ed., *Kautilya's Arthasastra* (Mysore: Mysore Publishers, 1967), 224.

12. Ibid., 166.

13. *Caraka-Samhita,* trans. Priyavrat Sharma, (Varanasi: Chaukhambha Orientalia, 1983) I, 315.

14. Ibid.

15. *Manusmriti (The Laws of Manu),* trans. G. Buhler, (Delhi: Motilal Banarsidass, 1975), 137.

16. Centre for Science and Environment, *The State of India's Environment 1984–85, the Second Citizens' Report* (New Delhi: CSE, 1985), 162.

17. Ibid., 164.

18. Chandi Prasad Bhatt, "The Chipko Andolan: Forest Conservation Based on People's Power" in eds. Anil Agrawal, Darryl D'Monte, and Ujwala Samarth *The Fight for Survival,* (New Delhi: Centre for Science and Environment, 1987), 51.

ISLAMIC ENVIRONMENTAL ETHICS, LAW, AND SOCIETY

Mawil Y. Izzi Deen (Samarrai)

Islamic environmental ethics, like all other forms of ethics in Islam, is based on clear-cut legal foundations which Muslims hold to be formulated by God. Thus, in Islam, an acceptance of what is legal and what is ethical has not involved the same processes as in cultures which base their laws on humanistic philosophies.

Muslim scholars have found it difficult to accept the term "Islamic Law," since "law" implies a rigidity and dryness alien to Islam. They prefer the Arabic word *Sharī'ah* (Shariah) which literally means the "source of water." The Shariah is the source of life in that it contains both legal rules and ethical principles. This is indicated by the division of the Shariah relevant to human action into the categories of: obligatory actions (*wājib*),—those which a Muslim is required to perform; devotional and ethical virtues (*mandūb*)—those actions a Muslim is encouraged to perform, the non-observance of which, however, incurs no liability; permissible actions (*mubāh*)—those in which a Muslim is given complete freedom of choice; abominable actions (*makrūh*)—those which are morally but not legally wrong; and prohibited actions (*haram*)—all those practices forbidden by Islam.

A complete separation into the two elements, law and ethics, is thus unnecessary in Islam. For a Muslim is obliged to obey whatever God has ordered, his philosophical questions having been answered before he became a follower of the faith.

THE FOUNDATION OF ENVIRONMENTAL PROTECTION

In Islam, the conservation of the environment is based on the principle that all the individual components of the environment were created by God, and that all living things were created with different functions, functions carefully measured and meticulously balanced by the Almighty Creator. Although the various components of the natural environment serve humanity as one of their functions, this does not imply that human use is the sole reason for their creation. The comments of the medieval Muslim scholar, Ibn Taymīyah, on those verses of the Holy Qur'ān which state that God created the various parts of the environment to serve humanity, are relevant here:

This essay was reprinted from *Ethics of Environment and Development*, edited by J. Ronald Engel and Joan Gibb Engel, Copyright 1990. Reprinted by permission of John Wiley & Sons. Ltd.

In considering all these verses it must be remembered that Allah in His wisdom created these creatures for reasons other than serving man, for in these verses He only explains the benefits of these creatures [to man].[1]

The legal and ethical reasons for protecting the environment can be summarized as follows:[2] First, the environment is God's creation and to protect it is to preserve its values as a sign of the Creator. To assume that the environment's benefits to human beings are the sole reason for its protection may lead to environmental misuse or destruction.

Second, the component parts of nature are entities in continuous praise of their Creator. Humans may not be able to understand the form or nature of this praise, but the fact that the Qur'ān describes it is an additional reason for environmental preservation:

> The seven heavens and the earth and all that is therein praise Him, and there is not such a thing but hymneth his praise; but ye understand not their praise. Lo! He is ever Clement, Forgiving (Sūrah 17: 44).[3]

Third, all the laws of nature are laws made by the Creator and based on the concept of the absolute continuity of existence. Although God may sometimes wish otherwise, what happens, happens according to the natural law of God (*sunnah*), and human beings must accept this as the will of the Creator. Attempts to break the law of God must be prevented. As the Qur'ān states:

> Hast thou not seen that unto Allah payeth adoration whosoever is in the heavens and whosoever is in the earth, and the sun, and the moon, and the stars, and the hills, and the trees, and the beasts, and many of mankind (Sūrah 22: 18).

Fourth, the Qur'ān's acknowledgment that humankind is not the only community to live in this world—"There is not an animal in the earth, nor a flying creature flying on two wings, but they are peoples like unto you" (Sūrah 6: 38)—means that while humans may currently have the upper hand over other "peoples," these other creatures are beings and, like us, are worthy of respect and protection. The Prophet Muhammad (peace be upon him) considered all living creatures worthy of protection (*hurmah*) and kind treatment. He was once asked whether there will be a reward from God for charity shown to animals. His reply was very explicit: "For [charity shown to] each creature which has a wet heart there is a reward."[4] Ibn Hajar comments further upon this tradition, explaining that wetness is an indication of life (and so charity extends to all creatures), although human beings are more worthy of the charity if a choice must be made.[5]

Fifth, Islamic environmental ethics is based on the concept that all human relationships are established on justice (*'adl*) and equity (*ihsān*): "Lo! Allah enjoineth justice and kindness" (Sūrah 16: 90). The prophetic tradition limits benefits derived at the cost of animal suffering. The Prophet Muhammad instructed: "Verily Allah has prescribed equity (*ihsān*) in all things.

Thus if you kill, kill well, and if you slaughter, slaughter well. Let each of you sharpen his blade and let him spare suffering to the animal he slaughters."

Sixth, the balance of the universe created by God must also be preserved. For "Everything with Him is measured" (Sūrah 13: 8). Also, "There is not a thing but with Us are the stores thereof. And We send it not down save in appointed measure" (Sūrah 15: 21).

Seventh, the environment is not in the service of the present generation alone. Rather, it is the gift of God to all ages, past, present and future. This can be understood from the general meaning of Sūrah 2:29: "He it is Who created for you all that is in the earth." The word "you" as used here refers to all persons with no limit as to time or place.

Finally, no other creature is able to perform the task of protecting the environment. God entrusted humans with the duty of viceregency, a duty so onerous and burdensome that no other creature would accept it: "Lo! We offered the trust unto the heavens and the earth and the hills, but they shrank from bearing it and were afraid of it. And man assumed it" (Sūrah 33: 72).

THE COMPREHENSIVE NATURE OF ISLAMIC ETHICS

Islamic ethics is founded on two principles—human nature, and religious and legal grounds. The first principle, natural instinct (*fitrah*), was imprinted in the human soul by God at the time of creation (Sūrah 91: 7–8). Having natural instinct, the ordinary individual can, at least to some extent, distinguish not only between good and bad, but also between these and that which is neutral, neither good nor bad.[6] However, an ethical conscience is not a sufficient personal guide. Due to the complexities of life an ethical conscience alone cannot define the correct attitude to every problem. Moreover, a person does not live in a vacuum, but is affected by outside influences which may corrupt the ability to choose between good and evil. Outside influences include customs, personal interests, and prevailing concepts concerning one's surroundings.[7]

The religious and legal grounds upon which Islamic ethics is founded were presented by the messengers of God. These messengers were possessed of a special nature, and since they were inspired by God, they were able to avoid the outside influences which may affect other individuals.

Legal instructions in Islam are not negative in the sense of forcing the conscience to obey. On the contrary, legal instructions have been revealed in such a way that the conscience approves and acknowledges them to be correct. Thus the law itself becomes a part of human conscience, thereby guaranteeing its application and its success.

An imported, alien law cannot work because, while it may be possible to make it legally binding, it cannot be made morally binding upon Muslims. Muslims willingly pay the poor-tax (*zakāh*) because they know that if they fail to do so they will be both legally and ethically responsible. Managing to avoid the legal consequences of failure to pay what is due will not help them to avoid the ethical consequences, and they are aware of this. Although a Muslim

Mawil Y Izzi Deen (Samarrai)

poacher may be able to shoot elephants and avoid park game wardens, if a framework based on Islamic principles for the protection of the environment has been published, he knows that he will not be able to avoid the ever-watchful divine Warden. The Muslim knows that Islamic values are all based on what God loves and wants: "And when he turns away [from thee] his effort in the land is to make mischief therein and to destroy the crops and the cattle; and Allah loveth not mischief" (Sūrah 2: 205).

When the Prophet Solomon and his army were about to destroy a nest of ants, one ant warned the rest of the colony of the coming destruction. When Solomon heard this he begged God for the wisdom to do the good thing which God wanted him to do. Solomon was obviously facing an environmental problem and needed an ethical decision; he begged God for guidance:

> Till, when they reached the Valley of the Ants, an ant exclaimed: O, ants! Enter your dwellings lest Solomon and his armies crush you, unperceiving.
>
> And [Solomon] smiled, laughing at her speech, and said: "My Lord, arouse me to be thankful for Thy favor wherewith Thou hast favored me and my parents, and to do good that shall be pleasing unto Thee, and include me among [the number of] Thy righteous slaves" (Sūrah 27: 18–19).

Ethics in Islam is not based on a variety of separate scattered virtues, with each virtue, such as honesty or truth, standing isolated from others. Rather virtue in Islam is a part of a total, comprehensive way of life which serves to guide and control all human activity.[8] Truthfulness is an ethical value, as are protecting life, conserving the environment, and sustaining its development within the confines of what God has ordered. When 'Āisha, the wife of the Prophet Muhammad, was asked about his ethics she replied: "His ethics are the whole Qur'ān." The Qur'ān does not contain separate scattered ethical values. Rather it contains the instructions for a complete way of life. There are political, social and economic principles side by side with instructions for the construction and preservation of the earth.

Islamic ethical values are based not on human reasoning, as Aristotle claimed values to be, nor on what society imposes on the individual, as Durkheim thought, nor on the interests of a certain class, as Marxists maintain. In each of these claims values are affected by circumstances. In Islam, ethical values are held to be based on an accurate scale which is unalterable as to time and place.[9] Islam's values are those without which neither persons nor the natural environment can be sustained.

THE HUMAN-ENVIRONMENT RELATIONSHIP

As we have seen, within the Islamic faith, an individual's relationship with the environment is governed by certain moral precepts. These originate with God's creation of humans and the role they were given upon the Earth. Our universe, with all its diverse component elements was created by God and the human being is an essential part of His Measured and Balanced Creation. The role of humans, however, is not only to enjoy, use and benefit from their surroundings. They are expected to preserve, protect and promote their fellow creatures. The Prophet Muhammad (peace be upon him) said: "All creatures are God's dependents and the best among them is the one who is most useful to God's dependents."[10] The Prophet of Islam looked upon himself as responsible for the trees and the animals and all natural elements. He also said: "The only reasons that God does not cause his punishment to pour over you are the elderly, the suckling babes, and the animals which graze upon your land."[11] Muhammad prayed for rain when he was reminded that water was short, the trees suffering from drought, and animals dying. He begged for God's mercy to fall upon his creatures.[12]

The relationship between human beings and their environment includes many features in addition to subjugation and utilization. Construction and development are primary but our relationship to nature also includes meditation, contemplation and enjoyment of its beauties. The most perfect Muslim was the Prophet Muhammad who was reported by Ibn 'Abbās to have enjoyed gazing at greenery and running water.[13]

When reading verses about the Earth in the Holy Qur'ān, we find strong indications that the Earth was originally a place of peace and rest for humans:

> Is not He [best] Who made the earth a fixed abode, and placed rivers in the folds thereof, and placed firm hills therein, and hath set a barrier between the two seas? Is there any God beside Allah? Nay, but most of them know not! (Sūrah 27: 61)

The Earth is important to the concept of interrelation. Human beings are made from two components of the Earth—dust and water.

> And Allah hath caused you to grow as a growth from the earth, And afterward He maketh you return thereto, and He will bring you forth again, a [new] forthbringing. And Allah hath made the earth a wide expanse for you That ye may thread the valleyways thereof. (Sūrah 71: 17–20)

The word "earth" (ard) is mentioned twice in this short quotation and in the Qur'ān the word occurs a total of 485 times, a simple measure of its importance.

The Earth is described as being subservient to humans: "He it is Who hath made the earth subservient unto you, so walk in the paths thereof and eat of His providence" (Sūrah 67: 15). The Earth is also described as a receptacle: "Have we not made the earth a receptacle both for the living and the dead" (Sūrah 77: 25–26).[14] Even more importantly, the Earth is considered by Islam to be a source of purity and a place for the worship of God. The Prophet Muhammad said: "The earth is made for me [and Muslims] as a prayer place (masjid) and as a purifier." This means that the Earth is to be used to cleanse oneself before prayer if water is unobtainable.[15] Ibn 'Umar reported that the Prophet of Islam said: "God is beautiful and loved everything beautiful. He is generous and loves generosity and is clean and loves cleanliness."[16]

Mawil Y Izzi Deen (Samarrai)

Thus it is not surprising that the Islamic position with regard to the environment is that humans must intervene in order to protect the Earth. They may not stand back while it is destroyed. "He brought you forth from the earth and hath made you husband it" (Sūrah 11: 61). For, finally, the Earth is a source of blessedness. And the Prophet Muhammad said: "Some trees are as blessed as the Muslim himself, especially palm."[17]

THE SUSTAINABLE CARE OF NATURE

Islam permits the utilization of the natural environment but this utilization should not involve unnecessary destruction. Squandering is rejected by God: "O Children of Adam! Look to your adornment at every place of worship, and eat and drink, but be not prodigal. Lo! He loveth not the prodigals" (Sūrah 7: 31). In this Qur'ānic passage, eating and drinking refer to the utilization of the sources of life. Such utilization is not without controls. The component elements of life have to be protected so that their utilization may continue in a sustainable way. Yet even this preservation must be undertaken in an altruistic fashion, and not merely for its benefit to human beings. The Prophet Muhammad said: "Act in your life as though you are living forever and act for the Hereafter as if you are dying tomorrow."[18]

These actions must not be restricted to those which will derive direct benefits. Even if doomsday were expected imminently, humans would be expected to continue their good behavior, for Muhammad said: "When doomsday comes if someone has a palm shoot in his hand he should plant it."[19] This *hadīth* encapsulates the principles of Islamic environmental ethics. Even when all hope is lost, planting should continue for planting is good in itself. The planting of the palm shoot continues the process of development and will sustain life even if one does not anticipate any benefit from it. In this, the Muslim is like the soldier who fights to the last bullet.

A theory of the sustainable utilization of the ecosystem may be deduced from Islam's assertion that life is maintained with due balance in everything: "Allah knoweth that which every female beareth and that which the wombs absorb and that which they grow. And everything with Him is measured" (Sūrah 13: 8). Also: "He unto Whom belongeth the sovereignty of the heavens and the earth, He hath chosen no son nor hath He any partner in the sovereignty. He hath created everything and hath meted out for it a measure" (Sūrah 25: 2).

Humans are not the owners, but the maintainers of the due balance and measure which God provided for them and for the animals that live with them.

> And after that He spread the earth,
> And produced therefrom water thereof and the pasture thereof,
> And He made fast the hills,
> A provision for you and for your cattle. (Sūrah 79: 30–33)

Mawil Y Izzi Deen (Samarrai)   169

The Qu'rān goes on to say:

> But when the great disaster cometh,
> The day when man will call to mind his [whole] endeavor. (Sūrah 79: 34–35)

Humans will have a different home (*ma'wā*) or place of abode, different from the Earth and what it contains. The word *ma'wā* is the same word used in modern Arabic for "environment." One cannot help but wonder if these verses are an elaboration on the concept of sustainable development, a task that humans will undertake until their home is changed.

Sayyid Qutb, commenting on these verses, observes that the Qur'ān, in referring to the origin of ultimate truth, used many correspondences (*muwāfaqāt*)—such as building the heavens, darkening the night, bringing forth human beings, spreading the earth, producing water and plants, and making the mountains fast. All these were provided for human beings and their animals as providence, and are direct signs which constitute proof as to the reality of God's measurement and calculation. Finally, Sayyid Qutb observes that every part of God's creation was carefully made to fit into the general system, a system that testifies to the Creator's existence and the existence of a day of reward and punishment.

At this point, one must ask whether it is not a person's duty to preserve the proof of the Creator's existence while developing it. Wouldn't the wholesale destruction of the environment be the destruction of much which testifies to the greatness of God?

The concept of the sustained care of all aspects of the environment also fits into Islam's concept of charity, for charity is not only for the present generation but also for those in the future. A story is told of 'Umar ibn al-Khattāb, the famous companion of the Prophet. He once saw that an old man, Khuzaymah ibn Thābit, had neglected his land. 'Umar asked what was preventing him from cultivating it. Khuzaymah explained that he was old and could be expected to die soon. Whereupon, Umar insisted that he should plant it. Khuzaymah's son, who narrated the story, added that his father and 'Umar planted the uncultivated land together.[20]

This incident demonstrates how strongly Islam encourages the sustained cultivation of the land. Land should not be used and then abandoned just because the cultivator expects no personal benefit.

In Islam, law and ethics constitute the two interconnected elements of a unified world view. When considering the environment and its protection, this Islamic attitude may constitute a useful foundation for the formulation of a strategy throughout, at least, the Muslim world. Muslims who inhabit so much of the developing world may vary in local habits and customs but they are remarkably united in faith and in their attitude to life.

Islam is a religion of submission to God, master of all worlds. The Earth and all its inhabitants were created and are dominated by God. All Muslims begin their prayers five times a day with the same words from the Holy Qur'ān: "Praise be to Allah, Lord of the Worlds" (Sūrah 1:1). These opening words of the Qur'ān have become not only the most repeated but also the most loved and respected words for Muslims everywhere. Ibn Kathīr, like many other Qur'ānic commentators, considers that the word "worlds" ('ālamī'n) means the different kinds of creatures that inhabit the sky, the land, and the sea. Muslims submit themselves to the Creator who made them and who made all other worlds. The same author mentions that Muslims also submit themselves to the signs of the existence of the Creator and His unity. This secondary meaning exists because "worlds" comes from the same root as signs; thus the worlds are signs of the Creator.[21]

A Muslim, therefore, has a very special relationship with those worlds which in modern times have come to be known as the environment. Indeed, that these worlds exist and that they were made by the same Creator means that they are united and interdependent, each a part of the perfect system of creation. No conflict should exist between them; they should exist in harmony as different parts of the whole. Their coexistence could be likened to an architectural masterpiece in which every detail has been added to complete and complement the structure. Thus the details of creation serve to testify to the wisdom and perfection of the Creator.

THE PRACTICE OF ISLAMIC ENVIRONMENTAL ETHICS

Islam has always had a great influence on the formation of individual Muslim communities and the policy making of Muslim states. Environmental policy has been influenced by Islam and this influence has remained the same throughout the history of the Islamic faith.

The concept of *himā* (protection of certain zones) has existed since the time of the Prophet Muhammad. *Himā* involved the ruler or government's protection of specific unused areas. No one may build on them or develop them in any way. The Mālikī school of Islamic law described the requirements of *himā* to be the following.[22] First, the need of the Muslim public for the maintenance of land in an unused state. Protection is not granted to satisfy an influential individual unless there is a public need. Second, the protected area should be limited in order to avoid inconvenience to the public. Third, the protected area should not be built on or cultivated. And fourth, the aim of protection (Zuhaylī 5:574) is the welfare of the people, for example, the protected area may be used for some restricted grazing by the animals of the poor.

The concept of *himā* can still be seen in many Muslim countries, such as Saudi Arabia, where it is practised by the government to protect wildlife. In a less formal way it is still practised by some bedouin tribes as a custom or tradition inherited from their ancestors.

The *harī'm* is another ancient institution which can be traced back to the time of the Prophet Muhammad. It is an inviolable zone which may not be used or developed, save with the specific permission of the state. The *harī'm* is usually found in association with wells, natural springs, underground water channels, rivers and trees planted on barren land or *mawāt*.[23] There is careful administration of the *harī'm* zones based on the practice of the Prophet Muhammad and the precedent of his companions as recorded in the sources of Islamic law.

At present the role of Islam in environmental protection can be seen in the formation of different Islamic organizations and the emphasis given to Islam as a motive for the protection of the environment.

Saudi Arabia has keenly sought to implement a number of projects aimed at the protection of various aspects of the environment, for example, the late King Khalid's patronage of efforts to save the Arabian oryx from extinction.

The Meteorology and Environmental Protection Administration (MEPA) of Saudi Arabia actively promotes the principles of Islamic environmental protection. In 1983 MEPA and the International Union for the Conservation of Nature and Natural Resources commissioned a basic paper on the Islamic principles for the conservation of natural environment.[24]

The Islamic faith has great impact on environmental issues throughout the Arab and Muslim world. The first Arab Ministerial Conference took as its theme "The Environmental Aspects of Development" and one of the topics considered was the Islamic faith and its values.[25] The Amir of Kuwait emphasized the fundamental importance of Islam when he addressed the General Assembly of the United Nations in 1988. He explained that Islam was the basis for justice, mercy, and cooperation between all humankind; and he called for an increase in scientific and technological assistance from the North to help conserve natural and human resources, combat pollution and support sustainable development projects.

Finally, it is imperative to acknowledge that the new morality required to conserve the environment which the World Conservation Strategy (Section 13.1) emphasizes, needs to be based on a more solid foundation. It is not only necessary to involve the public in conservation policy but also to improve its morals and alter its attitudes. In Muslim countries such changes should be brought about by identifying environmental policies with Islamic teachings. To do this, the public education system will have to supplement the scientific approach to environmental education with serious attention to Islamic belief and environmental awareness.

NOTES

1. Ahmad Ibn Taymīyah, *Majamū' Fatawā* (Rabat: Saudi Educational Attaché, n.d.), 11:96–97.

2. Mawil Y. Izzi Deen (Samarrai), "Environmental Protection and Islam," *Journal of the Faculty of Arts and Humanities, King Abdulaziz University* 5 (1985).

3. All references to the Holy Qur'ān are from *The Meaning of the Glorious Koran*, trans. Mohammed M. Pickthall, (New York: Mentor, n.d.).

4. Ibn Hajar al- 'Asqalānī, *Fath al-Bārī' bi-Sharh Sahīh al-Bukhāri*, edited by M. F. 'Abd al-Bāqī, M. al-Khātib, and A. B. Bāz 1959; 1970 (Beirut: Dār al-Ma'rifah, 195; 197), 5: 40.

5. Ibid., 5: 42.

6. Muhammad 'Abd Allah Draz, *La Morale du Koran*, trans. into Arabic by A. Shahin and S. M. Badāwī (Kuwait: Dār al-Risālah, 1973), 28.

7. Ibid.

8. Sayyid, Qutb, *Muqāwamāt al-Tasawwur al-Islāmī* (Cairo: Dār al-Shurūq, 1985), 289.

9. Ibid., 290.

10. Ismā'il Ibn Muhammad al-'Ajlūnī, *Kashf al-Khafā' wa Muzīl al-Ilbās*, edited by A. al-Qallash (Syria Damascus: Mu'assasat al-Risālah, 1983), 1: 458.

11. Ibid., 1:213.

12. Ibn Hajar, *Fath al Bārī*, 2: 512.

13. 'Ajlūnī, *Kashf al-Khafā'*, 1: 387.

14. N.J. Dawood, trans. *The Koran* (New York: Penguin, 1974): 54.

15. Muhammad Ibn Ismā'īl al-Bukhāri, *Sahīh al-Bukhāri*, (Istanbul: Dār al-Tiba'ah al-Amīrah, 1897), 1: 86.

16. Ajlūnī, *Kashf al-Khafā'*, 1: 260.

17. Bukhāri, *Sahīh al-Bukhāri*, 1: 22, 6: 211.

18. Ahmad Ibn al-Husayn al-Bayhāqī, *Sunan al-Bayhaqī al-Kubrā* (Hyderabad, India: n.d.), 3: 19.

19. Ibid., 3: 184.

20. Soūti, *al-Jāmi' al-Kabīr*, manuscript (Cairo: Egyptian General Committee for Publication, n.d.).

21. M. A. al-Sabunī, *Mukhtasar Tafsīr Ibn Kathīr* (Beirut: Dār al-Qur'ān al-Karīm, 1981), 1: 21.

22. Wahbah Mustafa Zuhayli, *al-Fiqh al-Islāmī wa 'Adilatuhu* (Damascus: Mu'assasat al-Risālah 1985).

23. Ibid., 5: 574.

24. A.H. Bakader, A. T. al-Sabbagh, M.A. al-Gelinid, and M.Y. Izzi Deen (Samarrai), *Islamic Principles for the Conservation of the Natural Environment* (Gland, Switzerland: International Union for the Conservation of Nature and MEPA, 1983).

25. *Habitat and the Environment* (Tunis: Economic Affairs Department of the Directorate of the Arab League, 1986).

"AFRICAN VIEWS OF THE UNIVERSE"

John S. Mbiti

ACCUMULATION OF IDEAS ABOUT THE UNIVERSE

As they went through life, African peoples observed the world around them and reflected upon it. They looked at the sky above with its stars, moon, sun and meteorites; with its clouds, rain, rainbows and the movement of the winds. Below they saw the earth with its myriad of life-forms, animals, insects, and plants, and its rivers and lakes, rocks and mountains. They saw the limits of man's powers and knowledge, and the shortness of human life. They experienced and witnessed the processes of birth, growth, procreation and death; they felt the agonies of the body and mind, hunger and thirst, the emotions of joy, fear, and love. All their five major senses (of hearing, seeing, feeling, tasting, and smelling) were open gates through which all kinds of experiences came upon them. These experiences stimulated them to reflect upon their life and the universe in which they lived. The result was a gradual building up of African views or ideas about the world and the universe at large.

No thinking person can live without forming some views about life and the world. Some of the ideas developed by individual reflection eventually spread among other people, through discussion, conversation, artistic expression and so on. The other people were stimulated to reflect further, extending old ideas, abandoning some of them, acquiring new ones and translating others into practical realities. And so the process gained momentum, people's ideas about the universe accumulated and definite views and systems of thought began to emerge. There can be no end to the development of people's views about the universe, as this process is a continuing one.

Obviously many ideas about the world have emerged among African peoples. It would be impossible to cover them in detail, but in this chapter we can give a broad summary of them in order to make us familiar with their general content. These views are expressed in myths, legends, proverbs, rituals, symbols, beliefs and wise sayings. There is no formal or systematized view of the universe, but when these various ideas are put together, a picture emerges. There are many mysteries in the universe and whenever possible people try to find an explanation for them, whether or not the explanation is final.

Reprinted with permission from *Introduction to African Religion: Second Edition* by John S. Mbiti, 1992, Heinemann Publishers Limited.

A CREATED UNIVERSE

It is generally believed all over Africa that the universe was created. The Creator of the universe is God. There is no agreement, however, on how the creation of the universe took place. But it seems impossible that the universe could simply have come into existence on its own. God is, therefore, the explanation for the origin of the universe, which consists of both visible and invisible realities. People often say that "God created all things." In many African languages, the name for God means "Creator"; even where there is another name, He is often called "the Creator" as well.

As we will see in the next chapter, the belief in God is found everywhere in Africa. When people explain the universe as having been created by God, they are automatically looking at the universe in a religious way. We can say, therefore, that the African view of the universe is profoundly religious. Africans see it as a religious universe, and treat it as such.

While there are many different accounts of the creation of the universe, it is commonly agreed that man has been put at its centre. We shall see that of all created things man is the most important and the most privileged. In some accounts of creation it is told that God made the heavenly part of the universe first, and then, standing on it, he created the earth. In other myths the order is reversed. Some accounts say that the entire universe was created in one act. It is also a widespread view among African peoples that God continues to create. Thus, the creation of the universe did not stop in the distant past: it is an ongoing process which will probably never end.

THE NATURE OF THE UNIVERSE

In many African societies it is believed that the universe is divisible into two. These are the visible and the invisible parts, or the heavens (or sky) and the earth. Some peoples, however, hold that the universe is in the form of a three-tier creation, namely: the heavens, the earth and the underworld, which lies below it. African peoples do not think of these divisions as separate but see them as linked together.

The heavenly part of the universe is the home of the stars, sun, moon, meteorites, sky, the wind and the rain, with all the phenomena connected with them such as thunder and lightning, storms, eclipses of the sun and the moon, "falling stars," and so on. It is also thought to be the home of God, although people cannot quite locate where he dwells, other than saying that he lives in "the sky," in "heaven," or "beyond the clouds," or they simply say that "God does not live on the earth like men." God is often believed to have other beings living with him or close to him. Some of these are in charge of different departments of the universe, others are his messengers and servants or ministers, and some are like his children. But there are other Africans who say that God dwells completely alone and does everything himself, since he is all-powerful.

It is generally held that the heavenly universe is not empty but that it has its own population. It is teeming with its own kinds of life in addition to the visible objects mentioned above. This means that it is more or less the counterpart of the earth, even though what goes on there is invisible to us.

The earth, too, is full of created things. Some African peoples regard it as a living being, and call it "Mother earth," "the goddess earth," or "the divinity of the earth." Symbolically it is looked on as the mother of the universe, while the heavenly part is the father. In some societies rituals are performed to show respect to the earth. For example, in Zambia, when the rains start, people have to refrain from working on the ground in the fields for a few days. In some parts of Africa when a major calamity like an earthquake or a murder befalls people, sacrifices may be made to the divinity of the earth. On the earth itself many things are held in great esteem for religious reasons, such as mountains, waterfalls, rocks, some forests and trees, birds, animals and insects.

The Link between Earth and Heaven

Man, who lives on the earth, is the centre of the universe. He is also like the priest of the universe, linking the universe with God its Creator. Man awakens the universe, he speaks to it, he listens to it, he tries to create a harmony with the universe. It is man who turns parts of the universe into sacred objects, and who uses other things for sacrifices and offerings. These are constant reminders to people that they regard it as a religious universe.

In many African myths it is told that at one time in the distant past, the heavens (or sky) and the earth were united as one. This union is pictured as being like the place where the earth and sky seem to touch each other at the end of the horizon. Other myths say that the union was formed by a ladder or rope between the two. These accounts go on to say how the separation took place. According to some, animals bit the leather rope into two, so that one part went up to the sky and the other fell to the ground, thus severing the heavens from the earth. Some myths say that it was through man's fault or error that the two parts of the universe were divided up. These are simply attempts to explain the fact that the universe is divided into two parts, as it appears to be to the ordinary person; and also to explain the fact that God and man are separated.

The Universe Is Seen as Eternal

The universe is considered to be unending in terms of both space and time. Nobody can reach the edge of the universe, since it has no known edge or rim. Just as there is no edge of the earth, so there is no edge to the universe. In terms of time, it makes sense for people to believe that there was a beginning for the universe, even though they do not know when it was. But nobody thinks that there will ever be an end to it. They say, "The world will never end." African ideas of time concern mainly the present and the past, and have little to say about the future, which in any case is expected to go on without end. Events come and go in the form of minor and major rhythms. The minor rhythms are found in the lives of the living things of this earth (such as men, animals and plants), in their birth, growth, procreation and death. These rhythms are thought to occur in the lives of everybody and everything that has physical life. The major rhythms of time are events like day and night, the months (reckoned on the basis of the phases of the moon), the seasons of rain and of dry weather, and the events of nature which come and go at greater intervals (such as the flowering of certain plants, the migration of certain birds and insects, famines, and the movement of certain heavenly bodies). All these rhythms of time suggest that the universe will never come to a halt, whatever changes there may be.

In many places, circles are used as symbols of the continuity of the universe. They are the symbols of eternity, of unendingness, of continuity. The circles may be used in rituals, in art, in rock paintings, as decorations on stools and domestic utensils and so on. In other places this unendingness is symbolized by drawings of a snake curled round sometimes with its tail in its mouth. The same idea is celebrated in rituals which re-enact birth, death and rebirth, showing that life is stronger than death. This can also be interpreted to mean that continuity on a large scale is more important than change in small details. People are aware that the laws of nature do not normally change, and so there is no ground for imagining that this entire universe might suddenly come to an end. Thus, the universe is considered to be permanent, eternal and unending.

In the African view, the universe is both visible and invisible, unending and without limits. Since it was created by God it is subsequently dependent on him for its continuity. God is the sustainer, the keeper and upholder of the universe. Man, on the other hand, is at the very centre of the universe. We may summarize these ideas in the form of a drawing:

ORDER AND POWER IN THE UNIVERSE

It is considered that the universe is orderly. As long as this order is not upset there is harmony. Order in the universe is seen as operating at several levels.

ORDER IN THE LAWS OF NATURE

First, there is order in the laws of nature. These function everywhere, and give a sense of security and certainty to the universe. If they were completely unpredictable and changed at random, there would be chaos in the world which would endanger the existence of both life and the universe itself.

Moral Order among People

Secondly, there is moral order at work among people. It is believed by African peoples that God gave moral order to people so that they might live happily and in harmony with one another. Through this moral order, customs and institutions have arisen in all societies, to safeguard the life of the individual and the community of which he is part. Moral order helps men to work out and know among themselves what is good and evil, right and wrong, truthful and false, and beautiful and ugly, and what people's rights and duties are. Each society is able to formulate its values because there is moral order in the universe. These values deal with relationships among people, and between people and God and other spiritual beings; and man's relationship with the world of nature.

Religious Order in the Universe

Thirdly, there is religious order in the universe. We saw earlier on in the chapter that Africans look at the universe in a religious way. Because of their basic belief that the universe is created and sustained by God, they interpret their life's experiences from that starting point. The laws of nature are regarded as being controlled by God directly or through his servants. The morals and institutions of society are thought to have been given by God, or to be sanctioned ultimately by him. Therefore any breach of such morals is an offence against the departed members of the family, and against God or the spirits, even if it is the people themselves who may suffer from such a breach and who may take action to punish the offender.

There are, therefore, taboos which strengthen the keeping of the moral and religious order. There may be taboos over any aspect of life: words, foods, dress, relations among people, marriage, burial, work, and so on. Breaking a taboo entails punishment in the form of social ostracism, misfortune and even death. If people do not punish the offender, then the invisible world will punish him. This view arises from the belief in the religious order of the universe, in which God and other invisible beings are thought to be actively engaged in the world of men.

Mystical Order in the Universe

Fourthly, there is a mystical order governing the universe. The belief in this order is shown clearly in the practice of traditional medicine, magic, witchcraft and sorcery. It is held in all African societies that there is power in the universe, and that it comes from God. It is a mystical power, in the sense that it is hidden and mysterious. This power is available to spirits and to certain human beings. People who have access to it are sometimes able to see the departed,

John S. Mbiti

hear certain voices, see certain sights (such as fire and light), have visions, communicate at a distance without using physical means, receive premonitions of coming events, foretell certain things before they happen, communicate with the invisible world, and perform "wonders" and "miracles" which other people may not ordinarily be able to do.

It is the knowledge of this mystical power which is used to help other people (especially in healing, rain-making, finding the cause of misfortunes and troubles, detecting thieves, and so on), or to harm them. When it is used harmfully, it is regarded as evil magic, witchcraft or sorcery; and it may also be used in curses. The ordinary people do not know much about this mystical power. It may take a long time for someone to be trained in the knowledge and use of mystical power; and such knowledge is often safeguarded and kept secret. In some cases the ability to use this mystical power is simply inherited or passed on without the conscious intention of those concerned. Once a person has discovered that he has some of this power, he may then proceed to undertake further training in using it, or he may just neglect it.

MAN AT THE CENTER OF THE UNIVERSE

As the Creator of the universe, God is outside and beyond it. At the same time, since he is also its sustainer and upholder, he is very close to the universe. But in African myths of creation, man puts himself at the centre of the universe.

Because man thinks of himself as being at the centre, he consequently sees the universe from that perspective. It is as if the whole world exists for man's sake. Therefore African peoples look for the usefulness (or otherwise) of the universe to man. This means both what the world can do for man, and how man can use the world for his own good. This attitude towards the universe is deeply engrained in African peoples. For that reason many people, for example, have divided animals into those which man can eat and those which he cannot eat. Others look at plants in terms of what can be eaten by people, what can be used for curative or medical purposes, what can be used for building, fire, and so on. Certain things have physical uses; some have religious uses (for ceremonies, rituals, and symbols); and other things are used for medicinal and magical purposes.

African peoples regard natural objects and phenomena as being inhabited by living beings, or having a mystical life. In religious language we speak of these beings as divinities and spirits. The idea behind this belief is to give man the ability to use or control some of these things and phenomena. For example, if people believe that there is a spirit or divinity of their local lake they will, through sacrifices, offerings or prayers, ask for the help of the divinity when fishing in the lake or crossing it in a canoe. This gives them a feeling of confidence and security, a feeling that they are in harmony with the lake (and with the life-agent personified by the lake or occupying that lake). In some societies it is believed that lightning and thunder are caused by a spirit; therefore people endeavour to be in harmony with that spirit, for fear that it might strike them dead or set their houses on fire.

We may say, therefore, that African people consider man to be at the centre of the universe. Being in that position he tries to use the universe or derive some use from it in physical, mystical and supernatural ways. He sees the universe in terms of himself, and endeavours to live in harmony with it. Even where there is no biological life in an object, African peoples attribute (mystical) life to it, in order to establish a more direct relationship with the world around them. In this way the visible and invisible parts of the universe are at man's disposal through physical, mystical and religious means. Man is not the master in the universe; he is only the centre, the friend, the beneficiary, the user. For that reason he has to live in harmony with the universe, obeying the laws of natural, moral and mystical order. If these are unduly disturbed, it is man who suffers most. African peoples have come to these conclusions through long experience, observation and reflection.

John S. Mbiti

PART III

ECOTHEOLOGY IN AN AGE OF ENVIRONMENTAL CRISIS

Transforming Tradition

The clear messages we see around us—the increased temperatures, the sickening die-off of species that may be as high as ten a day (ten chains of being stretching back to creation), the eroding ozone—these messages all tell us that we are badly out of balance. That we, the products of creation's later days, are destroying our elders. That having been given, in the words of Deuteronomy, a land of flowing streams, with springs and underground waters welling up in valleys and hills, a land of wheat and barely, of vines and fig trees and pomegranates . . . that having been given this land we are failing.

—Bill McKibben

In spite of all the worldwide concern with our deteriorating environment, very few people have yet got to grips with the deeper problems it raises. The implications are too revolutionary. They run counter to the ingrained ways of thought which have dominated the western world for the past two centuries.

The truth is that the goal of unlimited physical growth is no longer tenable. The only way out of the human predicament of our time lies in a complete and radical change, not of *methods,* but of *goals.* . . . There is only one way to avert the disaster which threatens to overwhelm mankind. *Material goals must be replaced by spiritual goals.*

—Aryeh Carmel

We told the native peoples of North America that their relationships with the land were worthless, primitive. Now we are a culture that spends millions trying to find this knowledge, trying to reestablish a sense of well-being with the earth.

—Barry Lopez

The High,
the low
all of creation,
God gives to humankind to use. If this privilege is misused,
God's Justice permits creation to punish humanity.

—Hildegard of Bingen

Lynn White's essay, which begins this part, helped initiate a fierce and searching discussion of the relation between Western religions and the environmental crisis. White's thesis—that Jewish and Christian "desacralization" of the Earth paved the way for the modern domination of nature—has been hotly debated and is referred to by many other authors in this book some of whom find in the *Bible* a model of stewardship for the land rather than domination over it.

Whatever the ultimate resolution of the debate, it is clear that a host of theologians are seriously wrestling with the need to reform their traditions to face the transition from nature to environment; that is, the fact that humanity has deeply altered and continues to threaten our natural surroundings.

In this part, a historical overview of the "Greening of the Church" is provided by Nash; and statements by Pope John Paul II, a report to the World Council of Churches, and messages by the Lutheran and Baptist churches all show a heightened awareness of issues that were rarely discussed even two decades ago. Essays by Sallie McFague, John F. Haught, Arthur Waskow, Arthur Green and Ken Jones reveal new religious sensibilities based in Christianity, Judaism and Buddhism. Old concepts are reinterpreted (as in the thought of an environmentally oriented "ecokosher") or challenging metaphors created (when Sallie McFague offers us the earth as the "body of God"). Green directly contests our everyday lives by supporting a religiously inspired vegetarianism. John F. Haught proposes a moderate reconceptualization of Christianity, which clings to basic tenets but opens to the severity of our environmental situation. Ken Jones examines some of the escapist tendencies of conventional Buddhism. Finally, Theodore Walker, Jr. looks to spiritual and ethical resources from the African-American experience to help forge a more liberating theology.

To all the varieties of contemporary ecotheology—as well as to ourselves—we may pose two essential questions: Will this body of thought remain merely an intellectual construct? Or will it, as in the case of the Civil Rights Movement, bring a religiously inspired vision into critical social struggles?

"THE HISTORICAL ROOTS OF OUR ECOLOGICAL CRISIS"

Lynn White

A conversation with Aldous Huxley not infrequently put one at the receiving end of an unforgettable monologue. About a year before his lamented death he was discoursing on a favorite topic: Man's unnatural treatment of nature and its sad results. To illustrate his point he told how, during the previous summer, he had returned to a little valley in England where he had spent many happy months as a child. Once it had been composed of delightful grassy glades; now it was becoming overgrown with unsightly brush because the rabbits that formerly kept such growth under control had largely succumbed to a disease, myxomatosis, that was deliberately introduced by the local farmers to reduce the rabbits' destruction of crops. Being something of a Philistine, I could be silent no longer, even in the interests of great rhetoric. I interrupted to point out that the rabbit itself had been brought as a domestic animal to England in 1176, presumably to improve the protein diet of the peasantry.

All forms of life modify their contexts. The most spectacular and benign instance is doubtless the coral polyp. By serving its own ends, it has created a vast undersea world favorable to thousands of other kinds of animals and plants. Ever since man became a numerous species he has affected his environment notably. The hypothesis that his fire-drive method of hunting created the world's great grasslands and helped to exterminate the monster mammals of the Pleistocene from much of the globe is plausible, if not proved. For six millennia at least, the banks of the lower Nile have been a human artifact rather than the swampy African jungle which nature, apart from man, would have made it. The Aswan Dam, flooding 5000 square miles, is only the latest stage in a long process. In many regions terracing or irrigation, overgrazing, the cutting of forests by Romans to build ships to fight Carthaginians or by Crusaders to solve the logistics problems of their expeditions, have profoundly changed some ecologies. Observation that the French landscape falls into two basic types, the open fields of the north and the *bocage* of the south and west, inspired Marc Bloch to undertake his classic study of medieval agricultural methods. Quite unintentionally, changes in human ways often affect nonhuman nature. It has been noted, for example, that the advent of the automobile eliminated huge flocks of sparrows that once fed on the horse manure littering every street.

Reprinted with permission from *Science*, Vol. 155, #3767, 10 March 1967, pp. 1203–1207. Copyright 1967 American Association for the Advancement of Science.

The history of ecologic change is still so rudimentary that we know little about what really happened, or what the results were. The extinction of the European aurochs as late as 1627 would seem to have been a simple case of overenthusiastic hunting. On more intricate matters it often is impossible to find solid information. For a thousand years or more the Frisians and Hollanders have been pushing back the North Sea, and the process is culminating in our own time in the reclamation of the Zuider Zee. What, if any, species of animals, birds, fish, shore life, or plants have died out in the process? In their epic combat with Neptune, have the Netherlanders overlooked ecological values in such a way that the quality of human life in the Netherlands has suffered? I cannot discover that the questions have ever been asked, much less answered.

People, then, have often been a dynamic element in their own environment, but in the present state of historical scholarship we usually do not know exactly when, where, or with what effects man-induced changes came. As we enter the last third of the 20th century, however, concern for the problem of ecologic backlash is mounting feverishly. Natural science, conceived as the effort to understand the nature of things, had flourished in several eras and among several peoples. Similarly there had been an age-old accumulation of technological skills, sometimes growing rapidly, sometimes slowly. But it was not until about four generations ago that Western Europe and North America arranged a marriage between science and technology, a union of the theoretical and the empirical approaches to our natural environment. The emergence in widespread practice of the Baconian creed that scientific knowledge means technological power over nature can scarcely be dated before about 1850, save in the chemical industries, where it is anticipated in the 18th century. Its acceptance as a normal pattern of action may mark the greatest event in human history since the invention of agriculture, and perhaps in nonhuman terrestrial history as well.

Almost at once the new situation forced the crystallization of the novel concept of ecology; indeed, the word *ecology* first appeared in the English language in 1873. Today, less than a century later, the impact of our race upon the environment has so increased in force that it has changed in essence. When the first cannons were fired, in the early 14th century, they affected ecology by sending workers scrambling to the forests and mountains for more potash, sulfur, iron ore, and charcoal, with some resulting erosion and deforestation. Hydrogen bombs are of a different order: a war fought with them might alter the genetics of all life on this planet. By 1285 London had a smog problem arising from the burning of soft coal, but our present combustion of fossil fuels threatens to change the chemistry of the globe's atmosphere as a whole, with consequences which we are only beginning to guess. With the population explosion, the carcinoma of planless urbanism, the now geological deposits of sewage and garbage, surely no creature other than man has ever managed to foul its nest in such short order.

There are many calls to action, but specific proposals, however worthy as individual items, seem too partial, palliative, negative: ban the bomb, tear down the billboards, give the

Hindus contraceptives and tell them to eat their sacred cows. The simplest solution to any suspect change is, of course, to stop it, or, better yet, to revert to a romanticized past: make those ugly gasoline stations look like Anne Hathaway's cottage or (in the Far West) like ghost-town saloons. The "wilderness area" mentality invariably advocates deep-freezing an ecology, whether San Gimignano or the High Sierra, as it was before the first Kleenex was dropped. But neither atavism nor prettification will cope with the ecologic crisis of our time.

What shall we do? No one yet knows. Unless we think about fundamentals, our specific measures may produce new backlashes more serious than those they are designed to remedy.

As a beginning we should try to clarify our thinking by looking, in some historical depth, at the presuppositions that underlie modern technology and science. Science was traditionally aristocratic, speculative, intellectual in intent; technology was lower-class, empirical, action-oriented. The quite sudden fusion of these two, towards the middle of the 19th century, is surely related to the slightly prior and contemporary democratic revolutions which, by reducing social barriers, tended to assert a functional unity of brain and hand. Our ecologic crisis is the product of an emerging, entirely novel, democratic culture. The issue is whether a democratized world can survive its own implications. Presumably we cannot, unless we rethink our axioms.

THE WESTERN TRADITIONS OF TECHNOLOGY AND SCIENCE

One thing is so certain that it seems stupid to verbalize it: both modern technology and modern science are distinctively *Occidental.* Our technology has absorbed elements from all over the world, notably from China; yet everywhere today, whether in Japan or in Nigeria, successful technology is Western. Our science is the heir to all the sciences of the past, especially perhaps to the work of the great Islamic scientists of the Middle Ages, who so often outdid the ancient Greeks in skill and perspicacity: al-Rāzī in medicine, for example; or ibn-al-Haytham in optics; or Omar Khayyám in mathematics. Indeed, not a few works of such geniuses seem to have vanished in the original Arabic and to survive only in medieval Latin translations that helped to lay the foundations for later Western developments. Today, around the globe, all significant science is Western in style and method, whatever the pigmentation or language of the scientists.

A second pair of facts is less well recognized because they result from quite recent historical scholarship. The leadership of the West, both in technology and in science, is far older than the so-called Scientific Revolution of the 17th century or the so-called Industrial Revolution of the 18th century. These terms are in fact outmoded and obscure the true nature of what they try to describe—significant stages in two long and separate developments. By A.D. 1000 at the latest—and perhaps, feebly, as much as 200 years earlier—the

Lynn White

West began to apply water power to industrial processes other than milling grain. This was followed in the late 12th century by the harnessing of wind power. From simple beginnings, but with remarkable consistency of style, the West rapidly expanded its skills in the development of power machinery, labor-saving devices, and automation. Those who doubt should contemplate that most monumental achievement in the history of automation: the weight-driven mechanical clock, which appeared in two forms in the early 14th century. Not in craftsmanship but in basic technological capacity, the Latin West of the later Middle Ages far outstripped its elaborate, sophisticated, and esthetically magnificent sister cultures, Byzantium and Islam. In 1444 a great Greek ecclesiastic, Bessarion, who had gone to Italy, wrote a letter to a prince in Greece. He is amazed by the superiority of Western ships, arms, textiles, glass. But above all he is astonished by the spectacle of waterwheels sawing timbers and pumping the bellows to blast furnaces. Clearly, he had seen nothing of the sort in the Near East.

By the end of the 15th century the technological superiority of Europe was such that its small, mutually hostile nations could spill out over all the rest of the world, conquering, looting, and colonizing. The symbol of this technological superiority is the fact that Portugal, one of the weakest states of the Occident, was able to become, and to remain for a century, mistress of the East Indies. And we must remember that the technology of Vasco da Gama and Albuquerque was built by pure empiricism, drawing remarkably little support or inspiration from science.

In the present-day vernacular of understanding, modern science is supposed to have begun in 1543, when both Copernicus and Vesalius published their great works. It is no derogation of their accomplishments, however, to point out that such structures as the *Fabrica* and the *De revolutionibus* do not appear overnight. The distinctive Western tradition of science, in fact, began in the late 11th century with a massive movement of translation of Arabic and Greek scientific works into Latin. A few notable books—Theophrastus, for example—escaped the West's avid new appetite for science, but within less than 200 years, effectively the entire corpus of Greek and Muslim science was available in Latin, and was being eagerly read and criticized in the new European universities. Out of criticism arose new observation, speculation, and increasing distrust of ancient authorities. By the late 13th century Europe had seized global scientific leadership from the faltering hands of Islam. It would be as absurd to deny the profound originality of Newton, Galileo, or Copernicus as to deny that of the 14th century scholastic scientists like Buridan or Oresme on whose work they built. Before the 11th century, science scarcely existed in the Latin West, even in Roman times. From the 11th century onward, the scientific sector of Occidental culture has increased in a steady crescendo.

Since both our technological and our scientific movements got their start, acquired their character, and achieved world dominance in the Middle Ages, it would seem that we cannot understand their nature or their present impact upon ecology without examining fundamental medieval assumptions and developments.

MEDIEVAL VIEW OF MAN AND NATURE

Until recently, agriculture has been the chief occupation even in "advanced" societies; hence, any change in methods of tillage has much importance. Early plows, drawn by two oxen, did not normally turn the sod but merely scratched it. Thus, cross-plowing was needed and fields tended to be squarish. In the fairly light soils and semi-arid climates of the Near East and Mediterranean, this worked well. But such a plow was inappropriate to the wet climate and often sticky soils of northern Europe. By the latter part of the 7th century after Christ, however, following obscure beginnings, certain northern peasants were using an entirely new kind of plow, equipped with a vertical knife to cut the line of the furrow, a horizontal share to slice under the sod, and a moldboard to turn it over. The friction of this plow with the soil was so great that it normally required not two but eight oxen. It attacked the land with such violence that cross-plowing was not needed, and fields tended to be shaped in long strips.

In the days of the scratch-plow, fields were distributed generally in units capable of supporting a single family. Subsistence farming was the presupposition. But no peasant owned eight oxen: to use the new and more efficient plow, peasants pooled their oxen to form large plow-teams, originally receiving (it would appear) plowed strips in proportion to their contribution. Thus, distribution of land was based no longer on the needs of a family but, rather, on the capacity of a power machine to till the earth. Man's relation to the soil was profoundly changed. Formerly man had been part of nature; now he was the exploiter of nature. Nowhere else in the world did farmers develop any analogous agricultural implement. Is it coincidence that modern technology, with its ruthlessness toward nature, has so largely been produced by descendants of these peasants of northern Europe?

This same exploitive attitude appears slightly before A.D. 830 in Western illustrated calendars. In older calendars the months were shown as passive personifications. The new Frankish calendars, which set the style for the Middle Ages, are very different: they show men coercing the world around them—plowing, harvesting, chopping trees, butchering pigs. Man and nature are two things, and man is master.

These novelties seem to be in harmony with larger intellectual patterns. What people do about their ecology depends on what they think about themselves in relation to things around them. Human ecology is deeply conditioned by beliefs about our nature and destiny—that is, by religion. To Western eyes this is very evident in, say, India or Ceylon. It is equally true of ourselves and of our medieval ancestors.

The victory of Christianity over paganism was the greatest psychic revolution in the history of our culture. It has become fashionable today to say that, for better or worse, we live in

Lynn White

"the post-Christian age." Certainly the forms of our thinking and language have largely ceased to be Christian, but to my eye the substance often remains amazingly akin to that of the past. Our daily habits of action, for example, are dominated by an implicit faith in perpetual progress which was unknown either to Greco-Roman antiquity or to the Orient. It is rooted in, and is indefensible apart from, Judeo-Christian teleology. The fact that Communists share it merely helps to show what can be demonstrated on many other grounds: that Marxism, like Islam, is a Judeo-Christian heresy. We continue today to live, as we have lived for about 1700 years, very largely in a context of Christian axioms.

What did Christianity tell people about their relations with the environment?

While many of the world's mythologies provide stories of creation, Greco-Roman mythology was singularly incoherent in this respect. Like Aristotle, the intellectuals of the ancient West denied that the visible world had had a beginning. Indeed, the idea of a beginning was impossible in the framework of their cyclical notion of time. In sharp contrast, Christianity inherited from Judaism not only a concept of time as nonrepetitive and linear but also a striking story of creation. By gradual stages a loving and all-powerful God had created light and darkness, the heavenly bodies, and earth and all its plants, animals, birds, and fishes. Finally, God had created Adam and, as an afterthought, Eve to keep man from being lonely. Man named all the animals, thus establishing his dominance over them. God planned all of this explicitly for man's benefit and rule: no item in the physical creation had any purpose save to serve man's purposes. And, although man's body is made of clay, he is not simply part of nature: he is made in God's image.

Especially in its Western form, Christianity is the most anthropocentric religion the world has seen. As early as the 2nd century both Tertullian and St. Irenaeus of Lyons were insisting that when God shaped Adam he was foreshadowing the image of the incarnate Christ, the Second Adam. Man shares, in great measure, God's transcendence of nature. Christianity, in absolute contrast to ancient paganism and Asia's religions (except, perhaps, Zoroastrianism), not only established a dualism of man and nature but also insisted that it is God's will that man exploit nature for his proper ends.

At the level of the common people this worked out in an interesting way. In Antiquity every tree, every spring, every stream, every hill had its own *genius loci,* its guardian spirit. These spirits were accessible to men, but were very unlike men; centaurs, fauns, and mermaids show their ambivalence. Before one cut a tree, mined a mountain, or dammed a brook, it was important to placate the spirit in charge of that particular situation, and to keep it placated. By destroying pagan animism, Christianity made it possible to exploit nature in a mood of indifference to the feelings of natural objects.

It is often said that for animism the Church substituted the cult of saints. True; but the cult of saints is functionally quite different from animism. The saint is not *in* natural objects; he may have special shrines, but his citizenship is in heaven. Moreover, a saint is entirely a man; he can be approached in human terms. In addition to saints, Christianity of course also had angels and demons inherited from Judaism and perhaps, at one remove, from Zoroastrianism. But these were all as mobile as the saints themselves. The spirits *in* natural objects, which formerly had protected nature from man, evaporated. Man's effective monopoly on spirit in this world was confirmed, and the old inhibitions to the exploitation of nature crumbled.

When one speaks in such sweeping terms, a note of caution is in order. Christianity is a complex faith, and its consequences differ in differing contexts. What I have said may well apply to the medieval West, where in fact technology made spectacular advances. But the Greek East, a highly civilized realm of equal Christian devotion, seems to have produced no marked technological innovation after the late 7th century, when Greek fire was invented. The key to the contrast may perhaps be found in a difference in the tonality of piety and thought which students of comparative theology find between the Greek and the Latin Churches. The Greeks believed that sin was intellectual blindness, and that salvation was found in illumination, orthodoxy—that is, clear thinking. The Latins, on the other hand, felt that sin was moral evil, and that salvation was to be found in right conduct. Eastern theology has been intellectualist. Western theology has been voluntarist. The Greek saint contemplates; the Western saint acts. The implications of Christianity for the conquest of nature would emerge more easily in the Western atmosphere.

The Christian dogma of creation, which is found in the first clause of all the Creeds, has another meaning for our comprehension of today's ecologic crisis. By revelation, God had given man the Bible, the Book of Scripture. But since God had made nature, nature also must reveal the divine mentality. The religious study of nature for the better understanding of God was known as natural theology. In the early Church, and always in the Greek East, nature was conceived primarily as a symbolic system through which God speaks to men: the ant is a sermon to sluggards; rising flames are the symbol of the soul's aspiration. This view of nature was essentially artistic rather than scientific. While Byzantium preserved and copied great numbers of ancient Greek scientific texts, science as we conceive it could scarcely flourish in such an ambience.

However, in the Latin West by the early 13th century natural theology was following a very different bent. It was ceasing to be the decoding of the physical symbols of God's communication with man and was becoming the effort to understand God's mind by discovering how his creation operates. The rainbow was no longer simply a symbol of hope first sent to Noah after the Deluge: Robert Grosseteste, Friar Roger Bacon, and Theodoric of Freiberg produced startlingly sophisticated work on the optics of the rainbow, but they did it as a venture in religious understanding. From the 13th century onward, up to and including Leibnitz and Newton, every major scientist, in effect, explained his motivations in religious terms. Indeed, if Galileo had not been so expert an amateur theologian he would have got into far less trouble: the professionals resented his intrusion. And Newton seems to have regarded himself more as a theologian than as a scientist. It was not until the late 18th century that the hypothesis of God became unnecessary to many scientists.

It is often hard for the historian to judge, when men explain why they are doing what they want to do, whether they are offering real reasons or merely culturally acceptable reasons. The consistency with which scientists during the long formative centuries of Western science said that the task and the reward of the scientist was "to think God's thoughts after him" leads one to believe that this was their real motivation. If so, then modern Western science was cast in a matrix of Christian theology. The dynamism of religious devotion, shaped by the Judeo-Christian dogma of creation, gave it impetus.

AN ALTERNATIVE CHRISTIAN VIEW

We would seem to be headed toward conclusions unpalatable to many Christians. Since both *science* and *technology* are blessed words in our contemporary vocabulary, some may be happy at the notions, first, that, viewed historically, modern science is an extrapolation of natural theology and, second, that modern technology is at least partly to be explained as an Occidental, voluntarist realization of the Christian dogma of man's transcendence of, and rightful mastery over, nature. But, as we now recognize, somewhat over a century ago science and technology—hitherto quite separate activities—joined to give mankind powers which, to judge by many of the ecologic effects, are out of control. If so, Christianity bears a huge burden of guilt.

I personally doubt that disastrous ecologic backlash can be avoided simply by applying to our problems more science and more technology. Our science and technology have grown out of Christian attitudes toward man's relation to nature which are almost universally held not only by Christians and neo-Christians but also by those who fondly regard themselves as post-Christians. Despite Copernicus, all the cosmos rotates around our little globe. Despite Darwin, we are *not,* in our hearts, part of the natural process. We are superior to nature, contemptuous of it, willing to use it for our slightest whim. The newly elected Governor of California, like myself a churchman but less troubled than I, spoke for the Christian tradition when he said (as is alleged), "when you've seen one redwood tree, you've seen them all." To a Christian a tree can be no more than a physical fact. The whole concept of the sacred grove is alien to Christianity and to the ethos of the West. For nearly two millennia Christian missionaries have been chopping down sacred groves, which are idolatrous because they assume spirit in nature.

What we do about ecology depends on our ideas of the man-nature relationship. More science and more technology are not going to get us out of the present ecologic crisis until we find a new religion, or rethink our old one. The beatniks, who are the basic revolutionaries of our time, show a sound instinct in their affinity for Zen Buddhism, which conceives of the man-nature relationship as very nearly the mirror image of the Christian view. Zen, however, is as deeply conditioned by Asian history as Christianity is by the experience of the West, and I am dubious of its viability among us.

Possibly we should ponder the greatest radical in Christian history since Christ: St. Francis of Assisi. The prime miracle of St. Francis is the fact that he did not end at the stake, as many of his left-wing followers did. He was so clearly heretical that a General of the Franciscan Order, St. Bonaventura, a great and perceptive Christian, tried to suppress the early accounts of Franciscanism. The key to an understanding of Francis is his belief in the virtue of humility—not merely for the individual but for man as a species. Francis tried to depose man from his monarchy over creation and set up a democracy of all God's creatures. With him the ant is no longer simply a homily for the lazy, flames a sign of the thrust of the soul toward union with God; now they are Brother Ant and Sister Fire, praising the Creator in their own ways as Brother Man does in his.

Later commentators have said that Francis preached to the birds as a rebuke to men who would not listen. The records do not read so: he urged the little birds to praise God, and in spiritual ecstasy they flapped their wings and chirped rejoicing. Legends of saints, especially the Irish saints, had long told of their dealings with animals but always, I believe, to show their human dominance over creatures. With Francis it is different. The land around Gubbio in the Apennines was being ravaged by a fierce wolf. St. Francis, says the legend, talked to the wolf and persuaded him of the error of his ways. The wolf repented, died in the odor of sanctity, and was buried in consecrated ground.

What Sir Steven Runciman calls "the Franciscan doctrine of the animal soul" was quickly stamped out. Quite possibly it was in part inspired, consciously or unconsciously, by the belief in reincarnation held by the Cathar heretics who at that time teemed in Italy and southern France, and who presumably had got it originally from India. It is significant that at just the same moment, about 1200, traces of metempsychosis are found also in western Judaism, in the Provençal *Cabbala*. But Francis held neither to transmigration of souls nor to pantheism. His view of nature and of man rested on a unique sort of pan-psychism of all things animate and inanimate, designed for the glorification of their transcendent Creator, who, in the ultimate gesture of cosmic humility, assumed flesh, lay helpless in a manger, and hung dying on a scaffold.

I am not suggesting that many contemporary Americans who are concerned about our ecologic crisis will be either able or willing to counsel with wolves or exhort birds. However, the present increasing disruption of the global environment is the product of a dynamic technology and science which were originating in the Western medieval world against which St. Francis was rebelling in so original a way. Their growth cannot be understood historically apart from distinctive attitudes toward nature which are deeply grounded in Christian dogma. The fact that most people do not think of these attitudes as Christian is irrelevant. No

Lynn White

new set of basic values has been accepted in our society to displace those of Christianity. Hence we shall continue to have a worsening ecologic crisis until we reject the Christian axiom that nature has no reason for existence save to serve man.

The greatest spiritual revolutionary in Western history, St. Francis, proposed what he thought was an alternative Christian view of nature and man's relation to it: he tried to substitute the idea of the equality of all creatures, including man, for the idea of man's limitless rule of creation. He failed. Both our present science and our present technology are so tinctured with orthodox Christian arrogance toward nature that no solution for our ecologic crisis can be expected from them alone. Since the roots of our trouble are so largely religious, the remedy must also be essentially religious, whether we call it that or not. We must rethink and refeel our nature and destiny. The profoundly religious, but heretical, sense of the primitive Franciscans for the spiritual autonomy of all parts of nature may point a direction. I propose Francis as a patron saint for ecologists.

"THE GREENING OF RELIGION"

Roderick Nash

A theology of the natural world . . . asserts the intrinsic worth of the non-human world. Such a theology declares that the non-human world has just as much right to its internal integrity as does the human world, that human beings transgress their divine authority when they destroy or fundamentally alter the rocks, the trees, the air, the water, the soil, the animals—just as they do when they murder other human beings.

—Allan R. Brockway, 1973

"Do people have ethical obligations toward rocks?" . . . To almost all Americans, still saturated with ideas historically dominant in Christianity . . . the question makes no sense at all. If the time comes when to any considerable group of us such a question is no longer ridiculous, we may be on the verge of a change of value structures that will make possible measures to cope with the growing ecologic crisis. One hopes that there is enough time left.

—Lynn White, Jr., 1973

As he concluded his pioneering delineation of a land ethic in *A Sand County Almanac,* Aldo Leopold despaired at the shallowness of the American conservation movement of the 1940s. Economic, not ethical, criteria still determined policy. "In our attempt to make conservation easy," Leopold wrote, "we have made it trivial." The reason, he believed, was that human beings were not prepared intellectually for "the extension of the social conscience from people to land." As proof Leopold submitted his opinion that "philosophy and religion have not yet heard" of including nature in an expanded morality. The next generation of theologians and philosophers, however, would pay a significant amount of attention to this problem. Indeed by the 1980s it is possible to discern, borrowing Charles Reich's word, a "greening" of both fields. Just as John Locke's ideas underlay the first wave of democratic revolutions, environmental philosophy and what is called "ecotheology" provided the intellectual foundations for a revolutionary expansion of the meaning of conservation.[1]

The church has always been the chief custodian of ethics. Even in the secular modern era, most Americans continue to derive their ideas of right and wrong, directly or indirectly, from one religion or another. Harold W. Wood, Jr., has noted, "insofar as ordinary people are concerned, it is religion which is the greatest factor in determining morality."[2] The morals of intellectual and political leaders also spring from a perception of reality that, if not related to established churches, could still be characterized as religious. Therefore when American religion began to consider the relations between humans and nature, it lent important support to environmental ethics. Formidable theological obstacles thousands of years old stood in the way of such a reorientation, but recognizing the obstacles was a start in the "greening" process.

The modern discussion of the resistance of Western religion to environmental ethics crystallized around a 1967 essay by the medieval historian Lynn White. In "The Historical Roots of Our Ecologic Crisis," White set himself the task of understanding why his civilization had exploited nature to such a degree that its own quality, if not its survival, was at stake. Granted that the rise of science and technology provided tools for wholesale ecological disruption, but why were they used so destructively? White found the explanation for this pattern in the history of ideas, in particular the concept that although it was wrong to exploit people, exploiting nature was perfectly right and proper. Where, then, did Western society find a dualistic ethical system that discriminated so sharply between people and the environment? White's answer was the Judeo-Christian tradition.[3]

Judaism and Christianity. White maintained, posited a dichotomy between people and nature. According to the sacred texts of these religions, people were masters, not members, of the natural world. Created in the likeness of God, unique in their possession of a soul and the expectation of salvation, humans clearly stood above other forms of life. Moreover, according to White, Jews and Christians traditionally believed that the rest of creation existed solely for human benefit. Referring to the creation account in the Bible, he wrote: "God planned all of this explicitly for man's benefit and rule; no item in the physical creation had any purpose save to serve man's purposes.... Christianity is the most anthropocentric religion the world has seen."[4] For evidence White needed to look no further than the first pages of the Old Testament where, after shaping man "in his own image," God commands his favorite artifact to "be fruitful and multiply, and fill the earth and subdue it; and have dominion over the fish of the sea and over the birds of the air and over every living thing that moves upon the earth."[5] Every creature was assumed to be created to serve a human need. Human beings were, quite literally, the kings of beasts; every other being was inferior in the Judeo-Christian hierarchy. In case any doubt remained, God reaffirmed his alleged promise of dominance to Noah after the great flood and the new beginning: "The fear of you and the dread of you shall be upon every beast of the field, and upon every bird of the air, upon everything that creeps on the ground, and all the fish of the sea; into your hand they are delivered ... I give you everything."[6] Human dominion, in other words, was complete and unqualified. Nature had good reason to fear humankind. As White saw it, this was all the rationale Christians and Jews needed to exploit nature at will. Meaningful change in human-nature relations would not occur "until we reject the Christian axiom that nature has no reason for existence save to serve man."[7]

Pausing at one point in his indictment, White observed that he seemed "to be headed toward conclusions unpalatable to many Christians."[8] In this opinion, at least, he had abundant support. Large numbers of environmentally conscious Jews and Christians challenged White's thesis. Frequently this response took on strong emotional overtones. White emerged in his critics' eyes as something of a heretic; they tended to forget that he was writing primarily as an historian.

As a scholar concerned with the history of ideas, White knew the relevant question was not, what does Christianity mean? but what did it mean to a particular society at a given time and place? His approach, in other words, was pragmatic: How was the Judeo-Christian tradition used? White was perfectly willing to concede that Christians of the 1960s might form a commitment to environmental responsibility from their reading of Genesis. He agreed that there was a biblical basis for environmentalism. But his point was that for nearly two thousand years the Christian tradition had not been so construed. Instead people used Scripture to justify the exploitation of nature in the same way that defenders of slavery used it to justify ownership and exploitation of certain classes of humans. Modern Christians, White observed, no longer viewed the Bible as a justification for holding slaves, and a similar reinterpretation with regard to nature might be under way. Revelation, after all, was supposed to be an unending process. "Perhaps," White concluded, "the Holy Ghost is whispering something to us."[9]

The best place to search for confirmation of Lynn White's contention that traditional Christianity opposed an ethical attitude toward nature is in the original significance of the language employed in the Bible. Hebrew linguists have analyzed Genesis 1:28 and found two operative verbs: *kabash,* translated as "subdue," and *radah,* rendered as "have dominion over" or "rule." Throughout the Old Testament *kabash* and *radah* are used to signify a violent assault or crushing. The image is that of a conqueror placing his foot on the neck of a defeated enemy, exerting absolute domination. Both Hebraic words are also used to identify the process of enslavement.[10] It followed that the Christian tradition could understand Genesis 1:28 as a divine commandment to conquer every part of nature and make it humankind's slave. Certainly such an interpretation proved useful over the centuries as intellectual lubrication for the exploitation of nature. Indeed, was this not one of the main reasons for its initial appearance and persistence in Christian thought?[11]

Along with positing a dualism that separated humans from nature and gave them the right to exploit it, the other principal argument in Lynn White's 1967 critique was Christianity's rejection of animism. This ancient body of ideas, typical of most pre-Christian cultures and persisting in non-Christian ones into the present era, held that every part of the environment, living and nonliving, had a consciousness or spirit. Pantheists, for example,

Roderick Nash

identified deities with natural objects and processes. The god of the sea—Poseidon to the Greeks and Neptune to the Romans—remains the best known of a full spectrum of gods. For people of this persuasion nature was holy. White reasoned that this belief conditioned human behavior toward nature in the direction of reverence and respect.

One way to understand animism is as an expanded circle of moral considerability. Ethical relevancy did not end with God, angels, saints, and other people. Everything had a sacred quality. Nothing, to use Martin Buber's terminology, was an "it." People thought of nature as something with which a personal relationship was possible, as with another human being. With animism what Buber called an "I-Thou" relationship characterized human interaction with the entire environment.[12]

Judaism and Christianity changed all this.[13] Rigidly monotheistic, the first commandment of these religions was to worship no other gods or idols or spirits except Yahweh/God/ the Heavenly Father. Even Jesus was the *son* of this supreme deity, and thus hierarchy (that villain of contemporary environmental and social reformers) was thoroughgoing in Christianity. Natural objects might be created by God, but they were not gods, nor did they possess souls or spirits of any sort. Modern Christians contend that the fact of divine creation of nonhuman beings and inanimate objects should be sufficient reason for respect and reverence, but their ancient and medieval predecessors took the absence of animism as a license to exploit. Since they had objectified nature and were now dealing with something outside their religious and ethical community, the restraints previously provided by fear or morality were no longer operative. As White put it, "by destroying pagan animism, Christianity made it possible to exploit nature in a mood of indifference to the feelings of natural objects."[14] Significantly, early Christian evangelists felled the sacred groves of northern Europe where pagans worshipped a multiplicity of deities. The contemporary custom of cutting Christmas trees may have vague ties to that ancient ritual.

White's brief 1967 essay could not involve more than a cursory examination of Christian ideas about the environment. He might have expatiated on that religion's deep hostility to metempsychosis. The soul of the good Christian was destined only for heaven, never for the body of a plant or animal. A grizzly bear or redwood tree could never be one's late grandmother reincarnated. This belief effectively removed another of the constraints that held pagan appetites for the exploitation of nature in check. Severed from the human community and its ethical protection, nature was fully exposed to human greed. Interestingly, one of the first American expositors of the rights of nature, Edward P. Evans, based part of his expanded moral philosophy on the possibility of metempsychosis.

White also said nothing about the traditional Christian view of wilderness as a cursed land, the antipode of paradise. But this idea, so pervasive in both the Old and New Testaments, contributed significantly to the absence of respect for the nonhumanized landscape for more than two thousand years. As the Puritans demonstrated at the beginning of the American experience, the only appropriate Christian response to wild country and its wild inhabitants was conquest, subjugation, and, in the case of the more fortunate Indians, conversion.[15]

Neither did Lynn White find space in his short essay to note the pervasive otherworldliness of Christianity. Christians' aspirations were fixed on heaven, the supposed place of their origins and, they hoped, their final resting. The earth was no mother but a kind of halfway house of trial and testing from which one was released at death. Ludwig Feuerbach, a nineteenth-century theologian, represented the Christian perspective that "nature, the world, has no value, no interest for Christians. The Christian thinks of himself and the salvation of his soul."[16] Indeed Christians expected that the earth would not be around for long. A vengeful God would destroy it, and all unredeemed nature, with floods or drought or fire. Obviously this eschatology was a poor basis from which to argue for environmental ethics in any guise. Why take care of what you expected to be obliterated?

Faced with growing misgivings about the environmental implications of the Judeo-Christian tradition, modern leaders of American religious thought and practice had essentially three options. They could turn to the East, to Asian faiths that had never abandoned a sense of the unity of nature and subscribed to an ethical philosophy that did not begin and end with people. They could incorporate the strong animist traditions of American Indians, which rendered the entire ecosystem sacred and therefore worthy of ethical consideration. Or the reformers could go back to basic Jewish and Christian beliefs and reinterpret them to accommodate demands for an ethical system that did not exclude nature. Most of the "greening" of recent American religion—the development of what is called ecotheology—involves the explication and, to some extent, the synthesis of these three options.

A starting point for exploring the theological frontiers of the new environmentalism might be Lynn White himself. Despite the comprehensiveness of his critique of Western religious traditions, he was not prepared to abandon them as a key to easing the ecologic crisis. He laughed at his reputation in conservative Christian circles as "a junior Anti-Christ, probably in the Kremlin's pay, bent on destroying the true faith." In fact, White's desire was to reform, not destroy, religion. "Since the roots of our [environmental] trouble are so largely religious," he noted at the conclusion of the 1967 essay, "the remedy must also be essentially religious." What he had in mind was a revolution in ethics with religion, as a basic determinant of morality, on its cutting edge. "Religious values," White's knowledge of history led him to believe, "are fundamental in the dynamics of cultural and social change."[17]

But what religious values could help the West work toward an environmental ethic? White knew that the concept of the rights of animals, plants, and even rocks was not foreign to many faiths. "To an ancient Greek, to an American Indian, or perhaps to certain kinds of Buddhists, the [idea] would have meaning." But from the traditional Christian perspective, White thought, the question "'Do people have ethical obligations toward rocks?' makes no sense at all." Yet it might if Christians like himself were willing to reinterpret their basic principles.[18]

Roderick Nash

White pointed to one possible direction for such rethinking in his proposal of Saint Francis of Assisi (1182–1226) as "a patron saint for ecologists." What led White to call Francis "the greatest spiritual revolutionary in Western history" was his forthright challenge to Christian anthropocentrism. Although the evidence from thirteenth-century Italy is fragmentary and interlaced with myth, it suggests that the saint subscribed to what might be called spiritual egalitarianism. Everything was equal in its derivation from God and its capacity to glorify God. Francis's thought held no hierarchies, no chains of being, no dualism. Worms and ants were just as much a part of his community of worshippers as the higher primates. And so, remarkably, were inanimate presences like rocks, water, fire, and wind. Expressing the ecological-like unity he perceived, Francis's canticles and prayers addressed nonhuman beings as "brother" and "sister." He preached sermons to birds, urging them as part of God's spiritual family to give thanks to their creator. Anticipating Albert Schweitzer by seven centuries, St. Francis commonly removed worms from paths where they might be crushed. In the village of Gubbio, Francis allegedly pacified a man-eating wolf by reminding him of his membership in the Christian community. And Francis used the adjective "mother" to characterize the earth. This way of thinking was completely unprecedented in Christian history, and it would be another seven centuries before religious leaders would recognize Francis's attitude toward nature as a starting point for an environmental ethic. In 1960 the University of Michigan zoologist, Marston Bates, declared that for Christians who loved nature, "St. Francis of Assisi rightfully is their patron." White's better-known proposal came seven years later. In 1980 the Vatican acted on these suggestions and officially dubbed the Assisi holy man the patron saint of ecologists.[19]

Francis of Assisi lived long before the age of the democratic revolutions, and he did not speak of the "rights" of birds, worms, wolves, and rocks. But he did remove them from the category of "things" by including them with humans in a single spiritual fellowship. Believing that they all independently praised and magnified God, Francis implicitly accorded to all creatures and natural processes a value entirely separate from human interest. Everything had a direct relationship with God. According to Francis the mere fact of something's existence was sufficient reason for its ethical consideration. While derived from sacred rather than secular premises, the thought of the medieval Christian radical paralleled that of later advocates of the rights of nature. But it is well to emphasize that within the Christian tradition Francis was unique in his point of view. He was the exception that proves the rule of Christian anthropocentrism. Had his Christian contemporaries fully recognized the radical quality of his ideas, Francis would quite likely have been condemned as a heretic rather than elevated to sainthood. As it was, orthodox Christians celebrated his love of God, his concern for the poor, and his disdain of things material while ignoring his bold challenge to other parts of the faith.

Lynn White, of course, was well aware that Francis of Assisi had failed in his attempt to persuade Christians to substitute "the idea of the equality of all creatures, including man, for the idea of man's limitless rule of creation." But White's study of Francis's thought inspired him to try again, and he felt he had an important ally in the new ecological perspective. "Fifteen years ago," White remarked in 1978, "almost no theologian knew what the word *ecology* meant." But with its axioms widely circulating in American thought, he hoped to construct a definition of Christian compassion grounded on "an ascetic and self-restraining conviction of man's comradeship with the other creatures." Perhaps, White reasoned, this concept of biological comradeship or interdependency could be "a viable equivalent to animism." If Christian-oriented Americans could not believe in the old pagan spirit of an organism, maybe they could acknowledge the importance of its presence in what White, following Aldo Leopold, called the "integrity" of the ecosystem. "Ecology," White felt, "provides us with new religious understandings of our own being, of other beings, and of being."[20]

In the manner of Joseph Wood Krutch, White believed that a meaningful ecotheology had to transcend prudence or enlightened self-interest. We should not protect the ecosystem and its component parts because they sustain us, he reasoned, just as "we should not be pleasant to people in order that they may treat us pleasantly." So much for the hallowed Golden Rule which underlay almost all ancient religious systems, including Judaism and Christianity. White even wondered "whether a prudential ethic can rightly be called an ethic." Instead he called for morality based on disinterested love of nature which, in turn, derived from nature's membership in God's world. St. Francis proved that this ethical system could emerge in a Christian individual; White called for its reappearance on a cultural scale. Indeed he believed that such an intellectual development was imperative if technological civilization was to have a chance of co-existing with the natural order that sustained it. This sense of urgency led White to conclude that "Christian ethics is in the greatest crisis of its history of two millennia."[21]

Most critics of Lynn White did not read beyond his 1967 condemnation. In point of fact, he was not anti-Christian. His later essays showed the potential for a Christian perspective to generate a far-reaching environmental ethic. Indeed, White's concept of a "spiritual democracy" stands out as one of the most radically inclusive ethical systems yet evolved. His sense of community literally knew no bounds. "We can sense our comradeship," he wrote in 1978, "with a glacier, a subatomic particle or a spiral nebula." All of these, as well as living things, were humankind's spiritual equals, with whom we needed to coexist. As a motive for self-restraint in the species with the most potential for disrupting the ecosystem, ethics could help. White looked forward to a world in which humans exercised their rights to satisfy biological needs with an eye to the identical rights of other organisms. He wrote about "spiritual . . . courtesy" and "cosmic manners" which would promote such coexistence.[22]

To cap his argument, White even dared to defend the rights of life-forms undeniably hostile to his own species, like the smallpox virus, *Variola.* At a time when ecologists were beginning to raise ethical questions about the extermination of germs, White asked theological ones. Noting in 1978 that modern medicine had reached the point of being able to extermi-

Roderick Nash

nate smallpox, White studied the implications. "From our standpoint, the advisability of the action is beyond debate. *Variola* could not be consulted because of a communication gap. What the God who created both *homo sapiens* and *Variola* thinks about all this, we do not yet know."[23] The implication was that a thoroughgoing Christian sense of morality must include smallpox, just as St. Francis included man-eating wolves. Perhaps White hoped for a latter-day saint who could instruct *Variola* in cosmic courtesy. More likely, he simply recognized that in killing people the smallpox virus was only performing its appointed role in the ecosystem God created.

Lynn White's theology stood out for its ethical egalitarianism. The more common approach of those who would make American religion environmentally responsible was to reinterpret traditional doctrine in light of the idea of stewardship. Rereading the Old Testament they found a directive to protect rather than a license to exploit nature. The "dominion" granted in Genesis 1:28 did not connote despotism, they said, but trusteeship. As God's most favored beings, humans were charged with overseeing the welfare of all the rest of creation—in a sense, completing creation. This halfway doctrine allowed for human superiority in the Christian hierarchy, acknowledged that God had "given" nature to humans, but used these concepts as reasons for protecting the natural world from exploitation. For biblical support the stewardship contingent went to Genesis 2:15, according to which God placed the first man in the Garden of Eden "to till it and keep it."[24] This, they contended, constituted a directive to humankind to take care of or serve the rest of God's creation.

Through their understanding of the creation myth, the stewards reinvested the environment with a sacredness once associated with animism and pantheism. Abuse of nature became, once again, sacrilegious. Of course abuse of nature also could endanger human existence, and the stewardship doctrine has been termed little more than enlightened self-interest. From a theological perspective, God could be thought of as punishing humans through the impact of neglected nature on human life. But the bottom line of stewardship was that the world belonged to God. Nature was holy. Therefore it was not only prudent but right to respect the environment. In a sense the myriad forms of life, as well as the earth itself, had rights that originated from their being the work of the deity. It followed that the stewards could interpret Christianity as being in league with environmental ethics.

Modern ecotheologians liked to point out that stewardship had an old and respected place in the Christian religion. The historical evidence for this characterization, however, is, at best, scanty. Still, it is interesting that René Dubos called attention to Benedict of Nursia as a pioneer practitioner of what Dubos called "a theology of the earth." A Christian of the sixth century, Saint Benedict founded the abbey of Monte Cassino in Italy. His followers spread the monastic system throughout medieval Europe. The busy monks drained swamps, cleared forests, improved fields, and tended their gardens with diligence and devotion. Dubos found them exemplifying the best of Christian stewardship and displaying an "ethical attitude" toward their environment. He added, in reply to Lynn White, "I believe that ecologists should select St. Benedict as a much truer symbol of the human condition than Francis of Assisi." What bothered Dubos about St. Francis was that he had rejected the hierarchical concept central to the idea of stewardly responsibility. Francis regarded all life-forms and even inanimate matter as brothers and sisters in the family of God. Dubos, on the contrary, accepted enlightened anthropocentrism as the basis of his ethical philosophy. Mankind was in charge of the world and could and should "manipulate nature to his best interests" but always with a feeling of reverence for what was ultimately not his possession but God's.[25]

Stewardship was notable chiefly by its absence in the thousand years of Christian thought following St. Benedict. Finally in the seventeenth century a minor motif of dissent to anthropocentrism began to surface in the work of John Ray and Alexander Pope. God, Pope wrote, had not created anything solely for the good of people. Humans were accountable to God for their treatment of his creation. Henry David Thoreau and John Muir in the nineteenth century and Edward Evans and Liberty Hyde Bailey in the early twentieth were the first Americans to apply this principle to human-environment relations.

Then in the 1930s a little-known forester and hydrologist named Walter C. Lowdermilk (1888–1974) used stewardship to rationalize the developing resource conservation movement. In 1922 Lowdermilk began a five-year residence in China to investigate problems of soil erosion and forest management. The Chinese, he concluded, had neglected intelligent land use to their extreme peril. In the next decade Lowdermilk became Assistant Chief of the Soil Conservation Service and traveled more than 25,000 miles by automobile in the Mediterranean Basin, the same ecologically depleted region that inspired George Perkins Marsh to call for a moral relationship to land. In June 1939, in the heart of the Holy Land, Lowdermilk made a speech on Jerusalem radio entitled "The Eleventh Commandment."[26] He reasoned that if God could have foreseen the ravages that centuries of thoughtless forestry and agriculture would bring to his creation, he would have been moved to add to the Ten Commandments. The eleventh, according to Lowdermilk, would "complete the trinity of man's responsibilities—to his Creator, to his fellow men, and to Mother Earth." The text Lowdermilk proposed for the new commandment read:

> XI. Thou shalt inherit the holy earth as a faithful steward, conserving its resources and productivity from generation to generation. Thou shalt safeguard thy fields from soil erosion, thy living waters from drying up, thy forests from desolation, and protect the hills from overgrazing by thy herds, that thy descendants may have abundance forever. If any shall fail in this stewardship of the land, thy fruitful fields shall become sterile stony ground and wasting gullies, and thy descendants shall decrease and live in poverty or perish from off the face of the earth.

Although Lowdermilk, writing in the utilitarian climate of the 1930s, grounded the appeal of his message in human self-interest, the concept of a commandment from God

Roderick Nash

through Moses to humankind carried with it a strong ethical implication. Drawing on the very source of Christian ethics (the human-God relationship), Lowdermilk succeeded in making conservation a moral matter. For him responsible land use was not just the key to "physical" progress but to "higher spiritual ... development" as well. Aldo Leopold had used ecology; Lowdermilk took religion to be the foundation of environmental ethics.[27]

A few American churches began to explore the implications of stewardship before the modern environmental era. The observance of Rogation Days, which dates to the Middle Ages and acknowledges human dependence on planting and harvesting, provided a conceptual basis for modern dedications such as Rural Life Sundays and Soil Stewardship Sundays. The dramatic exposure given soil erosion problems by the great dust storms that plagued the Middle West in the 1930s supported these tentative beginnings. In the 1940s the National Catholic Rural Life Commission of Des Moines, Iowa, endeavored to bring the force of religion behind careful land use. A decade later the National Council of Churches launched a program called "A Christian Ministry in the National Parks," but its emphasis was largely on human appreciation of the beauty of God's world. Few religious leaders or, for that matter, anyone took the rights of nature seriously before 1960. But the rising tide of interest in ecology and a parallel anxiety about environmental problems created new perspectives. In the 1970s and 1980s the ethics of the human-nature relationship became a major preoccupation of American theologians and, to a lesser extent, of ordinary churchgoers.

A necessarily brief history of this development can begin with Joseph Sittler, a professor of systematic theology at Chicago Lutheran Theological Seminary. Sittler was one of the first professional theologians in the United States to attempt to base an environmental ethic on Christian faith. He began the effort in 1954 in a key article entitled "A Theology for Earth." Rejecting the notion of mother earth (as a Christian Sittler had to accept God, not nature, as the creative power), he advocated, a decade before Lynn White, following St. Francis in regarding nature as "man's sister." The environment was part of the created community; there were no grounds for dualism in Sittler's reinterpretation of the Judeo-Christian tradition. "God-man-nature," he explained, had to be understood as a unity.[28] In 1960 Sittler presented the core of his theology in an address to the World Council of Churches. The purpose of God, he said, is "cosmic redemption." Not only human souls but "all things" were potential objects of God's saving grace. Extending this idea to the limit, Sittler argued that even atoms belonged within the circle of salvation. He opposed nuclear bombs for this reason, suggesting that the atoms used to destroy people and nature be "reclaimed for God."[29] Sittler's widely read 1962 sermon, "The Care of the Earth," drew a distinction between "use" and "enjoyment," and he urged Christians to let the latter guide them in their dealings with nature. The point was to take "joy in the things themselves," not in what they could do for people. Sittler believed that abuse of the environment was an insult to God; hence the care of the earth was a religious imperative. In this attitude Sittler was among the first theologians to rise above simple, anthropocentric stewardship. Environmental responsibility became a matter of obeying Christ, not providing for human needs.[30]

Theologians had not been common contributors to conservation journals, but in 1971 Joseph Sittler told the readers of the *National Parks and Conservation Magazine* that "dominion" meant not enslavement of but tender caring for nature. Another significant essay, "Ecological Commitment as Theological Responsibility," developed his early idea that nature was a participant in salvation along with humans. Consequently, ecological interdependence became not just a scientific description but the only appropriate worldview for Christians who accepted God's omnipresent love. According to Sittler the pantheism or animism that Lynn White regretted losing was not essential for environmental responsibility. Sittler dismissed pantheism and salvaged respect for nature in a single sentence: "The world is not God, but it is God's." All the thoughtful modern Christian needed as a reason to include nature in his or her moral circle was the belief that God, too, wanted it in the redeemed heavenly kingdom. Grace created the interlocked relationship of theology and ecology.[31]

Along with the writing of Charles Hartshorne[32] and Daniel Day Williams,[33] Joseph Sittler's work encouraged a number of younger theologians and clergymen to apply their faith to environmental problems. Richard A. Baer, Jr., is representative. Trained in the late 1950s at the Princeton Theological Seminary, Baer later added a Harvard doctorate in the history and philosophy of religion. In 1966, even before Lynn White's controversial essay, Baer published "Land Misuse: A Theological Concern" in *Christian Century,* one of the nation's oldest and most respected outlets of religious thought. His paper challenged American religion to become involved with environmental issues. "The church today," he wrote, "stands at a time of decision. If she is to remain true to her prophetic heritage, she must confront the power structures of society with a fresh and cogent ethic of land usage." He made it plain that he was not just interested in academic study but in "action—involvement." Significantly for the natural-rights tradition, Baer argued that religion's concern for race relations in the 1960s created a precedent for attention to exploitation of the environment.[34]

In welcome contrast to many of his colleagues, Baer took pains to simplify his case for deriving an environmental ethic from the Christian tradition. His first assumption was that "*the world belongs to God,*" not human beings. Baer developed the point in the language of political theory: Because God is the highest authority of earth, no member of his world can "dictate the destiny" of any other member. It was a clever stance, for it permitted Baer to retain the traditional Christian belief in human distinction from and superiority to nature but still argue for environmental responsibility. His point, in a nutshell, was that humans may be lords of nature but God is lord over humanity. It followed that "man's freedom to 'subdue' nature is always limited and under a higher authority." Baer believed that in this respect the Bible supported the same conclusion as "ecology texts" concerning the limits of the earth and the consequent necessity for human restraint.[35]

The second foundation of an ecotheology, according to Baer, is "*God likes the world he created.*" He cited passages from the Bible indicating that nature "praises and honors God," that it "witnesses to his glory and majesty" and that "God delights in nature and cares for it quite apart from its importance for man." As the clincher for this interpretation, Baer cited Genesis 1:31: "And God saw everything that he had made, and behold, it was very good." This meant for Baer that nature in its totality had intrinsic value for God, and he emphasized "*all* of nature, both the living and the non-living; the human and non-human; plants as well as animals; sticks, air, water, stones: *everything.*" Perhaps St. Francis of Assisi, but not many Christians before or since, would have understood Baer's universalism. Its implication was that the basic fact of their being created by God endowed every part of nature with rights that humans ought to respect. Americans familiar with their nation's history would immediately recognize the similarity of Baer's system to Lockean natural-rights liberalism, but for the theologian it stemmed from a sacred rather than a secular imperative and extended far beyond the limits of traditional liberal philosophy.[36]

Baer's third principle drew heavily on his knowledge of the ecological sciences. It held that not just every object in nature but the interrelationships between them were part of God's creation. God valued systems, processes, smoothly functioning wholes, and what Baer called the "web of life." The ethical precept Baer derived from this amalgamation of ecology and theology was that "wantonly to destroy the relational and holistic qualities of our environment is to sin against the very structure of the world which God has created." Here was another reason for religious condemnation of pollution and exploitation, another argument for involving the church in the environmental movement.[37]

Baer's three principles shed new light on the chronic Judeo-Christian "dominion" problem. As a practicing Christian he did not try to escape the central import of Genesis 1:26–28. Scripture clearly set humans apart from and placed them in dominance over nature. "Man cannot be man," he wrote in 1971, "and cease ruling over nature." The control of fire, the advent of herding and agriculture, and mechanical and electrical technology all proved to Baer that "whether he wants to or not man will rule over nature." But having thus stated what he knew would be "an obscenity for many environmentalists," Baer quickly reminded his readers that the important question was not the fact but the quality of human rule. Arrogance and anthropocentrism had to be avoided. Nature was not merely a utilitarian object with only instrumental value. As an antidote to this attitude, Baer suggested thinking of the environment as the home of a host and of humans as guests. Never forget that the earth is "property that does not belong to us." From Baer's perspective *Homo sapiens* rents an apartment called nature. God is, quite literally, the landlord. He expects compliance with basic "principles of etiquette" in the use of his creation. As Baer reinterpreted the controversial passage in Genesis, humankind does not have unconditional freedom to conquer and exploit what it could never, in the final analysis, own.[38]

Like others seeking to develop a modern ecotheology based on the reinterpretation of Christianity, Baer took the responsibility of stewardship very seriously. "Failure to fulfill our obligations as faithful trustees of the gifts of God's creation," he warned, "will inevitably bring God's judgment upon us. The earth itself will rebel against our greedy and thoughtless exploitation of nature and our irresponsible fecundity."[39] This linkage of ecological and theological catastrophe had the flavor of a jeremiad intermixed with new ecological insights. Baer spoke for a growing number of theologians who believed that environmental degradation, human suffering, and divine retribution were closely related.

Richard Baer also probed the meaning of the alleged desacralization of nature by the Christian faith. A year before Lynn White publicized the issue, Baer recognized that a fundamental change had occurred about 2,500 years ago when Greek philosophers and Jewish theologians substituted a single, supreme deity for the myriad gods earlier cultures had found in virtually every natural object. Baer was among the first American theologians to recognize that this switch from pantheism to monotheism brought about "the disenthronement of the nature deities" and a consequent callousness toward the environment that favored exploitation. But the remedy did not lie in restoring nature worship. Speaking again as a Christian, Baer reasoned that, although nature is not a deity, it is the creation of the supreme deity and therefore is holy. The import for human attitude and action is the same in either case; the spoliation of nature is "essentially irreligious." Baer concludes his argument with the observation that "a mature Christian position would permit one neither to worship nature nor to despise it."[40]

In his attitude toward monotheism, as in his ideas about hierarchy and dominion, Baer pointed the way for those who would save both their Christian faith and the environment. Working on the intellectual borderland of theology and ecology, he succeeded in giving new meaning to nonhuman rights and human moral obligations. But his interest extended beyond articulation to the implementation of a Christian land ethic. In his most optimistic moments Baer hoped that religious institutions could "draw into the conservation battle thousands, even millions, of committed churchmen."[41]

The Faith-Man-Nature Group, which Baer enthusiastically supported, was a notable institutional expression of this ideal. At one time or another it included most of the early environmental theologians. Taking shape in 1963 and 1964 within the National Council of Churches, the group's stated aim was "to understand man's relationship with nature in the light of religious faith, and to spell out ethical imperatives for the conservation of natural resources."[42] Philip N. Joranson, a biologist and consultant on forestry education, was the catalyst around which clergymen, theologians, and scientists gathered to discuss problems in human-environment relationships. Baer believed Joranson was "one of the first persons in America to see clearly the need for developing a new environmental ethic."[43] Debatable as this might be, Joranson had urged the church as early as 1954 to move beyond "standard stewardship" and recognize that the "moral activity of man is continuous with the process of the universe." He implied that the modern world needed reverence for, not simply conservation of, nature. Beginning in 1965 the Faith-Man-Nature Group convened at least annually to consider the possible contributions of religion to such concerns as population control, pollution, excessive resource consumption, and world community. It published the proceedings of its 1967 conference under the title *Christians and the Good Earth*. The 1969 meetings resulted in *A New Ethic for a New Earth*. In addition three regional gatherings produced written records.[44]

The primary message of the Faith-Man-Nature Group was that the earth and its resources are gifts of God which humans have thoughtlessly abused. The group's alternative recommendation was stewardship—human caretaking of God's good earth. Undeniably much of the force of this appeal stemmed from anthropocentric considerations. Time and again the clergymen and religious scholars anchored their case on the welfare of human beings, present and future. Several theologians, notably Conrad Bonifazi, argued that perception by the human mind was a necessary precondition for any object's having value. Yet an important theme in the Faith-Man-Nature books concerned God's creation and, in a sense, ownership of the earth. This viewpoint led some contributors to speak of stewardship as a "moral responsibility"—not of people to other people but of people to God.[45] A few went further. Citing St. Francis and Aldo Leopold, they argued for the transcendence of utilitarianism. "Things have a value and integrity in themselves," Daniel Day Williams of the Union Theological Seminary explained, because they are part of the process that is "ongoing reality." Environmental exploitation is therefore not only "bad for man" but also "bad for Nature" apart from any human interest.[46] This sense of the intrinsic worth of every part of the environment led one Faith-Man-Nature participant. H. Paul Santmire, to declare that "in the eyes of God nature has its own value, its own rights for life and fulfillment."[47] Such language indicates that theology was just as feasible a route to ethical egalitarianism as were ecology, philosophy, and environmental activism.

Despite its bold resolves to change the world, the Faith-Man-Nature Group did little other than prepare more studies and reports than it had originally condemned. In 1974, beset by the lack of regular funding and volunteer burnout, the organization disbanded.[48] But its leaders were justified in feeling that they had nourished a trend. Given the nearly total absence of environmental ethics in previous American religious life and thought, the simple fact that Faith-Man-Nature existed for a decade on a national level is remarkable enough. Philip Joranson continued to be active in ecotheology. In 1984 he published *Cry of the Environment: Rebuilding the Christian Creation Tradition*, which argued that the modern Christian's calling must be "to liberate the earth from the threat and the reality of its slow and steady execution at the hands of humanity." The idea of liberating nature from human domination linked environmental theology—or what Joranson called "eco-justice"—with earlier movements for human liberation.[49]

Paul Santmire, the most radical of the ecotheologians associated with Faith-Man-Nature, also went the farthest in developing and publishing his ideas on the Christian basis for environmental ethics. At Harvard, where Santmire took his doctorate in divinity in 1966, the reinterpretation of Christianity in the interest of ecological responsibility was a major preoccupation.[50] Richard Baer was a fellow graduate student, and Frederick Elder also did graduate work in Cambridge at the end of the 1960s. In 1970, while serving as chaplain of Wellesley College, Santmire published a popularized version of part of his Harvard thesis under the title *Brother Earth: Nature, God and Ecology in Time of Crisis*. This was the year of the National Environmental Policy Act and the first Earth Day, when America's obsession with the "Age of Ecology" approached cult proportions. Santmire's book reflects the new concerns. "The earth," he declares in his opening sentence, "is in danger of destruction." One of the reasons, we learn, is the state of human values, and Santmire pays the by then almost obligatory homage to Lynn White and his 1967 critique of Judeo-Christian morality. But the intent of *Brother Earth* is to salvage a basis for ecological responsibility from the West's dominant religious tradition. Santmire is convinced that the "ecological bankruptcy" of Western theology is indeed "alleged," and his writing constitutes proof of the point.[51]

The most creative part of Santmire's 1970 work is his adaptation of the old Judeo-Christian concept of the Kingdom of God to support ethical extension. Santmire contends that the kingdom idea, coupled with God's valuation of all nature, creates a theological basis for community embracing humanity and the environment. In making this point Santmire employs the language of political theory likely to appeal to Americans versed in natural-rights liberalism. Santmire's God is a ruler interested in the right treatment of all his subjects. According to the terms of the divine body politic, the dominant members of the community—humans—have no legitimate basis for oppressing and exploiting minority members, that is, nature. So when Santmire mentions "social justice" it is not in the usual sense of interpersonal relations but applies to the entire spectrum of life on earth. In this way Santmire gives a decidedly modern flavor to St. Francis's idea of mother earth.[52]

Santmire's argument depends heavily on the concept of rights. Rereading the account of creation in Genesis, he concludes that "nature . . . has its own rights before man." He adds that "the Kingdom of God validates the rights of both nature and civilization." This becomes an important point for Santmire. He is not attempting to divest humankind of its rights or even of its status as a special part of creation. But he is calling on people to recognize that other creatures are part of their community. "*Nature and civilization,*" Santmire states emphatically, "*are fellow citizens of the Kingdom of God.*" He takes this to mean that "each can enjoy certain inalienable rights."[53]

The problem of how humans are to live in a world of omnipresent rights occupied a substantial portion of Santmire's 1970 book and related essays. He made no effort to repudiate "dominion." Humans would and should use nature, but they must do so with full recognition of nature's intrinsic worth as part of God's kingdom. In effect, this limits human freedom with regard to nature. To enhance the point, Santmire used a metaphor from political theory. Humanity is like a mayor or governor over the populace of the environment but its authority is always subordinate to that of the king, whose concern is for the just treatment of all members of the realm. So "man's dominion is limited by the rights of nature."[54]

While Santmire endorsed the doctrine of stewardship, he gave it an unprecedented twist. Nature's membership in the Kingdom of God meant that humans were responsible to God for conducting themselves in such a way that nature can enjoy its own inherent rights to existence and, in Santmire's language, "fulfillment." The idea was not to care for nature for humankind's sake but to "take care of nature for nature's sake." Santmire did not fully develop the precise way in which humans can claim their own rights to material resources without violating nature's rights, but he suggested that the ecological concepts of balance and sustainability point in the proper direction. He was sure that a reduced level of affluence and environmental impact—a level determined by "justifiable human needs"—would be required.[55]

The defense of nature was also part of Santmire's concept of stewardship. He saw a Christian basis for preserving the wilderness. "One should so order one's life," he recommended, "that the whole of nature, including *wild* nature, can flourish. This means not only to respect nature's rights but to *act to preserve and to defend* those rights." People, then, have a God-directed "personal and social responsibility" for the welfare of every living thing. (Santmire did not extend his ethics to nonliving matter. Rocks apparently remained in the I-It category. "Nature," to Santmire, seems to mean nonhuman life.) Ethics, acting as a restraint, would allow "dominion without exploitation." The ecologists of Santmire's generation believed that this sort of environmental ethic stemmed from the membership of people in and their dependency on the natural community. Theologians of Santmire's persuasion, however, felt the important point was not that humans are part of nature but that both humans and nature are part of the Kingdom of God.[56]

The latest contribution of Santmire to environmental theology is *The Travail of Nature* (1985), a detailed history and analysis of the basic documents of the Christian tradition that bear on the meaning of nature. Santmire argues that an "ecological motif" exists in traditional Christianity which describes "a system of interrelationships between God, humanity, and nature." Nature is not merely irrelevant scenery against which the central drama of the human-God relationship is played out, but is a full participant in the basic Christian process of creation and redemption. *The Travail of Nature* thus stands as historical support for the vision of people and nature together as citizens in the Kingdom of God that Santmire broached fifteen years earlier.[57]

The "process" philosophy of Alfred North Whitehead and that of the French Catholic paleontologist-priest Pierre Teilhard de Chardin[58] stimulated several modern American theologians to investigate the consequences for nature of an expanded morality. Neither

Whitehead nor Teilhard specifically discussed environmental ethics or the rights of nature. Teilhard's thought is at best ambiguous on these matters; nature appears to have value for him primarily as a springboard for the emergence, through the evolution of consciousness, of the "Omega Point" of supreme human development. But both thinkers lay the philosophical groundwork for the intrinsic value of all matter that others would use to construct an environmental ethic. Charles Hartshorne, a student of Whitehead, and Hartshorne's student, Daniel Day Williams, pioneered this development. Conrad Bonifazi, an English-born professor at the Pacific School of Religion, extended it with the idea that "things" possessed an "inwardness" or intrinsic value that legitimized their being loved for their own sake. Borrowing Aldo Leopold's phrase, Bonifazi urged people to develop an "ecological conscience" as well as a social one.[59]

Of the modern Whiteheadians, John B. Cobb, Jr., made the greatest contribution to environmental theology. A professor at the School of Theology in Claremont, California, and a student of both Hartshorne and Williams, Cobb built upon Whitehead's notion that the universe is not composed of inert matter but is instead a continuous series of events or interactions; in other words, a process. Cobb understood Whitehead to mean that all things exist only in relation to their environment. Their very essence is determined by "taking account of" their surroundings, and this characteristic of all matter gives it "reality, value, and kinship." It followed, for Cobb, that everything from humans through the various forms of non-human life, right down to cells, atoms, and subatomic particles, had a purpose, a capability of being fulfilled or being denied that opportunity. God desires fulfillment as part of the requirement for divine perfection. Extrapolating from Whitehead's belief that all matter had significance for the universe, Cobb concluded that it also had intrinsic value in the eyes of God. In Cobb's view this fact invested the "subhuman world" with "rights" that humans, as the most intelligent form of life on earth, ought to respect.[60]

Cobb's conviction that human beings, alone among life-forms, are capable of love underlay his concept of ethical responsibility. People are partners with God in caring for nature. Cobb hastened to point out that in this sense "caring" had nothing to do with stewardship. He rejected enlightened self-interest and instrumental theories of value as a basis for ethics. As Cobb explained, "man will in fact care for the subhuman world sufficiently to heal it and to adjust himself to its needs only if he views it as having some claim upon him, some intrinsic right to exist and prosper." The basis of this claim, Cobb explained, is an extension of self-transcendent Christian love. Whitehead had made it possible to think of nature as having intrinsic value and being an appropriate object of love; Cobb demonstrated the potential of integrating Whitehead and traditional Christianity to build an environmental ethic.[61]

John Cobb wrote *Is It Too Late?* (1972) in the midst of what he called "the ecological crisis." His purpose, as a Christian, was to explore the role his faith might play in alleviating the "threat of doom" brought on by chronic environmental abuse. His first realization was that "the major past forms of Christianity are inadequate to our needs and must be superceded." But he also realized that "it is fruitless to seek the vision we need in primitive or Oriental religions." Instead Cobb proposed a "new Christianity" based on the expansion of morality to include recognition of the rights of nature. The modern Christian environmentalist, Cobb argued, should understand the significance to God of everything and every process in the universe. This is why it was possible to think of a "theology of ecology."[62]

At the conclusion of *Is It Too Late?* Cobb outlined his new vision. It renounced dualism in all its forms but still retained the conception, so necessary to Christianity, of human beings as the "apex and summation of nature." Cobb believed this self-image could coexist with environmental ethics because the fact that "man is of vastly greater worth than any other creature does not reduce the value of the others to nothing." Human life was sacred but only in the context of God's sacred world. Turning from theology to ecology to make the same point, Cobb employed Leopoldian terms to state that "the new Christianity must substitute a vision of a healthy biotic pyramid with man at its apex for the absoluteness of man." On these bases Cobb could finally contend that a Christian commitment to God necessarily involved a responsibility to cherish and promote life in all its forms. St. Francis and Albert Schweitzer, Cobb acknowledged, had pointed the way toward this environmentally sensitive Christianity while ecologists provided recent scientific grounding.[63]

In subsequent writings Cobb set forth the thesis that the "habitats" or "ecosystems" that sustain life also belong in the ethical circle.[64] In 1978, he stated that animals "have the right to have the value of their existence and happiness weighed seriously in the balance. They have the right not to be exploited casually for trivial human purposes."[65] Here was an emphasis on life and "happiness," and in 1981 Cobb added liberty. His book *The Liberation of Life,* co-authored with Australian process philosopher Charles Birch, took the widest possible view of ethical applicability. Cobb argued that all matter, from subatomic particles to human beings, had a "potential for richness of experience" that humans should respect. "If there is intrinsic value anywhere," he declared, "there is intrinsic value everywhere." Humans, obviously, had a lot of company in the ethical circle. Cobb's call for a "religion of life," and his willingness to extend his moral vision down to "cells" and up to "biospheres" and "ecosystems," marks a milestone in the greening of both Christianity and natural-rights liberalism.[66]

In view of the meager previous record, the early 1970s witnessed an impressively large religious contribution to the development and popularization of environmental ethics. Of course this was a time of unprecedented American concern in general for environment and ecology but the theologians, still smarting under Lynn White's critical lashes, were especially energetic. A whole generation of religious thinkers joined Richard Baer, Paul Santmire, and John Cobb in advancing the new moral vision. *Christian Century* devoted its entire October 7, 1970, issue to "The Environmental Crisis." *Time* magazine covered the Lynn White controversy on February 2, 1970, while *The New York Times* featured an essay on "The Link between

Faith and Ecology" in its January 4 issue. *The Nation* published the plea of a leading Episcopalian to expand the "circle of fellowship" to include other creatures and the earth. Scott I. Paradise went on to suggest that the growing appeal of an environmental ethic in the United States carried with it the "seeds of revolution."[67] Journals such as *Zygon* featured articles contending that "traditional theological or moral ideas must be extended to include not only man and society but nature itself." From this perspective "man's violence toward his surroundings is just as sinful as his violence toward his fellows."[68] Allan R. Brockway defined a theology of the natural world as one that "declares that the non-human world has just as much right to its internal integrity as does the human world, that human beings transgress their divine authority when they destroy or fundamentally alter the rocks, the trees, the air, the water, the soil, the animals—just as they do when they murder other human beings."[69] It would be hard to imagine a more direct application of natural-rights ideology to environmental relations.

While few ecotheologians went to such radical lengths as Brockway, concern was undeniably growing for the application of ethics to environmental problems. Conferences of clergymen resulted in publications such as *Ecology: Crisis and New Vision* (edited in 1971 by Richard Sherrell) and *This Little Planet* (1970, edited by Michael Hamilton). Francis A. Schaeffer wrote *Pollution and the Death of Man: The Christian View of Ecology* (1970) and Paul Folsom contributed *And Thou Shalt Die in a Polluted Land* (1971). Christopher Derrick's *The Delicate Creation: Towards a Theology of the Environment* (1972) contained an introduction by a prominent cardinal and by René Dubos. Ian Barbour edited two anthologies for college and university audiences, *Earth Might Be Fair* (1972) and *Western Man and Environmental Ethics* (1973). The latter exposed a large audience to the controversy engendered by Lynn White. The panicky mood of environmentalism at this time was reflected in books like Frederick Elder's *Crisis in Eden* (1970) and Henlee H. Barnette's *The Church and the Ecological Crisis* (1972). A student in Harvard's Divinity School when he wrote his book, Elder called for America's churches to emerge from "ethical parochialism" and, following the teachings of Aldo Leopold and Albert Schweitzer, to lead the nation "back from the brink of ecological disaster." As Elder understood it, this was nothing new; saving the world from disaster had always been the mission of religious institutions. But Christian churches would have to abandon their "exclusionist" position and recognize that humankind was part of nature as nature was part of God. Barnette argued that "the zone of ethics ... must be redefined to include man ... in his relation to all creatures and things, the organic and the inorganic."[70]

Eric C. Rust is an example of an older scholar of Judeo-Christian thought who became radicalized by the environmental movement and redirected his writing in the 1970s to advance environmental ethics. His *Man and Nature in Biblical Thought* (1953) had no prescriptive import. But twenty years later Rust contended that nature must be included, along with humankind, in the process of redemption and that it was humankind's responsibility to advance this end by right treatment of the environment. People were "co-workers with God in the redemption of nature." Rust concluded a 1971 essay in environmental theology with the observation that just as the churches had become involved in racial issues, they must now become "the conscience of the community" in ecological matters. He even added a section on "Christian Ecotactics."[71]

Not only did American religion become environmentally aware in the 1960s and 1970s, but environmentalism itself acquired some of the characteristics of a religion. The new environmentalists displayed an intensity of commitment and a tendency to conceptualize issues in terms of right and wrong. They could be said to subscribe to a "gospel of ecology."[72] Greenpeace, for example, regarded "ecology as religion."[73] The term "ecotheology" made the same point, and Henryk Skolimowski, for one, considered it "a religion for our times."[74] Peter Borrelli felt that "a sense of the sacred in nature" must be the "driving force … of environmentalism."[75] The National Council of Churches sponsored an "eco-justice agenda," regarding it as expressive of "a major new insight of our time."[76] John Carmody's *Ecology and Religion* (1983) argued that "every creature" is a "presence of God" and that therefore "nature has an independent right to exist, live and flourish." Carmody's ecological religion led him to call on Christians to "love nature like a neighbor or relative."[77] Jesus had once urged his followers to love their human neighbor as they loved themselves; by the 1980s some Christians had come to understand the neighborhood as the ecosystem.

A number of environmentally conscious modern Christians chose to focus their attention on farmland and farming. Viewing the former as sacred and the latter as holy work ("Farming for the Lord," one Minnesotan put it),[78] they combed Scripture for passages supporting stewardship. Wendell Berry's *The Unsettling of America* (1977) and *The Gift of Good Land* (1981) were the most visible statements. Berry summarized his thesis for the Sierra Club's 300,000 members: "If 'the earth is the Lord's' and we are His stewards, then obviously some livelihoods are 'right' and some are not." Berry doubted, for instance, that there could be a Christian strip mine or a Christian atomic bomb.[79] In the same tradition was John Hart's *The Spirit of the Earth: A Theology of the Land* (1984). Hart, a Catholic, described the awakening of the leaders of his faith to land-use problems and reforms. He detailed the preparation of two manifestos: *This Land Is Home to Me* (signed by twenty-five Appalachian bishops in 1975) and *Strangers and Guests* (signed by seventy-three bishops from Midwestern states in 1980). Their message was, by now, a familiar one: The land is God's and people have a sacred trust to be responsible custodians.[80] Berry, Hart, and others inspired endeavors such as the Land Stewardship Project based in St. Paul, Minnesota. Organized in 1983, its purpose is "to develop and encourage a public dialogue on a sustainable land ethic in the Midwest."[81]

A large part of the Christian stewardship argument was anthropocentric in character: take care of the earth (meaning, generally, productive soil) or you will either perish or be punished by an angry God. Guilt figured as a mainstay of the appeal. But latent in modern stewardship was the idea that because the environment was God's, not man's, it was morally wrong to abuse it regardless of the consequences for humanity. Some clergymen made this recognition of intrinsic value and the rights of nature their principal concern. Reverend Dennis G. Kuby's Berkeley-based Ministry of Ecology, for instance, functioned from 1973 to 1981 on a platform that emphasized "the interconnectedness inherent in the universe." Kuby's associates signed a pledge committing them "to moral accountability to . . . the biotic community."[82]

The Eleventh Commandment Fellowship picked up Walter Lowdermilk's earlier concept and the essence of Kuby's crusade in 1984. The additional commandment read: "The earth is the Lord's and the fullness thereof; thou shalt not despoil the earth nor destroy the life thereon." Reverend Vincent Rossi, who inspired the group, reminded it to transcend self-interested stewardship. "The *deep* ecological task is . . . to awaken in human souls the sharpest possible awareness that belief in the existence of God absolutely demands the deepest respect and reverence for the rights of the Earth."[83] The same message colored the concluding pages of *Earthkeeping: Christian Stewardship of Natural Resources,* which Loren Wilkinson edited in 1980 for Calvin College's Center for Christian Scholarship. Wilkinson pointed out that if "justice is done within a recognized community," then the ecological sciences have given people reason to think about new communities and new definitions of equity. It followed that "a society which meets all the subsistence and development needs of its people but which destroys or tortures all living things under its control is not a just society." Wilkinson was quick to add that he was not implying that "the needs of a tree, a wolf, or a cow are to be equated with the needs of a human," but "neither are they to be ignored." The needed balance seemed to lie in an appropriate level of human consumption that filled basic human needs while still respecting the rights of nonhumans to habitat and sustenance.

Finally, *Earthkeeping* turned to the question of why people should endeavor to implement environmental justice and concluded, "We are commanded by God to do so." We should seek justice for all the earth's creatures because "it is a working-out of our calling to be stewards. It is the command of the King—an obligation and a challenge placed on all Christians."[84]

While agriculture preoccupied Christian stewards, concern for the religious significance of wilder landscapes opened another ethical door. The idea that a place or particular environment was sacred had clear significance for traditional Native American beliefs. The American Transcendentalists, especially John Muir, understood wilderness appreciation as a religious act. But in the 1960s and 1970s increasing numbers of Americans began to think that wildernesses in general—and certain national parks in particular—were sacred spaces. People of this persuasion were inclined to believe that ethics should be extended to regulate action toward nature. A few even went so far as to suggest that freedom of religion connoted the right to worship where as well as how one chose. If wilderness was one's church, the argument ran, why not defend it on ethical grounds?[85]

Although less important in American thought than the reinterpretation of the Judeo-Christian tradition, another source of the greening of religion has been recent interest in the ethical implications of several Asian religions. Some Americans simply used non-Christian beliefs to inspire reassessment of their own faiths. Others, especially younger contributors to the countercultural energies of the 1960s, gladly exchanged discredited Christianity for Asian religions such as Taoism, Jainism, Shinto, Buddhism—particularly the Japanese variety known as Zen—and Hinduism. At the core of these faiths was a rejection of the dualism and anthropocentrism that so thoroughly colored traditional Christianity. Eastern religions assumed the ultimate oneness of all of nature's components. By advocating the submersion of the human self in a larger organic whole they cleared the intellectual way for environmental ethics. Ancient Eastern ideas closely paralleled the new assumptions of ecology. In both systems the biological and ethical gulf between humans and nature disappeared. "The ten thousand things," as Taoists phrased it, "are one with me."[86] The process of enlightenment (the Zen notion of *satori*, for example) included this perception as one of its major characteristics. Nature, as a consequence, could not be objectified, desacralized, or, in 1960s jargon, "used." These were precisely the grounds on which Lynn White and the others faulted Christianity.

Eastern religion and philosophy were notably devoid of the concept of individual rights which underlay much of environmental ethics in the West. The Oriental mind tended to regard nature as imbued with divinity rather than as something possessing rights. One root of the idea of rights in non-Asian cultures was the Judeo-Christian notion that all humans (but only humans) were made in the image of God;[87] therefore every human was sacred, possessed of a redeemable soul, and intrinsically valuable. The natural-rights philosophy of John Locke and Thomas Jefferson secularized this concept. In the East, on the other hand, intrinsic value extended to the limits of the universe. All beings and things, animate and inanimate, were thought to be permeated with divine power or spirit such as the Tao or, in Shinto, *kami*. Every one of Taoism's ten thousand things—that is, everything in nature—had a purpose, a potential, a significance for the universe. Mahayana Buddhists speak of the *dharma*, or Buddha-nature, of every object. The Eightfold Path of Buddhism uses this concept as a basis for outlining appropriate human conduct toward all creatures and things. It centers on the doctrine of harmlessness or *ahimsa* which the Jains carried to extremes in their desire to avoid the destruction of any life. In sharp contrast, the Ten Commandments, which anchor Western morality, concern themselves exclusively with human-to-God and human-to-human relationships. The notion of "neighbor" in Judeo-Christianity begins and ends with people. In the Asian doctrines, this circle of community knows no bounds.[88]

American interest in Asian religions began with Transcendentalists such as Henry David Thoreau, who read as widely as Harvard's English-language holdings permitted. According to Rick Fields's useful study of the history of Buddhism in America, "the Concordians were at odds with their age, and they looked to the Orientals as an example of what their own best lives might be."[89] The same analysis could be made of the dissident Americans of the 1960s and 1970s, with whom much of the new environmentalism originated. Both groups held ethical ideals concerning human-nature relationships that their contemporaries, in general, did not share. John Muir and Edward Evans might also be cited as Americans whose critical stance toward the ethics of their society led them to profess sincere if untutored Buddhist philosophy. Albert Schweitzer's all-embracing ethics derived in part from his doctoral studies of Asian religion.[90]

Much of the modern American attention to Oriental religion traces back to the remarkable Buddhist scholar and teacher Daisetz Teitaro Suzuki (1870–1966), who arrived in the United States from Japan in 1897. For a half century Suzuki wrote and taught the Zen philosophy to an increasingly receptive American audience.[91] Among those Suzuki inspired, the Englishman Alan W. Watts stood out for his influence on American thought about nature. Watts, a practicing Buddhist, moved to the United States in 1938. Twenty years before Lynn White's critique of Christian attitudes toward nature, Watts began explaining how Eastern and Western views differed in this regard. The most important of his twenty-five books, *The Way of Zen* (1957) and *Nature, Man and Woman* (1958), became paperback bestsellers and acquainted a generation with the idea that the world, humans included, was part of a "seamless unity."[92] Watts's readers came away with an unmistakable message: a fully developed moral sense must include everything in nature.

The rejection of Christianity in favor of Asian religions was a major component of the so-called beatnik mentality of the 1950s. Jack Kerouac's novels *On the Road* (1955) and *The Dharma Bums* (1959) popularized the rebellious new attitudes. Kerouac had a vision of a "great rucksack revolution" with "millions of young Americans" forsaking established churches and "going up to mountains to pray."[93] A leader in this new nature worship, and the inspiration for an important Kerouac character, was Gary Snyder. Born on the West Coast in 1930 and empathetic with wilderness, Snyder's chance encounter with D. T. Suzuki's books in 1951 and his friendship with both Kerouac and Watts led to ten years of study under a Zen master in Japan. Returning to the United States in the late 1960s, Snyder began to work out an ethic that combined Buddhist and Native American principles with American natural-rights ideology. The result was explicit personification of nature and its inclusion in a Lockean social contract. "Plants and animals are also people," Snyder wrote, and must be "given a place and a voice in the political discussions of the humans." He applauded Native American cultures that practiced "a kind of ultimate democracy." Nonhuman life was "represented," according to Snyder, through ritual, dance, and religion. It was essential, he noted, to rephrase the popular countercultural slogan, "Power to the people," as "Power to all the people." Snyder explained what he meant in 1970: "What we must . . . do . . . is incorporate the other people . . . the creeping people, and the standing people, and the flying people and the swimming people . . . into the councils of government." Aware of the American liberal tradition, Snyder carried this idea to its logical conclusion: If all these "people" were not represented, "they will revolt against us" just as the American colonists had revolted against a British government that refused them political equality. Snyder argued that an exploited environment would ultimately jeopardize human civilization just as colonial exploitation caused the disintegration of Great Britain's eighteenth-century empire. In Snyder's opinion an abused ecosystem was already submitting "nonnegotiable demands about our stay on earth." As a corrective he called for widening the moral community and incorporating "the rest of life in our democratic society."[94]

Snyder explicitly applied natural-rights liberalism to the human relationship with nature. He identified nature as an oppressed minority whose rights civilization violated. Snyder declared that as a poet and a Buddhist, he saw his role as that of spokesman "for a realm that is not usually represented either in intellectual chambers or in the chambers of government." His constituency would be "the wilderness," by which Snyder meant all nonhuman creatures and things.[95] Snyder came to this extrapolation of the American democratic tradition only after a long intellectual detour to the Orient. But he rooted his defense of nature in the bedrock of the American political tradition. Americans who were already aware of environmental problems were likely to be impressed by Snyder's logic. And in fact his statements became part of a collection, *Turtle Island,* that won the Pulitzer Prize for poetry in 1975. Just as Muir had been more popular than Thoreau, Gary Snyder received a degree of public acclaim notable for its absence three decades before when Aldo Leopold broached the idea of biotic rights in *A Sand County Almanac.* The times, as Bob Dylan told a generation, were changing, and environmental ethics was one beneficiary.

After winning the Pulitzer Prize, Snyder became a celebrated lecturer and a popular subject for interviews. In a 1976 interview he returned to the idea of being a spokesman for the rights of nature. Poets, Snyder thought, were uniquely positioned to "hear voices from trees." Poets could be the vehicles of expression that Christopher Stone was seeking in 1972 when he proposed that trees be given legal rights. Snyder was deeply interested in where this idea of "the rights of things, the potentiality of salvation of things" might lead. "Push it a generation or two in[to] the future," he felt, and you might produce people who "actually feel on a gut level that non-human nature has rights."[96] As a Buddhist, Snyder already held that conviction; as a poet he felt himself responsible for communicating the ideal to others.

Americans increasingly found Oriental religions a guide to improving human relationships to the environment. The bellwether periodical *Christian Century* began publishing articles on Zen as an alternative to Western attitudes.[97] In 1972 it printed an essay entitled "Ecology, Zen, and Western Religious Thought." The author, Hwa Yol Jung, disagreed with Lynn White and Frederick Elder, among others, in their feeling that Americans in search of environmental responsibility could not benefit from Eastern faiths and should, instead, revise Christianity. Zen Buddhism, Jung pointed out, could show any culture how to replace utilitarianism with reverence and respect. According to Jung, the most enlightened American environmentalists, such as Aldo Leopold, were articulating Zen principles in their affirmation of "the intrinsic value of land . . . and the right of every creature to live."[98] Robert Aitken, who learned about Zen Buddhism as a Japanese prisoner of war and later established a notable Zen center in Hawaii, wrote that "there is no barrier between human and non-human." All beings, even the grasses, were "in the process of enlightenment." Aitken took seriously "the right to life of stones and clouds." In his view environmental ethics must begin with "the cultivation of intimacy with all things." By "forgetting the self" the Buddhist made his or her mind open to close communal relations with everything in the universe.[99] Rajagopal Ryali contributed an examination of Hinduism's polytheism, mysticism, and transmigration of souls (reincarnation) as a basis of reverence for nature.[100] These arguments for looking to the East were persuasive, but some American theologians, notably Thomas Merton and John Cobb, attempted to remain firm in their Christian faith and still integrate Oriental wisdom. The most recent approach eschews "blaming" Christianity in favor of "constructive borrowing to the benefit of both East and West."[101]

On the more popular level, large numbers of American readers used Fritjof Capra's *The Tao of Physics* (1974) and *The Turning Point* (1980) as a start toward the development of alternatives to the Western world's mechanistic view of matter and the universe, a view traditionally hostile to environmental ethics. Capra was encouraged by the rise of ecology, which he took to be the Western equivalent of Taoism's organic sense of unity. Dolores La Chapelle provided guides to those who would build a sense of brotherhood and sisterhood with nature upon a rediscovery of religiously oriented celebrations and rituals.[102] The Universal Pantheist Society attracted people convinced that environmental ethics depended upon "a new recognition of the sacredness of the natural world." In a sense this neopantheism was a response to the criticism Lynn White leveled at Judeo-Christianity for its desacralization of nature.[103] On the institutional level, Zen Buddhism continued to grow as an American religion, particularly on the West Coast where the Zen Centers of Los Angeles and San Francisco instructed growing numbers in alternatives to Christianity's conception of nature.[104]

A widely distributed 1960s "ecology" poster featured a Native American contemplating the degraded condition of the continent after only a few centuries of white occupation. A single tear trickled down the man's cheek. The image expressed the new environmentalists' understanding that the first occupants of North America were better custodians of the ecosystem than the subsequent tenants. Like the Oriental varieties, Indian religions avoided the dualism that narrowed traditional Christian morality. Most white American environmentalists believed that nature had an important place in the Indians' moral community. This idea was subject to distortion—the first Americans were not "ecological saints"—but there is little doubt that they accepted more restraints in their relationship to their environment than did the people who displaced them.[105]

Roderick Nash

Central to most Indian religions and ethical systems was the idea that humans and other forms of life constituted a single society.[106] Indians regarded bears, for example, as the bear *people*. Plants were also people. Salmon constituted a nation comparable in stature and rights to human nations. A complex of rituals and ceremonies reinforced the familial bonds between Indians and their environment. Skins were, in effect, the outer coverings of a common being. Chief Seattle of the Suquamish tribe utilized these ideas in an 1853 oration. The version most familiar to environmentalists of the 1960s and 1970s, and probably modernized in meaning, contained the idea that "the rocky crests, the juices in the meadows, the body heat of the pony, and man—all belong to the same family." The demarcation between the animate and inanimate was not important to Seattle. "Every part of the earth is sacred to my people," he continued. "Rivers are our brothers," he explained; the sky was a sibling and the earth, almost universally in these cultures, a mother. "All things are connected," the chief concluded, "like the blood which unites one family."[107] Luther Standing Bear of the Lakotas or Sioux spoke in 1933, near the end of his life, of "a great unifying life force that flowed in and through all things." Taoists and Buddhists would have understood Standing Bear's belief that "all things were kindred and brought together by the same Great Mystery."[108]

It followed that restraints derived from ethics applied to every aspect of the human-environment relationship. Respect and courtesy were mandatory in all interactions with nature. Even when Indians took another life to sustain their own, it was done ritually with reverence and gratitude. Traditional tribal culture professed incredulity at the white tendency to objectify, desacralize, and exploit nature. The idea of owning the land was especially unthinkable. Buying and selling a piece of the earth was as foreign to most Indian cultures as marketing a brother or mother. This point of view may well have contributed to making Native Americans such easy targets for white treaty-makers. The natives never understood how a mark on a paper and the exchange of a few beads and tobacco could convert land to property. They balked at the notion of exchanging habitat for money. Ownership of nature appeared in their eyes morally wrong, a form of slavery. Standing Bear made this connection explicit with regard to domesticating and keeping animals. It was better to hunt wild creatures, he wrote, because herding "enslaved the animal" and deprived it of its basic rights: "the right to live, the right to multiply, the right to freedom."[109] This remarkable expression in 1933 deserves inclusion with Aldo Leopold's statement of a "conservation ethic" of the same year among the milestones in the American extension of natural-rights liberalism to include the rights of nature.

Whites' rediscovery of Native American religious and ethical beliefs became a characteristic of modern environmentalism. Seeking to disparage technological civilization. Theodore Roszak's widely read *The Making of a Counter Culture* (1969) publicized the remarks of a Wintu Indian woman who believed that not only trees but even rocks pleaded for respect. The white exploiters paid no attention and so "the spirit of the land hates them." Roszak called for a revitalization of the Native Americans' "shamanistic world view" that would guide alienated American society back to a moral relationship with sacred nature.[110] Secretary of the Interior Stewart Udall's history of American conservation characterized Native Americans as the first American ecologists. Understanding interdependency, they proclaimed an ethic of respect for nature.[111] By the time Udall wrote, Native Americans were becoming the most insightful publicists of their own moral philosophy. Along with Seattle and Standing Bear, Black Elk, Lame Deer, and Hyemeyohsts Storm published widely read accounts which left little doubt that Native Americans' ethical community included nature.[112] N. Scott Momaday, a Kiowa whose *House Made of Dawn* (1968) won a Pulitzer Prize, wrote "An American Land Ethic" in 1970. His point was that the "deep ethical regard for the land" of his ancestors needed to be resurrected and disseminated. Americans had to recover the feeling of love of the earth and the ethics attendant upon that emotional relationship. The Sierra Club featured the essay in a book about environmental protest and reform.[113] Vine Deloria, Jr., a Sioux, became the best-known Native American author of the 1970s with *Custer Died for Your Sins* (1969), *We Talk, You Listen* (1970), and *God Is Red* (1973). A vocal champion of Indian as well as environmental rights, Deloria predicted in 1971 that Indian ideas "are going to cut the country's whole value system to shreds."[114] In an unpublished 1974 essay he presented "the idea of legal rights of non-human nature" as an example. Adoption of this concept would, in Deloria's opinion, necessitate a radical and total change in the white American worldview. But, he explained, "the concept is self-apparent in the Indian scheme of things." It fit perfectly into the Indian sense of brotherhood with everything in the universe.[115]

In the 1960s American churches became concerned with the relevance of their message for social problems. Civil rights, the war in Vietnam, poverty, and women's liberation claimed a major share of clerical attention. The concern of religion for the rights of nonhuman life and of the earth in the 1970s and 1980s continued and extended this pattern. The reinterpretation of the Christian tradition and a simultaneous renaissance of interest in Oriental and Native faiths acquainted many Americans with environmental ethics. Theologians and clergymen became primary architects and publicists of the new idea that human ethical obligations must include nature.

To be sure, some highly placed religious leaders dissented. Even dedicated ecotheologians had serious blind spots, not altogether surprising in a field as new and radical as environmental ethics. For instance, Harold K. Schilling, the distinguished Pennsylvania State University scholar, could title an essay "The Whole Earth Is the Lord's: Toward a Holistic Ethic" and conclude it with the statement that mosquitoes, ticks, cockroaches, "rats that attack babies in their cribs" and "myriads of other kinds of vermin" are without useful purpose and are, in fact, "demonic." In Schilling's view there was "nothing good or sacred about them."[116] Evidently not quite the whole earth was the Lord's, and ethics was somewhat less than holistic.

In Los Angeles in 1973 Catholic Archbishop Robert Dwyer characterized "worship of the Environment" and "the new cult of Nature Unspoiled" as "anti-human." Follow the environmental theologians and "dogmatic Ecology," he warned, and humanity could succeed in self-extinction. Wilderness conditions would surely return to New York City and, at least in the archbishop's aroused imagination, mastodons would roam the ruins of Chicago. Better, he suggested, to maintain the view of "Nature as Enemy, the alien force, to be conquered and broken to man's will."[117] Richard Neuhaus contended that believers in the rights of nature were actually advocating a pagan nature-worshipping cult aimed at diminishing human rights. The environmental movement, according to Neuhaus, was an effort to distract radicalism from its proper concern—poor and oppressed people.[118] And it was still possible in 1983 to find occasional expressions such as one addressed to the newspaper column "Dear Abby." In the course of defending the trapping of fur-bearing animals for coats, the writer declared that "the Bible gave man dominance over animals, birds and fish. They are God's gifts to man—created for us to use."[119]

But by the 1980s such opinions sounded increasingly old-fashioned. From the seminaries to neighborhood churches, increasing numbers took it for granted that the human-nature relationship could not be excluded from the ethics of religious individuals. "Ecotheology" had not only become a new word but a compelling world view.

NOTES

1. Aldo Leopold, *A Sand County Almanac* (New York, 1949), 209–210; Charles A. Reich, *The Greening of America* (New York, 1970).

2. Harold W. Wood, Jr., "Modern Pantheism as an Approach to Environmental Ethics," *Environmental Ethics* 7 (Summer 1985), 151.

3. Lynn White, Jr., "The Historical Roots of Our Ecologic Crisis," *Science* 155 (March 10, 1967), 1203–1207. White anticipated his thesis twenty years earlier in "Natural Science and Naturalistic Art in the Middle Ages," *American Historical Review* 52 (April 1947), 421–435. Ian McHarg's well-known *Design with Nature* (Garden City, N.J., 1969), 24–26, 44, contained an apparently independent analysis of Christianity that paralleled White's. Morris Berman, *The Reenchantment of the World* (Ithaca, N.Y., 1981) is one of several recent elaborations of White's insights.

White's 1967 essay was initially a lecture and admittedly a suggestive rather than definitive study. It touched off a storm of controversy in the late 1960s which must be understood as a function of so-called countercultural disenchantment with established institutions as well as misgivings in the Christian community about its own contributions to contemporary social and environmental problems. Eugene C. Hargrove has recently called on theologians to move "beyond the Lynn White debate" and edited a collection of papers to that end: Eugene C. Hargrove, ed., *Religion and Environmental Crisis* (Athens, Ga., 1986).

Edward P. Evans was the first American writer to anticipate White's thesis (see above, pp. 50ff.). In the nineteenth century Arthur Schopenhauer recognized the "unnatural distinction" Christianity made between humankind and animals. "Christianity," he wrote, "contains in fact a great and essential imperfection in limiting its precepts to man, and in refusing rights to the entire animal world." Arthur Schopenhauer, *Religion: A Dialogue and Other Essays,* 2d ed. (London, 1890), 112.

4. White, "Historical Roots," 1205.

5. Genesis 1:27–28 as translated in *The Holy Bible: Revised Standard Edition,* Thomas Nelson and Sons edition (New York, 1953), 2.

6. Genesis 9:2–3, Ibid., 8.

7. White, "Historical Roots," 1207. For a rebuttal to White, contending that orthodox Christianity is ecologically responsible, see Vincent Rossi, "Church and Ecology: Ecological Reformation or Patristic Renewal?" *The Eleventh Commandment Newsletter* 4 (1986), 4–5.

8. White, "Historical Roots," 1206.

9. Lynn White, Jr., "Continuing the Conversation," in Ian G. Barbour, ed., *Western Man and Environmental Ethics* (Reading, Mass., 1973), 61.

10. W. Lee Humphreys, "Pitfalls and Promises of Biblical Texts as a Basis for a Theology of Nature," in Glenn C. Stone, ed., *A New Ethic for a New Earth,* Faith-Man-Nature Papers, no. 2 (Andover, Conn., 1971), 100–101. Humphreys concludes that "man of this century will not find a ready-made theology of nature in the Bible; he must create and recreate his own" (p. 115). For discussions that differ from White on the meaning of Genesis 1:28 see James Barr, "Man and Nature: The Ecological Controversy and the Old Testament," in David Spring and Eileen Spring, eds., *Ecology and Religion in History* (New York, 1959) and Thomas S. Deer, "Religious Responsibility for the Environmental Crisis: An Argument Run Amok," *Worldview* 18 (Jan. 1975), 30–45.

11. For details on the Christian view of nature, historically conceived, see Keith Thomas, *Man and the Natural World: A History of the Modern Sensibility* (New York, 1983), 17ff.; John Passmore, *Man's Responsibility for Nature: Ecological Problems and Western Traditions* (New York, 1974); and Clarence Glacken, *Traces on the Rhodian Shore: Nature and Culture in Western Thought from Ancient Times to the End of the Eighteenth Century* (Berkeley, Cal., 1967), especially ch. 4. H. Paul Santmire's *The Travail of Nature: The Ambiguous Ecological Promise of Christian Theology* (Philadelphia, 1985) is a recent, comprehensive study of the meaning of nature in Christian thought. See also Robin Attfield, "Christian Attitudes to Nature," *Journal of the History of Ideas* 44 (July–Sept. 1983), 369–386, and George H. Williams, "Christian Attitudes toward Nature," *Christian Scholars Review* 2 (Fall 1971 and Winter 1972), 33–35, and 112–126. Attfield's "Western Traditions and Environmental Ethics," in Robert Elliot and Arran Gare, eds., *Environmental Philosophy* (University Park, Pa., 1983), 201–228, is also useful, as is Robert S. Brumbaugh, "Of Man, Animals and Morals: A Brief History," in Richard Knowles Morris and Michael W. Fox, eds., *On the Fifth Day: Animal Rights and Human Ethics* (Washington, D.C., 1978), 6–25. Jewish attitudes toward nature, traditional and contemporary, are studied in Jonathan Helfand, "The Earth Is the Lord's: Judaism and Environmental Ethics," in Hargrove, ed., *Religion and Environmental Crisis,* 38–52; David Ehrenfeld and Joan Ehrenfeld, "Some Thoughts on Nature and Judaism," *Environmental Ethics* 7 (Spring 1985), 93–95; and Albert Vorspan, "The Crisis of Ecology: Judaism and the Environment," in *Jewish Values and Social Crisis* (New York, 1970).

12. Martin Buber, *I and Thou,* Walter Kaufmann, trans. (New York, 1970). Robert E. Wood's *Martin Buber's Ontology: An Analysis of I and Thou* (Evanston, Ill., 1969) is a helpful comment.

13. Among the many titles concerning the meaning of the Bible for human-nature relations, the following proved particularly useful: Martin LaBar, "A Biblical Perspective on Nonhuman Organisms: Values, Moral Considerability, and Moral Agency," in Hargrove, ed., *Religion and Environmental Crisis,* 76–93; Richard H. Hiers, "Ecology, Biblical Theology, and Methodology: Biblical Perspectives on the Environment," *Zygon* 19 (March 1984), 43–59; Susan Power Bratton, "Christian Ecotheology and the Old Testament," *Environmental Ethics* 6 (Fall 1984), 195–209; Gerhard Hasel, *Old Testament Theology: Basic Issues in the Current Debate* (Grand Rapids, Mich., 1972); Gordon D. Kaufman, "A Problem for Theology: The Concept of Nature," *Harvard Theological Review* 65 (1972), 337–366; John Black, *The Dominion of Man: The Search for Ecological Responsibility* (Edinburgh, 1970),

chs. 2–4; Walter Eichrodt, *Theology of the Old Testament* (Philadelphia, 1967); C. F. D. Moule, *Man and Nature in the New Testament* (Philadelphia, 1964); Gerhard von Rad, *Old Testament Theology* (New York, 1962); and Eric C. Rust, *Nature and Man in Biblical Thought* (London, 1953).

Mircea Eliade's *The Sacred and the Profane* (New York, 1959) remains an important investigation of what Eliade calls the "secularization of nature," while Berman, *The Reenchantment of the World* and Sam Keen, *Apology for Wonder* (New York, 1969) are more recent examinations of the same subject. D. H. Lawrence wrote a delightful essay on the implications of the end of animism: "Pan in America," in Edward D. McDonald, ed., *Phoenix: The Posthumous Papers of D. H. Lawrence* (New York, 1936), 22–31. According to Lawrence, the old Greek god of the mountain wilderness, called Pan, became the Christians' devil, complete with cloven hoofs and tail. There can be no more graphic evidence of Christians' attitude toward pantheism.

14. White, "Historical Roots," 1205.

15. Roderick Nash, *Wilderness and the American Mind* (New Haven, Conn., 1982), 13ff. 23ff.; George H. Williams, *Wilderness and Paradise in Christian Thought* (New York, 1962).

16. As quoted in Santmire, *Travail of Nature*, 3.

17. White, "Continuing the Conversation," 57, 60; White, "Historical Roots," 1207.

18. White, "Continuing the Conversation," 63.

19. White, "Historical Roots," 1207; Marston Bates, *The Forest and the Sea* (New York, 1960), 197. For the present purposes the most important studies of St. Francis of Assisi are Santmire, *Travail of Nature*, 106ff., and Edward A. Armstrong, *Saint Francis: Nature Mystic—The Derivation and Significance of the Nature Stories in the Franciscan Legend* (Berkeley, Cal., 1973). See also Roy Gasnick, *The Francis Book: Eight Hundred Years with the Saint from Assisi* (New York, 1980); J. R. H. Moorman, *Saint Francis of Assisi* (London, 1963); and C. W. Hume, *The Status of Animals in Christian Religion* (London, 1957). The most recent biography is Julien Green, *God's Fool* (New York, 1985). With reference to the legend of the wolf of Gubbio, Green reports that in 1873 construction workers in that Italian village unearthed the skull of an enormous wolf.

20. Lynn White, Jr., "The Future of Compassion," *Ecumenical Review* 30 (April 1978), 106–108; White, "Continuing the Conversation," 62.

21. White, "Future of Compassion," 107, 109; White, "Continuing the Conversation," 63.

22. White, "Continuing the Conversation," 61; White, "Future of Compassion," 107.

23. White, "Future of Compassion," 109.

24. Genesis 2:15, *Holy Bible*, 2. For commentary on stewardship in Christian history see Black, *Dominion of Man*, ch. 4. Evidence of stewardship in Judaism is discussed in Jonathan Helfand, "Ecology and the Jewish Tradition," *Judaism* 20 (Summer 1971), 330–335, and in Robert Gordis, "Judaism and the Spoliation of Nature," *Keeping Posted* 16 (Dec. 1970), 5–9.

25. René Dubos, *A God Within* (New York, 1972), 45, 153–74; René Dubos, "A Theology of the Earth," in Barbour, ed., *Western Man and Environmental Ethics*, 47. The first statement of Dubos's stewardship idea occurs in *So Human an Animal* (New York, 1968), 7–8; further development of the thesis may be found in his *The Wooing of Earth* (New York, 1980).

26. Walter Lowdermilk appears to be the first American to employ this concept in an argument for environmental responsibility. Subsequent uses include Roderick Nash, "An '11th Commandment' Vital to Our Environment," *Santa Barbara News Press* (June 22, 1969), A16–17; René Dubos, "The Eleventh Commandment," *Keeping Posted* 16 (Dec. 1970), 3–4; and the *Eleventh Commandment Newsletter*, which began publication in San Francisco in 1984. In 1986 two environmental educators proposed a series of ten "ecological commandments," patterned after the Bible's, that were designed to facilitate construction of a Leopoldian sense of community that includes nature: Paul A. Yambert and Carolyn F. Donow, "Are We Ready for Ecological Commandments?" unpublished manuscript submitted to the *Journal of Environmental Education*, March 1986.

27. Walter C. Lowdermilk, "The Eleventh Commandment," *American Forests* 46 (Jan. 1940), 12–15; J. Douglas Helms, "Walter Lowdermilk's Journey: From Forester to Land Conservationist," *Environmental Review* 8 (Summer 1984), 133–145; personal communication from Inez M. Lowdermilk, July 5, 1969.

28. Joseph Sittler, "A Theology for Earth," *Christian Scholar* 37 (Sept. 1954), 367–374.

29. Joseph Sittler, "Called to Unity," *Ecumenical Review* 14 (Jan. 1962), 177–179.

30. Joseph Sittler, *The Care of the Earth and Other University Sermons* (Philadelphia, 1964), 89, 97–98. The essay can be found more readily in Franklin H. Littell, ed., *Sermons to Intellectuals* (New York, 1963).

31. Joseph Sittler, "Two Temptations—Two Corrections," *National Parks and Conservation Magazine* 45 (Dec. 1971), 21; Sittler, "Ecological Commitment as Theological Responsibility," *Zygon* 5 (June 1970), 178. Additional statements of Sittler's theology appear in his *Essays on Nature and Grace* (Philadelphia, 1972). For analysis see Nathan A. Scott, Jr., "The Poetry and Theology of Earth: Reflections on the Testimony of Joseph Sittler and Gerard Manley Hopkins," *Journal of Religion* 54 (April 1974), 102–120.

32. For example, *A Natural Theology for Our Time* (LaSalle, Ill., 1967) and *Beyond Humanism: Essays in the New Philosophy of Nature* (Chicago, 1937). See also John B. Cobb and Franklin I. Gamwell, eds., *Existence and Actuality: Conversations with Charles Hartshorne* (Chicago, 1984).

33. Representative works are *God's Grace and Man's Hope* (New York, 1949) and *The Spirit and the Forms of Love* (New York, 1968).

34. Richard A. Baer, Jr., "Land Misuse: A Theological Concern," *Christian Century* 83 (Oct. 12, 1966), 1240. See also Baer's "Conservation: An Arena for the Church's Action," *Christian Century* 86 (Jan. 8, 1969), 40–43.

35. Richard A. Baer, Jr., "Higher Education, the Church, and Environmental Values," *Natural Resources Journal* 17 (July 1977), 485. A similar statement is Baer's "Ecology, Religion, and the American Dream," *American Ecclesiastical Review* 165 (Sept. 1971), 46–47. The essential ideas of both essays appeared initially in Baer's 1966 statement.

36. Baer, "Land Misuse," 1240; Baer, "Higher Education," 485–486; Baer, "Ecology," 47.

37. Baer, "Ecology," 49.

38. Ibid., 47, 53; Baer, "Higher Education," 486.

39. Richard A. Baer, Jr., "The Church and Man's Relationship to His Natural Environment," *Quaker Life* 12 (Jan. 1970), 421.

40. Baer, "Land Misuse," 1240; Richard A. Baer, Jr., "Conservation Problems More Human than Technological," *Conservation Catalyst* 2 (Summer 1967), 4–5.

41. Baer, "Conservation," 43.

42. "The Mission of the Faith-Man-Nature Group," n.d., and "Proceedings of Two Meetings which Led to the Formation of the Research Group on Theology and Ethics of Man-Nature-Resources," Nov. 1965, both in the Baer Papers in the possession of Richard A. Baer, Jr., Secretary, Faith-Man-Nature Group, Ithaca, N.Y.

43. Richard A. Baer, Jr., to Edward G. Zern, Nov. 30, 1977, Baer Papers, Ithaca, N.Y. Philip N. Joranson's work includes "Biological Development and the Christian Doctrine of Man," *Christian Scholar* 37 (Dec. 1954), 530, and "The Faith-Man-Nature Group and a Religious Environmental Ethic," *Zygon* 12 (June 1977), 175–179.

44. Joranson, "Biological Development," 530; Alfred Stefferud, ed., *Christians and the Good Earth,* "Faith-Man-Nature Papers," no. 1 (Alexandria, Va., 1968); Glenn C. Stone, ed., *A New Ethic for a New Earth,* "Faith-Man-Nature Papers," no. 2 (New York, 1971). The three regional publications are Donald Scherer, ed., *Earth Ethics for Today and Tomorrow: Responsible Environmental Trade-Offs* (Bowling Green, Ohio, 1974); Philip N. Joranson and C. Alan Anderson, eds., *Religious Reconstruction for the Environmental Future* (South Coventry, Conn., 1973); and Dave Stefferson, Walter J. Herrscher, and Robert S. Cook, eds., *Ethics for Environment: Three Religious Strategies* (Green Bay, Wis., 1973).

45. Donald Williams, "Christian Stewardship of the Soil," in Stefferud, ed., *Christians and the Good Earth*, 22.

46. Daniel Day Williams, "The Good of All," Ibid., 75.

47. H. Paul Santmire, "Reflections on the Alleged Ecological Bankruptcy of Western Theology," in Steffenson, Herrscher, and Cook, eds., *Ethics for Environment*, 36. The essay is more readily available under the same title in *Anglican Theological Review* 57 (April 1975), 131–152.

48. "Minutes of the Faith-Man-Nature Executive Committee," Jan. 3, 1975 and Philip N. Joranson, "To the Members of the Faith-Man-Nature Executive Committee," Feb. 5, 1976, Baer Papers.

49. Philip N. Joranson and Ken Butigan, eds., *Cry of the Environment: Rebuilding the Christian Creation Tradition* (Santa Fe, N. Mex., 1984), 8, 9, 127, 241.

50. H. Paul Santmire, "Creation and Nature: A Study of the Doctrine of Nature with Special Attention to Karl Barth's Doctrine of Creation" (Ph.D. diss., Harvard University, 1966).

51. H. Paul Santmire, *Brother Earth: Nature, God and Ecology in Time of Crisis* (New York, 1970), 6; Santmire, "Reflections on the Alleged Bankruptcy of Western Theology," *Anglican Theological Review* 57 (April 1975), 131–152.

52. Santmire, *Brother Earth*, 101.

53. Ibid., 98, 132–133. Extended, if sometimes abstruse, commentary on Santmire's ideas may be found in Claude Y. Stewart, Jr., *Nature in Grace: A Study in the Theology of Nature*, "National Association of Baptist Professors of Religion Dissertation Series," no. 3 (Macon, Ga. 1983), 39–88.

54. Santmire, *Brother Earth*, 146, 149. Several essays developed and publicized Santmire's ideas to a wide audience, at least in the Christian community. His most important statements are "Ecology, Justice and Theology: Beyond the Preliminary Skirmishes," *Christian Century* 93 (May 12, 1976, 460–464); "The Struggle for an Ecological Theology: A Case in Point," *Christian Century* 87 (March 4, 1970), 275–277; "The Integrity of Nature," in Stefferud, ed., *Christians and the Good Earth*, 128–133; and "A New Theology of Nature?" *Lutheran Quarterly* 20 (Aug. 1968), 290–308.

55. Santmire, *Brother Earth*, 151, 185–186, 188. On the need for a life-style revolution away from affluence and in the direction of ecstasy see H. Paul Santmire and Paul E. Lutz, *Ecological Renewal* (Philadelphia, 1972), 119ff.

56. Santmire, *Brother Earth*, 150, 160, 179, 191.

57. Santmire, *Travail of Nature*, 9, 13–29, 189–218.

58. Teilhard died in 1955, but his work was not well known in the United States until the 1960s. The most important translations in English appeared as *The Phenomenon of Man* (New York, 1961) and *The Divine Milieu* (New York, 1960). Commentary is available in Thomas Berry, *Teilhard in the Ecological Age* (Chambersburg, Pa., 1982).

59. Conrad Bonifazi, *A Theology of Things* (Philadelphia, 1967), 24. See also Bonifazi's *The Soul of the World: An Account of the Inwardness of Things* (Lanham, Md., 1978) and "Biblical Roots of an Ecologic Conscience," in Michael Hamilton, ed., *This Little Planet* (New York, 1970), 203–233.

60. John B. Cobb, Jr., *Is It Too Late? A Theology of Ecology* (Beverly Hills, Cal., 1972), 109–116; Cobb, "The Population Explosion and the Rights of the Subhuman World," in John A. Day, F. F. Fost and P. Rose, eds., *Dimensions of the Environmental Crisis* (New York, 1971), 19–32. Cobb's earlier work, such as *A Christian Natural Theology: Based on the Thought of Alfred North Whitehead* (Philadelphia, 1965), ignored the ethical status of nature, but by 1970 it had become one of his major preoccupations. On Cobb and his significance see Stewart, *Nature in Grace*, 89–160, and David Ray Griffin and Thomas J. J. Altizer, eds., *John Cobb's Theology in Process* (Philadelphia, 1977). Alfred North Whitehead's importance to Cobb and other modern theologians and organicists is the subject of Jay McDaniel, "Christian Spirituality as Openness to Fellow Creatures," *Environmental Ethics* 8 (Spring 1986), 33–46, and David Ray Griffen, "Whitehead's Contribution to a Theology of Nature," *Bucknell Review* 20 (Winter 1972), 3–24. For the modern statement of process philosophy see Jack R. Sibley and Pete A. Y. Gunter, eds., *Process Philosophy: Basic Writings* (Washington, D.C., 1978).

61. Cobb, *Is It Too Late?* 48–52; Cobb, "Population Explosion," 31. Cobb also rejected stewardship as a guide to human-nature relations in "The Local Church and the Environmental Crisis," *Christian Ministry* 4 (Sept. 1973), 7.

62. Cobb, *Is It Too Late?* vii.

63. Ibid., 51–52, 55–56, 125, 127.

64. John B. Cobb, Jr., "The Hierarchy of Rights," manuscript presented to The Conference on Nonhuman Rights, Claremont, Cal., April 18–20, 1974.

65. John B. Cobb, Jr., "Beyond Anthropocentrism," in Richard Knowles Morris and Michael W. Fox, eds., *On the Fifth Day,* 147.

66. John B. Cobb, Jr., and Charles Birch, *The Liberation of Life: From the Cell to the Community* (Cambridge, England, 1981), 152, 154, 168, 170. Cobb's most recent statement is "Christian Existence in a World of Limits," in Hargrove, ed., *Religion and Environmental Crisis,* 172–187.

67. Scott I. Paradise, "The Vandal Ideology," *The Nation* 209 (Dec. 29, 1969), 729–732.

68. Donald E. Engel, "Elements in a Theology of Environment," *Zygon* 5 (Sept. 1970), 223, 227.

69. Allan R. Brockway, "A Theology of the Natural World," *Engage/Social Action* 23 (July 1973), 37.

70. Frederick Elder, *Crisis in Eden: A Religious Study of Man and Environment* (Nashville, Tenn., 1970), 160–161; Henlee H. Barnette, *The Church and the Ecological Crisis* (Grand Rapids, Mich., 1972), 35.

71. Eric Charles Rust, *Nature—Garden or Desert? An Essay in Environmental Theology* (Waco, Tex., 1971), 132, 139–140.

72. Roderick Nash, *The American Environment: Readings in the History of Conservation* (Reading, Mass., 1976), 225ff.

73. Bob Hunter, "Environmentalism in the 1980s: Ecology as Religion," *Greenpeace Chronicles* 18 (Aug. 1979), 3.

74. Henryk Skolimowski, *Eco-Theology: Toward a Religion for Our Times* (Madras, India, 1985).

75. Peter Borrelli, "Epiphany: Religion, Ethics and the Environment," *Amicus Journal* 2 (Winter 1986), 35, 41.

76. *Land Stewardship Newsletter* 5 (Winter 1987), 3.

77. John Carmody, *Ecology and Religion: Toward a New Christian Theology of Nature* (New York, 1983), 119, 133, 166.

78. *Land Stewardship Newsletter* 4 (Spring 1986), 15.

79. Wendell Berry, "The Gift of Good Land," *Sierra* 64 (Nov.–Dec. 1979), 24. See also Wendell Berry, Wes Jackson, and Bruce Colman, eds., *Meeting the Expectations of the Land: Essays in Sustainable Agriculture and Stewardship* (San Francisco, 1984).

On the nuclear question Mark Hatfield, the Senator for Oregon and a devout Christian, proposed stewardship as the answer to those who would race toward nuclear armaments. It was wrong, he contended, for Christians to support something that could destroy God's creation. Mark O. Hatfield, "Finding the Energy to Continue," *Christianity Today* 24 (Feb. 8, 1980), 20–24.

80. John Hart, *The Spirit of the Earth: A Theology of the Land* (New York, 1984), 42–51, 122–123.

81. Joe Paddock and Nancy Paddock, eds., *The Land Stewardship Project Materials* (unpublished sourcebook, St. Paul, Minn., 1984). For a similar perspective applied internationally see Sean McDonagh, *To Care for the Earth: A Call for a New Theology* (Santa Fe, N. Mex., 1987).

82. *Ecology and Religion Newsletter* 1 (Jan. 1973); 47 (Nov. 1977); 78 (Summer, 1981).

83. Vincent Rossi, "The 11th Commandment: A Christian Deep Ecology," *The Eleventh Commandment Newsletter* 3 (1985), 3.

84. Loren Wilkinson, ed., *Earthkeeping: Christian Stewardship of Natural Resources* (Grand Rapids, Mich., 1980), 246–249. See also Loren Wilkinson, "Global Housekeeping: Lords or Servants?" *Christianity Today* 24 (July 27, 1980), 26–30.

85. The seminal study of sacred space is Mircea Eliade, *The Sacred and the Profane.* See also J. Donald Hughes and Jim Swan, "How Much of the Earth Is Sacred Space?" *Environmental Review* 10 (Winter 1986), 247–259; Robert S. Michaelsen, "Sacred Land in America," *Religion* 16 (1986), 249–268; J. Ronald Engel, *Sacred Lands: The Struggle for Community in the Indiana Dunes* (Middleton, Conn., 1983); Gary Snyder, "Good, Wild, Sacred," *Co-Evolution Quarterly* 39 (Fall 1983), 8–17; Roderick Nash, *Wilderness and the American Mind* (New Haven, Conn., 1982); Berman, *The Reenchantment of the World;* Ken Erickson, "Ceremonial Landscapes of the American West," *Landscapes* 22 (1977), 39–47; Linda H. Graber, *Wilderness as Sacred Space,* "Monograph Series of the Association of American Geographers," no. 8 (Washington, D.C., 1976); and Yi-Fu Tuan, *Man and Nature* (Washington, D.C., 1971).

86. The basic texts of Taoism are over two thousand years old. Americans of the 1960s popularized them as ethical guideposts in both social and natural relations. Two of the most popular American editions were Lao Tsu, *Tao Te Ching,* Gia-Fu Feng and Jane English, trans. (New York, 1972) and *Chuang Tze: Basic Writings,* Burton Watson, trans. (New York, 1964).

87. On this point see Ninian Smart, *Beyond Ideology: Religion and the Future of Western Civilization* (San Francisco, 1981), 290.

88. In making these broad generalizations I have relied upon J. Baird Callicott and Roger T. Ames, eds., *Environmental Philosophy: The Nature of Nature in Asian Traditions of Thought* (Albany, N.Y., 1988); Po-Keung Ip, "Taoism and Environmental Ethics," in Hargrove, ed., *Religion and Environmental Crisis,* 94–106; Peter Matthiessen, *Nine-Headed Dragon River: Zen Journals, 1969–1982* (New York, 1986); Huston Smith, "Tao Now: An Ecological Testament," in Ian G. Barbour, ed., *Earth Might Be Fair: Reflections on Ethics, Religion and Ecology* (Englewood Cliffs, N.J., 1972); 62–81; Theodore Roszak, *The Making of a Counter Culture* (Garden City, N.J., 1969), 124–154; Philip Kapleau, ed., *The Three Pillars of Zen* (Boston, 1967); Hajime Nakamura, *Ways of Thinking of Eastern Peoples,* Philip P. Wiener, ed., (Honolulu, 1964); Joseph Needham, *Science and Civilization in China,* 5 vols. (Cambridge, England, 1956); Daisetz T. Suzuki, "The Role of Nature in Zen Buddhism," in William Barrett, ed., *Zen Buddhism: The Selected Writings of D. T. Suzuki* (New York, 1956); and Herrlee Creel, *Sinism* (Chicago, 1929).

Particularly useful essays for the present purposes are Krishna Chaitanya, "A Profounder Ecology: The Hindu View of Man and Nature," *The Ecologist* 13 (1983), 127–135, and William La Fleur, "Sattva: Enlightenment for Plants and Trees in Buddhism," *Co-Evolution Quarterly* 19 (Fall 1978), 47–52. Recent scholarship includes the entire issues of *Philosophy East and West* 37 (April 1987) and of *Environmental Ethics* 8 (Winter 1986), as well as Holmes Rolston, "Can the East Help the West to Value Nature?" *Philosophy East and West* 37 (April 1987), 172–190.

The fact that Asians have not always been able to live up to their ideals concerning the environment is the subject of Vaclav Smil, *The Bad Earth: Environmental Degradation in China* (London, 1984); Yi-Fu Tuan, "Discrepancies between Environmental Attitudes and Behavior: Examples from Europe and China," in David Spring and Eileen Spring, eds., *Ecology and Religion in History* (New York, 1974), 91–113; and Lewis W. Moncrief, "The Cultural Basis of Our Environmental Crisis," *Science* 170 (Oct. 30, 1970), 508–512.

89. Rick Fields, *How the Swans Came to the Lake: A Narrative History of Buddhism in America* (Boulder, Colo., 1981), 60–61.

90. Albert Schweitzer, *Indian Thought and Its Development,* C. E. B. Russell, trans. (New York, 1936).

91. Fields, *Swans,* 136ff. Suzuki's important works include *The Training of the Zen Buddhist Monk* (New York, 1934); *Zen and Japanese Culture* (New York, 1959); *An Introduction to Zen Buddhism* (New York, 1964); and *Zen Buddhism,* Barrett, ed.

Roderick Nash

92. Alan W. Watts, *Nature, Man and Woman* (New York, 1958), 7–8. On Watts see John Stark, "Alan Watts: A Case Study in the Appropriation of Asian Religious Thought in Post-World War II America" (Ph.D. diss., University of California, Santa Barbara, 1983); Fields, *Swans,* 186ff.; and David K. Clark, *The Pantheism of Alan Watts* (Downers Grove, Pa., 1978).

93. Jack Kerouac, *The Dharma Bums* (New York, 1959), 78.

94. Gary Snyder, "Energy is Eternal Delight," *The New York Times,* Jan. 12, 1972, 43, which also appears in Snyder's *Turtle Island* (New York, 1974), 103–105; Gary Snyder, "The Wilderness," *Center Magazine* 3 (Aug. 1970), 70–71.

For Snyder's life and significance see Fields, *Swans,* 212ff.; L. Edwin Folsom, "Gary Snyder's Descent to Turtle Island: Searching for Fossil Love," *Western American Literature* 15 (Summer 1980), 103–121; Robert Kern, "Recipes, Catalogues, Open Form Poetics: Gary Snyder's Archetypal Voice," *Contemporary Literature* 18 (Spring 1977), 173–197; Bob Steuding, *Gary Snyder* (Boston, 1976); and Roy K. Okada, "Zen and the Poetry of Gary Snyder" (Ph.D. diss., University of Wisconsin-Madison, 1973).

95. Snyder, "Wilderness," 70. Exploring the Marxist dimensions of this idea on one occasion, Snyder proposed that we regard bacteria and simple plants as the proletariat of the ecological community. Disregard of their rights would bring down the entire capitalist structure. The *real* workers of the world would revolt. Snyder found this analogy effective in discussing environmental reforms with communists on his several visits to China. Interview with Gary Snyder, Santa Barbara, Cal., Feb. 21, 1985.

96. Gary Snyder, *The Real Work: Interviews and Talks, 1964–1979* (New York, 1980), 72. Snyder seems to have been aware since the 1960s that full subscription to Buddhist-inspired ethics entailed a revolutionary attitude with reference to many Western institutions. His essay "Buddhism and the Coming Revolution" appeared initially in Snyder, *Earth Household* (New York, 1969). It has since been extensively reprinted and slightly revised under the title "Buddhism and the Possibilities of a Planetary Culture," in Bill Devall and George Sessions, eds., *Deep Ecology* (Salt Lake City, Utah, 1985), 251–253.

97. William R. Hoyt, "Zen Buddhism and Western Alienation from Nature," *Christian Century* 87 (Oct. 7, 1970), 1194–1196.

98. Hwa Yol Jung, "Ecology, Zen and Western Religious Thought," *Christian Century* 89 (Nov. 15, 1972), 1155. Jung extended his analysis of Leopold in "The Splendor of the Wild: Zen and Aldo Leopold," *Atlantic Naturalist* 29 (Spring 1984), 5–11. See also D. Barash, "The Ecologist as Zen Master," *American Midland Naturalist* 89 (1973), 214–217 and Hwa Yol Jung, "The Ecological Crisis: A Philosophic Perspective, East and West," *Bucknell Review* 20 (Winter 1972), 25–44.

99. Robert Aitken, "Thoughts on Buddhist Ecology," *Blind Donkey* (1985) 9, 14, 17, 19, 21.

100. Rajagopal Ryali, "Eastern-Mystical Perspectives on Environment," in Steffenson, Herrscher, and Cook, eds., *Ethics for Environment,* 47–56.

101. Thomas Merton, *Zen and the Birds of Appetite* (New York, 1968); John B. Cobb, Jr., *Beyond Dialogue: Toward a Mutual Transformation of Christianity and Buddhism* (Philadelphia, 1982); Eugene C. Hargrove, "Religion and Environmental Ethics: Beyond the Lynn White Debate," in Hargrove, *Religion and Environmental Crisis,* xvii, xviii.

102. Dolores La Chapelle and Janet Bourque, *Earth Festivals: Seasonal Celebrations for Everyone Young and Old* (Silverton, Colo. 1977); Dolores La Chapelle, *Earth Wisdom* (Los Angeles, 1978); Dolores La Chapelle, *Ritual: The Pattern That Connects* (Silverton, Colo., 1981).

103. Harold W. Wood, "Modern Pantheism," 151. Representative statements are Bill Devall, "Nature Mysticism and Neo-Paganism" (unpublished essay, 1979) and Universal Pantheist Society, *Pantheism and Earthkeeping* (Big Pine, Cal., 1975).

104. Field, *Swans,* especially chs. 12–16.

105. On this point see Peter Steinhart, "Ecological Saints," *Audubon* 86 (July 1984), 8–9, and Calvin Martin, "The American Indian as Miscast Ecologist," in Robert C. Schultz and J. Donald Hughes, eds., *Ecological Consciousness* (Washington, D.C., 1981), 137–148.

106. The most useful secondary sources for Indian religion as it affected environmental attitudes are Gerard Reed, "A Native American Environmental Ethic," in Hargrove, ed., *Religion and Environmental Crisis,* 25–37; Peter Matthiessen, *Indian Country* (New York, 1984); Richard White, "Native Americans and the Environment," in William R. Swagerty, ed., *Scholars and the Indian Experience* (Bloomington, Ind., 1984), 179–204; J. Donald Hughes, *American Indian Ecology* (El Paso, Tex., 1983); J. Baird Callicott, "Traditional American Indian and Western European Attitudes toward Nature: An Overview," *Environmental Ethics* 4 (Winter 1982), 293–318; Peter Nabakov, "America as Holy Land," *North Dakota Quarterly* 48 (Autumn 1980), 9–20; Christopher Vecsey and Robert Venables, eds., *American Indian Environments* (Syracuse, N.Y., 1980); Calvin Martin, *Keepers of the Game* (Berkeley, Cal., 1978); Walter H. Capps, ed., *Seeing with a Native Eye: Essays on Native American Religion* (New York, 1976); and T. C. McLuhan, ed., *Touch the Earth* (New York, 1971). Hughes's bibliography, in particular, will lead to the most important related literature. Also valuable for its survey of recent scholarship is Richard White, "Native Americans and the Environment," in Swagerty, *Scholars and the Indian Experience,* 179–204.

107. Chief Seattle, "The Land Is Sacred," *Counseling and Values* 18 (Summer 1974), 275–277. The story behind the preservation of Seattle's remarks is told in Rudolph Kaiser, *Indians and Europe,* C. Feest, ed. (Aachen, West Germany, 1987). The original translation of Seattle's speech, which lacks some of the holistic language, appears in W. C. Vanderwerth, ed., *Indian Oratory: Famous Speeches by the Noted Indian Chieftains* (Norman, Okla., 1971), 118–122. Regardless of what the chief actually said in 1853, it is significant that modern white Americans wanted to credit him with a biocentric philosophy.

108. Luther Standing Bear, *Land of the Spotted Eagle* (Boston, 1933) 193.

109. Ibid.

110. Roszak, *Making of a Counter Culture,* 245, 264–268.

111. Steward Udall, *The Quiet Crisis* (New York, 1964), 4ff.

112. Black Elk, *Black Elk Speaks: Being the Life Story of a Holy Man of the Oglala Sioux,* John G. Niehardt, ed. (Lincoln, Neb., 1961, originally published 1932); John Fire Lame Deer, *Lame Deer, Seeker of Visions: The Life of a Sioux Medicine Man,* Richard Erdoes, ed. (New York, 1972); Hyemeyohsts Storm, *Seven Arrows* (New York, 1972).

113. N. Scott Momaday, "An American Land Ethic," in John G. Mitchell, ed., *Ecotactics: The Sierra Club Handbook for Environment Activists* (San Francisco, 1970), 97–106. A related statement is Momaday's "A First American Views His Land," *National Geographic* 150 (July 1976), 13–18.

114. Vine Deloria, Jr., "Introduction" in Sam Steiner, *The New Indians* (New York, 1968), x.

115. Vine Deloria, Jr., "Toward a Planetary Metaphysics," manuscript presented to The Conference on Nonhuman Rights, Claremont, Cal., April 18–20, 1974, 1, 18.

116. Harold K. Schilling, "The Whole Earth Is the Lord's," in Barbour, ed., *Earth Might Be Fair,* 115.

117. Robert Dwyer, "Worship of the Environment Is the New Religion," *Los Angeles Times,* August 10, 1973, 27.

118. Richard Neuhaus, *In Defense of People: Ecology and the Seduction of Radicalism* (New York, 1971).

119. Santa Barbara, Cal., *News Press,* Oct. 23, 1983, 12.

"THE ECOLOGICAL CRISIS: A COMMON RESPONSIBILITY"

Pope John Paul II

Message of His Holiness Pope John Paul II
For the Celebration of the World Day of Peace
1 January 1990
Vatican City
Peace with God the Creator, Peace with All of Creation

INTRODUCTION

1. In our day, there is a growing awareness that world peace is threatened not only by the arms race, regional conflicts and continued injustices among peoples and nations, but also by a lack of *due respect for nature,* by the plundering of natural resources and by a progressive decline in the quality of life. The sense of precariousness and insecurity that such a situation engenders is a seedbed for collective selfishness, disregard for others and dishonesty.

Faced with the widespread destruction of the environment, people everywhere are coming to understand that we cannot continue to use the goods of the earth as we have in the past. The public in general as well as political leaders are concerned about this problem, and experts from a wide range of disciplines are studying its causes. Moreover, a new *ecological awareness* is beginning to emerge which, rather than being downplayed, ought to be encouraged to develop into concrete programmes and initiatives.

2. Many ethical values, fundamental to the development of a *peaceful society,* are particularly relevant to the ecological question. The fact that many challenges facing the world today are interdependent confirms the need for carefully coordinated solutions based on a morally coherent world view.

For Christians, such a world view is grounded in religious convictions drawn from Revelation. That is why I should like to begin this Message with a reflection on the biblical account of creation. I would hope that even those who do not share these same beliefs will find in these pages a common ground for reflection and action.

Reprinted with permission of the Apostolic Nunciature, Washington, D.C.

I. "AND GOD SAW THAT IT WAS GOOD"

3. In the Book of Genesis, where we find God's first self-revelation to humanity (*Gen* 1–3), there is a recurring refrain: *"And God saw that it was good."* After creating the heavens, the sea, the earth and all it contains, God created man and woman. At this point the refrain changes markedly: "And God saw everything that he had made, and behold, *it was very good*" (*Gen* 1:31). God entrusted the whole of creation to the man and woman, and only then—as we read—could he rest "from all his work" (*Gen* 2:3).

Adam and Eve's call to share in the unfolding of God's plan of creation brought into play those abilities and gifts which distinguish the human being from all other creatures. At the same time, their call established a fixed relationship between mankind and the rest of creation. Made in the image and likeness of God, Adam and Eve were to have exercised their dominion over the earth (*Gen* 1:28) with wisdom and love. Instead, they destroyed the existing harmony *by deliberately going against the Creator's plan,* that is, by choosing to sin. This resulted not only in man's alienation from himself, in death and fratricide, but also in the earth's "rebellion" against him (cf. *Gen* 3:17–19; 4:12). All of creation became subject to futility, waiting in a mysterious way to be set free and to obtain a glorious liberty together with all the children of God (cf. *Rom* 8:20–21).

4. Christians believe that the Death and Resurrection of Christ accomplished the work of reconciling humanity to the Father, who "was pleased . . . through (Christ) to reconcile to himself *all things,* whether on earth or in heaven, making peace by the blood of his cross" (*Col* 1:19–20). Creation was thus made new (cf. *Rev* 21:5). Once subjected to the bondage of sin and decay (cf. *Rom* 8:21), it has now received new life while "we wait for new heavens and a new earth in which righteousness dwells" (*2 Pt* 3:13). Thus, the Father "has made known to us in all wisdom and insight the mystery . . . which he set forth in Christ as a plan for the fulness of time, to unite *all things* in him, all things in heaven and things on earth" (*Eph* 1:9–10).

5. These biblical considerations help us to understand better *the relationship between human activity and the whole of creation.* When man turns his back on the Creator's plan, he provokes a disorder which has inevitable repercussions on the rest of the created order. If man is not at peace with God, then earth itself cannot be at peace: "Therefore the land mourns and all who dwell in it languish, and also the beasts of the field and the birds of the air and even the fish of the sea are taken away" (*Hos* 4:3).

The profound sense that the earth is "suffering" is also shared by those who do not profess our faith in God. Indeed, the increasing devastation of the world of nature is apparent to all. It results from the behavior of people who show a callous disregard for the hidden, yet perceivable requirements of the order and harmony which govern nature itself.

People are asking anxiously if it is still possible to remedy the damage which has been done. Clearly, an adequate solution cannot be found merely in a better management or a more rational use of the earth's resources, as important as these may be. Rather, we must go to the source of the problem and face in its entirety that profound moral crisis *of which the destruction of the environment is only one troubling aspect.*

II. THE ECOLOGICAL CRISIS: A MORAL PROBLEM

6. Certain elements of today's ecological crisis reveal its moral character. First among these is the *indiscriminate application* of advances in science and technology. Many recent discoveries have brought undeniable benefits to humanity. Indeed, they demonstrate the nobility of the human vocation to participate *responsibly* in God's creative action in the world. Unfortunately, it is now clear that the application of these discoveries in the fields of industry and agriculture have produced harmful long-term effects. This has led to the painful realization that *we cannot interfere in one area of the ecosystem without paying due attention both to the consequences of such interference in other areas and to the well-being of future generations.*

The gradual depletion of the ozone layer and the related "greenhouse effect" has now reached crisis proportions as a consequence of industrial growth, massive urban concentrations and vastly increased energy needs. Industrial waste, the burning of fossil fuels, unrestricted deforestation, the use of certain types of herbicides, coolants and propellants: all of these are known to harm the atmosphere and environment. The resulting meteorological and atmospheric changes range from damage to health to the possible future submersion of low-lying lands.

While in some cases the damage already done may well be irreversible, in many other cases it can still be halted. It is necessary, however, that the entire human community—individuals, States and international bodies—take seriously the responsibility that is theirs.

7. The most profound and serious indication of the moral implications underlying the ecological problem is the lack of *respect for life* evident in many of the patterns of environmental pollution. Often, the interests of production prevail over concern for the dignity of workers, while economic interests take priority over the good of individuals and even entire peoples. In these cases, pollution or environmental destruction is the result of an unnatural and reductionist vision which at times leads to a genuine contempt for man.

On another level, delicate ecological balances are upset by the uncontrolled destruction of animal and plant life or by a reckless exploitation of natural resources. It should be pointed out that all of this, even if carried out in the name of progress and well-being, is ultimately to mankind's disadvantage.

Finally, we can only look with deep concern at the enormous possibilities of biological research. We are not yet in a position to assess the biological disturbance that could result from indiscriminate genetic manipulation and from the unscrupulous development of new forms of plant and animal life, to say nothing of unacceptable experimentation regarding the origins of human life itself. It is evident to all that in any area as delicate as this, indifference to fundamental ethical norms, or their rejection, would lead mankind to the very threshold of self-destruction.

Respect for life, and above all for the dignity of the human person, is the ultimate guiding norm for any sound economic, industrial or scientific progress.

The complexity of the ecological question is evident to all. There are, however, certain underlying principles, which, while respecting the legitimate autonomy and the specific competence of those involved, can direct research towards adequate and lasting solutions. These principles are essential to the building of a peaceful society; *no peaceful society can afford to neglect either respect for life or the fact that there is an integrity to creation.*

III. IN SEARCH OF A SOLUTION

8. Theology, philosophy and science all speak of a harmonious universe, of a "cosmos" endowed with its own integrity, its own internal, dynamic balance. *This order must be respected.* The human race is called to explore this order, to examine it with due care and to make use of it while safeguarding its integrity.

On the other hand, the earth is ultimately *a common heritage, the fruits of which are for the benefit of all.* In the words of the Second Vatican Council, "God destined the earth and all it contains for the use of every individual and all peoples" (*Gaudium et Spes,* 69). This has direct consequences for the problem at hand. It is manifestly unjust that a privileged few should continue to accumulate excess goods, squandering available resources, while masses of people are living in conditions of misery at the very lowest level of subsistence. Today, the dramatic threat of ecological breakdown is teaching us the extent to which greed and selfishness—both individual and collective—are contrary to the order of creation, an order which is characterized by mutual interdependence.

9. The concepts of an ordered universe and a common heritage both point to the necessity of a *more internationally coordinated approach to the management of the earth's goods.* In many cases the effects of ecological problems transcend the borders of individual States; hence their solution cannot be found solely on the national level. Recently there have been some promising steps towards such international action, yet the existing mechanisms and bodies are clearly not adequate for the development of a comprehensive plan of action. Political obstacles, forms of exaggerated nationalism and economic interests—to mention only a few factors— impede international cooperation and long-term effective action.

The need for joint action on the international level *does not lessen the responsibility of each individual State.* Not only should each State join with others in implementing internationally accepted standards, but it should also make or facilitate necessary socio-economic adjustments within its own borders, giving special attention to the most vulnerable sectors of society. The State should also actively endeavor within its own territory to prevent destruction of the atmosphere and biosphere, by carefully monitoring, among other things, the impact of new technological or scientific advances. The State also has the responsibility of ensuring that its citizens are not exposed to dangerous pollutants or toxic wastes. *The right to a safe environment* is ever more insistently presented today as a right that must be included in an updated Charter of Human Rights.

IV. THE URGENT NEED FOR A NEW SOLIDARITY

10. The ecological crisis reveals the *urgent moral need for a new solidarity,* especially in relations between the developing nations and those that are highly industrialized. States must increasingly share responsibility, in complimentary ways, for the promotion of a natural and social environment that is both peaceful and healthy. The newly industrialized States cannot, for example, be asked to apply restrictive environmental standards to their emerging industries unless the industrialized States first apply them within their own boundaries. At the same time, countries in the process of industrialization are not morally free to repeat the errors made in the past by others, and recklessly continue to damage the environment through industrial pollutants, radical deforestation or unlimited exploitation of non-renewable resources. In this context, there is urgent need to find a solution to the treatment and disposal of toxic wastes.

No plan or organization, however, will be able to effect the necessary changes unless world leaders are truly convinced of the absolute need for this new solidarity, which is demanded of them by the ecological crisis and which is essential for peace. *This need presents new opportunities for strengthening cooperative and peaceful relations among States.*

11. It must also be said that the proper ecological balance will not be found without *directly addressing the structural forms of poverty* that exist throughout the world. Rural poverty and unjust land distribution in many countries, for example, have led to subsistence farming and to the exhaustion of the soil. Once their land yields no more, many farmers move on to clear new land, thus accelerating uncontrolled deforestation, or they settle in urban centers which lack the infrastructure to receive them. Likewise, some heavily indebted countries are destroying their natural heritage, at the price of irreparable ecological imbalances, in order to develop new products for export. In the face of such situations it would be wrong to assign responsibility to the poor alone for the negative environmental consequences of their actions. Rather, the poor, to whom the earth is entrusted no less than to others, must be enabled to find a way out of their poverty. This will require a courageous reform of structures, as well as new ways of relating among peoples and States.

12. But there is another dangerous menace which threatens us, namely *war.* Unfortunately,

modern science already has the capacity to change the environment for hostile purposes. Alterations of this kind over the long term could have unforeseeable and still more serious consequences. Despite the international agreements which prohibit chemical, bacteriological and biological warfare, the fact is that laboratory research continues to develop new offensive weapons capable of altering the balance of nature.

Today, any form of war on a global scale would lead to incalculable ecological damage. But even local or regional wars, however limited, not only destroy human life and social structures, but also damage the land, ruining crops and vegetation as well as poisoning the soil and water. The survivors of war are forced to begin a new life in very difficult environmental conditions, which in turn create situations of extreme social unrest, with further negative consequences for the environment.

13. Modern society will find no solution to the ecological problem unless it *takes a serious look at its life style*. In many parts of the world society is given to instant gratification and consumerism while remaining indifferent to the damage which these cause. As I have already stated, the seriousness of the ecological issue lays bare the depth of man's moral crisis. If an appreciation of the value of the human person and of human life is lacking, we will also lose interest in others and in the earth itself. Simplicity, moderation and discipline, as well as a spirit of sacrifice, must become a part of everyday life, lest all suffer the negative consequences of the careless habits of a few.

An education in ecological responsibility is urgent: responsibility for oneself, for others, and for the earth. This education cannot be rooted in mere sentiment or empty wishes. Its purpose cannot be ideological or political. It must not be based on a rejection of the modern world or a vague desire to return to some "paradise lost." Instead, a true education in responsibility entails a genuine conversion in ways of thought and behaviour. Churches and religious bodies, non-governmental and governmental organizations, indeed all members of society, have a precise role to play in such education. The first educator, however, is the family, where the child learns to respect his neighbor and to love nature.

14. *Finally, the aesthetic value of creation cannot be overlooked.* Our very contact with nature has a deep restorative power; contemplation of its magnificence imparts peace and serenity. The Bible speaks again and again of the goodness and beauty of creation, which is called to glorify God (cf. *Gen* 1:4ff; *Ps* 8:2; 104:1ff; *Wis* 13:3–5; *Sir* 39:16, 33; 43:1, 9). More difficult, perhaps, but no less profound, is the contemplation of the works of human ingenuity. Even cities can have a beauty all their own, one that ought to motivate people to care for their surroundings. Good urban planning is an important part of environmental protection, and respect for the natural contours of the land is an indispensable prerequisite for ecologically sound development. The relationship between a good aesthetic education and the maintenance of a healthy environment cannot be overlooked.

V. THE ECOLOGICAL CRISIS: A COMMON RESPONSIBILITY

15. Today, the ecological crisis has assumed such proportions as to be *the responsibility of everyone.* As I have pointed out, its various aspects demonstrate the need for concerted efforts aimed at establishing the duties and obligations that belong to individuals, peoples, States and the international community. This not only goes hand in hand with efforts to build true peace, but also confirms and reinforces those efforts in a concrete way. When the ecological crisis is set within the broader context of *the search for peace* within society, we can understand better the importance of giving attention to what the earth and its atmosphere are telling us: namely, that there is an order in the universe which must be respected, and that the human person, endowed with the capability of choosing freely, has a grave responsibility to preserve this order for the well-being of future generations. I wish to repeat that *the ecological crisis is a moral issue.*

Even men and women without any particular religious conviction, but with an acute sense of their responsibilities for the common good, recognize their obligation to contribute to the restoration of a healthy environment. All the more should men and women who believe in God the Creator, and who are thus convinced that there is a well-defined unity and order in the world, feel called to address the problem. Christians, in particular, realize that their responsibility within creation and their duty towards nature and the Creator are an essential part of their faith. As a result, they are conscious of a vast field of ecumenical and interreligious cooperation opening up before them.

16. At the conclusion of this Message, I should like to address directly my brothers and sisters in the Catholic Church, in order to remind them of their serious obligation to care for all of creation. The commitment of believers to a healthy environment for everyone stems directly from their belief in God the Creator, from their recognition of the effects of original and personal sin, and from the certainty of having been redeemed by Christ. Respect for life and for the dignity of the human person extends also to the rest of creation, which is called to join man in praising God (cf. *Ps* 148:96).

In 1979, I proclaimed Saint Francis of Assisi as the heavenly Patron of those who promote ecology (cf. Apostolic Letter *Inter Sanctos:* AAS 71 [1979], 1509f.). He offers Christians an example of genuine and deep respect for the integrity of creation. As a friend of the poor who was loved by God's creatures, Saint Francis invited all of creation—animals, plants natural forces, even Brother Sun and Sister Moon—to give honor and praise to the Lord. The poor man of Assisi gives us striking witness that when we are at peace with God we are better able to devote ourselves to building up that peace with all creation which is inseparable from peace among all peoples.

It is my hope that the inspiration of Saint Francis will help us to keep ever alive a sense of "fraternity" with all those good and beautiful things which Almighty God has created. And may he remind us of our serious obligation to respect and watch over them with care, in light of that greater and higher fraternity that exists within the human family.

From the Vatican, 8 December 1989.
Joannes Paulus II

"CREATION AND THE COVENANT OF CARING"

American Baptist Churches, USA

Christians believe that the whole creation is God's handiwork and belongs to God (Psalm 24:1). The creation has value in itself because God created and values it (Proverbs 8:29–31). God delights in the creation and desires its wholeness and well-being.

God created the earth, affirmed that it was good, and established an everlasting covenant with humanity to take responsibility for the whole of creation. God declares all of creation good. Our proper perspective on all activity on the earth flows directly from our affirmation of God as Creator.

The earth belongs to God, as affirmed in Psalm 24:1. We are caretakers or stewards. Thus we are each related to God as one appointed to take care of someone else's possessions entrusted to us—our life, our home, the earth. The vast resources of the earth can provide for all its inhabitants, or they can be greedily swallowed up or poisoned by a few without regard for the impact of their actions.

The best understanding of the Biblical attitude of humanity's relationship with the Creation can be gained by a study of the Greek words which are the foundation of the New Testament. The word "stewardship" comes from the Greek words for house and management. The Greek word which is commonly translated "stewardship" is the root word for economics and ecology. The literal translation of steward is manager of the household. As such, we are all called to be managers of God's household, the earth and all that is in it.

Our responsibility as stewards is one of the most basic relationships we have with God. It implies a great degree of caring for God's creation and all God's creatures. The right relationship is embodied in the everlasting covenant to which Isaiah refers. There can be no justice without right relationships of creatures with one another and with all of creation. Eco-justice is the vision of the garden in Genesis—the realm and the reality of right relationship.

God has given humans tremendously creative capacities. The development of science has enabled us to understand the inherent capabilities of the resources God gave. Modern scientific technology has provided thousands of ways of applying scientific knowledge to improve our lives. It is a powerful tool, and one of the gifts God has given us.

Technology holds the possibility of both good and evil, life and death. We are given the responsibility to choose: "I set before you life or death, blessing or curse. Choose life, then so

Reprinted with permission of American Baptist Churches, USA.

that you and your descendants may live . . ." (Deuteronomy 30:19). It is our responsibility as stewards to require that technology be used for the good and that the harmful effects of its use (or misuse) be mitigated or prevented.

RESPONSIBILITY—INDIVIDUAL AND CORPORATE

The image of God within us makes it possible for people to be aware and responsive to God's self-revelation in the creation. We have the gift of God which enables us to perceive and reflect upon the life within us and around us. The distinctive human vocation is to bring creation's beauty and order to consciousness and to express God's image within us by caring for the creation.

In the ability God has given us to make choices also lies inherent danger. We can choose to disobey, to be irresponsible, to disrupt and disturb the peaceable relationship of creature and creation. We can choose to use nature's resources only for what we perceive is our own immediate interest. Such action is sin. It is a violation of the basic covenant wherein we are called to stewardship. It is an unfaithful refusal of the responsibility entrusted to us. Often we tend to think of sin in terms of individual actions. Yet decisions and actions which we make as groups, communities and societies constitute corporate sin. These corporate decisions and actions reflect values and interests which conflict with the vision of shalom and eco-justice consistent with created order. Our task is to discern the conflict and to choose ways of living which build an eco-just community and world.

JESUS—A MODEL FOR TAKING SIDES

Jesus' ministry provides a model for choosing sides. He is clear about where his loyalty lies. In his earliest reported reading of scripture in public, he chooses, Luke tells us, to read from the prophet Isaiah. He proclaims that his mission is to serve the poor, the captives, and the downtrodden—the victims of social injury. He further states that he will "proclaim the acceptable year of the Lord." This is the Jubilee Year of Leviticus 25, a year of land reform. It is a recognition that all land basically and ultimately belongs to God, and that no person or group has the right to destroy it or to use it unendingly for unjust personal or institutional gain.

AMERICAN BAPTIST POLICY STATEMENT ON ECOLOGY

The study of ecology has become a religious, social and political concern because every area of life is affected by careless use of our environment. The creation is in crisis. We believe that ecology and justice, stewardship of creation and redemption are interdependent. Our task is to proclaim the Good News of Jesus Christ until the coming of the Kingdom on Earth. All God's people must be guided by the balance of reverence, the acknowledgement of our interdependence, the integrity of divine wholeness and the need for empowerment by the Holy Spirit to image God by our dominion over creation (Mark 10:43–45). If we image God we will reflect in our dominion the love and the care that God has for the whole creation, "for God so loved the world . . ." (John 3:16, Romans 8:21–22, Matthew 5:43–48). Jesus told us to let your light so shine that others may see the good things you do and praise God (Matthew 5:16).

The Bible affirms, "The earth is the Lord's and the fullness thereof, the world and they that dwell therein" (Psalms 24:1). As Christians we believe that the whole universe reveals God's manifold works. God continues to create as well as to redeem. God asks us not only to call persons to redemption but also to teach them to be wise stewards, tenderly caring for God's creation.

Today the human race faces an unprecedented challenge to rediscover the role of steward in a time of extraordinary peril and promise. The explosive growth of population, the depletion of nonrenewable resources, tropical deforestation, the pollution of air, land, and water, waste of precious materials and the general assault on God's creation, springing from greed, arrogance and ignorance present the possibility of irreversible damage to the intricate, natural systems upon which life depends. At the same time nuclear weapons threaten the planet. They have the capability not only of destroying human life on a massive scale but also of poisoning and altering the environment in ways that would render much of the planet incapable of sustaining life. The danger is real and great. Churches and individual Christians must take responsibility to God and neighbor seriously and respond (Eph. 2:10).

Ironically, science and technology have multiplied many times the ecological threat. The very instruments that brought great blessing—and still hold much promise—now threaten to bring disaster unless they are used in concert rather than in conflict with the created order.

God made a world that is good in reality and potential, but our enslavement to modern industrial images of civilization hinders our ability to envision God's created order. According to our Native-American Christian sisters and brothers, we are causing the earth to self-destruct, and then we are dying of loneliness for our ruined lands. This loneliness is best understood as an alienation from Creator and creation (Job 41:1–11, 42:5–6). We are dealing with the classic theological issues of a good Creator and creation, human sin and the fall into evil which requires radical repentance in response to the saving Gospel of Jesus Christ. Salvation cannot come to creation unless we repent and turn away from former lifestyles (Romans 8:12–14, 18–23).

The Creator-Redeemer seeks the renewal of the creation and calls the people of God to participate in saving acts of renewal. We are called to cooperate with God in the transformation of a fallen world that has not fulfilled its divinely given potential for beauty, peace, health, harmony, justice and joy (Isa. 11:6–9, Micah 4:3–4, Eph. 2:10, Rev. 21:1–5). Our task is nothing less than to join God in preserving, renewing and fulfilling the creation. It is to relate to nature in ways that sustain life on the planet, provide for the essential material and physical needs of all humankind, and increase justice and well-being for all life in a peaceful world.

A wise and responsible people will recognize the increasing interdependence of all humankind in an emerging planetary society. In our time we must provide opportunities for all to grow and thrive. The fortunate who tolerate misery, strife and terrorism elsewhere, can stay safe themselves no longer. In a quest for survival, justice, and peace, we are "members one of another" (Rom. 12:5) The neighbor whom we are commanded to love is everyone (Luke 10:27), including those yet to be born who depend on us to leave them a habitable earth. Because God is our deliverer, we must recognize sin and refuse to participate in it.

Ecology and justice are inseparable. The threat to the global environment presents American Baptists with a call for prompt and vigorous response. As Christians and faithful stewards, we bear the responsibility to affirm and support programs, legislation, research and organizations that protect and restore the vulnerable and the oppressed, the earth as well as the poor. This responsibility for a habitable environment is not just for human life, but for all life. A stewardship that will fulfill this responsibility will be guided by the norms of solidarity, as we stand with the vulnerable creation and work with its defenders; sustainability, as we devise social systems that maintain the balance of nature, and sufficiency, as we give priority to basic sustenance for all life.

Therefore, we call on all of the members of the American Baptist Churches of the USA to:

1.—Affirm the goodness and beauty of God's creation.

2.—Acknowledge our responsibility for stewardship of the Creator's good earth.

3.—Learn of the environmental dangers facing the planet.

4.—Recognize that our practices and styles of life have had an effect on the environment.

5.—Pursue a lifestyle that is wise and responsible in light of our understanding of the problems.

6.—Exert our influence in shaping public policy and insisting that industries, businesses, farmers and consumers relate to the environment in ways that are sensible, healthy and protective of its integrity.

7.—Demonstrate concern with "the hope that is within us," as despair and apathy surround us in the world (Rom. 12:21).

8.—Become involved in organizations and actions to protect and restore the environment and the people in our communities.

We call upon the National Boards, Regions and institutions of our denomination to:

9.—Promote an attitude affirming that all nature has intrinsic value and that all life is to be honored and reverenced.

10.—Seek ways and means to alert the churches to present and impending environment threats.

Adopted by the General Board of the American Baptist Churches—June 1989, 157 For, 0 Against, 0 Abstentions (General Board Reference #7040:12/88)

"BASIS FOR OUR CARING"

Evangelical Lutheran Church in America

The world beset by environmental problems is the world created, redeemed and sustained by God. The earth system that knows many-sided crises is the earth system we are called to serve.

In the words of our responsive prayer, we know that "awesome things will you show us in your righteousness, O God of our Salvation, O hope of all the ends of the earth and of the seas that are far away" (*Lutheran Book of Worship* [*LBW*], p. 162). Since God is Lord of heaven and earth, our longing is "eager longing for the revealing of the children of God" (Rom 8:19).

GOD, EARTH AND ALL CREATURES

GOD THE CREATOR

Scripture witnesses to God as maker of the earth and all that dwells therein (Ps 24:1). The witness begins in Genesis, continues in the psalms and prophets, and stands behind the claim that Jesus Christ died and was raised for the salvation of the world.

The God revealed to us as LORD (Yahweh), the God who brought Israel out of Egypt, the God who sent Israel into exile and brought her out again, the God who spoke of old by the prophets but who has now spoken to us by a Son (Heb 1:1–2)—this is the Creator. The God who is faithful, righteous, just and loving (Ps 33:4–5; 89:8–14) attends to creation faithfully, righteously, justly and lovingly.

The creeds, which guide our reading of Scripture, proclaim God the Father of Jesus Christ to be maker of heaven and earth. Jesus Christ is also the one "through whom all things were made" (Nicene Creed; cf. Jn 1:3; 1 Cor 8:6; Col 1:16; Heb 1:2–3). And the Holy Spirit is "the Lord, the giver of life" (Nicene Creed; cf. Gen 1:2; Ps 104:30). It is the one and triune God who creates the cosmos.

VALUE OF THE WORLD

God blesses the world and calls it good. The parts of creation are "good" (Gen 1:4, 10, 12, 18, 21, 25), and the whole of creation is "very good" (Gen 1:31) solely because of the grace of its good Creator. Creation is given its own integrity. It is intact and healthy, and its parts work in harmony.

God calls aspects of creation "good" before humanity comes on the scene. *All creation, not just human beings, is declared good from a divine perspective.* And God continues to care not just for people but also for animals (Gen 6–9), plants (Ps 147:8), and even deserts and wastelands (Job 38–41, esp. 38:25–27). The New Testament, too, tells of God's faithful care for all creation (Mt 5:45; 6:26–30; Lk 12:6–7; Acts 14:17). God is at work, sustaining the world (Jn 5:17).

God is linked to all creation through covenant: to all living creatures (Gen 8–9); to beasts of the field, birds of the air, and creeping things of the ground (Hos 2:18); and to night and day (Jer 33:20). To say that God is linked to creation through covenant is also to say that God is linked to creation through promise. God's very word guarantees creation. We and all creation live by that promise.

GOOD, BUT NOT GOD

The world is good, but it is not God. Creation is good, but is nevertheless distinct from the Creator. Even though creation has honor as the work of God, those who worship it exchange truth for a lie (Rom 1:25; cf. Job 31:26–28). Creation worships the Creator (Ps 19; 96; 148).

God is "wholly other," the final reality beyond creaturely realities, the awesome and terrible mystery. Wholly other, God stands over and against creation as judge. Wholly other, God stands *for* creation as giver of free, sustaining and saving grace.

God's creation—very good but not divine—has the limitations observed in the current environmental crisis. A creation that is good but not God is finite, and lends itself to appropriate scientific analysis.

THE PRESENCE OF GOD IN CREATION

The God who is wholly other is very near. God is deeply and compassionately involved in what happens to the planet. God does not choose to dominate creation with tyrannical power, however, and works in and through natural forces (as in Ps 104) and history (as in 2 Chr 36:22–23) to lead it to fulfillment.

God is intimately and irreversibly connected to all creation through the Incarnation, where infinite grace is carried by finite creation. In Christ, God takes on the earthly material of human life. Through Christ, God is reconciled to "all things, whether on earth or in heaven" (Col 1:20). The Incarnation has saving significance for a creation that longs for fulfillment (Rom 8:18–25), seen elsewhere in the Bible as heaven coming down to earth (Rev 21).

The eternal Word of God became flesh and dwelled among us, teaching us how to live and move and have our being in creation. Unlike the foxes and birds, Jesus had nowhere to lay his head (Mt 8:20). Many of his parables, however, show he understood the land (Mt 13:32; Mk 4:26–29).

Jesus presents the world as a theatre of God's grace and glory, where lilies mirror God's glory (Mt 6:28–29) and birds display God's care (Mt 6:26). And Jesus acts in accordance with God's covenant to bring peace to creation, for example, by stilling the waters (Mk 4:35–41).

The eternal Word of God became human, lived as part of earthly creation, and comes to us in, with and under the elements of bread and wine. The sacraments underscore the intimate relationship between God and a nature that is neither unclean nor unspiritual. In a variety of ways, nature imparts God's faithfulness and loving kindness.

A Family Portrait

The Bible tells of the goodness of creation. The first photographs of the earth relayed from space a quarter of a century ago gave us a portrait of a good planet. On a seemingly endless and void background, the earth appeared as a shimmering planet glowing in the light of the sun.

An earth-bound audience now had a portrait of the planet God made: the blue oceans, the green and brown continents, the white clouds and ice caps. We now had a portrait of the family—diverse, often divided, bound together in one earth system where every part connects with every other part.

Our planet has been through a lot in its five billion years: continental drift, ice ages, volcanic eruptions. Changes in soil, air and water have meant the appearance or disappearance of various forms of life. Predators have lived at the expense of other creatures. They, too, have received their food from God (Ps 104:21).

The earth is very good. Neither demonic nor divine, neither meaningless nor sufficient unto itself, it receives its meaning and value from God. It is filled with God's glory and permeated by God's grace (Isa 6:3).

OUR VOCATION

Humanity as Part of Nature

Humanity (in Hebrew, 'adam) is formed from dust of the ground (in Hebrew, 'adamah) (Gen 2:7). Out of the same ground the Creator causes trees to grow and makes beasts and birds. In *creation*, humans are connected to the earth and other living things.

In Isaiah's vision of redeemed creation, animals of all kinds—wolves and lambs, lions and calves, bears and cows—live peaceably together with the child and the serpent in a world united and filled with knowledge of the LORD (Isa 11:6–9). While Isaiah's vision need not be understood literally as a prediction of the future, it does show that in *redemption,* too, the bonds between humanity and other creatures remain intact.

The great creation Psalm 104 finds people joining wild goats, lions and birds in looking to God for sustenance. The Psalmist is joined by modern scientists in a vision of human beings, in their *day to day life,* as part of the earth system.

Throughout Scripture, heaven and earth and all living creatures witness to God's lordship and power. They bless God and sing praises to their Creator (Ps 148). In our hymn of praise we "join in the hymn of all creation" (*LBW,* p. 61; cf. Easter preface).

Humans and the rest of creation are bound together in creation, redemption, sustenance, praise and thanksgiving. It is right, therefore, to include nature in our understanding of humanity's relationship to God.

We stand as God's creatures within an orderly creation, our lives woven from threads of dependence and interdependence. We depend upon God, who gives us existence through interdependence with other human beings and with the rest of creation. We cannot be persons without other persons; we cannot be humans apart from other creatures.

What God Expects of Us

Humans are a part of nature, but with a special role on behalf of the whole. We receive dignity and responsibility that distinguishes us from the rest of creation. Our status (Gen 1; 2; Deut 4:32; Ps 8; 115:16; Lk 12:6–7) is affirmed when God becomes human.

Humans relate to God in distinctive ways: we are spiritually aware and morally accountable. This includes awareness of the significance of all creation, and accountability for the earth on which we depend.

Called to Be Neighbors to Other Creatures

When we say God is Creator, we acknowledge ourselves to be part of creation. The command to love the LORD and the neighbor (Deut 6:5; Lev 19:18; Mt 22:37–40) implies love for neighbors who are the whole of creation.

Throughout Scripture we find an interplay between concern for human benefit, and concern for the land and other living things. Strongly connected to love of self and human neighbor is love of the rest of creation. Linked to social justice is care for the environment.

Leviticus 25 brings together regard for social justice and regard for the earth. Along with the admonition "you shall not wrong one another" comes a provision for the land's jubilee or sabbath rest (Lev 25:4). The Creator blesses creation through rest from work (Gen 2:2); we have a sabbath (Gen 2:3; Ex 20:8–10); the land also has sabbath rest. Additionally, jubilee and sabbath regulations seem to view the welfare of both wild and domestic animals (esp. Lev 25:6–7; cf. Ex 23:10–11).

Human beings are given some responsibility for other creatures (Gen 1:26–30;2:19). Humans are to respect trees (Deut 20:19–20) and animals (Ex 23:12; Deut 22:6–7; 25:4). God's promise is for all of creation (Gen 9); God's compassion is for all living things (cf. the deutero-canonical Sir 18:13). This implies humane treatment of living things in activities such as laboratory experimentation, meat production and hunting.

While trees may be harvested, and animals used for work and slaughtered for food (after the entrance of sin into the world), we are to care for them. Rules on slaughter of animals, especially in post-biblical Jewish tradition, may ensure humane treatment, as well as ritual correctness.

The Bible also acknowledges that God deals with creation in some ways unknown to, and independent of us (Job 39–41). Our wonder of God, whose purposes we cannot fathom, is thereby deepened. Our esteem for other creatures, who have a value apart from what we give them, is heightened.

Called to Live According to the Wisdom of God's Creation

Scripture invites us, in fact urges us as a matter of life and death, to live according to the wisdom of God—learning prudence, paying attention, ordering our lives and our society according to the wisdom present at creation (Prov 8). The New Testament amplifies this by identifying Christ as the true Wisdom and Word of God (1 Cor 1:24; Eph 1:9; Col 2:3).

As God has called humanity to care for the earth, so God has given us the faculty for investigating the underlying wisdom and patterns of creation. In that sense, science is a modern counterpart to the wisdom of ancient Israel.

Dependent and interdependent creatures, we act correctly when we respect the wisdom and integrity of an earth system where human and other sorts of life flourish. In wisdom we know the limits of the earth system. These limits determine what we can do, and necessitate wise political, social and economic courses of action.

Although the face of the earth has changed over the centuries, often through degradation by humans, the same scientific laws are in operation. Political, social and economic conditions to which we order our lives change radically over the centuries, but they, too, have a continuity. We are no less interdependent with creation than the people of ancient Israel, no less bound by God's demand for justice.

Called to Serve and Keep the Earth

Part of humanity's job description is given in Genesis 2. There, the newly created human is placed by God in the fruitful garden and instructed to serve (in Hebrew, *'abad*) and keep (in Hebrew, *shamar*) the garden (Gen 2:15). These very verbs, often translated as "to till and to keep," are also used for serving and guarding God's temple and the tent of meeting in the wilderness (Num 3:7, 8; 4:47; 16:9).

As with the Garden of Eden, God entrusts the earth to us to serve and to protect. Serving and protecting are sacred tasks: we care for the earth as God's temple, in gratitude for God's care for us (Ps 121). Stewardship, in this environmental context, means serving life-giving cycles and rhythms of creation through restrained and creative intervention.

Called to Be God's Representatives

The cultures that surrounded ancient Israel saw only their kings—sons of the god—as an image of the divine. For Israel, all humanity was created in the image of God, after God's likeness (Gen 1:26). The myths of neighboring cultures presented humans as slaves of the gods. For Israel to say that human beings have dominion over the earth (Gen 1:28; Ps 8) was to affirm the dignity of all human beings, not to debase the rest of creation.

Made in the image of God and designated royal children of God, humans have the task of caring for the earth as representatives of God. Their dominion is to be in the image of God's dominion. "Dominion," however, is frequently removed from its proper setting and used to justify uncaring attitudes and destructive behavior toward the earth and its people.

There are other facts about dominion, a biblical yet easily misused term. *First,* having dominion does not mean that humans cease to be part of creation. We may differ qualitatively from other creatures in our ability to understand and influence the world. But we are still interdependent with the rest of creation; our power is *with* creation.

Second, the language of dominion sounded different to ancient Israelites, as compared to people with modern science and high technology. The people of biblical times were far more vulnerable to the power *of* nature. We, on the other hand, unleash considerable power *upon* nature. They could not cause global environmental disaster; we can.

Third, as God's representatives we must follow God's way of being sovereign—serving justly, loyally, compassionately (2 Sam 23; Ps 89; Isa 42:1–2; 49:1–6; 50:4–11; 52:13–53:12). As we sing at vespers: "You [God] are merciful, and you love your whole creation" (*LBW,* p. 144). God's way of being sovereign is clearly shown on the cross; it is self-giving (Jn 3:16; Phil 2:5–11).

SIN

FALLEN HUMANITY

Humanity has been driven from the garden (Gen 3:24). We have placed our highest loyalty and trust in something other than God. We have looked to ourselves or to things of our own making for ultimate security, meaning and purpose. Sometimes we have presumed ourselves to be masters of the universe. Sometimes we have made a god of nature itself—viewing it as ultimate, and considering its welfare apart from human needs.

We have sinned. In our desire to be like God (Gen 3:5–6), we have rejected the fact that we are creatures. We have lost sight of our place in creation, and have not done what God has called us to do on behalf of creation.

Sinners all, we threaten the creation. We oppress human and other neighbors in the name of nation, race, gender or ideology. We wreak social injustice and environmental degradation upon the earth. Sloth or cowardice then prevent us from rising to defend a creation that includes ourselves from the prospect of destruction.

Some environmental destruction is the accidental consequence of well-intentioned, well-designed ideas. Even our best efforts can fail. But when ignorance becomes invincible through denial, when misinterpretation results from self-serving bias, when comfort and convenience take priority over care-giving, when demands arise from infinite greed rather than finite need—sin is at work.

Churches have often mistaken domination for dominion, and acquiesced to life-styles and structures of exploitation. By leaving unchallenged such distorted ideas of God's will for creation, or by actively promoting them, they have contributed to a sinful state of affairs.

DISRUPTION OF CREATION

Scripture sees human sin as disrupting the rest of creation. Nature witnesses to God's covenant with Israel; nature reacts to Israel's unfaithfulness (Deut 11:13–17). When Israel obeys God's commands and acts in justice, the earth is blessed. But when Israel forgets her part of the covenant and ignores God's command to do justice, all nature cries out. Curses replace blessing.

Perhaps the most dramatic reaction to human injustice is recorded in Jeremiah's haunting vision of a creation reversed so that the earth finally appears before him as wasted and void. There are no mountains or hills, no humans or birds, no fruitful land or cities, no light in the heavens. There is only desolation (Jer 4:23–28).

Today we know well the danger of desolation caused by human sin. Patterns of social injustice have led to chaos in the environment. And the converse is also true: environmental degradation has intensified social injustice.

HOPE

FORGIVENESS

Massive degradation, suffering by humanity and the rest of creation—such are the signs of our failure to follow God's call. Hope for creation is possible, nevertheless, because of God's promise. Working graciously within both natural forces and history, God overcomes our failure and brings the universe to its intended destiny.

Against the threat of desolation, God comes as Savior of the world. God loves the world, to the point of experiencing the evil and death brought about by sin. *Through the death and resurrection of Christ, God does not save us FROM the world, but saves us AND the world.*

Beginning at the cross of Christ, we give up our pursuit of security and our arrogance toward the rest of creation. God's forgiveness enables us to see what we have done to one another and to the earth. Freed by forgiveness from the paralysis of guilt, regret and remorse, we serve and protect the victims of environmental degradation.

Life in Christ gives us the vision and confidence to follow our vocation on behalf of all creation. As we live in hope, and care for creation, we know the Holy Spirit is at work within nature and history. "The Lord and giver of life" restores the broken bonds of community among people, and between human beings and the rest of creation.

FULFILLMENT

God does not just *heal* a creation wounded by human sin; God *perfects* that creation. Although nature itself has not sinned or "fallen," it looks forward to a final fulfillment. Once again: creation hopes for liberation (Rom 8:18–25); "all things" are reconciled to God through the cross (Col 1:15–20).

To say that Christ died for forests and fish as well as for human beings is admittedly rather surprising. The idea does not startle us so much when we remember our dependent and interdependent relationships. We are fully human only with our environment. Since we are saved, there must be a sense in which the environment is saved as well.

Christian hope is not for human destiny only. The Creator of all things is also the Redeemer of all things.

"LIBERATING LIFE: A REPORT TO THE WORLD COUNCIL OF CHURCHES"

Liberating Life

INTRODUCTION: THE HISTORICAL CONTEXT

The theme of the 1991 General Assembly at Canberra is "Come Holy Spirit, Renew the Whole Creation." There are many ways in which creation needs renewal. It needs renewal from the debilitating poverty, repression, and violence under which hundreds of millions of people now suffer. It needs renewal from the shrinking of its forests, the loss of its topsoil, the pollution of its atmosphere, and the contamination of its waters. It needs renewal from the abuse of individual animals in factory farms and scientific laboratories. It needs renewal from war and the threat of nuclear war. This renewal depends on us as empowered by God, the Holy Spirit, who works in and through the whole creation.

This report was produced at a consultation sponsored by the World Council of Churches held at Annecy, France, in September 1988. Fourteen theologians attended, representing different theological traditions and coming from different parts of the world. As is apparent from the introduction to the report, liberation theologies and non-Western theologies played a prominent role in discussion. All participants, including those from North America and Europe, came to realize that the theme of liberation can itself be a promising stimulus toward modes of Christian thought that free people, the earth, and other creatures from various forms of exploitations.

The report was composed by the participants after their papers, written for the consultation, had themselves been discussed.

The Annecy report is not an official report *of* the World Council of Churches. Rather it is a report *to* the World Council of Churches *by* people brought together by the World Council for the purpose of deliberating upon the integrity of creation. The members of the consulta-

Pages 273–290 reprinted from *Liberating Life: Contemporary Approaches to Ecological Theology* edited by Charles Birch, William Eakin, and Jay McDaniel, Orbis Books, 1990. Reprinted with permission of Orbis Books.

tion felt that the report should not be altered in any significant way before being considered before the appropriate bodies of the World Council (except by Charles Birch and Jay McDaniel for this volume). Charles Birch and Jay McDaniel have added a few additional paragraphs and sentences to the original as originally submitted to the World Council, though for the most part the report is precisely as produced at Annecy. The additional material is bracketed.[1]

Indeed, life, in all its forms, cries out for liberation, for freedom. People across the earth are fighting for liberation from the pain of oppression due to poverty, gender, race, handicapping conditions, and many other causes. Liberation needs to be extended to animals, plants, and to the very earth itself, which sustains all life. Thus "the liberation of life," which is the theme for this report, extends the worldwide plea for peace and justice to all creatures, whom we humans need in order to exist, but of equal importance, who are valuable in and for themselves and to God.

Exploitation of People and Destruction of Other Forms of Life Are Inseparable

Consider South Africa. In 1988 the Afrikaner minority celebrated the 150th anniversary of the white man's "trek" into "the North," which was described in the Piet Relief Manifesto as "a beautiful country teeming with game" of every kind. In fact it was a beautiful country, where grass grew as tall as humans and silver streams cascaded down to the oceans on either side. In spite of internecine conflict, humans lived together in community with nature, and children innocently played with crystals later identified as precious diamonds. The indigenous people felt the presence of what they called *Modimo,* the Source and Presence of life, which penetrates through plants, humans and other animals, dark caverns and tall mountains. With "industrialization" and "development" this land has now been divided and fenced into farms, and its surface scarred and scratched to make a few people rich and powerful. It has been disemboweled at points and left agape in a quest for minerals, coal, gold, diamonds, and uranium for nuclear power. For sport alone, animals are hunted as trophies and some species have been rendered extinct. In less than two centuries a land of pristine splendor has become a repository of human heartlessness, a victim of "progress" and "civilization." As if this were not enough, this relentless onslaught has spilled over to human beings themselves. By means of Land Acts, native reserves were created and then developed into tribal homelands, human movement restricted by influx control, homes and family life disrupted to serve the interests of industry and commerce.

Or consider Korea. For four thousand years the Korean peninsula and the island just south of it, Cheju, had been a homogenous community of people united with the land. People spoke of their home as "the land of morning calm." In 1910 the Japanese colonized Korea, after which Korean women were recruited into the military, then forced to be prostitutes. Over two hundred thousand women died of sexual abuse. Then, immediately after the liberation from Japanese rule in 1945, the United States and the Soviet Union divided the peninsula. The Korean people were not consulted. Family members were separated against their will, and eighty thousand of the three hundred thousand Cheju islanders who protested the division of the peninsula were killed by Korean soldiers under the Far East command of the United States. Most of the victims were male. Now the island is famous for three things, strong winds, volcanic rocks, and its many women. Indeed, Cheju has become a center of international sex tourism. There are houses of prostitution with three to five hundred women in each. Meanwhile, polluting industries have been exported to the southern parts of the peninsula. Not only the land, air, and water have been harmed. Not long ago tens of thousands of people mourned the death of a fifteen-year-old boy who died of toxic poisoning as a result of working for only six months in a mercury-producing factory. A once united land has become a land of violence, division, and exploitation.

In each of these and myriad other situations, integral communities of people, animals, plants, and land have been neglected and destroyed. [This is not to say that the communities existed in a state of perfection prior to the arrival of foreign powers. They did not. As with all communities, they were mixtures of good and evil. It is to say, however, that the good they had achieved—in terms of satisfying relations between humans, between humans and other animals, and between humans and the earth—has been dramatically disrupted by the arrival of foreign powers, bringing with them science, technology, and nonindigenous concepts of "development."

Increasingly we realize that "development" promoted by advances in science and technology has been a two-edged sword. It has freed human life from much superstition and has opened a Pandora's box of goods and services to enrich life. But with these obvious benefits have come setbacks and destruction. With every passing day the potential of science and technology for bringing swift and widespread benefits to humanity is matched by its potential for ever swifter and more widespread damage and destruction to life and the environment.]

In many cases in the past the foreign powers offering "development" came from the West. They were accompanied by inadequate Christian perspectives—what Korean Minjung theologians call "division theologies"—which themselves become a source of community disintegration. The disintegration of these communities as a result of this assault by foreign powers, sometimes with the collaboration of indigenous elites, has had tragic consequences.

What characterizes a "division theology"? In its neglect and disdain for living communities, it has at least two features. The first is an arrogant approach to nature. The land and its creatures are objectified as mere tools for human use. The value of plants, animals, and land in their own right—as expressions of the Source and dynamic Presence of life itself, called *Modimo* by some Africans, and *Hanulnim* in Korea—is forgotten. Moreover, those who see nonhuman life in this way also often see human life in a similar manner. People become objects. The second feature of "division theology" is that it is male-centered. This way of thinking subordinates nature to human exploitation, the poor and destitute to the privileged and powerful, and women to control by men.

In response to the massive destruction of all forms of life, a theology that serves the liberation of life is needed. Such a theology must offer a view of creation that moves beyond arrogant anthropocentrism and promotes respect for communities of life in their diversity and connectedness to God. Moreover, the needed theology should welcome contributions from many voices, from those who have been heard, and especially from those who have not. Finally, and perhaps paradoxically, this new theological vision must promise to liberate those who, often unwittingly, are parties to oppression. Just as it liberates the victimized, humans and other living beings, a theology for the liberation of life can liberate people of privilege and power from their complacency and isolation. A theology that so serves the liberation of life is a theology of justice, peace, and respect for the integrity of creation.

A THEOLOGY FOR THE LIBERATION OF LIFE

As just said, the current destruction of living communities demands conversion to new thinking and commitment, a theology for the liberation of life. Informed by the biblical witness, the insights of science, and our experience of the interdependence of life, this theology needs to address the brokenness of our world and its intricate web of life with a new statement of the healing words of Christian faith.

THE BIBLICAL WITNESS

Christian visions of the world and of salvation are profoundly shaped by the biblical story of creation. For many generations in the West, this story was read primarily in human-centered terms; human beings were created in the image of God, commanded to be fruitful and multiply, given dominion over the rest of creation, only to disobey God and fall. This one-sided interpretation led to reading the remainder of the Bible as the story of human salvation alone. It also supported exploitative attitudes and practices in relation to the remainder of creation and the destruction of the habitat of many species.

As the disastrous consequences of this exploitation, both for the rest of creation and for humanity as a whole, have become manifest, Christians have reread the creation story. We have found that it locates the story of humanity in a much wider context, as a cosmic one. Before and apart from the creation of human beings, God sees that the animals are good. When humanity is added creation as a whole is very good. The command to human beings to be fruitful and to multiply does not nullify the identical command to animals. The image of God with its associated dominion is not for exploitation of animals but for responsible care. The plants that are good in themselves are given to both animals and human beings for their food. This is the integrity of creation in its ideal form.

According to the biblical stories, human sin disrupts this integral creation. As a consequence, there emerges competition and war between farmers and pastoralists. Injustice and strife proceed so far that God repents having created the world. Nevertheless, God saves the Noah family from the deluge, and at God's command this human family exercises its rightful dominion in saving all animal species from a watery death. When the waters recede God makes a covenant with the animals. From this vision of creation and human sin there follows a longing for inclusive salvation. The whole creation praises God, but this whole creation also groans in travail. As human sin has caused the subjection of all creation to futility, so the liberation of all life can come about only through the liberation of humanity from its bondage to Mammon.

The ideas expressed in the creation and Noah stories and the consequent vision of universal salvation have profound relevance today. All creatures have value in themselves as well as for one another and for God. Each, therefore, claims respect from human beings. The whole creation in all its rich complexity has a special value that is diminished when forests are turned into grasslands and grasslands are turned into deserts. The Noah story highlights God's concern for the preservation of species.

From these stories we acquire a distinctive understanding of "the integrity of creation." *The value of all creatures in and for themselves, for one another, and for God, and their interconnectedness in a diverse whole that has unique value for God, together constitute the integrity of creation.*

As human beings who participate in this creation we have a unique responsibility to respect its integrity, but in fact we have violated it in many ways. Indeed, our violence against one another and against the rest of creation threatens the continuation of life on the planet. It is now our opportunity and our duty, by God's grace, to be restored to peace and justice both in our relations to one another and in our relations with the rest of creation. As long as human beings order their lives to short-sighted economic gain or increased wealth, there will be no end to violence, oppression, or to the exploitation of the other creatures. Only a society ordered to the regeneration of the earth will attain peace and justice. Only in such a world is the integrity of creation respected and achieved.

Within the message of Jesus we find a profound deepening of the importance of our treatment of one another and especially of the weak and oppressed. "Truly, I say to you as you did it to one of the least of these my brothers and sisters, you did it to me" (Mt 25:40). Primarily this refers to our treatment of human beings, but on the lips of the Jesus who speaks of God's care for the grass of the field and the fallen sparrow, these too are included among "the least of these." In the hunger of millions of children, in the loneliness and humiliation of the homeless, in the wretchedness of the raped, in the suffering of the tortured, and also in the pain of myriads of animals used for human gain without regard to their own worth, Christ is crucified anew (Eph 1:10).

THE CONTRIBUTIONS OF SCIENCE

The contributions of the sciences are also an essential part of a theology for the liberation of life. When they avoid the assumptions of scientism and materialism, they open up the mystery of the cosmos in a most impressive way. Indeed, while in one sense science diminishes the area of the unknown, in another sense it leads us deeper into incomprehensible mystery. Recent discoveries in physics, biology, and other sciences tell us the story of an evolving universe that needs to be put side by side with our religious narrative. According to recent astrophysics, the universe originated in an event known as the Big Bang. During the first few moments of our world's infancy its fundamental pre-atomic physical features acquired numerical values that would eventually allow for the origin and evolution of living, sentient, and thinking beings. The stellar production of elements that make up cells and organisms required a universe of sufficient breadth and temporal duration to make life possible. The specific physical properties, the immense size, and the age of the universe are intimately related to the existence of life.

The biological theory of evolution with its ingredients of chance and struggle for existence requires a deeper understanding of divine power. God is not a magician but one who lovingly invites the created world to participate in the unfolding of the cosmic story. Evolutionary thinking compels us to acknowledge more explicitly than ever before the continuity of the whole network of life with the universe as such. The evolutionary cosmic epic contributes to a deeper understanding of the universe as our origin and our home. We are made of the same stuff as the stars. Our existence is deeply embedded in the existence of the universe itself.

Of course, there are senses in which human life is unique. Our unique qualities lie, not in an ontological discontinuity between us and the rest of nature, but rather in the remarkable degrees to which we can realize certain evolutionary capacities. We humans are unique in the range of our sensibilities, in our degree of freedom, in our capacities to understand the world, and in our control of the world through cultural evolution. These capacities are themselves developments out of, rather than apart from, the evolutionary process.

As these remarks concerning evolution suggest, an ongoing dialogue between science and theology is indispensable for addressing environmental issues. Such a conversation will help science to understand its task in the service of the whole creation. And it will also enable theology to remain in contact with the real world and thus be faithful to the earth. The world of the sciences, including the social sciences, is of special significance for demonstrating the intricate interrelatedness and interdependence of the biosphere, human community, and the cosmic totality. Without constant attention to the latest developments in the sciences, Christian theology will become irrelevant to those who strive to preserve peace, justice, and the integrity of creation. For theology to do less than come to terms with our present scientific understanding, for it to accept outmoded assumptions about reality from a different time, seems blatantly wrong-headed, even allowing for the qualification that science is an evolving and fallible enterprise.

IMAGING THE NEW SENSIBILITY

A contemporary reading of Scripture suggests an interrelatedness of all creatures within the earth and with God. Likewise, the story of the universe emerging from the sciences indicates that all that exists is part of everything else. How should Christians image this sensibility when speaking of God and of world? Whenever human beings attempt to speak about God, we do so in the language of our own time, our various cultures, and from familiar and important relationships. In biblical times, this language was of God as king and lord, but also of God as creator, father, mother, healer, and liberator. As we think about the way to express the relationship of God to the world in our time, we realize that metaphors such as king and lord limit God's activity to the human sphere; moreover, these metaphors suggest that God is external to the world and distant from it.

The creation narrative of our time, the awesome story of the beginning of the universe some ten billion years ago, evolving into our incredibly complex and intricate cosmos in which "everything that is" is interrelated, suggests the need for different symbolic language. Instead of a king relating to his realm, we picture God as the creator who "bodies forth" all that is, who creates not as a potter or an artist does, but more as a mother. That is to say, the universe, including our earth and all its creatures and plants, "lives and moves and has its being" in God (cf. Acts 17:28), though God is beyond and more than the universe. Organic images seem most appropriate for expressing both the immanence of God in and to the entire creation as well as God's transcendence of it. In the light of the incarnation, the whole universe appears to us as God's "body." Just as we transcend our bodies, so also the divine spirit transcends the body of the universe. And, just as we are affected by what happens to our body, so also God is affected by what happens in the world. The sufferings and joys of people and other creatures are shared by God.

When we express the relationship between God and the world (or universe) in organic images, several things become clearer. First, all of us, humans and other living creatures, live together within this body—we are part of each other and can in no way exist separately. Second, unlike the king-realm image which is hierarchical and dualistic and encourages human beings to adopt similar postures toward other members of their own species as well as toward other species, the organic symbolism underscores the inherent worth of all the different parts of the body, different species as well as individuals within those species. Third, while the body metaphor has been used since the time of Paul to express Christ, the Church (1 Corinthians 12:12–26), extending it to the cosmos (we are all members of the body of God, the universe) places us in intimate relations with all our fellow human beings as well as with all other forms of life. We not only empathize with all who are oppressed and suffer— victims of war and injustice, both humans and other living creatures—but we also feel responsibility for helping to bring about peace and justice to the suffering members of God's "body." God's glory and God's closeness are expressed in this image. We stand in awe of the One upon whom this universe depends, whether we view it through a telescope in which its vastness enthralls and terrifies us or through a microscope in which the intricate patterns of the veins of a leaf amaze us. And at a molecular level of life, the complex and beautiful structure of the DNA molecule that can exist in an indefinite variety of forms gives us a sense of awe and wonder. We also, each of us, are part of this universe, this body, in which God is present to us. We feel God's presence here in our world as we touch one another, love and serve one another, that is, all the others that make up the fabric of existence.

Our scripture speaks of the cosmic Christ (Colossians 1), the presence of God in the cosmos, God's embodiment, God's "incarnation." In this image of divine embodiment, we have a helpful way of talking about creation that is biblical, consonant with contemporary science, and experientially illuminating. The universe, everything that is, each and every living thing and the ecosystem that supports all things, is bound together, intrinsically and inextricably, with its creator. Within this bond, the oppression of life is common history, the liberation of life is our common responsibility and our common hope.

AN ETHIC FOR THE LIBERATION OF LIFE

An ethic for the liberation of life calls for seeing the whole of creation in its integrity and therefore demands respect of every creature. Human respect for fellow creatures properly emphasizes individual members of the human community itself. Peace among nations and justice both within and between them are crucial. But this human community is part of a larger community of creatures whose health is essential for the well-being of human beings. An ethic for the liberation of life involves concern for this larger community not only because of its importance to human beings but also for the sake of its other members.

An ethic for the liberation of life would involve treating all of these topics in detail. Fortunately, the issues of peace and justice have been treated throughout the history of the World Council of Churches and vigorous discussion is continuing. Accordingly, section 1 is a brief statement pointing toward this larger discussion. Section 2 is a slightly longer statement building on earlier discussions of a sustainable society. Section 3 notes very briefly the special importance of drastically reducing the extinction of species caused by human actions. These three sections are not unrelated. When any of these levels of the discussion is pressed, the others appear. Although reflection about peace and justice begins with human relations, relations with other creatures are extricably involved. The health of the ecosystem is essential for animals and human beings alike, and violence against ecosystems involves the oppression of human beings and the decimation of species. The need to preserve species is for the sake of the creatures themselves and at the same time for the sake of human purposes.

Section 4 is somewhat different. It does not discuss the benefit to human beings of right treatment of animals. Indeed, it implies that even when respect for animals does not coincide with human benefit it is still required of Christians. Perhaps it is partly for this reason that this topic has been ignored by the World Council of Churches and by most of its member churches up to now. To bring this neglect to focused attention, this section is more extensive. It rejects anthropocentrism by affirming the integrity of creation with peculiar vividness. The themes that unite this fourth section to the others are two: first, that the integrity of creation requires human beings to abandon domination and exploitation as a style of relating both to one another and to the rest of creation, and, second, that respect for the integrity of creation calls upon us to expand our conviviality, that we live with other creatures in peace and justice.

PEACE AND JUSTICE

Much of the discussion of peace and justice has dealt with their interrelatedness: There is no peace without justice, no justice without peace. This means that the mere absence of war between the superpowers, essential as that is, is not peace, and that an egalitarianism enforced by violence is not justice. An ethic for the liberation of life expands on these familiar ideas. For there is no true peace when the wider community of life is violated, and there is no justice when its animal members are not respected.

The quest for peace between nations aims to end the enormous expenditures and preparations especially for war by the superpowers and their allies. These expenditures not only add to the threat of military destruction but also rob the earth of resources that could be used to meet pressing human needs and contribute to global pollution. In the United States the endless preparation for war gives grossly unjust power to the military-industrial-university complex. Even unaligned nations are drawn into arms races that distort their economies. The emphasis on arms often leads to military dominance of their governments and the oppression of their people.

Respect for the Integrity of the Ecological Community

The integrity of the ecological community is threatened when plants and animals are used exclusively as objects without due consideration for the long-term sustainability of the ecological community.

With the exception of minerals and petro-chemical products, modern civilization depends entirely upon products from four ecological systems: croplands, pastures, forests, and fisheries. Yet in most if not all countries today, each of these ecological systems shows symptoms of being overstressed. In the case of forests and fisheries, the stress is so great that global production itself is declining.

Below are some selected examples of ecological communities that are under threat. They are a few of any number of examples that might be chosen. In each of these examples ecological communities are used for food and other products. There is a conflict between the present self-interest of some people, the present public interests of many people, the interests of posterity, and the interests, present and future, of nonhuman nature itself. No one of these interests can become dominant without another suffering.

[The conception of the sustainable community is one that is helpful here. It envisions a management of ecological communities such that they continue to exist indefinitely into the future. This does not necessarily mean that they persist without change, but that such changes as do occur are within the limits that permit sustainability of the community as a whole. The sorts of changes in the Sahel regions of Africa in the last decade, for example, were such as to result in desertification and irreversible destruction of the ecological community that had persisted for numerous biological generations. These sorts of changes are unsustainable; what is needed are modes of human interaction with the rest of nature that are sustainable.]

Modern Agriculture—Croplands and Grasslands

Agricultural practices over the millennia have often proved unsustainable. Whole civilizations have collapsed when they exhausted the soils that supported them. Half the land that was available when farming began is now unstable. The pace at which desertification proceeds has greatly accelerated with capital-intensive agriculture in the past fifty years as much sustainable family farming has been replaced by corporate agriculture. This has driven millions of people off the land and into urban slums especially in the United States and in many third world countries. The laborers who replace the family farmers often suffer from the chemicals that also cause the soil to deteriorate. Nations formerly capable of feeding them-selves are now dependent upon imported food. For example, in parts of Brazil, mono-cultures of sugar cane have replaced the staple crops of rice and beans that formerly contributed to a staple diet.

One major cause of the unsustainability of modern agriculture, which is chemically intensive, energy intensive and mono-cultural, is the deterioration of soil structures. This in turn is caused by the intensive use of chemical fertilizers and pesticides, which deplete the soil of microorganisms that normally maintain soil structure. Another cause is rising water tables in irrigation areas with consequent salination of the soil. When the plants no longer cover the soil from these and other causes, wind often blows away much of the top soil. The violence of much industrialized agriculture to the life-support system is at the same time violence against the poor. It violates the integrity of creation.

Forestry

Tropical rain forests are now disappearing at the rate of one football field every second, mostly in Latin America and South East Asia. These forests sustain the greatest diversity of plants and animals known in any terrestrial habitat. The destruction of habitats is the main cause of extinction on earth today. Hence the destruction of rain forests is the main cause of the extinction of species in our own time. When the forests are cleared, soil erosion sets in and in many places the soil becomes useless. In other places attempts are made to replace the forest with farms, often with disastrous results. The chances of the forests returning are remote. So when the rain forest is gone, it is gone forever. The tragedy of the ecological community is paralleled time and time again by human tragedy. This is particularly so when the forests have been the home and livelihood of indigenous peoples. As in unsustainable agriculture, we find unsustainability of the ecological community due to human interference by one group of people leads to misery and tragedy for others.

Marine Communities

Much could be said about disrespect for the integrity of marine communities. A few examples will have to suffice. The major oceanic fisheries around the world have declining yields (for example, the anchovy fisheries off the coast of Peru and a number of fisheries in the North Atlantic). Two main causes of these declines seem to be over-fishing and pollution. In both cases we have good guidelines for preventing such interferences with the natural communities so that they may be sustained. But the implementation of such practices seem to be exceedingly difficult. Very often the people who suffer most are the poor who are dependent upon such fish as they can catch or buy cheaply. The greed and mismanagement of the few leads to the suffering of the many.

The recent deaths of seals in the North Sea and Baltic Sea illustrate a trail of interconnections that lead to ecological disaster. It seems that toxic wastes in the sea, resulting from industrial pollution, may cause an immune deficiency in the seals. This renders them susceptible to a virus or viruses to which they are normally immune. In a healthy environment seals do not succumb to such viruses. A greater respect for the health of their environment might well have avoided the death of the seals.

Experience tells us that if we look after nature, nature looks after us. That is a prudential reason for not turning ecologically sustainable communities into unsustainable ones. But an ethic for the liberation of life goes only part of the way if it ends there. It should be extended to the well-being of individual organisms. This is the subject of section 4.

The Maintenance of Biological Diversity

Throughout the history of life numerous species have become extinct. Human activity from early times has increased the rate of extinction. With the vast growth of human population and economic activity in this century the rate of extinction has accelerated.

There are many reasons to be concerned. Much of potential value to human beings is lost. Innumerable creatures that should be respected are being destroyed instead. The rich diversity of plant and animal life which, according to Genesis, God saw to be, in community with human beings, "very good," is being simplified. The life of God is impoverished.

Although attention is often focused on efforts to protect some endangered species, such as the California condor, by quite artificial means, the major cause of extinction is destruction of habitat. In general, habitat has been wilderness, and the human pressure on wilderness has greatly reduced it on every continent. The lessening of this pressure is a matter of moral urgency. Instead of viewing wilderness as empty or undeveloped, we must learn to see it as full of life, often far richer and more diverse than what we call "occupied" or "developed" land. Wilderness is usually able to sustain a vast diversity of life for tens of thousands of years, whereas "development" often leads to great reduction of this diversity and sometimes to the inability to sustain even that for extended periods. The attitude of conquest should give way to reverence toward the integrity of these parts of creation.

Respect for Individual Animals

The biblical and theological messages about the value of animals speak with one voice: Animals do not exist for the sake of the unbridled pursuit of human avarice and greed. And yet the increasingly powerful transnational corporations prefer that people not know, or not care, about the pain and death literally billions of animals are made to suffer every year in the name of corporate mass-production and consumer over-consumption. Some examples follow.

Cosmetics and Household Products

Many areas of the world have an abundance of toothpastes, colognes, after-shaves, deodorants, perfumes, powders, blushes, detergents, oven and window cleaners, furniture and floor polishes, and other cosmetics and household products. This is well-known. What is not well-known is that these items routinely are tested on animals in a variety of painful ways, including acute eye-irritance tests as well as so-called "lethal dose" tests, in which animals are force-fed a deodorant or floor polish, for example, until a specific number die. When we purchase the products of the major cosmetic and household products' corporations, we support massive animal pain and death—all of which is unnecessary. For there are alternatives. Attractive cosmetics and effective household products that are both safe and economical, that have *not* been tested on animals, already exist and are available, and others would be if enough consumers demanded them.

Fashion

Mass-production and over-consumption encourage ignorance and indifference in the name of fashion. Nowhere is this more evident than in the case of fur products (coats, capes, gloves, and the like). Fur-bearing animals trapped in the wild inevitably suffer slow, agonizing deaths, while those raised on "modern" fur-farms live in unnatural conditions that severely limit their ability to move, groom, form social units, and engage in other patterns of behavior that are natural to their kind. When we purchase the products of commercial furriers, we support massive animal pain and death—all of which is unnecessary. For there are alternatives. Many attractive coats, capes, gloves, and the like, which are not directly linked to the commercial exploitation of animals, already exist and are available, and others would be if enough consumers demanded them.

Food

Increasingly, the family farm is being replaced by national and often multi-national interests, business ventures void of any roots in the land on bonds to the animals they raise. The goal of mass-production is to raise the largest number of animals in the shortest time with the least investment. The "good shepherd" has given way to the corporate factory.

Corporate animal agriculture relies on what are called "close-confinement" or "intensive rearing" methods. The animals are taken off the land and raised permanently indoors. There is no sunlight, no fresh air, often not even room enough to turn around. In many cases six to eight laying hens are packed in a wire-mesh metal cage three-quarters of the size of a page of daily newspaper. For up to five years, many breeding sows are confined to stalls barely larger than their bodies. Veal calves (typically male calves born to dairy herds) routinely are taken from their mothers at birth and raised in permanent isolation. Increasingly even dairy cattle are being taken off the land and raised indoors.

Because of the massive numbers of farm animals raised for slaughter (upwards of 4 billion annually, just in the United States), huge amounts of grains are used as feed. More than 90 percent of the oats, corn, rye, barley and sorghum crops grown in the United States, for example, are fed to animals, and this use of food is enormously wasteful. Every pound of complete protein produced by beef cattle requires eight to nine pounds of complete vegetable protein, while every pound of complete protein supplied by hogs requires four to five pounds of complete vegetable protein. When more protein is being used to produce less, it is no exaggeration to say that we have a protein production system running in reverse.

On the corporate factory that is today's animal farm, virtually every natural form of behavior is thwarted, from preening and dust bathing in chickens to nursing and gamboling in veal calves. When we purchase the products of corporate factory farming, we support massive animal deprivation and death—all of which is unnecessary. For alternatives exist. People can choose to purchase the products of the remaining small-scale family farms or explore a dietary life-style free from all direct commercial connections with the suffering death of animals.

Entertainment

Many different animals are used for commercial purposes in entertainment. The forms of entertainment include circuses, stage and aquatic shows, rodeos, bullfights, and organized cock and dog fights. In whatever form, the animals are treated as mere means to human ends. Sometimes (as in the case of bull and bronco busting in rodeos) the animals are caused more than incidental pain. Sometimes (in the case of the housing and transportation of circus and other "performing" animals) the animals are subjected to severe and often protracted deprivation. Sometimes (as in the case of animals who perform "tricks" in stage and aquatic shows) the animals are rewarded for their ability to mimic human behavior (for example, by balancing themselves on balls or jumping through hoops). And sometimes (as in the case of bull, cock, and dog fights) some of the animals are killed and all are made to endure acute suffering.

When we patronize these forms of entertainment, we support those commercial interests that reduce the value of animals to the status of the purely instrumental, often at the cost of great pain (and sometimes even death) for the animals themselves—and all of this is unnecessary. For alternatives exist. We do not have to train, exploit, outwit, or outmuscle animals, or to support those who make a profit from doing so, in order to take pleasure in their presence or their beauty. Benign forms of recreation involving animals exist. For some people this may involve photography, scuba, and other forms of ocean diving, or the viewing of any one of the thousands of films about wildlife. For all people this can involve becoming attentive to and appreciative of many forms of animal life that live in community with us, wherever we live.

Education

A traditional rite-of-passage for children and adolescents in the affluent world is compulsory dissection of animals. Those students who resist or refuse for reasons of conscience routinely are ridiculed or punished for their moral sensitivity. Often they stand alone, abandoned even by their parents, ostracized by their peers. And yet this exercise in scholastic coercion is totally unnecessary. For alternatives exist. These include detailed drawings of animal anatomy and physiology, state-of-the art videos of relevant dissections, and even computer programs that enable students to "dissect" a frog, for example, on a screen rather than dissect a once living organism. When we support an educational system that callously punishes young people for being concerned about the integrity and value of animals, we tacitly support not only the unnecessary pain and death of countless numbers of animals but also the moral damage done to our children.

The examples given above are only that: examples. There are many other ways in which people fail to show minimal respect for animals as creatures of God. These include instances of wasteful, needlessly duplicative, and poorly executed scientific use of animals, the "sport" of hunting, and the killing of members of rare and endangered species, such as the African elephant and the black rhino. Like the previous examples, these further ones have a common denominator: A creature having intrinsic value is reduced to one having only instrumental value—as an object of mere scientific curiosity, a trophy, or a source of illegal profit.

The ethic of the liberation of life is a call to Christian action. In particular, how animals are treated is not "someone else's worry," it is a matter of our individual and collective responsibility. Christians are called to act respectfully towards "these, the least of our brothers and sisters." This is not a simple question of kindness, however laudable that virtue is. *It is an issue of strict justice.* In all our dealings with animals, whether direct or indirect, the ethic for the liberation of life requires that *we render unto animals what they are due, as creatures with an independent integrity and value.* Precisely because they cannot speak for themselves or act purposively to free themselves from the shackles of their enslavement, the Christian duty to speak and act for them is the greater, not the lesser.

In facing this new challenge—this challenge to liberate all life, the animals included—Christians should aspire to two ideals:

1. Seek knowledge.

2. Act justly.

The first ideal enjoins us to break the habit of ignorance when it comes to how animals are being treated. It bids us to ferret out truth, to make the invisible visible, to make the obscure clear. The second ideal bids us to make our own life a living expression of justice towards God's creation, to bring peace to our own lives even as we work to bring peace to the world. Indeed, we are unlikely to succeed in doing the latter if we fail in doing the former. There is little hope, that is, that we can change the world if we cannot even change ourselves: in the choice of the cosmetics and household products we use, the clothes we wear, the food we eat, and the entertainment we patronize. The ethic for the liberation of life begins at home.

Much else remains to be considered. Laws and institutions that permit or encourage the oppression of animals need to be identified and changed. The truth about the ways animals are oppressed needs to be made known, beginning in the church itself. Our children need to be sustained in their natural empathy with and compassion for animals, and this means that certain traditional practices in their education, including in particular compulsory dissection, will have to be altered. Clearly, the struggle to liberate life is not for the faint of heart.

Yet just as clearly it is a struggle no thoughtful Christian can avoid. When St. Paul says that "the whole creation has been groaning in travail together until now," he speaks to our time and our circumstances. For the animals have been groaning, though we have heard them not. We hear them now. They cry for justice. We cannot fail to answer.

CONCLUSION

The theme of this report is "the liberation of life." Increasingly during this century Christians have come to understand the gospel, the Good News, in terms of freedom, both freedom *from* oppression and freedom *for* life with God and others. Too often, however, this freedom has been limited to human beings, excluding most other creatures as well as the earth. This freedom *cannot* be so limited because if we destroy other species and the ecosystem, human beings cannot live. This freedom *should not* be so limited because other creatures, both species and individuals, deserve to live in and for themselves and for God. Therefore, we call on Christians as well as other people of good will to work toward the liberation of life, *all* life.

RECOMMENDATIONS

1. There is a real need to bring together persons of diverse emphasis and perspective from Latin American liberation theologies, feminist theologies, black theologies, ecological theologies, Minjung theologies, and African theology, those committed to animal rights, those struggling to free Christianity from its anti-Jewish tendencies and those involved in dialogue with persons of other living faiths.

The aim would be to go beyond the still somewhat fragmentary and divisive works of such thinkers to a consensual theological statement that would not be a specialized theology geared to particular issues, but a fresh statement of the heart of Christian faith for the whole community of believers.

We therefore request JPIC ("Justice, Peace, and Integrity of Creation") to organize such a meeting for the further development of Christian theology that expresses the convictions of persons concerned for justice, peace, and the integrity of creation.

2. We recommend that JPIC and the sub-unit on Church and Society of the World Council of Churches co-sponsor a series of conferences designed to envision in concrete terms what social, economic, agricultural, and industrial structures and practices would make possible ecologically sustainable modes of development and progress which take account of human respect for the integrity of creation, peace, and justice. Such conferences should include persons representing points of view similar to those identified in recommendation one. Those willing to think in new categories from such areas as political theory, sociology, anthropology, economics, agriculture, climatology, and oceanography should also be included.

3. We commend the sub-unit on Church and Society for its work in bringing together theologians and scientists for informative and critical dialogue. In the light of our description of the role of the sciences in the theology for the liberation of life, we recommend that these conferences continue.

4. In view of the ecologically unsustainable practices of modern agriculture and forestry we recommend to JPIC that these issues be priorities on the agenda of JPIC.

5. Seminary education is woefully lacking in basic courses in ecology and/or perspectives in science and religion. It is certainly not necessary for divinity students to have in-depth understanding of scientific procedures. What is imperative is a basic, even minimal, perspective of how contemporary science depicts reality. Many men and women preparing for the ordained ministry hold a Newtonian, individualistic, substantialist view of reality. It is this understanding that they attempt to correlate with Christian faith, resulting in an individualistic, otherworldly theology of salvation. We recommend to the sub-units of Theology and Education of the World Council of Churches that member churches of the WCC counsel their seminaries to require coursework in the contemporary scientific "picture" of reality, a picture that underscores the interdependence and interrelatedness of all reality. Such a view could profoundly influence how church leaders preach and teach in regard to the relationship of human beings to the environment.

6. In view of the widespread maltreatment of animals throughout the world and in view of the intrinsic value of individual animals to themselves and to God we recommend that Church and Society take appropriate steps to: (a) encourage the churches and their members to acquire knowledge about how animals are being treated and in what ways this treatment departs from respect for the intrinsic value to themselves and of animals as creatures of God and how abuses could be minimized through legislation and other means; (b) encourage members of the Christian community to act according to such guidelines as the following:

i. Avoid cosmetics and household products that have been cruelly tested on animals. Instead, buy cruelty-free items.

ii. Avoid clothing and other aspects of fashion that have a history of cruelty to animals, products of the fur industry in particular. Instead, purchase clothes that are cruelty-free.

iii. Avoid meat and animal products that have been produced on factory farms. Instead, purchase meats and animal products from sources where animals have been treated with respect, or abstain from these products altogether.

iv. Avoid patronizing forms of entertainment that treat animals as mere means to human ends. Instead, seek benign forms of entertainment, ones that nurture a sense of the wonder of God's creation and reawaken that duty of conviviality we can discharge by living respectfully in community with all life, the animals included.

7. We recommend that Church and Society encourage the member churches of the World Council of Churches to involve Christians in environmental causes and to cooperate with organizations which defend ecological communities at regional and parish levels.

8. We recommend that Church and Society sponsor a series of courses for church leaders on the emergent theme of our consultation: the liberation of life. In such courses church leaders from different parts of the world, selected by a subcommittee of the sub-unit in consultation with any additional sponsors, could be introduced to the environmental crises of our time, to problems of animal abuse, and to theological perspectives emerging out of the JPIC process, such as those proposed in this report, which encourage a constructive response to such issues.

A NOTE ON THE REPORT

1. The report has received considerable worldwide attention, not least because it represents one of the strongest statements ever produced by a Christian ecumenical body on respect for animals. While the participation at the Annecy Consultation felt the issue of animal rights is an important topic on which, unfortunately, the church has been all too silent for centuries, they did not feel this the only important issue addressed in the document. Equally important, from the point of view of the participants, is the report's emphasis on linking concerns for ecological sustainability with concerns for social justice; on moving beyond oppressive under-standings of God; on recognizing the deleterious effects of exclusively Western understand-ings of development on the peoples of Asia, Africa, Latin America, and Oceania; on recogniz-ing the importance of science for contemporary Christian thought; and on recognizing bibli-cal resources for affirming what the World Council has called the integrity of creation.

One important feature of the report is that it attempts to offer a biblically rooted, succinct definition of that phrase—*the integrity of creation*. According to the report: *The value of all creatures in and for themselves, for one another, and for God, and their interconnectedness in a diverse whole that has unique value for God, together constitute the integrity of creation.* The participants at Annecy thought that this definition invites Christians to recognize the ultimate inseparability, at least from God's point of view, of concerns for ecological sustainability, social justice, and animal protection. In any case the editors of this book hope that this report will stimulate constituent members of the World Council of Churches, as well as readers in general, to formulate their own positions on these important issues.

"CHRISTIANITY AND ECOLOGY"

John F. Haught

Precisely why should we care about the nonhuman natural world? Most of us probably believe that it is a good thing to do, and we can even give some very convincing pragmatic answers to the question. But theology is concerned with the religious justification of any ecological concern we might have. It is the task of environmental theology to spell out, from within the context of a particular religious tradition, the *ultimate* reasons why we should care about the cosmos. In my case, the tradition is Christian, and so in this and the following chapter I would like to draw out what I think are some distinctive contributions of Christian faith to the ecological movement.

I have already suggested that the threat of global ecological collapse need not lead us to abandon our religious traditions, but that it could be a major historical stimulus to their revitalization. Yet in the case of Christianity such a suggestion may seem too optimistic. Critics of this tradition, as well as some Christian authors themselves, have complained about Christianity's complicity in the western war against nature? Hasn't Christianity been too anthropocentric, too androcentric, too otherworldly and too cavalier about the intrinsic value of nature? Hasn't its theology so overemphasized the need to repair the "fall" of humanity that it has almost completely ignored the original goodness of creation? Hasn't it heard the words of Genesis about human "dominion" over the earth as an imperative to exploit and deface it?

Whether these accusations are justified or not, it is at least certain that many Christians, perhaps even the majority of them, continue to interpret the physical universe as though it were little more than a "soul school" wherein we are challenged to develop our moral character but which itself has little intrinsic significance and no share in human destiny. In this interpretation nonhuman nature is merely a set of props for the drama of human salvation or a way-station for the human religious journey.

Because of its traditionally longing so much for another world, British philosopher John Passmore doubts that Christian theology can ever reshape itself in an ecologically helpful way without ceasing thereby to be Christian. Since Christianity actually sanctions our hostility toward nature, he argues, the only healthy alternative is a radical secularism:

Reprinted from *The Promise of Nature* by John F. Haught © 1993 John F. Haught. Used by permission of Paulist Press.

Only if men see themselves ... for what they are, quite alone, with no one to help them except their fellowmen, products of natural processes which are wholly indifferent to their survival, will they face their ecological problems in their full implications. Not by the extension, but by the total rejection, of the concept of the sacred will they move toward that sombre realization.[1]

While Passmore's indictment of Christianity may be harsh, I think we have to admit that environmentally speaking this tradition, like many others, has been at best ambiguous.[2] While the doctrines of creation and incarnation clearly affirm the value of the cosmos, most Christian spiritualities, saints and scholars have been relatively indifferent to nature. The welfare of the natural world has seldom, if ever, been a dominant concern. We can boast of St. Francis of Assisi, or of Ignatius Loyola, who urged us to see God in all things (and that would have to include nature as well). But we cannot forget other saints like Martin and John of Ephesus, each at opposite ends of the Mediterranean during the rise of Christianity, both of whom are famous for their prowess in the art of deforestation.[3] And if expressions of a deep love of nature appear in some Christian hymnody and hagiography, there are just as many indications of a desire to escape from nature in other facets of the tradition.[4]

Concern for either local or global environmental welfare is not a very explicit part of the Christian tradition. Nevertheless, I agree with Paul Santmire that there is great promise for theological renewal in the ecologically ambiguous Christian tradition.[5] In fact a rethinking of Christianity in terms of the environmental crisis is already under way, and it is the cause for some optimism that this tradition may potentially be enlivened by an ecological transformation. The new theological reflection comes in several different strains, of which I shall discuss three. I will call these respectively the *apologetic,* the *sacramental* and the *eschatological* attempts to formulate an environmental theology. None of these can be found in a perfectly pure form, and aspects of all three may be found in the work of any single author. Nevertheless, they vary considerably in theological method, and so I hope it will prove illuminating to treat them here as distinct types.

THE APOLOGETIC APPROACH

The first, and the least revisionist of the three, is the more or less apologetic enterprise of trying to show that there is already a sufficient basis in scripture and tradition for an adequately Christian response to the environmental crisis. It is exemplified by recent statements of the pope and the American Catholic bishops,[6] as well as a number of theological articles and books published in the past decade or so.[7] According to this approach, which runs the range from biblical literalism to very sophisticated theological scholarship, we have simply ignored the wealth of ecologically relevant material in the tradition. Therefore, what we need to do now in order to have an adequate environmental theology is simply dig up the appropriate texts and allow them to illuminate the present crisis. Sometimes this apologetic method merely scours the scriptures for nuggets of naturalism in order to show that the Bible cares about the cosmos after all. At its most simplistic extreme it does little more than recite the psalms and other biblical passages that proclaim creation as God's handiwork. But at a more erudite level of interpretation it excavates the themes of incarnation and creation as theological warrants for an ecological theology. In addition it digs out environmentally sensitive, and previously overlooked passages in the early Christian and other theological writings.[8] More than anything else, though, the apologetic approach emphasizes the biblical notion that God has given humanity "dominion" and "stewardship" over creation, and that this is reason enough for us to take care of our natural environment.

This first type of ecological theology also argues that if only we practiced the timeless religious virtues we could alleviate the crisis. Since one of the main sources of our predicament is simple human greed, the solution lies in a renewed commitment to humility, to the virtue of detachment, and to the central religious posture of gratitude by which we accept the natural world as God's gift and treat it accordingly. If we allowed our lives to be shaped by genuinely Christian virtues, our relation to nature would have the appropriate balance, and we could avert the disaster that looms before us.

I call this approach apologetic because it defends the integrity of biblical religion and traditional theology without requiring their transformation. It holds, at least implicitly, that Christianity is essentially okay as it is, that environmental abuse stems only from perversions of pure faith and not from anything intrinsic to it, and therefore that Christianity does not need to undergo much of a change in the face of the present emergency. Rather, we need only to bring our environmental policies into conformity with revelation and time-tested doctrine. With respect to the present state of our environment, the fault is not with Christianity but with our failure to accept its message.

How are we to evaluate this apologetic approach (which is probably the one most Christians, and I suspect most Christian theologians, take today)? On the positive side, I would say that it does develop an indispensable component of an ecological theology: it turns our attention to significant resources in the Christian classics that have not been sufficiently emphasized. Its highlighting the environmental relevance of traditional teachings, forgotten texts and religious virtues is very helpful. We need this retrieval as we begin the work of shaping a theology appropriate to the contemporary crisis.

Moreover, a good dose of apologetics is certainly called for today in the face of many incredibly simplistic complaints by some historians that Christianity is the sole or major cause of the environmental crisis. A sober analysis of the historical roots of the crisis will show that some of the antinature attitudes associated with Christianity comprise only one aspect of a very complex set of ingredients leading to the present destruction of the ecosphere. An unbiased historical analysis can also demonstrate that major aspects of Christianity have firmly resisted the dominating practices that led us to the present situation. Thus, some defending of Christianity seems entirely appropriate.

However, I do not think that this apologetic type goes far enough in opening Christian faith to the radical renewal the ecological crisis seems to demand. I seriously doubt that we can adequately confront the problems factoring our natural environment, theologically speaking, simply by being more emphatic about familiar moral exhortations or by endlessly exegeting scriptural passages about the goodness of nature or the importance of stewardship. Such efforts are not insignificant; indeed they are essential. But I wonder if they are fundamental enough. In the face of the chastisement Christianity has received from secular environmentalists, the apologetic quest for relevant texts, teachings and virtues does not go far enough. I doubt that even the most impressive display of biblical or patristic passages about God and nature will allay this criticism or, for that matter, turn many Christians into serious environmentalists. In order to have an adequate environmental theology Christianity, I think, will need to undergo a more radical internal change.

THE SACRAMENTAL APPROACH

The beginnings of such a change are now taking place in what I shall call the sacramental approach to Christian ecological theology. This second type focuses less on normative religious texts or historical revelation than does the apologetic approach, and more on the allegedly sacral quality of the cosmos itself. It is more willing to acknowledge the revelatory character of nature. It comes in a variety of theological forms ranging from what has been called "natural theology," which focuses on the apparent evidence for God's existence in nature, to the cosmic spirituality of Thomas Berry[9] and Matthew Fox and their followers.[10] It is also found, in different ways and degrees, in non-Christian religions, as well as in the spirituality of eco-feminists and some so-called "deep ecologists."[11]

In its typical form this sacramental approach interprets the natural world as the primary symbolic disclosure of God. Religious texts and traditions are still important, but the cosmos itself is the primary medium through which we come to know the sacred. Today the sacramental approach usually accommodates evolutionary theory and aspects of contemporary physics. It embraces a holistic view of the earth as an organism comprised of a delicately balanced web of interdependent relationships. Rejecting mechanism, it regards the entire universe organismically, that is, as an intricate network of dynamic interconnections in which all aspects are internal to each other. Hence, it also places particular emphasis on the continuity of humans with the rest of the natural world.

Accordingly, it views our spiritual traditions not as activities that we humans "construct" on the face of the earth, but as functions that the cosmos performs through us. According to Thomas Berry, for example, the universe is the primary subject, and humanity is one of many significant developments of the universe. Cultures and religions are simply natural extensions of the cosmic process rather than unnatural creations of lonely human exiles on earth.

In the Christian context today I think this revisionist approach finds its most compelling expression in what has been called "creation-centered" theology. As the prime example of our second type it goes beyond the apologetic variety of environmental theology by arguing that our present circumstances require a whole new interpretation of what it means to be Christian. In the face of the environmental crisis it will not do simply to take more seriously our inherited texts and teachings. These are still important, but they must be carefully sifted and reinterpreted in terms of a cosmological, relational, nonhierarchical, nonpatriarchal, nondualistic and more organismic understanding of the universe. We must pay more attention to the sacral quality of the universe and not place such a heavy burden on premodern religious texts to give us the foundations of our environmental ethic.

In Christian circles this creation-centered outlook accepts the doctrines of the creed but gives them a cosmological interpretation. It may be helpful to look briefly at several of the results of its recosmologizing of traditional Christian teachings.

1.   As the label suggests, this new theological emphasis brings the biblical theme of *creation* to the center of theology instead of subordinating it, as it has been in the past, to the theme of redemption. Theology's focusing primarily on the redemption of a "fallen" world has distracted us from an adequate reverencing of the intrinsic goodness of nature. Moreover, our understanding of redemption has been too anthropocentric. We have been so obsessed with overcoming our human sinfulness and suffering, that we have forgotten about the travail of nature as a whole.

2.   Creation-centered theology also argues that we need a correspondingly broader understanding of that from which we are said to be redeemed, namely, *sin*. It insists that sin means not just our estrangement from God or from each other, but also the present condition of severe alienation of the cosmos from ourselves. Reconciliation then implies not only the restoration of human communion but, just as fundamentally, our reintegration with the earth-community and the whole of the universe. In order to experience this reconciliation we must abandon all forms of religious dualism which have sanctioned our self-distancing from nature.

3.   Creation-centered theology insists also that we need to rethink what we mean by *revelation*. Revelation is not just God's self-manifestation in history, let alone the communication of divine information in propositional form. We need to think of revelation in more cosmic terms. The universe itself is the primary revelation. In its 15 billion-year evolution the cosmos is the most fundamental mode of the unfolding of divine mystery. The mystery of God is revealed gradually in the evolution of matter, life, human culture and the religions of the world (and not just in biblical religion either). Viewed in terms of cosmic evolution our religions can no longer be explained or explained away as simple heartwarming gestures that

estranged humans engage in on an alien terrain as we look toward some distant far-off eternity. Rather, religions are something that the universe does through us as it seeks to disclose its mysterious depths. The fact of there being a plurality of religions is in perfect keeping with evolution's extravagant creation of variety and difference. Hence, an ecological spirituality should be no less committed to preserving the plurality of religions in the world than it is to the salvaging of biodiversity. We should lament the loss of religious diversity since religions are also products of cosmic evolution and just as deserving of conservation as the multiple species of plants and animals.

4.   Viewing things in this cosmological way, creation-centered theology appreciates both ancient and modern efforts to understand the *Christ* also as a cosmic reality, and not simply as a personal historical savior. Cosmic Christology, already present in ancient Christian theology, needs to be recovered today in terms of an evolutionary and ecological worldview. The entire cosmos (and not just human society) is the body of Christ. A cosmic Christology then provides the deepest foundations of a distinctively Christian environmental spirituality. And in keeping with this cosmic Christology the eucharistic celebration ideally represents the healing not only of severed human relationships, but also of the entire universe.

5.   The theological experiment of creation-centered theology culminates in an ecological understanding of *God*. Here the trinitarian God is the supreme exemplification of ecology, a term which refers to the study of relationships. Creation in the image of God then means that the world itself has being only to the extent that, like God, it exists in relationship. An ecological theology is congruent both with contemporary science and the classic doctrine of the Trinity, a doctrine which renounces the idea that God exists only in isolated aseity.

6.   This ecological contextualization of Christian teaching leads us in the direction of a whole new *spirituality*. Creation-centered theology encourages an enjoyment of the natural world as our true home. Traditional spiritualities, often characterized by a discomfort with bodily existence, received parallel expression simultaneously in the sense of humanity's fundamental homelessness in nature. The classic texts of Christianity have unfortunately been tainted by a dualistic bias that has sanctioned our hostility toward nature and the body. For this reason a purely apologetic type of environmental theology is inadequate, for it is not sufficiently alert to such ideological flaws in the classic sources.

7.   Moreover, an ecological spirituality requires its own kind of *asceticism*. This asceticism prescribes a renunciation not of the natural world but of the Enlightenment ideal of autonomous, isolated selfhood. It subjects us to the arduous discipline of taking into full account the fact of our being inextricably tied into a wider earth-community. A full life, one in which we acknowledge our complex relation to the universe, widens our sense of responsibility toward ourselves and others. Above anything else, this means adopting a continually expanding posture of inclusiveness toward all otherness that we encounter, including the wildness of the natural world.

8.   Creation-centered spirituality in turn inspires a restructuring of Christian *ethics* in terms of an environmental focus. Ethics cannot be grounded only in the classic moral traditions which usually left the welfare of the cosmos out of the field of concern. An environmental awareness gives a new slant to social ethics and life ethics. In place of (or alongside of) social justice, it advocates a more inclusive "eco-justice" according to which we cannot repair human inequities without simultaneously attending to the prospering of the larger earth-community. And being "pro-life" means going beyond the focus simply on the ethics of human reproduction. An environmentally chastened life ethic questions aspects of current moral teachings that tolerate policies which, while protective of human fertility, ignore the complex life-systems in which human fertility dwells.[12]

9.   Finally, creation-centered theology advocates the reshaping of *education* from the earliest years so that it pays closer attention to the natural world. At the level of secondary and college education, including the core curriculum, this would mean making environmental education central and not just an afterthought. Our students should be required to look carefully at what both science and religion have to say about the universe, and yet remain critical of scientism and materialism, both of which are no less ecologically disastrous ideologies than are dualistic and patriarchal forms of religion.

The most characteristic feature of this contemporary revision of theology is its focus on the sacramentality of nature. (By "sacrament," let us recall, we mean any aspect of the world through which a divine mystery becomes present to religious awareness.) Ever since the Old Stone Age aspects of nature such as clean water, fresh air, fertile soil, clear skies, bright light, thunder and rain, living trees, plants and animals, human fertility, etc., have symbolically mediated to religious people at least something of the reality of the sacred. As we saw in the previous chapter, sacramentalism recognizes the transparency of nature to the divine, and it therefore gives to the natural world a status that should evoke our reverence and protectiveness. The sacramental perspective reads in nature an importance or inherent value that a purely utilitarian or naturalist point of view cannot discern. Nature, then, is not primarily something to be used for human purposes or for technical projects. It is essentially the showing forth of an ultimate goodness and generosity.

In principle the sacramental features of Christianity (and of other religions) protect the integrity of the natural world. According to our second type of environmental theology, therefore, the nurturing of a sacramental vision is one of the most important contributions Christianity and other religions can make to the preservation of the natural world. If biodiversity eventually decays into a homogeneity similar, say, to the lunar landscape (and this is the direction in which things are now moving) we will lose the richness of our sacramental reference to God. And if we lose the environment, Thomas Berry is fond of saying, we will lose our sense of God as well.

By way of evaluation, I would say that this second type of environmental theology is another important step toward an acceptable Christian environmental theology. It goes beyond the more superficial efforts of our first type which consist primarily of an apologetic search for texts that allegedly contain a ready-made environmental theology adequate to our contemporary circumstances. Our second type seeks a radical transformation of all religious traditions, including Christianity, in the face of the present crisis. The creation-centered approach is aware that religious texts, like any other classics, can sometimes sanction policies which are socially unjust and ecologically problematic. So it allows into its interpretation of the classic sources of Christian faith a great deal of suspicion about some of the same motifs that our first approach holds to be normative.

To give one example, the ideal of human dominion or stewardship over creation, which is fundamental in our first type of environmental theology, turns out to be quite inadequate in the second. Stewardship, even when it is exegetically purged of the distortions to which the notion has been subjected, is still too managerial a concept to support the kind of ecological ethic we need today. Most ecologists would argue that the earth's life-systems were a lot better off before we humans came along to manage them. In fact, it is almost an axiom of ecology that these systems would not be in such jeopardy if the human species had never appeared in evolution at all. So, even if we nuance the notions of stewardship and dominion in the light of recent scholarship, the biblical tradition is still too anthropocentric. And since anthropocentrism is commonly acknowledged to be one of the chief causes of our environmental neglect, creation-centered theology seeks to play down those theological themes that make us too central in the scheme of things. In the shadow of the environmental crisis it seeks a more cosmic understanding of Christianity.

At the same time, this approach acknowledges that we humans still play a very important role in the total cosmic picture. Our presence enriches and adds considerable value to life on earth. However, the concept of dominion or stewardship, important as it is, fails to accentuate that we belong to the earth much more than it belongs to us, that we are more dependent on it than it is on us. If in some sense we "transcend" the universe by virtue of our freedom and consciousness, in another sense this same universe is taken up as our constant companion in our own transcendence of it. Christian theology now needs to emphasize more than ever before the inseparable and (as we shall develop in the next chapter) the everlasting connection between ourselves and the cosmos.[13]

THE ESCHATOLOGICAL APPROACH

As I have already hinted, I have much stronger sympathies with the second approach than with the first (although the exegetical work that accompanies the first is also quite fruitful).

Any attempt to construct a Christian environmental theology today must build on the sacramental interpretation of nature. Today Christianity desperately needs to bring the cosmos back into the center of its theology, and creation-centered theology is an important contribution to this process.

However, if we are looking for Christianity's possible significance in the global project of bringing an end to the crisis that threatens all of humanity as well as life on earth, I think in all honesty we have to ask whether the Bible's most fundamental theme, that of a divine promise for future fulfillment, is of any relevance here. In other words, we need to ask whether the *eschatological* dimension of Christianity, its characteristic hope for future perfection founded on the ancient Hebrew experience of God's promise and fidelity, can become the backbone of an environmentally sensitive religious vision. If a return to cosmology is theologically essential today, then from the point of view of Christian faith, we need assurance that this cosmology remains adequately framed by eschatology.

During the present century, we have rediscovered the central place of eschatology in Christian faith. Hope in God's promise upon which Israel's faith was built is now also seen to be the central theme in Christian faith as well, a fact that bonds Christianity very closely to its religious parent. The faith of Jesus and his followers was steeped in expectation of the coming of the reign of God. Reality is saturated with promise, and the authentic life of faith is one of looking to the fulfillment of God's promise, based on a complete trust that God is a promise keeper. True faith scans the horizon for signs of promise's fulfillment. For this faith present reality, including the world of nature in all of its ambiguity, is pregnant with hints of future fulfillment.

Until recently this way of looking at the cosmos, namely, as the embodiment of promise, had almost completely dropped out of Christian understanding. It had been replaced by a dualism that looked vertically above to a completely different world as the place of fulfillment. The cosmos itself had no future. Only the immortal human soul could look forward to salvation, and this in some completely different domain where all connection with nature and bodiliness would be dissolved. That such an interpretation of human destiny could arise in a community of faith which from the beginning professed belief in the resurrection of the body is indeed ironic. But more than that, it is tragic. For by suppressing awareness of the bodiliness of human nature dualism was inclined also to disregard the larger matrix of our bodiliness, the entire physical universe which is inseparable from our being. By excepting nature and its future from the ambit of human hope Christianity left the cosmos suspended in a state of hopelessness. It had forgotten St. Paul's intuition that the entire universe yearns for redemption. Fortunately theology has begun to retrieve this inspired idea. Now any ecological theology worked out in a Christian context must make this motif of nature's promise the very center of its vision.

John F. Haught

It is easy enough to argue that Christianity's sacramental quality, which it shares with many other religions, affirms the value of nature. But the Bible, because of the multiplicity of traditions it embodies, has an eschatologically nuanced view of sacramentality. It is aware, for example, that something is terribly wrong with the present world and that any sacraments based on the present state of nature inevitably participate in this imperfection. Pure sacramentalism, therefore, is not enough. Biblical faith looks less toward a God transparently revealed in present natural harmony than toward a future coming of God in the eschatological perfection of creation. It is especially this hopeful tone, and not just its sacramentalism, that can ground an ecological spirituality. As we seek a Christian theology of the environment, therefore, we need to ask how the future-oriented, promissory aspect of this tradition connects with contemporary ecological concern. Most recent attempts by Christians to build an environmental theology have made only passing reference to the eschatological vision of nature as promise.[14]

Hence, as an alternative to the apologetic and the sacramental types, I am proposing a more inclusive eschatological cosmology as the foundation of a Christian environmental theology. Here the cosmos is neither a soul-school for human existence nor a straightforward epiphany of God's presence. Rather, it is in its deepest essence a promise of future fulfillment. Nature is promise. If we are sincere in proposing a theology of the environment that still has connections with biblical religion, we need to make the topic of promise central, and not subordinate, in our reflections. In order to do this in an ecologically profitable way we must acknowledge that the cosmos itself is an installment of the future, and for that reason deserves neither neglect nor worship, but simply the kind of care proportionate to the treasuring of a promise.

A Christian environmental theology, I am maintaining, is ideally based on the promissory character of nature. But some religious thinkers will complain that the biblical theme of promise is not very helpful in theological efforts to ground ecological ethics. Following Arnold Toynbee, Thomas Berry, for example, argues that it is precisely the biblical emphasis on the future that has wreaked ecological havoc. For Berry the future orientation of the Bible has bequeathed to us the dream of progress, and it is the latter that has caused us to bleed off the earth's resources while we have uncritically pursued an elusive future state of perfection. Berry holds that biblical eschatology, with its unleashing of a dream of future perfection, is inimical to environmental concern. According to this leading creation-centered geologian, hoping in a future promise can lead us to sacrifice the present world for the sake of some far-off future fulfillment. Although he is a Catholic priest himself, Berry considerably distances himself from the prophetic tradition that many of us still consider to be the central core of biblical faith and the bedrock of Christian ethics.[15]

But would our environmental theology be consonant with biblical tradition if we left out the prophetic theme of future promise? The sacramental accent taken by Berry and many other religiously minded ecologists has the advantage of bringing the cosmos back into our theology, and this is essential today. But Berry seems to be embarrassed by eschatology. Hence, in spite of his many valuable contributions to environmental thinking, I would have to question whether his and some other versions of creation-centered theology have adequately tapped the ecological resources of biblical eschatology.

In the preceding chapter's general depiction of religion I argued that the sacramental component present in Christianity and other religions is ecologically significant. Preserving religion's sacramentality contributes to the wholeness of both nature and religion. But we cannot forget that in the Bible sacramentality is taken up into eschatology. Biblical hope diverts our religious attention away from exclusive enrapturement with any present world-harmony and from nature's alleged capacity to mediate an epiphany of the sacred through its present forms of beauty. Instead, the Bible's eschatology encourages us to look toward the future coming of God. In terms of this particular religious accent any reversion to pure sacramentalism is suspect. It has, in fact, been condemned outright by prophets and reformers as faithless idolatry.

Christianity, aided by its roots in biblical monotheism, and owing to its unique emphasis on the promise of history, may itself be partly responsible for the demotion of the sacramental attitude which some religious ecologists now wish to make paramount. By understanding the promising God of history to be alone holy, Judaism and Christianity (as well as Islam) seem to have divested any present state of nature of its supposedly sacral character. Belief in God's radical transcendence of nature, and the location of absolute reality in the realm of the historical or eschatological future—these seem to have relativized present cosmic realities, at times to the point of insignificance. The biblical desacralization of nature may even have helped open up the natural world to human domination and exploitation. Biblical religion expels the gods from the forests and streams once and for all, and because of its "disenchantment" of nature, along with its focus on the historical future, it is problematic to some religious ecologists of a more sacramental or cosmological persuasion.

Adding to this environmentally controversial character of biblical religion is the fact that, in terms of the fourfold typology of religion presented in the previous chapter, prophetic faith falls predominantly in the active or transformative type. The Bible not only gives thanks for present creation, but it also seeks to change it. It celebrates the Sabbath on one day, but it permits work on the other six. Because it is based fundamentally on the sense of promise it can never remain totally satisfied with present reality, including any present harmoniously balanced state of nature. This is because it looks toward the future perfection of creation. That is, it moves beyond any merely vertical sacramentalism that seeks to make the divine fully transparent in presently available nature. It acknowledges the imperfection of the present state of creation and seeks to reshape the world, including the natural world, so that it will come into conformity with what it takes to be God's vision of the future. Some writers

John F. Haught

have sensed herein an ecologically dangerous feature of Christianity. The Bible's prophetic tradition is then itself blamed for unleashing the dream of a transforming "progress" that has ended up wrecking the earth rather than perfecting it.

This is a serious charge, and I simply cannot respond to it adequately here. I might just point out that apologists of our first type rightly indicate that though the biblical texts emphasize God's transcendence of nature they do not sanction the kind of exploitation of nature that some historians have traced to this doctrine. Even so, it seems appropriate for us to ask whether a pure sacramentalism would itself guarantee that we will save the environment. And, on the other hand, is it self-evident that actively transforming nature will lead inevitably to its degradation? John Passmore, whom I quoted earlier, says that

> ... the West needs more fully to ... "glorify" nature. But it cannot now turn back [to a sacralization of nature]...; only by transforming nature can it continue to survive. There is no good ground, either, for objecting to transformation as such; it can make the world more fruitful, more diversified, and more beautiful.[16]

At the same time, he goes on to say that

> ... societies for whom nature is sacred have nonetheless destroyed their natural habitation. Man does not necessarily preserve ... the stream he has dedicated to a god; simple ignorance ... can be as damaging as technical know-how.[17]

Thus an immoderate sacramentalism may be not only religiously but also environmentally irresponsible. If carried to an extreme, Passmore insists, the sacramental view can even precipitate environmental neglect. It may do so by causing us naively to trust that nature can always take care of itself. And he argues that one of the main causes of ecological destruction is the human ignorance which only a heavy dose of scientific learning can help to dispel.[18]

While many ecologists will certainly take issue with Passmore on this matter, he helpfully forces us to ask whether we need to think of nature itself as sacred, as many religious environmentalists are now suggesting, in order to ground its intrinsic value. Can the sacramental vision proposed by Berry and creation-centered theology all by itself motivate us religiously to take care of our planet?

My own suggestion is that, without denying the ecological importance of the sacramental approach, we may follow the Bible's lead by holding close to the theme of promise. For to suppress the theme of hope and promise whenever we do any kind of theologizing from a Christian point of view, no matter what the occasion or the issue, is to fail to engage the heart and soul of this tradition. I am more sympathetic, therefore, with the theological program of Jürgen Moltmann who for almost three decades now has consistently argued that all Christian theology must be eschatology.[19] Theology must be saturated with hope for the future. And what this means for our purposes here is that environmental theology must also be future oriented, no matter how tendentious this may initially appear from the point of view of a pure sacramentalism.

I am afraid that the creation-centered approach, valuable as it is in retrieving the cosmos that has been tragically lost to our theology, has not paid sufficient attention to the radically eschatological, promise-laden, character of Christian faith. It has helpfully promulgated what has been called a "lateral transcendence," that is, a reaching out beyond the narrow boundaries of our isolated selfhood in order to acknowledge the ever-expanding field of present relationships that comprise the wider universe.[20] But this horizontal transcendence must be complemented by a looking-forward-beyond-the-present. Transcendence, understood biblically, means not only a movement beyond narrowness toward a wider inclusiveness, but also a reaching toward the region of what Ernst Bloch calls "not-yet-being," toward the novelty and surprise of an uncontrollable future.[21]

Consequently, I would like to persist in my suggestion that the distinctive contribution Christian theology has to offer to ecology (since many of its sacramental aspects are present in other traditions) is a vision of nature as promise. A biblical perspective invites us to root ecology in eschatology. It reads in cosmic and sacramental reality an intense straining toward the future. It obliges us to keep the cosmos in the foreground of our theology without removing the restlessness forced on the present by a sense of the yet-to-come.

The Bible, in fact, includes not only human history but also the entire cosmos in its vision of promise. The universe, as St. Paul insinuates, is not a mere point of departure, a *terminus a quo*, which we leave behind once we embark on the journey of hope. Modern science has also demonstrated that our roots still extend deep down into the earth and fifteen billion years back in time to the big bang. Hence, our own hoping carries with it the whole universe's yearning for its future.

The natural world is much more than a launching pad that the human spirit abandons as it soars off toward some incorporeal absolute. Through the sacramental emphasis of creation-centered spirituality (as well as the powerful voices of deep ecology, ecofeminism and the many varieties of contemporary naturalism) the cosmos now claims once again that it, too, shares in our hope. Billions of years before our own appearance in evolution it was already seeded with promise. Our own religious longing for future fulfillment, therefore, is not a violation but a blossoming of this promise.

Human hoping is not simply our own constructs of imaginary ideals projected onto an indifferent universe, as much modern and postmodern thought maintains. Rather, it is the faithful carrying on of the universe's perennial orientation toward an unknown future. By looking hopefully toward this future we are not being unfaithful to the cosmos, but instead we are allowing ourselves to be carried along by impulses that have always energized it. If we truly want to recosmologize Christianity then we do well also to "eschatologize" our cosmology. Eschatology invites us to make more explicit nature's own refusal to acquiesce in trivial forms of harmony. It persuades us to understand the universe as an adventurous journey toward the complexity and beauty of a future perfection.

IMPLICATIONS FOR ENVIRONMENTAL ETHICS

In the light of an eschatological cosmology let us then ask once again: why should we be concerned about our natural environment? Not only because it is sacramentally transparent to the sacred, but even more fundamentally because it is the incarnation of a promise yet to be fulfilled. It is because nature is not only sacrament but also promise that we are obliged to revere it. In the sacramental view we condemn environmental abuse because it is a sacrilege. But in the eschatological perspective the sin of environmental abuse is one of despair. To destroy nature is to turn away from a promise. What makes nature deserve our care is not that it is divine but that it is pregnant with a mysterious future. When looked at eschatologically its value consists not so much of its sacramentally mediating a divine "presence," as of its nurturing a promise of future perfection.

Nature is not yet complete, nor yet fully revelatory of God. Like any promise it lacks the perfection of fulfillment. To demand that it provide fulfillment now is a mark of an impatience hostile to hope. Nature is wonderful, but it is also incomplete. We know from experience that it can also be indifferent and ugly at times. A purely sacramental or creation-centered theology of nature cannot easily accommodate the shadow side of nature. By focusing on ecological harmony it expects us to see every present state of nature as an epiphany of God. This is a projection which neither our religion nor the natural world can bear.

An eschatological view of nature, on the other hand, allows ambiguity in as a partner to promise. Nature's harshness, which so offends both religious romantics and cosmic pessimists, is entirely in keeping with its being the embodiment of promise. The perspective of hope allows us to be realistic about what nature is. We do not have to cover up its cruelty. We can accept the fact that the cosmos is not a paradise but only the promise thereof.

The world, including that of nonhuman nature, has not yet arrived at the final peace of God's kingdom, and so it does not merit our worship. It does deserve our valuation, but not our prostration. If we adopt too naive a notion of nature's significance we will inevitably end up being disappointed by it. If we invest in it an undue devotion we will eventually turn against it, as against all idols, for disappointing us—as it inevitably will. For that reason an exclusively sacramental interpretation of nature is theologically inadequate, and it can even prepare the way for our violating the earth. I think that a biblical vision invites us to temper our devotion with a patient acceptance of nature's unfinished status. Understanding the cosmos as a promise invites us to cherish it without denying its ambiguity.

SUMMARY AND CONCLUSION

The Christian story of hope embraces the entirety of cosmic occurrence as part of its promise. Looking toward the future in hope requires that we preserve nature for the promise it carries. A religion of hope allows us to accept nature as imperfect precisely because it is promise. A sacramental theology is all by itself unable to accommodate the fact of nature's fragility. To accept nature's intrinsic value we can learn from primal sacramental traditions much that we had forgotten. But in order to accommodate both its ambiguity and its promise we are usefully instructed not only by the spirituality of primal traditions, but also by the story of Abraham.

NOTES

1. John Passmore, *Man's Responsibility for Nature* (New York: Scribner, 1974), p. 184.

2. See Paul Santmire, *The Travail of Nature* (Philadelphia, Fortress Press, 1985).

3. Robin Lane Fox, *Pagan and Christian* (San Francisco: Harper & Row, 1988), p. 44.

4. Very early in the history of Christianity there appeared the "heresies" of docetism and monophysitism, which denied the incarnation of God in Christ, and gnosticism, which advocated escape from the allegedly evil material world. In spite of their being officially condemned by the Christian church, however, docetism and monophysitism still hover over our Christology, and gnosticism continues to infect Christian spirituality. The previous failure of Christianity effectively to confront the ecological crisis is in part the result of its continuing flirtation with these excessively spiritualist perspectives, both of which are embarrassed at our historicity, our "naturality" and our embodied existence.

5. Paul Santmire, *The Travail of Nature* (Philadelphia: Fortress Press, 1985).

6. See the World Day of Peace Message by Pope John Paul II entitled *The Ecological Crisis: A Common Responsibility* (1990), and the American Catholic bishops' recent statement, *Renewing the Earth* (1992).

7. One of the best examples of the apologetic type, from a quite conservative Catholic standpoint, is Charles M. Murphy's *At Home on Earth* (New York: Crossroad, 1989). From a more "liberal" Catholic perspective, but still within the framework of what I am calling the apologetic kind of environmental theology, is John Carmody's provocative *Religion and Ecology* (New York: Paulist Press, 1983). Most current Christian theology of the environment is apologetic in nature.

8. See, for example, Bernard J. Przewozny, "Elements of a Catholic Doctrine of Humankind's Relation to the Environment," in B. J. Przewozny, C. Savini and O. Todisco, *Ecology Francescana* (Rome: Edizioni Micellanea Francescana, 1987), pp. 223–255.

9. Thomas Berry, *The Dream of the Earth.*

10. Matthew Fox, *Original Blessing* (Santa Fe: Bear & Co., 1983); and Brian Swimme, *The Universe Is a Green Dragon* (Santa Fe: Bear & Co., 1984).

11. For a compendium of such viewpoints see Charlene Spretnak, *States of Grace* (San Francisco: Harper & Row, 1991).

John F. Haught

12. Whenever it ignores the fact that overpopulation adds enormously to every kind of ecological degradation, Christian moral teaching ironically contributes to what the Irish missionary to the Philippines, Sean McDonagh, has called the "death of birth," and therefore does not deserve to be called "pro-life" in the deepest sense of the term. See his *The Greening of the Church* (Maryknoll: Orbis Books, 1990), pp. 38–73.

13. See Fritjof Capra and David Steindl-Rast, *Belonging to the Universe* (San Francisco: HarperCollins).

14. A major exception is Jürgen Moltmann, *God in Creation,* trans. Margaret Kohl (San Francisco: Harper & Row, 1985).

15. Berry, p. 204.

16. Passmore, p. 179.

17. Ibid., pp. 175–76.

18. Ibid.

19. Jürgen Moltmann, *Theology of Hope,* trans. James W. Leitch (New York: Harper & Row, 1967).

20. The concept of lateral transcendence is that of Linda Holler, cited by Spretnak, p. 155.

21. See Ernst Bloch, *The Principle of Hope,* Vol. I, trans. Neville Plaice, Stephen Plaice and Paul Knight (Oxford: Basil Blackwell, 1986).

"THE SCOPE OF THE BODY: THE COSMIC CHRIST"

Sallie McFague

The suffering of creation—undoubtedly the greater reality for most creatures, human as well as nonhuman—is addressed by the scope of the body or the cosmic Christ. *Whatever* happens, says our model, happens to God also and not just to us.[1] The body of God, shaped by the Christic paradigm, is also the cosmic Christ—the loving, compassionate God on the side of those who suffer, especially the vulnerable and excluded. All are included, not only in their liberation and healing, but also in their defeat and despair. Even as the life-giving breath extends to all bodies in the universe, so also does the liberating, healing, *and* suffering love of God. The resurrected Christ is the cosmic Christ, the Christ freed from the body of Jesus of Nazareth, to be present in and to all bodies.[2] The New Testament appearance stories attest to the continuing empowerment of the Christic paradigm in the world: the liberating, inclusive love of God for all is alive in and through the entire cosmos. We are not alone as we attempt to practice the ministry of inclusion, for the power of God is incarnate throughout the world, erupting now and then where the vulnerable are liberated and healed, as well as where they are not. The quiescent effect on human effort of the motif of sacrificial suffering in the central atonement theory of Christianity has made some repudiate any notion of divine suffering, focusing entirely on the active, liberating phase of God's relation to the world.[3] But there is a great difference between a sacrificial substitutionary atonement in which the Son suffers for the sins of the world and the model of the God as the body within which our bodies live and who suffers with us, feeling our pain and despair. When we have, as disciples of Jesus' paradigmatic ministry, actively fought for the inclusion of excluded bodies, but nonetheless are defeated, we are not alone, even here. And the excluded and the outcast bodies for which we fought belong in and are comforted by the cosmic Christ, the body of God in the Christic paradigm.

THE DIRECTION OF CREATION AND THE PLACE OF SALVATION

The immediate and concrete sense of the cosmic Christ—God with us in liberation and in defeat—is the first level of the scope or range of God's body. But there are two additional dimensions implied in the metaphor that need focused and detailed attention. One is the relationship between creation and salvation in which salvation is the *direction* of creation and creation is the *place* of salvation. The metaphor of the cosmic Christ suggests that the cosmos is moving *toward* salvation and that this salvation is taking place *in* creation. The other dimension is that God's presence in the form or shape of Jesus' paradigmatic ministry is available not just in the years 1–30 C.E. and not just in the church as his mystical body, but everywhere, in the cosmic body of the Christ. Both of these dimensions of the metaphor of the cosmic Christ are concerned with *place* and *space*, with where God's body is present in its Christic shape.[4] Christian theology has not traditionally been concerned with or interested in spatial matters, as we have already noted, priding itself on being a historical religion, often deriding such traditions as Goddess, Native, and "primitive" for focusing on place, on sacred spaces, on the natural world. But it is precisely place and space, as the common creation story reminds us, that must now enter our consciousness. An ecological sensibility demands that we broaden the circle of salvation to include the natural world, and the practical issues that face us will, increasingly, be ones of space, not time. On a finite, limited planet, arable land with water will become not only the symbol of privilege but, increasingly, the basis of survival. Geography, not history, is the ecological issue. Those in the Christian tradition who have become accustomed to thinking of reality in a temporal model—the beginning in creation; the middle in the incarnation, ministry, and death of Jesus Christ; and the end at the eschaton when God shall bring about the fulfillment of all things—need to modify their thinking in a spatial direction. We need to ask where is this salvation occurring here and now, and what is the scope of this salvation?

In regard to the first dimension of the cosmic Christ, what does it mean to say that salvation is the *direction* of creation and creation is the *place* of salvation? To say that salvation is the direction of creation is a deceptively simple statement on a complex, weighty matter. It is a statement of faith in the face of massive evidence to the contrary, evidence that we have suggested when we spoke of the absurdity of such a claim in light of both conventional standards and natural selection. Some natural theologies, theologies that begin with creation, try to make the claim that evolutionary history contains a teleological direction, an optimistic arrow, but our claim is quite different. It is a retrospective, not a prospective claim; it begins with salvation, with experiences of liberation and healing that one wagers are from God, and reads back into creation the hope that the whole creation is included within the divine liberating, healing powers. It is a statement of faith, not of fact; it takes as its standpoint a concrete place where salvation has been experienced—in the case of Christians, the paradigmatic ministry of Jesus and similar ministries of his disciples in different, particular places—and projects the shape of these ministries onto the whole. What is critical, then, in this point of view about the common creation story is not that this story tells us anything about God or salvation but, rather, that it gives us a new, contemporary picture with which to remythologize

Christian faith. The entire fifteen-billion-year history of the universe and the billions of galaxies are, from a Christian perspective, from this concrete, partial, particular setting, seen to be the cosmic Christ, the body of God in the Christic paradigm. Thus, the direction or hope of creation, all of it, is nothing less than what I understand that paradigm to be for myself and for other human beings: the liberating, healing, inclusive love of God.

To say that creation is the place of salvation puts the emphasis on the here-and-now aspect of spatiality. While the direction motif takes the long view, speaking of the difficult issue of an evolutionary history that appears to have no purpose, the place motif underscores the concrete, nitty-gritty, daily, here-and-now aspect of salvation. In contrast to all theologies that claim or even imply that salvation is an otherworldly affair, the place motif insists that salvation occurs *in* creation, in the body of God. The cosmic Christ is the physical, available, and needy outcast in creation, in the space where we live. In Christian thought creation is often seen as merely the backdrop of salvation, of lesser importance than redemption, the latter being God's main activity. We see this perspective in such comments as "creation is the prologue to history" or "creation provides the background and setting for the vocation of God's people,"[5] and in Calvin's claim that nature is the stage for salvation history. In this way of viewing the relation between creation and redemption, creation plays no critical role: it is only the stage on which the action takes place, the background for the real action. But in our model of the body of God as shaped by the Christic paradigm, creation is of central importance, for creation—meaning our everyday world of people and cities, farms and mountains, birds and oceans, sun and sky—is the place where it all happens and to whom it happens. Creation as the place of salvation means that the health and well-being of all creatures and parts of creation is what salvation is all about—it is God's place and our place, the one and only place. Creation is not one thing and salvation something else; rather, they are related as scope and shape, as space and form, as place and pattern. Salvation is for all of creation. The liberating, healing, inclusive ministry of Christ takes place *in* and *for* creation.

These two related motifs of the direction of creation and the place of salvation both underscore expanding God's liberating, healing, inclusive love to all of the natural world. This expansion does not eclipse the importance of needy, vulnerable human beings, but it suggests that the cosmic Christ, the body of Christ, is not limited to the church or even to human beings but, as coextensive with God's body, is *also* the direction of the natural world and the place where salvation occurs.

NATURE AND THE COSMIC CHRIST

These comments lead us into the second dimension of the metaphor of the cosmic Christ, which also concerns spatiality. The world in our model is the sacrament of God, the visible, physical, bodily presence of God. The cosmic Christ metaphor suggests that Jesus' paradig-

Sallie McFague

matic ministry is not limited to the years 1–30 C.E. nor to the church, as in the model of the church as the mystical body of Christ, but is available to us throughout nature. It is available everywhere, it is unlimited—with one qualification: it is mediated *through bodies.* Our model is unlimited at one end and restrictive at the other: the entire cosmos is the habitat of God, but we know this only through the mediation of the physical world. The world as sacrament is an old and deep one in the Christian tradition, both Eastern and Western. The sacramental tradition assumes that God is present not only in the hearing of the Word, in the preaching and reading of Scripture, and not only in the two (or seven) sacraments of the church, but also in each and every being in creation. While Christian sacramentalism derives from the incarnation ("the Word became flesh"), the sense of the extraordinary character of the ordinary or the sacredness of the mundane is scarcely a Christian insight. In fact, it is more prevalent and perhaps more deeply felt and preserved in some other religious traditions, including, for instance, Goddess, Native, and Buddhist ones.[6] Moreover, Christian sacramentalism has usually been utilitarian in intent, that is, using the things of the world as symbols of religious states. They are often not appreciated in their own integrity as having intrinsic value but rather as stepping stones on one's pilgrimage to God. This perspective is evident in a famous passage from Augustine's *Confessions,* in which all the delights of the senses are transmuted into symbols of divine ecstasy: "But what is it I love when I love You? Not the beauty of any bodily thing . . . Yet in a sense I do love light and melody and fragrance and food and embrace when I love my God—the light and the voice and the fragrance and the food and embrace in the soul. . . ."[7] This tradition is rich and powerful, epitomized in a sensibility that sees God in everything and everything full of the glory of God: the things of this earth are valuable principally as vehicles for communication with the divine. A different sensibility is evident in this Navajo chant:

> May it be delightful my house;
> From my head may it be delightful;
> To my feet may it be delightful;
> Where I lie may it be delightful;
> All above me may it be delightful;
> All around me may it be delightful.[8]

The delight here is in and not through the ordinary; the ordinary is not chiefly a symbol of the divine delight. The difference between these sensibilities is epitomized in two lines, one from Hildegard of Bingen, a medieval German mystic ("Holy persons draw to themselves all that is earthly") and one from Abraham Heschel, a contemporary Jewish theologian ("Just to be is a blessing, Just to live is holy").[9] The first perspective transmutes all things earthly into their holy potential, while the second finds ordinary existence itself to be holy.

Nevertheless, in spite of its limitations, traditional sacramentalism is an important perspective, for it is the major way Christianity has preserved and developed an appreciation for nature. It has encouraged Christians to look upon the world as valuable—indeed, as holy—and has served as a counterforce to two other perspectives on nature within Christian history, one that divorces it totally from God through secularizing it and one that dominates and exploits it. Traditional sacramentalism has, in its own way, supported the principal thesis of this essay: the model of the world (universe) as God's body means that the presence of God is not limited to particular times or places but is coextensive with reality, with all that is. It has been one of the few traditions within Christianity that has encouraged both a spatial and a historical perspective; that is, Christian sacramentalism has included nature as a concern of God and a way to God rather than limiting divine activity to human history. For these and other reasons Christian sacramentalism should be encouraged. It is a distinctive contribution of Christianity. From its incarnational base, it claims that in analogy with the body of Jesus the Christ all bodies can serve as ways to God, all can be open to and give news of the divine presence. But it does not claim, at least primarily, that bodies have intrinsic value. The great theologians and poets of the Christian sacramental tradition, including Paul, John, Irenaeus, Augustine, the medieval mystics (such as Julian of Norwich, Meister Eckhart, Hildegard of Bingen), Gerard Manley Hopkins, and Pierre Teilhard de Chardin, love the things of this world principally *as expressions of* divine beauty, sustenance, truth, and glory.[10] It is not a sensibility that in a homey phrase wants "to hold on hard to the huckleberries."[11] The value of huckleberries as huckleberries is not a major concern of Christian sacramentalism.

Again, we need to remind ourselves that for the purposes of the planetary agenda, no one tradition needs to claim universality or the whole truth. What is more helpful is to specify the *kind* of insights that are distinctive of different traditions. The Christian tradition does not underscore the intrinsic value of all things earthly but does express richly and deeply the symbolic importance of each and every body on the earth: each in its own way expresses divine reality and is valuable for this reason. Unfortunately, traditional sacramentalism is not a central concern for many Christians; in fact, some Protestant churches scarcely attend to it. Yet it can be a way that Christians, at least, might begin to change their exploitative, utilitarian attitudes toward nature—as well as toward other humans whose bodies are also expressions of God. As Hopkins puts it, "Christ plays in ten thousand places, lovely in limbs, lovely in eyes not his."[12] If use is to be made of our earth and its people and other creatures, it can only be a use, says Christian sacramentalism, for God's glory, not for our profit.

Nevertheless, we suggest two qualifications of traditional sacramentalism. The first is implicit in the direction of this entire essay: the need to replace the utilitarian attitude toward other beings that accompanies anthropocentrism with a perspective that values them intrinsically. If we are not the center of things, then other beings do not exist for our benefit—even for our spiritual growth as ways to God. They exist within the vast, intricate web of life in the cosmos, of which they and we are all interdependent parts, and each and every part has both utilitarian and intrinsic value. Within our model of the world as God's body, all of

Sallie McFague

us, human beings included, exist as parts of the whole. Some parts are not merely means for the purposes of other parts, for all parts are valued by God and hence should be valued by us. We do have a distinctive role in this body, but it is not as the ones who use the rest as a ladder to God; rather, it is as the ones who have emerged as the caretakers of the rest.

The second qualification of traditional sacramentalism picks up on this note of care and might be called "negative sacramentalism." It focuses on bodies not as expressions of divinity, but as signs of human sin and destruction. It is a perspective on the earth and its many bodies that sees them not as telling of the glories of God but of human destruction. The bodies of the earth, human and nonhuman, that are vulnerable and needy cry out for compassion and care. These bodies appear to us, in the closing years of the twentieth century, not primarily as expressions of divine loveliness, but as evidence of human neglect and oppression. The focus is not on their use to help us in our religious pilgrimage but on our misuse of them, our refusal to acknowledge these bodies as valuable in and for themselves and to God. One of the motifs of our analysis of the model of the world as God's body from the perspective of the common creation story is that all bodies are united in webs of interrelatedness and interconnectedness. This motif has been radicalized by the Christic paradigm that reaches out to include especially the vulnerable, outcast, needy bodies. Hence, I would suggest that a form of Christian sacramentalism for an ecological era should focus not on the use of all earthly bodies but on our care of them, in the ways that the Christic paradigm suggests. We are suggesting that the Christic shape to God's body be applied to the full scope of that body, especially to the new poor, the natural world. Nature, its flora and fauna, therefore would not simply be addenda to human salvation, avenues providing deeper communion between God and human beings; rather, the Christic salvific paradigm would also be applied to the earth and its many creatures. This is what a cosmological or ecological context for theological reflection demands: the whole cosmos is God's concern, not just its human inhabitants and not merely as our habitat.

In what ways, then, should the Christic paradigm be applied to the natural world? In the same ways as applied to other outcasts: the deconstructive phase (liberation from oppressive hierarchies as seen in the parables), the reconstructive (physical sustainability as suggested by the healing stories), and the prospective (inclusion of all as manifest in the eating practices). These primary, active dimensions of the Christic paradigm—the shape of the cosmic Christ given to God's body—are balanced by a secondary, passive phase, the suffering of God with the despairing and defeated. What does each of these themes suggest to us as we reflect on the deteriorating, needy body of our planet earth?

Just as, in the overturning of oppressive, dualistic hierarchies, poor people are liberated from their enslavement by the rich, people of color are liberated from discrimination by whites, so also the earth and its many nonhuman creatures are liberated from oppression and destruction by human beings. The dualistic hierarchy of people over nature is an old and profound one, certainly as ancient as the patriarchal era that stretches back some five thousand years.[13] Until the sixteenth-century scientific revolution, however, and the subsequent marriage of science with technology, human beings were not sufficiently powerful to wreak massive destruction on nature. But we now are. The first phase, then, of extending the Christic paradigm beyond human beings is the recognition, which involves a confession of sin, of our oppressive misuse of the major part of God's creation in regard to our planet, that is, everything and every creature that is *not* human. The destructive phase is a breaking down of our "natural" biases against nature; our prejudices that it is, at best, only useful for our needs; our rationalizations in regard to activities that profit us but destroy it. The hierarchy of humans over nature has been, at least in the West, so total and so destructive for the last several hundred years that many people would deny that nature merits a status similar to other oppressed "minorities." Nature is, of course, the *majority* in terms of both numbers and importance (it can do very well without us, but not vice versa). Bracketing that issue for the moment, however, many would still claim that it does not, like poor or oppressed people, deserve attention as intrinsically valuable. Nature is valuable insofar as and only insofar as it serves human purposes. Thus, in a telling phrase, many speak of wilderness as "undeveloped" land, that is, of course, undeveloped for human profit, though it is excellently developed for the animals, trees, and plants that presently inhabit it.

The liberation of nature from our oppressive practices, the recognition that the land and its creatures have rights and are intrinsically valuable, is by no means easy to practice, since immediately and inevitably, especially on a finite planet with limited resources and increasing numbers of needy human beings, conflicts of interest will occur. These conflicts are real, painful, and important, but the point that our model underscores is that the resolution of them from a Christian perspective cannot ignore the value and rights of 99 percent of creation on our planet. The model of the world as God's body denies this attitude, and the model of the cosmic Christ intensifies that denial. Whether we like it or not, these models say that all parts of the planet are parts of God's body and are included in the Christic liberation from dualistic hierarchies. It is for us to figure out what this must, can, mean in particular situations where conflicts arise. The preferential option for the poor is uncomfortable wherever it is applied; it will be no less so when applied to the new poor, nature.

The second phase of the Christic paradigm, the healing phase, is especially appropriate to the nonhuman dimensions of creation. It is increasingly evident that the metaphors of sickness, degeneration, and dysfunction are significant when discussing the state of our planet. The pollution of air and water, the greenhouse effect, the depletion of the ozone layer, the desertification of arable land, the destruction of rainforests are all signs of the poor health of the earth. One of the great values of the organic model is that it not only focuses on bodies and includes the natural world (unlike many models in the Christian tradition), but it also implies that salvation includes, as the bottom line, the health of bodies. While the model helps us to focus on basic justice issues for human beings—the need for food, clean air and water, adequate housing, education and medical benefits—it also insists that we focus on the basics for other creatures and dimensions of our planet. The organic model focuses on the basics of existence: the healthy functioning of all inhabitants and systems of the planet. Jesus' healing stories are extremely valuable in a time of ecological deterioration and destruction such as we are experiencing. They refuse any early and easy spiritualizing of salvation; they force us, as Christians, to face the deep sickness of the many bodies that make up the body of God. These embarrassing stories are part of the mud of our tradition, the blood-and-guts part of the gospel that insists that whatever more or else Christian faith might be and mean, it includes as a primary focus physical well-being. And nature, in our time, is woefully ill.

Most of us, most of the time, refuse to acknowledge the degree of that sickness. It is inconvenient to do so, since curing the planet's illnesses will force human inhabitants to make sacrifices. Hence, denial sets in, a denial not unlike the denial many people practice in relation to serious, perhaps terminal, illness when it strikes their own bodies. But denial of the planet's profoundly deteriorating condition is neither wise nor Christian: it is not wise because, as we increasingly know, we cannot survive on a sick planet, and it is not Christian because, if we extend the Christic healing ministry to all of creation, then we must work for the health of its many creatures and the planet itself.

This brings us to the third and final phase of the Christic paradigm as extended to the whole body of God: the inclusive fulfillment epitomized in Jesus' eating practices. As with the healing stories, the stories of Jesus feeding the multitudes and inviting the excluded to his table are embarrassments, perhaps scandals, in their mundanity and inclusivity. Neither conventional standards nor natural selection operates on the themes of sharing and inclusion; these stories are countercultural and counterbiological, but they are hints and clues of a new stage of evolution, the stage of our solidarity with other life-forms, especially with the needy and outcast forms. The time has come, it appears, when our competition with various other species for survival will not result in a richer, more complex and diverse community of life-forms. The human population is already so dominant that it is likely to wipe out many other forms and probably seriously harm its own, if predictions of our exponential growth prove true and the profligate life-style of many of us continues. The good life rests in part, then, on human decisions concerning sharing and inclusion, with food as an appropriate and powerful symbol of both bare existence as well as the abundant life. In the Christian tradition food has always served these dual functions, though the emphasis has often been on the latter meaning, especially in the eucharist as a foretaste of the eschatalogical banquet. But in our time, the value of food is precisely its literal meaning: sustainability for bodies, especially the many bodies on our planet that Christians as well as others in our society think of as superfluous. In a telling reversal of the need of all bodies for food, many people assume that other creatures not only do not *deserve* food but are themselves *only* food—food for us.[14]

The paradigmatic Christic shape of the body of the world, then, suggests some hints and clues for Christians as we, in an ecological age, extend that shape to be coextensive with the world, superimposing, as it were, the cosmic Christ on the body of God. We look at the world, our planet and all its creatures, through the shape of Christ. As we do so, we acknowledge the distinctive features of that form, especially liberation from our destructive oppression, the healing of its deteriorating bodies, and the sharing of basic needs with all the planet's inhabitants, that the Christian tradition can contribute to the planetary agenda.

But we are not left alone to face this momentous, indeed, horrendous, task. Ecological despair would quickly overwhelm us if we believed that to be the case. The cosmic Christ as the shape of God's body also tells us that God suffers with us in our suffering, that divine love is not only with us in our active work against the destruction of our planet but also in our passive suffering when we and the health of our planet are defeated. An attitude of sober realism, in view of the massiveness of ecological and human oppression that faces us in our time, is the appropriate—perhaps the only possible—attitude. We and our planet may, in fact, be defeated, or, at least life in community, life worth living, may no longer be possible. The situation we face is similar in many respects to that portrayed in Albert Camus's powerful allegorical novel, *The Plague,* in which a mysterious and devastating plague overwhelmed and destroyed most of the inhabitants of a contemporary Algerian town. It was a symbol of the modern malaise, but for our purposes "the plague" can serve as a literal description of deepening planetary sickness. The response of one of the book's chief activists fighting the plague is a soberly realistic one: "All I maintain is that on this earth there are pestilences and there are victims, and it's up to us, so far as possible, not to join forces with the pestilences."[15] When the work of healing fails in spite of all efforts to make it work, one must, Christians must, not "join forces with the pestilences." The cross in the Christic paradigm does not, in our model, promise victory over the pestilences, but it does assure us that God is with the victims in their suffering. That is the last word, however, not the first.

Actually, the cross is not the last word. The enigmatic appearance stories of the risen Christ, the Christ who appeared in bodily form to his disciples, is the witness to an ancient, indelible strain within the Christian community. It is the belief and the hope that diminishment and death are not the last word, but in some inexplicable manner, the way to new life that, moreover, is physical. This is an important point for an embodiment theology. The death and resurrection of Jesus Christ are paradigmatic of a mode of change and growth that only occurs on the other side of the narrow door of the tomb. Often that pattern has been absolutized as occurring completely and only in Jesus of Nazareth: his death and resurrection are the answer to all the world's woes. In his death all creation dies; in his resurrection all arise to new life. The absolutism, optimism, and universalism of this way of interpreting the ancient and recurring relationship between death and new life—a relationship honored in most religious traditions as well as in evolutionary biology—are problematic in a postmodern, ecological, and highly diverse cultural and religious era. What is possible and appropriate, however, is to embrace these strains in Christian thought as a deep pattern within existence to which we cling and in which we hope—often as the hope against hope. We must believe in the basic trustworthiness at the heart of existence; that life, not death, is the last word; that against all evidence to the contrary (and most evidence is to the contrary), all our efforts on behalf of the well-being of our planet and especially of its most vulnerable creatures, including human ones, will not be defeated. It is the belief that the source and power of the universe is on the side of life and its fulfillment. The "risen Christ" is the Christian way of speaking of this faith and hope: Christ is the firstborn of the new creation, to be followed by all the rest of creation, including the last and the least.

NOTES

1.   See John Hick's analysis of major theodicies; he supports the contemporary one in which God suffers with those who suffer (*Evil and the God of Love* [New York: Macmillan, 1966]).

2.   For a brief but excellent treatment of the cosmic Christ in the tradition, see Rosemary Radford Ruether, *Gaia and God: An Ecofeminist Theology of Earth Healing* (San Francisco: HarperCollins, 1992), 321ff. For two very different twentieth-century reconstructions of the cosmic Christ, see various works by Pierre Teilhard de Chardin, and Matthew Fox, *The Coming of the Cosmic Christ* (San Francisco: Harper and Row, 1988).

3.   This tendency is evident in some forms of liberation theology, especially reform feminism, which is understandably cautious about embracing motifs of divine sacrifice and suffering that might encourage similar passive behavior among the oppressed.

4.   One of the few instances of serious attention to the notion of space by a Christian theologian is interesting treatment by Jürgen Moltmann in *God in Creation: A New Theology of Creation and the Spirit of God* (San Francisco: Harper and Row, 1985), chap. 6.

5.   Bernhard W. Anderson, "Creation in the Bible," in *Cry of the Environment: Rebuilding the Christian Creation Story,* ed. Philip N. Joranson and Ken Butigan (Santa Fe, N. M.: Bear and Co., 1984), 25.

6.   Two collections of poems and prayers illustrate this point: Marilyn Sewell, ed., *Cries of the Spirit: A Celebration of Women's Spirituality* (Boston: Beacon Press, 1991); Elizabeth Roberts and Elias Amidon, eds., *Earth Prayers from Around the World* (San Francisco: Harpers, 1991).

7.   *The Confessions of St. Augustine,* Bks. I–X, trans. F. J. Sheed (New York: Sheed and Ward, 1942), 10.6.

8.   *Earth Prayers,* 366.

9.   *Earth Prayers,* 360, 365.

10. This is a complex issue to which we cannot here do justice. There are at least two directions within this tradition, one from Augustine's Neoplatonism, which tends to absorb the things of the world into God, and the other from Thomas's Aristotelianism, which supports greater substance for empirical reality. One sees the former epitomized in the extreme realism of the doctrine of transubstantiation in which the eucharistic elements are wholly converted into the body and blood of Christ, and the latter in a poet such as Gerard Manley Hopkins with his notion of "inscape," the particular, irreducible, concrete individuality of each and every aspect of creation that is

preserved and heightened in its sacramental role as a sign of God's glory. But between these poles are many other positions, with the unifying factor being that in some way or other the things of this world are valuable because of their connection to God.

11. The phrase is from an essay by the literary critic, R. W. B. Lewis, and refers to the "suchness" and "thereness" of ordinary things in the world that stand against all attempts to translate them into or use them for spiritual purposes.

12. Gerard Manley Hopkins, *Poems and Prose,* introd. by W. H. Gardner (London: Penguin Books, 1953), 51.

13. See an analysis by Gerda Lerner, *The Creation of Patriarchy* (New York: Oxford University Press, 1986).

14. On animal rights and vegetarianism, see the following: Carol J. Adams, *The Sexual Politics of Meat: A Feminist-Vegetarian Critical Theory* (New York: Continuum, 1991); Tom Regan, *The Case for Animal Rights* (Berkeley, Calif.: University of California Press, 1983).

15. Albert Camus, *The Plague,* trans. Stuart Gilbert (New York: Alfred A. Knopf, 1954), 229.

"WHAT IS ECO-KOSHER?"

Arthur Waskow

Over thousands of years, Judaism has evolved a series of precepts intended to govern the Jewish community and to keep it in internal harmony and in harmony with other peoples and the Earth. Twice in Jewish history, profound changes in society have required changes in the content of these precepts in order to achieve a new harmony in the new situation. One of those times was 2,000 years ago, when Hellenism swept across the Mediterranean basin, greatly increasing the ability of human beings to control their own history and the forces of nature, and dispersed the Jewish people into many lands.

The second time is now. Modernity has shattered the Jewish life that had become traditional, has liberated and empowered women, has transformed the very chemistry and biology of the Earth, and threatens to bring about a mass death of many species. Under these conditions, we must reexamine the content of the precepts that sought for harmony under old conditions, while drawing on the wisdom of the entire Jewish past in order to shape the new content.

Part of that wisdom was the code of eating kosher food in which only the meat of non-predatory animals and birds was kosher to eat; the food of mammalian life (milk) and mammalian death (meat) could not be eaten together; even this restricted kind of meat could only be eaten if the animal had been slaughtered in a painless way with prayerful consciousness and ritual; and vegetarianism was viewed as the higher, but not compulsory, path.

Today we must ask ourselves a broader question: Is it food alone that is subject to the precepts of a kosher life-path? If we wish to protect the Earth, then today we must explore a broader set of questions about what might be considered an "eco-kosher" life.

Are tomatoes that have been grown by drenching the earth in pesticides "eco-kosher" to eat at a wedding reception?

Is newsprint that has been made by chopping down an ancient and irreplaceable forest "eco-kosher" to use for a newspaper?

Are windows and doors so carelessly built that the warm air flows out through them and the furnace keeps burning all night "eco-kosher" for a home or a public building?

Is a bank that invests the depositors' money in an oil company that befouls the ocean an "eco-kosher" place to deposit money?

If by "kosher" we mean a broader sense of "good practice" that draws on the deep wellsprings of Jewish wisdom and tradition about protecting the Earth, then none of these ways of behaving is eco-kosher.

"Eco-kosher" might as an approach speak to two kinds of Jews—both those who now live by the traditional code of kosher food and those who have decided the traditional code is no longer important to them. It might speak to other communities as well.

Why does "eco-kosher" transcend these differences? Because the Earth and the human race are in serious danger. Not economic progress but the *way* we have pursued economic progress has brought this danger. For the sake of our children and our children's children, it is crucial to address the issues. And the Jewish people has its own wisdom on these matters, rooted in our own ancient tradition of ourselves as a pastoral and agricultural people that nourished the Earth, as well as in our modern efforts to nurture the Land of Israel. So it may be of value to the human race to examine and draw on this sense of sacred practicality.

Shabbat—the Sabbath—is the great challenge of the Jewish people to technology run amok. It asserts that although work can be good, it becomes good only when crowned by rest, reflection, re-creation, and renewal. The Sabbaths of the seventh day, the seventh month, the seventh year, and in principle the seventh cycle (the Jubilee at the fiftieth year) give not only human beings but animals and even plants and minerals, the entire Earth, the right to rest.

The modern age has been the greatest triumph of work, technology, in all of human history. This triumph deserves celebration. But instead of pausing to celebrate and reevaluate, we have become addicted to the work itself. For five hundred years, the human race has not made Shabbat, has not paused to reflect and reconsider, to take down this great painting from its easel and catch our breaths before putting up a new canvas to begin a new project.

Torah teaches that if we deny the Earth its Shabbats, the Earth will make Shabbat anyway—through desolation. The Earth *does* get to rest. Our only choice is whether the rest occurs with joy or disaster.

The Earth and the human race are now faced with such a moment of Shabbat denied. Triumphant human technology, run amok without Shabbat, brings the danger of impending desolation. We can quickly identify several specific areas in which these dangers are already clear:

The multiplication of thousands of nuclear-weapons warheads that, if exploded in a short period, could devastate the planet; the creation from nuclear energy plants of radioactive wastes that will need to be contained and controlled for thousands of years; the galloping destruction of the ozone layer; the overproduction of carbon dioxide from massive deforestations and the extensive burning of fossil fuels, in such a way as to make much more likely a major rise in world temperatures; the destruction of many species through destruction of their habitats.

Torah teaches not that we abandon technology but that we constrain it with Shabbat and all the implications of Shabbat. Instead, we have used technological progress to poison the earth and air and water, so that they poison us with cancer at the very moment when we take in their nourishment.

What we sow is what we reap.

If what we sow is poison, what we reap is also poison.

The planetary biosphere cannot long endure the treatment we are now giving it. Nor can the human race.

Our technology has also transformed the medium of the relationship between Earth and human earthling. Originally, food was the great connection. But that is no longer so. The human race has created an economy in which *energy, minerals,* and *money* take on many of the roles that land and food originally had.

That is why an eco-kosher approach to life requires us to look beyond food to such other consumable items as wood, oil, and aluminum, and to where and how we save and invest our money.

And the new conditions of the planet may also point toward changes in the content of precepts outside the arena of kosher or eco-kosher consuming of goods from the Earth.

The most important of these is the area of population and the sexual ethics that bear on population. Traditionally, Jewish sexual ethics operated under the rubric of "Be fruitful and multiply, and fill up the Earth." It strongly encouraged sexuality that was likely to procreate and rear more children, and frowned both on celibacy and on all sexuality outside a heterosexual marriage, and even then on sexual relations outside the two most fertile weeks of the woman's ovulation cycle. So traditional Jewish sexual precepts opposed gay or lesbian sexuality, masturbation, most forms of birth control, and sexual relations for the sake of loving pleasure between two adult, unmarried people.

But once the Earth is already "filled up" with human beings, where shall we look for a sexual ethic to balance one that is focused on bearing and nurturing children?

In the books of Jewish wisdom, one that looks to such a time is the *Song of Songs.* It celebrates a Garden of Eden that is no longer peopled by a childish human race that is just entering rebellious adolescence, but by adults.

Its sexual ethic is one of loving pleasure and flowing relationship between human beings and each other, and human beings and the Earth. Instead of opposing sexual expression except when it is focused on the bearing or rearing of children, the *Song of Songs* celebrates sexual expression except when it is coerced or demeaning.

In the new era of the Earth, the human race needs to balance a sexual ethic focused on children and the family with one focused on love and joy. The new "eco-kosher" sexual ethic might affirm sexual relationships between adults of any sexual orientation where there is honesty, caring, no coercion or other misuse of an imbalance in power between the parties, and no deceit of others or an attack on other relationships. And it might affirm as well the special relationship of two people who have decided to make a more permanent commitment, including one to have and rear children, so long as they have made a careful judgment in the light of the Earth's needs about how many children will suffice.

Why should the Jewish people and religious community bother to do all this, and why should other communities encourage the Jews to do it? Why is this a Jewish issue and why is it a Jewish-renewal issue? For two reasons:

We must draw on the wisdom, energy, and commitment of all peoples, each of them in the specificity and uniqueness of its own world view, if we are to heal the Earth, nurture all living beings, and protect our children from environmentally caused cancer, famine, and other disasters.

Just as every unique species of plant and animal brings a sacred strand into the sacred web of life, so does the unique wisdom of each human culture. Just as modernity threatens to narrow and crush the diversity of species, so it threatens to narrow and crush the diversity of cultures. Both Jews and others are helping to heal that web of life if they give new heart and new life to endangered cultures as well as endangered species. The Jewish people is one such endangered culture.

The shift from Biblical to Rabbinic Judaism is one of the most useful histories of how a culture can renew and transform itself without losing its own identity. Now when the world is being profoundly transformed, every religious tradition needs to examine how best to renew and transform itself, neither abandoning its own deepest wisdom nor getting stuck in the transient versions of itself that worked in a departed past. [For further information on "eco-kosher," write the author at ALEPH: Alliance for Jewish Renewal, 7318 Germantown Ave., Philadelphia, PA 19119, and see his book *Down-to-Earth Judaism* (Morrow, 1995).]

"VEGETARIANISM: A *KASHRUT* FOR OUR AGE"

Arthur Green

... I believe the time has come for us to reconsider the question of whether we should continue to consume animal flesh as food. Our tradition has always contained within it a certain
provegetarian bias, even though it has provided for the eating of meat. In the ideal state of
Eden, according to the Bible, humans ate only plants; we and the animals together were given
the plants as food. Only after the expulsion from Eden, when the urge overwhelmed humans
and led them toward evil, did the consumption of flesh begin. The very first set of laws given to
humanity sought to limit this evil by forbidding the flesh of a still-living creature, placing a
limit on acts of cruelty or terror related to the eating of animal flesh. The Torah's original insistence that domestic animals could be slaughtered only for purpose of sacrifice, an offering to
God needed to atone for the killing, was compromised only when the Book of Deuteronomy
wanted to insist that sacrifice be offered in Jerusalem alone. Realizing that people living at a
great distance could not bring all their animals to the Temple for slaughter, the "secular"
slaughter and eating of domestic animals was permitted. Even then, the taboo against consuming blood, and later, the requirement to salt meat until even traces of blood were removed, "for
the blood is the self" of the creature, represent a clear discomfort with the eating of animal
flesh. Most significantly, the forbidding of any mixing of milk and meat represents a protoveg-
etarian sensibility. Milk is the fluid by which life is passed on from generation to generation; it
may not be consumed with flesh, representing the taking of that life in an act of violence. The
fluid of life may not be mixed with that of death. As the Torah says of the hewn-stone altar:
"For you have waved your sword over it and have profaned it."

The reasons for acting upon this vegetarian impulse in our day are multiple and compelling, *just as compelling, I believe, as the reasons for the selective taboos against certain animals
must have been when the Community of Israel came to accept these as the word of God.* This is
what we mean, after all, when we talk about a *mitzvah* being "the word of God" or "God's
will." It is a form of human expression or a way of acting that feels compellingly right. This
rightness has both a moral and a spiritual dimension; it is an expression of values we choose,
but it also makes a more profound statement about who we are. We then come to associate it
with divinity, and it becomes a vehicle through which we express our spiritual selves. With the

---

Reprinted from *Seek My Face, Speak My Name: A Contemporary Jewish Theology* by Arthur Green. Reprinted by
permission of the author and the publisher, Jason Aronson Inc., Northvale, NJ © 1992.

passage of time, origins are shrouded in mystery, and the form becomes the "will of God." Israelites of ancient times felt that way about the taboos widely current in their society against the consumption of certain animals that they saw as repulsive, against the eating of blood, the mixing of milk and meat, and so forth. They associated this series of taboos with the God of Sinai. Over the centuries, *kashrut* as we know it became a *mitzvah*, a way in which Jews are joined to God.

Our situation has certain important parallels to this one. We are urgently concerned with finding a better way to share earth's limited resources. We know that many more human lives can be sustained if land is used for planting rather than for grazing of animals for food. We are committed also to a healthier way of living and are coming to recognize that the human is, after all, a mostly vegetarian species. But for us as Jews, the impulse is largely a moral and religious one. We have a long tradition of abhorring violence. Cruelty to animals has long been forbidden by Jewish law and sensibilities. Our tradition tells us that we must shoo a mother bird away from the nest before we take her eggs so that she does not suffer as we break the bond between them. We are told that a mother and her calf may not be slaughtered on the same day. The very next step beyond these prohibitions is a commitment to a vegetarian way of living.

We Jews in this century have been victims of destruction and mass slaughter on an unprecedented scale. We have seen every norm of humanity violated as we were treated like cattle rather than human beings. Our response to this memory is surely a complex and multi-textured one. But as we overcome the understandable first reactions to the events, some of us feel our abhorrence of violence and bloodshed growing so strong that it reaches even beyond the borders of the human and into the animal kingdom. We Jews, who always looked upon killing for sport or pleasure as something alien and repulsive, should now, out of our own experience, be reaching the point where we find even the slaughter of animals for food morally beyond the range of the acceptable. If Jews have to be associated with killing at all in our time, let it be only for the defense of human life. Life has become too precious in this era for us to be involved in the shedding of blood, even that of animals, when we can survive without it. This is not an ascetic choice, we should note, but rather a life-affirming one. A vegetarian Judaism would be more whole in its ability to embrace the presence of God in all of Creation.

"GETTING OUT OF OUR OWN LIGHT"

Ken Jones

"When I was little, my mother would teach me how to sew in the evenings, by the light of a table lamp. She used to say, 'If you keep getting in your own light, you'll never be able to do it.'"

Public perception of the ecological crisis, for the most part, is still at the level of environmentalism. It is limited to attempts at environmental clean up, to the Greening of consumerism, and to allegedly sustainable growth. Business is pretty much as usual, painted a pale shade of Green.

As the crisis bites deeper, it will become clearer that if we are to get through in good shape, caring for all our people as well as other planetary life, we shall have to undertake the most radical social transformation since the Neolithic Revolution modestly initiated the advent of agriculture five thousand years ago.

However, there is nothing inevitable about such a Green Liberation. History suggests that other and nastier scenarios are more probable, such as lifeboat authoritarianism or biotechnological elitism. How can we dissolve the age-old drives of oppression and exploitation (by class, sex, race, nation, or species) of the workings of Gaia? How can we engender the necessary public spiritedness, tolerance, trust, and capacity for nonviolence, cooperation, and conflict resolution? It seems clear that radical social transformation will need to be facilitated by personal psycho-spiritual shifts that go much deeper than the relatively superficial changes in beliefs, values, and attitudes that have marked the revolutions of the last three hundred years. Buddhism could make a unique contribution to an ecologically and socially grounded spirituality.

Buddhism focuses directly upon the development of insight into how things are beneath our habitual and delusive experience of reality. Even at the beginning of a meditative practice we start to see what frightened creatures we really are and to what extent our lives are a futile struggle to achieve security and satisfaction through the many different kinds of belongingness available to us. We engage in restless activity and achievement, the inward significance of which is continually to affirm ourselves to ourselves and to others. We begin to see how much

Reprinted from *Dharma Gaia: A Harvest of Essays in Buddhism and Ecology* edited by Allan Hunt Badiner (1990) with permission of Parallax Press, Berkeley, CA, USA.

the reality we experience is colored and distorted by self-need, and how much our responses to realities out there are at the same time responses to the problem of being who we are.

Through meditative awareness there comes acceptance born of a deepening inner peace that has no place for either hope or despair. However bleak the global outlook may be, the situation is nevertheless manageable. And we are better able to make positive and effective contributions to the dilemma when, through meditation, we accept ourselves and come to terms with our fears.

Although few may experience enlightenment and unity consciousness, most can certainly become more human in the above sense. We cannot liberate Gaia from ourselves or realize humanity's huge untapped potential for social good unless, at the same time, we liberate ourselves. And if we are aware and mindful in our work for eco-social liberation, the burden of fear and all that flows from it and masks it will lighten of its own accord. If we endeavor thus to actualize Green Liberation each day, both enlightenment and ecotopia can be left to take care of themselves.

Through awareness comes acceptance, and through acceptance comes empowerment and generosity of spirit. This is the perennial Way shared by the spiritual traditions of all the world's great religions. The particular value of Buddhism lies in its openness to humanistic and nontheistic approaches, with its emphasis on practice and experience rather than acceptance of an alternative body of belief. In this spirit, despair and empowerment workshops particularly directed toward the needs of social activists have been developed by Joanna Macy,[1] John Seed,[2] and others. Another cluster of practices is designed to prepare people for nonviolent direct action in the Gandhian and related traditions. Yet another has to do with conflict resolution and mediation. As for traditional Buddhist practice, it could be made more widely available, perhaps with adaptations, to people who are working to resolve the global crisis. Buddhism must open out beyond its image as otherworldly, cultic, exotic, mystical—and privatized.

Also relevant to the inner work needed to facilitate Green Liberation is the range of humanistic growth therapies which Ken Wilber has usefully arrayed in terms of levels of consciousness.[3] I believe that there is an urgent need for all of the above concerns to coordinate, popularize, and develop their activities through an inner-work network in which relevant social-action organizations also take part.

TOWARD AN ECO-SOCIAL BUDDHOLOGY

A second contribution to the Green Liberation process would be the development of an eco-social Buddhology (as distinct from traditional, scriptural Buddhology). By this I mean the intellectual development and application of root Dharma (for example the Madhyamika dialectic) to the explication of social and ecological phenomena.

My book *The Social Face of Buddhism*[4] is a preliminary attempt to sketch out such a Buddhology. For example, using phenomenological sociology, it offers a Buddhological understanding of how reality is socially constructed, evolving historically through karmic impulsion.

The metaphor of Indra's Net (*Avatamsaka Sutra*) is an excellent example of an expression of root Dharma of great ecological and social potential.[5] At each intersection of Indra's Net is a light-reflecting jewel (that is, a phenomenon, entity, thing), and each jewel contains another net, ad infinitum. The jewel at each intersection exists only as a reflection of all the others and therefore has no self-nature. Yet it also exists as a separate entity to sustain the others. Each and all exist only in their mutuality. In other words, all phenomena are identifiable with the whole, just as the phenomena that constitute a particular phenomenon are identifiable with it.

Indra's Net is a fruitful metaphor for exploring topics as varied as deep ecology, organizational networking, constitutional confederation, permaculture, and bioregionalism as well as for a fundamental understanding of Gaia. At the coarsest intellectual level it can help to wean us from logical (either this *or* that) thinking to dialectical (both this *and* that) thinking.

At the more subtle intellectual levels where Buddhology begins to merge with Dharmic insight, the metaphor takes on an experiential validation beyond theory, so that we really are able "to see the world in a grain of sand ... and eternity in an hour"[6] or "to think like a mountain." At each level it offers an ethical expression of how, human and non-human, we are all sisters and brothers of one another. At a lower level of consciousness Indra's Net is a concept for our use. At a higher level we *are* the Net, if we can but allow it.

To the extent that self-need has been filtered out of our experience of intellectual constructions, they will be experienced as provisional, situational, problematic, and paradoxical. They are devoid (sunyata) of manifestations of self. But to the extent that they must bear the weight of the need to believe, our intellectual constructions become reified and solidified as ideology. By ideology I mean a dogmatic and strenuously upheld belief system that exists as much to affirm our identity or religion as to throw explanatory light on the world.

The world in general, observed the Buddha, grasps after systems and is imprisoned in ideologies.[7] Asserting the insubstantiality and impermanence of all phenomena and particularly in the Madhyamika doctrine, their absolute relativity,[8] Buddhology is the ultimate solvent of ideology. And yet, as an intellectual construction, it too is in continual danger of solidifying into ideology.

BUDDHOLOGY AS IDEOLOGICAL SOLVENT

Discernible in the whole variegated Green/New Age movement are several ideological tendencies that would benefit from a Buddhological critique. First, there are the concepts that are solidified into dogmas. Thus E. F. Schumacher warned in vain against making a fetish of "Small is beautiful."[9] For him it was a situational principle emphasized only because of the current obsession with bigness. After the creative thinker follows the ideologist, like Leopold Kohr, who wrote in *Breakdown of Nations*, "Whenever something is wrong, something is too big." Similarly traditional and primal cultures are idealized without reservation, and bioregionalism, decentralization and other helpful Green notions become cure-alls. The complex, variable and situational potential of valuable ideas is laundered out in order to clothe emergent ideology, leaving not a speck of real muck on the starched hems of those three sirens Goodness, Truth and Beauty.

Ideology supports the believer with a reassuringly simple picture of where he or she stands. It centers absolutely upon a key issue that becomes the distorting organizing principle for all other phenomena, except for those that are ignored because they cannot be made to fit. For the ideological Marxist it is the class struggle. For the ideological feminist it is patriarchy. Similarly, ideological Greens see the world only in terms of degrees of Greenness, shading by degrees into the grayness of their adversaries. While it is true that everything does in fact depend upon the well-being of Gaia, it is also true that an exclusively ecological (or worse still, environmental) perspective can only give us a shallow and unhelpful understanding of the overall global crisis. For the ecological crisis is the dramatic outcome of cumulative economic, social and political forces at work. The ecological and the social are indivisible.

For example, the Amazonian rainforest crisis is about the disappearance of species and the arrival of multinational corporations. Why do these corporations behave as they do? Could they behave otherwise? And so on . . . But here as elsewhere in the tropics the ecological crisis is also about the arrival of hundreds of thousands of landless and desperate people who need to clear the forest in order to live. Or do they? In Latin America, for example, 97 percent of the farmland is owned by 7 percent of the population. Land redistribution is the hottest political issue, and the ruling and landowning elite hope to cool it by diverting pressure into the rainforests. In this and other ways the ecological disaster in the Amazon basin is political dynamite, as it is elsewhere in the Third World.

I have the impression that Buddhists prefer committing themselves to ethically unproblematic issues—like rainforests, whales, primal peoples, animal rights, even human rights and world peace—and to all forms of service, rather than involving themselves with the militant wretched of the Earth (especially close to home), and with the structural violence of our social system. For the anger of the powerless and oppressed really can get under our skin, especially if they are violent, narrow-minded, unreasonable and make us feel somehow guilty, helpless and ethically uncertain. Ecology is clean and safe.

I live close to what is perhaps the most polluted sea in Europe. Its once-famed dolphins are now being killed off by a toxic cocktail of nuclear, industrial, and domestic wastes. Because there is nowhere further west to run, there are people who tend to get washed up in our little town. Mary, for example, was in her late thirties and had been deprived and put down in so many ways, and for so often, that her health and her spirit seemed entirely bro-

Ken Jones

ken. Mary was being slowly killed by a toxic cocktail also. It is a political and economic poison with a long pedigree, currently called Thatcherism. Mary and the dolphins on the shore bear the same witness.

We are strengthened and confirmed when our *this* is opposed to their *that*, even when *this* is no more than a paradigm of New Age concepts set against the mechanistic, dualistic, anthropocentric listing alongside it. It is not that I disagree with the paradigms, but rather I am unhappy about the dualistic weight often given them and the confrontational way in which they are sometimes used. (Yin/yang are also sometimes explained incorrectly, as if they were dualistic opposites.)

And then there is the assurance of the millennial vision—the ecotopian heaven as contrasted with the contemporary hell. But history suggests that if and when we do get there it will not be what we expected (or not for long), that we won't live happily ever after and the work will have to go on. The road is the goal and the goal is the road. Meanwhile, the UK Green Party argues (often vehemently) over every jot and tittle of what they will do when the Queen asks them for a government! If we could but cherish some uncertainty and ignorance about where we are going and what we are going to do, we will gain access to a certain spaciousness in which new possibilities can open up.

When an idea begins to harden into ideology, a theory, or a belief system, its proponents lose sight of the inherent paradoxes and seeming contradictions that could really be its growing points. For example, deep ecology has transcended anthropocentric humanism by asserting that nonhuman life has a value in itself, independent of its usefulness to mankind. But deep ecologists have been accused of inadequate recognition of the needs of millions of powerless and impoverished humans and of otherwise failing to relate ecology to social justice. Ultimately the disagreement turns on the paradoxical nature of humankind; each side is holding on to half the truth. We do have a unique responsibility for other creatures and the whole ecosystem, and yet we are at the same time an integral part of that system. As with the jewels in Indra's Net, to become fully human is to accept being qualitatively different and yet the same as the rest of planetary life; to accept full responsibility while remaining unreservedly at one with nature.

An astounding new perspective is attained when we make the leap out of an anthropocentric humanism and, following St. Francis, enjoy and value other life forms with which we feel equal and as one. But we still delude ourselves unless there is a further leap up the spiral and return to our human responsibility at a higher level. I suggest that next time deep ecologists hold one of their workshops centered upon a role-playing Council of All Beings they also allow the wretched of the Earth to turn up, with their large families and their chain saws. For the social ecology that challenges deep ecology is really the cutting edge and the growing point of a deep ecology yet to come of age.

Buddhology also reminds us of how fellowship, which can support our cultivation of *awareness*-identity, can slide all too easily into propping up a delusive *belongingness*-identity.

The network becomes a movement which feeds on itself, enabling us to dress up in everything we need without ever leaving the theme park. Ideology takes itself deadly seriously. But our present situation is surely much too serious to be taken seriously! Irony, black comedy and playfulness are all inherent in it and keep us sane. That's the Wise Fool's way of empowerment.

In conclusion, through meditative self-awareness we can "get out of own light" and respond positively and openly to what the situation requires of us. Through a self-critical Buddhology we can do the same for our intellectual and organizational endeavors. Both enable us to work for a Green Liberation that is our own liberation as well.

NOTES

1. Joanna Rogers Macy, *Despair and Personal Power in the Nuclear Age* (Philadelphia: New Society Publishers, 1983).

2. John Seed *et al.*, *Thinking Like a Mountain* (Philadelphia: New Society Publishers, 1988).

3. Ken Wilber, *No Boundary: Eastern and Western Approaches to Personal Growth* (Boston: Shambhala, 1981).

4. Ken H. Jones, *The Social Face of Buddhism: An Approach to Political and Social Activism* (Boston: Wisdom Publications, 1989).

5. A very attractive and approachable introduction to Indra's Net can be found in Francis Cook, *Hua-yen Buddhism* (University Park: Pennsylvania State University Press, 1977).

6. From William Blake's poem *Auguries of Innocence*.

7. *Samyutta Nikaya*, xii, 15.

8. See, for example, T. R. V. Murti, *The Central Philosophy of Buddhism: a Study of the Madhyamika System*, 2nd ed., (Boston: Allen & Unwin, 1960).

9. E. F. Schumacher, *Small is Beautiful* (New York: Harper & Row, 1973), pp. 63 and 236.

"AFRICAN-AMERICAN RESOURCES FOR A MORE INCLUSIVE LIBERATION THEOLOGY"

Theodore Walker, Jr.

Black theology is a form of liberation theology which holds that we are morally obliged to contribute to the well-being of all, and most especially to the well-being of the poor and oppressed. Black theology, on account of its appropriation of the philosophy of black power, sometimes describes contribution to the well-being of others in terms of empowerment. And most often, black theology's main social ethical concern is with the well-being and empowerment of people, i.e., "power to the people." This essay emphasizes what is occasionally but not frequently emphasized by black and other liberation theologians, that our moral obligation to contribute to the well-being and empowerment of others includes obligation to plants and animals.

In the foreword to Jay B. McDaniel's *Of God and Pelicans: A Theology of Reverence for Life*, John B. Cobb, Jr., notes that until recently the church was largely silent in regard to environmental issues. Cobb accounts for this "deafening silence" in terms of churchly fear that "attention to ecological issues would distract from that given to justice" (p. 11). But, as Cobb notes, "this has changed" because the church is coming to see that both justice and ecological sustainability "are essential and that in fact neither is possible without the other" (p. 11).

Like other churches and theologies, black churches and black theologians have been less than consistently outspoken about support for ecological and animal rights issues. Again, it would be correct to account for this relative silence by reference to the need for increased attention to human rights issues, and while it is true that John Cobb, Jay McDaniel, Sallie McFague, Thomas Berry, Tom Regan and others have done much to increase the conceptual and moral ground for unity between concern with justice and concern with the environment, there are some causes of black churchly and theological reluctance to adopt ecological and animal rights agenda which have yet to be overcome. From the perspective of many black and colored peoples, there are racial and racist aspects of modern white ecological/animal rights

Reprinted from *Good News for Animals?: Christian Approaches to Animal Well-Being* edited by Charles Pinches and Jay B. McDaniel, © 1993, by permission of the author and Orbis Books.

thinking which make it somewhat more difficult for us to adopt their ecological/animal rights agenda as our own. One recent example from the literature of environmental and animal rights/protection will serve to illustrate our difficulty.

Douglas H. Chadwick's "Elephants—Out of Time, Out of Space," in *National Geographic* (vol. 179, no. 5, May 1991) includes a photograph of two white persons shooting a family of elephants in Zimbabwe (pp. 44–45). In the text we are told that the riflemen are members of a "culling team," and: "Culling, unlike poaching and trophy hunting, attempts to maintain the herd's natural age and gender balance. Still, critics emphasize the inevitable loss of genetic diversity and the horror of slaughtering great and intelligent beings" (p. 45).

Here it is reported that regard for the well-being of elephants and a sense of horror over their slaughter, produces criticism of shooting elephants, even when killing individual elephants is thought to benefit elephant life in general. In this very same article, there is a photograph of black men shooting black men. The text tells us this is Richard Leakey's "anti-poaching unit in Kenya," and that they are armed with automatic rifles, helicopter gunships, and "shoot-to-kill orders" (pp. 30–31). And we are told that as a result of Leakey's command; "more than a hundred poachers have been killed, giving Kenya's elephants a fighting chance" (p. 31). *National Geographic* reports nothing horrible, regrettable, or even critical of killing more than a hundred humans.

Obviously, this example of animal protection policy is morally problematic. Moreover, the fact that Mr. Leakey's anti-poaching unit has shoot-to-kill orders that pertain to predominantly if not exclusively black poachers in Africa, but no such homicidal power over the predominantly nonblack buyers and distributors of ivory, indicates that this valuing of elephant life over human life is helped by the fact that the humans being shot are black. This uncritical valuing of elephant life over black human life is helped by the fact that the modern West is victim of a racist heritage that regards black and colored humans as less than fully human. For instance, at one point in United States legal history, a black man was counted as "three-fifths of a man." This racist heritage no doubt helps to enable white environmentalists and animal rights advocates to experience no horror when Mr. Leakey's unit shoots to kill black humans for the sake of elephants, when in fact they do experience horror when elephants are shot for the sake of elephants, and when in fact they would be much horrified if Mr. Leakey's antipoaching unit were to start shooting to kill the white consumers, investors, and distributors who profit from this and other destruction of wildlife.

From our perspective, many calls by white persons for an extension of the range of moral concern so as to include regard for the well-being of plants and animals are morally suspect on account of failure to include adequate regard for the well-being of black and colored humans—such as, for example, the more than one hundred persons killed by Mr. Leakey's antipoaching unit. When those who value the lives of black humans less than they value the lives of elephants, and less than they value the lives of white humans, ask us to join them in expressing their newfound concern for the well-being and rights of animals, we are not overly eager to join them. When we see environmentalists and animal rights proponents expressing criticism and concern with the well-being of elephants and other life while at the same time being utterly unconcerned about human life, just as when we see "right-to-life" activists showing much concern for the well-being of the unborn and no concern for the already born, we find it difficult, even impossible at times, to adopt their social ethical agenda as our own. Too often what passes for a wider concern inclusive of the environment is in fact a white racially gerrymandered concern which reaches out to include plants and animals while continuing to exclude black and colored peoples. These difficulties have yet to be overcome, and they must be overcome if white environmentalists and animal rights activists expect to receive the support of black and colored peoples.[1]

In the meantime, it is important for black theologians to consult nonracist traditions and resources in order to develop our own independent black churchly environmental agenda. Moreover, we must work to help our white sisters and brothers in the various environmental and ecological movements overcome the racial exclusions that continually retard the development of more inclusive efforts to contribute to ecological sustainability and liberation of other life.

Katie Geneva Cannon has an essay in a book titled *Inheriting Our Mothers' Gardens,* the language of mothers' gardens being an inheritance from Alice Walker's black womanist *In Search of Our Mothers' Gardens.* In her essay, Katie Cannon speaks about "surviving the blight" of hard times and oppression by attending to the inheritance from our mothers' gardens.[2] When black theologians attend to the inheritance from the gardens of Mother Africa, we learn that righteous social ethical reflection must take due account of the cross-generational character of human existence.

According to traditional African thought, we are morally obliged to remember and venerate the contributions of previous generations, most notably the ancestors; we are morally obliged to contribute to the well-being of our neighbors in this generation, and our neighborhood includes other life, human and nonhuman; and we have a moral responsibility to contribute to the well-being of future life (including our own future lives) and future generations. Traditional African social ethical reflection is characterized by a strong emphasis upon the need to contribute to the well-being of future life, including especially the well-being of those who are called "the beautiful ones" by Ayi Kwei Armah in his classic novel *The Beautyful Ones Are Not Yet Born.*[3] We have a moral responsibility to contribute to the well-being and empowerment of the beautiful ones who are not yet born.

This cross-generational vision of social ethical obligation is an important resource for black theological social ethical reflection. It is also a very much needed resource for modern western ethical thought. For it is clear that much of modern western ecological irresponsibility is a function of the failure to consider the well-being of future life and future generations.

The well-being of other life and of future generations is regularly sacrificed for the sake of immediate monetary gain. Modern western ethical calculus seldom reaches beyond consequences which obtain for the present generation. Let us, then, cultivate among ourselves and others the habit of being explicitly attentive to the cross-generational aspects of human existence and social ethical responsibility. This is essential to the development of more ecologically responsible social ethical reflection and behavior.

Another insight essential to more ecologically responsible social ethical reflection and behavior which we can glean from traditional African sources is a more holistic vision of life and of our place within the web of life. Harvey Sindima's essay "Community of Life: Ecological Theology in African Perspective" teaches us that traditional African thought offers an alternative to the traditional western "mechanistic perspective that views all things as lifeless commodities to be understood scientifically and to be used for human ends."[4] Sindima describes the African alternative to this western-mechanistic-commodity-oriented way of seeing the world as "a life-centered way" which "stresses the bondedness, the interconnectedness, of all living beings" (p. 137). According to this African alternative, the nonhuman world of nature is not merely a collection of exploitable lifeless commodities; instead, the whole world (including nonhuman animals, plants, the earth, and its ecosystem) is seen as a living and sacred part of one divine life. Specifically, Sindima says that for Malawians, "nature and persons are one, woven by creation into one texture or fabric of life, a fabric or web characterized by an interdependence between all creatures. This living fabric of nature—including people and other creatures—is sacred" (p. 143).

For Sindima, this traditional African perspective upon the community of life calls for a more inclusive understanding of justice. Sindima defines justice in terms of "how we live in the web of life in reciprocity with people, other creatures, and the earth, recognizing that they are part of us and we are part of them" (p. 146).

Also among the important resources inherited from the gardens of Mother Africa are the ancient and antiquitous religions on North Africa, greater North Africa, and the Afro-Mediterranean world, including ancient Egyptian, Hebrew, Christian, and Moslem religions. Scripture scholars and historians of religion are already teaching us that according to these sources, the modern western habit of excluding and failing to reverence other life, including nonhuman and future life, is contrary to right relationship to God. According to early religious insights that grew out of Afro-Mediterranean soil and water, right relation to God entails right relation to creation. We must contribute to the well-being of those who are and will be loved by God, and God's love includes all creation. No creature, species, race, or gender is excluded.

The philosophy of black power is another important resource for black theological social ethical reflection. The philosophy of black power is defined by an attempt to answer the question, What must we black folk do with the resources that we control in order to contribute to the well-being and empowerment of all the people? The most recent scholarly reflection upon this question includes an attempt to correct what Harold Cruse identifies as the failed tradition of "noneconomic liberalism."[5] Noneconomic liberalism is a social strategy which focuses upon political empowerment without adequate attention to economic empowerment. During the 1980s, Cruse and other black social analysts became increasingly critical of failure to give adequate attention to economic empowerment. We should remain mindful of this criticism when thinking about environmental issues and animal rights.

Social ethical reflection upon contribution to ecological sustainability and animal protection must take account of the fact that pollution and environmental exploitation and oppression of animals and other life are financially profitable. Noneconomic or financially unprofitable environmental animal-protection policies are likely to be no more successful than noneconomic liberalism has been for African-Americans. Given the relentless pursuit of short-term financial profit, significant improvement cannot be achieved until it becomes financially profitable to be ecologically responsible. Like with struggles for human liberation, the quest for liberation of other life requires serious attention to economic matters.

Another resource related to the philosophy of black power is the inclusive conception of freedom symbolized by our liberation colors—red, black, green, and gold. Our red-black-green liberation flag was first popularized in the United States by Marcus Garvey (1887–1940) and the Universal Negro Improvement Association.[6] The color red is a symbol for blood, especially blood sacrificed in the struggle for liberty. Black symbolizes people. Green symbolizes land, particularly the motherland of Africa, and, more broadly, the whole earth. During the 1980s, African-Americans in the United States and other black people became increasingly inclined to add a fourth liberation color—gold. Gold is for the wealth and resources stolen from Mother Africa and from the earth as a whole. These colors—red, black, green, gold—symbolize a conception of freedom and a black liberation agenda which includes concern for the well-being of Mother Earth and all her creatures. Other life and life-forms—including our own future lives, the lives of the beautiful ones not yet born, the earthly ecosystem, and nonhuman lives or creatures inclusive of plants and animals—are important parts of the liberation agenda called for by our black liberation flag and colors.

Our black liberation flag and colors are conceptual resources also in that by inviting our attention to the land and its wealth, they remind us to be attentive to the plight of our farmers. Green is for the land. Gold is for the wealth and resources stolen from the land, most especially from the land of Africa. We Africans in the Americas are part of that stolen wealth. We were stolen from the land of Africa so that we could be forced to work the land that was stolen from red people in the Americas. When we were emancipated from slavery, we were driven from the rural land we had worked and farmed for others, and into the cities. Some few of us were able to stay on the land as landowners and farmers, but, in recent years, the forces of racial oppression and exploitation have joined with the forces of agribusiness and factory farming to drive us from farmland and from farming altogether. In 1910 there were approximately one million minority farmers in the United States. By 1978, there were only 57,000 black farmers in the United States. Between 1910 and 1978, African-American farmers suffered the loss of over nine million acres of land. Given the continuation of these trends, it is estimated that there will be virtually no black farmowners in the United States by the year 2000.[7]

Of course, one of the most basic resources available to us is data from the black experience of suffering and oppression. The witness of our people is that the experience of suffering is such as to entail desire to be liberated from suffering. Insofar as animals suffer, there is no doubt that they experience desire to be free of suffering. There is, then, no good reason for failure to take account of this experience in our social ethical reflection and behavior. Howard Thurman made the point about animals experiencing desire to be free of suffering and oppression by narrating an experience from his youth in Daytona Beach, Florida. Thurman recalled that on one occasion during his childhood, he happened upon a tiny green snake crawling along a dirt path. In the mischievous way that is typical of a boy child, he pressed his bare foot on top of the little snake. Immediately, the little snake began to struggle against this oppression. Young Thurman felt the tremor of the snake's struggle as it vibrated up his leg and through his body. Thurman reasoned that struggle against suffering and oppression is divinely given to the nature of all living creatures, including even little green snakes.[8]

Attention to the cross-generational character of existence and moral obligation; a more holistic vision of life, and a more inclusive understanding of justice; the ancient and antiquitous religions of North Africa, greater North Africa, and the Afro-Mediterranean world; the philosophy of black power, including attention to economic empowerment; the conception of freedom and the inclusive liberation agenda called for by our liberation colors, including attention to the land, especially farmland; and the witness of the black experience of suffering and of other experiences of suffering are all important resources for developing a liberation agenda that includes concern for the well-being of other and future life. The religious and moral reflection of Native American peoples, Korean Minjung theologies, Buddhism, process/neoclassical philosophies, and many other helpful resources are also available. The harvest is plentiful, and there is great need for our labor in these fields and gardens. It is important that black churches and black theology contribute to the growth of more ecologically responsible reflection and behavior. We African-Americans in the United States are not without a measure of responsibility for the global ecological crisis. While it is historically true that through recent generations we have been and continue to be victim of the same Euro-American oppression that has victimized the global environment, nonetheless, it is also true that at this time and in this generation and for our social location in the Euro-American world, many of us are beneficiaries of environmental exploitation. Our piano keys also contain ivory. We also drive cars, eat butchered animal flesh, use animal-tested cosmetics, and otherwise benefit from the misuse and abuse of other and future life.

Moreover, the well-being of earthly creatures and the life-sustaining capacity of the ecosystem are much too important for us to leave entirely to the resources of white people. Given the unfortunate heritage of much Western thought, they are not likely to do well without help. Environmental and animal-protection efforts are very much in need of contributions from Native Americans, Latin American campesinos, traditional Africans, and other colored and black peoples. I believe, for example, the Environmental Protection Agency would be a more diligent protector of the environment if it were heavily peopled with Native Americans. Given sufficient economic resources, native South Americans could protect the Amazon rain forests from the destruction that is presently financed by North Atlantic interests. And I am certain that African elephants would be better served if Africans were paid more to protect elephants than they are paid for ivory. For the sake of other life, including elephants, pelicans, buffalo, and humans—black and white and colored, born and yet to be born—and for the sake of right relation to God, all of us are called to help in this important work.

NOTES

1. Cain Hope Felder provides another example of ecological concern failing to include the well-being of black and colored humans in an unpublished paper—"Technology, Ecology, and the Eclipse of the Biblical Vision: Theological Reflections on the State of the Environment"—presented at the Fourth Annual Theodore Roosevelt Environment and Conservation Symposium, October 23, 1989. Felder says "It is proper to highlight President Theodore Roosevelt's concern about aspects of the natural environment.... Yet, we cannot forget his safaris nor those thousands of Blacks imported to Panama as cheap labor to build the Panama Canal. Anonymous hundreds of them were killed in the blasting areas, their bodies in pieces buried under the soil, unmarked; while others were crushed under boulders or became victims of malaria. Rarely does anyone dare to mention the lack of human ecology for/of African Americans during his presidency. In the area of moral human ecology, the Roosevelt legacy itself is quite mixed" (pp. 3, 4).

2. See Katie Geneva Cannon, "Surviving the Blight," *Inheriting Our Mothers' Gardens: Feminist Theology in Third World Perspective*, Letty M. Russell, Kwok Puilan, Ada Maria Isasi-Diaz, Katie Geneva Cannon, eds. (Philadelphia: Westminster Press, 1988). And see Alice Walker, "In Search of Our Mothers' Gardens," in *Black Theology: A Documentary History, 1966–1979*, Gayraud S. Wilmore and James H. Cone, eds. (Maryknoll, N. Y.: Orbis Books, 1984) (originally published in *MS.*, vol. 2, no. 11, May 1974), and Alice Walker, *In Search of Our Mothers' Gardens: Womanist Prose* (San Diego: Harcourt Brace Jovanovich, 1983).

3. See Ayi Kwei Armah, *The Beautyful Ones Are Not Yet Born* (New York: Collier Books, 1969).

4. Harvey Sindima's "Community of Life: Ecological Theology in African Perspective" appears in *Liberating Life: Contemporary Approaches to Ecological Theology*, edited by Charles Birch, William Eakin, and Jay B. McDaniel (Maryknoll, N.Y.: Orbis Books, 1990), p. 137.

5. See Harold Cruse, *Plural But Equal: Blacks and Minorities in America's Plural Society* (New York: William Morrow, 1987).

6. In March 1921, the Universal Negro Improvement Association (UNIA) issued a "Universal Negro Catechism" prepared by the Reverend George Alexander McGuire (founder of the African Orthodox Church). According to this catechism, red, black, and green were established as the "National Colors of the Negro Race" at the UNIA's First International Negro Convention in New York in August 1920. See Robert Hill, ed., *Marcus Garvey Universal Negro Improvement Association Papers,* vol. 3. (Los Angeles: University of California Press, 1984), p. 319.

7. These statistics come from David M. Graybeal's 1986 film, "From This Valley: On Defending the Family Farm" (Jo Bales Gallagher, executive producer). Drawing upon data from the March 1986 report to Congress by the Office of Technology Assessment, Graybeal reports a national trend toward the increase of large corporate farms and toward decreasing numbers of medium and small family farms. In the U.S. generally, there were 7 million family farms in 1930. By 1986 that had become 2.2 million. The Office of Technology Assessment expects that very large farms will get larger, with only 50,000 of them producing three-fourths of all U.S. agricultural output, while on the other hand, moderate size and smaller farms will decline in number, market share, and net income. The plight of black and minority farmers is a very much more severe instance of this general trend. Graybeal reports that churches are coming to recognize that defense of family farming, including defense of black and minority farming, is an important item on the churchly liberation agenda. Here we are told that: "The churches are concerned by the centralization of coperate control over the national supplies of food and fiber, and by the transformation of agriculture into agribusiness. They are concerned by the pushing of dispossessed farmers into an economy that already has much unemployment. This is especially painful for black and other minority farm families and workers. The churches are concerned about a democracy in which nearly all the land is owned by the white race. They are concerned by tax policies that reward speculation in farm land by investors interested only in quick gains. . . . In short, the churches are concerned about future generations and the sustainability of a food production system when land, water, and other natural resources are threatened. . . . The churches intend to resist the growth of a new feudalism."

8. Howard Thurman narrated this story on the occasion of his visit to Livingstone College in Salisbury, North Carolina, during the spring of 1978.

PART IV

ECOTHEOLOGY IN AN AGE OF ENVIRONMENTAL CRISIS

Ecofeminist Spirituality

The Goddess in all her manifestations was a symbol of the unity of all life in Nature. Her power was in water and stone, in tomb and cave, in animals and birds, snakes and fish, hills, trees, and flowers. Hence the holistic and mythopoetic perception of the sacredness and mystery of all there is on Earth.

... The Goddess gradually retreated into the depths of forests or onto mountaintops, where she remains to this day in beliefs and fairy stories. Human alienation from the vital roots of earthly life ensued, the results of which are clear in our contemporary society. But the cycles never stop turning, and now we find the Goddess reemerging from the forests and mountains, bringing us hope for the future, returning us to our most ancient human roots.

—Marija Gimbutas

People often ask me if I *believe* in the Goddess. I reply, "Do you believe in rocks?" ... In the Craft, we do not *believe* in the Goddess—we connect with Her; through the moon, the stars, the ocean, the earth, through trees, animals, through other human beings, through ourselves. She is here. She is within us all.

—Starhawk

... for more than twenty thousand years, a Great Goddess existed in our mythic and religious imagination, art, rituals, and lives. What these images tell us is that in earliest periods of human consciousness, the creative impulse was imagined as female. ... In clay, bone, and stone, her body is sculpted with great egg shapes—breast, belly, and buttocks—images of fullness and potential becoming.

—Patricia Reis

The mother of us all,
the oldest of all,
hard,
      splendid as rock

Whatever there is that is of the land
          it is she
             who nourishes it,
     It is the Earth
     that I sing.

         —Homer

In the beginning, people prayed to the Creatress of Life, the Mistress of Heaven. At the very dawn of religion, God was woman. Do you remember?

         —Merlin Stone

Since the 1960s a worldwide feminist movement has called into question virtually every cherished institution and belief system of patriarchal culture. In 1974, French feminist Françoise d'Eaubonne coined the term "ecofeminism" to express a theoretical perspective that sees critical links between the domination of nature and the exploitation of women. Early texts by Carolyn Merchant (*The Death of Nature*) and Susan Griffin (*Women and Nature*) documented how modern Western culture associated women and nature, contrasting both to the self-proclaimed rationality, moral superiority and scientific prowess of "man."

Simultaneously, thinkers such as Mary Daly, Rosemary Radford Ruether, Carol Christ and Judith Plaskow—as well as countless grassroots activists—brought feminist claims into the realm of established religions. They questioned male power in religious institutions, sexist teachings about gender relationships, and exclusively male images of divinity.

These two tendencies are connected in spiritual ecofeminism, which builds on the premise that patriarchal society dominates women and nature with parallel ideologies and practices. Further, ecofeminism self-consciously values those aspects of women's social and natural experience which allow them to sense and value their connections to the nonhuman world. Ecofeminist spirituality tends to celebrate the body and the earth. It is highly critical of the familiar hierarchies of Western metaphysics, which privilege the eternal, the immaterial and the (supposedly) rational over the changing, the physical body and the realm of emotional response and empathic connection.

Part IV begins with Rosemary Radford Ruether's overview of the subject, as she traces the lineage of patriarchy in the history of Western religion. Anna Primavesi argues for the necessity of redefining the essential texts of Christianity. Shamara Shantu Riley relates ecofeminism to the social situation of African-Americans, reminding us that while all people share environmental concerns, the experience of racism, no less than sexism, is often instrumental in determining how and to what degree those concerns are manifest. Paula Gunn Allen and Susan Griffin offer poetic meditations expressing a fundamentally empathic sensibility towards nature. Selections by Riane Eisler and Vandana Shiva highlight the feminist attempt to recover in the worship of the goddess a religious form that treasures both women and the earth. Brooke Medicine Eagle describes her own spiritual initiation. Finally Terry Tempest Williams and Carol Adams make difficult and highly charged connections between the oppression of women in religious settings and various concrete forms of violence against women and other forms of life.

A comparatively recent perspective, spiritual ecofeminism (like all bold new philosophies) faces serious questions. For instance, is the turn to Goddess worship really a rediscovery of the past or simply an invention of the present? Is the association of women with nature likely to support rather than weaken patriarchy's devaluation of women's capacity for instrumental reason and public power? How much of traditional religious life can be transformed by feminism, and how much is beyond redemption?

"ECOFEMINISM: SYMBOLIC AND SOCIAL CONNECTIONS OF THE OPPRESSION OF WOMEN AND THE DOMINATION OF NATURE"

Rosemary Radford Ruether

What is ecofeminism? Ecofeminism represents the union of the radical ecology movement, or what has been called "deep ecology," and feminism. The word "ecology" emerges from the biological science of natural environmental systems. It examines how these natural communities function to sustain a healthy web of life and how they become disrupted, causing death to the plant and animal life. Human intervention is obviously one of the main causes of such disruption. Thus ecology emerged as a combined socioeconomic and biological study in the late sixties to examine how human use of nature is causing pollution of soil, air, and water, and destruction of the natural systems of plants and animals, threatening the base of life on which the human community itself depends (Ehrlich et al. 1973).

Deep ecology takes this study of social ecology another step. It examines the symbolic, psychological, and ethical patterns of destructive relations of humans with nature and how to replace this with a life-affirming culture (Devall and Sessions 1985).

Feminism also is a complex movement with many layers. It can be defined as only a movement within the liberal democratic societies for the full inclusion of women in political rights and economic access to employment. It can be defined more radically in a socialist and liberation tradition as a transformation of the patriarchal socioeconomic system, in which male domination of women is the foundation of all socioeconomic hierarchies (Eisenstein 1979). Feminism can be also studied in terms of culture and consciousness, charting the symbolic, psychological, and ethical connections of domination of women and male monopolization of resources and controlling power. This third level of feminist analysis connects closely with deep ecology. Some would say that feminism is the primary expression of deep ecology (see Doubiago 1989, 40–44).

Yet, although many feminists may make a verbal connection between domination of women and domination of nature, the development of this connection in a broad historical,

---

social, economic, and cultural analysis is only just beginning. Most studies of ecofeminism, such as the essays in *Healing the Wounds: The Promise of Ecofeminism,* are brief and evocative, rather than comprehensive (Plant 1989).

Fuller exploration of ecofeminism probably goes beyond the expertise of one person. It needs a cooperation of a team that brings together historians of culture, natural scientists, and social economists who would all share a concern for the interconnection of domination of women and exploitation of nature. It needs visionaries to imagine how to construct a new socioeconomic system and a new cultural consciousness that would support relations of mutuality, rather than competitive power. For this, one needs poets, artists, and liturgists, as well as revolutionary organizers, to incarnate more life-giving relationships in our cultural consciousness and social system.

Such a range of expertise certainly goes beyond my own competence. Although I am interested in continuing to gain working acquaintance with the natural and social sciences, my primary work lies in the area of history of culture. What I plan to do in this essay is to trace some symbolic connections of domination of women and domination of nature in Mediterranean and Western European culture. I will then explore briefly the alternative ethic and culture that might be envisioned, if we are to overcome these patterns of domination and destructive violence to women and to the natural world.

PRE-HEBRAIC ROOTS

Anthropological studies have suggested that the identification of women with nature and males with culture is both ancient and widespread (Ortner 1974, 67–88). This cultural pattern itself expresses a monopolizing of the definition of culture by males. The very word "nature" in this formula is part of the problem, because it defines nature as a reality below and separated from "man," rather than one nexus in which humanity itself is inseparably embedded. It is, in fact, human beings who cannot live apart from the rest of nature as our life-sustaining context, while the community of plants and animals both can and, for billions of years, did exist without humans. The concept of humans outside of nature is a cultural reversal of natural reality.

How did this reversal take place in our cultural consciousness? One key element of this identification of women with nonhuman nature lies in the early human social patterns in which women's reproductive role as childbearer was tied to making women the primary productive and maintenance workers. Women did most of the work associated with child care, food production and preparation, production of clothing, baskets, and other artifacts of daily life, cleanup, and waste-disposal (French 1985, 25–64).

Although there is considerable variation of these patterns cross-culturally, generally males situated themselves in work that was both more prestigious and more occasional, demanding bursts of energy, such as hunting larger animals, war, and clearing fields, but allowing them more space for leisure. This is the primary social base for the male monopolization of culture, by which men reinforced their privileges of leisure, the superior prestige of their activities, and the inferiority of the activities associated with women.

Perhaps for much of human history, women ignored or discounted these male claims to superiority, being entirely too busy with the tasks of daily life and expressing among themselves their assumptions about the obvious importance of their own work as the primary producers and reproducers (Murphy and Murphy 1974, 111–41). But, by stages, this female consciousness and culture was sunk underneath the growing male power to define the culture for the whole society, socializing both males and females into this male-defined point of view.

It is from the perspective of this male monopoly of culture that the work of women in maintaining the material basis of daily life is defined as an inferior realm. The material world itself is then seen as something separated from males and symbolically linked with women. The earth, as the place from which plant and animal life arises, became linked with the bodies of women, from which babies emerge.

The development of plow agriculture and human slavery very likely took this connection of woman and nature another step. Both are seen as a realm, not on which men depend, but which men dominate and rule over with coercive power. Wild animals which are hunted retain their autonomy and freedom. Domesticated animals become an extension of the human family. But animals yoked and put to the plow, driven under the whip, are now in the new relation to humans. They are enslaved and coerced for their labor.

Plow agriculture generally involves a gender shift in agricultural production. While women monopolized food gathering and gardening, men monopolize food production done with plow animals. With this shift to men as agriculturalists comes a new sense of land as owned by the male family head, passed down through a male line of descent, rather than communal landholding and matrilineal descent that is often found in hunting-gathering and gardening societies (Martin and Voorhies 1975, 276–332).

The conquest and enslavement of other tribal groups created another category of humans, beneath the familiar community, owned by it, whose labor is coerced. Enslavement of other people through military conquest typically took the form of killing the men and enslaving the women and their children for labor and sexual service. Women's work becomes identified with slave work (Lerner 1986, ch. 4). The women of the family are defined as a higher type of slave over a lower category of slaves drawn from conquered people. In patriarchal law, possession of women, slaves, animals, and land all are symbolically and socially linked together. All are species of property and instruments of labor, owned and controlled by male heads of family as a ruling class (see Herlihy 1988, 1–28).

As we look at the mythologies of the Ancient Near Eastern, Hebrew, Greek, and early Christian cultures, one can see a shifting symbolization of women and nature as spheres to be conquered, ruled over, and finally, repudiated altogether.

In the Babylonian Creation story, which goes back to the third millennium B.C.E., Marduk, the warrior champion of the gods of the city states, is seen as creating the cosmos by conquering the Mother Goddess Tiamat, pictured as a monstrous female animal. Marduk kills her, treads her body underfoot, and then splits it in half, using one half to fashion the starry firmament of the skies, and the other half the earth below (Mendelsohn 1955, 17–46). The elemental mother is literally turned into the matter out of which the cosmos is fashioned (not accidentally, the words *mother* and *matter* have the same etymological root). She can be used as matter only by being killed; that is, by destroying her as "wild," autonomous life, making her life-giving body into "stuff" possessed and controlled by the architect of a male-defined cosmos.

THE HEBRAIC WORLD

The view of nature found in Hebrew Scripture has several cultural layers. But the overall tendency is to see the natural world, together with human society, as something created, shaped, and controlled by God, a God imaged after the patriarchal ruling class. The patriarchal male is entrusted with being the steward and caretaker of nature, but under God, who remains its ultimate creator and Lord. This also means that nature remains partly an uncontrollable realm that can confront human society in destructive droughts and storms. These experiences of nature that transcend human control, bringing destruction to human work, are seen as divine judgment against human sin and unfaithfulness to God (see Isaiah 24).

God acts in the droughts and the storms to bring human work to naught, to punish humans for sin, but also to call humans (that is, Israel) back to faithfulness to God. When Israel learns obedience to God, nature in turn will become benign and fruitful, a source of reliable blessings, rather than unreliable destruction. Nature remains ultimately in God's hands, and only secondarily, and through becoming servants of God, in male hands. Yet the symbolization of God as a patriarchal male and Israel as wife, son, and servant of God, creates a basic analogy of woman and nature. God is the ultimate patriarchal Lord, under whom the human patriarchal lord rules over women, children, slaves, and land.

The image of God as single, male, and transcendent, prior to nature, also shifts the symbolic relation of male consciousness to material life. Marduk was a young male god who was produced out of a process of theogony and cosmogony. He conquers and shapes the cosmos out of the body of an older Goddess that existed prior to himself, within which he himself stands. The Hebrew God exists above and prior to the cosmos, shaping it out of a chaos that is under his control. Genesis 2 gives us a parallel view of the male, not as the child of woman, but as the source of woman. She arises out of him, with the help of the male God, and is handed over to him as her Master.[1]

THE GREEK WORLD

When we turn to Greek philosophical myth, the link between mother and matter is made explicit. Plato, in his creation myth, the *Timaeus,* speaks of primal, unformed matter as the receptacle and "nurse" (Plato, 29). He imagines a disembodied male mind as divine architect, or Demiurgos, shaping this matter into the cosmos by fashioning it after the intellectual blueprint of the Eternal Ideas. These Eternal Ideas exist in an immaterial, transcendent world of Mind, separate from and above the material stuff that he is fashioning into the visible cosmos.

The World Soul is also created by the Demiurgos, by mixing together dynamics of antithetical relations (the Same and the Other). This world soul is infused into the body of the cosmos in order to make it move in harmonic motion. The remnants of this world soul are divided into bits, to create the souls of humans. These souls are first placed in the stars, so that human souls will gain knowledge of the Eternal Ideas. Then the souls are sown in the bodies of humans on earth. The task of the soul is to govern the unruly passions that arise from the body.

If the soul succeeds in this task, it will return at death to its native star and there live a life of leisured contemplation. If not, the soul will be reincarnated into the body of a woman or an animal. It will then have to work its way back into the form of an (elite) male and finally escape from bodily reincarnation altogether, to return to its original disincarnate form in the starry realm above (Plato, 23). Plato takes for granted an ontological hierarchy of being, the immaterial intellectual world over material cosmos, and, within this ontological hierarchy, the descending hierarchy of male, female, and animal.

In the Greco-Roman era, a sense of pessimism about the possibility of blessing and well-being within the bodily, historical world deepened in Eastern Mediterranean culture, expressing itself in apocalypticism and gnosticism. In apocalypticism, God is seen as intervening in history to destroy the present sinful and finite world of human society and nature and to create a new heaven and earth freed from both sin and death.[2] In gnosticism, mystical philosophies chart the path to salvation by way of withdrawal of the soul from the body and its passions and its return to an immaterial realm outside of and above the visible cosmos.[3]

CHRISTIANITY

Early Christianity was shaped by both the Hebraic and Greek traditions, including their alienated forms in apocalypticism and gnosticism. Second-century Christianity struggled against gnosticism, reaffirming the Hebraic view of nature and body as God's good creation. The second-century Christian theologian Irenaeus sought to combat gnostic anticosmism

Rosemary Radford Ruether

and to synthesize apocalypticism and Hebraic creationalism. He imaged the whole cosmos as a bodying forth of the Word and Spirit of God, as the sacramental embodiment of the invisible God.

Sin arises through a human denial of this relation to God. But salvific grace, dispensed progressively through the Hebrew and Christian revelations, allows humanity to heal its relation to God. The cosmos, in turn, grows into being a blessed and immortalized manifestation of the divine Word and Spirit, which is its ground of being (Richardson 1953, 1:387–98).

However, Greek and Latin Christianity, increasingly influenced by Neoplatonism, found this materialism distasteful. They deeply imbibed the platonic eschatology of the escape of the soul from the body and its return to a transcendent world outside the earth. The earth and the body must be left behind in order to ascend to another, heavenly world of disembodied life. Even though the Hebrew idea of resurrection of the body was retained, increasingly this notion was envisioned as a vehicle of immortal light for the soul, not the material body, in all its distasteful physical processes, which they saw as the very essence of sin as mortal corruptibility.[4]

The view of women in this ascetic Christian system was profoundly ambivalent. A part of ascetic Christianity imagined women becoming freed from subordination, freed both for equality in salvation and to act as agents of Christian preaching and teaching. But this freedom was based on woman rejecting her sexuality and reproductive role and becoming symbolically male. The classic Christian "good news" to woman as equal to man in Christ was rooted in a misogynist view of female sexuality and reproduction as the essence of the sinful, mortal, corruptible life (see Vogt, 1990).

For most male ascetic Christians, even ascetic woman, who had rejected her sexuality and reproductive role, was too dangerously sexual. Ascetic women were increasingly deprived of their minor roles in public ministry, such as deaconess, and locked away in convents, where obedience to God was to be expressed in total obedience to male ecclesiastical authority. Sexual woman, drawing male seminal power into herself, her womb swelling with new life, became the very essence of sin, corruptibility, and death, from which the male ascetic fled. Eternal life was disembodied male soul, freed from all material underpinnings in the mortal bodily life, represented by woman and nature.

Medieval Latin Christianity was also deeply ambivalent about its view of nature. One side of medieval thought retained something of Irenaeus's sacramental cosmos, which becomes the icon of God through feeding on the redemptive power of Christ in the sacraments of bread and wine. The redeemed cosmos as resurrected body, united with God, is possible only by freeing the body of its sexuality and mortality. Mary, the virgin Mother of Christ, assumed into heaven to reign by the side of her son, was the representative of this redeemed body of the cosmos, the resurrected body of the Church (Semmelroth 1963, 166–68).

But the dark side of Medieval thought saw nature as possessed by demonic powers that draw us down to sin and death through sexual temptation. Women, particularly old crones with sagging breasts and bellies, still perversely retaining their sexual appetites, are the vehicles of the demonic power of nature. They are the witches who sell their souls to the Devil in a satanic parody of the Christian sacraments (Summers 1928).

THE REFORMATION
AND THE SCIENTIFIC REVOLUTION

The Calvinist Reformation and the Scientific Revolution in England in the late sixteenth and seventeenth centuries represent key turning points in the Western concept of nature. In these two movements, the Medieval struggle between the sacramental and the demonic views of nature was recast. Calvinism dismembered the Medieval sacramental sense of nature. For Calvinism, nature was totally depraved. There was no residue of divine presence in it that could sustain a natural knowledge or relation to God. Saving knowledge of God descends from on high, beyond nature, in the revealed World available only in Scripture, as preached by the Reformers.

The Calvinist reformers were notable in their iconoclastic hostility toward visual art. Stained glass, statues, and carvings were smashed, and the churches stripped of all visible imagery. Only the disembodied Word, descending from the preacher to the ear of the listener, together with music, could be bearers of divine presence. Nothing one could see, touch, taste, or smell was trustworthy as bearer of the divine. Even the bread and wine were no longer the physical embodiment of Christ, but intellectual reminders of the message about Christ's salvific act enacted in the past.

Calvinism dismantled the sacramental world of Medieval Christianity, but it maintained and reinforced its demonic universe. The fallen world, especially physical nature and other human groups outside of the control of the Calvinist church, lay in the grip of the Devil. All who were labeled pagan, whether Catholics or Indians and Africans, were the playground of demonic powers. But, even within the Calvinist church, women were the gateway of the Devil. If women were completely obedient to their fathers, husbands, ministers, and magistrates, they might be redeemed as goodwives. But in any independence of women lurked heresy and witchcraft. Among Protestants, Calvinists were the primary witch-hunters (Perkins 1590, 1596; see also Carlsen 1980).

The Scientific Revolution at first moved in a different direction, exorcizing the demonic powers from nature in order to reclaim it as an icon of divine reason manifest in natural law (Easlea 1980). But, in the seventeenth and eighteenth centuries, the more animist natural science, which unified material and spiritual, lost out to a strict dualism of transcendent intellect and dead matter. Nature was secularized. It was no longer the scene of a struggle between

Rosemary Radford Ruether

Christ and the Devil. Both divine and demonic spirits were driven out of it. In Cartesian dualism and Newtonian physics, it becomes matter in motion, dead stuff moving obediently, according to mathematical laws knowable to a new male elite of scientists. With no life or soul of its own, nature could be safely expropriated by this male elite and infinitely reconstructed to augment its wealth and power.

In Western society, the application of science to technological control over nature marched side by side with colonialism. From the sixteenth to the twentieth centuries, Western Europeans would appropriate the lands of the Americas, Asia, and Africa, and reduce their human populations to servitude. The wealth accrued by this vast expropriation of land and labor would fuel new levels of technological revolution, transforming material resources into new forms of energy and mechanical work, control of disease, increasing speed of communication and travel. Western elites grew increasingly optimistic, imagining that this technological way of life would gradually conquer all problems of material scarcity and even push back the limits of human mortality. The Christian dream of immortal blessedness, freed from finite limits, was translated into scientific technological terms (Condorcet 1794).

ECOLOGICAL CRISIS

In a short three-quarters of a century, this dream of infinite progress has been turned into a nightmare. The medical conquest of disease, lessening infant mortality and doubling the life span of the affluent, insufficiently matched by birth limitation, especially among the poor, has created a population explosion that is rapidly outrunning the food supply. Every year 10 million children die of malnutrition.[5] The gap between rich and poor, between the wealthy elites of the industrialized sector and the impoverished masses, especially in the colonized continents of Latin America, Asia, and Africa, grows ever wider (Wilson and Ramphele 1989).

This Western scientific Industrial Revolution has been built on injustice. It has been based on the takeover of the land, its agricultural, metallic, and mineral wealth appropriated through the exploitation of the labor of the indigenous people. This wealth has flowed back to enrich the West, with some for local elites, while the laboring people of these lands grew poorer. This system of global affluence, based on exploitation of the land and labor of the many for the benefit of the few, with its high consumption of energy and waste, cannot be expanded to include the poor without destroying the basis of life of the planet itself. We are literally destroying the air, water, and soil upon which human and planetary life depend.

In order to preserve the unjust monopoly on material resources from the growing protests of the poor, the world became more and more militarized. Most nations have been using the lion's share of their state budgets for weapons, both to guard against one another and to control their own poor. Weapons also become one of the major exports of wealthy nations to poor nations. Poor nations grow increasingly indebted to wealthy nations while buying weapons to repress their own impoverished masses. Population explosion, exhaustion of natural resources, pollution, and state violence are the four horsemen of the new global apocalypse.

The critical question of both justice and survival is how to pull back from this disastrous course and remake our relations with one another and with the earth.

TOWARD AN ECOFEMINIST ETHIC AND CULTURE

There are many elements that need to go into an ecofeminist ethic and culture for a just and sustainable planet. One element is to reshape our dualistic concept of reality as split between soulless matter and transcendent male consciousness. We need to discover our actual reality as latecomers to the planet. The world of nature, plants, and animals existed billions of years before we came on the scene. Nature does not need us to rule over it, but runs itself very well, even better, without humans. We are the parasites on the food chain of life, consuming more and more, and putting too little back to restore and maintain the life system that supports us.

We need to recognize our utter dependence on the great life-producing matrix of the planet in order to learn to reintegrate our human systems of production, consumption, and waste into the ecological patterns by which nature sustains life. This might begin by revisualizing the relation of mind, or human intelligence, to nature. Mind or consciousness is not something that originates in some transcendent world outside of nature, but is the place where nature itself becomes conscious. We need to think of human consciousness not as separating us as a higher species from the rest of nature, but rather as a gift to enable us to learn how to harmonize our needs with the natural system around us, of which we are a dependent part.

Such a reintegration of human consciousness and nature must reshape the concept of God, instead of modeling God after alienated male consciousness, outside of and ruling over nature. God, in ecofeminist spirituality, is the immanent source of life that sustains the whole planetary community. God is neither male nor anthropomorphic. God is the font from which the variety of plants and animals well up in each new generation, the matrix that sustains their life-giving interdependency with one another (McFague 1987, 69–77).

In ecofeminist culture and ethic, mutual interdependency replaces the hierarchies of domination as the model of relationship between men and women, between human groups, and between humans and other beings. All racist, sexist, classist, cultural, and anthropocentric assumptions of the superiority of whites over blacks, males over females, managers over workers, humans over animals and plants, must be discarded. In a real sense, the so-called superior pole in each relation is actually the more dependent side of the relationship.

Rosemary Radford Ruether

But it is not enough simply to humbly acknowledge dependency. The pattern of male-female, racial, and class interdependency itself has to be reconstructed socially, creating more equitable sharing in the work and the fruits of work, rather than making one side of the relation the subjugated and impoverished base for the power and wealth of the other.

In terms of male-female relations, this means not simply allowing women more access to public culture, but converting males to an equal share in the tasks of child nurture and household maintenance. A revolution in female roles into the male work world, without a corresponding revolution in male roles, leaves the basic pattern of patriarchal exploitation of women untouched. Women are simply overworked in a new way, expected to do both a male workday, at low pay, and also the unpaid work of women that sustains family life.

There must be a conversion of men to the work of women, along with the conversion of male consciousness to the earth. Such conversions will reshape the symbolic vision of salvation. Instead of salvation sought either in the disembodied soul or the immortalized body, in a flight to heaven or to the end of history, salvation should be seen as continual conversion to the center, to the concrete basis by which we sustain our relation to nature and to one another. In every day and every new generation, we need to remake our relation with one another, finding anew the true nexus of relationality that sustains, rather than exploits and destroys, life (Ruether 1984, 325–35).

Finally, ecofeminist culture must reshape our basic sense of self in relation to the life cycle. The sustaining of an organic community of plant and animal life is a continual cycle of growth and disintegration. The western flight from mortality is a flight from the disintegration side of the life cycle, from accepting ourselves as part of that process. By pretending that we can immortalize ourselves, souls and bodies, we are immortalizing our garbage and polluting the earth. In order to learn to recycle our garbage as fertilizer for new life, as matter for new artifacts, we need to accept our selfhood as participating in the same process. Humans also are finite organisms, centers of experience in a life cycle that must disintegrate back into the nexus of life and arise again in new forms.

These conversions, from alienated, hierarchical dualism to life-sustaining mutuality, will radically change the patterns of patriarchal culture. Basic concepts, such as God, soul-body, and salvation will be reconceived in ways that may bring us much closer to the ethical values of love, justice, and care for the earth. These values have been proclaimed by patriarchal religion, yet contradicted by patriarchal symbolic and social patterns of relationship.

These tentative explorations of symbolic changes must be matched by a new social practice that can incarnate these conversions in new social and technological ways of organizing human life in relation to one another and to nature. This will require a new sense of urgency about the untenability of present patterns of life and compassionate solidarity with those who are its victims.

NOTES

1. Phyllis Trible (1973) views the story of Eve's creation from Adam as essentially egalitarian. For an alternative view from the Jewish tradition, see Reik 1960.

2. For the major writings of inter-testamental apocalyptic, see Charles 1913.

3. For the major gnostic literature, see Robinson 1977.

4. Origen (1966, Bk. 2, ch. 3, 83–94). Also Nyssa, 464–65.

5. Cited in a talk in London, May 29, 1989, by Dr. Nafis Sadik, head of the United Nations Fund for Population Activities. See Broder, 1989.

BIBLIOGRAPHY

Broder, David. 1989. *Chicago Tribune* (May 31), sec. 1, 17.

Carlsen, Carol F. 1980. *The Devil in the Shape of a Woman: The Witch in 17th-Century New England.* Ph.D. Diss. New Haven, Conn.: Yale University.

Charles, R. H. 1913. *The Pseudepigrapha of the Old Testament.* Oxford: Clarendon Press.

Condorcet, Antoine-Nicholas de. 1794. *Sketch for a Historical Picture of the Progress of the Human Mind.*

Devall, Bill, and George Sessions. 1985. *Deep Ecology: Living as if Nature Mattered.* Salt Lake City: Peregrine Smith Books.

Doubiago, Sharon. 1989. "Mama Coyote Talks to the Boys." In Judith Plant, ed. *Healing the Wounds: The Promise of Ecofeminism.* Philadelphia, Pa.: New Society Publishers.

Easlea, Brian. 1980. *Witchhunting, Magic and the New Philosophy.* Highlands, N.J.: Humanities Press.

Ehrlich, Paul R., et al. 1973. *Human Ecology: Problems and Solutions.* San Francisco: W. H. Freeman Co.

Eisenstein, Zillah, ed. 1979. *Capitalist Patriarchy and the Case for Socialist Feminism.* New York: Monthly Review Press.

French, Marilyn. 1985. *Beyond Power: On Women, Men and Morals.* New York: Summit Books.

Herlihy, David. 1988. *Medieval Households.* Cambridge, Mass.: Harvard University Press.

Lerner, Gerda, ed. 1986. *The Creation of Patriarchy.* New York: Oxford University Press.

McFague, Sallie. 1987. *Models of God: Theology for an Ecological, Nuclear Age.* Philadelphia: Fortress Press.

Martin, M. Kay, and Barbara Voorhies. 1975. *Female of the Species.* New York: Columbia University Press.

Mendelsohn, Isaac, ed. 1955. *Religion in the Ancient Near East.* New York: Liberal Arts Press.

Murphy, Yolanda, and Robert Murphy. 1974. *Women of the Forest.* New York: Columbia University Press.

Nyssa, Gregory, 1893. *On the Soul and the Resurrection.* In *Nicene and Post-Nicene Fathers.* 2nd series, vol, 5. New York: Parker.

Origen. G. W. Butterworth, ed. 1966. *On First Principles.* New York: Harper and Row.

Ortner, Sherry. 1974. "Is Female to Male as Nature Is to Culture?" In Michelle Zimbalist Rosaldo and Louise Lamphere, eds. *Woman, Culture and Society.* Stanford, Calif.: Stanford University Press.

Perkins, William. 1590. *Christian Oeconomie.* London.

Plant, Judith, ed. 1989. *Healing the Wounds: The Promise of Ecofeminism.* Philadelphia: New Society Publishers; Toronto: Between the Lines.

Plato. 1937. Timaeus. In B. Jowett, ed. *The Dialogues of Plato.* vol. 2. New York: Random House.

Reik, Theodor. 1960. *The Creation of Woman.* New York: McGraw-Hill.

Richardson, Cyril, ed. 1953. *Early Christian Fathers* 1. Philadelphia: Westminster Press.

Robinson, James M., ed. 1977. *The Nag Hammadi Library.* San Francisco: Harper and Row.

Ruether. 1984. "Envisioning Our Hope: Some Models for the Future." In Janet Kalven and Mary Buckley, eds. *Women's Spirit Bonding.* New York: Pilgrim Press.

Semmelroth, Otto. 1963. *Mary: Archetype of the Church.* New York: Sheed and Ward.

Summers, Montague, ed. 1928. *Malleus Maleficarum.* London: J. Rodker.

Trible, Phyllis. 1973. "Depatriarchalizing in Biblical Interpretation." *Journal of the American Academy of Religion* 41(1) (March).

Vogt, Kari. 1990. "Becoming Male: A Gnostic and Early Christian Metaphor." In Kari Borresen, ed. *Image of God and Gender Models in Judaeo-Christian Tradition.* Oslo: Solum Forlag.

Wilson, Francis, and Mamphela Ramphele. 1989. *Uprooting Poverty: The South African Challenge.* Capetown: David Philip.

"ECOFEMINISM AND CANON"

Anne Primavesi

[I argue] for the inclusion of feminine and natural imagery in the Christian tradition, and for women's right to participate in the making of that tradition. Interpretation of the Bible plays a crucial part in any decision made about the exclusion or inclusion of women. Up to now, it has worked against them by canonizing the perpetuation of patriarchy and by making male metaphors for God absolute. A new perception of what is involved in the process of canonizing may help open up the tradition to include women's experience as an integral part of it.

WHAT IS THE CANON?

An interplay between Bible, tradition and interpretation was the dominant force in Christianity's development in self-understanding. This development is reflected in the process usually called the formation of the *canon*: the process by which certain historical records of the religious past were chosen as authoritative. This canon was defined in the fifth century as: "that which has been believed everywhere, always and by all."[1] The process is a living one, and its development has rested on the acceptance by believers that the choice of record made in canonization (the Bible as we have it today, with or without certain writings of the church Fathers and conciliar pronouncements) was inspired by the Spirit. Furthermore, it presupposes that the interpretation of these records is definitively propounded through the authority of the Spirit handed on (*traditio*) from one generation to the next. The exclusion of some books from the Protestant canon and their inclusion by the Catholic hierarchy does not affect the notion of canon itself. Rather, it emphasizes it, since both actions were intended to be seen as claims to the authority to define what it means to be Christian. Outside ecclesiastical government circles, the ordinary believer generally accepts that the books of the Bible as printed constitute the basic written record of the revelation of God given to the Church.

This is true even of the Roman Catholic Church, which until the Second Vatican Council would have taught that there were two distinct sources of revelation, Scripture and Tradition (the recorded authorized interpretations). In 1965, in the document on revelation, the Council devoted its two opening chapters to revelation and its transmission without explicitly distinguishing them as separate sources. Four of the six chapters in the document deal expressly with the Bible. In it, the document says, God revealed himself to men, spoke to men out of the abundance of his love and invited them into fellowship with himself. By this revelation the deepest truth about God and the Salvation of man is made clear to us in Christ. After speaking in many places and various ways through the prophets, God last of all has spoken to us by his Son, the Word made flesh, sent as "a man to men."[2]

The Protestant position in regard to the revelation of God was stated briefly by Barth when he described Holy Scripture as an entity which stands superior in order to the church, temporal like it, yet different from it. This is because it is the canon of the church, that is, the regulation, the pattern, what is fixed in the church as authoritative. From the fourth century on, he says, the word "canon" has developed into the list of books in the Bible recognized in the church as authoritative, because recognized as apostolic.[3]

The complex process of the formation of the canon is a study in its own right, and it is impossible to give an adequate outline of its development here. What I want to focus on is simply the fact that such a thing as the canon exists, and then to follow up some questions raised by its existence and by the way in which it came to exist. Whether it is ever formally invoked or not, it is taken by ordinary Christians to mean that the Bible is the foundation stone upon which is built the security of faith and practice which comes from having God's will for the world made explicit. Its authenticity is seen as guaranteed by the authority of those to whom Christ handed on his own unique perception of that will, the apostles. The Catholic and Protestant positions come together here by making the apostles the link between the handing on of the truth of God in Christ ("the Word made flesh, sent as a man to men") and the authoritative reading of the Bible in churches today.

QUESTIONS RAISED BY THE CANON

The first question raised by the existence of the canon is its dependence on the hierarchical paradigm of Christianity. The power to interpret what is contained in it is assumed to be given "from above," from the Spirit handed on by Jesus to certain men who have the power to delegate it to others. The authority to interpret the Scriptures definitively is attributed to the "highest" level of church government, from which and on which all others depend.

The corollary to this is that the Spirit is confined to hierarchical relationships within this structure, both between the Father and Son and between them and the church. The Spirit is boxed in between Father and Son, Son and apostles, apostles and church. The personal role of the Spirit within the life of the Trinity is confined to empowering the love between Father and Son, or the mission of the Father and Son to the world through the church. The hierarchical church thus makes itself the cause of grace in the world and the means of dispensing the Spirit, rather than simply being the occasion and context where these may take place. The freedom of the Spirit to act as and when and where it pleases, intimated by the image of the wind used for it by Jesus, is lost in the superimposed image of it as a possession of men, handed on, literally, to other men, through the laying-on of hands.

Then there is the question of those who heard, proclaimed, recorded or wrote the texts as they now appear. Neither they, nor today's readers and proclaimers, can isolate themselves and their personal contexts from the interpretative process. They are part of it, not least by the questions they pose and the answers they expect. Their attitudes to women and Nature cannot be isolated from their enquiries into the complex life systems presented to us in the Bible and other canonical sources. . . .

There is the further question of how balanced a view of the world we can expect to find in the records. The Bible and the interpretations of it which came from a patriarchal church necessarily failed to integrate the contribution women could have made to the canon. Male dominance permeates it. To recognize this is difficult and painful: our personal stories are involved, our deepest identity called into question. For male readers it is especially difficult, and one man, a biblical scholar, accepted the analysis, but said it made him feel as if he were being asked to accept castration.[4] How do women feel?

On the basis of these and allied questions, ecofeminists refuse to take the canonical record of male relationship with God and the world, centered on one small group of people in a particular time and culture, as normative for the whole of humanity. They refuse to accept as God's will the continuance of the patriarchal power structures enshrined within this record. These have ensured that women's voices have been omitted from the ongoing interpretative process and that a particular attitude to Nature has been canonized. Therefore ecofeminist theologians claim the right from now on to include women's experience as part of that process which keeps the canon alive as a source of inspiration and strength within the Church.

Therefore they seek contemporary meaning within the texts in a dialogical relationship between them and the primary system of the world we live in. The dialogue is always open-ended, for the meaning emerges in the act of struggling for it in a relational rather than an oppositional way. Therefore it is constantly open to revision through fresh input, for example from the data of scientific ecology.

Starting from these premises, ecofeminist theology challenges the present assumptions behind the canonicity of Scripture. Why these texts and not others? What texts were omitted when it was decided that these were the only revealed truth about God's dealings with the world? Who made the decisions? What effects has this partiality had on Christianity's relationship with the world?

In raising the first question, why these texts and not others, we note that the Hebrew scriptures come from sources removed both hierarchically and demographically from the lives of most Israelites. This is hardly surprising, since in a largely pre-literate or illiterate society, the possibility of keeping records was necessarily confined to certain classes. Those parts of the canon most concerned with human relationships with the land (the Pentateuch) are by the large the product of a priestly, all-male, hereditary group with its leadership based on the Temple, located in the capital city, Jerusalem. Virtually all of the historical writings—the so-

Anne Primavesi

called Deuteronomic history, which runs from Joshua through to Kings and constitutes the core of the Hebrew Bible—were probably based on court records or traditions circulating in royal circles. The post-exilic chronicles were compiled at the behest of governors like Ezra and Nehemiah. (The point at issue here is the common acceptance of this attribution, and not its truth, falsity or the possibility of exceptions to it within the Wisdom tradition.) This attribution to official ruling classes, whether royal, priestly or gubernatorial, excluded most men and the vast majority of Israelite women. The governing establishment was unrepresentative of the population as a whole. Yet the experience of this male part of the nation Israel, even today, has been taken as representing the whole history of God's relationship with this people.[5]

This is equally true of those texts written after the death of Jesus. Paul's education and the evangelists' literary skills were important factors in the acceptance of their writings as normative. Paul was a city person. The city breathes through his language. When he constructs a metaphor of olive trees or gardens, the Greek is fluent and evokes schoolroom more than farm; he seems at home with the clichés of Greek rhetoric, drawn from gymnasium, stadium or workshop. He depended on the city for his livelihood, supporting himself as an artisan in distinction both from the workers of the farms, both slave and free, and from the few whose wealth and status depended on their agricultural estates. When Paul rhetorically catalogues the places where he has suffered danger, he divides the world into city, wilderness, and sea (2 Cor. 11:26). His world does not include the *chora*, the productive countryside; outside the city there is nothing—*eremia*. Since his world consisted, practically speaking, only of the cities of the Roman Empire, he makes the extraordinary claim that from Jerusalem and as far round as Illyricum, he has fully preached the Gospel of Christ, so that he no longer has work in these regions. What he had actually done was to plant small cells of Christians in scattered households in some of the strategically located cities of the north-east Mediterranean basin.[6]

The authors of the Gospel records may or may not have included a countryman. Popular attribution ascribes them to a physician (Luke), a philosopher theologian (John), a Hellenistic catechist (Matthew) and a disciple of Peter's who made his way to Rome and became recorder of the community there (Mark). Whoever they were, their accounts concentrate almost exclusively on what is commonly called the "public" life of Jesus, centred on town and city, and on his debates with the ruling classes in the context of his trial and death at the hands of spiritual and imperial elites.

The Pauline Epistles and Acts record Paul's own battles with these as well as with the male ruling council of the emerging church. Attribution to him was enough for the so-called "Pastoral" letters to the churches to be taken as authoritative, especially where they lay down rules for the "normative" relationships within church hierarchies which, for example, exclude women from spiritual authority. The pseudo-Pauline letter to Timothy gives an inaccurate gloss of Genesis in its attempt to justify the male right to exclude (cf. 1 Cor. 11:3, 5; 14:34f; 2 Tim. 2:11–14). This appeal to a flawed male hermeneutic of Genesis was to have lasting consequences for the role of women and Nature within Christianity.

This process within the canonized Bible of using interpretations of existing Scriptures to reinforce certain religious and cultural assumptions must be seen for what it is, a literary and interpretative device. Then the internal dialogue in the New Testament between the Jewish scriptures and the nascent Christian community after the death of Jesus will be seen as aspects of this system of reinforcing the authority to interpret. They are not master codes possessing the ability to bring about the truth. Seen like this, the Pauline emphasis on Jesus as Lord is respected as no more than that, a vital personal relationship and not a universal one to be given dominance over all others.

THE PARTIALITY OF THE CANON

From an ecofeminist theological viewpoint, priests, prophets, kings, officers, bureaucrats and apostles are seen to be small élite groups within masses of population, both male and female, all of whom have a relationship with their creator God. The biblical concentration on these élites, to the exclusion of the rest, has necessarily given us a partial picture of our religious origins which has taken such groups out of their metacontexts and raised them to the status of the whole. This goes some way towards answering the question about which records were kept and which discarded. However small in number these groups were, they had enormous power and influence, not least because of their ability to articulate the meaning of their relationship with God and the world around them.

So their ideologies, in the sense of their religious understanding of events and ideas, came to be considered as normative by everyone. Not only that, but they also became the apparent divine norm, and certain social and religious structures (notably monarchy and ecclesiastical hierarchy) were established on this basis. Not only must we acknowledge the relative status of these writings. We also need to analyze the positions of power which underlay their circulation.

We must also keep in mind the group of theologians (the church Fathers) who up to and since the fourth century have kept certain interpretations of these writings in a position of dominance over the Christian imagination. They shared a Greek culture and transmitted their teaching through the concepts and categories of Greek philosophy. They also shared the reverence for Scriptural authority manifest in the Christian records written after Jesus' death. So when Denys, the author of *The Celestial Hierarchy* wanted to give his vision authority, he wrote under the pseudonym "Denys the Areopagite." Denys was the first of Paul's converts in Athens, and Athens meant philosophy, and more precisely, Plato. Denys the Athenian convert stands at the point where Christ and Plato meet. The pseudonym expressed the author's belief that the truths that Plato grasped belong to Christ, and are not abandoned by embracing faith in Christ.[7] This view was shared, as we have seen, by some of the most influential shapers of the Christian tradition.

Returning to the Israelite stage of the tradition for the moment, those who shaped it were not only exclusive in number and education. They were separated from most of their fellow Israelites in that as residents of Jerusalem or of other major cities, they participated in an urban pattern of life. This is of more than passing consequence for assessing the effects of those texts included or excluded. For a start, most people lived in the non-urban settings under-represented in the Bible. Its androcentric bias and also its urban, élite orientation mean that even the information it does contain about agrarian life may be a distortion or misrepresentation. So the highly stylized Leviticus texts, for instance, cannot be taken as universally applicable norms in respect to women and Nature.[8] Indeed, even within the Christian canon there is a notable outburst attributed to God, no less, against such stereotyping when Peter is reminded forcibly that no creature created by God can be classified as unclean (Acts 10).

Such partiality toward urban society, its relationships with and its distancing from the land, has been hard-programmed into the Christian interpretation of the biblical sources in all sorts of covert ways. Until recently, biblical archaeology concentrated disproportionately on the urban sites most likely to provide verification or illumination of the political history recorded in the Bible. Consequently the sites chosen tended to be major cities assumed to have been cultic and administrative centers. Archaeologists concentrated on fortification systems, palaces, villas, and public buildings. In doing so, they chose features of urban life related to the military, to the governing elite, and to the cultic establishment. This contributed further to the lack of visibility of the middle and lower echelons of society, and of all those whose realm of activity was oriented to private or domestic affairs. Insofar as women's lives were typically confined to the domestic realm, biblical archaeology has offered virtually nothing that could be used to reconstruct the social or religious role of women or anyone else belonging to the non-urban, non-élite or non-specialist segment of the population.[9] In short, almost nothing was done up to now to recover a balanced understanding of early Israelite society or the "ordinary" person's relationship with God.

The same invisibility cloaks the life of the early Christian communities, but is often compensated for by haggling over visible sites associated with the life and death of Jesus. In the Christian Diaspora imperial basilicas are studied to provide ground plans and scale maps for Christian worship. By the late second century, the episcopal model of leadership had developed into an urban hierarchy in which the bishop became the presiding pastor at the major congregation of the city and supervised others. The pattern of episcopal hierarchy expanded in the next two centuries into provincial and imperial forms by which the presiding bishops at major sees supervised bishops and elders under them. Gradually, the church began to duplicate the political structures of the late Roman Empire and to evolve an ecclesiastical counterpart to the Roman system of urban and provincial governors.[10]

In such ways, the very notion of church became identified with visible structures designed and built by men, and church membership appeared synonymous with attendance in them. Churchgoers, that is, those who went out of the home to worship, were counted as "the Church."

EFFECTS OF THE CANON ON WOMEN AND NATURE

One obvious effect of this split in religious consciousness was that the home, woman-centered in its rituals of bringing forth and nourishing life, became desacralized. Instead of ritualizing natural birth through the water and blood of the mother, baptism in church became the religious rite by which one rejects one's natural life, derived from and nourished by the waters of the mother's womb, and undergoes a "rebirth" through "holy" water blessed by men hierarchically chosen to possess the Spirit. Women's experience of life-giving was alienated from the sacred and excluded from canonical authority.

If it were included, it would integrate the mother and child into a community representing the whole of human relationality. The experience of naturally giving birth is intrinsically linked with the nourishment and sustaining of life through food. Women's continuous experience of lifegiving centers on the nurture and growth of bodies through food shared at meals. This is the central symbolic act of Christianity known as Eucharist. Yet it has been most radically alienated from its natural setting by being literally taken out of women's hands and transferred to a church sanctuary. There the symbolic act of blessing and giving food and drink has been "elevated" into a symbol of the power to control divine or redeeming life, a power that the clergy claim to possess in a way that is beyond the access of "natural" human beings.[11]

This tendency to reserve Eucharistic actions to those males in churches seen as sole possessors of the Spirit has contributed much to the desacralizing of our attitudes to "ordinary" food and the acceptance of "consumerism" instead. . . . [T]he theological and ecological implications of this will be discussed at some length. An ecological Christianity would seek to heal the division between Eucharist and home by restoring a sense of the sacred to every meal, and by re-valuing women's role in bearing the Spirit of a God who continually sustains us through eating.

This bias toward church buildings in the city incorporated an important shift not only in the perception of home but also of Nature. Certain man-made edifices became isolated sanctuaries, holy places dotted about a natural, profane world. The sacred was sequestered within the walls of a public building made with hands. Human activities were classified as "holy" according to whether or not they took place within a "consecrated" place. Implicitly, therefore, one stepped outside such a place into a world that was not sacred. The accepted reason for the "profanity" of Nature was that it became corrupted through Adam's Sin.[12] But whereas humanity was redeemed within these buildings through baptism into Christ the second Adam, outside them Nature remained unredeemed.

In such ways the foundations were laid for a dualistic modelling of Christian society into two kinds of activity, the private and the public, which came to be seen as corresponding to the profane and the sacred. The private domestic sphere revolved around home and field and the reproductive processes centred on women and the natural world. While not explicitly excluded from the realm of the sacred, it was definitely not its primary locus either. The public sphere was everything outside the home environment: collective rituals, legal or judicial regulation of supradomestic matters, and official worship.

Theologically as well as culturally then, female identity was linked with the domestic and male identity with the public. Women were associated with the "natural" functions taking place in the domestic contexts, and men more closely identified with public functions.[13] Consciously and unconsciously, the female natural habitat, whether of humankind or beast, was linked with the profane, and the male public sphere was the area of encounter with the sacred. In regard to the non-human world, any possibility of locating the divine there was repudiated.

Today it is official Christian teaching that Nature is desacralized, "fallen."[14] Yet hardly a day goes by without someone reminding us that unless we recover a sense of reverence for Nature, we are not going to win the battle for its and our survival. How is this sense to be recovered in a tradition which has consistently denied Nature the possibility of its own relationship with the divine and the right to reverence for its own sake?[15]

A start must be made by acknowledging the endemic partiality of Christianity. This runs right through its canonical tradition. It is based in texts which make small sections of the community representative of the whole and it allows that community to believe itself to be the isolated recipient of the whole of God's revelation to the whole of creation. That self-perception turns all too easily into one which knowingly displaces the rest of creation, whether women, non-Christians, non-human species or inert matter, into a desacralized zone. This continues as long as Christian assertions are made (for example, that no one comes to the Father except through the Son, or that no one is saved outside the church), in ways which seemingly accept that God has created the whole world in order to save a very small number of baptized human beings out of it.

So far this book has given a glimpse of some of the covert and overt effects on women and Nature wherever it is assumed that the male part of humanity's experience of God can be taken for the whole. It has left us with a few further questions here: who decided which part of the tradition should be so taken? Why these records and not others? The recent discovery of so much "non-canonical, inter-testamental and pre-Christian literature, such as the Nag Hammadi texts and the Qumran scrolls, poses the question with renewed force.

THE CANON AND THE SPIRIT

The Christian canonization of Scripture, begun in the second century C.E., assigned authority to certain writings chosen out of those circulating among Christians at the time. The men who chose these and rejected others claimed absolute authority for themselves to decide which books were authoritative. They based their claim on their possession of the Spirit. In all Christian churches, including the non-episcopal ones, this claim to possession of the Spirit in order to choose and interpret the essential books of the Bible continues to constitute that church's claim to be a Christian church, and guarantees its members' belonging to Christ's Body. In episcopal churches, the claim is made that the Holy Spirit is passed on to ordained ministers through the bishop, the successor of the apostles. An up-to-date statement of this claim is found in the Vatican II Dogmatic Constitution on the Church, *Lumen Gentium*, 24–8.[16]

This claim on behalf of one section of the community gradually absorbed (or eroded) any counter-claim to possession of the Spirit. Traditional theology held that the spiritual phenomena of the early times had disappeared because they were no longer needed. The strength of the church made them unnecessary for confirming the faith of the people. The liberation theologian José Comblin asks: "Was it not rather the opposite; that the (human) strength of the churches closed the doors on the Spirit and its gifts?"[17]

The closure is exemplified in the first centuries of the Church by the exclusion of Christian women from spiritual authority. This was justified by a "canonized" interpretation of the Genesis narratives (cf. the reference from 2 Tim. 2) which blamed the daughters of Eve for the fall of man. This interpretation was legalized in the twelfth century canons of Gratian (*Corpus iuris Canonici*, Pt. II. C.33. q.5, c.12, 13, 17, 18).

With this interpretation of the fall of man through woman's weakness as its major presupposition, all traditional Christian efforts have been directed at finding a remedy for this fall. The resulting doctrines of salvation have elevated man twice over above women and Nature. They are agents neither of their own damnation nor salvation. It is the fall of Adam that is credited (!) with the corruption of all succeeding generations. In him we are all fallen. Correlatively, it is the second Adam, Jesus Christ, who is credited with the salvation of both man and woman. Only a male can save us from the sin generated by a male. This logic denies women the power to be agents of salvation for themselves or others. They have access to redemption only through men.

This effectively blocks them from any relationship with the Spirit other than through male mediation. It also effectively blocks any relationship with the Spirit other than a utilitarian one, useful for human salvation. Comblin remarks dryly that the domination of the poor of Latin America was accepted for so long because of the traditional view that the clergy hold the keys of the kingdom of heaven, so those who wish to be saved have to accept the whims of the clergy—outwardly at least. But their present experience of liberation through the Spirit is of a new sense of responsibility for themselves, of being capable of acting on their own initiative. So they are now expressing their own opinions about sin, life and death. As are women.[18]

The doctrine of salvation from sin through the power invested in the clergy was seen to be effective for human beings alone. Yet Adam's fall was deemed sufficient cause for Nature's corruption. When he fell, so did the whole natural world. Augustine adduced postlapsarian thorns and thistles as evidence for this. But when the man Jesus Christ redeemed humanity from that fall, the thorns still flourished and the thistles spread: Nature remained corrupt, condemned to be subdued and exploited by men. There was no recognition of its own relationship with its Creator, nor any effective mediation of salvation through the church offered to it.

Therefore St. Francis's preaching to the birds is usually regarded as a pious aberration, and blessings of animals are generally treated as either certifiable or suspicious, on the grounds that they have no souls. The Rogation Day blessing of fields has withered away, and while there are some attempts to revive harvest festivals in a meaningful way, their success is limited in the Northern Hemisphere by the fact that most churchgoers shop for their food, and the festival is set in the context of the Eucharistic celebration with its emphasis on a different sort of food again.

As long as sin/salvation rituals dominate Christian practice, this cutting off of the non-human world from the church's ministry will continue. Its own perception of its role in salvation, as sole mediator between God and the world through its possession of the Spirit, effectively breaks the relationship between the Spirit and the whole of creation.

Therefore it also breaks the bond between the Trinity and creation, a bond traditionally expressed in the doctrine of the "economic" Trinity. This treats of the process of God's self-disclosure addressed to creation in the three-fold aspect of Father, Son and Spirit.

While this notion of economy seems to bear little relation to what is now understood by the word, among its original meanings was the popular understanding of it as distribution, organization and arrangement of a number of factors; in this case, the ordering of right relationships between the whole of creation and different aspects of God recorded in the tradition (Father, Son and Spirit). It is also noteworthy that the earliest reference to the "divine economy" occurs in Ignatius's Epistle to the Ephesians (XVIII, 2), where the words *oikonomia theou* refer to what one might call "God's management of the divine household." The Greek original has the same root (*oikos*: house, home, inhabited world) as ecology and ecumenism. It seems fair to say that the department marked "human salvation" appears not only to have taken over all the others but has effectively closed them down.

ECOFEMINIST CRITIQUE OF CANON

Ecofeminism calls for their re-opening as a matter of priority. It asks that human beings positively assert their relationship with Nature, and their common relationship with God, in particular under the aspect of the Spirit. What if we spoke of the Spirit of God the housekeeper? What would happen then to Christian attitudes to home and garden, to meals and housework?

Such a shift in perception can happen only if we integrate women's lives into the living canon of Christianity. We must reject the common demotion of women, their bodies, work and habitat, to all that is not divine. In company with the figure of Wisdom in the Jewish scriptures, women must again raise their voices to recount their role in the fashioning, in the sustaining of the world.

How can they be heard in a church which includes 2 Timothy in its canon? The violence with which Quaker women were treated in the seventeenth century (from whippings to hangings and burnings) when they dared raise their voices to interpret scripture is evidence of how well this male prohibition had worked until then. Is it so different now? The physical violence may appear to have gone, but psychological and pseudotheological barriers remain firmly in place. So unless women's interpretations of the book of Genesis are given authority, rather than the biassed views of a pseudo-Pauline author or an Augustine, their desacralization together with that of Nature will continue under the name of Christian orthodoxy. So too will Christian theology continue to be obsessed with fall/redemption doctrines which start from the premise that Nature is condemned to live in fear and dread of humanity because of its complicity in that fall.

The inclusion in the canon of women's experience of the Spirit takes account of the fact that the scriptures evolved through a process kept going by the tension between different points of view, different cultures, different theologies and the attempt to include them in some fashion. A re-valuing of this process will be based on the knowledge that the Spirit gives a diversity of gifts, to women and men alike, and that a new manifestation of the Spirit's power from within Christianity is found in women's speech. Their silence within the tradition was a commonplace. They talked elsewhere, in the home, in the fields, in the shops, and latterly in offices and civil institutions. But in the presence of church authority, they were silent.

Now, however, the Spirit sustains them in their access to God. The Spirit enables them to say worthwhile things of themselves and of Nature. The Spirit enlightens them in their study of the formation of the canon. They become aware that what it testifies to *directly* is not the religion of the whole of Israel or of Christianity, but of individuals and groups attempting, with varying degrees of success, to make their vision emerge in the wider society. What it testifies to *indirectly*, especially in the legislation, the historical narratives and prophetic denunciations, is that the whole relationship between God and Israel, God and Christianity, was something quite different. It becomes clear that the canon does not contain its own self-justification, especially in its hierarchical patterning, but rather directs our attention to the living tradition which it mediates partially.[19]

Without this tradition, partial as it is, there is for Christians no shared memory, no meta-context for our religious metaphor and no believing community in which to express our relationship with God. Without this tradition there is no structure against which the prophetic Spirit can react. Without it, the process does not continue whereby we are led as an ecological community to the truth about the world, the truth about God and the truth about ourselves; the economic, ecochristian truth. Without it, once its partiality has been recognized, there is no clear task of reconstruction in the light of the present.

Part of that task today is a re-interpretation of the Genesis texts as a decisive event in the life of the tradition, as the basis for a sustainable theology. Such a theology sustains hope in the face of ecological apocalypse, sustains life in the face of decomposition and death. It is sustainable also because it remains open to the hard data of science, to feminine imaginative consciousness and to the vision of thinkers and doers in other disciplines. It unites us all in a common purpose: to work with the divine economy of creation and sustain the life of the earth.

NOTES

1. This is usually known as the Vincentian canon, formulated by Vincent of Lérins. See Henry Bettenson, ed., *The Documents of the Christian Church* (Oxford, 1963), p. 82.

2. Walter Abbott, ed., *Documents of Vatican II* (London and Dublin, 1966), pp. 112f. On the implications of this for the relationship between Scripture and Tradition, see Gabriel Moran, *Theology of Revelation* (London, 1967).

3. Karl Barth, *The Doctrine of the Word of God* (Edinburgh, 1936), p. 113. For a discussion of the formation of the Hebrew canon, see Joseph Blenkinsopp, *Prophecy and Canon* (Notre Dame, 1977).

4. Brian Wren, *What Language Shall I Borrow?* (London, 1989), p. 6.

5. Carol Meyers, *Discovering Eve: Ancient Israelite Women in Context* (London, 1988), p. 12.

6. Wayne Meeks, *The First Urban Christians: The Social World of the Apostle Paul* (Yale, 1983), p. 9.

7. See Andrew Louth, *Denys the Areopagite* (London, 1989), pp. 10–11.

8. See Mary Douglas, *Purity and Danger* (London, 1966), pp. 41–57. See also the interesting discussion on the cultural basis of purity codes in L. W. Countryman, *Dirt, Greed and Sex* (London, 1989), p. 12. See also the distinctions he makes between the Israelite notion of the family and its subversion in the teachings of Jesus, pp. 168f.

9. Meyers, *Discovering Eve*, p. 18.

10. See Rosemary Radford Ruether, *Women-Church: Theology and Practice* (San Francisco, 1985), p. 12.

11. Ibid., pp. 78f. See suggestions for baptismal ceremonies, pp. 183f., and other liturgies celebrating the life cycle of living beings. See also Huub Oosterhuis, *Prayers, Peoms and Songs* (London, 1971), pp. 123f. for an imaginative baptismal liturgy.

12. See Elaine Pagels, *Adam, Eve, and the Serpent* (London, 1990). She brings out the implications for nature of Augustine's doctrine of the fall of Adam in his debate with Julian of Eclanum, and goes into some of the reasons why Augustine's negative assessment was adopted as official orthodox teaching from then on.

13. See Susan Thistlethwaite, *Sex, Race and God* (London, 1990), p. 85, for an interesting and challenging expansion of this notion in terms of differences between black and white women.

14. Arthur Peacocke, *Creation and the World of Science* (Oxford, 1979), p. 279.

15. See R. C. Zaehner, *Mysticism Sacred and Profane* (London, 1957), p. 33. Defining strictly religious mysticism, he says it means a total and absolute detachment from Nature, from "all that is not God."

16. See the discussion of the historic basis for these claims formulated by Irenaeus in Pagels, *The Gnostic Gospels* (New York, 1979), pp. 23f.

17. José Comblin, *The Holy Spirit and Liberation* (Tunbridge Wells and Maryknoll, N.Y., 1989), p. xiv.

18. Ibid., pp. 25f.

19. Blenkinsopp, *Prophecy and Canon*, p. 152.

"ECOLOGY IS A SISTAH'S ISSUE TOO: THE POLITICS OF EMERGENT AFROCENTRIC ECOWOMANISM"

Shamara Shantu Riley

Black womanists, like everyone in general, can no longer overlook the extreme threat to life on this planet and its particular repercussions on people of African descent.[1] Because of the race for increased "development," our world continues to suffer the consequences of such environmental disasters as the Chernobyl nuclear meltdown and Brazil's dwindling forests. Twenty percent of all species are at risk of extinction by the year 2000, with the rate of plant and animal extinction likely to reach several hundred per day in the next ten to thirty years (Worldwatch 1987, 3). Manufacturing chemicals and other abuses to the environment continue to weaken the ozone layer. We must also contend with the phenomenon of climate change, with its attendant rise in sea levels and changes in food production patterns.

Along with these tragic statistics, however, are additional environmental concerns that hit far closer to home than many Black people realize. In the United States, poor people of color are disproportionately likely to be the victims of pollution, as toxic waste is being consciously directed at our communities. The nation's largest hazardous-waste dump, which has received toxic material from 45 states, is located in predominantly black Sumter County, Alabama (de la Pena and Davis 1990, 34). The mostly African-American residents in the 85-mile area between Baton Rouge and New Orleans, better known as Cancer Alley, live in a region which contains 136 chemical companies and refineries. A 1987 study conducted by the United Church of Christ's Commission for Racial Justice found that two-thirds of all Blacks and Latinos in the United States reside in areas with one or more unregulated toxic-waste sites (Riley 1991, 15). The CRJ report also cited race as the most significant variable in differentiating communities with such sites from those without them. Partly as a result of living with toxic waste in disproportionate numbers, African-Americans have higher rates of cancer, birth defects, and lead poisoning than the United States population as a whole.[2]

On the African continent, rampant deforestation and soil erosion continue to contribute to the hunger and poverty rates in many countries. The elephant population is rapidly being reduced as poachers kill them to satisfy industrialized nations' ivory trade demands (Joyce 1989, 22). Spreading to a dozen African nations, the Green Belt Movement is seeking to reverse the environmental damage created by the European settlers during colonialism, when the settlers brought nonindigenous trees on the continent. As with United States communities of color, many African nations experience "economic blackmail," which occurs when big business promises jobs and money to "impoverished areas in return for these areas' support of or acquiescence to environmentally undesirable industries" (Meyer 1992, 32).

The extinction of species on our ancestral continent, the "mortality of wealth," and hazardous-waste contamination in our backyards ought to be reasons enough for Black womanists to consider the environment as a central issue of our political agendas.[3] However, there are other reasons the environment should be central to our struggles for social justice. The global environmental crisis is related to the sociopolitical systems of fear and hatred of all that is natural, nonwhite, and female that has pervaded dominant Western thought for centuries.[4] I contend that the social constructions of race, gender, class and nonhuman nature in mainstream Western thought are interconnected by an ideology of domination. Specific instances of the emergent Afrocentric ecowomanist activism in Africa and the United States, as well as West African spiritual principles that propose a method of overcoming dualism, will be discussed in this paper.

THE PROBLEM OF NATURE FOR BLACK WOMANISM

Until recently, few Black womanists gave more than token attention to environmental issues. At least in the United States, the origins of such oversight stem from the traditional Black association of environmentalism as a "white" concern. The resistance by many United States Blacks to the environmental movement may partly originate from a hope of revenge. Because of our acute oppression(s), many Blacks may conclude that if the world comes to an end because of willful negligence, at least there is the satisfaction that one's oppressors will also die. In "Only Justice Can Stop a Curse," author Alice Walker discusses how her life experiences with the Eurocentric, masculinist ideology of domination have often have often caused her to be indifferent to environmental issues:

> I think . . . *Let the earth marinate in poisons. Let the bombs cover the ground like rain. For nothing short of total destruction will ever teach them anything.* (Walker 1983b, 341)

However, Walker later articulates that since environmental degradation doesn't make a distinction between oppressors and the oppressed, it should be very difficult for people of color to embrace the thought of extinction of all life forms simply for revenge.

In advocating a reformulation of how humans view nonhuman nature, ecofeminist theorist Ynestra King states that from the beginning, women have had to grapple with the historical projection of human concepts onto the natural, which were later used to fortify masculinist notions about females' nature (King 1989, 118). The same problem is applicable to people of color, who have also been negatively identified with the natural in white supremacist ideologies.

Black women in particular have historically been associated with animality and subsequently objectified to uphold notions of racial purity. bell hooks articulates that since the 1500s, Western societies have viewed Black women's bodies as objects to be subdued and controlled like nonhuman nature:

> From slavery to the present day, the Black female body has been seen in Western eyes as the quintessential symbol of a "natural" female presence that is organic, closer to nature, animalistic, primitive. (hooks and West 1991, 153)

Patricia Hill Collins asserts that white exploitation of Black women as breeders during the Slave Era "objectified [Black women] as less than human because only animals can be bred against their will" (Collins 1990, 167). Sarah Bartmann, an African woman also known as the Hottentot Venus, was prominently displayed at elite Parisian parties. While being reduced to her sexual parts, Bartmann's protruding buttocks were often offered as "proof" that Blacks were closer to animals than whites. After her death in 1815, Bartmann was dissected, and her genitalia and buttocks remain on display in Paris (Gilman 1985). Bartmann's situation was similar to the predicament of Black female slaves who stood on auction blocks as masters described their productive body parts as humans do cattle. The historical dissection of Black women, be it symbolic or actual, to uphold white supremacist notions is interconnected with the consistent human view of nonhuman animals as scientific material to be dissected through an ideology that asserts both groups are inferior.

Because of the historical and current treatment of Blacks in dominant Western ideology, Black womanists must confront the dilemma of whether we should strive to sever or reinforce the traditional association of Black people with nature that exists in dominant Western thought. However, what we need is not a total disassociation of people from nature, but rather a reformulation of *everyone's* relationship to nature by socially reconstructing gender, class, and ethnic roles.

Environmentalism is a women's issue because females (especially those of color) are the principal farm laborers around the world, as well as the majority of the world's major consumers of agricultural products (Bizot 1992, 36). Environmentalism is also an important issue for people of color because we disproportionately bear the brunt of environmental degradation. For most of the world's population, reclaiming the Earth is not an abstract state of affairs but rather is inextricably tied to the survival of our peoples.

Womanism and ecology have a common theoretical approach in that both see all parts of a matrix as having equal value. Ecology asserts that without each element in the ecosystem, the biosphere as a whole cannot function properly. Meanwhile, womanism asserts the equality of races, genders, and sexual preferences, among other variables. There is no use in womanists advocating liberation politics if the planet cannot support people's liberated lives, and it is equally useless to advocate saving the planet without addressing the social issues that determine the structure of human relations in the world. If the planet as a whole is to survive, we must all begin to see ourselves as interconnected with nonhuman nature and with one another.

THE POLITICS OF NATURE-CULTURE DUALISM

At the foundation of dominant Western thought exists an intense ambivalence over humankind's place in the biosphere, not only in relation to one another, but also in relation to nonhuman nature. The systematic denigration of men of color, women, and nonhuman nature is interconnected through a nature-culture dualism. This system of interconnectedness, which bell hooks labels "the politic of domination," functions along interlocking axes of race, gender, species, and class oppression. The politic of domination "refers to the ideological ground that [the axes] share, which is a belief in domination, and a belief in the notions of superior and inferior, which are components of all those systems" (hooks 1989, 175). Although groups encounter different dimensions of this matrix based on such variables as species or sexual orientation, an overarching relationship nevertheless connects all of these socially constructed variables.

In discussing the origins of Western dualism, Dona Richards articulates the influence of dominant Jewish and Christian thought on Western society's conceptions about its relationship to nonhuman nature:

> Christian thought provides a view of man, nature, and the universe which supports not only the ascendancy of science, but of the technical order, individualism and relentless progress. Emphasis within this world view is placed on humanity's dominance over *all* other beings, which become "objects" in an "objectified" universe. Humanity is separated from nature. (Richards 1980, 69)

With dualistic thinking, humans, nonhuman nature, and ideas are categorized in terms of their difference from one another. However, one part is not simply deemed different from its counterpart; it is also deemed intrinsically *opposed* to its "Other" (Collins 1990, 69). For instance, speciesists constantly point to human neocortical development and the ensuing civilization that this development constructs as proof of human superiority over nonhuman animals. Women's position as other in Western patriarchies throughout the histories of both psychological theory and Christian thought has resulted in us being viewed as defective men.

Women, the nonelite, and men of color are not only socially constructed as the "Others," but the elite, white, male-controlled global political structure also has the power—through institutions such as the international media and politics—to extensively socialize us to view ourselves as others to be dominated. By doing so, the pattern of domination and subjugation is reinforced. Objectification is also central to the process of oppositional difference for all entities cast as other. Dona Richards claims that in dominant Western thought, intense objectification is a "prerequisite for the despiritualization of the universe and through it the Western cosmos was made ready for ever increasing materialization" (Richards 1980, 72). Since one component is deemed to be the other, it is simultaneously viewed as an object to be controlled and dominated, particularly through economic means.

Because nature-culture dualism conceives of nature as an other that (male) human undertakings transcend and conquer, women, nonhuman nature, and men of color become symbolically linked in Eurocentric, masculinist ideology. In this framework, the objectification of the other also serves as an escape from the anxiety of some form of mortality. For instance, white supremacists fear that it will be the death of the white race if people of color, who comprise the majority of the world's population, successfully resist the current global relations of power. Objectifying nonhuman nature by technology is predicated on an intense fear of the body, which reminds humans of death and our connection with the rest of nature. By making products that make tasks easier, one seeks to have more opportunities to live one's life, with time and nature converted into commodities.

World history can be seen as one in which human beings inextricably bind the material domination of nonhuman nature with the economic domination of other human beings. The Eurocentric, masculinist worldview that dominates Western thought tends to only value the parts of reality that can be exploited in the interest of profit, power and control. Not only is that associated with nature deemed amenable to conquest, but it is also a conquest that requires no moral self-examination on the part of the prospective conqueror. For instance, there is very little moral examination by research laboratories that test cosmetics on animals, or by men who assault women. There was also very little moral examination on the part of slave owners on the issue of slavery or by European settlers on colonialism in "Third World" nations.

By defining people of color as more natural and animalistic, a political economy of domination has been historically reinforced. An example of this phenomenon is the founding of the United States and the nation's resultant slave trade. In order for the European colonialists to exploit the American land for their economic interests, they first needed to subjugate the Native American groups who were inhabiting the land. While this was being accomplished, the colonists dominated Blacks by utilizing Africans as slave labor (and simultaneously appropriating much of Mexico) in order to cultivate the land for profit and expand the new capitalist nation's economy. Meanwhile, the buffalo almost became extinct in the process of this nation building "from sea to shining sea."

A salient example of the interconnectedness of environmental degradation and male supremacy is the way many societies attach little value to that which can be exploited without (economic) cost. Because nonhuman nature has historically been viewed by Westerners as a free asset to be possessed, little value has been accredited to it. Work traditionally associated with women via cultural socialization has similarly often been viewed as having little to no value. For instance, in calculating the Gross Domestic Product, no monetary value is attached to women's contributions to national economies through reproduction, housework, or care of children.

THE ROLE OF THE ENVIRONMENTAL-ISMS IN PROVIDING THE FOUNDATION FOR AN AFROCENTRIC WOMANIST AGENDA

While serving as executive director of the United Church of Christ's Commission for Racial Justice in 1987, Reverend Benjamin Chavis, Jr., coined the term *environmental racism* to explain the dynamics of socioeconomic inequities in waste-management policies. Peggy Shephard, the director of West Harlem Environmental Action, defines United States environmental racism as "the policy of siting potentially hazardous facilities in low-income and minority communities" (Day and Knight 1991, 77). However, environmental racism, which is often intertwined with classism, doesn't halt at the boundaries of poor areas of color. Blacks in Africa and the United States often have to contend with predominantly white environmental groups that ignore the connection between their own values and the struggles of people of color to preserve our future, which is a crucial connection in order to build and maintain alliances to reclaim the earth. For instance, because the Environmental Protection Agency is often seen as another institution that perceives elite white communities' complaints as more deserving of attention than poor communities of color, many United States social activists are accusing the EPA of "environmental apartheid" (Riley 1991, 15).

In "Granola Boys, Eco-Dudes, and Me," Elizabeth Larsen articulates how race, class, and gender politics are interconnected by describing the overwhelmingly white middle-class male leadership of mainstream United States environmental groups. In addition to being indifferent to the concerns of people of color and poor whites, the mainstream organizations often reinforce male supremacy by distributing organizational tasks along traditional gender roles (Larsen 1991, 96). The realization that only we can best represent our interests, an eco-identity politics, so to speak, lays the foundation for an Afrocentric ecowomanist agenda.[5] Even though many Black women have been active in the environmental movement in the past, there appears not to be much *published* analysis on their part about the role of patriarchy in environmental degradation. The chief reason for this sentiment may stem from perceiving race as the "primary" oppression. However, there is an emergent group of culturally identified

Black women in Africa and the United States who are critically analyzing the social roles of white supremacy, patriarchy, and classism in environmental degradation.

EMERGENT AFROCENTRIC ECOWOMANISM: ON THE NECESSITY OF SURVIVAL

There are several differences between ecofeminism and Afrocentric ecowomanism. While Afrocentric ecowomanism also articulates the links between male supremacy and environmental degradation, it lays far more stress on other distinctive features, such as race and class, that leave an impression markedly different from many ecofeminists' theories.[6]

Many ecofeminists, when analyzing the links between human relations and ecological degradation, give primacy to gender and thus fail to thoroughly incorporate (as opposed to mere tokenism) the historical links between classism, white supremacy, and environmental degradation in their perspectives. For instance, they often don't address the fact that in nations where such variables as ethnicity and class are a central organizing principle of society, many women are not only viewed in opposition to men under dualism, but also to other women. A salient example of this blind spot is Mary Daly's *Gyn/Ecology*, where she implores women to identify with nature against men and live our lives separately from men. However, such an essentialist approach is very problematic for certain groups of women, such as the disabled and Jews, who must ally themselves with men (while simultaneously challenging them on their sexism) in order to combat the isms in their lives. As writer Audre Lorde stated, in her critique of Daly's exclusion of how Black women use Afrocentric spiritual practices as a source of power against the isms while connecting with nonhuman nature:

> to imply, however, that women suffer the same oppression simply because we are women, is to lose sight of the many varied tools of patriarchy. It is to ignore how these tools are used by women without awareness against each other. (Lorde 1983, 95)

Unlike most white women, Black women are not limited to issues defined by our femaleness but are rather often limited to questions raised about our very humanity.

Although they have somewhat different priorities because of their different environments, Afrocentric ecowomanists in the United States and Africa nevertheless have a common goal—to analyze the issues of social justice that underlie environmental conflict. Not only do Afrocentric ecowomanists seek to avoid detrimental environmental impacts, we also seek to overcome the socioeconomic inequalities that led to the injustices in the first place.

EMERGENT UNITED STATES AFROCENTRIC ECOWOMANIST ACTIVISM

Contrary to mainstream United States media claims, which imply that African-Americans are not concerned about ecology, there has been increased environmental activism within

Black communities since the early 1980s. Referred to as the environmental equity movement by Robert Bullard, predominantly Black grassroots environmental organizations tend to view environmentalism as an extension of the 1960s civil rights movement. In *Yearning*, bell hooks links environmentalism with social justice while discussing Black radicals and revolutionary politics:

> We are concerned about the fate of the planet, and some of us believe that living simply is part of revolutionary political practice. We have a sense of the sacred. The ground we stand on is shifting, fragile, and unstable. (hooks 1990, 19)

On discussing how the links between environmental concerns and civil rights encouraged her involvement with environmentalism, arts writer and poet Esther Iverem states:

> Soon I began to link civil rights with environmental sanity. . . . Because in 1970 Black folks were vocally fighting for their rightful share of the pie, the logical question for me became "What kind of shape will that pie be in?" (Iverem 1991, 38)

Iverem's question has been foremost in many African-American women's minds as we continue to be instrumental in the Black communities' struggle to ensure that the shape of the social justice pie on our planet will not be increasingly carcinogenic. When her neighborhood started to become dilapidated, Hattie Carthan founded the Magnolia Tree Earth Center of Bed-Stuy in Brooklyn in 1968, to help beautify the area. She planted more than 1,500 trees before her death in 1974. In 1986, the city council of Los Angeles decided that a 13-acre incinerator, which would have burned 2,000 tons of city waste daily, was to be built in a low-income Black and Latino neighborhood in South Central Los Angeles. Upon hearing this decision, residents, mostly women, successfully organized in opposition by forming Concerned Citizens of South Central Los Angeles. While planning direct actions to protest the incinerator, the grass roots organization didn't have a formal leadership structure for close to two years. Be it a conscious or unconscious decision, Concerned Citizens accepted a relatively nonhierarchical, democratic process in their political activism by rotating the chair's position at meetings, a form of decision making characteristic of many ecofeminist groups.[7]

The Philadelphia Community Rehabilitation Corporation (PCRC), founded by Rachel E. Bagby, operates a village community to maintain a nonhierarchical relationship between human and nonhuman nature for its working-class-to-poor urban Black residents. About 5,000 reside in the community, and there is communalistic living, like that of many African villages. PCRC has a "repeopling" program that renovates and rents more than 50 previously vacant homes and also created a twelve-unit shared house. PCRC also takes vacant lots and recycles them into gardens to provide food, and oversees literacy and employment programs. Hazel and Cheryl Johnson founded People for Community Recovery (PCR), which is operated from a storefront at the Altgeld Gardens housing project, after they became aware that their community sits atop a landfill and has the greatest concentration of hazardous waste in the nation. In its fight against environmental racism, PCR has insisted that the Chicago Housing Authority remove all asbestos from the Altgeld homes and has helped lobby city government to declare a moratorium on new landfill permits. PCR also successfully prevented the establishment of another landfill in Altgeld Gardens.

One Black women's organization that addresses environmental issues is the National Black Women's Health Project. The NBWHP expresses its Afrocentric ecowomanist sentiment primarily through its SisteReach program, which seeks to connect the NBWHP with various Black women's organizations around the world. On urging African-American women to participate in the environmental movement and analyze the connections between male supremacy and environmental degradation, Dianne J. Forte, the SisteReach coordinator, makes the following statement:

> At first glance and with all the major problems demanding our energy in our community we may be tempted to say, "this is not my problem." If however, we look at the ominous connection being made between environmental degradation and population growth; if we look at the same time at trends which control women's bodies and lives and control the world's resources, we realize that the same arguments are used to justify both. (Forte 1992, 5)

For instance, women are increasingly being told that we should not have control over our own bodies, while the Earth is simultaneously deemed feminine by scientists who use sexual imagery to articulate their plans to take control over the Earth. Meanwhile, dominant groups often blame environmental degradation on overpopulation (and with their privileged status, usually point at poor women of color), when industrial capitalism and patriarchal control over women's reproduction are among the most pronounced culprits.

The most salient example of practical United States Afrocentric ecowomanism combating such claims is Luisah Teish, a voodoo priestess. In connecting social justice issues with spiritual practices rooted in the West African heritage, Teish articulates the need for everyone to actively eliminate patriarchy, white supremacy, and classism, along with the domination of nonhuman nature. Members of Teish's altar circle have planned urban gardening projects both to supply herbs for their holistic healing remedies and to assist the poor in feeding themselves. They have also engaged in grassroots organizing to stop gentrification in various communities.

EMERGENT AFROCENTRIC ECOWOMANIST ACTIVISM IN AFRICA

On the African continent, women have been at the forefront of the movement to educate people about environmental problems and how they affect their lives. As with much of the African continent, environmental problems in Kenya particularly influence rural women's lives, since they comprise 80 percent of that nation's farmers and fuel gatherers (Maathai 1991, 74). Soil erosion directly affects the women, because they depend on subsistence agriculture for their families' survival. The lack of firewood in many rural areas of Kenya because of deforestation disproportionately alters the lives of women, who must walk long distances to fetch firewood. The lack of water also makes a negative imprint on Kenyan women's lives, because they have to walk long distances to fetch the water.

However, many Kenyan women are striving to alter these current realities. The most prominent Afrocentric ecowomanist in Africa is Wangari Maathai, a Kenyan microbiologist and one of Africa's leading activists on environmental issues. Maathai is the founder and director of the Green Belt Movement (GBM), a fifteen-year-old tree-planting project designed to help poor Kenyan communities stop soil erosion, protect their water systems, and overcome the lack of firewood and building materials.

Launched under the auspices of the National Council of Women of Kenya, the majority of the Green Belt Movement's members are women. Since 1977, these women have grown 10 million trees, 80 percent of which have survived, to offset Kenya's widespread deforestation.[8] Although the Green Belt Movement's primary practical goal is to end desertification and deforestation, it is also committed to promoting public awareness of the relationship between environmental degradation and social problems that affect the Kenyan people—poverty, unemployment, and malnutrition. However, one of the most significant accomplishments of the GBM, Maathai asserts, is that its members are "now independent; had acquired knowledge, techniques; had become empowered" (Maathai 1991, 74).

Another Kenyan dedicated to environmental concerns is Wagaki Mwangi, the founder and coordinator of the International Youth Development and Environment Network. When she visited the University of Illinois at Urbana-Champaign, Mwangi discussed how Kenya suffers economic and environmental predicaments primarily because her homeland is trying to imitate Western cultures. "A culture has been superimposed on a culture," Mwangi said, but there are not enough resources for everyone to live up to the new standards of the neocolonial culture (Schallert 1992, 3). She asserted that in attempts to be more Western, "what [Kenyans] valued as our food has been devalued, and what we are valuing is what they value in the West" (Schallert 1992, 3). For instance, Kenyans used to survive by eating a variety of wild foods, but now many don't consider such foods as staples because of Western influences. In the process, many areas of Kenya are deemed to be suffering from food shortages as the economy has been transformed to consumer capitalism with its attendant mechanization of agriculture.

In Kourfa, Niger, women have been the primary force behind preventing the village from disappearing, a fate that many surrounding villages have suffered because of the Sahel region's desertification. Reduced rainfall and the drying up of watering places and vegetation, combined with violent sandstorms, have virtually deprived Kourfa of harvests for the past five years. As a result, the overwhelming majority of Kourfa's men have had to travel far away for long periods of time to find seasonal work.

With the assistance of the Association of Women of Niger and an agricultural advisor, the women have laid out a small marketgarden around the only well in Kourfa. Despite the few resources at their disposal, the Kourfa women have succeeded in supporting themselves, their children, and the village elders. In response to the survival of the village since these actions, the Kourfa women are now calling for increased action to reverse the region's environmental degradation so "the men won't go away" from the village (Ouedraogo 1992, 38).

AFROCENTRIC ECOMOTHERISTS: ECOWOMANIST POTENTIAL?

The environmental activism of some Black women brings up the question of whether community-oriented Black women who are addressing environmental issues are genuinely Afrocentric ecowomanists or possibly Afrocentric ecomotherists.[9] According to Ann Snitow, motherists are women who, for various reasons, "identify themselves not as feminists but as militant mothers, fighting together for survival" (Snitow 1989, 48). Snitow also maintains that motherism usually arises when men are absent or in times of crisis, when the private sphere role assigned to women under patriarchy makes it impossible for the collective to survive. Since they are faced with the dictates of traditional work but face a lack of resources in which to fulfill their socially prescribed role, motherists become a political force.

Since they took collective action to secure the survival of the village's children and elders only after the necessary absence of Kourfa's men, the activism of the Kourfa women may possibly be based on a motherist philosophy. One can only conjecture whether the Kourfa women criticized the social role of motherhood in Niger as they became a political force, or if womanist consciousness emerged after their political experiences. Because of their potential to transform into ecowomanists after they enter the political realm, Afrocentic ecomotherists shouldn't be discounted in an analysis of Black women's environmental activism. For instance, Charlotte Bullock contends that she "did not come to the fight against environmental problems as an intellectual but rather as a concerned mother" (Hamilton 1990, 216). However, she and other women in Concerned Citizens of South Central Los Angeles began to notice the sexual politics that attempted to discount their political activism while they were protesting. "I noticed when we first started fighting the issue how the men would laugh at the women ... they would say, 'Don't pay no attention to them, that's only one or two women ... they won't make a difference.' But now since we've been fighting for about a year the smiles have gone" (Hamilton 1990, 215). Robin Cannon, another member of Concerned Citizens, asserts that social relations in her home, specifically gender roles on caretaking, were transformed after she began participating in the group's actions (Hamilton 1990, 220).

Shamara Shantu Riley

MOVING BEYOND DUALISM:
AN AFROCENTRIC APPROACH

In utilizing spiritual concepts to move beyond dualism, precolonial African cultures, with their both/and perspectives, are useful forms of knowledge for Afrocentric ecowomanists to envision patterns toward interdependence of human and nonhuman nature. Traditional West African cultures, in particular, which also happen to be the ancestral roots of the overwhelming majority of African-Americans, share a belief in nature worship and view all things as being alive on varying levels of existence (Haskins 1978, 30). One example of such an approach in West African traditions is the *Nyam* concept. A root word in many West African languages, *Nyam* connotes an enduring power and energy possessed by all life (Collins 1990, 220). Thus, all forms of life are deemed to possess certain rights, which cannot be violated at will.

In *Jambalaya,* Luisah Teish writes of the *Da* concept, which originates from the Fon people of Western Africa. *Da* is "the energy that carries creation, the force field in which creation takes place" (Teish 1985, 61). In the Fon view, all things are composed of energy provided by *Da.* For example, "the human is receptive to the energy emanating from the rock and the rock is responsive to human influence" (Teish 1985, 62). Because West Africans have traditionally viewed nonhuman nature as sacred and worthy of praise through such cultural media as song and dance, there is also a belief in *Nommo. Nommo* is "the physical-spiritual life force which awakens all 'sleeping' forces and gives physical and spiritual life" (Jahn 1961, 105).

However, with respect for nonhuman nature comes a different understanding of *Ache,* the Yoruba term for human power. *Ache* doesn't connote "power over" or domination, as it often does in mainstream Western thought, but rather power *with* other forms of creation. With *Ache,* Teish states that there is "a regulated kinship among human, animal, mineral, and vegetable life" (Teish 1985, 63). Humans recognize their *Ache* to eat and farm, "but it is also recognized that they must give back that which is given to them" (Teish 1985, 63). In doing so, we respect the overall balance and interdependence of human and nonhuman nature.

These concepts can be useful for Afrocentric ecowomanists not only in educating our peoples about environmental issues, but also in reclaiming the cultural traditions of our ancestors. Rachel Bagby states the positivity of humans connecting with nonhuman nature, a view that is interwoven in her organization's work:

> If you can appreciate the Earth, you can appreciate the beauty of yourself. The same creator created both. And if I learned to take care of that I'll also take care of myself and help take care of others. (Bagby 1990, 242)

Illustrating an outlook of planetary relations that is parallel to the traditional West African worldview, Bagby simultaneously reveals the continuous link between much of the African-American religious tradition and African spirituality.

In light of the relations of power and privilege that exist in the world, the appropriation of indigenous cultures by some ecofeminists must be addressed. Many womanists, such as Andy Smith and Luisah Teish, have criticized cultural feminists for inventing earth-based feminist spiritualities that are based on the exploitation of our ancestral traditions, while we're struggling to reclaim and defend our cultures from white supremacy. In "For All Those Who Were Indian in Another Life," Smith asserts that this appropriation of non-Western spiritual traditions functions as a way for many white women to avoid taking responsibility for being simultaneously oppressive as well as oppressed (see her article, pp. 168–71). White ecofeminists can reclaim their own pre-Christian European cultures, such as the Wiccan tradition, for similar concepts of interconnectedness, community, and immanence found in West African traditions.[10]

Adopting these concepts would transform humans' relationship to nonhuman nature in a variety of ways. By seeing all components of the ecosystem affecting and being affected by one another, such a world perspective demonstrates a pattern of living in harmony with the rest of nature, instead of seeking to disconnect from it. By viewing ourselves as a part of nature, we would be able to move beyond the Western disdain for the body and therefore not ravage the Earth's body as a result of this disdain and fear. We would realize that the Earth is not merely the source of our survival, but also has intrinsic value and must be treated with respect, as it is our elder.

The notion of community would help us to appreciate the biological and cultural diversity that sustains life. Because every entity is viewed as embodying spirituality under immanence, culture wouldn't be viewed as separate from, and superior to, nature, as it is seen in mainstream Western religions. Communalism would also aid us in reformulating the social constructions of race, gender, species, class (among other variables), which keep groups separate from one another. And finally, the environmental movement in particular would view politics as rooted in community and communally take actions to reclaim the Earth and move toward a life of interdependence for generations to come.

NOTES

I would like to acknowledge the help that Carol Adams has given me with this essay. Her reading suggested valuable changes in the structure of the paper as well as clearing up minor flaws in writing. She also suggested some references that would augment my claims.

1. Alice Walker's definition of womanist is a feminist of color who is "committed to the survival and wholeness of entire people, male *and* female" (Walker 1983a, xi–xii). University of Ibadan (Nigeria) English senior lecturer Chikwenye Okonjo Ogunyemi contends that "black womanism is a philosophy that celebrates black roots ... It concerns itself as much with the black sexual power tussle as with the world power structure that subjugates

Shamara Shantu Riley

blacks" (Ogunyemi 1985, 72). Since feminism often gives primacy to gender, and race consciousness often gives primacy to race, such limitations in terminology have caused many women of color to adopt the term *womanist,* which both Walker and Ogunyemi independently coined in the early 1980s. Although some of the women in this paper refer to themselves as feminists rather than womanists, or use both terms interchangeably, I am using the term *womanist* in an interpretative sense to signify a culturally identified woman of color who also critically analyzes the sexual politics within her respective ethnic group.

2. For a discussion of how toxic waste has affected the environmental health of United States Black communities, see Day and Knight (1991).

3. Robert Bullard (1990) contends that the mortality of wealth involves toxic-waste dumping to pursue profits at the expense of others, usually low-income people of color in the United States. Because this demographic group is less likely to have economic resources and political clout, it can't fight back as easily as more affluent communities that possess white skin privileges. I think this term is also applicable to the economic nature of toxic dumping in "Third World" countries, which are basically disempowered in the global political process.

4. For an ecofeminist text that makes a similar claim, see King (1989).

5. My definition of an Afrocentric ecowomanist is a communalistic-oriented Black woman who understands and articulates the interconnectedness of the degradation of people of color, women, and the environment. In addition to articulating this interconnectedness, an Afrocentric ecowomanist also strives to eradicate this degradation. For an extensive discussion of Afrocentrism, see Myers (1988).

6. An example of this distinction can be seen in Davies (1988). In her article, Davies only discusses the interconnections between gender and nature and completely avoids analyzing how such variables as ethnicity and class influence the experience of gender in one's life.

7. For several descriptions of the political decision making within feminist peace organizations, see the essays in Harris and King (1989).

8. It is noteworthy that the seedlings come from over 1,500 tree nurseries, 99 percent of which are operated by women. In addition, the women are given a small payment for the trees that survive.

9. In comparison to an Afrocentric ecowomanist, I define an Afrocentric ecomotherist as a communalistic-oriented Black woman who is involved in saving the environment and challenging white supremacy, but who does not challenge the fundamental dynamics of sexual politics in women's lives.

10. For instance, Starhawk, a practitioner of the Wiccan tradition, has written about her spiritual beliefs (1990).

BIBLIOGRAPHY

Bagby, Rachel. 1990. "Daughters of Growing Things." In Irene Diamond and Gloria Feman Orenstein, eds. *Reweaving the World: The Emergence of Ecofeminism.* San Francisco: Sierra Club Books.

Bullard, Robert. 1990. *Dumping in Dixie: Race, Class and Environmental Quality.* Boulder, Colo.: Westview Press.

Collins, Patricia Hill. 1990. *Black Feminist Thought: Knowledge, Consciousness, and the Politics of Empowerment.* Boston: Unwin Hyman.

Davies, Katherine. 1988. "What Is Ecofeminism?" *Women and Environments* 10(3): 4–6.

Day, Barbara, and Kimberly Knight. 1991. "The Rain Forest in Our Back Yard." *Essence* 21 (Jan.): 75–77.

de la Pena, Nonny, and Susan Davis. 1990. "The Greens Are White: And Minorities Want In." *Newsweek* 116 (Oct. 15): 34.

Forte, Dianne J. 1992. "SisteReach . . . Because 500 Years Is Enough." *Vital Signs: News from the National Black Women's Health Project* 1 (Spring): 5.

Gilman, Sander L. 1985. "Black Bodies, White Bodies: Toward an Iconography of Female Sexuality in Late Nineteenth-Century Art, Medicine and Literature." *Critical Inquiry* 12 (Autumn): 205–43.

Hamilton, Cynthia. 1990. "Women, Home and Community: The Struggle in an Urban Environment." In Irene Diamond and Gloria Feman Orenstein, eds. *Reweaving the World: The Emergence of Ecofeminism.* San Francisco: Sierra Club Books.

Harris, Adrienne, and Ynestra King, eds., 1989 *Rocking the Ship of State: Toward a Feminist Peace Politics.* Boulder, Colo.: Westview Press.

hooks, bell. 1989. *Talking Back: Thinking Feminist, Thinking Black.* Boston: South End Press.

———. 1990. *Yearning: Race, Gender and Cultural Politics.* Boston: South End Press.

hooks, bell, and Cornell West. 1991. *Breaking Bread: Insurgent Black Intellectual Life.* Boston: South End Press.

Iverem, Esther. 1991. "By Earth Obsessed." *Essence* 22 (Sept.): 37–38.

Jahn, Janheinz. 1961. *Muntu: The New African Culture.* New York: Grove Press.

Joyce, Christopher. 1989. "Africans Call for End to the Ivory Trade." *New Scientist* 122 (June 10): 22.

King, Ynestra. 1989. "Healing the Wounds: Feminism, Ecology, and the Nature/Culture Dualism." In Alison M. Jaggar and Susan R. Bordo, eds. *Gender/Body/Knowledge: Feminist Reconstructions of Being and Knowing.* New Brunswick, N.J.: Rutgers University Press.

Larsen, Elizabeth. 1991. "Granola Boys, Eco-Dudes, and Me." *Ms.* 2 (July/Aug.), 96–97.

Lorde, Audre. 1983. "An Open Letter to Mary Daly." In Cherríe Moraga and Gloria Anzaldua, eds. *This Bridge Called My Back: Writings by Radical Women of Color.* New York: Kitchen Table Press.

Maathai, Wangari. 1991. "Foresters Without Diplomas." *Ms.* 1 (Mar./Apr.), 74–75.

Meyer, Eugene L. 1992. "Environmental Racism: Why Is It Always Dumped In Our Backyard? Minority Groups Take a Stand." *Audubon* 94 (Jan./Feb.): 30–32.

Myers, Linda James. 1988. *Understanding an Afrocentric Worldview: Introduction to an Optimal Psychology.* Dubuque, Iowa: Kendall/Hunt.

Ogunyemi, Chikwenye Okonjo. 1985. "Womanism: The Dynamics of the Contemporary Black Female Novel in English." *Signs: Journal of Women in Culture and Society* 11 (Autumn): 63–80.

Ouedraogo, Josephine. 1992. "Sahel Women Fight Desert Advance." *UNESCO Courier* 45 (March): 38.

Richards, Dona. 1980. "European Mythology: The Ideology of 'Progress.'" In Molefi Kete Asante and Abdulai Sa Vandi, eds. *Contermporary Black Thought.* Beverly Hills, Calif.: Sage.

Riley, Shay. 1991. "Eco-Racists Use Fatal Tactics." *Daily Illini* 121 (Sept. 4), 15.

Schallert, K. L. 1992. "Speaker Examines Impact of the West on Africa" (Wagaki Mwangi). *Daily Illini* 121 (April 3), 3.

Smith, Andy. 1991. "For All Those Who Were Indian in Another Life." *Ms.* (Nov./Dec.), 44–45.

Snitow, Ann. 1989. "A Gender Diary." In Adrienne Harris and Ynestra King, eds. *Rocking the Ship State: Towards a Feminist Peace Politics.* Boulder, Colo: Westview Press.

Starhawk. 1990. "Power, Authority, and Mystery: Ecofeminism and Earth-Based Spirituality." In Irene Diamond and Gloria Feman Orenstein, eds. *Reweaving the World: The Emergence of Ecofeminism.* San Francisco: Sierra Club Books.

Teish, Luisah. 1985. *Jambalaya: The Natural Woman's Book of Personal Charms and Practical Rituals.* San Francisco: Harper & Row.

———. 1983b. "Only Justice Can Stop a Curse." In *In Search of Our Mothers' Gardens: Womanist Prose.* New York: Harcourt Brace Jovanovich.

Walker, Barbara. 1983. *The Woman's Encyclopedia of Myths and Secrets.* San Francisco: Harper & Row.

Worldwatch. 1987. "On the Brink of Extinction." Quoted in *World Development Forum* 5 (Nov.), 3.

from *WOMAN AND NATURE: THE ROARING INSIDE HER*

Susan Griffin

PROLOGUE

He says that woman speaks with nature. That she hears voices from under the earth. That wind blows in her ears and trees whisper to her. That the dead sing through her mouth and the cries of infants are clear to her. But for him this dialogue is over. He says he is not part of this world, that he was set on this world as a stranger. He sets himself apart from woman and nature.

And so it is Goldilocks who goes to the home of the three bears, Little Red Riding Hood who converses with the wolf, Dorothy who befriends a lion, Snow White who talks to the birds, Cinderella with mice as her allies, the Mermaid who is half fish, Thumbelina courted by a mole. *(And when we hear in the Navaho chant of the mountain that a grown man sits and smokes with bears and follows directions given to him by squirrels, we are surprised. We had thought only little girls spoke with animals.)*

We are the bird's eggs. Bird's eggs, flowers, butterflies, rabbits, cows, sheep; we are caterpillars; we are leaves of ivy and sprigs of wallflower. We are women. We rise from the wave. We are gazelle and doe, elephant and whale, lilies and roses and peach, we are air, we are flame, we are oyster and pearl, we are girls. We are woman and nature. And he says he cannot hear us speak.

But we hear.

※

HIS POWER

He Tames What Is Wild

The Hunt

> Is it by its indefiniteness it shadows forth the heartless voids and immensities of the universe, and thus stabs us from behind with the thought of annihilation when beholding the milky way?
> —Herman Melville, *Moby-Dick*

❧

And at last she could bear the burden of herself no more. She was to be had for the taking. To be had for the taking.

—D. H. Lawrence, Lady Chatterley's Lover

She has captured his heart. She has overcome him. He cannot tear his eyes away. He is burning with passion. He cannot live without her. He pursues her. She makes him pursue her. The faster she runs, the stronger his desire. He will overtake her. He will make her his own. He will have her. (The boy chases the doe and her yearling for nearly two hours. She keeps running despite her wounds. He pursues her through pastures, over fences, groves of trees, crossing the road, up hills, volleys of rifle shots sounding, until perhaps twenty bullets are embedded in her body.) She has no mercy. She has dressed to excite his desire. She has no scruples. She has painted herself for him. She makes supple movements to entice him. She is without a soul. Beneath her painted face is flesh, are bones. She reveals only part of herself to him. She is wild. She flees whenever he approaches. She is teasing him. (Finally, she is defeated and falls and he sees that half of her head has been blown off, that one leg is gone, her abdomen split from her tail to her head, and her organs hang outside her body. Then four men encircle the fawn and harvest her too.) He is an easy target, he says. He says he is pierced. Love has shot him through, he says. He is a familiar mark. Riddled. Stripped to the bone. He is conquered, he says. (The boys, fond of hunting hare, search in particular for pregnant females.) He is fighting for his life. He faces annihilation in her, he says. He is losing himself to her, he says. Now, he must conquer her wildness, he says, he must tame her before she drives him wild, he says. (Once catching their prey, they step on her back, breaking it, and they call this "dancing on the hare.") Thus he goes on his knees to her. Thus he wins her over, he tells her he wants her. He makes her his own. He encloses her. He encircles her. He puts her under lock and key. He protects her. (Approaching the great mammals, the hunters make little sounds which they know will make the elephants form a defensive circle.) And once she is his, he prizes his delight. He feasts his eyes on her. He adorns her luxuriantly. He gives her ivory. He gives her perfume. (The older matriarchs stand to the outside of the circle to protect the calves and younger mothers.) He covers her with the skins of mink, beaver, muskrat, seal, raccoon, otter, ermine, fox, the feathers of ostriches, osprey, egret, ibis. (The hunters then encircle that circle and fire first into the bodies of the matriarchs. When these older elephants fall, the younger panic, yet unwilling to leave the bodies of their dead mothers, they make easy targets.) And thus he makes her soft. He makes her calm. He makes her grateful to him. He has tamed her, he says. She is content to be his, he says. (In the winter, if a single wolf has leaped over the walls of the city and terrorized the streets, the hunters go out in a band to rid the forest of the whole pack.) Her voice is now soothing to him. Her eyes no longer blaze, but look on him serenely. When he calls to her, she gives herself to him. Her ferocity lies under him. (The body of the great whale is strapped with explosives.) Now nothing of the old beast remains in her. (Eastern Bison, extinct 1825; Spectacled Cormorant, extinct 1852; Cape Lion, extinct 1865; Bonin Night Heron, extinct 1889; Barbary Lion, extinct 1922; Great Auk, extinct 1944.) And he can trust her wholly with himself. So he is blazing when he enters her, and she is consumed. (Florida Key Deer, vanishing; Wild Indian Buffalo, vanishing; Great Sable Antelope, vanishing.) Because she is his, she offers no resistance. She is a place of rest for him. A place of his making. And when his flesh begins to yield and his skin melts into her, he becomes soft, and he is without fear; he does not lose himself; though something in him gives way, he is not lost in her, because she is his now: he has captured her.

THE LION IN THE DEN OF THE PROPHETS

She swaggers in. They are terrifying in their white hairlessness. She waits. She watches. She does not move. She is measuring their moves. And they are measuring her. Cautiously one takes a bit of her fur. He cuts it free from her. He examines it. Another numbers her feet, her teeth, the length and width of her body. She yawns. They announce she is alive. They wonder what she will do if they enclose her in the room with them. One of them shuts the door. She backs her way toward the closed doorway and then roars. "Be still," the men say. She continues to roar. "Why does she roar?" they ask. The roaring must be inside her, they conclude. They decide they must see the roaring inside her. They approach her in a group, six at her two front legs and six at her two back legs. They are trying to put her to sleep. She swings at one of the men. His own blood runs over him. "Why did she do that?" the men question. She has no soul, they conclude, she does not know right from wrong. "Be still," they shout at her. "Be humble, trust us," they demand. "We have souls," they proclaim, "we know what is right," they approach her with their medicine, "for you." She does not understand this language. She devours them.

"THE WOMAN I LOVE IS A PLANET; THE PLANET I LOVE IS A TREE"

Paula Gunn Allen

Our physicality—which always and everywhere includes our spirituality, mentality, emotionality, social institutions and processes—is a microform of all physicality. Each of us reflect, in our attitudes toward our body and the bodies of other planetary creatures and plants, our inner attitude toward the planet. And, as we believe, so we act. A society that believes that the body is somehow diseased, painful, sinful, or wrong, a people that spends its time trying to deny the body's needs, aims, goals, and processes—whether these be called health or disease—is going to misunderstand the nature of its existence and of the planet's and is going to create social institutions out of those body-denying attitudes that wreak destruction not only on human, plant, and other creaturely bodies but on the body of the Earth herself.

The planet, our mother, Grandmother Earth, is *physical* and therefore a spiritual, mental, and emotional being. Planets are alive, as are all their by-products or expressions, such as animals, vegetables, minerals, climatic and meteorological phenomena.

Believing that our mother, the beloved Earth, is inert matter is destructive to yourself. (There's little you can do to her, believe it or not.) Such beliefs point to a dangerously diseased physicality.

Being good, holy, and/or politically responsible means being able to accept whatever life brings—and that includes just about everything you usually think of as unacceptable, like disease, death, and violence. Walking in balance, in harmony, and in a sacred manner requires staying in your body, accepting its discomforts, decayings, witherings, and blossomings and respecting them. Your body is also a planet, replete with creatures that live in and on it. Walking in balance requires knowing that living and dying are twin beings, gifts of our mother, the Earth, and honoring her ways does not mean cheating her of your flesh, your pain, your joy, your sensuality, your desires, your frustrations, your unmet and met needs, your emotions, your life. In the end you can't cheat her successfully, but in the attempt to do so you can do great harm to the delicate and subtle balance of the vital processes of planetary being.

Reprinted from *Reweaving the World: The Emergence of Ecofeminism* edited by Irene Diamond and Gloria Feman Orenstein with permission of Sierra Club Books.

A society based on body hate destroys itself and causes harm to all of Grandmother's grandchildren.

In the United States, where milk and honey cost little enough, where private serenity is prized above all things by the wealthy, privileged, and well-washed, where tension, intensity, passion, and the concomitant loss of self-possession are detested, the idea that your attitudes and behaviors vis-à-vis your body are your politics and your spirituality may seem strange. Moreover, when I suggest that passion—whether it be emotional, muscular, sexual, or intellectual—IS spirituality, the idea might seem even stranger. In the United States of the privileged, going to ashrams and centers to meditate on how to be in one's immediate experience, on how to be successful at serenity when the entire planet is overwrought, tense, far indeed from serene, the idea that connected spirituality consists in accepting overwroughtness, tension, yes, and violence, may seem not only strange but downright dangerous. The patriarchs have long taught the Western peoples that violence is sin, that tension is the opposite of spiritual life, that the overwrought are denied enlightenment. But we must remember that those who preached and taught serenity and peacefulness were teaching the oppressed how to act—docile slaves who deeply accept their place and do not recognize that in their anguish lies also their redemption, their liberation, are not likely to disturb the tranquillity of the ruling class. Members of the ruling class are, of course, utterly tranquil. Why not? As long as those upon whose labor and pain their serenity rests don't upset the apple cart, as long as they can make the rules for human behavior—in its inner as well as its outer dimensions—they can be tranquil indeed and can focus their attention on reaching nirvanic bliss, transcendence, or divine peace and love.

And yet, the time for tranquillity, if there ever was time for it, is not now. Now we have only to look, to listen, to our beloved planet to see that tranquillity is not the best word to describe her condition. Her volcanic passions, her hurricane storms of temper, her tremblings and shakings, her thrashings and lashings indicate that something other than serenity is going on. And after careful consideration, it must occur to the sensitive observer that congruence with self, which must be congruence with spirit, which must therefore be congruence with the planet, requires something more active than serenity, tranquillity, or inner peace.

Our planet, my beloved, is in crisis; this, of course, we all know. We, many of us, think that her crisis is caused by men, or White people, or capitalism, or industrialism, or loss of spiritual vision, or social turmoil, or war, or psychic disease. For the most part, we do not recognize that the reason for her state is that she is entering upon a great initiation—she is becoming someone else. Our planet, my darling, is gone coyote, *heyoka*, and it is our great honor to attend her passage rites. She is giving birth to her new consciousness of herself and her relationship to the other vast intelligences, other holy beings in her universe. Her travail is not easy, and it occasions her intensity, her conflict, her turmoil—the turmoil, conflict, and intensity that human and other creaturely life mirror. And as she moves, growing and learning ever closer to the sacred moment of her realization, her turmoil, intensity, agony, and conflict increase.

We are each and all a part of her, an expression of her essential being. We are each a small fragment that is not the whole but that, perforce, reflects in our inner self, our outer behavior, our expressions and relationships and institutions, her self, her behaviors, her expressions and relationships, her forms and structures. We humans and our relatives the other creatures are integral expressions of her thought and being. We are not her, but we take our being from her, and in her being we have being, as in her life we have life. As she is, so are we.

In this time of her emergence as one of the sacred planets in the Grandmother galaxy, we necessarily experience, each of us in our own specific way, our share or form of her experience, her form. As the initiation nears completion we are caught in the throes of her wailings and contractions, her muscular, circulatory, and neurologic destabilization. We should recognize that her longing for the culmination of the initiatory process is at present nearly as intense as her longing to remain as she was before the initiation ceremony began, and our longing for a new world that the completion of the great ceremony will bring, almost as great as our longing to remain in the systems familiar to us for a very long time, correspond. Her longing for completion is great, as is ours; our longing to remain as we have been, our fear that we will not survive the transition, that we will fail to enter the new age, our terror at ourselves becoming transformed, mutated, unrecognizable to ourselves and all we have known correspond to her longing to remain as she has been, her fear that she will fail the tests as they arise for her, her terror at becoming new, unrecognizable to herself and to all she has known.

What can we do in times such as these? We can rejoice that she will soon be counted among the blessed. That we, her feathers, talons, beak, eyes, have come crying and singing, lamenting and laughing, to this vast climacteric.

I am speaking of all womankind, of all mankind. And of more. I am speaking of all our relatives, the four-leggeds, the wingeds, the crawlers; of the plants and seasons, the winds, thunders, and rains, the rivers, lakes, and streams, the pebbles, rocks, and mountains, the spirits, the holy people, and the Gods and Goddesses—of all the intelligences, all the beings. I am speaking even of the tiniest, those no one can see; and of the vastest, the planets and stars. Together you and I and they and she are moving with increasing rapidity and under ever increasing pressure toward transformation.

Now, now is the time when mother becomes grandmother, when daughter becomes mother, when the living dead are released from entombment, when the dead live again and walk once again in her ways. Together we all can rejoice, take up the tasks of attending, take up the joy of giving birth and of being born, of transforming in recognition of the awfulness of what is entailed, in recognition of what it is we together can and must and will do. I have said that this is the time of her initiation, of her new birth. I could also say it is the time of mutation, for transformation means to change form; I could also say it is the climacteric, when the beloved planet goes through menopause and takes her place among the wise women planets that dance among the stars.

At a time such as this, what indeed can we do? We can sing *Heya-hey* in honoring all that has come to pass, all that is passing. Sing, honoring, *Heya-hey* to all the beings gathering on all the planes to witness this great event. From every quadrant of the universe they are coming. They are standing gathered around, waiting for the emergence, the piercing moment when she is counted among those who are counted among the wise. We can sing *Heya-hey* to the familiar and the estranged, to the recognized and the disowned, to each shrub and tree, to each flower and vine, to each pebble and stone, to each mountain and hill. We can sing *Heya-hey* honoring the stars and the clouds, the winds and the rains, the seasons and the temperature. We can think with our hearts, as the old ones do, and put our brains and muscles in the service of the heart, our Mother and Grandmother Earth, who is coming into being in another way. We can sing *Heya-hey,* honoring.

What can we do, rejoicing and honoring, to show our respect? We can heal. We can cherish our bodies and honor them, sing *Heya-hey* to our flesh. We can cherish our being—our petulances and rages, our anguishes and griefs, our disabilities and strengths, our desires and passions, our pleasures and delights. We can, willingly and recognizing the fullness of her abundance, which includes scarcity and muchness, enter inside ourselves to seek and find her, who is our own dear body, our own dear flesh. For the body is not the dwelling place of the spirit—it is the spirit. It is not a tomb, it is life itself. And even as it withers and dies, it is born; even as it is renewed and reborn, it dies.

Think: How many times each day do you habitually deny and deprive her in your flesh, in your physicality? How often do you willfully prevent her from moving or resting, from eating or drinking what she requests, from eliminating wastes or taking breath? How many times do you order your body to produce enzymes and hormones to further your social image, your "identity," your emotional comfort, regardless of your actual situation and hers? How many of her gifts do your spurn, how much of her abundance do you deny? How often do you interpret disease as wrong, suffering as abnormal, physical imperatives as troublesome, cravings as failures, deprivation and denial of appetite as the right thing to do? In how many ways do you refuse to experience your vulnerability, your frailty, your mortality? How often do you refuse these expressions of the life force of the Mother in your lovers, your friends, your society? How often do you find yourself interpreting sickness, weakness, aging, fatness, physical differences as pitiful, contemptible, avoidable, a violation of social norm and spiritual accomplishment? How much of your life is devoted to avoiding any and/or all of these? How much of her life is devoted to avoiding any and all of these?

The mortal body is a tree; it is holy in whatever condition; it is truth and myth because it has so many potential conditions; because of its possibilities, it is sacred and profane; most of all, it is your most precious talisman, your own connection to her. Healing the self means honoring and recognizing the body, accepting rather than denying all the turmoil its existence brings, welcoming the woes and anguish flesh is subject to, cherishing its multitudinous forms and seasons, its unfailing ability to know and be, to grow and wither, to live and die, to mutate, to change. Healing the self means commiting ourselves to a wholehearted willingness to be what and how we are—beings frail and fragile, strong and passionate, neurotic and balanced, diseased and whole, partial and complete, stingy and generous, safe and dangerous, twisted and straight, storm-tossed and quiescent, bound and free.

What can we do to be politically useful, spiritually mature attendants in this great transformation we are privileged to participate in? Find out by asking as many trees as you meet how to be a tree. Our Mother, in her form known as Sophia, was long ago said to be a tree, the great tree of life: Listen to what they wrote down from the song she gave them:

> I have grown tall as a cedar on Lebanon,
> as a cypress on Mount Hermon;
> I have grown tall as a palm in Engedi,
> as the rose bushes of Jericho;
> as a fine olive on the plain,
> as a plane tree I have grown tall.
> I have exhaled perfume like cinnamon and acacia;
> I have breathed out a scent like choice myrrh,
> like galbanum, onzcha and stacte,
> like the smoke of incense in the tabernacle.
> I have spread my branches like a terebinth,
> and my branches are glorious and graceful.
> I am like a vine putting out graceful shoots,
> my blossoms bear the fruit of glory and wealth.
> Approach me, you who desire me,
> and take your fill of my fruits.

"MESSAGES FROM THE PAST: THE WORLD OF THE GODDESS"

Riane Eisler

What kind of people were our prehistoric ancestors who worshiped the Goddess? What was life like during the millennia of our cultural evolution before recorded or written history? And what can we learn from those times that is relevant to our own?

Because they left us no written accounts, we can only infer, like Sherlock Holmes turned scientist, how the people of the Paleolithic and of the later, more advanced Neolithic thought, felt, and behaved. But almost everything we have been taught about antiquity is based on conjecture. Even the records we have from early historic cultures, such as Sumer, Babylon, and Crete, are at best scanty and fragmentary and largely concerned with inventories of goods and other mercantile matters. And the more detailed later written accounts about both prehistory and early history from classical Greek, Roman, Hebrew, and Christian times are also mainly based on inferences—made without even the aid of modern archaeological methods.

Indeed, most of what we have learned to think of as our cultural evolution has in fact been interpretation. Moreover, as we saw in the preceding chapter, this interpretation has more often than not been the projection of the still prevailing dominator worldview. It has consisted of conclusions drawn from fragmentary data interpreted to conform to the traditional model of our cultural evolution as a linear progression from "primitive man" to so-called "civilized man," who, despite their many differences, shared a common preoccupation with conquering, killing, and dominating.

Through scientific excavations of ancient sites, archaeologists have in recent years obtained a great deal of primary information about pre-history, particularly about the Neolithic, when our ancestors first settled in communities sustained by farming and the breeding of stock. Analyzed from a fresh perspective, these excavations provide the data base for a re-evaluation, and reconstruction, of our past.

One important source of data is excavations of buildings and their contents—including clothing, jewelry, food, furniture, containers, tools, and other objects used in daily life. Another is the excavation of burial sites, which tell us not only about people's attitudes about death but also about their lives. And overlapping both of these data sources is our richest source of information about prehistory: art.

Even when there is a written as well as an oral literary tradition, art is a form of symbolic communication. The extensive art of the Neolithic—be it wall paintings about daily life or about important myths, statuary of religious images, friezes depicting rituals, or simply vase decorations, pictures on seals, or engravings on jewelry—tells us a great deal about how these people lived and died. It also tells us a great deal about how they thought, for in a very real sense Neolithic art is a kind of language or shorthand symbolically expressing how people in that time experienced, and in turn shaped, what we call reality.[1] And if we let this language speak for itself, without projecting on it prevailing models of reality, it tells a fascinating—and in comparison to the stereotype, a far more hopeful—story of our cultural origins.

NEOLITHIC ART

One of the most striking things about Neolithic art is what it does *not* depict. For what a people do not depict in their art can tell us as much about them as what they do.

In sharp contrast to later art, a theme notable for its absence from Neolithic art is imagery idealizing armed might, cruelty, and violence-based power. There are here no images of "noble warriors" or scenes of battles. Nor are there any signs of "heroic conquerors" dragging captives around in chains or other evidences of slavery.

Also in sharp contrast to the remains of even their earliest and most primitive male-dominant invaders, what is notable in these Neolithic Goddess-worshiping societies is the absence of lavish "chieftain" burials. And in marked contrast to later male-dominant civilizations like that of Egypt, there is here no sign of mighty rulers who take with them into the afterlife less powerful humans sacrificed at their death.

Nor do we here find, again in contrast to later dominator societies, large caches of weapons or any other sign of the intensive application of material technology and natural resources to arms. The inference that this was a much more, and indeed characteristically, peaceful era is further reinforced by another absence: military fortifications. Only gradually do these begin to appear, apparently as a response to pressures from the warlike nomadic bands coming from the fringe areas of the globe, which we will examine later.

In Neolithic art, neither the Goddess nor her son-consort carry the emblems we have learned to associate with might—spears, swords, or thunderbolts, the symbols of an earthly sovereign and/or deity who exacts obedience by killing and maiming. Even beyond this, the art of this period is strikingly devoid of the ruler-ruled, master-subject imagery so characteristic of dominator societies.

What we do find everywhere—in shrines and houses, on wall paintings, in the decorative motifs on vases, in sculptures in the round, clay figurines, and bas reliefs—is a rich array of symbols from nature. Associated with the worship of the Goddess, these attest to awe and wonder at the beauty and mystery of life.

There are the life-sustaining elements of sun and water, for instance, the geometric patterns of wavy forms called meanders (which symbolized flowing waters) incised on an Old European altar from about 5000 B.C.E. in Hungary. There are the giant stone heads of bulls with enormous curled horns painted on the walls of Catal Huyuk shrines, terra-cotta hedgehogs from southern Romania, ritual vases in the form of does from Bulgaria, egg-shaped stone sculptures with the faces of fish, and cult vases in the form of birds.[2]

There are serpents and butterflies (symbols of metamorphosis) which are in historic times still identified with the transformative powers of the Goddess, as in the seal impression from Zakro, in eastern Crete, portraying the Goddess with the wings of an eyed butterfly. Even the later Cretan double axe, reminiscent of the hoe axes used to clear farm lands, was a stylization of the butterfly.[3] Like the serpent, which sheds its skin and is "reborn," it was part of the Goddess's epiphany, yet another symbol of her powers of regeneration.[4]

And everywhere—in murals, statues, and votive figurines—we find images of the Goddess. In the various incarnations of Maiden, Ancestress, or Creatrix, she is the Lady of the waters, the birds, and the underworld, or simply the divine Mother cradling her divine child in her arms.[5]

Some images are so realistic that they are almost lifelike, like the slithering snake on a dish found in an early fifth millennium B.C.E. cemetery in western Slovakia. Others are so stylized that they are more abstract than even our most "modern" art. Among these are the large stylized sacramental vase or chalice in the shape of an enthroned Goddess incised with ideograms from the Tisza culture of southeastern Hungary, the pillar-headed Goddess with folded arms from 5000 B.C.E. Romania, and the marble Goddess figurine from Tell Azmak, central Bulgaria, with schematized arms and an exaggerated pubic triangle, dating from 6000 B.C.E. Still other images are strangely beautiful, such as an 8000-year-old horned terra-cotta stand with female breasts, somehow reminiscent of the classical Greek statue called the Winged Victory, and the painted Cucuteni vases with their graceful shapes and rich geometric snake-spiral designs. And others, such as the crosses incised on the navel or near the breasts of the Goddess, raise interesting questions about the earlier meanings of some of our own most important symbols.[6]

There is a sense of fantasy about many of these images, a dreamlike and sometimes bizarre quality suggestive of arcane rituals and long-forgotten myths. For example, a bird-faced woman on a Vinca sculpture and a bird-faced baby she is holding would seem to be masked protagonists of ancient rites, probably enacting a mythological story about a bird Goddess and her divine child. Similarly, a terra-cotta head of a bull with human eyes from 4000 B.C.E. Macedonia suggests a masked protagonist of some other Neolithic ritual and myth. Some of these masked figures seem to represent cosmic powers, either benevolent or threatening. Others have a humorous effect, such as the masked man with padded knickers and exposed belly from fifth millennium B.C.E. Fafkos, described by Gimbutas as probably a comic actor. There are also what Gimbutas calls cosmic eggs. These too are symbols of the Goddess, whose body is the divine Chalice containing the miracle of birth and the power to transform death into life through the mysterious cyclical regeneration of nature.[7]

Indeed, this theme of the unity of all things in nature, as personified by the Goddess, seems to permeate Neolithic art. For here the supreme power governing the universe is a divine Mother who gives her people life, provides them with material and spiritual nurturance, and who even in death can be counted on to take her children back into her cosmic womb.

For instance, in the shrines of Catal Huyuk we find representations of the Goddess both pregnant and giving birth. Often she is accompanied by powerful animals such as leopards and particularly bulls.[8] As a symbol of the unity of all life in nature, in some of her representations she is herself part human and part animal.[9] Even in her darker aspects, in what scholars call the chthonic, or earthy, she is still portrayed as part of the natural order. Just as all life is born from her, it also returns to her at death to be once again reborn.

It could be said that what scholars term the chthonic aspect of the Goddess—her portrayal in surrealistic and sometimes grotesque form—represented our forebears' attempt to deal with the darker aspects of reality by giving our human fears of the shadowy unknown a name and shape. These chthonic images—masks, wall paintings, and statuettes symbolizing death in fantastic and sometimes also humorous forms—would also be designed to impart to the religious initiate a sense of mystical unity with both the dangerous as well as the benign forces governing the world.

Thus, in the same way that life was celebrated in religious imagery and ritual, the destructive processes of nature were also recognized and respected. At the same time that religious rites and ceremonies were designed to give the individual and the community a sense of participation in and control over the life-giving and preserving processes of nature, other rites and ceremonies attempted to keep the more fearful processes at bay.

But with all of this, the many images of the Goddess in her dual aspect of life and death seem to express a view of the world in which the primary purpose of art, and of life, was not to conquer, pillage, and loot but to cultivate the earth and provide the material and spiritual wherewithal for a satisfying life. And on the whole, Neolithic art, and even more so the more developed Minoan art, seems to express a view in which the primary function of the mysterious powers governing the universe is not to exact obedience, punish, and destroy but rather to give.

We know that art, particularly religious or mythical art, reflects not only peoples' attitudes but also their particular form of culture and social organization. The Goddess-centered art we have been examining, with its striking absence of images of male domination or warfare, seems to have reflected a social order in which women, first as heads of clans and priestesses and later on in other important roles, played a central part, and in which both men and

Riane Eisler

women worked together in equal partnership for the common good. If there was here no glorification of wrathful male deities or rulers carrying thunderbolts or arms, or of great conquerors dragging abject slaves about in chains, it is not unreasonable to infer it was because there were no counterparts for those images in real life.[10] And if the central religious image was a woman giving birth and not, as in our time, a man dying on a cross, it would not be unreasonable to infer that life and the love of life—rather than death and the fear of death—were dominant in society as well as art.

THE WORSHIP OF THE GODDESS

One of the most interesting aspects of the prehistoric worship of the Goddess is what the mythologist and religious historian Joseph Campbell calls its "syncretism."[11] Essentially, what this means is that the worship of the Goddess was both polytheistic and monotheistic. It was polytheistic in the sense that she was worshiped under different names and in different forms. But it was also monotheistic—in the sense that we can properly speak of faith in the Goddess in the same way we speak of faith in God as a transcending entity. In other words, there are striking similarities between the symbols and images associated in various places with the worship of the Goddess in her various aspects of mother, ancestress or creatrix, and virgin or maid.

One possible explanation for this remarkable religious unity could be that the Goddess appears to have been originally worshiped in all ancient agricultural societies. We find evidence of the deification of the female—who in her biological character gives birth and nourishment just as the earth does—in the three main centers for the origins of agriculture: Asia Minor and southeastern Europe, Thailand in Southeast Asia, and later on also Middle America.[12]

In many of the earliest known creation stories from very different parts of the world, we find the Goddess-Mother as the source of all being. In the Americas, she is the Lady of the Serpent Skirt—of interest also because, as in Europe, the Middle East, and Asia, the serpent is one of her primary manifestations. In ancient Mesopotamia this same concept of the universe is found in the idea of the world mountain as the body of the Goddess-Mother of the universe, an idea that survived into historic times. And as Nammu, the Sumerian Goddess who gives birth to heaven and earth, her name is expressed in a cuneiform text of circa 2000 B.C.E. (now in the Louvre) by an ideogram signifying sea.[13]

The association of the feminine principle with the primal waters is also a ubiquitous theme. For example, in the decorated pottery of Old Europe, the symbolism of water—often in association with the primal egg—is a frequent motif. Here the Great Goddess, sometimes in the form of the bird or snake Goddess, rules over the life-giving force of water. In both Europe and Anatolia, rain-bearing and milk-giving motifs are interwoven, and ritual containers and vases are standard equipment in her shrines. Her image is also associated with water containers, which are sometimes in her anthropomorphic shape. As the Egyptian Goddess

Nut, she is the flowing unity of celestial primordial waters. Later on, as the Cretan Goddess Ariadne (the Very Holy One), and the Greek Goddess Aphrodite, she rises from the sea.[14] In fact, this image was still so powerful in Christian Europe that it inspired Botticelli's famous Venus rising from the sea.

Although this too is rarely included in what we are taught about our cultural evolution, much of what evolved in the millennia of Neolithic history is still with us today. As Mellaart writes, "it formed the basis on which all later cultures and civilizations have built."[15] Or as Gimbutas put it, even after the world they represented was destroyed, the mythic images of our Goddess-worshiping Neolithic forebears "lingered in the substratum which nourished further European cultural developments," enormously enriching the European psyche.[16]

Indeed, if we look closely at the art of the Neolithic, it is truly astonishing how much of its Goddess imagery has survived—and that most standard works on the history of religion fail to bring out this fascinating fact. Just as the Neolithic pregnant Goddess was a direct descendant of the full-bellied Paleolithic "Venuses," this same image survives in the pregnant Mary of medieval Christian iconography. The Neolithic image of the young Goddess or Maiden is also still venerated in the aspect of Mary as the Holy Virgin. And of course the Neolithic figure of the Mother-Goddess holding her divine child is still everywhere dramatically in evidence as the Christian Madonna and Child.

Images traditionally associated with the Goddess, such as the bull and the bucranium, or horns of the bull, as symbols of the power of nature, also survived well into classical, and later Christian, times. The bull was appropriated as a central symbol of later "pagan" patriarchal mythology. Still later, the horned bull god was in Christian iconography converted from a symbol of male power to a symbol of Satan or evil. But in Neolithic times, the bull horns we now routinely associate with the devil had a very different meaning. Images of bull horns have been excavated in both houses and shrines at Catal Huyuk, where horns of consecration sometimes form rows or altars under representations of the Goddess.[17] And the bull itself is here also still a manifestation of the ultimate power of the Goddess. It is a symbol of the male principle, but it is one that, like all else, issues from an all-giving divine womb—as graphically depicted in a Catal Huyuk shrine where the Goddess is shown giving birth to a young bull.

Even the Neolithic imagery of the Goddess in two simultaneous forms—such as the twin Goddesses excavated in Catal Huyuk—survived into historic times, as in the classical Greek images of Demeter and Kore as the two aspects of the Goddess: Mother and Maid as symbols of the cyclical regeneration of nature.[18] Indeed, the children of the Goddess are all integrally connected with the themes of birth, death, and resurrection. Her daughter survived into classical Greek times as Persephone, or Kore. And her son-lover/husband likewise survived well into historic times under such diverse names as Adonis, Tammutz, Attis—and finally, Jesus Christ.[19]

This seemingly remarkable continuity of religious symbolism becomes more understandable if we consider that in both the Neolithic-Chalcolithic of Old Europe and the later

Minoan-Mycenaean Bronze Age civilization the religion of the Great Goddess appears to have been the single most prominent and important feature of life. In the Anatolian site of Catal Huyuk the worship of the Goddess appears to permeate all aspects of life. For example, out of 139 rooms excavated between 1961 and 1963, more than 40 appear to have served as shrines.[20]

This same pattern prevails in Neolithic and Chalcolithic Europe. In addition to all the shrines dedicated to various aspects of the Goddess, the houses had sacred corners with ovens, altars (benches), and offering places. And the same holds true for the later civilization of Crete, where, as Gimbutas writes, "shrines of one kind or another are so numerous that there is reason to believe that not only every palace but every private house was put to some such use.... To judge by the frequency of shrines, horns of consecration, and the symbol of the double-axe, the whole palace of Knossos must have resembled a sanctuary. Wherever you turn, pillars and symbols remind one of the presence of the Great Goddess."[21]

To say the people who worshiped the Goddess were deeply religious would be to understate, and largely miss, the point. For here there was no separation between the secular and the sacred. As religious historians point out, in prehistoric and, to a large extent, well into historic times, religion was life, and life was religion.

One reason this point is obscured is that scholars have in the past routinely referred to the worship of the Goddess, not as a religion, but as a "fertility cult," and to the Goddess as an "earth mother." But though the fecundity of women and of the earth was, and still is, a requisite for species survival, this characterization is far too simplistic. It would be comparable, for example, to characterizing Christianity as just a death cult because the central image in its art is the Crucifixion.

Neolithic religion—like present-day religious and secular ideologies—expressed the worldview of its time. How different this worldview was from ours is dramatically illustrated if we contrast the Neolithic religious pantheon with the Christian one. In the Neolithic, the head of the holy family was a woman: the Great Mother, the Queen of Heaven, or the Goddess in her various aspects and forms. The male members of this pantheon—her consort, brother, and/or son—were also divine. By contrast, the head of the Christian holy family is an all-powerful Father. The second male in the pantheon—Jesus Christ—is another aspect of the godhead. But though father and son are immortal and divine, Mary, the only woman in this religious facsimile of patriarchal family organization, is merely mortal—clearly, like her earthly counterparts, of an inferior order.

Religions in which the most powerful or only deity is male tend to reflect a social order in which descent is patrilinear (traced through the father) and domicile is patrilocal (the wife goes to live with the family or clan of her husband). Conversely, religions in which the most powerful or sole deity is female tend to reflect a social order in which descent is matrilinear (traced through the mother) and domicile is likewise matrilocal (a husband goes to live with his wife's family or clan).[22] Moreover, a male-dominated and generally hierarchic social structure has historically been reflected and maintained by a male-dominated religious pantheon and by religious doctrines in which the subordination of women is said to be divinely ordained.

IF IT ISN'T PATRIARCHY IT MUST BE MATRIARCHY

Applying these principles to the mounting evidence that for millennia of human history the supreme deity had been female, a number of nineteenth- and early twentieth-century scholars came to a seemingly earthshaking conclusion. If prehistory was not patriarchal, it must have been matriarchal. In other words, if men did not dominate women, women must have dominated men.

Then, when the evidence did not seem to support this conclusion of female dominance, many scholars returned to the more conventionally accepted view. If there never was a matriarchate, they reasoned, male dominance must, after all, always have been the human norm.

The evidence, however, supports neither one of these conclusions. To begin with, the archaeological data we now have indicate that in its general structure prepatriarchal society was, by any contemporary standard, remarkably equalitarian. In the second place, although in these societies descent appears to have been traced through the mother, and women as priestesses and heads of clans seem to have played leading roles in all aspects of life, there is little indication that the position of men in this social system was in any sense comparable to the subordination and suppression of women characteristic of the male-dominant system that replaced it.

From his excavations of Catal Huyuk, where the systematic reconstruction of the life of the city's inhabitants was the primary archaeological goal, Mellaart concluded that though some social inequality is suggested by sizes of buildings, equipment, and burial gifts, this was "never a glaring one."[23] For example, there are in Catal Huyuk no major differences between houses, most of which show a standardized rectangular plan covering about twenty-five square meters of floor space. Even shrines are not structurally different from houses, nor are they necessarily larger in size. Moreover, they are intermingled with the houses in considerable numbers, once again indicating a communally based rather than a centralized, hierarchic social and religious structure.[24]

The same general picture emerges from an analysis of Catal Huyuk burial customs. Unlike the later graves of Indo-European chieftains, which clearly bespeak a pyramidal social structure ruled by a feared and fearful strongman on the top, those of Catal Huyuk indicate no glaring social inequalities.[25]

As for the relationship between men and women, it is true, as Mellaart points out, that the divine family of Catal Huyuk is represented "in order of importance as mother, daughter, son, and father,"[26] and that this probably mirrored the human families of the city's inhabitants, which were evidently matrilineal and matrilocal. It is also true that in Catal Huyuk and other Neolithic societies the anthropomorphic representations of the Goddess—the young Maid, the mature Mother, and the old Grandmother or Ancestress, all the way back to the original Creatrix—are, as the Greek philosopher Pythagoras later noted, projections of the various stages of the life of woman.[27] Also suggesting a matrilineal and matrilocal social organization is that in Catal Huyuk the sleeping platform where the woman's personal possessions and her bed or divan were located is always found in the same place, on the east side of the living quarters. That of the man shifts, and is also somewhat smaller.[28]

But despite such evidence of the preeminence of women in both religion and life, there are no indications of glaring inequality between women and men. Nor are there any signs that women subjugated or oppressed men.

In sharp contrast to the male-dominated religions of our time, in which in almost all cases until quite recently only men could become members of the religious hierarchy, there is here evidence of both priestesses and priests. For instance, Mellaart points out that although it seems likely that it was primarily priestesses who officiated at the worship of the Goddess in Catal Huyuk, there is also evidence pointing to the participation of priests. He reports that two groups of objects found only in burials in shrines were mirrors of obsidian and fine bone belt fasteners. The former were found only with the bodies of women, the latter only with men. This led Mellaart to conclude that these were "attributes of certain priestesses and priests, which would explain both their rarity and their discovery in shrines."[29]

It is also revealing that sculptures of elderly men, sometimes fashioned in a position reminiscent of Rodin's famous *The Thinker*, suggest that old men as well as old women had important and respected roles.[30] Equally revealing is that the bull and the bucranium, or horns of consecration, which have a central place in the shrines of Neolithic Anatolia, Asia Minor, and Old Europe and later in Minoan and Mycenaean imagery, are symbols of the male principle, as are the images of phalluses and boars, which make their appearance in the later Neolithic, particularly in Europe. Moreover, some of the earlier Goddess figurines are not only hybrids of human and animal features, but often also have features, such as exaggerated long necks, that can be interpreted as androgynous.[31] And of course the young god, the son-consort of the Goddess, plays a recurring part in the central miracle of pre-patriarchal religion, the mystery of regeneration and rebirth.

Clearly, then, while the feminine principle as the primary symbol of the miracle of life permeated Neolithic art and ideology, the male principle also played an important role. The fusion of these two principles through the myths and rituals of the Sacred Marriage was in fact still celebrated in the ancient world well into patriarchal times. For example, in Hittite Anatolia, the great shrine of Yazilikaya was dedicated to this purpose. And even later, in Greece and Rome, the ceremony survived as the *hieros gamos*.[32]

It is interesting in this connection that there is Neolithic imagery indicating an understanding of the joint roles of women and men in procreation. For example, a small stone plaque from Catal Huyuk shows a woman and man in a tender embrace; immediately next to them is the relief of a mother holding a child, the offspring of their union.[33]

All this imagery reflects the markedly different attitudes prevailing in the Neolithic about the relationship between women and men—attitudes in which linking rather than ranking appears to have been predominant. As Gimbutas writes, here "the world of myth was not polarized into female and male as it was among the Indo-Europeans and many other nomadic and pastoral peoples of the steppes. Both principles were manifest side by side. The male divinity in the shape of a young man or male animal appears to affirm and strengthen the forces of the creative and active female. Neither is subordinate to the other: by complementing one another, their power is doubled."[34]

Again and again we find that the debate about whether there once was or was not a matriarchate, which still periodically erupts in academic and popular works, seems to be more a function of our prevailing paradigm than of any archaeological evidence.[35] That is, in our culture built on the ideas of hierarchy and ranking and in-group versus out-group thinking, rigid differences or polarities are emphasized. Ours is characteristically the kind of if-it-isn't-this-it-has-to-be-that, dichotomized, either/or thinking that philosophers from earliest times have cautioned can lead to a simplistic misreading of reality. And, indeed, psychologists today have discovered it is the mark of a *lower* or less psychologically evolved stage of cognitive and emotional development.[36]

Mellaart apparently tried to overcome this either/or, if-it-isn't-patriarchy-it-has-to-be-matriarchy tangle when he wrote the following passage: "If the Goddess presided over all the various activities of the life and death of the Neolithic population of Catal Huyuk, so in a way did her son. Even if his role is strictly subordinate to hers, the males' role in life seems to have been fully realized."[37] But in the contradiction between a "fully realized" and a "strictly subordinate" role we again find ourselves tangled up in the cultural and linguistic assumptions inherent in a dominator paradigm: that human relations must fit into some kind of superior-inferior pecking order.

However, looked at from a strictly analytical or logical viewpoint, the primacy of the Goddess—and with this the centrality of the values symbolized by the nurturing and regenerating powers incarnated in the female body—does not justify the inference that women here dominated men. This becomes more apparent if we begin by analogizing from the one human relationship that even in male-dominant societies is not generally conceptualized in superiority-inferiority terms. This is the relationship between mother and child—and the way we perceive it may actually be a remnant of the prepatriarchal conception of the world. The larger, stronger adult mother is clearly, in hierarchic terms, superior to the smaller, weaker child. But this does not mean we normally think of the child as inferior or less valued.

Riane Eisler

Analogizing from this different conceptual framework, we can see that the fact that women played a central and vigorous role in prehistoric religion and life does not have to mean that men were perceived and treated as subservient. For here both men and women were the children of the Goddess, as they were the children of the women who headed the families and clans. And while this certainly gave women a great deal of power, analogizing from our present-day mother-child relationship, it seems to have been a power that was more equated with responsibility and love than with oppression, privilege, and fear.

In sum, in contrast to the still prevailing view of power as the power symbolized by the Blade—the power to take away or to dominate—a very different view of power seems to have been the norm in these Neolithic Goddess-worshiping societies. This view of power as the "feminine" power to nurture and give was undoubtedly not always adhered to, for these were societies of real flesh-and-blood people, not make-believe utopias. But it was still the normative ideal, the model to be emulated by both women and men.

The view of power symbolized by the Chalice—for which I propose the term *actualization power* as distinguished from *domination power*—obviously reflects a very different type of social organization from the one we are accustomed to.[38] We may conclude from the evidence of the past examined so far that it cannot be called matriarchal. As it cannot be called patriarchal either, it does not fit into the conventional dominator paradigm of social organization. However, using the perspective of Cultural Transformation theory we have been developing, it does fit the other alternative for human organization: a partnership society in which neither half of humanity is ranked over the other and diversity is not equated with inferiority or superiority.

. . . [T]hese two alternatives have profoundly affected our cultural evolution. Technological and social evolution tend to become more complex regardless of which model prevails. But the *direction* of cultural evolution—including whether a social system is warlike or peaceful—depends on whether we have a partnership or a dominator social structure.

NOTES

1. Marija Gimbutas, *Goddesses and Gods of Old Europe, 7000–3500 B.C.* (Berkeley and Los Angeles: University of California Press, 1982), 37–38.

2. See illustrations in James Mellaart, *Catal Huyuk* (New York: McGraw-Hill, 1967); Gimbutas, *Goddesses and Gods of Old Europe.*

3. *Goddesses and Gods of Old Europe,* plate 17 and text figure 148.

4. Nicolas Platon, *Crete* (Geneva: Nagel Publishers, 1966), 148.

5. For examples, see illustrations in Erich Neumann, *The Great Mother* (Princeton, NJ: Princeton University Press, 1955); Mellaart, *Catal Huyuk*; Gimbutas, *Goddesses and Gods of Old Europe.*

6. Gimbutas, *Goddesses and Gods of Old Europe,* examples (in order) from plates 58, 59, 105–7, 140, 144; plate 53, text figures 50–58 on pp. 95–103; 114, 181, 173, 108, 136.

7. Ibid., 66; plates 132, 341, 24, 25; pp. 101–7.

8. Mellaart, *Catal Huyuk,* 77–203.

9. Gimbutas, *Goddesses and Gods of Old Europe,* see, e.g., plates 179–81 for bee Goddess, plates 183–85 for Goddess with animal mask, p. 146 for Minoan snake Goddess with a bird's beak.

10. The absence of these images is also striking in the art of Minoan Crete. See, e.g., Jacquetta Hawkes, *Dawn of the Gods: Minoan and Mycenaean Origins of Greece* (New York: Random House, 1968), 75–76. The double ax of the Minoan Goddess is reminiscent of the hoe axes used to clear farmland and was, according to Gimbutas, also a symbol of the butterfly, part of the Goddess's epiphany. As Gimbutas notes, the image of the Goddess as a butterfly continued to be engraved on double axes (Gimbutas, *Goddesses and Gods of Old Europe,* 78, 186).

11. Joseph Campbell, "Classical Mysteries of the Goddess" (workshop at Esalen Institute, California, May 11–13, 1979). The cultural historian Elinor Gadon also stresses this aspect of the prehistoric worship of the Goddess but takes it one important step further. Gadon writes that the reemergence of the Goddess in our time is a key to "the radical pluralism so urgently needed to counteract the prevailing ethnocentrism and cultural imperialism" (prospectus for Elinor Gadon, *The Once and Future Goddess: A Symbol for Our Time* [San Francisco: Harper & Row, 1988]; and private communications with Gadon, 1986).

12. Ibid.

13. See, e.g., Joseph Campbell, *The Mythic Image* (Princeton, NJ: Princeton University Press, 1974), 157, 77.

14. Gimbutas, *Goddesses and Gods of Old Europe,* 112–50, 112, 145; figs. 87, 88, 105, 106, 107; p. 149.

15. Mellaart, *Neolithic of the Near East* (New York: Scribner, 1975), 279.

16. Gimbutas, *Goddesses and Gods of Old Europe,* 238.

17. Mellaart, *Catal Huyuk.* See, e.g., 108–9.

18. Ibid., 113.

19. See, e.g., Neumann, *The Great Mother.*

20. Mellaart, *Catal Huyuk,* 77.

21. Gimbutas, *Goddesses and Gods of Old Europe,* 80.

22. See, e.g., Jane Harrison, *Prolegomena to the Study of Greek Religion* (London: Merlin Press, 1903, 1962), 260–63.

23. Mellaart, *Catal Huyuk,* 225.

24. Mellaart, *Neolithic of the Near East,* 100; Mellaart, *Catal Huyuk,* chap. 6.

25. Mellaart, *Catal Huyuk,* chap. 9.

26. Ibid., 201.

27. Harrison, *Prolegomena to the Study of Greek Religion,* 262.

28. Mellaart, *Catal Huyuk,* 60.

29. Ibid., 202, 208.

30. Gimbutas, *Goddess and Gods of Old Europe,* 232, fig. 248. See also figs. 84–91 in Mellaart, *Catal Huyuk,* for examples of male figurines.

31. Gimbutas, *Goddesses and Gods of Old Europe,* 217, where Gimbutas notes that seventh and sixth millennium B.C.E. Goddess figurines often had long, cylindrical necks reminiscent of a phallus, that there were also phallic representations in the form of simple clay cylinders that sometimes had female breasts, and that the combining of female and male characteristics in one figure did not completely die out after the sixth millennium B.C.E.

32. Edwin Oliver James, *The Cult of the Mother Goddess* (London: Thames & Hudson, 1959), 87.

33. Mellaart, *Catal Huyuk,* 184.

34. *Gimbutas, Goddesses and Gods of Old Europe, 237.*

35. See, e.g., "the caveat that such a social order need not imply the domination of one sex, which the term 'matriarchy' would by its semantic analogue to patriarchy infer," in Kate Millett, *Sexual Politics* (New York: Doubleday, 1970), 28, n. 9; or Adrienne Rich's comment that "the terms 'matriarchy,' 'mother-right,' or 'gynocracy' tend to be used imprecisely, often interchangeably," in *Of Woman Born* (New York: Bantam, 1976), 42–43. Rich also notes that "Robert Briffault goes to some pains to show that matriarchy in primitive societies was not simply patriarchy with a different sex in authority" (p. 43). For a discussion of how the term *gylany* avoids this semantic confusion, see chapter 8.

36. Abraham, Maslow, *Toward a Psychology of Being,* 2d ed. (New York: Van Nostrand-Reinhold, 1968).

37. Mellaart, *Catal Huyuk,* 184.

38. This distinction will be discussed at length in Riane Eisler and David Loye, *Breaking Free* (forthcoming). It is a distinction that is central to the new feminist ethic now being developed by many thinkers. See, e.g., Jean Baker Miller, *Toward a New Psychology of Women* (Boston: Beacon, 1976); Carol Gilligan, *In a Different Voice* (Cambridge: Harvard University Press, 1982); Wilma Scott Heide, *Feminism for the Health of It* (Buffalo: Margaretdaughters Press, 1985). Of particular interest in this context is Anne Barstow, "The Uses of Archaeology for Women's History: James Mellaart's Work on the Neolithic Goddess at Catal Huyuk," *Feminist Studies* 4 (October 1978): 7–18, who independently arrived at a similar conclusion about the way power was probably conceptualized in the societies that worshiped the Goddess (see p. 9).

from "STAYING ALIVE"

Vandana Shiva

NATURE AS THE FEMININE PRINCIPLE

Women in India are an intimate part of nature, both in imagination and in practise. At one level nature is symbolised as the embodiment of the feminine principle, and at another, she is nurtured by the feminine to produce life and provide sustenance.

From the point of view of Indian cosmology, in both the exoteric and esoteric traditions, the world is produced and renewed by the dialectical play of creation and destruction, cohesion and disintegration. The tension between the opposites from which motion and movement arises is depicted as the first appearance of dynamic energy (Shakti). All existence arises from this primordial energy which is the substance of everything, pervading everything. The manifestation of this power, this energy, is called nature (Prakriti).[1] Nature, both animate and inanimate, is thus an expression of Shakti, the feminine and creative principle of the cosmos; in conjunction with the masculine principle (Purusha), Prakriti creates the world.

Nature as Prakriti is inherently active, a powerful, productive force in the dialectic of the creation, renewal and sustenance of *all* life. In *Kulacudamim Nigama*, Prakriti says:

> There is none but Myself
> Who is the Mother to create.[2]

Without Shakti, Shiva, the symbol for the force of creation and destruction, is as powerless as a corpse. "The quiescent aspect of Shiva is, by definition, inert ... Activity is the nature of Nature (Prakriti)."[3]

Prakriti is worshipped as Aditi, the primordial vastness, the inexhaustible, the source of abundance. She is worshipped as Adi Shakti, the primordial power. All the forms of nature and life in nature are the forms, the children, of the Mother of Nature who is nature itself born of the creative play of her thought.[4] Hence Prakriti is also called Lalitha,[5] the Player because *lila* or play, as free spontaneous activity, is her nature. The will-to-become many (Bahu-Syam-Prajayera) is her creative impulse and through this impulse, she creates the diversity of living forms in nature. The common yet multiple life of mountains, trees, rivers, animals is an expression of the diversity that Prakriti gives rise to. The creative force and the

Reprinted from *Staying Alive: Women, Ecology, and Development* by Vandana Shiva, (London: Zed Books, 1989). Reprinted by permission of Zed Books.

created world are not separate and distinct, nor is the created world uniform, static and fragmented. It is diverse, dynamic and inter-related.

The nature of Nature as Prakriti is activity *and* diversity. Nature symbols from every realm of nature are in a sense signed with the image of Nature. Prakriti lives in stone or tree, pool, fruit or animal, and is identified with them. According to the *Kalika Purana*:

> Rivers and mountains have a dual nature. A river is but a form of water, yet is has a distinct body. Mountains appear a motionless mass, yet their true form is not such. We cannot know, when looking at a lifeless shell, that it contains a living being. Similarly, within the apparently inanimate rivers and mountains there dwells a hidden consciousness. Rivers and mountains take the forms they wish.[6]

The living, nurturing relationship between man and nature here differs dramatically from the notion of man as separate from and dominating over nature. A good illustration of this difference is the daily worship of the sacred tulsi within Indian culture and outside it. Tulsi (*Ocimum sanctum*) is a little herb planted in every home, and worshipped daily. It has been used in Ayurveda for more than 3,000 years, and is now also being legitimized as a source of diverse healing powers by western medicine. However, all this is incidental to its worship. The tulsi is sacred not merely as a plant with beneficial properties but as Brindavan, the symbol of the cosmos. In their daily watering and worship women renew the relationship of the home with the cosmos and with the world process. Nature as a creative expression of the feminine principle is both in ontological continuity with humans as well as above them. Ontologically, there is no divide between man and nature, or between man and woman, because life in all its forms arises from the feminine principle.

Contemporary Western views of nature are fraught with the dichotomy or duality between man and woman, and person and nature. In Indian cosmology, by contrast, person and nature (Purusha-Prakriti) are a duality in unity. They are inseparable complements of one another in nature, in woman, in man. Every form of creation bears the sign of this dialectical unity, of diversity within a unifying principle, and this dialectical harmony between the male and female principles and between nature and man, becomes the basis of ecological thought and action in India. Since, ontologically, there is no dualism between man and nature and because nature as Prakriti sustains life, nature has been treated as integral and inviolable. Prakriti, far from being an esoteric abstraction, is an everyday concept which organizes daily life. There is no separation here between the popular and elite imagery or between the sacred and secular traditions. As an embodiment and manifestation of the feminine principle it is characterised by (*a*) creativity, activity, productivity; (*b*) diversity in form and aspect; (*c*) connectedness and inter-relationship of all beings, including man; (*d*) continuity between the human and natural; and (*e*) sanctity of life in nature.

Conceptually, this differs radically from the Cartesian concept of nature as "environment" or a "resource." In it, the environment is seen as separate from man: it is his surrounding, not his substance. The dualism between man and nature has allowed the subjugation of the latter by man and given rise to a new world-view in which nature is (*a*) inert and passive; (*b*) uniform and mechanistic; (*c*) separable and fragmented within itself; (*d*) separate from man; and (*e*) inferior, to be dominated and exploited by man.

The rupture within nature and between man and nature, and its associated transformation from a life-force that sustains to an exploitable resource characterizes the Cartesian view which has displaced more ecological world-views and created a development paradigm which cripples nature and woman simultaneously.

The ontological shift for an ecologically sustainable future has much to gain from the world-views of ancient civilizations and diverse cultures which survived sustainably over centuries. These were based on an ontology of the feminine as the living principle, and on an ontological continuity between society and nature—the humanisation of nature and the naturalization of society. Not merely did this result in an ethical context which excluded possibilities of exploitation and domination, it allowed the creation of an earth family.

The dichotomised ontology of man dominating woman and nature generates maldevelopment because it makes the colonizing male the agent and model of "development." Women, the Third World and nature become underdeveloped, first by definition, and then, through the process of colonization, in reality.

The ontology of dichotomization generates an ontology of domination, over nature and people. Epistemologically, it leads to reductionism and fragmentation, thus violating women as subjects and nature as an object of knowledge. This violation becomes a source of epistemic and real violence—I would like to interpret ecological crises at both levels—as a disruption of ecological perceptions of nature.

Ecological ways of knowing nature are necessarily participatory. Nature herself is the experiment and women, as sylviculturalists, agriculturists and water resource managers, the traditional natural scientists. Their knowledge is ecological and plural, reflecting both the diversity of natural ecosystems and the diversity in cultures that nature-based living gives rise to. Throughout the world, the colonization of diverse peoples was, at its root, a forced subjugation of ecological concepts of nature and of the Earth as the repository of all forms, latencies and powers of creation, the ground and cause of the world. The symbolism of Terra Mater, the earth in the form of the Great Mother, creative and protective, has been a shared but diverse symbol across space and time, and ecology movements in the West today are inspired in large part by the recovery of the concept of Gaia, the earth goddess.[7]

The shift from Prakriti to "natural resources," from Mater to "matter" was considered (and in many quarters is still considered) a progressive shift from superstition to rationality. Yet, viewed from the perspective of nature, or women embedded in nature, in the production and preservation of sustenance, the shift is regressive and violent. It entails the disruption of

Vandana Shiva

nature's processes and cycles, and her inter-connectedness. For women, whose productivity in the sustaining of life is based on nature's productivity, the death of Prakriti is simultaneously a beginning of their marginalization, devaluation, displacement and ultimate dispensability. The ecological crisis is, at its root, the death of the feminine principle, symbolically as well as in contexts such as rural India, not merely in form and symbol, but also in the everyday processes of survival and sustenance.

NOTES

1. "Prakriti" is a popular category, and one through which ordinary women in rural India relate to nature. It is also a highly evolved philosophical category in Indian cosmology. Even those philosophical streams of Indian thought which were patriarchal and did not give the supreme place to divinity as a woman, a mother, were permeated by the prehistoric cults and the living "little" traditions of nature as the primordial mother goddess.

2. For an elaboration of the concept of the feminine principle in Indian thought see Alain Danielon, *The Gods of India,* New York: Inner Traditions International Ltd., 1985; Sir John Woodroffe, *The Serpent Power,* Madras: Ganesh and Co., 1931; and Sir John Woodroffe, *Shakti and Shakta,* London: Luzaz and Co., 1929.

3. Woodroffe, *op. cit.,* (1931), p 27.

4. W. C. Beane, *Myth, Cult and Symbols in Sakta Hinduism: A Study of the Indian Mother Goddess,* Leiden: E.J. Brill, 1977.

5. *Lalitha Sahasranama,* (Reprint), Delhi: Giani Publishing House, 1986.

6. *Kalika Purana,* 22.10–13, Bombay: Venkateshwara Press, 1927.

THE RAINBOW BRIDGE

Brooke Medicine Eagle

I found some dry, bleached bones today,
and gathered them to put into a bag
for casting to ask the future,
when modern means have failed me.

The vision quest that I have done was with my teacher who is a Northern Cheyenne woman. She is eighty-five years old and is known as The Keeper of the Sacred Buffalo Hat. Her people call her The Woman Who Knows Everything. She and a younger medicine woman took me to a place called Bear Butte, South Dakota; it's plains country that goes up into the Black Hills. That's the traditional fasting, vision-questing place of the Sioux and Cheyenne and has been for centuries and centuries. What is usually done among the Cheyenne is that you fast and cleanse yourself bodily, emotionally, and psychically. Then you go atop a mountain for four days and nights with just a breechcloth on and a buffalo robe, and you stay there without food or water, praying for vision. This is the kind of quest that I did.

The younger medicine woman took me up the butte. She prepared and blessed a bed of sagebrush on a very rocky hill halfway up the mountain. This was to be my bed. After we smoked a pipe and offered prayers, she left me. So I spent the time there fasting and praying for vision.

It was just getting to be dark. Up on the mountain, I can look down over the country: There's a lake down below me; in the far-off distance are the Black Hills, and I can see the lights of Rapid City. I'm hoping it won't rain because I really don't want to be rained on up here. A few little clouds are flitting across the sky, but it is relatively warm, the late fall. I'm just lying here very peacefully. And beside me there comes a woman, older than me, but not really an old woman. She's dressed very simply, buckskin. And I'm surprised that she doesn't have beading on her dress. She has raven black hair in long braids. And she stands beside me and begins to talk to me. As she talks to me, her words come, but not in my ears; I don't really hear her say anything. It's as though she's feeding something in at my navel, and it comes through me, and I can interpret part of it in words but not all of it, like she's giving me something through my stomach and letting it come up. So the words that I put to it have to be my own, and I have discovered more and more of what she told me as time has gone on.

Reprinted by permission of the author. This essay appeared in *Shamanic Voices: A Survey of Visionary Narratives* edited by Joan Halifax (Dutton, 1979).

Just then the little clouds that were over the moon move off, and as they move away, the moonlight shining on her dress creates a flurry of rainbows, and I can see that her dress is beaded with crystal beads, hundreds of tiny crystal beads; the slightest movement she makes sends little flurries of soft rainbows all over. About this time, something else starts to happen. Down off the high part of the mountain, it starts to become light, and I hear soft drumbeats begin, very soft. There's a kind of dance that the women do that is very soft. And down off that mountain in a slow, soft, and gentle step come the old women, spirits of that land, that mountain, old gray-haired women, Indian women, dancing down. They either *are* light or carry light. They wind down the mountain and then circle around the hill I am on. And as they dance around in a circle, very quickly, into that circle comes another circle, this of young women, of my age and time, young women that I know, and they, too, are dancing. Those two circles are dancing and moving, and then they begin to weave in and out of each other, sway in and out of each other. And then inside of that circle comes another circle of seven old grandmothers, white-haired women, women who are significant to me, powerful old women.

In the Native American tradition, there is an amazing amount of humor. And the humor comes when all this very solemn, very slow, and very beautiful ceremony is taking place. Running off the mountain, with her hair flying, is this friend of mine. She's always late. She is a very high person, but she is very unstable. Into the circle comes Dianne, flying, with her hair streaming, late as always. And on her hand she is carrying a dove. The Rainbow Woman looks down on me and says, "Her name is Moon Dove," and she smiles. Dianne then lets the dove fly. The circles around me disappear, and I am again alone with the Rainbow Woman.

She said to me that the earth is in trouble, that the land is in trouble, and that here on this land, this Turtle Island, this North American land, what needs to happen is a balancing. She said that the thrusting, aggressive, analytic, intellectual, building, making-it-happen energy has very much overbalanced the feminine, receptive, allowing, surrendering energy. She said that what needs to happen is an uplifting and a balancing. And because we are out of balance, we need to put more emphasis on surrendering, being receptive, allowing, nurturing. She was speaking to me as a woman, and I was to carry this message to women specifically. But not only do women need to become strong in this way; we all need to do this, men and women alike.

Women are born into that kind of space. It's more natural for us to be receptive and nurturing. That's what being a woman in this body is about. But even the women in our society don't do that very well. None of us has ever been taught how to do that. We know how to *do* something; we know how to *make* something, how to *do*, how to *try*. But we need to allow, to be receptive, to surrender, to serve. These are things we don't know very well. So she told me that women especially need to find that place, to find the strength of their place, and that also the whole society, men and women, need that balance to bring ourselves into balance.

Another thing she said to me was that we on this North American continent are all children of the rainbow, all of us; we are mixed-bloods. And especially me she was speaking to, saying that she felt that I would be a carrier of the message between the two cultures, across the rainbow bridge, from the old culture to the new, from the Indian culture to the dominant culture, and back again. And in a sense, all of us in this generation can be that. We can help bridge that gap, build that bridge into the new age of balance.

Those are the kind of things that she talked about, about cleansing ourselves so that we can allow love and light and surrender to come through us. And when she finished talking, she stood quietly for a moment. Her feet stayed where they were, but she shot out across the sky in a rainbow arc that covered the heavens, her head at the top of that arc. And then the lights that formed that rainbow began to die out, almost like fireworks in the sky, died out from her feet and died out and died out. And she was gone.

When I woke up the next morning, on the other side of the sky was the completion of the rainbow that had started the night before. And for days and days after that, rainbows kept appearing in my life.

There are very few women who are on the path of the shaman, and yet, this is my way. I was raised on the Crow Reservation in Montana. My blood is Sioux and Nez Percé. The Indian tradition was very much hidden when I was growing up on the reservation. However, I am getting back, more and more, to the tribal way. This happened as I began to have visions; I was drawn back to the old ways by my visions. I did not choose it outwardly. It just came about.

One of the things that I feel about the quest for vision: The traditional Indians, when they prayed, their prayers were always "Not only for myself do I ask this, but that the people may live, the people may live." Any of us can dream, but when you seek a vision, you do this not only for yourself but that the people may live, that life might be better for all of us, not only for me but for all people.

I feel my purpose is to help in any way I can to heal the earth. I feel that we are in a time when the earth is in dire need of healing. We see it everywhere, the droughts, earthquakes, storms, pollution. Yes, the earth itself is in need of healing. And I feel that any way that I can help, that is my mission: to make it whole, to pay attention to that wholeness, not only in ourselves but also in relation to the earth.

The Indian people are the people of the heart. When the white man came to this land, what he was to bring was the intellect, that analytic, intellectual way of being. And the Indian people were to develop the heart, the feelings. And those two were to come together to build the new age, in balance, not one or the other.

It has been only a couple of hundred years now, and I think we're beginning to see the force of this land, that receptive force, come back again, and that balance is beginning to happen. And I feel that what we are is that land. We are those children Rainbow Woman talked about. We are the ones who are going to have to do it. We are that blend.

In the philosophy of the true Indian people, Indian is an attitude, a state of mind; Indian is a state of being, the place of the heart. To allow the heart to be the distributor of energy on

Brooke Medicine Eagle

this planet; to allow your heart, your feelings, your emotions to distribute your energy; to pull that energy from the earth, from the sky; to pull it down and distribute it from your heart, the very center of your being—that is our purpose.

Several different traditions talk about four or five different worlds and say that the Creator made all these worlds with one simple law: that we shall be in harmony and in balance with all things, including the sun. And time and again people have destroyed that harmony; we have destroyed that harmony. And we have done it again needlessly. Unless we bring about that balance again, this is our last chance.

We need to achieve a clarity and lack of resistance before we seek vision—a surrendering, a relinquishing. If you are unwilling to be in your experience now, then vision will not open for you. You need to get on that circle where there is no resistance, no up, no down, where there are no square corners to stumble on. Then, someday, you become that circle.

THE CLAN OF
ONE-BREASTED WOMEN

Terry Tempest Williams

I belong to a Clan of One-Breasted Women. My mother, my grandmothers, and six aunts have all had mastectomies. Seven are dead. The two who survive have just completed rounds of chemotherapy and radiation.

I've had my own problems: two biopsies for breast cancer and a small tumor between my ribs diagnosed as a "borderline malignancy."

This is my family history.

Most statistics tell us breast cancer is genetic, hereditary, with rising percentages attached to fatty diets, childlessness, or becoming pregnant after thirty. What they don't say is living in Utah may be the greatest hazard of all.

We are a Mormon family with roots in Utah since 1847. The "word of wisdom" in my family aligned us with good foods—no coffee, no tea, tobacco, or alcohol. For the most part, our women were finished having their babies by the time they were thirty. And only one faced breast cancer prior to 1960. Traditionally, as a group of people, Mormons have a low rate of cancer.

Is our family a cultural anomaly? The truth is, we didn't think about it. Those who did, usually the men, simply said, "bad genes." The women's attitude was stoic. Cancer was part of life. On February 16, 1971, the eve of my mother's surgery, I accidentally picked up the telephone and overheard her ask my grandmother what she could expect.

"Diane, it is one of the most spiritual experiences you will ever encounter."

I quietly put down the receiver.

Two days later, my father took my brothers and me to the hospital to visit her. She met us in the lobby in a wheelchair. No bandages were visible. I'll never forget her radiance, the way she held herself in a purple velvet robe, and how she gathered us around her.

"Children, I am fine. I want you to know I felt the arms of God around me."

We believed her. My father cried. Our mother, his wife, was thirty-eight years old.

A little over a year after Mother's death, Dad and I were having dinner together. He had just returned from St. George, where the Tempest Company was completing the gas lines that would service southern Utah. He spoke of his love for the country, the sandstoned landscape, bare-boned and beautiful. He had just finished hiking the Kolob trail in Zion National Park.[1] We got caught up in reminiscing, recalling with fondness our walk up Angel's Landing on his fiftieth birthday and the years our family had vacationed there.

Over dessert, I shared a recurring dream of mine. I told my father that for years, as long as I could remember, I saw this flash of light in the night in the desert—that this image had so permeated my being that I could not venture south without seeing it again, on the horizon, illuminating buttes and mesas.

"You did see it," he said.

"Saw what?"

"The bomb. The cloud. We were driving home from Riverside, California. You were sitting on Diane's lap. She was pregnant. In fact, I remember the day, September 7, 1957. We had just gotten out of the service. We were driving north, past Las Vegas. It was an hour or so before dawn when this explosion went off. We not only heard it, but felt it. I thought the oil tanker in front of us had blown up. We pulled over and suddenly, rising from the desert floor, we saw it, clearly, this golden-stemmed cloud, the mushroom. The sky seemed to vibrate with an eerie pink glow. Within a few minutes, a light ash was raining on the car."

I stared at my father.

"I thought you knew that," he said. "It was a common occurrence in the fifties."

It was at this moment that I realized the deceit I had been living under. Children growing up in the American Southwest, drinking contaminated milk from contaminated cows, even from the contaminated breasts of their mothers, my mother—members, years later, of the Clan of One-Breasted Women.

It is a well-known story in the Desert West, "The Day We Bombed Utah," or more accurately, the years we bombed Utah: above-ground atomic testing in Nevada took place from January 27, 1951, through July 11, 1962. Not only were the winds blowing north covering "low-use segments of the population" with fallout and leaving sheep dead in their tracks, but the climate was right. The United States of the 1950s was red, white, and blue. The Korean War was raging. McCarthyism was rampant. Ike was it, and the cold war was hot.[2] If you were against nuclear testing, you were for a communist regime.

Much has been written about this "American nuclear tragedy." Public health was secondary to national security. The Atomic Energy Commissioner, Thomas Murray, said, "Gentlemen, we must not let anything interfere with this series of tests, nothing."

Again and again, the American public was told by its government, in spite of burns, blisters, and nausea, "It has been found that the tests may be conducted with adequate assurance of safety under conditions prevailing at the bombing reservations." Assuaging public fears was simply a matter of public relations. "Your best action," an Atomic Energy Commission booklet read, "is not to be worried about fallout." A news release typical of the times stated, "We find no basis for concluding that harm to any individual has resulted from radioactive fallout."

On August 30, 1979, during Jimmy Carter's presidency, a suit was filed, *Irene Allen v. The United States of America*. Mrs. Allen's case was the first on an alphabetical list of twenty-four test cases, representative of nearly twelve hundred plaintiffs seeking compensation from the United States government for cancers caused by nuclear testing in Nevada.

Irene Allen lived in Hurricane, Utah. She was the mother of five children and had been widowed twice. Her first husband, with their two oldest boys, had watched the tests from the roof of the local high school. He died of leukemia in 1956. Her second husband died of pancreatic cancer in 1978.

In a town meeting conducted by Utah Senator Orrin Hatch, shortly before the suit was filed, Mrs. Allen said, "I am not blaming the government, I want you to know that, Senator Hatch. But I thought if my testimony could help in any way so this wouldn't happen again to any of the generations coming up after us . . . I am happy to be here this day to bear testimony of this."

God-fearing people. This is just one story in an anthology of thousands.

On May 10, 1984, Judge Bruce S. Jenkins handed down his opinion. Ten of the plaintiffs were awarded damages. It was the first time a federal court had determined that nuclear tests had been the cause of cancers. For the remaining fourteen test cases, the proof of causation was not sufficient. In spite of the split decision, it was considered a landmark ruling. It was not to remain so for long.

In April 1987, the Tenth Circuit Court of Appeals overturned Judge Jenkins's ruling on the ground that the United States was protected from suit by the legal doctrine of sovereign immunity, a centuries-old idea from England in the days of absolute monarchs.

In January 1988, the Supreme Court refused to review the Appeals Court decision. To our court system it does not matter whether the United States government was irresponsible, whether it lied to its citizens, or even that citizens died from the fallout of nuclear testing. What matters is that our government is immune: "The King can do no wrong."

In Mormon culture, authority is respected, obedience is revered, and independent thinking is not. I was taught as a young girl not to "make waves" or "rock the boat."

"Just let it go," Mother would say. "You know how you feel, that's what counts."

For many years, I have done just that—listened, observed, and quietly formed my own opinions, in a culture that rarely asks questions because it has all the answers. But one by one, I have watched the women in my family die common, heroic deaths. We sat in waiting rooms hoping for good news, but always receiving the bad. I cared for them, bathed their scarred bodies, and kept their secrets. I watched beautiful women become bald as Cytoxan, cisplatin, and Adriamycin[3] were injected into their veins. I held their foreheads as they vomited greenblack bile, and I shot them with morphine when the pain became inhuman. In the end, I witnessed their last peaceful breaths, becoming a midwife to the rebirth of their souls.

The price of obedience has become too high.

The fear and inability to question authority that ultimately killed rural communities in Utah during atmospheric testing of atomic weapons is the same fear I saw in my mother's body. Sheep. Dead sheep. The evidence is buried.

I cannot prove that my mother, Diane Dixon Tempest, or my grandmothers, Lettie Romney Dixon and Kathryn Blackett Tempest, along with my aunts developed cancer from nuclear fallout in Utah. But I can't prove they didn't.

My father's memory was correct. The September blast we drove through in 1957 was part of Operation Plumbbob, one of the most intensive series of bomb tests to be initiated. The flash of light in the night in the desert, which I had always thought was a dream, developed into a family nightmare. It took fourteen years, from 1957 to 1971, for cancer to manifest in my mother—the same time Howard L. Andrews, an authority in radioactive fallout at the National Institute of Health, says radiation cancer requires to become evident. The more I learn about what it means to be a "down-winder," the more questions I drown in.

What I do know, however, is that as a Mormon woman of the fifth generation of Latter-Day Saints, I must question everything, even if it means losing my faith, even if it means becoming a member of a border tribe among my own people. Tolerating blind obedience in the name of patriotism or religion ultimately takes our lives.

When the Atomic Energy Commission described the country north of the Nevada Test Site as "virtually uninhabited desert terrain," my family and the birds at Great Salt Lake were some of the "virtual uninhabitants."

One night, I dreamed women from all over the world circled a blazing fire in the desert. They spoke of change, how they hold the moon in their bellies and wax and wane with its phases. They mocked the presumption of even-tempered beings and made promises that they would never fear the witch inside themselves. The women danced wildly as sparks broke away from the flames and entered the night sky as stars.

And they sang a song given to them by Shoshone[4] grandmothers:

Ah ne nah, nah	Consider the rabbits
nin nah nah—	How gently they walk on the earth—
ah ne nah, nah	Consider the rabbits
nin nah nah—	How gently they walk on the earth—
Nyaga mutzi	We remember them
ah ne nay—	We can walk gently also—
Nyaga mutzi	We remember them
oh ne nay—	We can walk gently also—

The women danced and drummed and sang for weeks, preparing themselves for what was to come. They would reclaim the desert for the sake of their children, for the sake of the land.

A few miles downwind from the fire circle, bombs were being tested. Rabbits felt the tremors. Their soft leather pads on paws and feet recognized the shaking sands, while the roots of mesquite and sage were smoldering. Rocks were hot from the inside out and dust devils hummed unnaturally. And each time there was another nuclear test, ravens watched the desert heave. Stretch marks appeared. The land was losing its muscle.

The women couldn't bear it any longer. They were mothers. They had suffered labor pains but always under the promise of birth. The red-hot pains beneath the desert promised death only, as each bomb became a stillborn. A contract had been made and broken between human beings and the land. A new contract was being drawn by the women, who understood the fate of the earth as their own.

Under the cover of darkness, ten women slipped under a barbed-wire fence and entered the contaminated country. They were trespassing. They walked toward the town of Mercury,[5] in moonlight, taking their cues from coyote, kit fox, antelope squirrel, and quail. They moved quietly and deliberately through the maze of Joshua trees. When a hint of daylight appeared they rested, drinking tea and sharing their rations of food. The women closed their eyes. The time had come to protest with the heart, that to deny one's genealogy with the earth was to commit treason against one's soul.

At dawn, the women draped themselves in mylar,[6] wrapping long streamers of silver plastic around their arms to blow in the breeze. They wore clear masks, that became the faces of humanity. And when they arrived at the edge of Mercury, they carried all the butterflies of a summer day in their wombs. They paused to allow their courage to settle.

The town that forbids pregnant women and children to enter because of radiation risks was asleep. The women moved through the streets as winged messengers, twirling around each other in slow motion, peeking inside homes and watching the easy sleep of men and women. They were astonished by such stillness and periodically would utter a shrill note or low cry just to verify life.

The residents finally awoke to these strange apparitions. Some simply stared. Others called authorities, and in time, the women were apprehended by wary soldiers dressed in desert fatigues. They were taken to a white, square building on the other edge of Mercury. When asked who they were and why they were there, the women replied, "We are mothers and we have come to reclaim the desert for our children."

The soldiers arrested them. As the ten women were blindfolded and handcuffed, they began singing:

You can't forbid us everything
You can't forbid us to think—
You can't forbid our tears to flow
And you can't stop the songs that we sing.

The women continued to sing louder and louder, until they heard the voices of their sisters moving across the mesa:

Ah ne nah, nah
nin nah nah—
Ah ne nah, nah

nin nah nah—
Nyaga mutzi
oh ne nay—
Nyaga mutzi
oh ne nay—

"Call for reinforcements," one soldier said.

"We have," interrupted one woman, "we have—and you have no idea of our numbers."

I crossed the line at the Nevada Test Site and was arrested with nine other Utahns for trespassing on military lands. They are still conducting nuclear tests in the desert. Ours was an act of civil disobedience. But as I walked toward the town of Mercury, it was more than a gesture of peace. It was a gesture on behalf of the Clan of One-Breasted Women.

As one officer cinched the handcuffs around my wrists, another frisked my body. She did not find my scars.

We were booked under an afternoon sun and bused to Tonopah, Nevada. It was a two-hour ride. This was familiar country. The Joshua trees standing their ground had been named by my ancestors, who believed they looked like prophets pointing west to the Promised Land. These were the same trees that bloomed each spring, flowers appearing like white flames in the Mojave. And I recalled a full moon in May, when Mother and I had walked among them, flushing out mourning doves and owls.

The bus stopped short of town. We were released.

The officials thought it was a cruel joke to leave us stranded in the desert with no way to get home. What they didn't realize was that we were home, soul-centered and strong, women who recognized the sweet smell of sage as fuel for our spirits.

NOTES

1. Located in southwestern Utah, mainly in Washington County.

2. Events and figures of the 1950s: the Korean War (1950–53) pitted the combined forces of the Republic of Korea and the United Nations against the invading armies of Communist North Korea; McCarthyism, after

Republican senator Joseph S. McCarthy, refers to the Communist "witch hunt" led by the senator, which intensified a fear of Communism and in turn stimulated the buildup of nuclear weapons; "Ike" is the nickname of Dwight D. Eisenhower, president from 1953 to 1961; the Cold War refers to the power struggle from the end of World War II to the late 1980s between Communist countries under the influence of the USSR and the capitalist bloc represented by the United States and Western Europe.

3. Substances used in chemotherapy for cancer patients.

4. Shoshonean Indians share a common linguistic heritage, and except for a few tribes, they live between the Rocky Mountains and the Sierra Nevada in semidesert, range, and sagebrush regions.

5. Town in southern Nevada bordering the Nuclear Test Site.

6. A filmy synthetic material.

"DESTABILIZING PATRIARCHAL CONSUMPTION"

Carol Adams

> The eating of animal flesh, an easy matter of course for most people unless made complex by ritual warnings, may yet turn out to be a problem of psycho-social evolution when humankind comes to review and reassess the inner and outer consequences of having assumed the life of an armed hunter, and all the practical and emotional dead ends into which this has led us. Only then will it be possible to separate the superstitious, neurotic and faddish aspects of vegetarianism from its possible ethical persuasiveness.
>
> —Erik H. Erikson, *Gandhi's Truth*

Beneath the equivocations and the hedges in the above passage that cloak his criticism of meat, Erik Erikson acknowledges that vegetarianism has ethical meaning; its meaning is connected with the implications of killing animals, the consequences of which are experienced internally and externally. Like many meat eaters, Erikson perceives that vegetarianism is burdened by numerous associations, the superstitious, the neurotic, and the faddish; he fails to admit that so is meat eating. The eating of animal flesh is burdened by superstitions regarding our needs for animal protein and the equation of meat with strength; neurotic aspects of meat eating are revealed in the reactions of meat eaters to the threat of vegetarianism. Erikson's statement, though acknowledging the troubling dimension of killing animals for food, which has equipped our culture to be armed hunters even when this is no longer necessary, exemplifies the fact that one cannot be an objective viewer of one's own meat eating. Thus he raises questions about the texts of meat but stays firmly committed to them, as well.

Because of the dominant discourse which approves of meat eating, we are forced to take the knowledge that we are consuming dead animals and accept it, ignore it, neutralize it, repress it. What are the costs of this? What are the implications of repressing facts about the absent referent whose death enables meat eating?

For women in patriarchal culture, additional concerns arise as well. For we have been swallowed *and* we are the swallowers. We are the consumers *and* the consumed. We are the ones whose stomachs do not listen—having no ears—and we are the ones who seek to be heard from within the stomach that has no ears.

Eating animals acts as mirror and representation of patriarchal values. Meat eating is the re-inscription of male power at every meal. The patriarchal gaze sees not the fragmented flesh of dead animals but appetizing food. If our appetites re-inscribe patriarchy, our actions regarding eating animals will either reify or challenge this received culture. If meat is a symbol of male dominance then the presence of meat proclaims the disempowering of women.

Many cultural commentators have observed that the rituals that attend the consumption of animals in nontechnological societies occur because meat eating represents patricide. What is consumed is the father. The men are said to resolve their hostility toward their father through the killing of animals.[1] The dead animal represents the father whose power has been usurped by the sons, yet, who, as ancestor forgives them. In this typology, the worst fears of a patriarchy—fathers being deposed by sons—are displaced through ritual and the killing of animals. Meat becomes a metaphor for the resolution of the tension between father and son for power; meat is viewed as male. The question arises: do we ritually enact primal patricide whenever we sit down to a meal of meat?[2]

Though we are eating "father-food" we are not consuming the father. How can that which we eat be father when we rarely eat normal, adult male animals? The metaphor that whatever is killed becomes father screens the reality behind the metaphor. The reality is the structure of the absent referent. We are continuously eating mothers. The fact is that we proclaim and reinforce the triumph of male dominance by eating female-identified pieces of meat.

Kate Millet remarked that "every avenue of power" is male dominated. This includes the "power" we think we absorb from dead victims who are still bleeding. Meat is a "power-structured relationship" in which power is thought to transfer to the consumer.[3] The concept that meat gives physical strength derives from this symbolic power. Meat reflects back male power every time it is consumed. From symbolically defeated females flows the imagined power that is assimilated by the victor. Thus meat is both animalized *and* masculinized.

A reconceptualization of power has occured. Power, mana, was imagined to exist in dead animals. Power would be absorbed through the consumption of the animal, and since fathers had power, the power being absorbed was considered to be the power of the father. We have been convinced to surrender part of our concept of power to the consummable, dead animal. We then think we absorb this power as we consume the dead. We are giving back to ourselves the power we think was in the victim.

How do we overthrow patriarchal power while eating its symbol? Autonomous, antipatriarchal being is clearly vegetarian. To destabilize patriarchal consumption we must interrupt patriarchal meals of meat.

Virginia Woolf seems to suggest that it is when thinking about women that we will forget

Carol Adams

the meat. Buried within the significant events of Woolf's *Jacob's Room* is a small interchange between mother and son. Betty Flanders, Woolf tells us, was thinking of

> responsibility and danger. She gripped Archer's hand. On she plodded up the hill.
>
> "What did I ask you to remember?" she said.
>
> "I don't know," said Archer.
>
> "Well, I don't know either," said Betty, humorously and simply, and who shall deny that this blankness of mind, when combined with profusion, mother wit, old wives' tales, haphazard ways, moments of astonishing daring, humour and sentimentality—who shall deny that in these respects every woman is nicer than any man?
>
> Well, Betty Flanders, to begin with.
>
> She had her hand upon the garden gate.
>
> "The meat!" she exclaimed, striking the latch down.
>
> She had forgotten the meat.[4]

But how, precisely, do we forget meat once our appetites are acclimated to her? The Yanomano of South America have two words for hunger: one word means that you have an empty stomach; the other word declares that you have a full stomach that craves meat. As the narrator in Colette's *Break of Day* discovered—despite seeing the reality of meat, the broken joints, the mutilations, imagining the life that only this morning enjoyed running and scratching, attempting to determine the difference between this and cooking a child, too—the aroma of the delicate flesh dripping on the charcoal gives one a yawning hunger, a hunger that begs that she forget her objections to meat.

The codes of the texts of meat must be broken down. They cannot be broken down while meat is present for it reifies all of the old codes. We must admit that there will be a destruction of the pleasure of meals as we now know it. But there awaits the discovery of the pleasure of vegetarian meals as well.

To forget the meat we begin by naming and claiming the absent referent, restoring to animals their individual beings. We must consider our own appetites and whether we wish to be dependent on them; we place the importance of acceding to these appetites within the symbolic patriarchal order that they will either accept or challenge.

One way by which we accept the eating of animal flesh is by creating a symbolic order, a cosmology, which reifies meat eating. Patriarchal values are expressed by appropriating images of animals' deaths into our symbolism. As Joseph Campbell describes this imagery:

> the paramount object of experience is the beast. Killed and slaughtered, it [*sic*] yields to people its [*sic*] flesh to become our substance, teeth to become our ornaments, hides for clothing and tents, sinews for ropes, bones for tools. The animal life is translated into human life entirely, through the medium of death, slaughter, and the arts of cooking, tanning, sewing.

The killed and slaughtered animal yields as well imagery of ferociousness, territorial imperative, armed hunting, aggressive behavior, the vitality and virility of meat eating. Carnivorous animals provide a paradigm for male behavior. Through symbolism based on killing animals, we encounter politically laden images of absorption, control, domain, and the necessity of violence. This message of male dominance is conveyed through meat eating—both in its symbolism and reality.

According to Campbell, the plant world, in contrast to the animal world, supplies "the food, clothing and shelter of people since time out of mind, but also our model of the wonder of life—in its cycle of growth and decay, blossom and seed, wherein death and life appear as transformations of a single, superordinated, indestructible force."[5] The plant world yields imagery of tending, nurturing, slow evolutionary change, harmony with the seasons. Political implications are derived from a sense of organic unity rather than disjunction; harvest rather than violence; living in harmony rather than having domain over. This is the challenge that the uniting of feminist and vegetarian insights offers: political symbolism based on an affirmation of a diet drawn from the plant world.

Deriving meaning from plant imagery, we can say we wilt if we eat flesh; we will feed on the grace of vegetables. Virginia de Araújo describes such a perspective, that of a friend, who takes the barrenness of a cupboard, filled only with "celery threads, chard stems, avocado skins" and creates a feast, a grace:

> & says, On this grace I feed, I wilt
> in spirit if I eat flesh, let the hogs,
> the rabbits live, the cows browse,
> the eggs hatch out chicks & peck seeds.[6]

The creation of vegetarian rituals that celebrate the grace of eating plants will contribute to destablizing patriarchal consumption. In place of the ritual of the fatted calf for the return of the prodigal son, the celebration of the return of a daughter would be vegetarian. Maxine Hong Kingston suggests this in describing her welcome home: "My parents killed a chicken and steamed it whole, as if they were welcoming home a son, but I had gotten out of the habit of meat." She ate rice and vegetables instead.[7]

To destabilize patriarchal consumption, eat rice have faith in women. By doing so we release Metis, and all who have been swallowed, from the belly of Zeus; we restore wholeness to our fragmented relationships with each other and the other animals. The question before us is, which images of the universe, of power, of animals, of ourselves, will we represent in our food? Of that which has preceded us, what shall remain?

Eat Rice Have Faith in Women. Our dietary choices reflect and reinforce our cosmology, our politics. It is as though we could say, "Eating rice *is* faith in women."

On this grace may we all feed.

NOTES

Epigraph: Erik H. Erikson, *Gandhi's Truth: On the Origins of Militant Nonviolence* (New York: W. W. Norton & Co. Inc., 1969), p. 142. (Sexist language has been changed.)

1. See for instance Joseph Campbell's use of Géza Róheim's statement that "whatever is killed becomes father" to explain "the rites of the paleolithic hunters in connection with the killing and eating of their totem beasts." Joseph Campbell, *The Masks of God: Volume I Primitive Mythology* (New York: The Viking Press, 1959, New York: Penguin Books, 1978), pp. 77, 129.

2. This is a paraphrase of a question posed by Rynn Berry, Jr., in his book *The Vegetarians* (Brookline, MA: Autumn Press, 1979), p. 83.

3. Kate Millet, *Sexual Politics* (Garden City, NY: Doubleday & Co., 1970), pp. 25, 23.

4. Virginia Woolf, *Jacob's Room* (Hogarth Press, 1922, Hammondsworth, England: Penguin Books, 1971), p. 9.

5. Campbell, *The Masks of God*, pp. 129, 137. Sexist language has been changed.

6. Virginia de Araújo, "The Friend . . .," *Sinister Wisdom* no. 20 (1982), p. 17.

7. Maxine Hong Kingston, *The Woman Warrior: Memoirs of a Girlhood Among Ghosts* (New York: Alfred A. Knopf, 1977), p. 34.

PART V

ECOTHEOLOGY IN AN AGE OF ENVIRONMENTAL CRISIS

Spiritual Deep Ecology

Love animals, God has given them the rudiments of thought and joy untroubled. Do not trouble their joy, don't harass them, don't deprive them of their happiness.

—Fyodor Dostoyevsky

The deep ecology sense of self-realization goes beyond the modern Western sense of "self" as an isolated ego striving for hedonistic gratification.... Self, in this sense, is experienced as integrated with the whole of nature.

—Bill Devall and George Sessions

Familiarity with basic ecology will permanently change your world view. You will never again regard plants, microorganisms, and animals (including people) as isolated entities. Instead you will see them—more accurately—as parts of a vast complex of natural machinery—as, in the dictionary definition, "related elements in a system that operates in a definable manner."

—Paul Ehrlich

Being rock, being gas, being mist, being Mind,

Being the mesons traveling among the galaxies with the speed of light,

You have come here, my beloved one . . .

You have manifested yourself as trees, as grass, as butterflies, as single-celled beings, and as chrysanthemums;

but the eyes with which you looked at me this morning tell me you have never died.

—Thich Nhat Hanh

Deep ecology is both an orientation within environmental ethics and a spiritually based rethinking of human identity. The term was first used by environmental philosopher Arne Naess to signal the view that nature has value in its own right, and is not simply an instrument to meet human needs.

For deep ecology people's "selves" are not bounded solely by individuality or social group, but partly constituted by our connections to and at times identity with the natural world. In this regard, spiritual deep ecology echoes religious perspectives that ask us to "love our neighbor as ourselves," or that deny the essential reality of the isolated ego. Here, however, the expansion of identity has to do with connections to the nonhuman. As Joanna Macy writes in *World as Lover, World as Self*:

> In our infancy as a species, we felt no separation from the natural world around us. Trees, rocks, and plants surrounded us with a living presence as intimate and pulsing as our own bodies. . . . Now . . . having gained distance and sophistication of perception, we can turn and recognize who we have been all along . . . we are our world knowing itself.

The selections which follow express a variety of deep ecological perspectives. In a piece written well before the term was coined, Albert Schweitzer extends Christianity into a comprehensive "reverence" for all of life. Thomas Berry, a Catholic monk cited by many as a leading teacher of deep ecology, tells a new story about humanity's place in the universe. Joanna Macy, whose perspective is rooted in Buddhism as well as deep ecology, continues here her profoundly important "despair and empowerment work"—in which she seeks to have us acknowledge both the pain and the healing power of our emotional responses to the environmental crisis. Marianne Karsh, Nik Ansell and Brian Walsh provide a scientifically oriented spiritual understanding of forests. Warwick Fox carefully explores deep ecological ways of conceiving selfhood.

The great gift of a deep ecological sensibility—whether it goes under that term or not—is to acquaint us with our most profound connections to the natural world, and to suggest a way beyond the limitations of the conventional social ego. Nevertheless, deep ecology faces some significant dilemmas. Even if we accept every deep ecological claim, that does not tell us how we should interact with the natural world in any given situation. While nature may be sacred, a person must eat to live, and must necessarily displace other parts of nature in order to dwell in a house, warm his body, feed her children and cultivate the land. To live is to use and be used. Further, is reverence for all of nature to be extended to ghetto rats and the AIDS virus? Is personal or human survival necessarily human centered rather than nature-loving?

Perhaps a deep ecological point of view can simply ask us to question carefully before we consume and displace; and to experience our utilization of nature as a sacred exchange rather than as casual consumption in a cosmic shopping mall.

"THE FAWN"

Edna St. Vincent Millay

There it was I saw what I shall never forget
And never retrieve.
Monstrous and beautiful to human eyes, hard to believe,
He lay, yet there he lay,
Asleep on the moss, his head on his polished cleft small ebony hooves,
The child of the doe, the dappled child of the deer.

Surely his mother had never said, "Lie here
Till I return," so spotty and plain to see
On the green moss lay he.
His eyes had opened; he considered me.
I would have given more than I care to say
To thrifty ears, might I have had him for my friend
One moment only of that forest day:

Might I have had the acceptance, not the love
Of those clear eyes;
Might I have been for him the bough above
Or the root beneath his forest bed,
A part of the forest, seen without surprise.

Was it alarm, or was it the wind of my fear lest he depart
That jerked him to his jointy knees,
And sent him crashing off, leaping and stumbling
On his new legs, between the stems of the white trees?

"MAN AND CREATURE"

Albert Schweitzer

The ethics of reverence for life makes no distinction between higher and lower, more precious and less precious lives. It has good reasons for this omission. For what are we doing, when we establish hard and fast gradations in value between living organisms, but judging them in relation to ourselves, by whether they seem to stand closer to us or farther from us. This is a wholly subjective standard. How can we know what importance other living organisms have in themselves and in terms of the universe?

In making such distinctions, we are apt to decide that there are forms of life which are worthless and may be stamped out without its mattering at all. This category may include anything from insects to primitive peoples, depending on circumstances.

To the truly ethical man, all life is sacred, including forms of life that from the human point of view may seem to be lower than ours. He makes distinctions only from case to case, and under pressure of necessity, when he is forced to decide which life he will sacrifice in order to preserve other lives. In thus deciding from case to case, he is aware that he is proceeding subjectively and arbitrarily, and that he is accountable for the lives thus sacrificed.

The man who is guided by the ethics of reverence for life stamps out life only from inescapable necessity, never from thoughtlessness. He seizes every occasion to feel the happiness of helping living things and shielding them from suffering and annihilation.

Whenever we harm any form of life, we must be clear about whether it was really necessary to do so. We must not go beyond the truly unavoidable harm, not even in seemingly insignificant matters. The farmer who mows down a thousand flowers in his meadow, in order to feed his cows, should be on guard, as he turns homeward, not to decapitate some flower by the roadside, just by way of thoughtlessly passing the time. For then he sins against life without being under the compulsion of necessity.

Those who carry out scientific experiments with animals, in order to apply the knowledge gained to the alleviation of human ills, should never reassure themselves with the generality that their cruel acts serve a useful purpose. In each individual case they must ask themselves whether there is a real necessity for imposing such a sacrifice upon a living creature. They must try to reduce the suffering insofar as they are able. It is inexcusable for a scientific institution to omit anesthesia in order to save time and trouble. It is horrible to subject animals to torment merely in order to demonstrate to students phenomena that are already familiar.

The very fact that animals, by the pain they endure in experiments, contribute so much to suffering humanity, should forge a new and unique kind of solidarity between them and us. For that reason alone it is incumbent upon each and every one of us to do all possible good to nonhuman life.

When we help an insect out of a difficulty, we are only trying to compensate for man's ever-renewed sins against other creatures. Wherever animals are impressed into the service of man, every one of us should be mindful of the toll we are exacting. We cannot stand idly by and see an animal subjected to unnecessary harshness or deliberate mistreatment. We cannot say it is not our business to interfere. On the contrary, it is our duty to intervene in the animal's behalf.

No one may close his eyes and pretend that the suffering that he does not see has not occurred. We must not take the burden of our responsibility lightly. When abuse of animals is widespread, when the bellowing of thirsty animals in cattle cars is heard and ignored, when cruelty still prevails in many slaughterhouses, when animals are clumsily and painfully butchered in our kitchens, when brutish people inflict unimaginable torments upon animals and when some animals are exposed to the cruel games of children, all of us share in the guilt.

As the housewife who has scrubbed the floor sees to it that the door is shut, so that the dog does not come in and undo all her work with his muddy paws, so religious and philosophical thinkers have gone to some pains to see that no animals enter and upset their systems of ethics.

It would seem as if Descartes, with his theory that animals have no souls and are mere machines which only seem to feel pain, had bewitched all of modern philosophy. Philosophy has totally evaded the problem of man's conduct toward other organisms. We might say that philosophy has played a piano of which a whole series of keys were considered untouchable.

To the universal ethics of reverence for life, pity for animals, so often smilingly dismissed as sentimentality, becomes a mandate no thinking person can escape.

The time will come when public opinion will no longer tolerate amusements based on the mistreatment and killing of animals. The time will come, but when? When will we reach the point that hunting, the pleasure in killing animals for sport, will be regarded as a mental aberration? When will all the killing that necessity imposes upon us be undertaken with sorrow?

Albert Schweitzer   409

"INTO THE FUTURE"

Thomas Berry

Since the appearance of *Silent Spring* by Rachel Carson in 1962 we have been reflecting on the tragic consequences of the plundering industrial society that we have brought into existence during these past few centuries. That we should have caused such damage to the entire functioning of the planet Earth in all its major biosystems is obviously the consequence of a deep cultural pathology.

Just as clearly there is need for a deep cultural therapy if we are to proceed into the future with some assurance that we will not continue in this pathology or lapse into the same pathology at a later date. We still do not have such a critique of the past or a therapy for the present. Yet even without such evaluation of our present situation we must proceed with the task of creating a viable future for ourselves and for the entire planetary process.

The two things needed to guide our judgment and to sustain the psychic energies required for the task are a certain terror at what is happening at present, and a fascination with the future that is available to us if only we respond creatively to the urgencies of the present.

I am concerned in this chapter with the second of these requirements. I wish especially to outline the conditions for entering onto a future that will lead to that wonderful fulfillment for which the entire planet as well as ourselves seems to be destined.

The first condition for achieving this objective is to realize that the universe is a communion of subjects, not a collection of objects. The devastation of the planet can be seen as a direct consequence of a loss of this capacity for human presence to the nonhuman world. This reached its most decisive moment in the seventeenth-century proposal of René Descartes that the universe is composed simply of "mind and mechanism." In this single stroke he, in a sense, killed the planet and all its living creatures with the exception of the human.

The thousandfold voices of the natural world suddenly became inaudible to the human. The mountains and rivers and the wind and the sea all became mute insofar as humans were concerned. The forests were no longer the abode of an infinite number of spirit presences but were simply so many board feet of timber to be "harvested" as objects to be used for human benefit. Animals were no longer the companions of humans in the single community of existence. They were denied not only their inherent dignity, but even their rights to habitat.

As we recover our awareness of the universe as a communion of subjects a new interior experience awakens within the human. The barriers disappear. An enlargement of soul takes place. The excitement evoked by all natural phenomena is renewed. Dawn and sunset are once again transforming experiences as are all the sights and sounds and scents and tastes and the feel of the natural world about us, the surging sea, the sound of the wind, the brooding forests. All this could be continued in a never-ending listing of the experiences that take place constantly throughout the planet, experiences that have been lost to large segments of the human community in recent centuries—not because the phenomena do not surround us constantly, but that we have become autistic, as though large segments of the human mind have become paralyzed. It is no wonder that humans have devastated the planet so extensively. It was only a collection of objects to be used.

Associated with this attitude is the loss of realization that the planet Earth is a onetime endowment. It came into being at a moment that will never occur again. It was given a structure and a quantum of energy for its self-shaping processes whereby it could bring forth all those remarkable geological formations and all those magnificent modes of life expression that we see about us. The Earth was caught up in an inner dynamism that is overwhelming in its impact on human consciousness. These energies have been functioning throughout these past millennia with remarkable genius in a sequence of transformations on this planet that will never take place again. The quantum of energy needed has been expended. Species that we wantonly extinguish will never appear again. The quantum of energy involved in their historical existence has been expended.

There does exist at present a quantum of energy available for a creative movement from the terminal Cenozoic era to the emergent Ecozoic. Yet it will be available only for a brief period of time. Such transformation moments arise in times of crisis that need resolution immediately. So with the present the time for action is passing. The devastation increases. Yet the time is limited. The Great Work remains to be done. This is not a situation that can be remedied by trivial or painless means. A largeness of vision and a supreme dedication are needed.

Our only hope for such a renewal is our awakening to the realization that the Earth is primary and that humans are derivative. That this relation should be so obvious and yet so consistently violated is beyond all understanding. This primacy of the Earth community applies to every mode of human activity: economics, education, law, medicine, religion. The human is a subsystem of the Earth system. The primary concern in every phase of human activity must be to preserve the integrity of the Earth system. Only then can the subsystems function with any efficacy. Yet no phase of human activity is so directly violated as this relation of the human to the Earth.

In the realm of jurisprudence, the English Common Law tradition that has claimed such superiority in its conceptions of the human and the dignity of the human, has little sense of the larger governing principles of the universe or of the planet. This tradition lays great emphasis on the rights of humans. In this context the nonhuman world has become property to be used by the human. A governance and a jurisprudence founded in the supremacy of the already-existing Earth governance is needed. An interspecies jurisprudence is needed. The primary community is not the human community but the Earth community. The primary obligations are to the success of this larger community.

Especially in religion the human depends on the natural system. For it is the wonder and majesty of the universe that evokes the sense of the divine and the sensitivity to the sacred. For the universe is a mysterious reality. We can know only the marginal aspects of how the universe or the Earth functions. Once the divine is perceived through written Scriptures there is then a tendency to exclude the evidences of the natural world of things, for these, it is thought, do not communicate the sense of the sacred except in some minor way. Yet we can never replace our need for a resplendent natural world if we are to respond effectively to the exaltation of the divine or our sense of the sacred.

Since the discovery of the universe as an evolutionary process there is the need to establish a new sense of the revelatory experience. That this new mode of experiencing the universe carries with it a new modality in the manifestation of the ultimate mysteries of the universe implies that future generations will need to be religious within this context. Our traditional Scriptures will probably not be effective in awakening future generations to a sense of the sacred as they have done in past generations. This will involve a serious process of adaptation, a new awakening to the divine not only through the awesome qualities of the universe as experienced immediately, but also through the immense story of the universe and its long series of transformations.

We also need to establish rituals for celebrating these transformation moments that have enabled the universe and the planet Earth to develop over the past many years. This would involve celebrating the primordial moment of emergence of the universe and such other transformation moments as the supernova collapse of the first generation of stars whereby the ninety-some elements needed for life and consciousness came into existence. We should especially celebrate that star out of which our own solar system was born and the various life forms of Earth became possible.

The discovery of sexual reproduction upon which the evolutionary process depends so directly, the discovery of photosynthesis, of respiration, the emergence of life out of the sea and its venturing onto the land, the appearance of the first trees, the first flowering plants, the transition to the Cenozoic period, the emergence of the human—all these are sacred moments. To celebrate these occasions would renew our sense of the sacred character of the universe and of the planet Earth.

Another condition for entering a viable relationship of the human with the Earth community is a realization that the planet Earth will never again function in the future in the manner that it has functioned in the past. A decisive transformation has taken place, for

Thomas Berry

whereas the human had nothing to say in the emergent period of the universe prior to the present, in the future the human will be involved in almost everything that happens. We have passed over a threshold. While we cannot make a blade of grass, there is liable not to be a blade of grass in the future unless it is accepted, protected, and fostered by the human. Sometimes, too, there is a healing that can be brought about by human assistance.

Just now our modern world with its scientific technologies, its industrial processes, and its commercial establishments functions with amazing arrogance in our human attitude toward the natural world. The assumption is that the human is the supreme reality and that every other being is available for exploitation in the service of the human. The supreme law of economics is to take as much as possible of the Earth's resources to be processed, passed through the consumer economy as quickly as possible, and then deposited as residue on the waste heap. The greater amount of natural resources consumed in this manner, the greater the Gross Domestic Product or the Gross Human Product, the more successful the human enterprise is thought to be, although the final consequence of such an economic program is to turn the entire planet into a wasteland. Any sense of the sacred, any restraints in favor of the inner coherence and resplendence of the natural world, these are thought of as the expression of an unendurable romanticism.

Yet the planet now exists in a more intricate relation with the human than ever before. The very devastation wrought by the human has brought about a new type of violence in human-Earth relationships. Yet this apparent control by the human does not imply that the human can, as it were, run the planet or bring the planet into any context that the human wishes. The human can bring about extinction on a broad scale, but it cannot bring about life through its own power. It can only assist in some limited way in evoking life through the processes inherent in the Earth itself.

The ultimate goal of any renewal process must be to establish a "mutually enhancing mode of human presence on the Earth." While this mutual enhancement can be achieved only within limits, since the human, as every other being, in some manner places stress upon the larger process, it is something that can make the gains and the losses more proportional and more acceptable within the larger context of the planetary community.

What can be hoped for is a sense of the human joining in the larger liturgy of the universe itself. The very cosmological patterns of universe-functioning that were established in much earlier times can be considered as a primordial liturgy. This liturgy inherent in the ancient mystique of the Earth and its functioning might be established once again—this time, however, not simply in the traditional sequence of seasonal renewal, but also in the sequence of irreversible transformations that can now be identified as the larger story of the planetary process.

This story of the universe now becomes the basic context for education. This comprehensive context includes all education, from the earliest period of schooling through to professional schools. The story of the universe expresses a functional cosmology that needs to be taught at every level of training. To be educated is to know the story and the human role in the story. Through this story we come to know the manner whereby we ourselves came into being and the role that we should be fulfilling in the story. Because our capacity to tell this story in its full dimensions in space and in its sequence of transformations in time is only recently attained, we are only now beginning to understand its significance.

Through this story we can now guide our way through this transition phase of our history, from the terminal Cenozoic into the emerging Ecozoic. This emergent phase of Earth history can be defined as that period when humans would be present to the Earth in a mutually enhancing manner. This story evokes not only the guidance but also the psychic energy needed to carry out the sequence of transformations that is now required of us as we move into the future.

Throughout its vast extent in space and its long sequence of transformations in time the universe constitutes a single, multiform, sequential, celebratory event. Every being in the universe is intimately present to and influencing every other being in the universe. Every being contributes to the magnificence of the whole. Because the universe is the only self-referent mode of being in the phenomenal world it constitutes the norm of all reality and value. The universe is the only text without context. Every particular mode of being is universe-referent and its meaning is established only within this comprehensive setting. This is the reason why this story of the universe, and especially of the planet Earth, is so all-important. Through our understanding of this story our own role in the story is revealed. In this revelation lies our way into the future.

FAITH, POWER, AND ECOLOGY

Joanna Macy

Yesterday morning at this time I was standing for about an hour in the sweet, gentle, English drizzle. I was in a large meadow with about forty men and women; three of them held toddlers. We stood in a circle and at the center of the circle were two ancient, sacred standing stones. We had come there at the close of a five-day workshop on ecology, and our band included activists from all over the island—social workers, civil servants, artisans, teachers, homemakers—drawn together by a common concern for the fate of our planet.

In the presence of those stones, thousands of years old, we seemed to find ourselves in two dimensions of time simultaneously. One was vast and immeasurable. As we tried to reach back to the ancient Earth wisdom of the culture that erected the stones, we sensed the long, long journey of the unfolding of life on this planet. At the same time, given the focus of the workshop, we were acutely aware of this particular historical moment when forces our culture has unleashed seem to be destroying our world.

Among us were Christians, Jews, Buddhists, Pagans. Yet, despite the differing belief systems to which we belonged, the prayers and affirmations that spontaneously arose in that circle expressed a common faith and fueled a common hope. They bespoke a shared commitment to engage in actions and changes in lifestyle on behalf of our Earth and its beings. They expressed a bonding to this Earth, where we go beyond feeling sorry for the Earth or scared for ourselves, to experience relationship—relationship that can be spiritually as well as physically sustaining, a relationship that can empower.

Fresh from that experience, it seems fitting to address the issue of faith and ecology. Faith is an elusive and questionable commodity in these days of a dying culture. Where do you find it? If you've lost a faith, can you invent one? Which faith to choose? Some of us have retained a faith in a just creator God or in a lawful, benevolent order to the universe. But some of us find it hard, even obscene, to believe in an abiding providence in a world of such absurdity as ours where, in the face of unimaginable suffering, most of our wealth and wits are devoted to preparing a final holocaust. And we don't need nuclear bombs for our holocaust, it is going on right now in the demolition of the great rainforests and in the toxic contamination of our seas, soil, and air.

Reprinted from *World as Lover, World as Self* by Joanna Macy (1991) with permission of Parallax Press, Berkeley, CA.

Faith, in a world like this? The very notion can appear distasteful, especially when we frequently see faith used as an excuse for denial and inaction. "God won't let it happen." Or even, as we hear in some circles today, "It may be God's will," a fearful assertion indeed when it refers to nuclear war itself, seen as the final just and holy battle to exterminate the wicked. The radical uncertainties of our time breed distortions of faith, where fundamentalist beliefs foster self-righteousness and deep divisions, turning patriotism into xenophobia, inciting fear and hatred of dissenters, and feeding the engines of war. If we are allergic to faith, it is with some reason.

Another option opens, however, that can lead to a more profound and authentic form of faith. We can turn from the search for personal salvation or some metaphysical haven and look instead to our actual experience. When we simply attend to what we see, feel, and know is happening to our world, we find authenticity. Going down into a darkness where there appears to be no faith, we can make three important discoveries. I see them as redeeming discoveries that can ground us in our ecology and serve as our faith; and I believe that our survival depends on our making them. These three are: (1) the discovery of what we know and feel, (2) the discovery of what we are, and (3) the discovery of what can happen through us or, as one might express it, grace.

DISCOVERING WHAT WE KNOW AND FEEL

To discover what we know and feel is not as easy as it sounds, because a great deal of effort in contemporary society is devoted to keeping us from being honest. Entire industries are focused on maintaining the illusion that we are happy, or on the verge of being happy as soon as we buy this toothpaste or that deodorant or that political candidate. It is not in the self-perceived interests of the state, the multinational corporations, or the media that serve them both, that we should stop and become aware of our profound anguish with the way things are.

None of us, in our hearts, is free of sorrow for the suffering of other beings. None of us is indifferent to the dangers that threaten our planet's people, or free of fear for the generations to come. Yet when we are enjoined to "keep smiling," "be sociable," and "keep a stiff upper lip," it is not easy to give credence to this anguish.

Suppression of our natural responses to actual or impending disaster is part of the disease of our time, as Robert Jay Lifton, the American psychiatrist who pioneered the study of the psychological effects of nuclear bombs, explains. The refusal to acknowledge or experience these responses produces a profound and dangerous splitting. It divorces our mental calculations from our intuitive, emotional, and biological imbeddedness in the matrix of life. That split allows us passively to acquiesce in the preparations for our own demise.

Joel Kovel, a psychiatrist teaching at Albert Einstein College, says that we are kept subservient and passive by "the state of nuclear terror." This terror is not the fear of nuclear weapons and other means of mass annihilation so much as our fear of experiencing the fear that we might break apart or get stuck in despair if we open our eyes to the dangers. So the messages we tend to hear or give are: "Don't talk to me about acid rain, or the arms race. There is nothing I can do about it. I have a family to support, a job to keep. If I were to take it all in and allow myself to think about it and to *feel* it, I wouldn't be able to function."

The first discovery, opening to what we know and feel, takes courage. Like Gandhi's *satyagraha,* it involves "truth-force." People are not going to find their truth-force or inner authority in listening to the experts, but in listening to themselves, for everyone in her or his way is an expert on what it is like to live on an endangered planet. To help this happen and counter habits of suppression, Interhelp, an international network, has evolved methods and workshops for people to come together to find their own inner authority. Without mincing words, without apology, embarrassment, or fear of causing distress, participants find they can simply tell the truth about their experience of this world. A boy talks about the dead fish in a stream he loves; a young couple wonders about the Strontium 90 in the bones of their children.

Justin Kenrick, an Interhelper in Great Britain, has said:

> We need permission in our minds and hearts and guts to accept that we are destroying the Earth and to feel the reality of who we are in that context; isolated, desperate, and powerless individuals, defeated by our old patterns of behavior before we have even begun to try to heal our lives and the Earth. Only then can we give ourselves permission to feel the power our culture denies us, to regain our intuitive sense of everything being in relation rather than in opposition, to regain our intuitive sense of the deep miraculous pattern to life that opens to us as we accept it.

When we come to the authority of what we know and feel, when we acknowledge our pain for the world, we remember the original meaning of *compassion,* "to suffer with." Suffering with our world, we are drawn now into the cauldron of compassion. It is there; it awaits us; and as Kenrick's words suggest, it can reconnect us with our power.

DISCOVERING WHAT WE ARE

Acknowledging the depths and reaches of our own inner experience, we come to the second discovery: the discovery of what we are. We are experiencers of compassion. Buddhism has a term for that kind of being—it is *bodhisattva.* The bodhisattva is the Buddhist model for heroic behavior. Knowing there is no such thing as private salvation, she or he does not hold aloof from this suffering world or try to escape from it. It is a question rather of returning again and again to work on behalf of all beings, because the bodhisattva knows there is no healing or transformation without connection.

The *sutras,* or scriptures, tell us that we are all bodhisattvas, and our fundamental interconnections are portrayed in the beautiful image of the Jeweled Net of Indra. It is similar to the holographic model of the universe we find emerging from contemporary science. In the cosmic canopy of Indra's Net, each of us, each jewel at each node of the net, reflects all the others and reflects the others reflecting back. That is what we find when we listen to the sounds of the Earth crying within us—that the tears that arise are not ours alone; they are the tears of an Iraqi mother looking for her children in the rubble; they are the tears of a Navajo uranium miner learning that he is dying of lung cancer. We find we are interwoven threads in the intricate tapestry of life, its deep ecology.

What happens for us then is what every major religion has sought to offer—a shift in identification, a shift from the isolated "I" to a new, vaster sense of what we are. This is understandable not only as a spiritual experience, but also, in scientific terms, as an evolutionary development. As living forms evolve on this planet, we move not only in the direction of diversification, but toward integration as well. Indeed, these two movements complement and enhance each other. Open systems self-organize and integrate by virtue of their differentiation, and, vice-versa, they differentiate by virtue of their interactions. As we evolved we progressively shed our shells, our armor, our separate encasements; we grew soft, sensitive, vulnerable protuberances, like eyes, lips, and fingertips, to better connect and receive information, to better know and interweave our knowings. If we are all bodhisattvas, it is because that thrust to connect, that capacity to integrate with and through each other, is our true nature.

In his book *Ecology and Man,* Paul Shepard writes: "We are hidden from ourselves by patterns of perception. Our thought forms, our language, encourage us to see ourselves or a plant or an animal as an isolated sac, a thing, a contained self, whereas the epidermis of the skin is ecologically like a pond surface or a forest soil, not a shell so much as a delicate interpenetration." Paul Shepard is calling us to a faith in our very biology. He goes on to say, "Affirmation of its own organic essence will be the ultimate test of the human mind."

We begin to see that a shift of identification can release us not only from the prison cell of ego, but also from the tight compartment of a solely human perspective. As John Seed, Director of the Rainforest Information Center in Australia, points out, it takes us "beyond anthropocentrism." In his essay by that title, he says that anthropocentrism or human chauvinism is similar to sexism, but substitute "human race" for man and "all other species" for woman. And he says,

> When humans investigate and see through their layers of anthropocentric self-cherishing, a most profound change in consciousness begins to take place. Alienation subsides. The human is no longer an outsider apart. Your humanness is then recognized as being merely the most recent stage of your existence; as you stop identifying exclusively with this chapter, you start to get in touch with yourself as vertebrate, as mammal, as species only recently emerged from the rainforest. As the fog of amnesia disperses, there is a transformation in your relationship to other species and in your commitment to them ... The thousands of years of imagined separation are over and we can begin to recall our true nature; that is, the change is a spiritual one—thinking like a mountain, sometimes referred to as deep ecology.

As your memory improves ... there is an identification with all life ... Remember our childhood as rocks, as lava? Rocks contain the potentiality to weave themselves into such stuff as this. We are the rocks dancing.

BEING ACTED THROUGH

That leads us to the third discovery we can make in our ecological *Pilgrim's Progress:* the discovery of what can happen through us. If we are the rocks dancing, then that which evolved us from those rocks carries us forward now and sustains us in our work for the continuance of life.

When I admired a nurse for her strength and devotion in keeping long hours in the children's ward, she shrugged off my compliment as if it were entirely misplaced. "It's not *my* strength, you know. I get it from them," she said, nodding at the rows of cots and cribs. "They give me what I need to keep going." Whether tending a garden or cooking in a soup kitchen, there is the sense sometimes of being sustained by something beyond one's own individual power, a sense of being acted "through." It is close to the religious concept of grace, but distinct from the traditional Western understanding of grace, as it does not require belief in God or a supernatural agency. One simply finds oneself empowered to act on behalf of other beings—or on behalf of the larger whole—and the empowerment itself seems to come "through" that or those for whose sake one acts. This phenomenon, when approached from the perspective of ecology, can be understood as synergy. This is an important point because it leads us to reconceptualize our very notion of what power is.

From the ecological perspective, all open systems—be they cells or organisms, cedars or swamps—are seen to be self-organizing. They don't require any external or superior agency to regulate them, any more than your liver or your apple tree needs to be told how to function. In other words, order is implicit in life; it is integral to life processes. This contrasts with the hierarchical worldview our culture held for centuries, where mind is set above nature and where order is assumed to be something imposed from above on otherwise random, material stuff. We have tended to define power in the same way, seeing it as imposed from above. So we have equated power with domination, with one thing exerting its will over another. It becomes a zero-sum, or win-lose, game, where to be powerful means to resist the demands or influences of another, and strong defenses are necessary to maintain one's advantage.

In falling into this way of thinking, we lost sight of the fact that this is not the way nature works. Living systems evolve in complexity, flexibility, and intelligence through interaction with each other. These interactions require openness and vulnerability in order to process the flow-through of energy and information. They bring into play new responses and new possibilities not previously present, increasing the capacity to effect change. This interdependent release of fresh potential is called synergy. It is like grace, because it brings an increase of power beyond one's own capacity as a separate entity.

THE POWER TO CONNECT

I see the operation of this kind of grace or synergy everywhere I go. For example, I see it in the network of citizens that has sprung up along the tracks of the "white train" that carries the nuclear warheads from the Pantex plant in Amarillo, Texas, up to the Trident base in the northwest on Puget Sound and across the south to the Charleston Naval Base on the Atlantic. Sitting up late at night to watch the tracks they telephone to alert each other that the train is coming their way; then these ordinary citizens come out of their homes, to stand by the railroad line and vigil with lighted candles or, on occasion, put their bodies on the tracks to stop the train. Even though this network is scattered across thousands of miles and relatively few of its members have met face to face, it calls itself now the Agape community; for these people have learned to feel each other's presence and support. And the tracks that bear the weapons for the ultimate war have become arteries interconnecting people and eliciting new dimensions of caring and courage.

I see this grace in the Sanctuary movement, where local churches and groups give protective asylum to refugees from the U.S.-supported violence in Central America. In January 1985, the FBI, in an effort to break the movement, which then included 105 centers, brought a number of its members to court and some were jailed. Although the local citizens who participated in decisions to grant sanctuary are largely law-abiding people—middle-aged, middle-class, respected and respectable—the FBI crackdown discouraged few of them. A year and a half later, the number of groups offering protection to Central American refugees, against the will of the Administration, had doubled.

The members of a small Quaker Meeting I know near Philadelphia hesitated to take this step, because they feared they might not be numerous enough or strong enough to provide the constant care and vigilance that is required when you adopt an illegal alien. But, inspired by similar actions elsewhere, they took the risk and granted sanctuary to a young Salvadoran woman. When I visited them a year later, Paz was still with them and the membership of the Meeting itself had become far larger and more active than ever before. By risking action together, action that made them more vulnerable, their power had increased.

There are countless such innovative grassroots actions; they do not make headlines, but taken all together, they amount to an unprecedented silent explosion of people who are quietly putting the interests of the planet ahead of their personal profit or pleasure. I see it in the growing number of citizens who are refusing to pay taxes for weapons of war; I see it in the thousands of Americans who have been paying their own way to the USSR, simply to connect with their Soviet counterparts so they might begin to know and comprehend each other firsthand. I see it in the bands of eco-warriors who risk their lives to protect marine mammals, and old-growth forests. I see it among the Vietnam veterans who fasted publicly to protest America's undeclared war on Nicaragua, and among the many other veterans across the

United States who rallied to support them. As they do this, they expand our understanding of patriotism, demonstrating that love for one's country does not have to exclude the other beings of our planet.

These people show us what can happen through us when we break free of the old hierarchical notions of power. They show that grace happens when we act with others on behalf of our world.

ROOTS OF POWER

What can we do to nourish these efforts and strengthen the bodhisattva in ourselves? Two ways that I know are community and practice.

The liberation struggles in Latin America and the Philippines have demonstrated the efficacy of spiritually-based communities for nonviolent action. These tough networks of trust arise on the neighborhood level, as people strive together to understand, in their own terms and for their own situation, what they need to do to live without fear and injustice. These groups need be neither residential nor elite, just ordinary people meeting regularly in a discipline of honest searching and mutual commitment.

In our own society, too, such communities have been arising in the form of local support and action groups. Here neighbors or co-workers, parents or professionals organize and meet regularly to support each other in action—be it in responding to the poisons leaching from a nearby dump or to the need for a peace curriculum in the local school. Those of us who participate in such "base communities" know that they enhance both personal integrity and our belief in what is possible.

In addition to such external support, we need, in this time of great challenge and change, the internal support of personal practice. I mean practice in the venerable spiritual sense of fortifying the mind and schooling its attitudes. Because for generations we have been conditioned by the mechanistic, anthropocentric assumptions of our mainstream culture, intellectual assent to an ecological vision of life is not enough to change our perceptions and behaviors. To help us disidentify from narrow notions of the self and experience our interexistence with all beings in the web of life, we turn to regular personal practices that range from meditation to the recycling of our trash.

Spiritual exercises for cultivating reverence for life arise now out of many traditions and are welcomed by people regardless of their religious affiliation. I have found adaptations from Buddhist practices particularly helpful because they are grounded in the recognition of the dependent co-arising or deep ecology of all things. Similarly, Native American prayers and ritual forms, evoking our innate capacity to know and live our Earth, are increasingly adapted and included in gatherings for work and worship.

This is a prayer from the Laguna Pueblo people:

I add my breath to your breath
that our days may be long on the Earth,
That the days of our people may be long,
that we shall be as one person,
that we may finish our road together.

Joanna Macy

TREES, FORESTRY, AND THE RESPONSIVENESS OF CREATION

Brian J. Walsh
Marianne B. Karsh
Nik Ansell

In *Crossing the Postmodern Divide,* Albert Borgmann contrasts his own version of postmodern realism with the epistemological despair of postmodernity. He claims that the "postmodern theorists have discredited ethnocentrism and logocentrism so zealously that they have failed to see their own anthropocentrism. Why reject a priori the very possibility that things may speak to us in their own right?"[1] What Borgmann intends by "postmodern realism" is not the naive and aggressive realism of modernity, but, rather, an attending to what he terms "the eloquence of reality." Aggressive realism has silenced creation: "Rivers are muted when they are dammed; prairies are silenced when they are stripped for coal; mountains become torpid when they are logged."[2] Nor has the postmodern concern for hearing the voice of the other been extended to the nonhuman other. Yet without such a hearing, there can be no response to the other's cry and no learning from the other's wisdom.

What follows is our exploration into hearing the voices of creation. We will begin with a short discussion of what Thomas Berry has described as our "cultural autism."[3] Why are we unable to "hear" the voices of creation, and what is necessary for us to be able to hear again? Then we will strive to listen to one particular kind of creature—the tree. We choose trees from the myriad of possibilities because one of us, Marianne Karsh, is a forester. Can we listen to trees, and through new paradigms in forestry and tree biology facilitate such a listening?

TREES AS THOU

Descartes summed up the modern spirit well when he said that the goal of its devotees was to become nothing less than "the masters and possessors of nature."[4] Mastery and posssession, however, require a silencing of the other. If we allow the other to speak to us, if we allow ourselves to hear the cry of the other, we can no longer continue our oppressive

Reprinted from *Cross Currents: A Journal of Religion and Intellectual Life*, Summer 1994, Vol. 44, No. 2, pp. 149–62 by permission of *Cross Currents*.

mastery. What is true in human affairs is also true in the context of the broader ecosphere.

Many of us first began instinctively to realize that there was something profoundly wrong with modernity's objectification of reality when we read Martin Buber's *I and Thou.*[5] We received this enigmatic book of poetic and relational epistemology as a wonderful liberation from the constricting categories of the rationalistically oriented philosophy and scientistic ethos that have dominated Western culture and scholarship. Although Buber's wise Jewish philosophy took us beyond the limiting overemphasis on I-It relationships in both society and the academy, there was a problem with Buber. When he suggested very early in the text that we could enter into an I-Thou relationship with a tree, many of us waved off the statement as some sort of weird Hasidic mysticism:

> I contemplate a tree.... I can feel it as movement: the flowing veins around the sturdy, striving core, the sucking of the roots, the breathing of the leaves, the infinite commerce with earth and air.... I can assign to it a species and observe it as an instance, with an eye to its construction and its way of life.... I can overcome its uniqueness and form so rigorously that I recognize it only as an expression of the law.... I can dissolve it into a number, into a pure relation between numbers, and eternalize it.

Further reflecting on this process of contemplation, Buber noted that "throughout all of this the tree remains my object and has its place and its time span, its kind and condition." Then he wrote words that many of us could not hear, or would not listen to:

> But it can also happen, if will and grace are joined, that as I contemplate the tree I am drawn into a relation, and the tree ceases to be an It.

For Buber, if something ceased to be an It, it thereby must have become a Thou. An I-Thou relationship with a tree! We may have been weary of much of Western rationalism but to give up on our culture's anthropocentric bias—its assumption that creatures such as trees were mere biotic objects that could be observed, analyzed, and acted upon—was more than many of us were willing to do. To use Buber's terms, "grace and will" have, by and large, not been "joined." We have not been drawn into such a relationship with trees.

The problem was that even though Buber insisted that such a relation does not require us to forego other modes of contemplation, he nonetheless clearly said that we "should not try to dilute the meaning of the relation: relation is reciprocity."[6] And, of course, this means that if we did enter into I-Thou relations with trees, doing so would not be a romanticist projection of relatedness, but a conviction that in some important way trees reciprocate the relationship; that not only do we relate to trees, but they also relate to us. This was not a welcome prospect for those of us raised in the context of an Enlightenment worldview.

Now, however, the worldview that presupposed an objectified nature has run its disastrous course and we are open to a different way of relating, a different way of life, beyond the

Brian J. Walsh / Marianne B. Karsh / Nik Ansell

subject/object dualism, beyond the I-It relationship. As we have come to see the profound truth that, "in the beginning is the relation,"[7] we have realized that relation entails reciprocity. Recognizing the dead end of an anthropology of the autonomous and imperial ego[8] and convinced that in the context of the present ecological brokenness we must strive anew for contact, for reciprocity—and that our striving must aim at what Buber called "tenderness"[9]—we find ourselves revisiting Buber's I-Thou relationship with trees. We want to *listen* to Buber again. Even more, we want to learn to *listen* to the trees.

Wanting to listen, however, does not mean that we *can* listen. By construing nature as deaf and dumb, we have made ourselves deaf and dumb in relation to that nature. This construal, this social construction, constricts our imagination and closes us to precisely the reciprocal relationship that we now seek.[10] We also find our imaginations held captive by a mechanistic worldview that makes it impossible to access profound resources of our own traditions that may open up such relationships. We refer to the Hebrew and Christian Scriptures.

DISENCHANTING THE BIBLICAL TRADITION

Buber's language of I-Thou relationships with trees sounds alien, perhaps even infantile, to modernist ears. So does the aboriginal language of kinship and communication with trees and other creatures.[11] To the degree that we are unable to countenance this language, however, we also find ourselves alienated from much of the biblical tradition. While not all Christians embraced Bultmann's demythologizing project earlier in this century, almost all Western Christians have been influenced by the demythologizing and disenchanting tendencies of post-Enlightenment scientism in their relation to nonhuman creatures, thereby alienating themselves from the Scriptures and engaging in a *de facto* act of demythologization. We can take trees as our example.

When trees are referred to as part of God's good creation (e.g., Gen. 1 or Ps. 104), or are spoken of symbolically as in "the tree of life" (Gen. 2:9, 3:22, 24; Prov. 3:18, 11:30, 13:12, 15:4; Rev. 22:2, 14), and "the tree of the knowledge of good and evil" (Gen. 2:9, 3:3), Christians of various persuasions have little interpretive difficulty. And while the way that Jesus relates to a certain fig tree might be somewhat puzzling for us (Mk. 11:12–14, 20–25), his frequent use of trees in his parables and teachings presents no problem. What becomes almost impossible for our modern Western minds is language that refers to trees exercising some form of agency not unlike the kind of agency that can be noted in aboriginal worldviews.

All of creation is portrayed as engaging in acts of groaning in Romans 8:22–23, and in many psalms all of creation is called upon to sing praise. As Jesus tells the Pharisees during the entry into Jerusalem that if his disciples' loud hosannas are silenced even "the stones will cry out" (Lk. 19:40), so also does David sing during the festivities surrounding the return of the ark of the covenant: "The trees of the forest will sing, they will sing for joy before the

Lord, for he comes to judge the earth" (1 Chron. 16:33). This connection between the trees singing and judgment is also found in Ps. 96:12–13:

> Then all the trees of the forest will sing for joy;
> they will sing before the Lord, for he comes,
> he comes to judge the earth.
> He will judge the world in righteousness
> and the peoples in his truth.

While prophetic literature speaks of forests being destroyed as part of the judgment upon a particular nation (cf. Is. 10:18–19; Jer. 7:20; 20:45ff), an even more common theme appears to be the place of trees in prophecies of restoration. Ezekiel's *covenant of peace* envisions creational harmony and mutual responsiveness as trees of the field joyously yield their crop (34:27; 36:30). And Isaiah's vision of the wilderness blossoming includes the growth of cedar, acacia, myrtle, olive, pine, fir, and cypress trees (41:19):

> You will go out in joy
> and be led forth in peace;
> the mountains and hills
> will burst into song before you,
> and all the trees of the field
> will clap their hands.
> Instead of the thornbush will grow
> the pine tree,
> and instead of briers the myrtle will grow.
> This will be for the Lord's renown,
> for an everlasting sign,
> which will not be destroyed. (Is. 55:12–13)

This kind of language, so creative in providing a biblical foundation for theological reflection in our context of ecological crisis, is also somewhat problematic. That trees have a place in God's restorative plan is not itself surprising, given the depth of creation theology that the Scriptures display. Nor should we be surprised that language of judgment is good news for trees since the whole created order has been, in the words of Walter Brueggemann, "terribly skewed and scarred by injustice"; God's judgment refers "to God's action of intervention to look after the rightful claims of the weak ones who have no power to make their own claim or look after themselves."[12]

Trees are among the weak ones. But what are we to make of the language that attributes agency to trees? What does this language about trees singing praise and clapping their hands mean? We are not, of course, appealing to a naive literalism in the biblical text; we know full well the meaning and use of metaphor. We modern readers must be careful, however, not to use metaphor as a way of distancing ourselves, in these instances, not only from the biblical text but also from trees themselves. If we speak of metaphor only as a way of saying that trees don't "really" sing praise, but rather that we, in moments of religious ecstasy, imaginatively attribute such activities to trees, we keep trees and humans in an I-It relationship; our attitude remains hopelessly anthropocentric. Our question here is, in what manner is it appropriate to use such metaphors in relation to trees, or, for that matter, in relation to other nonhuman creatures? We suggest that the metaphors are appropriate only if they are disclosing real dimensions of these creatures' subjectivity. Of course trees don't have hands, but it does make sense to speak of hands metaphorically in relation to trees, since trees do, in fact, in their own fashion, respond to their Creator, both with deep groans of longing and pain and with songs of praise. If we are to learn from our own scriptural tradition then we will need to learn how to listen to the trees and to respond to them appropriately. We need the ears to hear the "eloquence" of these creatures. Perhaps only then will we be able to hear the Scriptures anew.

TREES AS RESPONSIVE

As responsive creatures, trees display a high level of cooperation with other life forms, going beyond what is necessary or expected. Take, for example, the association between trees and fungus. It may be adequately explained as a biological evolutionary adaptation, but it is intriguing that "although both the trees and the fungus benefit from the association that forms, the trees can live without the fungus and the fungus without the tree."[13] Moreover, not every group of trees forms these associations. They appear to be optional; their sole purpose appears to be only to better the growth of one another. "The fungus assists the green plant in absorbing nitrogen and phosphorus and in return receives some of the plant's surplus carbohydrates."[14] Further, the fungi not only form associations with trees in their immediate vicinity but, like the vast train systems in Europe, they run for hundreds of miles, interconnecting with other trees and amassing large pockets of nutrients at various junctions. As Lewis Thomas comments:

> The most inventive and novel of all schemes in nature, and perhaps the most significant in determining the great landmark events in evolution, is symbiosis, which is simply cooperative behavior carried to its extreme. But something vaguely resembling symbiosis, less committed and more ephemeral, a sort of wish to join up, pervades the biosphere.[15]

Such a wish, we suggest, is indicative of a responsiveness, perhaps even of will.

Secondly, trees as responsive creatures display a remarkable ability to survive and adapt in spite of impossible circumstances. Who can but marvel that trees in our cities manage to survive in conditions of intense noise, vibration, pollution, and high dosages of salt. They have also been patient of and adaptable to other ways in which we have systematically mistreated them. We are now coming to realize that we have been wrongfully pruning trees for about as long as arboriculturists have been in existence. The treatments given to help trees have followed too closely the treatments given to people—"cover the wound with a dressing, cut deep into the wood and clean the cavity, stimulate healing by stimulating callus, prune trees by cutting branches flush to the stem. . . ."[16]

The problem is that all of these techniques cause the trees' most distinctive defense system to break down while the tree is still alive—the analogy to AIDS comes to mind. Yet the trees have adapted even to this mistreatment. Their strong survival capacity inspires wonder in us. Could it be that trees have a type of intentionality that we have previously not discerned?

Thirdly, trees display qualities totally inexplicable if considered solely from a mechanistic, nonresponsive viewpoint. For example, a mechanical model could lead us reasonably to expect that tree growth could be predicted accurately and that foresters could create an "ideo-type" or model tree. The fact that foresters cannot do this and that trees of the same species growing in the same soil, climate, and spacing conditions seem to respond individually to the same stimuli suggests that there is something else in trees—a selfhood, or subjectivity, or a factor "x"—contributing to their infinite variability.

Variability of tree growth is an established fact. Oddly enough, the more productive a site, the greater the variability and the greater the error in prediction, a great frustration to foresters who prefer conformity and standardization. The diversity of trees is especially apparent when one formulates concepts of quality which require identifying all the characteristics that produce a model tree. Researchers have long been struggling to define the illusive concept of "seedling quality" because, in spite of all our expertise in growing seedlings, we still cannot identify the factors in a young tree that will produce a healthy surviving adult.[17] To assess seedling quality, there is a need to incorporate, along with genetics and background data, an "x" factor (call it "will" or "motivation") whose existence would be difficult to prove. Yet, since trees do exhibit different rates of responsiveness that cannot be measured mechanistically, it seems valid to hypothesize an "x" factor.

Fourthly, trees as responsive creatures affirm life, an adaptation especially apparent where acid rain is a problem. In acidic conditions trees begin to show symptoms from the top down or from the outer extremities inward, suggesting that the tree maintains the core and roots in order to preserve its life for as long as possible. Even in the most extreme of acidic conditions (such as the fog-covered mountains of Germany) conifer trees will bear a huge cone crop in the last year of life.[18] There is no apparent biological reason for this except that a cone crop ensures that a seed source will survive in case conditions get better. It should be noted that cone production in trees depends on a lot of factors, including tree age and growing conditions. Cone production may also be cyclical, with a cone crop occurring every seven years or so. Further, it takes a special channeling of energy within the tree

Brian J. Walsh / Marianne B. Karsh / Nik Ansell

to grow a reproductive structure; in these areas where concentrated acid mists and fogs cover trees for most of the growing season, every last ounce of the tree's last bit of energy goes into producing a cone crop. Why? In these conditions, a cone crop would seem to be a wasteful use of the tree's energy. However, as the proponents of the nonmechanistic worldview tell us, nature is not wasteful. Perhaps the cone crop is a sign of hope. In symbolic terms this tree behavior says, "We believe in God's redemptive covenant to us, do you?" Even more interestingly, a proportion of trees do not produce a cone crop and die rather quickly. Perhaps they were under more stress than the others (no one has done research on this), or maybe they just did not have the same "will to live." It remains to be explained why trees under similar acidic conditions respond differently, some not only affirming life, but seeming to do so individually, thereby suggesting some form of individual agency.

FORESTRY AND THE FUTURE

The conclusion that trees are "responsive agents" challenges traditional forestry with something amounting to a paradigm change. Although forestry has moved from an era of exploitive extraction to various types of forest management, trees are still treated as indifferent and distant objects. Practicing foresters are governed today by inventory philosophies which perpetuate the idea that a little data collected everywhere will provide a sound basis for forest management. It will not. Moreover certain forestry practices lack credibility. For example, to put data into classes and simply to move the classes forward for the next twenty-year period so that foresters can have a normally distributed forest "makes sense economically but not biologically."[19] Paul Hawken's general comments about contemporary shifts in science need to be heeded in forestry:

> The new scientific paradigm is a bright blossom in a world dominated by the technology of the old, a science which treated life as mechanical, where living organisms responded to fixed laws which man discovered and applied. Unwillingness in the plant world to completely cooperate has always been met with new technologies, new ways to assert dominance over a life form which we approached as one to subjugate and control.[20]

A new approach is needed—an approach of listening and involvement.

Such involvement with plants characterized the work of Barbara McClintock, who was awarded a Nobel prize for her discoveries in gene transposition work with corn plants. She views the corn plant as "a unique individual," "as a mysterious other," and "as a kindred subject." This "kindred subjectivity" is a "special kind of attention that most of us experience only in relation to other persons"; as J. B. McDaniel explains, corn plants to McClintock "are distant, perhaps very distant cousins: strange but lovable kin."[21]

Similarly A. L. Shigo, states that, "the only way to get common sense about trees is to give them your attention, touch them, and watch them grow, wane and die."[22] For John Muir, whose special gift was listening to plants (he sat down beside an unfamiliar plant for a minute a day to hear what it had to tell), "listening included analytical scrutiny from his botanical training, along with sensitivity to the plant's environmental relationships. Muir's listening to a plant also involved cultivating empathy—that intuitive projection by which we imagine the character of another. Together these techniques create the kind of understanding we hope for in human relationships: recognition of another's living integrity."[23] Of trees he said, "I could distinctly hear the varying tones of individual trees—Spruce, and Fir, and Pine, and leafless Oak. Each was expressing itself in its own way—singing its own song, and making its own particular gestures. . . ."[24]

This kind of listening to the individuality and responsiveness of trees opens forestry up to a broader data base and it provides a perspective, an orientation, a worldview, through which to interpret that data. The responsiveness of trees to acid rain, for example, combined with global warming, now becomes relative data for forestry and calls forth new modes of interpretation.

Will the forestry of the future emerge as large-scale agriculture on a smaller land base, as some foresters fear, or will it become something else? *If will and grace be joined,* the new forestry will be characterized by a relationship of listening and communion.[25] Neither a naive preservationism nor a distanced objective management, it will be a stewardship of care that attends to trees in all their rich and nuanced diversity, variability, and individuality. Instead of reducing trees to economic objects that can be explained from a distance through quantifying measurements, the new forestry, rooted in "kindred subjectivity," will attempt to understand trees as eloquent others who have wisdom to impart.

Trees have been telling us that monocultural planting of trees with an eye only to profit is neither economically productive nor ecologically sound. They have been telling us, too, that deforestation will contribute to global warming. Charles Birch and John Cobb note that in tropical Africa, "the forest teaches diversity, the constant cover over the soil, and sustainability," and the people who are listening have been "achieving a natural control of pests and freedom from fertilizers."[26] Universally, trees are saying, "View us as gift, tend us, and keep us healthy." We ignore their impassioned cries at the risk not only of the sustainability of the ecosystem, but also at the risk of losing our own souls in the morass of I-It relationships.

TREES AS AGENTS

But this raises another question. What kind of claim are we making when we say, with Buber, that we can enter into I-Thou relationships with trees? Is our claim that trees are responsive creatures a scientific claim? We have appealed to the scientific evidence in forestry concerning the survival capacities, adaptivity, cooperation, variability, diversity, and individuality of trees to point to something which suggests a responsiveness, volition, or motivation in trees; it points us as well to a position which discerns agency in trees.

Nonetheless, our claim that trees are responsive creatures who have things to say to us is not, at its foundation, scientific. Rather, this claim functions for us prescientifically as part of the tacit dimension of our knowing, part of the conceptual, or even preconceptual framework that we bring to our scientific and theological reflection.[27] Following Michael Polanyi's contention that tacit knowing is both profoundly personal and an indispensable foundation of all knowing, we happily confess that we begin with a deep conviction concerning the meaningfulness of metaphors that portray trees clapping their hands, groaning, singing, or praising. This conviction functions in our thought, we must confess, as something which is argued from, not argued to. Indeed, it is the nature of such convictions that they cannot be successfully and conclusively argued to; scientific and theoretic argument meets its limitations when it comes to such convictions.[28] One vision of life reduces trees to a mechanistic notion of biotic functioning. Another sees only their value as economic resources. Our foundational worldview perceives them as creatures responding to their Creator-God.[29]

The orientation of one's limit convictions will give paradigmatic direction to one's science. Intuition, humility, feeling, connectedness, and relatedness become key words. If trees are responsive creatures, they will need to be respected in their responsiveness, with all of their individuality and variability. While traditional forestry attempts to overcome such individuality in order better to control the forest, the new forestry will respect variability and difference. Epistemologically this kind of science functions as "an invitation to engagement with nature,"[30] an engagement that calls for nothing less than a love for the subject "that allows an intimacy without the annihilation of difference." And such intimacy requires "a lifetime of cultivated attentiveness."[31]

The limit convictions that give rise to such science are formed in multidimensional ways. Our conviction that we need to rehear what trees are saying to us has been formed through the grief of seeing trees mistreated, the joy of a walk in the forest, the evocative wonder of listening to native stories, the shame of our oppression and exploitation of trees, the scientific inadequacy of older models of forestry and biology, the creative excitement generated by a science of connectedness, and personal momentary hearings of the trees' voices. For the authors of this article, the biblical witness has also been influential in our attempts to heed Buber's call to I-Thou relationships with trees. The model that we present is formed by all of these influences. But it is to the distinctiveness of the biblical tradition and its contrast to a more typically modern and Western worldview that we finally turn.

MUTUALITY WITH CREATION

Both the very nature of trees *qua* trees and the present ecological crisis require us to relate to trees in a way which goes beyond economic or even ecological self-interest. We need to go beyond notions of dutiful stewardship of resources to a relationship of coresponsiveness, intimacy, communion, mutuality, fellowship, and love with the trees themselves. A tree is not "merely an object in our world of experience but also a subject of relations in its own right. It is acted upon and it acts."[32] Only through a subject/subject relationship with trees can true understanding be achieved: an I-Thou relationship is both the heuristic foundation and epistemological goal of authentic science.

If trees function as responsive subjects capable of I-Thou relationships, then we need to find some way to talk meaningfully about trees possessing agency. To have agency is to have will, volition, intentionality, and selfhood. This means that an agent's behavior is not mechanistically determined but contingently directed by the agent's will. Trees do not merely react, but act on and interact with us, other creatures, and, we would contend, God.

The business of agency remains the central stumbling block to being able to embrace Buber's vision. How can trees have agency in the way in which we have been speaking of it here? To begin to answer this question requires that we be clear about what we mean by the exercise of agency. Does agency require that the agent be able to exercise some sort of *will?* This would appear to be the case. But if we confine our understanding of "will" to rational decision-making, it becomes ridiculous to speak of creatures that lack higher intellectual capabilities as exercising such will. This has been perhaps the greatest stumbling block to perceiving agency in plant life. The problem is that this is a false stumbling block. Human agency and will cannot be understood primarily in terms of rational decision-making. We are multidimensional creatures and our intellectual capabilities are but one factor in the exercise of our wills: an intellectualistic conception of will cannot adjudicate the claims of our volition, let alone those of nonhuman creation.

To say, as the Bible does, that trees praise, sing, clap, and rejoice is to say that trees, *as trees,* in their whole physical, chemical, spatial, biotic functioning can fully respond to their Creator when that functioning is uninhibited and free. To say that trees groan is to say that trees experience and respond to conditions of human abuse or neglect that inhibits and closes down their responsiveness. In this way, metaphors of praising and groaning enable us to "hear" what the trees have to "say."

But metaphors do not just disclose and identify the meaning of tree-responsiveness— they also are, in their own way, productive of reality. Metaphors are world-formative, they engage in world-construction. The metaphor of trees clapping their hands, for example, functions in the world-constructing activity of people who employ it in a way drastically different from that in which the metaphor of trees as economic resources (or "timber") functions for

Brian J. Walsh / Marianne B. Karsh / Nik Ansell

other people.[33] The metaphors we use mediate the worldviews by which we live; they function, therefore, both as visions *of* the world (or interpretive frameworks) and as visions *for* the world (providing an orientation for cultural and ecological praxis).[34]

"Hearing" trees through appropriate metaphors and allowing those metaphors to have a world-constructing role in our lives calls forth a response to what the trees are saying and what kind of world our metaphors envision. To hear the groaning of the trees is to be called by the trees to participate in that groaning. To hear the trees praise is to be invited to join in that creational liturgy. Such hearing also calls us to acts of stewardly empowerment. When trees groan they ask us to take away that which inhibits their praise. We are called to be partners with the trees in the coming shalom of God's creation. We suggest that such a partnership is what Buber envisaged with his I-Thou relationship with a tree—an eloquent creature in a responsive creation.

NOTES

1. Albert Borgmann, *Crossing the Postmodern Divide* (Chicago: University of Chicago Press, 1992), 117. See also his article, "Texts and Things," in Timothy Casey and Lester Embree, eds., *Lifeworld and Technology* (Washington, D.C.: University Press of America, 1990), 93–116.

2. Ibid., 118–19.

3. Thomas Berry, *The Dream of the Earth* (San Francisco: Sierra Club Books, 1988), chap. 3.

4. From his *Discourse on Method,* chap. 6. See *Essential Works of Descartes,* trans. Lowell Bair (New York: Bantam, 1961), 37.

5. Martin Buber, *I and Thou,* trans. Walter Kaufmann (New York: Charles Scribner's Sons, 1970).

6. Ibid. All of these quotes can be found on pp. 57–58.

7. Ibid., 69.

8. Buber notes that "the basic word I-It is made possible only by . . . the detachment of the I" (p. 73).

9. Ibid., 79.

10. On the construal of nature see Neil Evernden, *The Social Creation of Nature* (Baltimore: Johns Hopkins University Press, 1992); and Roderick Nash, *Wilderness and the American Mind,* 3d ed. (New Haven: Yale University Press, 1967, 1982).

11. Buber knew well that I-Thou relationships were not problematic for native peoples (see pp. 69–73). For a sampling of aboriginal approaches to nature see David Young, Grant Ingram, and Lise Swartz's fine study of the work of medicine man Russell Willier: *Cry of the Eagle: Encounters with a Cree Healer* (Toronto: University of Toronto Press, 1989); Thomas W. Overholt and J. Baird Callicott, *Clothed in Fur and Other Tales: An Introduction to an Ojibwa Worldview* (Washington, D.C.: University Press of America, 1982); James Redsky, *Great Leader of the Ojibway: Mis-quona-queb* (Toronto: McLelland and Stewart, 1972); and James R. Stevens, ed., *Legends of the Forest: Told by Chief Thomas Fiddler* (Moonbeam, Ont.: Penumbra Press, 1985).

12. Walter Brueggemann, *The Message of the Psalms: A Theological Commentary,* Augsburg Old Testament Studies (Minneapolis: Augsburg, 1984), 145.

13. Roger B. Swain, *Earthly Pleasures: Tales from a Biologist's Garden* (Markham, Ont.: Penguin, 1981), 134.

14. Ibid., 132.

15. Lewis Thomas, *The Fragile Species* (New York: Macmillan Publishing, 1992), 140.

16. Ibid., 502, 511.

17. The matter of seedling quality is addressed at greater length in an unpublished paper by Marianne Karsh, "How to Assess Seedling Stock Quality" (University of Toronto Faculty of Forestry, 1988).

18. These observations were pointed out by researchers at a Forest Decline Conference, Toronto, 1987.

19. Don MacIver, *Jack Pine Growth Model: A Brief Progress Report* (Ontario Ministry of Natural Resources, 1985), 16.

20. Paul Hawken, *The Magic of Findhorn* (New York: Harper and Row, 1975), 118–19.

21. Jay McDaniel, *Of God and Pelicans: A Theology of Reverence for Life* (Louisville: Westminster/John Knox Press, 1989), 86–87. All the quotes in this paragraph are from this book.

22. Alex Shigo, *A New Tree Biology: Facts, Photos, and Philosophies on Trees and Their Problems and Proper Care* (Durham: Shigo and Trees Associates, 1986), 51.

23. Richard Austin, *Baptized into Wilderness: A Christian Perspective on John Muir* (Atlanta: John Knox Press, 1987), 17.

24. Cited by Austin, ibid., 29.

25. We employ the phrase "new forestry" in full awareness of the movement that goes by that name. The New Forestry movement is attempting to foster a forestry practice that is rooted in a concern for ecological wholeness. Our project attempts to do the same thing but pushes the issues one step further to engender a "listening forestry." Indeed, only if there is such listening, we suggest, will ecological wholeness be attainable. On the New Forestry see Chris Maser, *The Redesigned Forest* (San Pedro, Calif.: R. and E. Miles, 1989).

26. C. Birch and J. B. Cobb, *The Liberation of Life: From the Cell to the Community* (Cambridge: Cambridge University Press, 1981), 305.

27. See Michael Polanyi, *The Tacit Dimension* (Garden City, N.Y.: Doubleday, 1966).

28. See Langdon Gilkey, *Religion and the Scientific Future: Reflections on Science, Myth and Theology* (New York: Harper and Row, 1970), chaps. 2 and 3. An excellent discussion of contemporary philosophies of science that corroborates the position taken here is found in Clarence Joldersma, "Beliefs and Scientific Enterprise: A Framework Model Based Upon Kuhn's Paradigms, Polanyi's Commitment Framework, and Radnitzky's Internal Steering Fields," unpublished M.Phil. thesis, Toronto: Institute for Christian Studies, 1982.

29. Brian Walsh (with Richard Middleton) has discussed worldviews at greater length in *The Transforming Vision: Shaping a Christian World View* (Downers Grove, Ill.: InterVarsity Press, 1984); and "Worldviews, Modernity and the Task of Christian College Education," *Faculty Dialogue* 18 (Fall 1992): 13–35.

30. Evelyn Fox Keller, *Reflections on Gender and Science* (New Haven: Yale University Press, 1985), 163. The context of Keller's comments is a discussion of Barbara McClintock.

31. Ibid., 164. Keller goes on to make the methodological observation that "questions asked about objects with which one feels kinship are likely to differ from questions asked about objects one sees as unalterably alien" (167). Also instructive are Douglas John Hall's comments about an "ontology of communion" and "being-with" in

Imaging God: Dominion as Stewardship (New York and Grand Rapids: Friendship Press and Eerdmans, 1986), chaps. 5–6.

32. Birch and Cobb, *The Liberation of Life: From the Cell to the Community,* 123.

33. Indeed, Walter Brueggemann notes that "world-creation also includes world-delegitimation of other worlds." *Israel's Praise: Doxology Against Idolatry and Ideology* (Philadelphia: Fortress, 1988), 27.

34. See James H. Olthuis, "On Worldviews," *Christian Scholar's Review* 14, no. 2 (1985): 153–64.

"TRANSPERSONAL ECOLOGY AND THE VARIETIES OF IDENTIFICATION"

Warwick Fox

THREE BASES OF IDENTIFICATION

How does one realize, in a this-worldly sense, as expansive a sense of self as possible? The transpersonal ecology answer is: through the process of identification. As Naess says: "The ecological self of a person is that with which this person identifies. This key sentence (rather than definition) about the self, shifts the burden of clarification from the term 'self' to that of 'identification,' or rather 'process of identification.'"[1] "How, then, does one proceed in realizing a way of being that sustains the widest and deepest possible identification? I suggest that there are three general kinds of bases for the experience of commonality that we refer to as identification; three general kinds of ways in which we may come to identify more widely and deeply. I refer to these bases of identification as *personal, ontological,* and *cosmological.*

Personally based identification refers to experiences of commonality with other entities that are brought about through personal involvement with these entities. This is the way in which most of us think of the process of identification most of the time. We generally tend to identify most with those entities with which we are often in contact (assuming our experiences of these entities are of a generally positive kind). This applies not only to concrete entities (e.g., the members of our family, our friends and more distant relations, our pets, our homes, our teddy bear or doll) but also to those more abstract kinds of entities with which we have considerable personal involvement (our football or basketball club, the individual members of which may change from year to year; our country). We experience these entities as part of "us," as part of our identity. An assault upon their integrity is an assault upon our integrity.

In contrast to personally based identification, ontologically and cosmologically based forms of identification are transpersonal in that they are not primarily a function of the personal contacts or relationships of this or that particular person. There is, of course, a sense in which *all* forms of identification beyond one's egoic, biographical, or personal sense of self can be described as *transpersonal.* However, the point here is that personally based identifica-

Reprinted from *Towards a Transpersonal Ecology* by Warwick Fox by permission of the State University of New York Press, and Green Books Ltd., Devon, England.

tion is, as its name suggests, a far more personal—or, alternatively, a far less *trans*personal—form of identification than either ontologically or cosmologically based identification, since it is a function of the personal contacts or relationships of this or that particular person, whereas, as we shall see below, the latter two forms of identification are not.

Ontologically based identification refers to experiences of commonality with all that is that are brought about through deep-seated realization of the fact *that* things are. (I am using the complex and variously employed term *ontology* in this context to refer to the fact of existence per se rather than to refer to the question of what the basic aspects of existence are or how the world is.) This is not a simple idea to communicate in words! Moreover, I do not intend to say very much about this idea since, in my view, it properly belongs to the realm of the training of consciousness (or perception) that is associated, for example, with Zen Buddhism, and those who engage in such training continually warn about the limits of language in attempting to communicate their experientially based insights. Martin Heidegger is a notable Western philospher who does attempt to convey such insights in words, but then, although deeply rewarding, he is also notorious for the difficulty of his language. It is interesting to note in this connection, however, that upon reading a book by the Zen master D. T. Suzuki, Heidegger is reported to have said, "If I understand this man correctly, this is what I have been trying to say in all my writings."[2]

The basic idea that I am attempting to communicate by referring to ontologically based identification is that the fact—the utterly astonishing fact—that things *are* impresses itself upon some people in such a profound way that all that exists seems to stand out as foreground from a background of nonexistence, voidness, or emptiness—a background from which this foreground arises moment by moment. This sense of the specialness or privileged nature of all that exists means that "the environment" or "the world at large" is experienced not as a mere backdrop against which our privileged egos and those entities with which they are most concerned play themselves out, but rather as just as much an expression of the manifesting of Being (i.e., of existence per se) as we ourselves are. We have perhaps all experienced this state of being, this sense of commonality with all that is simply by virtue of the fact *that* it is, at certain moments. Things *are!* There is something rather than nothing! Amazing! If we draw upon this experience we can then gain some insight into why it is that people who experience the world in this way on a regular or semi-regular basis (typically as the result of arduous spiritual discipline) find themselves tending to experience a deep but impartial sense of identification with *all* existents. We can gain some insight into why such people find themselves spontaneously inclined "to be open for the Being [the sheer manifesting] of [particular] beings" and, hence, why, for them, "the best course of 'action' is to let beings be, to let them take care of themselves in accord with their own natures."[3]

For those who cannot see any logical connection between deep-seated realization of the fact that things *are* and the experience of deep-seated commonality with—and thus respect for—all that is, I can only reiterate that these remarks cannot and should not be analyzed through a logical lens. We are here in the realm of what Wittgenstein referred to as the mystical when he said, "It is not *how* things are in the world that is mystical, but *that* it exists."[4] If one seriously wishes to pursue the question of ontologically based identification then one must be prepared to undertake arduous practice of the kind that is associated with certain kinds of experientially based spiritual disciplines. (Roger Walsh captures what is of central interest about these disciplines in this context by referring to them as *consciousness disciplines* in order to distinguish them "from the religious dogma, beliefs, and cosmologies to which most religious devotees adhere, and from the occult popularisms of both East and West."[5] Those who are not prepared to do this—that is, most of us—are no more in a position to dismiss the fruits of such practice than are people who would dismiss the fruits of scientific research without being prepared to undertake the training that is necessary to become a scientist or at least to understand the general features of scientific procedure.[6]

Cosmologically based identification refers to experiences of commonality with all that is that are brought about through deep-seated realization of the fact that we and all other entities are aspects of a single unfolding reality. This realization can be brought about through the empathic incorporation of *any* cosmology (i.e., any fairly comprehensive account of *how* the world is) that sees the world as a single unfolding process—as a "unity in process," to employ Theodore Roszak's splendid phrase.[7] This means that this realization can be brought about through the empathic incorporation of mythological, religious, speculative philosophical, or scientific cosmologies.[8] I am not meaning to assert by this that these various kinds of accounts of how the world is are equal in epistemological status, only that each is *capable* of provoking a deep-seated realization that we and all other entities are aspects of a single unfolding reality. Consider, for example, the world-views of certain indigenous peoples (e.g., of some North American Indians), the philosophy of Taoism, or the philosophy of Spinoza.

For many people in the modern world the most viable—perhaps the only truly viable—source of cosmological ideas is science. Yet, despite this, there are many other people (including many who are formally trained in science or who simply have a general interest in science) who seem unable or unwilling to see science in a cosmological light. For them, science is all about prediction, manipulation, and control ("instrumental rationality") and cosmology is seen as something that belongs to mythology, religion, or speculative philosophy, or else as a highly specialized sub-discipline of physics that deals with the evolution and structure of the physical universe. But the anthropocentrically fueled idea that science is all about prediction, manipulation, and control is only half the story. As George Sessions says, "Modern science . . . [has] turned out to be a two-edged sword."[9] The other side of science is its importance for understanding our place in the larger scheme of things (and it is scarcely necessary to add that this aspect has had profoundly *non*anthropocentric implications). This side of science is its cosmological aspect. Considered from this side, modern science can be seen as providing an account of creation that is the equal of any mythological, religious, or speculative philosophical account in terms of scale, grandeur, and richness of detail. More specifically, modern science is providing an increasingly detailed account of the physical and biological evolution of the universe that compels us to view reality as a single unfolding process.[10]

The most obvious feature of the physical and biological evolution of the universe as revealed by modern science is the fact that it has become increasingly differentiated over time. This applies not just at the level of biological evolution but also at the level of the physical evolution of the cosmos. If we think of this process of increasing differentiation over time diagrammatically then it is natural to depict it as a branching tree. Indeed, this is precisely the way in which evolutionary theorists think of biological evolution.[11] In general terms, ancestral species do not change *into* newer species; rather, newer species radiate out (branch away) from ancestral species, which can continue to exist alongside the newer species. This "budding off" process occurs when populations of a particular kind of organism become in any way reproductively isolated (e.g., through geographical divergence or through divergence in breeding seasons) and then undergo changes in their genetic composition, primarily as a result of natural selection, to the point where members of one population are no longer capable of interbreeding with members of the other population.[12] But it is not only phylogenetic development (the evolution of species) that must be depicted as a continually branching tree. The image of a branching tree is just as relevant to other forms of development that involve increasing differentiation over time, whether it be ontogenetic development (the evolution of individual organisms from a cell to maturity) or the evolution of the universe itself from *nothing* to its present state some fifteen billion years later.[13] As the science writer Stephen Young explains in a brief recent introduction to the importance of the tree metaphor in science generally: "Trees are indispensable to science. From physics to physiology, they serve as metaphors, expressing in a word details that would otherwise occupy a paragraph.... The theory of evolution is unthinkable without trees. Elsewhere within science, afforestation continues apace. If trees did not exist, scientists would have to invent them."[14]

Even if our present views on cosmological evolution (including phylogenetic and ontogenetic evolution) turn out to stand in need of modification in crucial respects, we still have every reason to believe that the particular views that supersede these views will be entirely in conformity with the far more general idea that all entities in the universe are aspects of a single unfolding reality that has become increasingly differentiated over time. The justification for such confidence lies not only in the fact that *all* the evidence that bears on this question across *all* scientific disciplines points in this general direction, but also in the fact that even the most radical scientific (i.e., empirically testable) challenges to our present scientific views also point in this general direction. What is at issue in scientifically framed debates about the evolution of the universe or the evolution of life is only the question of the *mechanisms* of evolution (i.e., the mechanisms that underlie the increasing differentiation of the universe over time), not the fact of evolution per se.

A good illustration of this general point is provided by Rupert Sheldrake's *hypothesis of formative causation,* which constitutes a fundamental challenge to our present understanding of the development of form in ontogenetic, phylogenetic, and cosmological evolution.[15] Sheldrake's hypothesis suggests that the form that every entity takes is shaped by, and in turn contributes to the shaping of, a formative field—Sheldrake calls it a *morphic field*—that is associated with that particular kind of entity. Thus, the physical forms of crystals, daisies, and elephants are supposed to be influenced by the morphic fields that have been built up by earlier examples of their own kind. Even the *behavior* of organisms is supposed to be influenced by the morphic fields that have been built up by the behaviors of earlier examples of their own kind. This suggests that people who have never learned Morse code, for example, ought to learn real Morse code faster or more accurately than a comparable group of people who are asked to learn a newly created version of Morse code. In Sheldrake's view this would be expected simply because many people have previously learned the real version of Morse code, and thereby contributed to the creation of a morphic field for the learning of that code, whereas no morphic field exists for the newly created code. As it happens, this experiment has been performed and the results support Sheldrake's hypothesis.[16]

Now if Sheldrake's fascinating but presently highly controversial hypothesis turns out to be supported by a wide range of experimental findings, then this would, I think, cause the biggest revolution in biology, and in the sciences generally, since Darwin's theory of evolution by means of natural selection. But the point in this context is this: even if Sheldrake's ideas were accepted, we would still find ourselves living in an evolutionary, "branching tree" universe because, as Sheldrake explains, the idea of formative causation does not reject Darwinian evolution but rather "greatly extends Darwin's conception of natural selection to include the natural selection of morphic fields."[17] Thus, even when we consider a challenge to mainstream science that is as broad and as profound in its implications as Sheldrake's, we find, as I have already stated, that what is at issue is still only the question of the *mechanisms* that underlie evolutionary processes, not the fact of evolution per se. Evolutionary development, in other words, is the great unifying theme of modern science.[18]

If we empathically incorporate (i.e., have a lived sense of) the evolutionary, "branching tree" cosmology offered by modern science then we can think of ourselves and all other presently existing entities as leaves on this tree—a tree that has developed from a single seed of energy and that has been growing for some fifteen billion years, becoming infinitely larger and infinitely more differentiated in the process. A deep-seated realization of this cosmologically based sense of commonality with all that is leads us to identify ourselves more and more with the entire tree rather than just with our leaf (our personal, biographical self), the leaves on our twig (our family), the leaves we are in close proximity to on other twigs (our friends), the leaves on our minor sub-branch (our community), the leaves on our major sub-branch (our cultural or ethnic grouping), the leaves on our branch (our species), and so on. At the limit, cosmologically based identification, like ontologically based identification, therefore leads to impartial identification with *all* particulars (all leaves on the tree).

Having said this, it must immediately be noted that, as with ontologically based identification, the fact that cosmologically based identification tends to be more *impartial* than personally based identification does not mean that it need be any less deeply felt. Consider the Californian poet Robinson Jeffers! For Jeffers, "This whole [the universe] is *in all its parts* so beautiful, and is felt by me to be so intensely in earnest, that I am *compelled* to love it" (emphases added).[19] Although Jeffers may represent a relatively extreme exemplar of cosmologically based identification, it should nevertheless be clear that this form of identification issues at least—perhaps even primarily?—in an orientation of steadfast (as opposed to fair-weather) friendliness. Steadfast friendliness manifests itself in terms of a clear and steady expression of positive interest, liking, warmth, goodwill, and trust; a steady predisposition to help or support; and, in the context of these attributes, a willingness to be firm and to criticize constructively where appropriate. Indeed, if a particular entity or life form imposes itself unduly upon other entities or life forms, an impartially based sense of identification may lead one to feel that one has no real choice but to *oppose*—even, in extreme cases, to terminate the existence of—the destructive or oppressive entity or life form. Even here, however, an impartially based sense of identification leads one to oppose destructive or oppressive entities or life forms in as educative, least disruptive, and least vindictive a way as possible.

Over time, steadfast friendliness often comes to be experienced by the recipient as a deep form of love precisely because it does not cling or cloy but rather gives the recipient "room to move," room to be themselves. In the context of this book, it may be of particular interest to add here that Arne Naess seems to me to be an exemplar of steadfast friendliness—and of course I am not only talking here about his relationship with me over the years, but of his orientation toward the world in general. It is also interesting to note that Naess has himself written a paper on the importance of the concept of friendship in Spinoza's thinking in which he notes that "the intellectual sobriety of Spinoza favours *friendship rather than worship*" and that, for Spinoza, "friendship is the basic social relation" between members of a free society.[20] Naess concludes this paper by explicitly linking the theme of friendship in Spionza's philosophy with "the ecological concept of symbiosis as opposed to cutthroat competition." "Both in Spinoza and in the thinking of the field ecologist," says Naess, "there is respect for an extreme diversity of beings capable of living together in an intricate web of relations."[21]

Notwithstanding the eloquent testimonies to cosmologically based identification that have been offered by Spinoza, Gandhi, Jeffers, Naess, and many others (even Einstein, for example), many people find it difficult to think of identification in anything other than personally based terms. For these people, cosmologically based identification approximates to something like going out, encountering every entity in the universe (or, at least, on the planet) on a one-to-one basis, and coming to identify with each entity on the basis of that contact. But this simply represents an example of personally based identification that has been blown up into universal (or global) proportions. In contrast, cosmologically based identification means having a lived sense of an overall scheme of things such that one comes to feel a sense of commonality with all other entities (whether one happens to encounter them personally or not) in much the same way as, for example, leaves on the same tree would feel a sense of commonality with each and every other leaf if, say, we assumed that these leaves were all conscious and had a deep-seated realization of the fact that they all belonged to the same tree. In summary, then, personally based identification proceeds from the person—and those entities that are psychologically, and often physically, closest to the person—and works outward to a sense of commonality with other entities. In contrast, cosmologically based identification proceeds from a sense of the cosmos (such as that provided by the image of the tree of life) and works inward to each particular individual's sense of commonality with other entities. In vectorial terms, this contrast in approaches means that we can think of personally based identification as an "inside-out" approach and cosmologically based identification as an "outside-in" approach.

One may gain or seek to cultivate a cosmologically based sense of identification in a wide variety of ways. Even if we exclude mythological, religious, and speculative philosophical cosmologies and restrict ourselves to the cosmology of modern science, these ways of coming to embody a cosmologically based sense of identification can range from approaches such as the ritualized experientially based work being developed by John Seed and Joanna Macy under the title "Council of All Beings"[22]; to participation in theoretical scientific work (a number of the very best scientists have had a profound sense of cosmologically based identification); to more practically oriented involvement in natural history (many naturalists and field ecologists, for example, effectively come to experience themselves as leaves on the tree of life and seek to defend the unfolding of the tree in all its aspects as best they can); to simply developing a deeper personal interest in the scientific world model and in natural history along with one's other interests.

NOTES

1. Arne Naess, "Self-realization: An Ecological Approach to Being in the World," p. 35.

2. Quoted in William Barrett, "Zen for the West," in *Zen Buddhism: Selected Writings of D. T. Suzuki*, ed. William Barrett (Garden City, N.Y.: Doubleday/Anchor Books, 1956), p. xi. There is a whole literature on the similarities between Heidegger's thought and Eastern thought, especially Zen. For a guide to much of this literature, see the

papers and books listed at note 3 in Michael Zimmerman, "Heidegger and Heraclitus on Spiritual Practice," *Philosophy Today* 27 (1983): 87–103. Special mention should be made here of Zimmerman's own book on Heidegger entitled *Eclipse of the Self: The Development of Heidegger's Concept of Authenticity* (Athens: Ohio University Press, 1981), which explores the relationship between Heidegger's thought and Zen in its final section (pp. 255–76). In addition to the papers and books cited by Zimmerman in "Heidegger and Heraclitus," see the following inspirational papers by Hwa Jol Jung: "The Ecological Crisis: A Philosophic Perspective, East and West," *Bucknell Review* 20 (1972): 25–44; and "The Paradox of Man and Nature: Reflections on Man's Ecological Predicament," *The Centennial Review* 18 (1974): 1–28.

3. Michael Zimmerman, "Toward a Heideggerean Ethos for Radical Environmentalism," *Environmental Ethics* 5 (1983): 99–131, pp. 102 and 115.

4. Ludwig Wittgenstein, *Tractatus Logico-Philosophicus,* trans. D. F. Pears and B. F. McGuiness (London: Routledge and Kegan Paul, 1961), proposition 6.44.

5. Roger Walsh, "The Consciousness Disciplines and the Behavioral Sciences: Questions of Comparison and Assessment," *American Journal of Psychiatry* 137 (1980): 663–73, p. 663.

6. On this general point, see Ken Wilber's insightful essays "Eye to Eye" and "The Problem of Proof," which constitute the first two chapters of his book *Eye to Eye: The Quest for the New Paradigm* (Garden City, N.Y.: Anchor Books, 1983).

7. Theodore Roszak, *Where the Wasteland Ends: Politics and Transcendence in Postindustrial Society* (London: Faber and Faber, 1973), p. 400.

8. On the general question of the empathic incorporation of cosmologies or "world models," see Alex Comfort, *Reality and Empathy: Physics, Mind, and Science in the 21st Century* (Albany: State University of New York Press, 1984). By *empathy,* Comfort means an "incorporation going beyond intellectual assent" (p. xviii). See also Stephen Toulmin, *The Return to Cosmology: Postmodern Science and the Theology of Nature* (Berkeley: University of California Press, 1982), esp. the final chapter in which Toulmin explicitly links the cultivation of a cosmological sense of things—or what I am referring to as cosmologically based identification—with the development of "a genuine piety . . . toward creatures of other kinds: a piety that goes beyond the consideration of their usefulness to Humanity as instruments for the fulfillment of human ends" (p. 272).

9. George Sessions, "Ecocentrism and the Greens: Deep Ecology and the Environmental Task," *The Trumpeter* 5 (1988): 65–69, p. 67.

10. One could drown in the number of semi-popular and more technical books that could be cited at this point! A gentle approach might be more effective; thus, for a highly readable, comprehensive, *single* volume overview of the scientific view of the world, see Isaac Asimov's exemplary guide *Asimov's New Guide to Science,* rev. ed. (Harmondsworth, Middlesex: Penguin Books, 1987). For an excellent systems-oriented overview of the scientific view of the world, see Ervin Laszlo, *Evolution: The Grand Synthesis* (Boston: Shambhala, 1987).

11. See, for example, Richard Dawkins, *The Blind Watchmaker* (London: Penguin Books, 1988), esp. ch. 10: "The One True Tree of Life."

12. See Mark Ridley, *The Problems of Evolution* (Oxford: Oxford University Press, 1985), ch. 8: "How Can One Species Split into Two?"

13. For overviews of recent work on the origins of the physical cosmos, see Paul Davies, *God and the New Physics* (Harmondsworth, Middlesex: Penguin Books, 1984); Paul Davies, *Superforce: The Search for a Grand Unified Theory of Nature* (London: Unwin Paperbacks, 1985); John Gribbin, *In Search of the Big Bang: Quantum Physics and Cosmology* (London: Corgi Books, 1987); Alan H. Guth and Paul J. Steinhardt, "The Inflationary Universe," *Scientific American,* May 1984, pp. 90–102; Stephen W. Hawking, *A Brief History of Time: From the Big Bang to Black Holes* (New York: Bantam Books, 1988); and Heinz R. Pagels, *Perfect Symmetry: The Search for the Beginning of Time* (New York: Bantam Books, 1986).

14. Stephen Young, "Root and Branch in the Groves of Academe," *New Scientist,* 23/30 December 1989, pp. 58–61, at pp. 58 and 61.

15. Rupert Sheldrake, *A New Science of Life: The Hypothesis of Formative Causation,* 2nd ed. (London: Paladin/Grafton Books, 1987); and Rupert Sheldrake, *The Presence of the Past: Morphic Resonance and the Habits of Nature* (New York: Vintage Books, 1989).

16. Arden Mahlberg, "Evidence of Collective Memory: A Test of Sheldrake's Theory," *Journal of Analytical Psychology* 32 (1987): 23–34. Sheldrake's two books provide overviews of the experimental work that has been performed to test his hypothesis thus far. The appendix in the second edition of *A New Science of Life* also contains an overview of the controversy that greeted the original publication of his hypothesis.

17. Sheldrake, *The Presence of the Past,* p. 294.

18. See Ervin Laszlo, *Evolution: The Grand Synthesis* (Boston: Shambhala, 1987).

19. Quoted in Bill Devall and George Sessions, *Deep Ecology: Living as if Nature Mattered,* p. 101.

20. Arne Naess, "Friendship, Strength of Emotion, and Freedom," in *Spinoza Herdacht 1677–1977,* pp. 11–19, at p. 13.

21. Ibid., p. 19.

22. See John Seed, Joanna Macy, Pat Fleming, and Arne Naess, *Thinking Like a Mountain: Towards a Council of All Beings* (Santa Cruz: New Society Publishers, 1988).

PART VI

RELIGIOUS PRACTICE FOR A SACRED EARTH

In safety and in Bliss
May all creatures be of a blissful heart
Whatever breathing beings there may be
Frail or firm . . . long or small
Seen or unseen, dwelling far or near
Existing or yet seeking to exist
May all creatures be of a blissful heart.

—Sutta Nipata (Buddhist Scriptures)

Training began with children who were taught to sit still and enjoy it. They were taught to use their organs of smell, to look when there was apparently nothing to see, and to listen intently when all seemingly was quiet. A child that cannot sit still is a half-developed child.

—Standing Bear, Lakota Indian Chief

In order to serve God, one needs access to the enjoyment of the beauties of nature, such as the contemplation of flower-decorated meadows, majestic mountains, flowing rivers. For all these are essential to the spiritual development of even the holiest of people.

—Moses Maimonides

To Plant a tree is to say Yes to life:
It is to affirm our faith in the future.
To plant a tree is to acknowledge our debt to the past:
Seeds are not created out of nothing.
To plant a tree is a token of sorrow for past mistakes:
When we took life's gifts for granted.

—Reverend Francis Simons

I feed thee, Spirit of the Earth
Spirit of the Forest, of the Green Trees,
Spirit of the Forest,
Spirit of the Village Sites;
decree that the Paddy grow,
that the Fire devour.
Leading my younger brothers,
leading my elder brothers,
tomorrow, and the day after tomorrow, I will again act
in the same way.

—Prayer of the Mnong Gar, Vietnam

For many people, the heart of religious life resides not in abstract theology, but in rites and ceremonies. The repetitive nature of rituals can provide a comforting constancy in an often uncontrollable world. The symbolic material of candles or wine, special foods or familiar melodies may reach our emotional center in a way that little else does. If they have become authentic for us, religious rituals soothe our spirits or raise them to ecstasy, giving us a brief taste of the indwelling Spirit of God, Goddess or Life.

What follows here is a brief sampling of religious practices that are designed to help us honor the earth and feel the depth and sacred character of our connection to it. The content of these practices once again expresses the twofold character now indelibly stamped on the nonhuman world. On the one hand, as *nature*, the nonhuman world has an integrity, beauty and majesty that leads us to see it as a gift from God or as a Sacred Presence. On the other hand, as the *environment*, we see something threatened and polluted by human action. We feel awe as we stand before nature, but anxiety and concern as we confront the environment.

Of the practices which follow, some are taken from or are adaptations of long-established religious forms. Thich Nhat Hanh's "Earth Gathas" are meant to bring mindfulness to our everyday transactions with nature. Ellen Bernstein and Dan Fink examine traditional Jewish prayers and concepts that directly bear on our attitudes towards nature, and provide a framework to study those materials. "A Service of Worship" from the National Council of Churches and Kenneth Kraft's account of "The Greening of Buddhist Practice" are examples of how Christian prayer services and Buddhist meditation techniques express environmental concerns. The meditations by John Seed, Pat Fleming and Joanna Macy reflect a deep ecological sensibility, while Marina Lachecki has reoriented a familiar Christian practice. Finally, Black Elk's account of the Sun Dance should remind us that the spiritual practices of many indigenous peoples contain a long-established wealth of environmental wisdom.

"EARTH GATHAS"

Thich Nhat Hanh

The green Earth   (first step of the day)
is a miracle!
Walking in full awareness,
the wondrous Dharmakaya is revealed.

Water flows from the high mountains.   (turning on water)
Water runs deep in the Earth.
Miraculously, water comes to us
and sustains all life.

Water flows over my hands.   (washing hands)
May I use them skillfully
to preserve our precious planet.

As I mindfully sweep the ground of enlightenment   (sweeping)
A tree of understanding springs from the Earth.

In this plate of food,   (eating)
I see the entire universe
supporting my existence.

The mind can go in a thousand directions.   (walking)
But on this beautiful path, I walk in peace.
With each step, a gentle wind.
With each step, a flower.

Earth brings us into life and nourishes us.   (gardening)
Countless as the grains of sand
in the River Ganges,
all births and deaths are present in each breath.

Water and sun green these plants.   (watering garden)
When the rain of compassion falls
even the desert becomes an immense, green ocean.

Garbage becomes rose.   (recycling)
Rose becomes compost—

Reprinted from *Dharma Gaia: A Harvest of Essays in Buddhism and Ecology* edited by Allan Hunt Badiner (1990) with permission of Parallax Press, Berkeley, CA, USA.

Everything is in transformation.
Even permanence is impermanent.
Dear plant, do not think you are alone.   (watering plants)
This stream of water comes from Earth and sky.
This water is the Earth.
We are together for countless lives.
I entrust myself to Buddha;   (planting trees)
Buddha entrusts himself to me.
I entrust myself to Earth;
Earth entrusts herself to me.

"BLESSINGS AND PRAISE"

and

"BAL TASHCHIT"

Ellen Bernstein and Dan Fink

"BLESSINGS AND PRAISE"

INTRODUCTION

Our busy lives, our need or desire to get ahead—all of our seemingly important obligations—often pull us away from life's simple daily miracles. Staying aware of the purpose and meaning of things, remembering their interconnections and knowing that all of our actions have consequences is not easy. Yet these may be our most important tasks in becoming *shomrei adamah*. If we do not remember who we are and what our place is, the human tendency to become masters and controllers of our universe can get the better of us.

It takes practice to learn to "see" and value all of life, just as it takes practice to become a good athlete, musician, artist, doctor or student. Judaism provides us with a multitude of practices to help us remember our place in the web of nature. Our rabbis understood the human condition and the tendency toward arrogance. They provided us with a wide range of practices to keep us on track, in harmony with God's creation. Reciting *brachot* (blessings) is one such practice. *Brachot* remind us that ultimately we humans are not the ones in charge. *Brachot* remind us to stop and pay attention to the world around us at times when we might otherwise take things for granted. In this way, *brachot* can train our eyes and our minds and enrich our lives.

Objectives

- Participants will understand where *brachot* and giving thanks fit into the Jewish way of life, and how they are basic to an ecological perspective.

- Participants will have an opportunity to express their thanks for an aspect of creation.

Reprinted from *Let the Earth Teach You Torah*, 1992, with permission of the author and Shomrei Adamah.

- A loaf of bread or challah.

- Copies of Readings & Worksheets

- Paper and fine-point markers.

BLESSINGS AND PRAISE

Opening

Invite participants to say the blessing over the bread with you. Break the bread and share it.

ברוך אתה ד׳ אלקינו מלך העולם המוציא לחם מן הארץ.

Baruch Atah Adonai Eloheynu Melech Ha-olam ha-mo-tzi lehem min ha-aretz.
Praise to You *Adonai,* our God and Universal Ruler, Who brings forth bread from the earth.

Discussion Questions

- What is the purpose of *brachot*?

   Brachot *are a Jewish way of telling us to slow down and pay attention—something special is happening that we don't want to miss. Brachot can help us to know our place in the universe and to know that God has given everything a purpose (whether or not we are aware of that purpose).*

   Brachot *are a momentary pause between the awareness of an act and the act itself. From a naturalist perspective, this pause may be considered unnatural; animals do not contemplate their food before eating. In this way brachot remind us of our humanity, and the distinctions between humans and the animal world.*

   Have a volunteer read the selection from *God in Search of Man* by Abraham Joshua Heschel (see Readings & Worksheets). Rabbi Abraham Joshua Heschel was a modern theologian and important Jewish thinker who taught at the Jewish Theological Seminary. He wrote numerous books and was renowned for his work in the civil rights movement.

- Have you ever looked at *brachot* in the same way that Heschel does?

- Do you agree with Heschel? Could you imagine any change in your life if you looked differently at *brachot*?

- According to the *Talmud* (Brachot 35), "Man may not take pleasure in [or derive benefit from] any worldly thing until he has recited a blessing over it. Anyone who takes pleasure [or derives benefit] from this world without making a blessing is guilty of misappropriating sacred property [a sin punishable by death]." What does this mean?

   Everything in nature is a gift from God; it does not belong to us. If we use something of nature without thanking God, we are, in effect, stealing. Giving thanks is our way of recognizing the Creator who gave us the gift.

- Can you think of traditions similar to *brachot* in any other cultures or religions, in which giving back to the earth is considered of critical importance?

  Native American tradition: One always utters thanks when using anything from nature.

- Many people may have had the wonderful and important experience of noticing how magnificent or beautiful a tree is. Is there a difference between saying, "Oh wow, nice tree," and "Praise to You, God, who has created the trees"?

  Both are personal expressions that praise and honor the life of the tree. One uses the Jewish vehicle for praise and appreciation, but both exclamations may stem from the same intentions.

Text Study: The *Brachot*

There is a whole set of *brachot* which are less familiar to many Jews. These *brachot* are recited when a person experiences various natural phenomena.

After the Bible was written, the early rabbis interpreted and expanded upon the biblical laws. Around 200 C.E., Rabbi Judah the Prince collected all the rabbis' discussions and interpretations of the Bible's laws and wrote them down in a book called the *Mishnah.*

It is in the *Mishnah* that we will find the roots of the *brachot* we say today. It is traditional for Jews to study the *Mishnah* in pairs called *Hevrutot* (sing. *Hevrutah*). Participants will study a selection from the first *masechet* (division): *Brachot* (Blessings), of the first *seder* (order): *Zeraim* (Seeds) 9:2.

Divide the group into *Hevrutah* pairs and hand out copies of the text and questions (see Readings & Worksheets). Allow ten minutes to study the texts and answer the questions. Regroup and discuss the texts, using the questions as a guide.

Points to Emphasize

By giving us these *brachot* to recite, the *Mishnah* is training us to appreciate the wonders of the daily world that have become commonplace to most of us.

Through the *brachot,* the *Mishnah* is teaching us of God's presence in nature—even in the frightening, powerful aspects of nature.

Many people feel closest to God outdoors; that is why we have a custom of putting windows in our synagogues. For some of us, praying indoors feels unnatural; we prefer the mountains for our temples.

Athletes, artists and musicians all exercise to improve their skills. *Brachot* are spiritual exercises that we can do to help us remember the source and the Eternal in everything. Reciting *brachot* can expand our appreciation and joy in life. With an expanded awareness of the inherent value of all life, can we still exploit the earth?

The Jewish people did not stop composing *brachot* after the *Mishnah* was compiled. Like Rabbi Judah, many sages believed that some natural phenomena were special enough to merit a new, unique *brachah* (sing for *brachot*).

Examples of these post-*Mishnaic brachot* include:

•   The blessing over a rainbow, the sign of God's covenant with Noah:

ברוך אתה ד׳ אלקינו מלך העולם זוכר הברית ונאמן בבריתו וקים במאמרו.

Baruch Atah Adonai Eloheynu Melech ha-olam, zocher ha-brit v'neeman b'vreeto v'kayam b'mamaro.

Praise to You *Adonai,* our God and Universal Ruler, Who remembers the covenant and keeps its promise faithfully with all creation.

•   The blessing over fruit trees in bloom in Spring (this may be recited only once a year):

ברוך אתה ד׳ אלקינו מלך העולם שלא חסר בעולמו דבר וברא בו בריות
טובות ואילנות טובים להנות בהם בני אדם.

Baruch Atah Adonai, Eloheynu Melech Ha-olam, she'lo chiser ba'olamo davar, oobarah bo briyot tovot v'eelanot tovim, l'hanot bahem b'nai adam.

Praise to You *Adonai,* our God and Universal Ruler, Who created a universe lacking in nothing, and who has fashioned goodly creatures and trees that give people pleasure.

Brachot are one way in which the Rabbis taught us to honor nature and God. Can you think of others?

The following story is told of Rabbi Nachman of Bratslav. He was raised in a city and never spent time in a natural setting until he was married (at age 14) and went to live with his wife in her village. Her village was in the midst of a beautiful countryside, and when he first got there, he couldn't believe how wonderful it felt to be in nature. He felt that outside, he could easily pray and talk to God. There was no one to bother him, and all the animals and plants helped his prayers reach heaven. He spent much time outdoors. When he became a rabbi, he told his congregants to spend one hour a day outdoors to commune with God. Have a volunteer recite Rabbi Nachman's prayer (see Readings & Worksheets).

Ask participants to also create their own *brachot and prayers*. Have them choose a part of nature for which they would like to compose a *brachah* or poem (for example: thunder, snowstorms, an eclipse, clouds, flowers, bird songs).

If it is to be a *brachah,* it should begin with the words "Praise to You *Adonai,* our God and Universal Ruler." Tell the class to think about how the part of nature they have chosen makes them think and feel about God. The *brachah* can be simple ("Praise to You, *Adonai* ... Who makes grasshoppers") or more elaborate ("Praise to You, Eternal ... Who creates flying insects that sing in the summer night"). The *brachot* should say something about God's presence in nature. Encourage participants to use a name for God that speaks to them, like "Eternal" or "Source of Life," and so on.

BRACHOT SHEETS

Hand out paper and fine-point markers. Have participants write their newly-created *brachot* and prayers along with some of the traditional *brachot* we have discussed. Encourage them to decorate their "*brachot* sheets" with drawings and designs.

[Note: According to some traditional Jewish legal teachings, it is no longer permissible to create our own *brachot*. If you take this stance, explore this and talk about the possible rationale for this position. Then, go ahead and have participants write on their sheets and illustrate them, using the traditional *brachot* only.]

BRINGING IT HOME

Brachot help us see God as part of everything in the world. When we view nature as connected with God we are less likely to mistreat or destroy it. Rabbi Meir said that "it is a *mitzvah* (commandment) to recite 100 blessings every day" (Babylonian *Talmud, Menahot* 43b). Could this help you in your life today? Is it appropriate to expect people to do this? Would it make a difference in the world if people did this? Try to notice the number of times a day you feel appreciation for anything. How do you feel when you are appreciative? What does it feel like on a day when you forget to appreciate things? It takes work to be conscious of your world and to be appreciative of it. Try over the next week to bless things in whatever way is comfortable to you. Compare notes next time and see if the work pays off.

For Further Reading: Abraham Joshua Heschel, *God in Search of Man.*

BLESSINGS AND PRAISE

OPENING: FROM ABRAHAM JOSHUA HESCHEL, *GOD IN SEARCH OF MAN,* pp. 48–51.

Reading

Three times a day we pray:

We Thank Thee . . .

For Thy miracles which are daily with us,

For thy continual marvels . . .

In the evening liturgy we recite the words of Job (9:10):

Who does great things past finding out,
Marvelous things without number.

Every evening we recite: "He creates light and makes the dark." Twice a day we say: "He is One." What is the meaning of such repetition? A scientific theory, once it is announced and accepted, does not have to be repeated twice a day. The insights of wonder must be constantly kept alive. Since there is a need for daily wonder, there is a need for daily worship.

The sense for the "miracles which are daily with us," the sense for the "continual marvels," is the source of prayer. There is no worship, no music, no love, if we take for granted the blessings or defeats of living. No routine of the social, physical, or physiological order must dull our sense of surprise at the fact that there is a social, a physical, or a physiological order. We are trained in maintaining our sense of wonder by uttering a prayer before the enjoyment of food. Each time we are about to drink a glass of water, we remind ourselves of the eternal mystery of creation, "Blessed be Thou . . . by Whose word all things come into being." A trivial act and a reference to the supreme miracle. Wishing to eat bread or fruit, to enjoy a pleasant fragrance or a cup of wine; on tasting fruit in season for the first time; on seeing a rainbow, or the ocean; on noticing trees when they blossom; on meeting a sage in Torah or in secular learning; on hearing good or bad tidings—we are taught to invoke His great name and our awareness of Him. Even on performing a physiological function we say "Blessed be Thou . . . who healest all flesh and *doest wonders.*"

This is one of the goals of the Jewish way of living: to experience commonplace deeds as spiritual adventures, to feel the hidden love and wisdom in all things.

> . . . The belief in "the hidden miracles is the basis for the entire Torah. A man has no share in the Torah, unless he believes that all things and all events in the life of the individual as well as in the life of society are miracles. There is no such thing as the natural course of events. . . ." (Nachmanides).

BLESSINGS AND PRAISE

TEXT STUDY: THE *BRACHOT. MISHNAH BRACHOT 9:2*

Reading
A. Upon seeing shooting stars, earthquakes, lightning, thunder, and storms, one says:

ברוך אתה ד׳ אלקינו מלך העולם שכחו וגבורתו מלא עולם.

Baruch . . . she'kocho oog'voortoh maleh olam.
Praise to You . . . Whose strength and power fill the entire world.

Ellen Bernstein and Dan Fink

B. Upon seeing mountains, valleys, oceans, rivers, and wilderness, one says:

ברוך אתה ד׳ אלקינו מלך העולם עשה בראשית.

Baruch . . . oseh breisheet.
Praise to You . . . making Creation work.

C. Rabbi Yehudah taught: One who sees the Great Sea (the Mediterranean) very rarely says:

ברוך אתה ד׳ אלקינו מלך העולם שעשה את הים הגדול.

Baruch . . . she'asah et ha-yam ha-gadol.
Praise to You . . . Who made the Great Sea.

D. Over rain and over good news, one says:

ברוך אתה ד׳ אלקינו מלך העולם הטוב והמטיב.

Baruch . . . ha-tov v'ha-mateev.
Praise to You . . . Who is Good and does Goodness.

BLESSINGS AND PRAISE

Text Study: The *Brachot. Mishnah Brachot 9:2*

Participant Worksheet

1. What do the items in section A have in common? What do the items in section B have in common? How do the items in section A differ from those in section B?

2. Are the blessings in sections A and B appropriate for the items over which they are said? What do the blessings make us think about in each case? Why do you think the Rabbis chose these blessings for these items?

3. What items could you add to the lists in sections A and B?

4. Even though we already have a blessing for oceans, in section C, Rabbi Judah assigns the Great Sea its own *brachah*. Why do you think he does this? Are there any events or parts of nature that you believe deserve their own special blessing? Why?

5. Why do you think the blessing for rain is the same as the one for good news, and not the one for storms and thunder? This blessing would make a great deal of sense in a time of drought; should we still recite it in a time of flood?

6. Why do you think the *Mishnah* instructs someone who sees these things every day not to recite the blessing each time?

7. If we observed this tradition and recited blessings on a regular basis, how might it change the way we looked at the world around us?

Ellen Bernstein and Dan Fink

457

8. Based on these blessings, the Rabbis seem to feel that when we look closely enough, every part of nature tells us something about God (examples: God's power, God's creative force). How might looking at nature in this way change the way we treat the natural world?

BLESSINGS AND PRAISE

TEXT STUDY: THE *BRACHOT*. *MISHNAH BRACHOT 9:2*

Leader Worksheet

1. What do the items in section A have in common? What do the items in section B have in common? How do the items in section A differ from those in section B?

All the items in section A are powerful, even frightening or destructive events. They are not everyday occurrences. The items in section B are common but beautiful, natural features. These items are constant—so constant that we often take them for granted.

2. Are the blessings in sections A and B appropriate for the items over which they are said? What do the blessings make us think about in each case? Why do you think the Rabbis chose these blessings for these items?

Yes. In the first case, the blessing speaks of God's power and in the second, the blessing speaks of evidence of God's amazing creativity. The first section's items are powerful and even frightening. They might seem to represent God's power. The second list of items might not seem special until we remember that God made them.

3. What items could you add to the lists in sections A and B?

A: volcanic eruptions; tidal waves; an eclipse
B: flowers; rocks; waterfalls

4. Even though we already have a blessing for oceans, in section C, Rabbi Judah assigns the Great Sea its own *brachah*. Why do you think he does this? Are there any events or parts of nature that you believe deserve their own special blessing? Why?

The Mediterranean had a special importance and meaning in the life of the Jewish people; it is the largest body of water close to the land of Israel. In the ancient world, the Mediterranean helped to define the boundaries of the "known" world.

5. Why do you think the blessing for rain is the same as the one for good news, and not the one for storms and thunder? This blessing would make a great deal of sense in a time of drought; should we still recite it in a time of flood?

As we all know (although we may not appreciate it all the time), rain is good news, providing sustenance for the crops, insuring that our tables will be full. What could be better than the knowledge that we will be able to eat another meal, and will be able to experience another day!! In the ancient Middle East, as well as in many parts of the world today, rain was unpredictable

Ellen Bernstein and Dan Fink

and often scarce. During a time of floods, we can pray for gentle, nourishing rains instead of destructive torrents.

6. Why do you think the *Mishnah* instructs someone who sees these things every day not to recite the blessing each time?

If one recited the same blessing every day, it could become rote and meaningless. Someone who has never seen the mountains or ocean before will undoubtedly be impressed on first viewing them.

7. If we observed this tradition and recited blessings on a regular basis, how might it change the way we looked at the world around us?

We may notice more, we may appreciate the beauties of nature more, we may be more careful about preserving the natural world, and we may feel closer to God more often.

8. Based on these blessings, the Rabbis seem to feel that when we look closely enough, every part of nature tells us something about God (examples: God's power, God's creative force). How might looking at nature in this way change the way we treat the natural world?

We would see the world as holy (connected with God) and therefore treat it with more respect and concern.

BLESSINGS AND PRAISE

Your Own *Brachot* and Praises: Rabbi Nachman's Prayer

Reading
Master of the Universe, grant me the ability to be alone:
May it be my custom to go outdoors each day, among the trees and grasses, among all growing things, there to be alone and enter into prayer.
There may I express all that is in my heart, talking with You, to Whom I belong.
And may all grasses, trees and plants awake at my coming.
Send the power of their life into my prayer, making whole my heart and my speech through the life and spirit of growing things.

"BAL TASHCHIT"

Introduction

Humans are guests on earth; God is our host. We are part of the web of life, and simultaneously, we have a unique task: the responsibility to preserve this beautiful gift of the earth for the next generation. This responsibility is a part of what it means to be human. For Jews, caring for the earth is our birthright and responsibility: we need only remember the most intimate relationship between *adam* (earthling) and *adamah* (earth).

The goal of this lesson is to demonstrate how a Jewish law, *bal tashchit*, "Do Not Destroy," is applicable to the contemporary environmental crisis.

Objectives

- Participants will be able to articulate the law of *bal tashchit* and its rabbinic genesis.

- Participants will examine their own behaviors in terms of *bal tashchit.* and will learn to decrease the waste in their lives.

Materials and Preparation

- Bring the following for the Opening exercise: Paper bag, a sandwich wrapped in plastic, soda can or foil, some prepackaged food like chips, juice pack and a sample of an unpackaged food like an apple.

- Each group member should bring in one item of what they normally consider garbage.

- Art supplies including glue, paints, glitter.

- Copies of Readings & Worksheets.

- Speak to your institution's administrators and ascertain whether your group may perform an environmental audit (see "Detective Work").

BAL TASHCHIT

OPENING

Our American society is the most wasteful society in the history of humanity. The value of the resources that we throw away is higher than the GNP (Gross National Product) of many other countries. In the average American's lifetime, he or she will throw out 45 tons of garbage. The problem of garbage is worsened by our inadequate means of disposal. Most landfills are filling up fast, and other means, such as incineration, are not considered environmentally sound. Waste reduction through the use of the three R's, **R**educe waste, **R**euse products and **R**ecycle, is considered the intelligent way to approach the waste problem.

Take out a paper lunch bag filled with what would be a typical lunch and proceed to take out each item. The lunch should contain the following types of items:

> Paper: the bag itself
> Plastic: a sandwich wrapped in plastic
> Aluminum: soda can or foil
> Packaged food: chips, juice pack
> Unpackaged food: fruit

Take out each food item and the packaging associated with it.

Ellen Bernstein and Dan Fink

Where does plastic come from, and where does it go after lunch is over? Repeat this question for each of the the items in the lunch.

- Plastic: Every year 50 billion pounds of plastic are made in the United States (see "The Path of Plastic" in Readings & Worksheets).

- Aluminum: Every three months we throw away enough aluminum to replace all the commercial airplanes in the U.S.

- Paper: The paper equivalent of 500,000 trees is used every Sunday to print the Sunday paper in the U.S.

- Packaged food: Thirty-three percent of our garbage is just unnecessary packaging.

TEXT STUDY: THE LAW OF *BAL TASHCHIT*

There are two concerns about waste expressed in Deuteronomy. Ask volunteers to read the following passages:

> There will be an area beyond the military camp where you can relieve yourself. You will have a spade among your weapons; and after you have squatted, you will dig a hole and cover your excrement.
> —Deuteronomy 23:13–15

> When you lay siege and battle against a city for a long time in order to capture it, *you must not destroy its trees*, wielding an ax against them. You may eat of them, but you must not cut them down. Are the trees of the field human to withdraw before you into the besieged city? Only trees which you know do not yield food may be destroyed; you may cut them down for constructing siege works against the city that is waging war on you, until it has been captured.
> —Deuteronomy 20:19–20

Discussion Questions

- The first passage is rather explicit. Are you surprised to hear such things in the Bible? How does this law make you feel (do you find it repulsive, fascinating, etc.)?

    Judaism is concerned with all aspects of life in this world. One of the beauties of the tradition is its attention to the small details we often take for granted.

- The second passage is more difficult. We will be studying this in detail. What does this law mean?

    In wartime we may eat from fruit trees, but are forbidden to cut them down. This law is referred to as Bal Tashchit.

    In general, fruit trees serve no other purpose but to bear fruit. Compare fruit trees to other trees: oak, maple, cedar. These trees are much larger, and are solid. They are excellent for build-

ing. They could serve well to construct the siege works. Fruit trees, on the other hand, are not useful for building. They serve primarily to bear fruit. Animals and humans can benefit from the fruit. The Torah is telling us we cannot cut down trees senselessly, simply for convenience, because we don't like them or because we want to harm the enemy. A scorched earth policy is forbidden according to the Bible. If not, it would be wasteful or destructive.

The Rabbis used many different interpretive tools in order to understand the Bible. One tool is called *kal v'homer* (literally, from hard to easy). *Kal v'homer* means that we infer from a difficult situation how to behave in an easier situation. In other words, if you find one law in a specific biblical context the rabbis can extend its application to other related situations. An example of this is reciting a blessing before eating. The only blessing that we are commanded to make is the blessing after eating. The Rabbis reasoned that if we are commanded to recite a blessing after eating, when our appetite is satiated, when we are tired and do not feel compelled to make a blessing, then there is all the more reason to say a blessing before we have eaten, when we are eager to eat and making a blessing would be a simple act.

Deuteronomy 20:19–20 was extended to other situations based on the law of *kal v'homer*. In this activity, we'll be thinking about how we can apply *kal v'homer* to *bal tashchit*.

Divide the group into pairs. Hand out the text and questions on *bal tashchit* (see Readings & Worksheets). Have participants answer the questions, using the text study sheet as a reference. Reconvene after ten minutes and discuss the material using the study questions as a guide.

[Note: Leader may use current and local environmental issues for a more up-to-date and inspiring discussion.]

Garbage Art

When you throw something away, where is "away"? *There is no such thing as "away." Garbage always goes somewhere.* The only way to deal with the problem of garbage is through the three R's. To demonstrate how we can reduce the amount of waste by reusing what would normally go into the waste stream, the class will make an art project out of the waste items they have brought in with them.

What Do You Know About Waste?
Ask participants to take the "What Do You Know Quiz" (see Readings & Worksheets). Go over answers. Participants will be astonished at how much we ourselves and our country waste or unnecessarily destroy.

Detective Work: Conducting an Audit of Your School or Institution
Invite participants to be *bal tashchit* detectives and investigate where their institution wastes; submit suggestions to the administration to decrease waste. Begin this activity now.

Ellen Bernstein and Dan Fink

Participants will need to take on the responsibility to research more on their own. After hours or during lunch, participants could examine the trash generated in various offices and classrooms. Participants can give a booby prize to the greatest offenders, and an award to the most creative conserver.

Begin with a brainstorming session. Have a volunteer write on the blackboard, while participants offer suggestions of areas that use resources and produce waste. Ask for suggestions on how waste can be decreased in each area. If after brainstorming they have not come up with the following ideas, you can offer them.

- Do they recycle paper, plastics and metals? Check the packaging of the toilet paper and paper towels used. Is there a "recycled" label?

- Is recycled paper used for photocopying and office needs? Hold the paper up to the light; if it is recycled, there will probably be a watermark of the recycling sign.

- What is the volume of paper used for fliers and newsletters? Can it be consolidated? Are memos written on the backs of old letters?

- Does the institution use non-recyclable items? Can recyclables or reusables be substituted (for instance, cheap silverware instead of plastic throw-away eating utensils)? What is thrown away that can be reused or can be replaced with a recyclable alternative?

- What is the energy source of the institution? Are there alternatives? What is the usual heat setting? Are excess lights left on at night?

- How much energy is used? Can energy be reduced? What sort of light bulbs are used? How is the insulation?

- Is the institution making maximal use of its space? Are unused rooms heated? What happens in the space at night, and in the summer?

- What is the air conditioner's usual setting? Will a fan suffice? Are there trees planted around the facility that could cool the building, eliminating the need for air conditioning?

- Are carpooling, public transportation, or bike riding encouraged?

- Are cleaning supplies or lawn products toxic?

- What sort of toxics are thrown away? How are they disposed of?

- How much food is thrown away at events?

- Where does the waste water (dishwater) go?

At this point focus on a few of the items and come up with a plan on how the institution can follow *bal tashchit*.

When planning, be sure to:

- Choose a plan of action that the administration will allow

- Set a reasonable goal

- Determine how to measure waste

- Assign tasks to participants, and follow through with your plan!

(This activity may be substituted for the audit if you feel it is more appropriate. Many of the same questions will apply.)

We must realize that we have the ability and power to make changes in the world. Good stewardship (caring for the earth) begins at home. Therefore the participants must look at their habits and the habits of their families to determine what needs to be changed. Spend a few minutes discussing participants' own personal habits in reference to *bal tashchit*. Discuss areas where they waste resources. Decide how they may be able to improve these behaviors and habits. Have participants perform a week-long project at home, recording everything that is thrown away or used up (such as gallons of gasoline for the cars, gallons of water for the lawn or garden, gallons of bathwater, gallons of toilet bowl water, gallons of dishwater). Encourage them to work out plans for following the commandment of *bal tashchit* at home.

For Further Reading: The Earthworks Group, *50 Simple Things You Can Do to Save the Earth.*

BAL TASHCHIT

OPENING: THE PATH OF PLASTIC

Reading

Fossil fuels are the remains of plants and animals (organic matter) that died millions of years ago. Over the millennia, layers upon layers of sediment were deposited, compressing the remains with their enormous weight. Under this pressure, heat was generated. This heat, along with chemical and bacterial activity, gradually reformed the organic matter into the compounds of hydrogen and carbon we know as petroleum (when distilled, petroleum produces oil).

In order to obtain petroleum, the land must be "cleared": stripped of all plants and guarded against the return of indigenous animals. The land is then graded—bulldozed to accommodate derricks. Often roads must be built to make the area accessible to heavy equipment and workers. Sometimes a larger area is cleared in order to establish nearby housing for the oil field workers.

After the oil is pumped and shipped to a factory, chemicals and heat are added to transform it into plastic. The heat causes the molecules in oil to move around rapidly, and the

Ellen Bernstein and Dan Fink

chemicals cause the carbon molecules to bond in various formations. The fraction of carbon molecules that bond determines whether the plastic is hard or soft.

BAL TASHCHIT

TEXT STUDY: THE LAW OF BAL TASHCHIT

Readings

When in your war against a city you have to besiege it for a long time in order to capture it, you must not destroy its fruit trees, wielding an ax against them. You may eat of them, but you must not cut them down. Are the trees of the city human to withdraw from you into the besieged city? Only trees which you know do not yield food may be destroyed; you may cut them down for constructing siege works against the city that is waging war on you, until it has been captured.

—Deuteronomy 20:19–20

Whoever breaks vessels or rips up garments, destroys a building, stops up a fountain, or ruins food is guilty of violating the prohibition of bal tashchit.

—Babylonian *Talmud Kiddushin* 32a

It is forbidden to cut down fruit-bearing trees outside a [besieged] city, nor may a water channel be deflected from them so that they wither, as it is said: "You must not destroy its trees" [Deut. 20:19]. It [a fruit-bearing tree] may be cut down, however, if it causes damage to other trees or to a field belonging to another man or if its value for other purposes is greater [than that of the fruit it produces]. The law forbids only wanton destruction.

—Maimonides, *Mishnah Torah;* Judges, Laws of Kings and Their Wars 6:8–10.

... [D]estruction does not only mean making something purposelessly unfit for its designated use; it also means trying to attain a certain aim by making use of more things and more valuable things when fewer and less valuable ones would suffice; or if this aim is not really worth the means expended for its attainment. [For example] kindling something which is still fit for other purposes for the sake of light; ... wearing down something more than is necessary ... consuming more than is necessary ...

On the other hand, if destruction is necessary for a higher and more worthy aim, then it ceases to be destruction and itself becomes wise creating. [For example] cutting down a fruit tree which is doing harm to other more valuable plants, [and] burning a vessel when there is a scarcity of wood in order to protect one's weakened self from catching cold ...

—Reprinted and adapted with permission of the publisher from Hirsch, Samson Raphael, *Horeb: A Philosophy of Jewish Laws and Observances,* translated from the German by I. Grunfeld, (New York: Soncino Press) 1962, 1968, 1972, 1981, pp. 280–281.

BAL TASHCHIT

Participant Worksheet

1) Read Deuteronomy 20:19–20 again. Using *kal v'homer* reasoning, how do you think the Rabbis may have extended this law?

2) What might have been the Rabbis' reason to extend this law?

3) What does a fruit tree symbolize? What is its importance?

4) Jews have invoked the principle of *bal tashchit* in all instances of wanton destruction. It is said that there was a Rabbi who used to cry whenever his students would pick a leaf off of a tree unnecessarily. But what happens when there is a more pressing human need at stake? What if you need to cut down a fruit tree because it is on the site that you have purchased to build a synagogue or a hospital?

5) Can you spray dandelions because you don't like them?

6) Can you weed your garden?

BAL TASHCHIT

Text Study: The Law of *Bal Tashchit*

Reader Worksheet

1) Read Deuteronomy 20:19–20 again. Using *kal v'homer* reasoning, how do you think the Rabbis may have extended this law?

They extended the prohibition of cutting down trees in time of war (hard situation) to any unnecessary destruction of anything (easier situation). Specifically, the Rabbis said that "Whoever breaks vessels or rips up garments, destroys a building, stops up a fountain, or ruins foods is guilty of violating the prohibition of *bal tashchit*."

2) What might have been the Rabbis' reason to extend this law?

If the destruction of fruit trees is prohibited in a time of war, when one would most likely destroy them (we are all familiar with the scorched earth policy of many armies: at wartime, opponents become demoralized through the total destruction of the environment), then it is certainly prohibited to cut fruit trees down in times of peace, when one is not likely to do so.

3) What does a fruit tree symbolize? What is its importance?

To the rabbinic mind, the fruit tree is a gift from God that is useful to humans. It has a purpose: to bear fruit that serves the rest of creation. A fruit tree should be used for the purpose of feeding people and other creatures. To use a fruit tree for any other purpose would be needless

Ellen Bernstein and Dan Fink

waste and destruction. Furthermore, the trees are harmless and vulnerable, and should be allowed to live in most situations.

4) Jews have invoked the principle of *bal tashchit* in all instances of wanton destruction. It is said that there was a Rabbi who used to cry whenever his students would pick a leaf off of a tree unnecessarily. But what happens when there is a more pressing human need at stake? What if you need to cut down a fruit tree because it is on the site that you have purchased to build a synagogue or a hospital?

Rabbis have often made the choice that is best for the community. If destruction is needed for a higher goal, then it ceases to be destruction; it is then "wise use." The challenge, then, is to determine what is the "common good."

5) Can you spray dandelions because you don't like them?

Not if it is purely for your convenience.

6) Can you weed your garden?

Yes, this insures the greater good of the garden; with fewer weeds, your vegetables will receive ample sunlight and nutrients, and will grow more successfully.

BAL TASHCHIT

WHAT DO YOU KNOW ABOUT WASTE?

Participant Worksheet
What Do You Know Quiz

1. What percentage of paper used yearly in the United States is used just for packaging?

a. 8%   b. 23%   c. 50%

2. If you are an average adult who weighs 150 pounds, how much garbage will you generate in your lifetime?

a. 1 ton (2,000 lbs.)   b. 10 tons (20,000 lbs.)   c. 45 tons (90,000 lbs.)

3. If all the aluminum thrown away in the U.S. were recycled, how long would it take to gather enough aluminum to rebuild all the commercial airliners in the U.S.?

a. 10 years.   b. 2 years   c. 3 months

4. How much of your garbage is packaging that you throw out immediately?

a. 10%   b. 18%   c. 33%

5. The paper equivalent of how many trees is used each week to supply U.S. citizens with the Sunday newspaper?

a. 10,000 trees   b. 50,000 trees   c. 500,000 trees

6. What is the percentage of newspapers that are thrown away and not recycled?

a. 25%   b. 48%   c. 71%

7. Which of the following breaks down first in a landfill?

a. paper cup   b. plastic cup   c. aluminum can   d. none of the above

8. Which country uses half as many resources as we do in the U.S. to produce a single manufactured item?

a. Japan   b. Germany   c. Sweden   d. all of the above

BAL TASHCHIT

WHAT DO YOU KNOW ABOUT WASTE?

Reader Worksheet
What Do You Know Quiz

1. What percentage of paper used yearly in the United States is used just for packaging?

a. 8%   b. 23%   c. 50%

2. If you are an average adult who weighs 150 pounds, how much garbage will you generate in your lifetime?

a. 1 ton (2,000 lbs.)   b. 10 tons (20,000 lbs.)   c. 45 tons (90,000 lbs.)

3. If all the aluminum thrown away in the U.S. were recycled, how long would it take to gather enough aluminum to rebuild all the commercial airliners in the U.S.?

a. 10 years   b. 2 years   c. 3 months

4. How much of your garbage is packaging that you throw out immediately?

a. 10%   b. 18%   c. 33%

5. The paper equivalent of how many trees is used each week to supply U.S. citizens with the Sunday newspaper?

a. 10,000 trees   b. 50,000 trees   c. 500,000 trees

6. What is the percentage of newspapers that are thrown away and not recycled?

a. 25%   b. 48%   c. 71%

7. Which of the following breaks down first in a landfill?

a. paper cup   b. plastic cup   c. aluminum can   d. none of the above

8. Which country uses half as many resources as we do in the U.S. to produce a single manufactured item?

a. Japan   b. Germany   c. Sweden   d. all of the above

Ellen Bernstein and Dan Fink

Answers: 1. a, 2. c, 3. c, 4. c, 5. c, 6. c, 7. d (most landfill contents are "mummified" because there is no air to catalyze the breakdown), 8. d

Source of Information: *50 Simple Things You Can Do to Save the Earth*

"WIWANYAG WACHIPI: THE SUN DANCE"

Black Elk

The *wiwanyag wachipi* (dance looking at the sun) is one of our greatest rites and was first held many, many winters after our people received the sacred pipe from the White Buffalo Cow Woman. It is held each year during the Moon of Fattening (June) or the Moon of Cherries Blackening (July), always at the time when the moon is full, for the growing and dying of the moon reminds us of our ignorance which comes and goes; but when the moon is full it is as if the eternal light of the Great Spirit were upon the whole world. But now I will tell you how this holy rite first came to our people and how it was first made.

Our people were once camped in a good place, in a circle, of course, and the old men were sitting having a council, when they noticed that one of our men, Kablaya (Spread), had dropped his robe down around his waist, and was dancing there all alone with his hand raised towards heaven. The old men thought that perhaps he was crazy, so they sent someone to find out what was the matter; but this man who was sent suddenly dropped his robe down around his waist, too, and started dancing with Kablaya. The old men thought this very strange, and so they all went over to see what could be the matter. Kablaya then explained to them:

"Long ago *Wakan-Tanka* told us how to pray with the sacred pipe, but we have now become lax in our prayers, and our people are losing their strength. But I have just been shown, in a vision, a new way of prayer; in this manner *Wakan-Tanka* has sent aid to us."

When they heard this the old men all said, *"How!"* and seemed very pleased. They then had a conference and sent two men to the keeper of the sacred pipe, for he should give advice on all matters of this sort. The keeper told the men that this was certainly a very good thing, for "we were told that we would have seven ways of praying to *Wakan-Tanka*, and this must certainly be one of them, for Kablaya has been taught in a vision, and we were told in the beginning that we should receive our rites in this manner."

The two messengers brought this news back to the old men, who then asked Kablaya to instruct them in what they must do. Kablaya then spoke to the men, saying: "This is to be the sun dance; we cannot make it immediately but must wait four days, and during this time we shall prepare, as I have been instructed in my vision. This dance will be an offering of our bodies and souls to *Wakan-Tanka* and will be very *wakan*. All our old and holy men should

From *The Sacred Pipe: Black Elk's Account of the Seven Rites of the Oglala Sioux* recorded and edited by Joseph Epese Brown. Copyright © 1953, 1989 by the University of Oklahoma Press.

gather; a large tipi should be built and sage should be placed all around inside it. You must have a good pipe, and also all the following equipment:

Ree twist tobacco	a tanned buffalo calf hide
bark of the red willow	rabbit skins
Sweet grass	eagle plumes
a bone knife	red earth paint
a flint axe	blue paint
buffalo tallow	rawhide
a buffalo skull	eagle tail feathers
a rawhide bag	whistles from the wing bones of the Spotted Eagle.

After the people had secured all these sacred things, Kablaya then asked all those who could sing to come to him that evening so that he could teach them the holy songs; he said that they should bring with them a large drum made from a buffalo hide, and they should have very stout drum sticks, covered at the end with buffalo hide, the hair side out.

Since the drum is often the only instrument used in our sacred rites, I should perhaps tell you here why it is especially sacred and important to us. It is because the round form of the drum represents the whole universe, and its steady strong beat is the pulse, the heart, throbbing at the center of the universe. It is as the voice of *Wakan-Tanka*, and this sound stirs us and helps us to understand the mystery and power of all things.

That evening the singers, four men and a woman, came to Kablaya, who spoke to them in this manner: "O you, my relatives, for a very long time we have been sending our voices to *Wakan-Tanka*. This He has taught us to do. We have many ways of praying to Him, and through this sacred manner of living our generations have learned to walk the red path with firm steps. The sacred pipe is always at the center of the hoop of our nation, and with it the people have walked and will continue to walk in a holy manner.

"In this new rite which I have just received, one of the standing peoples has been chosen to be at our center; he is the wagachun (the rustling tree, or cottonwood); he will be our center and also the people, for the tree represents the way of the people. Does it not stretch from the earth here to heaven there?[1] This new way of sending our voices to *Wakan-Tanka* will be very powerful; its use will spread, and, at this time of year, every year, many people will pray to the Great Spirit. Before I teach you the holy songs, let us first offer the pipe to our Father and Grandfather, *Wakan-Tanka*."

"O Grandfather, Father, *Wakan-Tanka*, we are about to fulfill Thy will as You have taught us to do in my vision. This we know will be a very sacred way of sending our voices to You; through this, may our people receive wisdom; may it help us to walk the sacred path with all the Powers of the universe! Our prayer will really be the prayer of all things, for all are really one; all this I have seen in my vision. May the four Powers of the universe help us to do this rite correctly; O Great Spirit, have mercy upon us!"

The pipe was smoked by all, and then Kablaya began to teach the songs to the five people. Many other people had gathered around the singers, and to these Kablaya said that while they listen they should frequently cry "O Grandfather, *Wakan-Tanka,* I offer the pipe to You that my people may live!"

There were no words to the first song that Kablaya taught the singers; it was simply a chant, repeated four times, and the fast beat on the drum was used. The words to the second song were:

> *Wakan-Tanka, have mercy on us,*
> *That our people may live!*

And the third song was:

> *They say a herd of buffalo is coming;*
> *It is here now!*
> *Their blessing will come to us.*
> *It is with us now!*

The fourth song was a chant and had no words.

Then Kablaya taught the men who had brought their eagle-bone whistles how they should be used, and he also told the men what equipment they should prepare and explained the meaning of each ritual object.

"You should prepare a necklace of otter skin, and from it there should hang a circle with a cross in the center. At the four places where the cross meets the circle there should hang eagle feathers which represent the four Powers of the universe and the four ages. At the center of the circle you should tie a plume taken from the breast of the eagle, for this is the place which is nearest to the heart and center of the sacred bird. This plume will be for *Wakan-Tanka,* who dwells at the depths of the heavens, and who is the center of all things.

"You all have the eagle-bone whistles, and to the ends of each of these an eagle plume should be tied. When you blow the whistle always remember that it is the voice of the Spotted Eagle; our Grandfather, *Wakan-Tanka,* always hears this, for you see it is really His own voice.

"A *hanhepi wi* [night sun, or moon] should be cut from rawhide in the shape of a crescent, for the moon represents a person and, also, all things, for everything created waxes and wanes, lives and dies. You should also understand that the night represents ignorance, but it is the moon and the stars which bring the Light of *Wakan-Tanka* into this darkness. As you know the moon comes and goes, but *anpetu wi,* the sun, lives on forever; it is the source of light, and because of this it is like *Wakan-Tanka.*

"A five-pointed star should be cut from rawhide. This will be the sacred Morning Star who stands between the darkness and the light, and who represents knowledge.

"A round rawhide circle should be made to represent the sun, and this should be painted red; but at the center there should be a round circle of blue, for this innermost center represents

Wakan-Tanka as our Grandfather. The light of this sun enlightens the entire universe; and as the flames of the sun come to us in the morning, so comes the grace of *Wakan-Tanka,* by which all creatures are enlightened. It is because of this that the four-leggeds and the wingeds always rejoice at the coming of the light. We can all see in the day, and this seeing is sacred for it represents the sight of that real world which we may have through the eye of the heart. When you wear this sacred sign in the dance, you should remember that you are bringing Light into the universe, and if you concentrate on these meanings you will gain great benefit.

"A round circle should be cut and painted red, and this will represent Earth. She is sacred, for upon Her we place our feet, and from Her we send our voices to *Wakan-Tanka.* She is a relative of ours, and this we should always remember when we call Her "Grandmother" or "Mother." When we pray we raise our hand to the heavens, and afterwards we touch the earth, for is not our Spirit from *Wakan-Tanka,* and are not our bodies from the earth? We are related to all things: the earth and the stars, everything, and with all these together we raise our hand to *Wakan-Tanka* and pray to Him alone.

"You should also cut from rawhide another round circle, and this should be painted blue for the heavens. When you dance you should raise your head and hand up to these heavens, looking at them, for if you do this your Grandfather will see you. It is He who owns everything; there is nothing which does not belong to Him, and thus it is to Him alone that you should pray.

"Finally, you should cut from rawhide the form of *tatanka,* the buffalo. He represents the people and the universe and should always be treated with respect, for was he not here before the two-legged peoples, and is he not generous in that he gives us our homes and our food? The buffalo is wise in many things, and, thus, we should learn from him and should always be as a relative with him.

"Each man should wear one of these sacred symbols on his chest, and he should realize their meanings as I have explained to you here. In this great rite you are to offer your body as a sacrifice in behalf of all the people, and through you the people will gain understanding and strength. Always be conscious of these things which I have told you today; it is all *wakan!"*

The next day it was necessary to locate the sacred rustling tree which was to stand at the center of the great lodge, and so Kablaya told his helper of the type of tree which he should find and mark with sage, that the war party will be able to locate it and bring it back to camp. Kablaya also instructed the helpers how they must mark out the ground where the sacred sun-dance lodge will be set up, around the holy tree, and how they should mark the doorway at the east with green branches.

The following day the scouts, who had been chosen by the spiritual leaders, went out and pretended to scout for the tree. When it was found they returned immediately to camp, and after circling sun-wise around the place where the lodge was to be, they all charged for the doorway, trying to strike a coup on it. These scouts then took up a pipe, and, after offering it to the six directions, they swore that they would tell the truth. When this had been done, Kablaya spoke to the men in this manner:

"You have taken up the holy pipe, and so you must now tell us with truth all that you have seen. You know that running through the stem of the pipe there is a little hole leading straight to the center and heart of the pipe; let your minds be as straight as this Way. May your tongues not be forked. You have been sent out to find a tree that will be of great benefit to the people, so now tell us truthfully what you have found."

Kablaya then turned the pipe around four times, and pointed the stem towards the scout who was to give the report.

"I went over a hill, and there I saw many of the sacred standing peoples."

"In which direction were you facing, and what did you see beyond the first hill?"

"I was facing the west," the scout replied, "and then I went further and looked over a second hill and saw many more of the sacred standing people living there."

In this manner the scout was questioned four times, for as you know with our people all good things are done in fours; and then this is the manner in which we always question our scouts when we are on the warpath, for you see we are here regarding the tree as an enemy who is to be killed.

When the scouts had given their report, they all dressed as if they were going on the warpath; and then they left the camp as if to attack the enemy. Many other people followed behind the scouts. When they came to the chosen tree, they all gathered around it; then, last of all, Kablaya arrived with his pipe, which he held with its stem pointing towards the tree; he spoke in this manner:

"Of all the many standing peoples, you O rustling cottonwood have been chosen in a sacred manner; you are about to go to the center of the people's sacred hoop, and there you will represent the people and will help us to fulfill the will of *Wakan-Tanka*. You are a kind and good-looking tree; upon you the winged peoples have raised their families; from the tip of your lofty branches down to your roots, the winged and four-legged peoples have made their homes. When you stand at the center of the sacred hoop you will be the people, and you will be as the pipe, stretching from heaven to earth. The weak will lean upon you, and for all the people you will be a support. With the tips of your branches you hold the sacred red and blue days. You will stand where the four sacred paths cross—there you will be the center of the great Powers of the universe. May we two-leggeds always follow your sacred example, for we see that you are always looking upwards into the heavens. Soon, and with all the peoples of the world, you will stand at the center; for all beings and all things you will bring that which is good. *Hechetu welo!*"

Kablaya then offered his pipe to Heaven and Earth, and then with the stem he touched the tree on the west, north, east, and south sides; after this he lit and smoked the pipe.

Black Elk

I think it would be good to explain to you here why we consider the cottonwood tree to be so very sacred. I might mention first, that long ago it was the cottonwood who taught us how to make our tipis, for the leaf of the tree is an exact pattern of the tipi, and this we learned when some of our old men were watching little children making play houses from these leaves. This too is a good example of how much grown men may learn from very little children, for the hearts of little children are pure, and, therefore, the Great Spirit may show to them many things which older people miss. Another reason why we choose the cottonwood tree to be at the center of our lodge is that the Great Spirit has shown to us that, if you cut an upper limb of this tree crosswise, there you will see in the grain a perfect five pointed star, which, to us, represents the presence of the Great Spirit. Also perhaps you have noticed that even in the very lightest breeze you can hear the voice of the cottonwood tree; this we under-stand is its prayer to the Great Spirit,[2] for not only men, but all things and all beings pray to Him continually in differing ways.

The chiefs then did a little victory dance there around the tree, singing their chief's songs, and as they sang and danced they selected the man who was to have the honor of counting coup on the tree; he must always be a man of good character, who has shown him-self brave and self-sacrificing on the warpath. Three other men were also chosen by the chiefs, and then each of these four men stood at one of the four sides of the tree—the leader at the west. This leader then told of his great deeds in war, and when he had finished the men cheered and the women gave the tremulo. The brave man then motioned with his axe three times towards the tree, and the fourth time he struck it. Then the other three men in turn told of their exploits in war, and when they finished they also struck the tree in the same manner, and at each blow all the people shouted "*hi! hey!*" When the tree was nearly ready to fall, the chiefs went around and selected a person with a quiet and holy nature, and this person gave the last blow to the tree; as it fell there was much cheering, and all the women gave the tremulo. Great care was taken that the tree did not touch the ground when it fell, and no one was permitted to step over it.

The tree was then carried by six men towards the camp, but before they reached camp they stopped four times, and after the last stop they all howled like coyotes—as do the war-riors when returning from the warpath; then they all charged into camp and placed the sacred tree up upon poles—for it must not touch the ground—and pointed its base towards the hole which had already been prepared, and its tip faced towards the west. The lodge around the tree had not yet been set up, but all the poles had been prepared, and all the equipment for constructing the *Inipi* had been gathered.

The chief priest, Kablaya, and all those who were to take part in the dance, then went into a large tipi where they were to prepare themselves and receive instructions. The lodge was shut up very tightly, and leaves were even placed all around the base.

Kablaya, who was seated at the west, scraped a bare place on the ground in front of him, and here a coal was placed; as Kablaya burned sweet grass upon the coal, he said: "We burn this sacred herb for *Wakan-Tanka*, so that all the two-legged and winged peoples of the universe will be relatives and close to each other. Through this there shall be much happiness."

A small image of a drying rack was then made from two forked sticks and one straight one, and all were painted blue, for the drying rack represents heaven, and it is our prayer that the racks always be as full as heaven. The pipe was then taken up, and after being purified over the smoke, it was leaned against the rack, for in this way it represents our prayers and is the path leading from earth to heaven.

All the sacred things to be used in the dance were then purified over the smoke of the sweet grass: the hide figures; the sacred paints; the calf skin; and the buckskin bags; and the dancers, also, purified themselves. When this had been done, Kablaya took up his pipe, and, raising it to heaven, he prayed.

"O Grandfather, *Wakan-Tanka*, You are the maker of everything. You have always been and always will be. You have been kind to your people, for You have taught us a way of prayer with the pipe which You have given us; and now through a vision You have shown to me a sacred dance which I must teach to my people. Today we will do Thy will."

"As I stand upon this sacred earth, upon which generations of our people have stood, I send a voice to You by offering this pipe. Behold me, O *Wakan-Tanka*, for I represent all the people. Within this pipe I shall place the four Powers and all the wingeds of the universe; together with all these, who shall become one, I send a voice to You. Behold me! Enlighten my mind with Your never fading Light!"

"I offer this pipe to *Wakan-Tanka*, first through You O winged Power of the place where the sun goes down; there is a place for You in this pipe. Help us with those red and blue days which make the people holy!"

Kablaya then held up a pinch of tobacco, and after motioning with it to Heaven, Earth, and the four Powers, he placed it in the bowl of the pipe. Then after the following prayers, he placed pinches of tobacco in the pipe for each of the other directions.

"O winged Power of the place where *Waziah* lives, I am about to offer this pipe to *Wakan-Tanka*; help me with the two good red and blue days which You have—days which are purifying to the people and to the universe. There is a place for You in the pipe, and so help us!

"O You, Power there where the sun comes up; You who give knowledge and who guard the dawn of the day, help us with Your two red and blue days which give understanding and Light to the people. There is a place for You in this pipe which I am about to offer to *Wakan-Tanka*; help us!

"O You, most sacred Power at the place where we always face; You who are the source of life, and who guard the people and the coming generations, help us with Your two red and blue days! There is a place for You in the pipe.

"O You, Spotted Eagle of the heavens! we know that You have sharp eyes with which you see even the smallest object that moves on Grandmother Earth. O You, who are in the depths of the heavens, and who know everything, I am offering this pipe to *Wakan-Tanka!* Help us with Your two good red and blue days!

"O You, Grandmother Earth, who lie outstretched, supporting all things! upon You a two-legged is standing, offering a pipe to the Great Spirit. You are at the center of the two good red and blue days. There will be a place for You in the pipe and so help us!"

Kablaya then placed a small grain of tobacco in the pipe for each of the following birds: the kingbird; the robin; the lark, who sings during the two good days; the woodpecker; the hawk, who makes life so difficult for the other winged peoples; the eagle hawk; the magpie, who knows everything; the blackbird; and many other wingeds. Now all objects of creation and the six directions of space have been placed within the bowl of the pipe. The pipe was sealed with tallow and was leaned against the little blue drying rack.

Kablaya then took up another pipe, filled it, and went to where the sacred tree was resting. A live coal was brought, and the tree and the hole were purified with the smoke from sweet grass.

"O *Wakan-Tanka,*" Kablaya prayed as he held his pipe up with one hand, "behold this holy tree-person who will soon be placed in this hole. He will stand with the sacred pipe. I touch him with the sacred red earth paint from our Grandmother and also with the fat from the four-legged buffalo. By touching this tree-person with the red earth, we remember that the generations of all that move come from our Mother the Earth. With your help, O tree, I shall soon offer my body and soul to *Wakan-Tanka,* and in me I offer all my people and all the generations to come."

Kablaya then took the red paint, offered it to the six directions, and again spoke to the sacred tree: "O tree, you are about to stand up; be merciful to my people, that they may flourish under you."

Kablaya painted stripes of red on the west, north, east, and south sides of the tree, and then he touched a very little paint to the tip of the tree for the Great Spirit, and he also put some at the base of the tree for Mother Earth. Then Kablaya took up the skin of a buffalo calf, saying: "It is from this buffalo person that our people live; he gives to us our homes, our clothing, our food, everything we need. O buffalo calf, I now give to you a sacred place upon the tip of the tree. This tree will hold you in his hand and will raise you up to *Wakan-Tanka.* Behold what I am about to do! Through this, all things that move and fly upon the earth and in the heavens will be happy!"

Kablaya next held up a small cherry tree, and continued to pray: "Behold this, O *Wakan-Tanka,* for it is the tree of the people, which we pray will bear much fruit."

This little tree was then tied upon the sacred cottonwood, just below the buffalo hide, and with it there was tied a buckskin bag in which there was some fat.

Kablaya then took up the hide images of a buffalo and a man, and, offering them to the six directions, he prayed: "Behold this buffalo, O Grandfather, which You have given to us; he is the chief of all the four-leggeds upon our sacred Mother; from him the people live, and with him they walk the sacred path. Behold, too, this two-legged, who represents all the people. These are the two chiefs upon this great island; bestow upon them all the favors that they ask for, O *Wakan-Tanka!*"

These two images were then tied upon the tree, just underneath the place where the tree forks; after this Kablaya held up a bag of fat to be placed underneath the base of the tree, and he prayed in this manner:

"O Grandfather, *Wakan-Tanka,* behold this sacred fat, upon which this tree-person will stand; may the earth always be as fat and fruitful as this. O tree, this is a sacred day for you and for all our people; the earth within this hoop belongs to you, O tree, and it is here underneath you that I shall offer up my body and soul for the sake of the people. Here I shall stand, sending my voice to You, O *Wakan-Tanka,* as I offer the sacred pipe. All this may be difficult to do, yet for the good of the people it must be done. Help me, O Grandfather, and give to me courage and strength to stand the sufferings which I am about to undergo! O tree, you are now admitted to the sacred lodge!"

With much cheering and many shrill tremulos, the tree was raised, very slowly, for the men stopped four times before it was straight and dropped into the hole prepared for it. Now all the people—the two-leggeds, four-leggeds, and the wingeds of the air—were rejoicing, for they would all flourish under the protection of the tree. It helps us all to walk the sacred path; we can lean upon it, and it will always guide us and give us strength.

A little dance was held around the base of the tree, and then the surrounding lodge was made by putting upright, in a large circle, twenty-eight forked sticks, and from the fork of each stick a pole was placed which reached to the holy tree at the center.

I should explain to you here that in setting up the sun dance lodge, we are really making the universe in a likeness; for, you see, each of the posts around the lodge represents some particular object of creation, so that the whole circle is the entire creation, and the one tree at the center, upon which the twenty-eight poles rest, is *Wakan-Tanka,* who is the center of everything. Everything comes from Him, and sooner or later everything returns to Him. And I should also tell you why it is that we use twenty-eight poles. I have already explained why the numbers four and seven are sacred; then if you add four sevens you get twenty-eight.[3] Also the moon lives twenty-eight days, and this is our month; each of these days of the month represents something sacred to us: two of the days represent the Great Spirit; two are for Mother Earth; four are for the four winds; one is for the Spotted Eagle; one for the sun; and one for the moon; one is for the Morning Star; and four for the four ages; seven are for our seven great rites; one is for the buffalo; one for the fire; one for the water; one for the rock; and finally one is for the two-legged people. If you add all these days up you will see that they come to twenty-eight. You should also know that the buffalo has twenty-eight ribs, and that in our war bonnets we usually use twenty-eight feathers. You see, there is a significance for everything, and these are the things that are good for men to know, and to remember.

NOTES

1. In the *Atharva Veda Samhita* of the Hindu scriptures, we find a description of the significance of their World Tree, which is quite identical to the symbolism of the tree for the Lakota: "The World Tree in which the trunk, which is also the sun pillar, sacrificial post, and *axis mundi,* rising from the altar at the navel of the earth, penetrates the world door and branches outo above the root of the world (A. V. X. 7. 3.); as the 'non-existent (unmanifested) branch that yonder kindreds know as the Supernal' (A. C. X. 7. 21.)." (Translated by A. K. Coomaraswamy, "Svayamatrna: Janua Coeli," *Zalmoxis.*)

For a full explanation of the symbolism of the tree, see René Guénon, *Le Symbolisme de la Croix,* Les Edition Vega (Paris, 1931); especially Chap. IX, "L'Arbre du Milieu."

2. An interesting parallel to this attitude towards trees is found in an Islamic source: "[Holy] men dance and wheel on the [spiritual] battlefield: From within them musicians strike the tambourine: at their ecstacy the seas burst into foam. You see it not, but for *their* ears the leaves too on the boughs are clapping hands ... one must have the spiritual ear, not the ear of the body." (Jalaluddin Rumi, *The Mathnawi* [R. A. Nicholson translation, 8 vols., Cambridge University Press, Cambridge, 1926], III 9.)

3. Editor's note: For discussion of the number seven as sacred, please see *The Sacred Pipe: Black Elk's Account of the Seven Rites of the Oglala Sioux,* Joseph E. Brown, ed., (New York: Viking Penguin, 1971).

"A SERVICE OF WORSHIP: THE EARTH IS THE LORD'S— A LITURGY OF CELEBRATION, CONFESSION, THANKSGIVING, AND COMMITMENT"

National Council of Churches of Christ

CALL TO WORSHIP

Reader: The Earth is the Lord's and the fullness thereof, the world and all that dwells therein.

All: We live in God's world, we are not alone. We share this life with the heavens and the earth, with the waters and the land, with trees and grasses, with fish, birds, and animals, with creatures of every form, and with all our brothers and sisters.

Reader: God saw all that was made, and behold, it was very good.

HYMN

celebrating the beauty and mystery of creation

ACT OF CONFESSION

CALL TO CONFESSION (*USING DIFFERENT VOICES*)

God's creation is being abused and violated.
We as human beings often see ourselves as separate
from creation, not woven into the web of life.
The reference to having "dominion over the earth" is used
to exploit and destroy the earth.

Reprinted from *God's Earth Our Home*, National Council of Churches of Christ.

As individuals and as societies, we become dependent on
a lifestyle of limitless growth.
We are quick to blame and judge others rather than
accept responsibility for the part that we play
in destroying our environment.
We use more than our share of earth's resources.
We are responsible for massive pollution of earth, water,
and sky.
We thoughtlessly drop garbage around our homes,
schools, churches, places of work, and places of play.
Much of the world struggles for survival—good food, clean
water, adequate homes.
We squander resources on technologies of destruction.
Bombs come before bread.

All: We are killing the earth:

Voices: as mountains of garbage pile up

as uranium and nuclear wastes threaten life for centuries to come

as we use trees faster than they can regrow

as our precious agricultural land loses its fertility.

All: We are killing the waters:

Voices: as toxic chemicals and human wastes are

dumped into lakes, rivers and oceans

as fish and plants die from acid rain

as groundwater is poisoned.

All: We are killing the skies:

Voices: as the global atmosphere heats up from chemical gases

as the ozone layer is destroyed

as clean air is poisoned by car and truck pollution.

PRAYER OF CONFESSION

All: We confess these sins to you our God, Creator of the universe. You have set before us
life and death. Too often we have chosen death. We have not loved the earth as you love it.

PERIOD OF SILENT MEDITATION

ASSURANCE OF PARDON

Reader: Know that our God is a God of love as well as of judgment. God promises to be with
us as we struggle to be faithful. Thanks be to God.

PRAYER OF GRACE

All: Holy and great Creator, we recognize as your people that these problems will not easily be solved. Give us the courage to truly repent and change our ways. May we genuinely ask for forgiveness from you, from the earth and from future generations. May we live this day faithfully loving your creation as you love it. May we walk together toward the future with hope.

PERIOD OF SILENT MEDITATION

Participants may offer their own prayers for grace.

EXPERIENCING THE WORD

SCRIPTURES

MEDITATION

ACT OF THANKSGIVING

Voice: We are thankful for the passion of the children and youth among us who push us to recognize the urgency of the environmental crisis.

All: Thank you creator and giver of passion.

Voice: We are thankful for the wisdom of the aged among us who remind us of what it means to respect the earth and to live in community with one another.

All: Thank you creator and giver of wisdom.

Voice: We are thankful for the insights of the native brothers and sisters among us who draw on their tradition and teach us about the sacredness of all creation and how to live in kinship with it.

All: Thank you creator and giver of insight.

Voice: We are thankful for the inspiration of those among us who have already begun to live their lives in ways that show a caring for the earth, water, and the skies.

All: Thank you creator and giver of inspiration.

Participants may offer other thanksgivings in word or deed.

All: We thank you God for all signs of hope that keep us from despairing and point us toward new ways of living.

ACT OF COMMITMENT

Reader: We have confessed our part in hurting the earth. We have expressed our thanks for creation and those who care for it. We are ready to commit ourselves to a new way of living.

Let us think about the hard questions that can lead to this kind of change, such as:

How do we leave behind the ways that have abused the earth?

How do we show that we care for all creation?

What can we do to stop those whose actions cause great pollution problems?

PERIOD OF SILENT MEDITATION

OFFERINGS

HYMN

COMMISSIONING

Reader: God said: "I have seen the affliction of my people in Egypt; their loud cry of complaint against their slave drivers I have heard. I know well their suffering" (Exodus 3:7). In the power of the Spirit go forth, seeing the affliction of the earth as God sees it, hearing creation's cry of complaint as God hears it, knowing its suffering as God knows it.

All: We commit ourselves anew to seeing the affliction of the earth, hearing its cry, and knowing its suffering. We commit ourselves to learning more about the changes that are needed. We commit ourselves to embarking on that long and difficult road toward life lived in harmony with all God's creation.

In covenant with God and with the wisdom of the Holy Spirit, we are called to action in the name of Jesus the Christ.

Amen

A SERVICE OF WORSHIP
THE EARTH IS THE LORD'S

SUGGESTIONS FOR USE

The environmental crisis is a threat to today's world and to future generations. For congregations and groups using this liturgy, it is suggested that readers of various ages be involved and that nature and our destruction of it be represented through different media, symbols, and images. You are encouraged to approach the liturgy with imagination. You may wish to use it in part or in its entirety. Groups could use it or their own variations on regular occasions throughout the year.

"THE GREENING
OF BUDDHIST PRACTICE"

Kenneth Kraft

On January 5, 1993, a Japanese ship called the *Akatsuki Maru* returned to port with a contro-versial cargo: an estimated 1.5 metric tons of plutonium. Its 134-day voyage was the first step in a Japanese plan to send spent nuclear fuel to Europe to be reprocessed as plutonium, which will then be reused as fuel in nuclear reactors. However, the *Akatsuki Maru*'s 20,000-mile round trip provoked expressions of concern in more than forty countries, including public demonstrations in France and Japan. Experts charged that such voyages could not adequately be shielded from the risks of a nuclear accident or a terrorist attack. Editorial writers ques-tioned Japan's commitment to its own nonnuclear principles (reactor-grade plutonium can also be used to make nuclear weapons). Pointing to the nuclear aspirations of North Korea and other countries, some observers called for a worldwide halt in the recovery of plutonium from spent fuel.

Plutonium (named after Pluto, the Greek god of the underworld) is one of the deadliest substances known to humankind. A single speck ingested through the lungs or stomach is fatal. Plutonium-239 has a half-life of 24,400 years, but it continues to be dangerous for a quar-ter of a million years. If we think in terms of human generations, about twenty-five years, we are speaking of 10,000 generations that will be vulnerable unless the radioactivity is safely con-tained. In Buddhism, the number 10,000 is a concrete way of indicating something infinite. That may also be the unpleasant truth about plutonium: it is going to be with us forever.

The American scholar-activist Joanna Macy has suggested that our most enduring legacy to future generations may be the decisions we make about the production and disposal of radioactive materials. Our buildings and books may not survive us, but we will be held accountable for what we do with the toxic substances (nuclear and nonnuclear) that we con-tinue to generate in such great quantities. Buddhists have long believed that the present, the past, and the future are inextricably linked and ultimately inseparable. "Just consider whether or not there are any conceivable beings or any conceivable worlds which are not included in this present time," a thirteenth-century master asserted.[1] For human beings at least, to sabotage the future is also to ravage the past and undermine the present. Although the threat of nuclear holocaust appears to have abated, we are beginning to see that the ongoing degradation of the

Reprinted from *Cross Currents: A Journal of Religion and Intellectual Life*, Summer 1994, Vol. 44, No. 2, pp. 163–179, by permission of *Cross Currents*.

environment poses a threat of comparable danger. As the *Akatsuki Maru* ships plutonium to Japan, it is also carrying a radioactive cargo, a "poison fire," into our common future.

I am reminded of a Zen *kōan* still used in the training of monks. The master says to the student: "See that boat moving way out there on the water? How do you stop it?" To give a proper answer the student must be able to demonstrate that he has "become one" with the boat. Just as one must penetrate deeply into a *kōan* to solve it, Buddhists around the world have begun to immerse themselves in environmental issues, attempting to approach urgent problems from the inside as well as the outside. An increasing number of practitioner-activists believe that the only way to stop the boat of ecological disaster is to deepen our relationship to the planet and all life within it.

In this essay I would like to survey some of the ways in which Buddhists are responding to the environmental issues faced by so many countries today. I will concentrate on spiritual/religious practices and forms of activism that take place in a spiritual context. Although many Buddhists in Asia and elsewhere are becoming increasingly aware of ecology, I focus principally on North American Buddhists, who seem to be taking the lead in the "greening" of Buddhism. Of course, what we need most are *human* responses to the environmental crisis rather than "Buddhist" ones; when the Buddhist label is used here, it is almost always used in that spirit.

INDIVIDUAL PRACTICES
RELATED TO THE ENVIRONMENT

A list of individual practices must begin with traditional forms of Buddhist meditation (and closely related practices such as chanting). Meditation can serve as a vehicle for advancing several ends prized by environmentalists: it is supposed to reduce egoism, deepen appreciation of one's surroundings, foster empathy with other beings, clarify intention, prevent what is now called burnout, and ultimately lead to a profound sense of oneness with the entire universe. "I came to realize clearly," said a Japanese Zen master upon attaining enlightenment, "that Mind is not other than mountains and rivers and the great wide earth, the sun and the moon and the stars."[2]

For some Buddhists, meditation alone is regarded as a sufficient expression of ecological awareness. Others supplement time-honored forms of meditation with new meditative practices that incorporate nature imagery or environmental themes. For example, the following verse by the Vietnamese Zen teacher Thich Nhat Hanh is widely used by his American students, who recite it mentally in seated meditation:

Breathing in, I know that I am breathing in.
Breathing out, I know that I am breathing out.

Breathing in, I see myself as a flower.
Breathing out, I feel fresh.

Breathing in, I see myself as a mountain.
Breathing out, I feel solid.

Breathing in, I see myself as still water.
Breathing out, I reflect things as they are.

Breathing in, I see myself as space.
Breathing out, I feel free.[3]

Thich Nhat Hanh has helped to popularize another method of individual practice—short poems (*gāthā*) that can prompt us to maintain awareness in daily life. Many of these "mindfulness verses" also function as reminders of our interconnectedness with the earth. The verses may be memorized or posted in appropriate locations. For example, when turning on a water faucet, a person following this practice will mentally recite:

Water flows from high in the mountains.
Water runs deep in the Earth.
Miraculously, water comes to us,
and sustains all life.

Washing one's hands can become an occasion for renewing one's dedication to the environment:

Water flows over these hands.
May I use them skillfully
to preserve our precious planet.[4]

The following verse, meant to be used when getting into a car, again evokes a twofold mindfulness—for the moment and for interrelatedness:

Entering this powerful car,
I buckle my seatbelt
and vow to protect all beings.[5]

The cultivation of intimacy with nature is a central aim for many Buddhist environmentalists. Buddhist activist Stephanie Kaza, who has written about her "conversations" with trees, suggests other ways to develop empathy with the natural environment:

One may engage in relationship with the moon, observing its waxing and waning cycle, position in the sky, and effect on one's moods and energy. One may cultivate relationships with migrating shorebirds, hatching dragonflies, or ancient redwoods. One may learn the topography of local rivers and mountains. These relations are not one-time encounters; rather they are ongoing friendships.[6]

The deepening sense of connectedness with our surroundings sometimes acquires an emotional intensity comparable to that of love or marriage. One practitioner writes, "This kind of in-love-ness—passionate, joyful—stimulates action in service to our imperiled planet. Walking in the world as if it were our lover leads inevitably to deep ecology."[7]

GROUP PRACTICES

When we turn our attention to group practices, we find that new and diverse forms are being created at a rapid rate. For American Buddhists, the family has become fertile ground for the potential elaboration of spiritual practice in daily life, and environmental concerns are often addressed in this setting. A parent from Colorado treats recycling as a "family ecological ritual," using it "to bring out the meaning of interbeing."[8] At most American Buddhist centers, conservation of resources and reduction of waste is a conscious part of communal practice. The responsibilities of the "ecological officer" at one center include: "educating workers and management about waste, recycling, conservation, etc.; evaluating operational procedures in terms of waste and efficiency; and investigating ecologically correct product lines."[9]

The Zen Center of Rochester, New York, conducts an "earth relief ceremony" that includes chanting, circumambulation, devotional offerings, prostrations, and monetary donations. Buddhist rituals traditionally end with a chant that "transfers the merit" of the event to a designated recipient. The earth relief ceremony ends with the following invocation:

> Tonight we have offered candles, incense, fruit, and tea,
> Chanted sutras and *dharani.*
> Whatever merit comes to us from these offerings
> We now return to the earth, sea, and sky.
> May our air be left pure!
> May our waters be clean!
> May our earth be restored!
> May all beings attain Buddhahood![10]

The Rochester Zen Center also sponsors rites specifically on behalf of animals. Ducks and other animals are purchased from pet stores or breeders and released in their natural habitats, and relief ceremonies for endangered species are held.

In northern California the Ring of Bone Zendo has found ways to integrate backpacking, pilgrimage, and *sesshin,* the intensive meditation retreat that undergirds formal Zen training. First conceived by poet and Zen pioneer Gary Snyder in the 1970s, this "mountains and rivers sesshin" emphasizes long hours of silent, concentrated walking in the foothills of the Sierra Mountains. "The wilderness pilgrim's step-by-step breath-by-breath walk up a trail," writes Snyder, "is so ancient a set of gestures as to bring a profound sense of body-mind joy."[11] The daily schedule also includes morning and evening periods of seated meditation and a morning lecture by the teacher, who expounds on the "Mountains and Rivers Sutra" chapter of *The Treasury of the True Dharma Eye*, by Zen master Dōgen. This text includes the following passage:

> It is not just that there is water in the world; there are worlds in the realm of water. And this is so not only in water—there are also worlds of sentient beings in clouds, there are worlds of sentient beings in wind, there are worlds of sentient beings in fire, there are worlds of sentient beings in earth. . . . Where there are worlds of sentient beings, there must be the world of Buddhas and Zen adepts.[12]

The Ring of Bone Zendo conducts weeklong backpacking sesshins twice a year, and the practice has spread to other West Coast Zen groups.

In March 1991, Thich Nhat Hanh inaugurated another kind of group practice in a six-day meditation retreat specifically for environmentalists. The two hundred people who traveled to Malibu, California, for the event included members of Greenpeace, Earth First!, Earth Island Institute, Rainforest Action Network, Natural Resources Defense Council, and other environmental organizations. Some were practicing Buddhists; others had little previous exposure to Buddhism or meditation. The retreat interposed periods of meditation with lectures by Nhat Hanh, silent walks through the Malibu hills, and gentle singing. In his talks, Nhat Hanh stressed the value of "deep, inner peace" for environmental activists: "The best way to take care of the environment is to take care of the environmentalist."[13]

One of the sites administered by the San Francisco Zen Center is Green Gulch Farm, a sizeable tract of land in scenic Marin County, California. Green Gulch functions as a semi-rural Zen center, complete with a large meditation hall, guest rooms, an abbot's cottage, and a Japanese-style tea house. But Green Gulch is best known for its extensive organic garden, which has been lovingly cultivated for two decades by numerous Zen practitioners, newcomers and veterans alike. On Earth Day, April 22, 1990, over a hundred friends of Green Gulch participated in special celebratory rituals that concluded with a dedication to the animals and plants that had died in the garden. The text read in part:

> Plants and Animals in the Garden,
> We welcome you—we invite you in—we ask your forgiveness and your understanding.
> Listen as we invoke your names, as we also listen for you:
> Little sparrows, quail, robins, and house finches who have died in our strawberry nets;
> Young Cooper's hawk who flew into our sweet pea trellis and broke your neck;
> Numerous orange-bellied newts who died in our shears, in our irrigation pipes, by our cars, and by our feet . . . ;
> Gophers and moles, trapped and scorned by us, and also watched with love, admiration, and awe for your one-mindedness . . . ;

And all plants we have shunned: poison hemlock, pigweed, bindweed, stinging nettle, bull thistle;

We call up plants we have removed by dividing you and separating you, and by deciding you no longer grow well here. ‾

We invoke you and thank you and continue to learn from you. We dedicate this ceremony to you. We will continue to practice with you and for you.[14]

This dedication follows ritual conventions that are found not only in Buddhism but also in other traditions. It directly addresses unseen beings or spirits, invites them into a sacred space, expresses sentiments ranging from grief to gratitude to awe, and concludes with a pledge of continued spiritual striving. The admission that many animals and plants had to be sacrificed for the garden to flourish should not be construed as hypocrisy; rather, the passage acknowledges the mystery of life and death, and it affirms—realistically, amid complexity—the cardinal precept not to kill. In the complete text, the detailed naming of animals and plants recreates a rich natural realm, elicits renewed attentiveness to that realm, and generates the cumulative power that ritual invocations require.

Another consciously created group ritual that illustrates the greening of Buddhist practice is called the Council of All Beings. It began in 1985 as a collaboration between Joanna Macy and John Seed, an Australian who embraced Buddhism and then became a passionate advocate of rainforest preservation. According to Seed, the Council of All Beings helps people to move "from having ecological ideas to having ecological identity, ecological self. . . . In the end, what we want to do is to turn people into activists."[15] The Council is usually presented as a daylong workshop or longer retreat in a setting with access to the outdoors; participants vary from a dozen to a hundred.

The ritual begins with shared mourning. Participants are encouraged to express their sense of grief and loss in response to the degradation of the earth. "One by one, people bring forward a stone or twig or flower, and laying it in the center, name what it represents for them. . . . In the ritual naming of these losses, we retrieve our capacity to care."[16] The premise is that we ordinarily refrain from expressing our anguish about the planet because we fear that we may be overwhelmed by sadness, or because we assume that such feelings are socially unacceptable. In the second phase of a Council, called "remembering," participants are led through exercises that reinforce their sense of connectedness with the earth. Methods include guided meditations and visualizations, body movement, drumming, and "sounding"—imitating the voices of animals or other natural sounds. Macy once had an opportunity to demonstrate part of a "remembering" exercise to the Dalai Lama. Taking his hand in hers, she said:

Each atom in each cell in this hand goes back to the beginning of time, to the first explosion of light and energy, to the formation of the galaxies and solar systems, to the fires and rains that bathed our planet, and the life-forms that issued from its primordial seas. . . . We have met and been together many times.

"Yes, of course," said the Dalai Lama. "Very good."[17]

For the culmination of the ritual, each participant chooses a nonhuman life-form, imaginatively identifies with it, and then speaks on its behalf before the group. The form chosen may be an animal, a plant, a river, or a mountain. Circumstances permitting, the participants make masks or breastplates to reinforce their adopted identity. Gathering to form the Council of All Beings, the recreated life-forms describe their plight, how they have been affected by humans, and their chances of survival. At a signal from the leader, some of the participants shed their selected identities to become human listeners inside the circle. Each of the life-forms is then asked what strengths it has to offer human beings in this time of planetary crisis. Here are some typical responses, as paraphrased by Macy:

> "I, lichen, work slowly, very slowly. Time is my friend. This is what I give you: patience for the long haul and perseverance."
>
> "It is a dark time. As deep-diving trout I offer you my fearlessness of the dark."
>
> "I, lion, give you my roar, the voice to speak out and be heard."[18]

The Council of All Beings expresses in modern terms the trans-species compassion that has long been a Buddhist ideal. Council participants not only mourn the loss of animals and plants (as at Green Gulch); they also strive to listen to other beings and imaginatively become them. In a ritual context, this crossing of human/nonhuman boundaries is not meant to answer complex questions about the relative value of species; its thrust is to enable participants to reconnect with an ecocentric (non-anthropocentric) world. Although the Council's format is still being modified, and its dissemination seems to have been hampered by a dearth of talented facilitators, it offers a foretaste of what Gary Snyder once called "a kind of ultimate democracy," in which "plants and animals . . . are given a place and a voice in the political discussions of the humans."[19]

GREEN BUDDHISM'S GLOBAL REACH

With increased communication and cooperation among Buddhists around the globe, Buddhist-inspired environmentalism is also becoming manifest in national and international arenas. Thailand, for example, has been the source of several influential projects. The Buddhist Perception of Nature Project, founded in 1985, uses traditional Buddhist doctrines and practices to teach environmental principles to ordinary villagers and city-dwellers. The International Network of Engaged Buddhists (INEB), established in 1989 by Nobel Peace Prize nominee Sulak Sivaraksa, puts environmental concerns high on its agenda, with special emphasis on Third-World issues. In rural Thailand, environmentally conscious monks have

Kenneth Kraft

helped protect endangered forests and watersheds by "ordaining" trees: villagers are loath to chop down trees that have been symbolically accepted into the Buddhist monastic order.

An unusual example of a Buddhist program with global repercussions is found in a successful baking business run by the Zen Community of Yonkers, New York. Since the late 1980s the Zen Community has cooperated with Ben and Jerry's ice cream company to produce Rainforest Crunch cookies. The product uses certain nuts and nut flour in an ecologically sustainable way, so it helps to protect Amazonian rainforests and support Brazilian farming cooperatives. A percentage of profits is donated to groups like the Rainforest Action Network. With $1.6 million in annual sales (1991), the bakery has also provided employment to about two hundred local residents, some of them formerly homeless. The advertising slogan for this popular product is a cheerful reminder of interconnectedness: "Eat a Cookie. Save a Tree."

The best-known international spokesperson for Buddhism, the Dalai Lama, has made many statements in support of environmental responsibility on a global scale. Strictly speaking, the Dalai Lama's teachings may not qualify as environmental "activism," but his ideas and his example are important sources of inspiration for socially engaged Buddhists. With his usual directness, he says, "The Earth, our Mother, is telling us to behave."[20] The Dalai Lama has proposed a five-point peace plan for Tibet that extends the notion of peace to the entire Tibetan ecosystem. He first presented his peace plan in 1987, speaking before the United States Congress, and he restated it in his 1989 Nobel Peace Prize address and again at the 1992 Earth Summit in Rio. On these occasions he has said, in part:

> Prior to the Chinese invasion, Tibet was an unspoiled wilderness sanctuary in a unique natural environment. Sadly, in the past decades the wildlife and the forests of Tibet have been almost totally destroyed by the Chinese. The effects on Tibet's delicate environment have been devastating. . . .
>
> It is my dream that the entire Tibetan plateau should become a free refuge where humanity and nature can live in peace and in harmonious balance. . . . The Tibetan plateau would be transformed into the world's largest park or biosphere. Strict laws would be enforced to protect wildlife and plant life; the exploitation of natural resources would be carefully regulated so as not to damage relevant ecosystems; and a policy of sustainable development would be adopted in populated areas.[21]

A decade ago the Dalai Lama supported nuclear power as a possible way to improve living conditions for the world's poor, but since then his thinking has changed. As part of his peace plan, he now rejects any use of nuclear energy in Tibet, not to mention "China's use of Tibet for the production of nuclear weapons and the dumping of nuclear waste."[22]

Even if the Dalai Lama's ambitious plan seems unrealistic by the standards of realpolitik, his proposal has exposed a worldwide audience to a Buddhist vision of a desirable society. Central to that vision is the attempt to extend the ideal of nonviolence *(ahimsa)* to all forms of life. Some people come to embrace environmentalism as an extension of their commitment to nonviolence, just as others come to embrace nonviolence via their commitment to the environment.

A final example of Buddhist-inspired environmental activity that is finding expression on a national and international scale is called the Nuclear Guardianship Project (NGP). Its targeted problem is radioactive waste, which brings us back to the *Akatsuki Maru* and its 1.5 metric tons of dangerous cargo. The concept of nuclear guardianship, advocated most forcefully by Joanna Macy, begins with the premise that current technological expertise does not offer a certifiably safe method for the disposal of nuclear waste: plans to bury the waste underground overlook known risks; transmutation and glassification schemes have not yet been perfected; and other proposals (such as shooting the waste into space) are even less realistic. From these assumptions, Macy and other project participants argue that nuclear waste should be stored in an accessible manner using the best available technology, monitored with great care, and recontained in new ways as technology advances.

But the thinking of NGP strategists is not limited to scientific and political calculations. If we are to succeed in protecting future generations from lethal radioactivity, they claim, people must also be inspired mythically and spiritually. Without a grander vision and deeper motivation, we might not even be able to implement whatever technical solutions become available. For Macy, one possible way to foster new attitudes would be to turn each nuclear site into a center of activity related to guardianship. She describes the genesis of this idea:

> It started with a kind of vision I had in England in 1983, when I visited the peace camps that had spontaneously arisen around nuclear bases. . . . I sensed that I was on sacred ground. I had a feeling of *déjà vu*. I thought, "Oh, maybe I'm being reminded of the monasteries that kept the flame of learning alive in the Middle Ages." People made pilgrimages to those places too. But then I realized, "No, this is about the *future*. This is how the radioactive remains are going to be guarded for the sake of future beings."[23]

Because such sites would require unwavering vigilance, they would entail a social version of the mindfulness practice that is so central to Buddhism. "We can contain the radioactivity if we pay attention to it," writes Macy. "That act of attention may be the last thing we want to do, but it is the one act that is required."[24] She goes on to suggest that surveillance communities built around today's nuclear facilities could also become centers for various activities beyond the technical process of containment: pilgrimage, meditation retreats, rituals "of acceptance and forgiveness," even a kind of monastic training. One hopeful NGP participant declares, "Let us build beautiful shrines, life-affirming shrines, with gardens and rooms for meditation."[25]

Not content merely to outline the possibilities, Macy and others are experimenting with ritual forms to be used in study groups and public workshops. They are even willing to modify the traditional four vows taken by Mahayana Buddhists, by adding a fifth vow:

Sentient beings are numberless; I'll do the best I can to save them.

Desires are inexhaustible; I'll do the best I can to put an end to them.

The Dharmas are boundless; I'll do the best I can to master them.

The Poison Fire lasts forever; I'll do the best I can to contain it.

The Buddha way is unsurpassable; I'll do the best I can to attain it.[26]

An NGP event often begins with an invocation to beings of the past, present, and future, welcoming them as companions and allies in a time of need. Future beings are summoned with these words:

All you who will come after us on this Earth, be with us now. All you who are waiting to be born in the ages to come, it is for your sakes too that we work to heal our world. We cannot picture your faces or say your names—you have none yet—but we would feel the reality of your claim on life.[27]

During a three-day NGP retreat in Mendocino County, California, seventy-five participants enacted a future pilgrimage to a guardian site, half of them playing the role of pilgrims, the rest posing as resident guardians. Some of the texts that are used in these NGP exercises look back at the present from an imagined future. One passage reads in part:

Pilgrims, Guardians, we are gathered here at the Great Guardian Site of Rancho Seco a brief two hundred years since the turning from the Times of Nuclear Peril. Here in the Silkwood Pavilion we are engaged in the essential practice of Remembering. We must remember, because we cannot uninvent the nuclear technology that almost killed our planet. . . .

Oh, what power it unleashed! Yes, the poison fire was first used for weapons, against great cities of a great people. And we know the names, and you can say them in your heart—we shall not forget them: Hiroshima, Nagasaki. A quarter of a million people burned at once, then many more sickened slowly, for that is how it destroys—slowly, hidden. Yet still our ancestors built bombs with the poison fire, scores of thousands more, and called them "war heads."

And then our ancestors of that time—this is also painful to remember—they took that poison fire to make electricity. We know how easy it is to share the power of the sun and the wind. But they took the poison fire and used it to boil water. And the signs of sickening grew. . . .

And the Governments tried to bury it. There were places called Carlsbad, Yucca Mountain: deep holes half a mile down. They wanted to bury it as if the Earth were not alive. . . .

Yet among our ancestors in those dark times were those whose practice of mindfulness allowed them to look directly at the poison fire. They looked into their hearts and thought: "We can guard the poison fire. We can overcome our fear of guarding it and be mindful. Only in that way can the beings of the future be protected." They remembered us![28]

Chapters of the Nuclear Guardianship Project have been formed in Germany, Switzerland, and Russia. The NGP has also been introduced to Japan, where one cannot help but note that major reactors have already been given religious names that would fit a guardian site perfectly: "Monju"—bodhisattva of wisdom, "Fugen"—bodhisattva of compassionate action, and "Jōyō"—eternal light.

The Nuclear Guardianship Project is difficult to assess. It has not yet made inroads among nuclear engineers, much less been tested in the public domain. To some observers it seems wildly fanciful, because it expects to transform deep-seated psychological responses to nuclear waste: denial of responsibility ("not in my backyard") and denial of danger ("it's not making us sick"). The NGP must contend with lingering disagreement among scientists on technical issues, and it must deal with the economic realities of implementing accessible containment on a massive scale. However, the greatest source of resistance may be our apparent unwillingness to reduce our material standard of living voluntarily. The best way to limit future nuclear waste is simply to stop producing it, but that course would call for radical social changes that few citizens anywhere are willing to contemplate. It is one thing to recognize the risks of nuclear energy, but quite another to change the systems and personal habits that currently demand it.

Regardless of the NGP's potential to influence affairs in the political realm, the concept of nuclear guardianship is certainly intriguing as a religious vision. This is not the first time that Buddhists have believed that the world is coming to an end in some significant way, and that an unprecedented response is required. In past eras, predictions about the imminent disappearance of the Buddha's teachings led to a revitalization of religion and sometimes to major shifts in society. By directing attention to the distant future, Macy invites us to "reinhabit" a deep, mythological sense of time; such a perspective is a welcome antidote to the impoverished, constricted sense of time that prevails in industrial societies. In a similar manner, the NGP calls for a dramatic extension of our sense of ethical responsibility. The notion of guardianship begins with plutonium but goes on to embrace numberless unborn beings and the planet as a whole.

POINTS OF DEPARTURE FROM BUDDHISM'S PAST

It is clear that an ecologically sensitive Buddhism exhibits significant continuities with traditional Buddhism, continuities that can be demonstrated textually, doctrinally, historically, and by other means. Sustained inquiry by scholars and practitioners will continue to elucidate those links. It is also instructive to consider the ways in which today's green Buddhism may depart from Buddhism's past. The individual and group activities surveyed here are not only innovative on the level of practice; in many cases they also embody consequential shifts in Buddhists' perceptions of nature and society.

In several contexts we have seen ecobuddhists struggling to think and act globally; that breadth of commitment is itself a trait that distinguishes today's activists from most of their

Buddhist predecessors. Just as current environmental problems are planetary as well as local, present-day Buddhism has become international as well as regional. For centuries, classic Buddhist texts have depicted the universe as one interdependent whole, and elegant doctrines have laid the conceptual foundation for a "cosmic ecology."[29] Contemporary Buddhist environmentalists are seeking to actualize that vision with a concreteness that seems unprecedented in the history of Buddhism.

The increased awareness of the sociopolitical implications of spiritual practice is another feature that might qualify as a departure from earlier forms of Buddhism. Socially engaged Buddhism is one of the notable developments in late twentieth-century Buddhism, and environmental Buddhism is an important stream within this larger movement. There is a well-known Zen story in which a master rebukes a monk for discarding a single chopstick. The original point is that even if the chopstick's mate is lost, it still has intrinsic value and can be put to use in some other way. In today's world, the widespread use of disposable chopsticks might suggest other lessons about the far-reaching environmental impact of daily actions.[30] Green Buddhists no longer assume that spiritual practice can take place in a social or environmental vacuum. Moreover, they believe that an overly individualistic model of practice may actually impede cooperative efforts to improve social conditions.

The importance of women and of women's perspectives is another characteristic of ecobuddhism that distinguishes it from more traditional forms of Buddhism. Today's environmentally sensitive Buddhists want to free themselves and others from sexist patterns of thought, behavior, and language. Women, no less than men, are the leaders, creative thinkers, and grassroots activists of green Buddhism. The influence of women also manifests itself in an aversion to hierarchy, an appreciation of the full range of experience, and an emphasis on the richness of relationships (human and nonhuman). Out of this milieu, the notion of the world "as lover" has emerged as a model for a new bond between humanity and nature. The ancient Greek goddess Gaia, who has been reclaimed by many people as a symbol of the earth, is also embraced by Buddhist environmentalists, men and women alike. Even the Buddha is sometimes feminized, as in the following gatha by Thich Nhat Hanh:

> I entrust myself to Earth;
> Earth entrusts herself to me.
> I entrust myself to Buddha;
> Buddha entrusts herself to me.[31]

Shifting perceptions of nature denote another area in which past Buddhism and present Buddhism diverge. Buddhists have long been sensitive to the transitory nature of things. In Japan, for example, generations of poets have "grieved" over the falling of cherry blossoms. Yet according to the premodern Buddhist view, nature's impermanence is also natural, part of the way things are, so the process of extinction (in a paradoxical way) is also reassuring. The grief of Buddhist environmentalists is prompted not by falling cherry blossoms but by the actual loss of entire species of living beings, and by the continuing devastation of the planet. A new dimension of meaning has been added to the time-honored Buddhist notion of impermanence. Gary Snyder writes:

> The extinction of a species, each one a pilgrim of four billion years of evolution, is an irreversible loss. The ending of the lines of so many creatures with whom we have traveled this far is an occasion for profound sorrow and grief. . . . Some quote a Buddhist teaching back at us: "all is impermanent." Indeed. All the more reason to move gently and cause less harm.[32]

Perennial assumptions about nature's power to harm human beings have been augmented by a fresh appreciation of humans' power to harm nature. In an early text the Buddha gives his monks a prayer which reads in part:

> My love to the footless, my love to the twofooted, my love to the four footed, my love to the manyfooted. Let not the footless harm me, let not the twofooted harm me, let not the four-footed harm me, let not the manyfooted harm me. All sentient beings, all breathing things, creatures without exception, let them all see good things, may no evil befall them.[33]

This passage expresses generous concern for other beings, yet it also serves as a protective charm against dangerous animals (especially poisonous snakes)—if I don't harm them, they won't harm me. In contrast, the ceremonial texts from Green Gulch Farm or the Nuclear Guardianship Project are most concerned about human threats to nature. Religious power is invoked in each case, but in the new texts that power is summoned to protect the environment from us and to atone for our depredations.

In many Buddhist cultures, nature has functioned as the ideal setting in which to seek salvation. Traditionally, movement toward nature was regarded as a type of *withdrawal:* one retreated to the mountains or the jungle to be free of society's defilements and distractions. But for contemporary Buddhists a deepening relation with nature is usually associated with a spirit of *engagement.* Even if the experience of heightened intimacy with nature is private and contemplative, that experience is commonly interpreted as a call to action. In this new context nature nonetheless retains its potential soteric power. For many Buddhist activists, preservation of the environment doubles as a spiritual path to personal and planetary salvation.

CONCLUSION

Critics and supporters of contemporary Buddhist environmentalism have already raised a number of provocative questions. Seasoned Buddhist practitioners suspect that the comparisons between "ecological awakening" and a true enlightenment experience are too facile. Buddhist scholars in North America and Japan ask if there a point at which the distance from traditional Buddhism becomes so great that the Buddhist label is no longer appropriate. Others express concern about the New Age elements that seem to be part of ecobuddhism (such as NGP rituals evoking the future), and they are not sure how to assess such elements. Buddhist environmentalists take these issues seriously and raise further questions. In daily life, how can traditional Buddhist practices and new ecologically oriented practices be meaningfully integrated? To what degree can a modern environmental ethic be extrapolated from these individual and group practices? What is the relation of green Buddhism to other forms of environmentalism, including deep ecology? Such questions will continue to generate discussion and reflection as the various forms of socially engaged Buddhism evolve and mature.

From certain perspectives it may seem that Buddhist environmentalism is marginal, especially in the United States. After all, "green politics" has appealed only to a minority in the culture at large; Buddhism captures only a percentage point or two in the national religious census; and even within American Buddhist communities, not everyone is interested in environmental issues or their relation to practice. If there is a way to communicate the key ideas and basic practices of green Buddhism to a wider public, it has not yet been found. Granted, Buddhists may have affected the outcome in a number of local campaigns, saving an old-growth forest in Oregon, protecting a watershed in northern California, blocking a proposed nuclear dump in a California desert. In such cases, however, it is hard to isolate distinctively "Buddhist" influences.

The potential significance of green Buddhism can also be considered from a religious standpoint. Even if there is little visible evidence of impact, Buddhism may nonetheless be contributing to a shift in the lives of individuals or the conduct of certain groups. Some would argue that if only one person's life is changed through an ecological awakening, the repercussions of that transformation have important and continuing effects in realms seen and unseen. An abiding faith in the fundamental interconnectedness of all existence provides many individual activists with the energy and focus that enable them to stay the course. Simply to return to a unitive experience is often enough: "We don't need to call it Buddhism —or Dharma or Gaia. We need only to be still and open our senses to the world that presents itself to us moment to moment to moment."[34]

NOTES

1. Dōgen, in Philip Kapleau, *The Three Pillars of Zen*, rev. ed. (New York: Doubleday, 1989), 310.

2. Quoted in Kapleau, *The Three Pillars of Zen*, 215.

3. Thich Nhat Hanh, *Touching Peace: Practicing the Art of Mindful Living* (Berkeley: Parallax Press, 1992), 11–12.

4. Thich Nhat Hanh, *Present Moment, Wonderful Moment: Mindfulness Verses for Daily Living* (Berkeley: Parallax Press, 1990), 9, 10.

5. *The Mindfulness Bell* 1:3 (Autumn 1990): 16.

6. Stephanie Kaza, "Planting Seeds of Joy" (unpublished paper, 1992), 13.

7. Lenore Friedman, "Book Reviews," *Turning Wheel* (Fall 1991): 39.

8. *The Mindfulness Bell* 4 (Spring 1991): 17.

9. *The Ten Directions* 11:1 (Spring/Summer 1990): 15.

10. Rochester Zen Center, "Earth Relief Ceremony" (unpublished manual, 1992).

11. Gary Snyder, *The Practice of the Wild* (San Francisco: North Point Press, 1990), 94.

12. Thomas Cleary, trans., *Shōbōgenzō: Zen Essays by Dōgen* (Honolulu: University of Hawaii Press, 1986), 98.

13. *The Mindfulness Bell* 7 (Summer/Fall 1992): 6.

14. "Earth Day Ceremony at Green Gulch Zen Center," *Buddhist Peace Fellowship Newsletter* (Summer 1990): 32–33.

15. Rik Scarce, *Eco-Warriors: Understanding the Radical Environmental Movement* (Chicago: Noble Press, 1990), 227.

16. Joanna Macy, *World as Lover, World as Self* (Berkeley: Parallax Press, 1991), 200.

17. Ibid., 202.

18. Ibid., 205.

19. Gary Snyder, *Turtle Island* (New York: New Directions, 1974), 104.

20. Allan Hunt Badiner, *Dharma Gaia: A Harvest of Essays in Buddhism and Ecology* (Berkeley: Parallax Press, 1990), v.

21. The Dalai Lama, "Five-Point Peace Plan for Tibet," in Petra K. Kelly, Gert Bastian, and Pat Aiello, eds., *The Anguish of Tibet* (Berkeley: Parallax Press, 1991), 291; the Dalai Lama, "A Zone of Peace," in Martine Batchelor and Kerry Brown, eds., *Buddhism and Ecology* (London: Cassell, 1992), 112–13.

22. Kelly, Bastian, and Aiello, *The Anguish of Tibet,* 288.

23. "Guardians of the Future," *In Context* 28 (Spring 1991): 20.

24. "Technology and Mindfulness," *Nuclear Guardianship Forum* 1 (Spring 1992): 3.

25. N. Llyn Peabody, "A Summary of the Council Discussion," *Buddhist Peace Fellowship Newsletter* 10:3/4 (Fall 1988): 23.

26. "Buddhist Vows for Guardianship," *Nuclear Guardianship Forum* 1 (Spring 1992): 2.

27. Macy, *World as Lover, World as Self,* 207.

28. The Fire Group, "Remembering at a Future Guardian Site," *Buddhist Peace Fellowship Newsletter* (Winter 1991): 18–19.

29. Francis H. Cook, *Hua-yen Buddhism: The Jewel Net of Indra* (University Park: Pennsylvania State University Press, 1977), 2.

30. Even if disposable chopsticks do not contribute to the destruction of rainforests (experts disagree), comparable examples are abundant.

31. Nhat Hanh, *Present Moment, Wonderful Moment,* 59.

32. Snyder, *The Practice of the Wild,* 176.

33. *Aṅguttara Nikāya*, Pali Text Society Publications 2, 72–73.

34. Nina Wise, "Thâystock at Spirit Rock," *The Mindfulness Bell* 5 (Autumn 1991): 19.

"INVOCATION"

John Seed

We ask for the presence of the spirit of Gaia and pray that the breath of life continues to caress this planet home.

May we grow into true understanding—a deep understanding that inspires us to protect the tree on which we bloom, and the water, soil and atmosphere without which we have no existence.

May we turn inwards and stumble upon our true roots in the intertwining biology of this exquisite planet. May nourishment and power pulse through these roots, and fierce determination to continue the billion-year dance.

May love well up and burst forth from our hearts.

May there be a new dispensation of pure and powerful consciousness and the charter to witness and facilitate the healing of the tattered biosphere.

We ask for the presence of the spirit of Gaia to be with us here. To reveal to us all that we need to see, for our own highest good and for the highest good of all.

We call upon the spirit of evolution, the miraculous force that inspires rocks and dust to weave themselves into biology. You have stood by us for millions and billions of years—do not forsake us now. Empower us and awaken in us pure and dazzling creativity. You that can turn scales into feathers, seawater to blood, caterpillars to butterflies, metamorphose *our* species, awaken in us the powers that we need to survive the present crisis and evolve into more aeons of our solar journey.

Awaken in us a sense of who we truly are: tiny ephemeral blossoms on the Tree of Life. Make the purposes and destiny of that tree our own purpose and destiny.

Fill each of us with love for our true Self, which includes all of the creatures and plants and landscapes of the world. Fill us with a powerful urge for the well-being and continual unfolding of *this* Self.

May we speak in all human councils on behalf of the animals and plants and landscapes of the Earth.

May we shine with a pure inner passion that will spread rapidly through these leaden times.

May we all awaken to our true and only nature—none other than the nature of Gaia, this living planet Earth.

Reprinted from *Thinking Like A Mountain: Towards a Council of All Beings* edited by John Seed by permission of New Society Publishers.

We call upon the power which sustains the planets in their orbits, that wheels our Milky Way in its 200-million-year spiral, to imbue our personalities and our relationships with harmony, endurance and joy. Fill us with a sense of immense time so that our brief, flickering lives may truly reflect the work of vast ages past and also the millions of years of evolution whose potential lies in our trembling hands.

O stars, lend us your burning passion.

O silence, give weight to our voice.

We ask for the presence of the spirit of Gaia.

John Seed

"GAIA MEDITATIONS"

John Seed and Joanna Macy

What are you? What am I? Intersecting cycles of water, earth, air and fire, that's what I am, that's what you are.

Water—blood, lymph, mucus, sweat, tears, inner oceans tugged by the moon, tides within and tides without. Streaming fluids floating our cells, washing and nourishing through endless riverways of gut and vein and capillary. Moisture pouring in and through and out of you, of me, in the vast poem of the hydrological cycle. You are that. I am that.

Earth—matter made from rock and soil. It too is pulled by the moon as the magma circulates through the planet heart and roots suck molecules into biology. Earth pours through us, replacing each cell in the body every seven years. Ashes to ashes, dust to dust, we ingest, incorporate and excrete the earth, are made from earth. I am that. You are that.

Air—the gaseous realm, the atmosphere, the planet's membrane. The inhale and the exhale. Breathing out carbon dioxide to the trees and breathing in their fresh exudations. Oxygen kissing each cell awake, atoms dancing in orderly metabolism, interpenetrating. That dance of the air cycle, breathing the universe in and out again, is what you are, is what I am.

Fire—Fire, from our sun that fuels all life, drawing up plants and raising the waters to the sky to fall again replenishing. The inner furnace of your metabolism burns with the fire of the Big Bang that first sent matter-energy spinning through space and time. And the same fire as the lightning that flashed into the primordial soup catalyzing the birth of organic life.

You were there, I was there, for each cell of our bodies is descended in an unbroken chain from that event. Through the desire of atom for molecule, of molecule for cell, of cell for organism. In that spawning of forms death was born, born simultaneously with sex, before we divided from the plant realm. So in our sexuality we can feel ancient stirrings that connect us with plant as well as animal life. We come from them in an unbroken chain— through fish learning to walk the land, feeling scales turning to wings, through the migrations in the ages of ice.

We have been but recently in human form. If Earth's whole history were compressed into twenty-four hours beginning at midnight, organic life would begin only at 5 p.m. . . . mammals emerge at 11:30 . . . and from amongst them at only seconds to midnight, our species.

Reprinted from *Thinking Like A Mountain: Towards a Council of All Beings* edited by John Seed by permission of New Society Publishers.

In our long planetary journey we have taken far more ancient forms than these we now wear. Some of these forms we remember in our mother's womb, wear vestigial tails and gills, grow fins for hands.

Countless times in that journey we died to old forms, let go of old ways, allowing new ones to emerge. But nothing is ever lost. Though forms pass, all returns. Each worn-out cell consumed, recycled . . . through mosses, leeches, birds of prey. . . .

Think to your next death. Will your flesh and bones back into the cycle. Surrender. Love the plump worms you will become. Launder your weary being through the fountain of life.

Beholding you, I behold as well all the different creatures that compose you—the mitochondria in the cells, the intestinal bacteria, the life teeming on the surface of the skin. The great symbiosis that is you. The incredible coordination and cooperation of countless beings. You are that, too, just as your body is part of a much larger symbiosis, living in wider reciprocities. Be conscious of that give-and-take when you move among trees. Breathe your pure carbon dioxide to a leaf and sense it breathing fresh oxygen back to you.

Countless times in that journey we died to old forms, let go of old ways, allowing new ones to emerge. But nothing is ever lost. Though forms pass, all returns.

Remember again and again the old cycles of partnership. Draw on them in this time of trouble. By your very nature and the journey you have made, there is in you deep knowledge of belonging. Draw on it now in this time of fear. You have earth-bred wisdom of your interexistence with all that is. Take courage and power in it now, that we may help each other awaken in this time of peril.

"EVOLUTIONARY REMEMBERING"

John Seed and Pat Fleming

PART ONE:
FROM THE BEGINNING OF THE UNIVERSE

Let us go back, way back before the birth of our planet Earth, back to the mystery of the universe coming into being. We go back 13,500 million years to a time of primordial silence . . . of emptiness . . . before the beginning of time . . . the very ground of all being . . . From this state of immense potential, an unimaginably powerful explosion takes place . . . energy travelling at the speed of light hurtles in all directions, creating direction, creating the universe. It is so hot in these first moments that no matter can exist, only pure energy in the form of light . . . thus time and space are born.

All that is now, every galaxy, star and planet, every particle existing comes into being at this great fiery birthing. Every particle which makes up you and me comes into being at this instant and has been circulating through countless forms ever since, born of this great cauldron of creativity. When we look at a candle flame or a star, we see the light of that fireball. Your metabolism burns with that very same fire now.

After one earth year, the universe has cooled down to some 13 billion degrees centigrade. It now occupies a sphere of perhaps 17 billion miles in diameter . . . This continues to expand and stream outward. . . .

Some 300,000 years pass while space grows to about one billionth of its present volume and cools to a few thousand degrees—about as hot and bright as the visible surface of the sun. The electrons are now cool enough for the electric force to snare, cool enough for matter to take form.

Matter begins to assume its familiar atomic form for the first time. The first atoms are of hydrogen, then helium and then other gases.

These gases exist as huge swirling masses of super-hot cosmic clouds drawn together by the allure of gravity . . . these slowly condense into forms we know as galaxies and our own galaxy; the Milky Way dances among them. Purged of free electrons, the universe becomes highly transparent by its millionth birthday.

Reprinted from *Thinking Like A Mountain: Towards a Council of All Beings* edited by John Seed by permission of New Society Publishers.

Within the Milky Way, our sun was born about 5 billion years ago, near the edge of this galaxy while the cosmic dust and gas spinning around it crystalized into planets. The third planet from the sun, our own earth, came into being about 4½ billion years ago.

The ground then was rock and crystal beneath which burned tremendous fires. Heavier matter like iron sank to the center, the lighter elements floated to the surface forming a granite crust. Continuous volcanic activity brought up a rich supply of minerals, and lifted up chains of mountains.

Then, about 4 billion years ago, when the temperature fell below the boiling point of water, it began to rain. Hot rain slowly dissolved the rocks upon which it fell and the seas became a thin salty soup containing the basic ingredients necessary for life.

Finally, a bolt of lightening fertilized this molecular soup and an adventure into biology began. The first cell was born. You were there. I was there. For every cell in our bodies is descended in an unbroken chain from that event.

Through this cell, our common ancestor, we are related to every plant and animal on the earth.

PART TWO:
MEDITATION ON THE EVOLUTION OF ORGANIC LIFE

Remember that cell awakening. BE that cell awakening (as indeed you are). We are all composed of that cell which grew, diversified, multiplied and evolved into all the biota of the earth.

What does it feel like to reproduce by dividing into two parts that were me and now we go our separate ways?

Now, some hundreds of millions of years have passed. First we were algae, the original green plants, then the first simple animals. The algae started to produce oxygen as a byproduct of photosynthesis and this over a billion years or so created a membrane of ozone, filtering out some of the fiercest solar rays.

Now I am a creature in the water. For 2½ billion years, simple forms of life washed back and forth in the ocean currents. Imagine them as I speak their names: coral, snails, squid, worms, insects, spiders. Imagine yourself as perhaps a simple worm or an early coral living in the warm sea. Feel your existence at this time for it remains within each of your cells, the memories of this period in your childhood.

Fish: This was followed by the evolution of fish and other animals with backbones. How does it feel to have a flexible backbone? . . . How do you move through the water as a fish?

Lying belly down, staying in one place, begin to experience gentle side-to-side rolling, with your head, torso and lower body moving all as one. How does the world look, feel . . . sound? Be aware of your backbone, your head and gills. What does it feel like to move through the ocean, to listen through the ocean?

John Seed and Pat Fleming

Amphibian: Finally about 450 million years ago the first plants emerged from the water and began to turn the rock into soil, preparing the ground for animals to follow. The first animals to emerge from the seas were the amphibians . . . slowly use your forearms to drag your body along. Pull with your left and right together . . . as amphibians we are still very dependent on the water, especially for our reproductive cycle.

Reptile: It wasn't until the evolution of the reptilian amniotic egg that we were liberated from our dependence on water and able to move completely onto dry land . . . still crawling on your belly start to use legs coordinated with arms, alternating from one side to the other. Notice how our range of movement and perception changes . . . By 200 million years ago, we had successfully moved onto the land.

Early mammal: As mammals we became warm-blooded. Remember how as a reptile you used to have to wait, sluggish, for the sun to warm you? The sun now fuels your metabolism in a more complex way. What are the advantages of this?

Living in holes, alert, sense of smell, sampling molecules from the air. To breed before being consumed. All of us are descended from this pedigree for 4 billion years. At every step billions fell by the wayside but each of us was there. In this game, to throw tails once is to fall by the wayside, extinct, a ghost.

Imagine yourself as a lemur, or perhaps as a small cat . . . Notice how supple your spine feels . . . Now with your belly off the floor, begin crawling on your hands and knees. How does this new-found freedom feel? How does your head move?

Now our young need to be looked after until they can fend for themselves.

Early monkey: Begin moving on hands and feet with greater lightness, leaping and climbing. Discover more flexibility in movement of the spine, head and neck. Make sounds. Notice increasing playfulness and curiosity. We move through the trees, running along branches and swinging through them, our strong opposable thumbs giving us the grip we need. Our sensitive fingertips (with nails instead of claws) able to judge the ripeness of fruit or groom. Agile balance and keen vision develop. We eat food on the spot where we find it.

Great ape: Our body becomes heavier and stronger. We can squat erect but use knuckles to walk. Experiment with balancing. How does the world look and smell? Communication?

Ten million years ago a major climatic change began and the forests, home of the ape, began to retreat to the mountains and were replaced by woodland and open savannah.

Early human: It is here on the open savannah that we first learned to walk on two legs . . . standing on two feet with strong jaw thrust forward. How does it feel? Vulnerable but inventive and adaptable. Able to look up and easily see the sky. We postpone eating food until it can be brought back to camp and shared. We live in families, discover language, catch fire, make art, music, tools . . . the complexities and subtleties of cooperating successfully with others in a group involves the development of language, the telling of stories, the use of tools, the making of fires.

About 100,000 years ago during the warm interglacial period, a new hominid species emerged called Neanderthal. They bury their dead, sometimes with flint tools—many in a fetal position suggesting a return to the womb of Mother Earth for rebirth, often in graves lying on an east/west axis—on the path of the sun which is reborn every day—their practice of burying the dead shows a dramatic increase in human self-consciousness. Now physical evolution stands still and cultural evolution takes over.

Modern human: Developing farming, working on the land, in market places, moving to town—seeing houses, temples, skyscrapers, walking through busy streets, driving in cars, what do you see and hear and smell and feel? How does it feel to be dwelling more often in cities? How have you become more separate from the earth? Now you are pushing your way through a crowded street, you are in a hurry . . . everyone is in your way.

Future human: The possible human: to the extent that we can surrender our tiny self to our actual, biological being, we can then manifest the powerful erotic energy of evolution and then our personalities slowly come to partake of the nature of evolution, the nature of this planet home.

Sitting down quietly by yourself . . . in your mind's eye, open to any glimpses, images, forms that are waiting to emerge as future human life . . . potential in us that is waiting to awaken a larger ecological Self, living fully as part of nature expressing our full potential in whatever way may occur to us . . . form.

Now slowly come back and, opening your eyes, find a partner close by and sit with them. Taking turns speaking, going back over the stages you remember, describing in the first person what you experienced, what you noticed about each life form. Use the present tense—"I am a single cell and I notice . . ." You are now recounting your evolutionary journey, recounting how the cosmic journey has been for you so far.

"THE BLESSING
OF THE WATER"

Marina Lachecki

> May the blessings of the Jordan be upon this water.
> May the blessings of the Jordan be upon this water.
> May the blessings of the Jordan be upon this water.

Three times I dipped the processional cross in the winter waters of Lake Superior. A circle of college students, wrapped in scarves and bedecked with mittens and winter coats, kept the wind to our backs on this day observing the Epiphany. After I raised the cross the final time, I took a cedar branch and dipped it in the now blessed water of the largest freshwater lake in the world. I blessed the four corners of the earth, and then individually, each student. I invited them to dip their hands in this renewed water of the earth. Many drew the water to their lips, their eyes, their ears, and their noses.

In planning for this worship experience, I wanted to celebrate a ritual which spoke to the care of God's creation, a primary value at the institution which I serve as campus minister. Northland College is a liberal arts/environmental college in northern Wisconsin which is affiliated with the United Church of Christ. In my search, I discovered a number of religious customs and rituals from the early liturgical tradition of the church.

While Christians in the Western tradition celebrate the Epiphany as the visitation of the Magi, priestly scholars from Asia, churches in the Eastern tradition observe January 5 and 6 as the Blessing of the Waters. Their appointed readings for this day tell of the baptism of Jesus in the river Jordan. As His divinity was pronounced, there was a subsequent sanctification of the waters by His immersion in them.

St. John Chrysotom delivered a homily with this understanding in 387. "For this is the day on which He was baptized and sanctified the natures of the waters. Therefore also on this solemnity in the middle of the night all who are gathered, having drawn the water, set the liquid aside in their houses and preserve it throughout the year, for today the waters are sanctified."[1] By the 6th century in communities along the Mediterranean, Christians gathered at midnight for this ritual. After the water had been blessed, they would boat out to pan aromatic substances into the water. Afterwards, they drew the water in jars and urns to later use in

---

Reprinted with permission of the author. This essay appeared in *Creation Spirituality Magazine*, P.O. Box 8749, Emeryville, CA 94662.

blessing their homes and fields. In their understanding, the waters of the earth were renewed in this blessing. Waters of the blessed rivers and seas were stirred by the winds and transported by the waves throughout the earth.

As centuries passed, the blessing of the waters turned away from flowing water, and became a ritual celebrated in the fountains in the atria of churches, and then with vessels small enough to be carried in procession from the rivers, lakes and seas which were then placed on the altars. On this winter day, we returned this ancient ritual to its place alongside the waters of the earth.

Prayers from several liturgies were used in re-creating this ritual. The students and I gathered outside the Religious Life Center, a residence for students who want to live in an intentional community focused on spiritual concerns. They are students who are struggling with faith questions, rediscovering their Christian or Jewish heritage, or finding a new way with Buddhism or American Indian spiritualities. We began with an invocation from a Milanese liturgy.

> Eternal God, you revealed yourself from heaven in the sound of thunder over the river Jordan
> in order to make known the Savior of the world and show yourself the God of Eternal Light.
> You opened the heavens, blessed the air, purified the water-springs, and pointed out your only
> Son by sending the Holy Spirit in the form of a dove.[2]

A student then read from Genesis. We listened to this ancient creation story and heard the rhythm of God's voice bringing forth life into the world and pronouncing what was created "good."

Following a processional cross, we journeyed the mile from the campus to the shores of Lake Superior. The mood was festive on this cold January day when students returned from their Christmas break. Friends were greeted and stories shared as we marched behind the cross. Along the way a few others were drawn into our procession and joined our ranks. At one point in our pilgrimage, we were stopped by a car of Ojibwe women who were also students on our campus. They asked us what we were doing. When I told them we were traveling to the lake to pray for the waters of the earth, they told me that they had a ceremony like that, too.

Upon our arrival, I led the students in an Orthodox litany:

> Today, the grace of the Spirit, in the likeness of a dove, comes down upon the waters; today,
> there shines the Sun that never sets, and the world is sparkling with the light of God;
>
> today, the moon is bright, together with the earth, in the glowing radiance of its beams;
>
> today the clouds from heaven shed upon us a shower of justice;
>
> today the hole universe is refreshed with mystical streams;
>
> today, we are delivered from the ancient mourning;
>
> today, the whole creation is brightened from on high . . .

In reading this litany, I was awestruck at the appropriateness of these ancient words to the plight of our world in the 20th century.

As the prayers were concluded, the students began to chip a hole in the two-foot thick ice which covered the bay. The blue-green ice gave way to the sharp edge of an ice pick. No words were spoken during this time. We listened to the call of the wind, and were drawn back into the story of Jesus' baptism in the Jordan. For time stopped then as John anticipated the baptism of the son of God. Tiny ice fragments were taken from the deepening hole and piled inside this circle of students. We awaited the water breaking forth as the scripture from Isaiah foretells. And the water did indeed break forth in the dryness of the winter ice. The vacuum we had created when we chipped out this ice vase was swiftly filled. We cheered in celebration. A student then proclaimed the promised renewal of the earth in the words of the prophet Isaiah, the 35th chapter.

> . . . for water gushes in the desert, streams in the wasteland, the scorched earth becomes a lake, the parched land springs of water . . . and through it will run a highway undefiled which shall be called the Sacred Way. (Isaiah 35.6–8)

These words were familiar to the students who gathered on the shores of Lake Superior. They are proclaimed at each convocation and graduation at the college. It was a reading from the scripture the college adopted when it was founded in 1892.

A college freshman, new to the school that January, then took the Holy Book and read the story of Jesus' baptism from the gospel of Mark. As the processional cross was raised above the water, an Armenian litany was shared:

> Today the grace of the Holy Spirit descends upon the waters in the form of a dove.
>
> Today the waters of the Jordan are changed into a remedy by the presence of the Lord.
>
> Today sins are wiped away in the waters of the Jordan.
>
> Today paradise is opened to us, and the Sun of Justice shines.

And then I immersed the cross, symbolic of the baptismal immersion of Jesus and reminiscent of more ancient fertility rites of the Canaanite people, into the water.

> And may we who partake of it be cleansed and purified, blessed and sanctified, healed and made whole, so that we may be filled with the fullness of God who is all in all.

Our liturgy did not end with its ancient conclusion. In today's world, the cry of the earth called us to pray for its healing. I asked students to call to mind the places on this earth where the water needs to be healed: the places of pollution, of drought, and of degradation. As each student visualized a specific place, we prayed for its healing. We prayed for the spirit of renewal to wash over the face of the earth. We prayed for the people of the earth that they would recognize the sacred gift of the land which was created by the word of God. We prayed for teachers and healers to come forth with a prophetic voice. And then we paused in a sacred moment.

The winds at the end of a winter's day encircled us again. And we closed with these words:

> The voice of God cries upon the waters, saying, "O come and receive all the Spirit of wisdom, the Spirit of understanding, the Spirit of the fear of God."

We journeyed back to campus in a winter silence, mindful of the grace and hope of God for all of creation.

NOTES

1. *Origins of the Liturgical Year* by Thomas J. Talley. Pueblo Publishing Company. New York, 1986.

2. Liturgical prayers were found in *A Christmas Sourcebook,* edited by Mary Ann Simcoe, Liturgical Training Publications, 1984.

PART VII

ECOLOGY, RELIGION, AND SOCIETY

A disenchanted world is, at the same time, a world liable to control and manipulation. Any science that conceives of the world as being governed according to a universal theoretical plan that reduces its various riches to the drab application of general laws thereby becomes an instrument of domination. And man, a stranger to the world, sets himself up as its master.

—Ilya Prigogine and Isabelle Stengers

All the streams have dried up or become muddy. The fish we used to catch have disappeared. The water is not clear anymore. And the birds of paradise have also disappeared; they have flown away to other places.

—Moi Tribesman, Indonesia

We the indigenous Peoples of the world, united in this corner of our Mother the Earth in a great assembly of men of wisdom, declare to all nations:

We glory in our proud past:

when the earth was our nurturing mother,

when the night sky formed our common roof,

when Sun and Moon were our parents,

when all were brothers and sisters,

when our great civilizations grew under the sun,

when our chiefs and elders were great leaders,

when justice ruled the Law and its execution.

—from the World Council
of Indigenous Peoples, 1977

As a child I understood how to give; I have forgotten this grace since I became civilized. I lived the natural life, whereas I now live the artificial. Any pretty pebble was valuable to me then; every growing tree an object of reverence. Now I worship with the white man before a painted landscape whose value is estimated in dollars! Thus the Indian is reconstructed, as the natural rocks are ground to powder and made into artificial blocks which may be built into the walls of modern society.

—Ohiyesa

The FBI says we are from a radical, secretive, loosely organized Animal Liberation Front. We are not radical, we choose to conserve life, not destroy it. We are not secretive, our voice has been heard since the harmonic balance of nature was first broken by human domination. Yes, we are the animal liberation front, but we are also the earth, air and water liberation front. We are one people. We are bound together by a 500 years resistance to ecological and cultural genocide.... Our beliefs are not the product of twentieth-century European philosophers. Our fight is the same fight as the Mohawk, Dine, Blackfoot, Lakota and Apache.... In Earth First! we see ourselves. In the American Indian Movement, we see ourselves. Red, brown, white, fur, feathers, and fins, we are all sisters and brothers. For a rebirth of the harmonious relationship with all life, let us no longer stand apart, but TOGETHER.

—Ron Coronado,

Animal Rights and Native American activist

There is a racial divide in the way the U.S. government cleans up toxic waste sites and punishes polluters. White communities see faster action, better results, and stiffer penalties than communities where blacks, Hispanics, and other minorities live. The unequal protection often occurs whether the community is wealthy or poor.

—*National Law Journal*

We are all victims. Not just blacks. Whites are in this thing, too. We're all victimized by a system that puts the dollar before everything else. That's the way it was in the old days when the dogs and whips were masters, and that's the way it is today when we got stuff in the water and air we can't even see that can kill us deader than we ever thought we could die.

—Amos Favorite,

resident of Louisiana's "Cancer Alley"

The passions we feel for the environment direct us to try to alter humanity's current mode of life. To paraphrase Marx: the point is not just to worship nature, but to save it! Furthermore, the religious vision of a sacred earth can be a powerful presence in the environmental movement; and the attempt to bring about social change can pose deeply troubling but also highly fruitful occasions for religious reflection.

Once we leave the temples and prayer circles, however, matters become infinitely more complex and difficult. To actually change social conduct towards nature involves changing our personal lives, to be sure, but also impels us to confront the entrenched interests of governments and corporations, and the dynamics of class, racial, national and gender inequality.

In this part, essays by myself, Charlene Spretnak, Max Oelschlaeger, and Bron Taylor provide overviews of relations between religious concern for the environment and political life. These essays focus in turn on a possible reconciliation between spiritual deep ecology and left politics; the role of spirituality in both Green political organizations and the radical activist group Earth First!; and the place of organized churches in American political life. B. D. Sharma, in an address to the 1992 Earth Summit, provides a deeply critical view of the advanced industrial nations from the perspective of the Third World. Bruce Sullivan and M. L. Daneel examine concrete political and environmental struggles in Asia and Africa. Catherine Ingram and Judith Scoville focus on agriculture: Scoville from the point of view of implications for ecotheology; Ingram, through her interview with Cesar Chavez, on the connections between Christian nonviolence and the struggle against chemical pesticides. David Spangler and Dieter T. Hessel bridge the gap between religion, modern science and society. Spangler inquires into the spiritual appropriateness of the scientifically inspired Gaia hypothesis, in which the entire earth is thought of as a living entity. Hessel examines the dilemmas posed by our capacity to literally invent new life-forms. In two poignant meditations, Paul Gorman (responding in some ways to Thomas Berry's essay in Part V) and Melody Ermachild reflect on what it is like to try to live an ecologically responsible and spiritually aware life in the midst of urban poverty. Their pieces remind us that we must be wary of a "spiritual bypass" that will see God only in the pleasant.

This Sacred Earth concludes with a series of public documents intended to reorient social practice. They embody an awareness of environmental racism, of the congruence of scientific information and religious concern, and end with some concrete steps that may be taken by a local parish.

The writings of Part VII leave off where the real work begins. If we are to save the earth and ourselves, religious ideals had better be translated into political action. It is to be hoped that such action will keep in mind both our collective human plight and our fundamental differences. *Everyone* is threatened by global warming and the hole in the ozone layer. By contrast, however, some people make a great deal of money selling pesticides, while others who work the fields die from exposure to them.

Yet we cannot let either the complications of political life or the virtually overwhelming scope of the task before us deflect our efforts. As bleak as the present is, it may yet be that the tide is turning. We cannot know now what the effects of today's acts will be. In that ignorance may be our greatest hope.

"SPIRITUAL DEEP ECOLOGY AND THE LEFT: AN ATTEMPT AT RECONCILIATION"

Roger S. Gottlieb

> I can see the bright green strip of grass beneath the wall, and the clear blue sky above the wall, and sunlight everywhere. Life is beautiful. Let the future generations cleanse it of all evil, oppression, and violence, and enjoy it to the full.[1]
>
> —Leon Trotsky

Often developed in isolation, and frequently opposed, it is actually the case that the more spiritual forms of deep ecology and the left political tradition need each other's insights and sensitivities. They are, I believe, mutually necessary to help us learn how to manifest respect for human and non-human nature alike. Uniting their contributions could help mobilize a political response to the poisoning of our environment, and root that response in an encompassing spiritual framework that will alter the fundamental ways in which we think about politics, our own identity, and nature.

A fruitful exchange between deep ecology and the left, however, requires that adherents of both perspectives suspend certain entrenched prejudices. Leftists need to open themselves to the possibility that a spiritually oriented perspective might actually have something to teach them: in this case, something about the ultimate sources of value in our lives and about limitations in our conventional sense of self. Deep ecologists, on the other hand, would do well to suspend their ahistorical arrogance about their own wisdom, their pretensions to being above or beyond political struggles and their too facile dismissal of left movements as unremitting agents of the exploitation of nature.

IDENTITY

Deep ecology, as I shall describe it here, is not solely about the environment, about protecting the rainforest or saving spotted owls. Paradoxically, what may be most important about deep

Reprinted with permission of the author. This essay originally appeared in *Capitalism, Nature, Socialism: A Journal of Socialist Ecology*, Vol. 6., No. 3, Fall 1995.

ecology is not just what it says about *non*-human nature, but what it says about people. For deep ecology, human identity—who we really are—is not constituted solely by either psychological and physical individuality or collective social experience. Rather, deep ecology asserts the direct and ultimate importance of humanity's connection to and identification with other forms of life and being. In preserving, respecting and even loving nature, then, we are not deferring to an Other, but overcoming a kind of alienation from essential aspects of our own selves. This is a potentially revolutionary claim, because both common sense and philosophical theory have for centuries concentrated on the isolated individual or the social group as the centers of our personal, social, and political selfhood.

By contrast to deep ecology, liberalism, socialism, feminism and other social movements have focused on resistance to tyranny, exploitation and injustice, putting individual freedom and/or group interests at the heart of their sense of the human.

Thus, to begin to understand how these two views need each other and how both are essential elements of our political response to ecocide, we need first to reflect on our understanding of human identity.

Who are we?

We come to answer this question not (or not *just*) by thinking about ourselves, but by learning particular ways of talking and concrete social practices. From infancy to adulthood, the manner in which human beings are taught to speak of themselves and to act cultivates very specific forms of self-understanding.

In the "modern" age of the last three centuries or so, forms of discourse and social practices have evolved to teach us to think and act as individuals—to live as if the central truth about ourselves is that we are isolated, and that connections with others follow from rather than make up who we are. Political philosophy and psychotherapy, educational competition and the nuclear family all cultivate self-interested autonomy. In other settings we may learn to evaluate beliefs and morality with independence of mind, to take personal responsibility for our own moral failings, and to see the possibility of autonomous and creative insights in art, science or technological development.

Existing in uneasy symbiosis—and at times conflicting—with both the positive and pernicious aspects of individualism, are varieties of group identity based in characteristics such as economic class, nation, race, ethnic history, religion, and gender. As members of groups we know ourselves through particular historical "fates": Jews who have faced the Holocaust or blacks with a legacy of slavery. And we know ourselves by the songs, stories, prayers and food that have shaped *our* communities and which are strange or unknown to others.[2]

Taken together, modern society's individualism and the continuing identification with socially differentiated groups have sharply demarcated human beings from the rest of the natural world. As *individuals* we seem to stand out—to be separable from—the biological context that makes our lives possible. We can know it, try to control it, approve of it or resist it. Similarly, as members of racial/ethnic/religious *groups,* our identity is constituted by cultural traditions, beliefs expressed in language, and our own special histories. Social groups define themselves, commemorate their history, compare and distinguish themselves from others. Such processes are found only among humans.[3]

THE VALUE(S) OF DEEP ECOLOGY

The above practices and discourses teach us, then, that we are individuals and members of groups. And that we are little else.

"Deep ecology" challenges these notions of human identity, seeking to add to them by enlarging our sense of our own selfhood. Denying that our essential identity includes only our individuality and our membership in social groups, deep ecology rejects many of the ethical, religious or "scientific" distinctions between humanity and non-human nature. This rejection is the hallmark of deep ecology—and is sometimes called biocentrism or ecocentrism.

A deep ecological perspective begins by claiming that non-human nature is not here solely to be of use to humanity. Individual animals and plants, as well as entire ecosystems of wetland, tundra or mountain range, have their own integrity, meaning, and importance. Yet deep ecology is not aiming to oppose the value of non-human nature to that of people. Rather, it roots the *value* of both in a fundamental sense of the *identity* of both. Water and air, earth and humans, are and can be experienced as strands of an infinite web of life and being where no part has inherent priority over the rest—just because there is no clear way to demarcate one part from another.

This view has been expressed in various forms.[4] My focus here is on versions that stress a revised view of human identity rather than emphasize nature's "rights" or our "obligations" to preserve it. Their point is that we can recognize, experience and honor our natural surroundings as essential to who we are. Care for nature is not a matter of deferring to the rights of strangers, but of loving a dimension of oneself.

> . . . ecological thinking requires a kind of vision across boundaries. The epidermis of the skin
> is ecologically like a pond surface or a forest soil, not a shell so much as a *delicate interpenetra-*
> *tion.* It reveals the self ennobled and extended rather than threatened as part of the landscape
> and ecosystem because the beauty and complexity of nature *are continuous with ourselves.*[5]

Of course to a confirmed anthropocentric, one who feels that human groups stand isolated from nature in the center of historical or cosmic importance, these claims about our connection to nature may seem either false or trivial. While we need air and we like furry animals, they might say, that does not make either air or kittens *part of ourselves.*

Perhaps the closest thing to an "argument" that the deep ecologist might offer the anthropocentric is to point to the many situations in which individuals feel, beyond doubt, a direct

Roger S. Gottlieb

and absolutely essential connection *to other people*. Mothers and infants, comrades in wartime, companions in political, spiritual, intellectual or artistic journeys may well experience each other with a kind of intimate solidarity, based in care, love, and empathy. In such contexts our regard for fellow humans is not based on their "rights," but on our bonds with them as companions on this earth, whose lives and well-being are intimately tied to our own. Similar feelings, deep ecology claims, are both possible and appropriate when we regard air that we breathe, water that we drink or the other species with whom we share this planet. Our regard for non-human nature can spring from an awareness of it as our companion, fellow traveler, and friend; or more profoundly as the very matrix which in fundamental ways enables our lives to be what they are. We "identify" with nature when we realize it is what makes our existence possible; and therefore no longer conceive of our "selves" as bounded by our skin.[6]

It is easy to show that humans depend on non-human nature. And the most confirmed anthropocentric thinker will readily allow that poisoned earth and water are "bad" for people. Agreement on this point, however, will not logically compel any emotional and ethical openness to the environment.

Yet we *can* describe the social practices and historical developments that give rise to either anthropocentrism or bio-centrism—just as we could with the beliefs and practices that gave rise to individualism and group identification. We can see, that is, the fundamental shifts in social practices and human experience that have created either a human-centered or a deep ecological vision.

We may suppose that their interdependence with the non-human natural world was evident to the hunter-gatherers of the Paleolithic (40,000–15,000 B.C.E.) and early agricultural settlements of the Neolithic (12,000–5,000 B.C.E.). The living earth provided food to gather or hunt, herbs for medicine, and revealed cycles of birth, maturation, and decay. Much of life was spent under open sky and whatever happened to come down from it. Viewing their artistic/religious artifacts, we can suppose they felt a strong sense of continuity and community with animals and plants; and that they were in awe of the powers of birth and death. This identification can be traced in the rich and varied symbolism of the mother goddess, which continued in cultural rituals and beliefs after these societies were themselves supplanted.[7]

In short, the daily experience of humans in these settings *itself* gives rise to a particular attitude towards nature.

Yet along with connection to and reverence for nature, there probably existed a certain amount of dread and fear, stimulated by the lack of predictability of the environment, a desire for "easier" ways of meeting human biological needs, and expanding populations. These feelings and conditions may have motivated new attitudes towards our natural surroundings; especially, they gave rise to the view of non-human nature as alien or separate and the desire to *control* it.

Whatever the initial causes, history from c. 3000 B.C.E. to the present witnessed the development of more advanced agriculture, increasingly complex social divisions of labor and relations of exploitation, and the continual creation of tools to delve and shape the earth and its products. Part of this development is the devaluation of "nature," the creation of exclusively masculine symbols for divinity, and the subjugation of women by patriarchal control over their reproductive and sexual status.

The continuous growth of technological and social power—and the attendant religious and political ideologies that supported them—promoted the illusion of our fundamental difference from nature. And it gave rise to the desire for *control* in and of itself, as a good thing. This desire played an essential role in the evolving interlocked systems of military, religious, economic, and ideological domination.[8]

Like all deeply embedded illusions, this one was based in a certain kind of truth: humanity did, in certain short-run ways, dramatically increase its capacity to dominate non-human nature. Mass agriculture produced mass surpluses, supporting cultural elites and a complex division of labor. Control first of fire, and then of water, steam, electricity and even atomic power perpetuated the image that nature had become our dominion. With the rise of modern science, mastery has seemed to be virtually limitless. Daily life in the industrialized world now depends on hyper-technological substitutions for and controls over previously natural processes: the ways in which we travel, dress, eat, communicate, labor and amuse ourselves, require an intricate technological system that seems to rely only on human knowledge and organization. Nature obeys our will.

At the same time, our powers over nature have always been embedded in gender- and class-dominated societies in which hard labor, power, status, and wealth are unequally and unjustly distributed; and in which "man-made" poverty and exploitation supplant droughts or floods as the greatest threats to material well-being. While we may be told that "man" controls nature, that control is ultimately vested in ruling elites.

And now the dreadful consequences of our presumption of separation from and superiority over non-human nature have become clear. Human "control" has evolved into a series of feedback loops in which the controller himself is controlled.[9] The "green revolution" in agriculture depletes the soil and leaves cancer-causing pesticide residues. The convenience of modern refrigeration threatens the ozone layer. The Environmental Protection Agency declares that ninety-nine major metropolitan areas in the U.S. have unhealthful air. Wilderness and species vanish. Some who experience these losses no longer trust in yet another technological fix. They want to turn away from the forms of individualism and group identity that fund the juggernaut of technological destruction, and turn toward a sense of community with the non-human world.[10]

Along with our emerging sense of what we have done to the non-human world, and how those actions are affecting us, there are other sources of deep ecology. For one thing, our societies seem increasingly inhumane. Violence haunts streets, offices and homes and is

Roger S. Gottlieb

echoed horribly in both popular culture and the military-industrial complex. Against such "man-made" threats, non-human nature may feel much more like "home" than where we in fact live. Further, the heroes of modern rationality—the scientist, the professional, the expert—do not seem to have produced either reasonable societies or models of personal wisdom. The "scientific" culture that was to have remade the world in the human image now gives us little comfort.

Consequently, many people have turned to other metaphors and narratives on which to construct ideals of how to live and whom to respect. Instead of the democratic republic of the Welfare State, we turn to the biotic community as both more attractive and more ultimately plausible. Instead of the scientific "expert" or the detached professional, we may look to the "wisdom of nature" or the ecological traditions of indigenous peoples.

DEEP ECOLOGY AND SPIRITUALITY

Because of the way it expands our sense of what people are, deep ecology can be considered a *spiritual* perspective.

While this term may be alienating to some, I wish to stress that it need not refer either to conventional organized religion or to faith in a vengeful Divine Father. Rather, the sense of spirituality I intend here begins with the belief that it is a grave error to understand ourselves solely in terms of our social role, possessions, personal successes and failures, individual achievements or purely social group identity. Some sources of contentment and inspiration are more lasting, powerful, and benign than anything that can be purchased, measured, evaluated, or socially calculated; in short, than anything which can be possessed or accomplished by a purely social being. A spiritual perspective suggests that only with this discovery of a sense of selfhood beyond the ego can we become released from the ego's compulsions and inevitable disappointments. Our social identity itself is not to be completely eliminated, but integrated into a more comprehensive selfhood. We are not to quit our jobs or surrender our zip codes, blending into some faceless, personality-less tapioca pudding of bliss. Our sense of personal identity continues. The difference, however, is that now we have another perspective on the conventional social ego and its foibles.

This sense of spirituality does not require a conventional (Western) religious attachment to a personal God. Nor does it require, as, unfortunately, many have supposed, a spiritual *denial* of the manifest horrors of human experience from concentration camps to violence against women. Traditional religion and pop spirituality frequently ignore social injustice, and radicals have rightly rejected their politically conservative and sexist tendencies.[11]

But we can no more fully comprehend spirituality if we focus on its lowest manifestations than we can fully understand Marxism if we only look at Stalinism. The model of spirituality I am developing must be understood as distinct from dogmatic religious attachments to particular rituals, creeds, or organizations. From this perspective, the concrete form of spiritual practice or belief is a means to self-transformation, not a way of deciding who to hate. Further, an authentic spirituality does not ignore social suffering. The more powerful, enduring and credible spiritual messages counsel openness to the truth: not the rosy security of a blissful avoidance, but a committed involvement with others.[12]

For instance, when we take action on behalf of threatened nature, we may see ourselves, in John Seed's words, not simply as individuals defending the rainforest, but as "*part of the rainforest defending itself.*" Such a view may well expand our selfhood beyond the conventionalities of status, money, power, possessions, physical beauty and purely human narrower forms of self or group interest; and it can help shape political action that transcends the simple pursuit of increased entitlements for particular social groups. In this vein we see that a spiritual deep ecology can help counter our society's addictive preoccupation with individual consumption and ownership and provide an alternative, non-commodity-centered framework of "self-realization." All it asks is that we give up the illusion that we are *only* our social selves.[13]

As we sense our continuity with leaf, stream, and butterfly, we manifest a global or ecological consciousness far from the domineering and consumptive obsessions of modernity. The compulsive accumulation of real money or the symbolic capital of status, endless self-evaluation or crippling high anxiety, paralyzing despair or entrenched loneliness—are soothed by the reassuring sense of our participation in the web of life.

As promising as such personal changes might be, there is also the profound effect that a spiritual deep ecology could have on some of the basic ways in which we think about politics. It can help overcome the limitations of progressive or radical political organizations whose aims seem to be stuck in attempting to satisfy the conventional egos of individuals or collectivities.

Although committed to overturning unjust systems and ending oppression, leftist or progressive political movements have often reproduced, rather than opposed, the conventional ego. Classical liberalism emphasized personal rights, enshrined individual economic activity at the heart of its system, and believed the central purpose of society was to protect and further ownership and consumption. Surely this view will not help us face the environmental crisis.

Sadly, more "radical" political movements of the West—despite their emphasis on community, class or racial experience, and their attempt to generate an ethic of collective solidarity and struggle—have *also* too often presupposed an individualistic, consumerist ego. The practical politics of the left have frequently aimed to provide more things, money, and prestige. They have too often represented the interest of one segment of the oppressed while claiming to represent all. And they have repeatedly failed to challenge the individualist premise that a higher standard of living will make for greater happiness. It has been a rare progressive party that called for less, not more, consumption—at least until the Green Parties of Europe came into being; and there has been little assertion that human fulfillment may be directly opposed to high-consumption lifestyles.

Moreover, concern for nature as a dimension of being in its own right has been absent in most progressive politics. The left has usually opposed consumerism for reasons of "pollution and conservation." The individual rights of the Lockean agrarian capitalist are, in this sense, pretty much the same as the overthrow of alienation sought by the Marxian communist. One grows crops for cash, and the other seeks fulfillment in an egalitarian and rationally ordered society. Both seek justice; yet both have little or no sense that there also may be norms for which the fulfillment of human beings is not the sole goal.

The exceptions to these trends—from Michael Lerner's "politics of meaning" to the hippies "turn on, tune in, drop out," from certain elements of early Socialist-Zionism to radical elements of spiritual feminism—have been minority currents on the left.

For the radical tradition—even at its best, when it sees the integral connections between humans and their environment—non-human nature has value or integrity only by reference to its relation to human beings. We should use it for our own good; if we pollute it we will suffer; and our access to scientific knowledge gives us the right of mastery. Ultimately, however, our destruction of it carries meaning just insofar as it affects us.[14] The problematic consequences of such views are revealed not only with every breath we take, but also in our inability to feel at home in our own world. Our dominion over the earth and its creatures leaves a bitter taste.

I do not mean to invalidate the enormous courage and self-sacrifice expended in trying to bring either the working class or oppressed minorities into a reasonable standard of living, protect their political and social rights, or give them a "place" in capitalist society. Nor do I wish to ignore the way ecological issues center at least as much on structures of production— over which the mass of the population have virtually no control—as on consumerist personal orientations. I am suggesting, however, that a politics that identifies human good purely or mainly with the acquisition of things or the achieving of social status of whatever kind is no longer adequate. The economism that has always pacified mass left movements—from the craft workers in the early decades of this century to the industrial unions of the 1930s to the inner-city insurgency of the 1960s—not only spells the inevitable continuity of ecocide but is self-defeating for the movements themselves.[15]

Thus, when progressive political movements take the conventional social ego for granted and seek to fulfill it, they are typically unable to counter our society's suicidal preoccupation with success, consumption and spectacle. Without an attempt to construct a sense of identity along more spiritual lines—as something not reducible to the ego of social consumption, social status or active control—the left may have little to offer individuals or groups whose main preoccupation is greater wealth and power. Such "progressive" groups are unable to progress beyond the unending use of—and so alienation from—nature. There is no consistent alternative vision of a form of life that is either ecologically sustainable (or even sane) and personally fulfilling. We see examples of the left's failure here in the way the political uproar of the 1960s too often devolved simply into demands for more transfer payments. Comparably, the vibrant movements for democracy and human rights, which toppled the tyrannies of communism, are now tripping over each other in their haste to effect a capitalist restructuring. One hopes that the emerging ecologically oriented left will continue to develop sensitivities in all these areas. Strands of the left that have stressed the material and spiritual costs of consumerism already will surely be strengthened and broadened by an infusion of deep ecological thinking.

With the acceptance of an essentially human-centered model of identity, rights, and fulfillment, the traditional left has also accepted models of interpersonal relations based on self-righteousness and rage. There has been little critical distance from the driving emotional force of entitlement: to justice, goods, or power. Within progressive organizations, these failings have too frequently given rise to relational styles that make interpersonal cooperation and organizational coalitions impossible. While a spiritual view stresses compassion and the transcendence of desire, the endless emphasis on personal and group entitlement, flavored with generous helpings of self-righteousness and pretentiousness, fracture every attempt to hold together an elusive "rainbow" of oppressed social groups. Competition over who is most oppressed, masculine leaders who pump up their own egos and position at the expense of the group, endless controversy and conflict leading to endless splits—all these riddle the history of progressive organizations.[16]

Spiritual deep ecology can help us begin to understand ourselves as natural, rather than purely psychic, social, and symbolic beings. We not only come to value non-human nature, we also come to think of *ourselves* in radically different ways. In doing so we may realize that we live not just socially but also in an ecologically bound biotic community. The particular needs and interests defined by our place in social life may no longer exhaust our vision of what we want or deserve.

Spiritually, this means that basic values such as birth and death (rather than murder or destructive consumption or commodification), identifying with other life forms, a sense of connection to and participation in one's place, may begin to inform not just spiritual reflection and mystical experience, but our prophetic political demands. We can enter into political life with a greater compassion for both comrade and opponent. We can see the goal not as endlessly raising consumption, but as reorienting the distribution of wealth and the process of production and consumption so that future generations of plants, animals, and people can live simply and in harmony. We can begin to be self-critical about ourselves, our particular ethnic, religious, or economic group—for we find our identity is not totally rooted in any human location or connection. We are part of nature, of tree and sky, as much as we are our bank account or racial history. Surely this realization will help free us emotionally from some of our compulsions to dominate other people or the earth, to be forever and in every instance "right," "in control," in "power." Surely this will help us learn to live with others—and with our own fears and greeds—in a much more sustainable, and even loving, way.[17]

THE RETURN OF THE SOCIAL

Yet thinking of nature alone will not do. We are creatures of history and society as well as of earth and air. We hunger for justice as we hunger for food and water. And without a compelling memory of class, gender, racial, and national forms of oppression, spirituality in general and deep ecology in particular will be blind to complex and painful issues of social injustice and political reorganization.[18]

To begin, one must observe that just as it is morally significant that species are made extinct or habitats poisoned, so it is critical to remember that humans are *also* sickened by environmental degradation, and that the contamination disproportionately affects the poor, people of color, and the "third world." There is surely a terrible "human" folly in using carcinogenic pesticides in agriculture. But while ultimately that folly affects us all, in the short run the toxins surround the migrant farmworkers in the fields, and their sale makes money for owners of the chemical companies who produce them, owners who work and live far from the contaminated substances they create.

The difference between the farmworker and the chemical company industrialist, between the World Bank executive who supports a destructive "development" loan for a massive dam and the indigenous tribes whose villages are destroyed by it, between the timber companies eager to clearcut and the native peoples whose lives and culture depend on the forest—these differences must be kept in mind when we speak of what "humanity" has done to the earth.[19] Clearly, the responsibility for the domination of nature does not lie equally on all humans—any more than racism, sexism or colonialism are equally the work of all whites, men, or Europeans.

Of course, the complexities of coercion and cooptation may make it difficult to decipher how responsibility is distributed. When peasants deforest a hillside because they have no other source of firewood, are they no different from clearcutting timber companies? When a housewife flushes a toxic cleaner down the sink, how is she like—and unlike—a negligent oil company in a major oil spill? How do the greenhouse gases released by our daily commute—including my own—compare to DuPont's continued production of ozone-destroying CFCs a full decade after their effects were known?

These questions are not easy to answer. Yet in a world of ruling elites and ideological mystification, in which some genders and races are identified with nature while others are considered nature's masters, it is necessary to approach ecological devastation with an understanding of the distribution of social power that makes a small number of people initiate and—to an extreme degree—profit from it; and of the social constraints that lead the mass of people to accept it.

Another problem arises when deep ecologists suggest that because humans are a *part* of the natural world we can therefore discover how we ought to live by observing how non-human nature operates. It is suggested, sometimes directly, sometimes indirectly, that were we simply to live "naturally" we should thereby end the environmental crisis. The wisdom of nature would guide us, replacing the follies of a purely human view.

This approach faces several difficulties. First, it should be recognized that "nature," for all its seeming self-sufficiency and objectivity, is *also* a social category. Our sense of what is "nature" rather than human, "natural" rather than artificial, is partly a product of social factors. The particular conceptual system out of which any sense of "nature" emerges will reflect, as do all such systems, a particular distribution of power and a pattern of social experience. Perhaps the most obvious historical example of such a mistake occurred when "Social Darwinists" applied the notion of the "survival of the fittest" to social life and thus identified the existing social elite with the genetically most successful animal species. Comparable errors arise when our supposedly immutable biological nature is used to justify some form of social domination; e.g., militarist aggression or patriarchy. In all these cases, the meaning given to "nature" is pretty clearly a product of social interests.

A deep ecologist who uses a politically unanalyzed sense of "nature" may well make similar errors. A lack of attention to class privilege may be a reason why some deep ecologists put so much stress on the existence and experience of wilderness—a locale and an encounter of limited cultural and economic accessibility—as the hallmark of a deep ecological sensibility. An authentic, as opposed to a self-indulgent, deep ecology will find "nature" in city pigeons or slum children playing in a vacant lot as well as in an old-growth forest. Equally important, the ultimate fate of the wilderness depends at least as much on relations among human beings as it does on our attitudes towards non-human nature itself.

Another fallacy of an uncritical reliance on the idea of "nature" is revealed if we ask why non-human nature cannot itself follow *our* rules, live as we do, since after all it is "connected" or a part of us as surely as we are a part of it. Why cannot we ask predators to consider the justice of their kill, or bacteria to think twice before they invade someone's throat? Why can't sharks and smaller fish, robins and worms, spiders and flies, make peace with each other?

These questions reveal that different things may be "part" of each other and still have their own distinct principles of organization, structural necessities, and proper states of being. Non-human nature and humans are, for all their connections and similarities, in some ways fundamentally different. (So are stars and beetles.) What humans have, and what non-human nature does not, is the capacity to interrogate both self and other, to raise questions of moral or cognitive validity, to examine purposes, to organize and *re*-organize the way we interact with nature. People do not live solely by instinct or need, but by rules, norms, values. We seek

Roger S. Gottlieb

to understand and evaluate our lives, and to alter them in accord with changes in our understanding and judgment.

Thus, human self-realization is (alas?) more complex, dangerous and troubling than that of animals, plants or rivers. Unlike other life forms, we can ask for justice, for compassion, for decency—and respond with rage or grief when they are absent. Thus, the "proper" state of being of humanity is not simply to act "naturally" in an ecosystem, but also to manifest *justice* among humans.[20]

Justice *is* our proper condition, the fitting form our nature should take.[21] Paradoxically, it is a nature we often fail to achieve. This ability to fail shows that our nature is "ours" in a very different way than the "nature" of a rosebush or a wolf is theirs. Roses and wolves *live* their nature. From those lives we can determine what their natures are. Humans, by contrast, strive to *fulfill* their nature; that is, to organize a social form that meets the implicit demands of our unique—and historically evolving—capacities and drives.

We are beings who need others and can also question the rightness of the way our needs are met. Because we have the gift of language, we can make claims to power and property— and also challenge those claims. We manifest complex emotional states that emerge—as the fulfillment of love and trust or as violations that give rise to hatred and anger—out of our natural social bonds. In these ways the anticipation of a just society is built into our basic physical, emotional and cognitive need for others and our basic capacity to speak. These are the elements of our existence that make us distinctly "human."[22]

The longing to realize our nature can be found in our dreams and prayers, our critical reflections on society, and our dissident movements. From the prophets of the *Bible* to the Bodhisattva ideal of Mahayana Buddhism, from Plato's ethics to Marx's critique of capitalism, in countless well-known and anonymous rebellions, uprisings and acts of resistance, we have sought love and justice. It is this importunate longing—and our sadness for our failures—which non-human nature cannot have, and therefore which no amount of deep ecological reflection can ever fully assuage.

Thus, our membership in cities, tribes, communities, nations, races, genders—and not merely our "natural" identity—is critical in our response to the environmental crisis. And if that crisis represents a profound failure of all basic social and cultural systems, then a tremendous amount of temporary pain must follow any attempt to set things right.

Who will bear the brunt of the pain? Who will initiate it? Who will resist? Who should be forced to pay the greatest price?

When we demand that logging be curtailed to save a rainforest, concern for the unemployed loggers must accompany our passion for owls and trees. Only if the costs of the transition to ecological sustainability and respect for nature are truly *socialized,* can such issues not take their present form of desperate, win-lose battles. Without a radical democratic political system and a rational economy, efforts to create a sustainable society will place vastly unequal burdens on the socially powerless. If technology is not shaped by the needs of the human and the ecosystem community as a whole, ruling elites will continue to combine the domination of nature with the domination of human beings. The choice between loggers and owls is like some of the bogus choices forced by affirmative action programs in which working-class whites and minorities are pitted against each other. When conflicts are posed in these ways, deep ecologists will always lose, because they will always be a tiny minority.

To further complicate matters, consider Bill McKibben's claim that our present alteration of the global climate gives all life on this planet a human imprint.[23] As we change the world's temperature, we change the growth conditions of every living thing. Further, man-made pollutants are found in the depth of the oceans and on top of the tallest mountains, in the most isolated deserts and glaciers. All areas designated as "wild" now exist as such only on the sufferance of some nation or community. Forests and species and ecosystems must have our blessing to live, otherwise they will go the way of the buffalo, the vast redwood forests of 19th-century California, or the long-lost wildlands of Western Europe.

In this most practical of ways, then, humanity and nature have truly become one. With the poisoning of the environment, plagues such as cancer, immune-system disorders and hunger take great tolls on humanity. With the use of the environment as an infinite source of expanding economic accumulation, and a source of commodities designed to compensate otherwise empty lives, non-human nature will be continually and increasingly degraded. Unjust power, private wealth without social responsibility, rulers who sustain themselves by military terror or the promise of more "things" to a demoralized population—none of these can do anything but continue to destroy the earth. Ecocide is their stock in trade.

Because of the necessary interdependence of all that lives, there are fundamental connections between respect for ecosystems and respect for people. As stated by the loose coalition of popular environmental and social justice groups in the Philippines, ultimately "The environmental movement is a struggle for equity in the control and management of natural resources." Such equity means that economic development must be fully participatory. Therefore, to work for "environmentally sustainable development requires working for human rights."[24] Similar conclusions are reached in a detailed study of efforts to save African wildlife.

> The two most successful conservation programs in Africa . . . are two of the least expensive. What makes them successful is that they are premised on the needs of people. All we have to do to preserve Africa's wildlife heritage is care about the people as much as we care about the wildlife.[25]

As Ramachandra Guha puts it, the grassroots Indian environmental movements focus not on "environmental protection" in itself, but on who should use and who should benefit from the environment.

If colonial and capitalist expansion has both accentuated social inequalities and signaled a precipitous fall in ecological wisdom, an alternate ecology must rest on an alternate society and polity as well.[26]

These quotations derive from movements of people who are far more *immediately* connected to non-human nature than those thinkers of the industrialized world who created deep ecology. In fact, however, every person must exchange with non-human nature every moment of an individual lifetime. Even the most devout deep ecologist must relate to nature by some degree of consumption and displacement—or else die of starvation and exposure. We can choose to make that exchange one of rapacious folly or respectful community, but we cannot exempt nature from its effects. We cannot, in Edward Abbey's desperate cry about Yosemite, "Keep it like it was."[27]

Conversely, however, deep ecology's struggles to preserve at least some of the pristine, pre-human wild should not be dismissed as the self-indulgence of the privileged. The wilderness has its own integrity and purpose, and the world would be a poorer place for us all if that were lost. A balance *can* be struck between *preserving* the wild and *reorganizing* our transactions in cities, suburbs, and countryside. Properly grounded in the social world as well as the wilderness, our reverence for non-human nature can be lavished on the birch tree next to my house in Boston as well as on the ones in the White Mountain National forest, the vegetables I ate for dinner as much as the wildflowers of the rainforest.

PROSPECTS

The reconciliation of deep ecology and radical politics, then, must not stress non-human nature *at the expense* of human beings. This would simply continue the painful history of divisiveness of left movements, in which suffering groups are pitted against each other in self-destructive competition over needs, degrees of self-righteousness, and entitlement. The goal, rather, is to widen our sense of community, including but going beyond our current human limits of race, class, gender or nationality.

There remain, of course, daunting social sources of experience which impede the rise of a deep ecological consciousness—just as there are comparable experiences obstructing the development of socialist/progressive group consciousness. In the case of ecological awareness, at least two barriers are crucially difficult to overcome, which I can mention here only in passing.

First, there is in the industrialized world the addictive quality of our relation to consumption. The idea of a form of life in which consumption plays an increasingly diminished part seems to threaten our very selfhood. Our anthropocentric economy offers so much to so many—and tantalizes the rest with the possibility that they too might one day enter the golden land of consumerist bliss—that the inevitably more austere prospect of a sustainable, ecologically respectful society is deeply troubling. It is difficult to imagine the success of a political party calling for fewer jobs, and lower production energy use and consumption; or that Americans, Europeans, or Japanese would willingly part with air conditioners, cars, nuclear power or the freedom to shop till you drop.

Second, our economies are so tied to an endlessly exploitative relation to non-human nature, that altering them involves a confrontation with our ultimate economic—and hence social and political—powers. Any brief glimpse of what deep ecological society might look like is immediately clouded by the dark shadows of the powers that depend on the exploitation of people and nature. These powers include not only the capitalist state and the corporations, but also entrenched authorities in science, technology, and culture.

As difficult as these obstructions are, they at least reveal once again the commonality of interest between deep ecology and the left, for surely these two barriers to deep ecology also deflect attempts to imagine or put into existence a democratic, socialist-feminist society.

NOTES

This essay benefited greatly from suggestions by Bettina Bergo, Miriam Greenspan, and the Boston area *Capitalism, Nature, Socialism* editorial group. Daniel Faber and John Wooding were kind enough to respond to two different drafts.

1. Leon Trotsky, shortly before his assassination. Quoted in Isaac Deutscher, *The Prophet Outcast: Trotsky: 1929–1940* (New York: Vintage, 1963), p. 479.

2. I have discussed social differentiation in *History and Subjectivity: The Transformation of Marxist Theory* (Atlantic Highlands, N.J.: Humanities Press, 1993), Chapters 12–14.

3. Even gender, which appears to some to be given by nature, varies so much over history and culture that it is clearly in many ways a social product itself.

4. Sources here include Joanna Macy, Warwick Fox, Theodor Roszak, Starhawk, Aldo Leopold, Dave Foreman, Gary Snyder, and Riane Eisler. Despite my support of deep ecology, I reject the way some of its voices have placed undue primacy on wilderness preservation, promoted an apolitical understanding of population issues, and been blind to political and social inequalities.

5. Paul Shepard, "Ecology and Man—a Viewpoint," in *The Subversive Science*, edited by Paul Shepard and Daniel McKinley, (Boston: Houghton Miflin, 1969), p. 2, emphasis mine.

6. Even such a bounded self involves non-human nature, for our health requires the presence of billions of microbes that function *within* our bodies.

7. See Riane Eisler, *The Chalice and the Blade* (New York: Harper and Row, 1987); and Marija Gimbutas, *The Goddesses and Gods of Old Europe* (Berkeley: University of California Press, 1982).

8. For sources describing the simultaneous emergence of patriarchy, class society, and dominating attitudes towards nature see Gerda Lerner, *The Creation of Patriarchy,* (New York: Oxford University Press, 1986), Marilyn French, *Beyond Power* (New York: Ballantine, 1985), Robert Pogue Harrison, *Forests: The Shadow of Civilization* (Chicago: University of Chicago Press, 1992) pp. 13–60; and Michael Mann, *The Sources of Social Power: Volume I* (New York: Cambridge University Press, 1987), pp. 34–129.

9. Andrew McLaughlin, "Marxism and the Mastery of Nature: An Ecological Critique," in Roger S. Gottlieb, ed., *Radical Philosophy: Tradition, Counter-Tradition, Politics* (Philadelphia: Temple University Press, 1993).

10. Theorists describing new forms of social organization—including bioregionalism, organic farming, ecological educational practices, tax codes restricting pollution, etc.—are thus depicting social practices which can further a deep ecological perspective.

11. Too many spiritual traditions also enshrine hierarchy and power within their own organizations.

12. For a fuller account of spirituality, see my Introduction to Roger S. Gottlieb, ed., *A New Creation: America's Contemporary Spiritual Voices,* (New York: Crossroad, 1990); and *Marxism 1844–1990: Origins, Betrayal, Rebirth* (New York: Routledge, 1992), pp. 197–220.

13. Adopting a deep ecological view will not solve particular conflicts of interests between humanity and nature; it will not tell us which houses or dams or diets are necessarily justified. But in this way it is no different from either liberalism or socialism, neither of which can exclude painful conflicts among legitimate interests.

14. Marx, Engels and Marxism's views on nature are more complex and controversial than I can do justice to here. Clearly, the major strength of the Marxist tradition's account of environmental issues lies in its analysis of the causes of ecological devastation. As for Marx's own attitudes to nature: even a defender of his ecological wisdom such as Howard Parsons notes that "Marx . . . shared the faith of a spectacularly successful nineteenth-century capitalism in material and technological progress" and "called for a *social mastery of nature* for the sake of *man.*" In Parsons, ed., *Marx and Engels on Ecology* (Greenwood, CT: Greenwood Press, 1977) p. 69. Much more negative critics, such as Stanley Aronowitz, Murray Bookchin, and Isaac Balbus, consider Marx to be a full-fledged representative of the worst excesses of Western philosophy's and modernity's attempt to endlessly dominate and exploit nature. See, e.g., Isaac Balbus, *Marxism and Domination* (Princeton: Princeton University Press, 1983).

15. This position is developed at some length in my treatment of the Communist Party and the CIO in *History and Subjectivity.*

16. I have discussed these problems at length in both *History and Subjectivity* and *Marxism 1844–1990.*

17. A deep ecological sensibility thus corresponds to forms of interaction stressed by feminism.

18. I have explored relations between spiritual and political viewpoints in "Heaven on Earth: A Dialogue between a Political Radical and a Spiritual Seeker," in *A New Creation.*

19. As others have observed: cf., Murray Bookchin, *Remaking Society: Pathways to a Green Future,* (Boston: South End Press, 1990); Tim Luke, "The Dreams of Deep Ecology," *Telos* 76 (1988); Ariel Salleh, "The Ecofeminism/Deep Ecology Debate: A Reply to Patriarchal Reason," *Environmental Ethics,* Vol 14, Fall 1992.

20. Sadly, these two conditions do not entail each other. We have seen cultures that practice a high degree of ecological sustainability—and even reverence for non-human nature—and are also quite patriarchal.

21. "Justice" here includes both institutional norms and face-to-face interpersonal relations, and is founded both in abstract principles and the cultivation of the capacity for care.

22. I am drawing here on both the communicative ethics perspective of Jurgen Habermas and the stress on emotional interdependency and care developed by feminist ethicists and psychologists such as Carol Gilligan, Jean Baker Miller, and Nel Noddings.

23. Bill McKibben, *The End of Nature,* (New York: Anchor, 1989).

24. Robin Broad, *Plundering Paradise: The Struggle for the Environment in the Philippines,* (Berkeley: University of California Press, 1993), pp. 137–9.

25. Raymond Bonner, *At the Hands of Man: Peril and Hope for Africa's Wildlife* (New York: Knopf, 1993) p. 286.

26. Ramachandra Guha, "Radical American Environmentalism and Wilderness Preservation: A Third World Critique," in Lori Gruen and Dale Jamieson, eds., *Reflecting on Nature: Readings in Environmental Philosophy,* (New York: Oxford University Press, 1994), p. 249.

27. Edward Abbey, *The Long Journey Home: Some Words in Defense of the American West,* (New York: Penguin, 1991), p. 145.

"BEYOND HUMANISM, MODERNITY, AND PATRIARCHY"

and

"TEN KEY VALUES OF THE AMERICAN GREEN MOVEMENT"

Charlene Spretnak

"BEYOND HUMANISM, MODERNITY, AND PATRIARCHY"

Any delineation of spiritual values within the vision of Green politics must reflect three essential elements of the cultural direction in which the movement is growing. First, Green politics rejects the anthropocentric orientation of humanism, a philosophy which posits that humans have the ability to confront and solve the many problems we face by applying human reason and by rearranging the natural world and the interactions of men and women so that human life will prosper. We need only consider the proportions of the environmental crisis today to realize the dangerous self-deception contained in both religious and secular humanism. It is *hubris* to declare that humans are the central figures of life on Earth and that we are in control. In the long run, *Nature is in control.*

Commenting on the delusion of our anthropocentric self-aggrandizement, the biologist Lewis Thomas has written

> Except for us, the life of the planet conducts itself as though it were an immense, coherent body of connected life, an intricate system, an organism. Our deepest folly is the notion that we are in charge of the place, that we own it and can somehow run it. We are a living part of Earth's life, owned and operated by the Earth, probably specialized for functions on its behalf that we have not yet glimpsed.

In rejecting humanism, Green politics separates itself from much of the "New Age" movement and the belief that humans are the epitome of creation rather than being *part* of the far more glorious unfolding universe. Our goal is for human society to operate in a learning mode and to cultivate biocentric wisdom. Such wisdom entails a sophisticated understanding of how the natural world—including us—works.

I disagree with most critics of humanism when they declare that our problem has been too much reliance on "reason" and not enough on emotion. In fact, we have been employing merely the truncated version of reason used in mechanistic thinking to focus attention on only the most obvious "figures" in a situation while ignoring the subtle, intricate field around them. In the area of human systems, emotions are always part of the field. If we valued a comprehensive grasp of the context, or *gestalt*, of various situations, we civilized humans would not have to stumble along ignoring most of the contextual data, arriving at inadequate conclusions, and congratulating ourselves on our powers of "reason." In Germany I sometimes heard fears that any turn away from rationalist solutions is extremely dangerous because it could lead to the kind of mass manipulation the Nazis employed so successfully. The essential point is that holistic, or ecological, thinking is not a retreat from reason; it is an enlargement of it to more comprehensive and hence more efficient means of analysis.

Green politics goes beyond not only the anthropocentric assumptions of humanism but also the broader constellation of values that constitute modernity. Modern culture—as we all recognize since we live in the belly of the beast—is based on mechanistic analysis and control of human systems as well as Nature, rootless cosmopolitanism, nationalistic chauvinism, sterile secularism, and monoculture shaped by mass media. Some critics of modernity have noted that it consists of revolt against traditional values even to the extent of being "an unyielding rage against the official order." An enthusiast of modernity has little use for the traditional institutions that further human bonding—the family, the church or synagogue, community groups, ethnic associations—championing instead an "individual-liberationist stance."

The values of modernity inform both socialist and capitalist nation-states. It is not surprising that citizens' resistance networks in socialist countries often find a resonant home in the churches, that both liberal and conservative churches in capitalist countries are rethinking religion's contemporary role as an inconsequential observer who is to make accommodations to the modern world and not interfere with "progress."

Many critics of modernity, while unable to suggest a comprehensive alternative, conclude that the transformation of modern society is "going to have something to do with religion." Whatever the particulars of postmodern culture, it will not signify an uncritical return to the values of the medieval world that immediately preceded the Enlightenment or those of the Gilded Age preceding World War I and the aggressive burst of modernism that followed it. The pioneers of modernity were right to reject certain conventions and restrictions that were stultifying to the human spirit. But, with the impulses of a rebellious adolescent, they destroyed too much and embraced a radical disregard for limits, especially concerning the natural world. What we need now is the maturity to value freedom *and* tradition, the individual *and* the community, science *and* Nature, men *and* women.

The third cultural force that Green politics counters is patriarchal values. In a narrow sense these entail male domination and exploitation of women. But in a broader sense the term "patriarchal culture" in most feminist circles connotes not only injustice toward women but also the accompanying cultural traits: love of hierarchical structure and competition, love of dominance-or-submission modes of relating, alienation from Nature, suppression of empathy and other emotions, and haunting insecurity about all of those matters. These traits usually show up in anyone, male or female, who opts to play by the rules of patriarchal culture.

"TEN KEY VALUES OF THE AMERICAN GREEN MOVEMENT"

1. **Ecological Wisdom** How can we operate human societies with the understanding that we are *part* of nature, not on top of it? How can we live within the ecological and resource limits of the planet, applying our technological knowledge to the challenge of an energy-efficient economy? How can we build a better relationship between cities and countryside? How can we guarantee the rights of nonhuman species? How can we promote sustainable agriculture and respect for self-regulating natural systems? How can we further biocentric wisdom in all spheres of life?

2. **Grassroots Democracy** How can we develop systems that allow and encourage us to control the decisions that affect our lives? How can we ensure that representatives will be fully accountable to the people who elect them? How can we develop planning mechanisms that would allow citizens to develop and implement their own preferences for policies and spending priorities? How can we encourage and assist the "mediating institutions"—family, neighborhood organization, church group, voluntary association, ethnic club—to recover some of the functions now performed by government? How can we relearn the best insights from American traditions of civic vitality, voluntary action, and community responsibility?

3. **Personal and Social Responsibility** How can we respond to human suffering in ways that promote dignity? How can we encourage people to commit themselves to lifestyles that promote their own health? How can we have a community-controlled education system that effectively teaches our children academic skills, ecological wisdom, social responsibility, and personal growth? How can we resolve interpersonal and intergroup conflicts without just turning them over to lawyers and judges? How can we take responsibility for reducing the crime rate in our neighborhoods? How can we encourage such values as simplicity and moderation?

4. **Nonviolence** How can we, as a society, develop effective alternatives to our current patterns of violence, at all levels, from the family and the street to nations and the world? How can we eliminate nuclear weapons from the face of the Earth without being naive about the intentions of other governments? How can we most constructively use nonviolent methods to oppose practices and policies with which we disagree and in the process reduce the atmosphere of polarization and selfishness that is itself a source of violence?

5. **Decentralization** How can we restore power and responsibility to individuals, institutions, communities, and regions? How can we encourage the flourishing of regionally-based culture rather than a dominant monoculture? How can we have a decentralized, democratic society with our political, economic, and social institutions locating power on the smallest scale (closest to home) that is efficient and practical? How can we redesign our institutions so that fewer decisions and less regulation over money are granted as one moves from the community toward the national level? How can we reconcile the need for community and regional self-determination with the need for appropriate centralized regulation in certain matters?

6. **Community-Based Economics** How can we redesign our work structures to encourage employee ownership and workplace democracy? How can we develop new economic activities and institutions that will allow us to use our new technologies in ways that are humane, freeing, ecological, and accountable and responsive to communities? How can we establish some form of basic economic security, open to all? How can we move beyond the narrow "job ethic" to new definitions of "work," "jobs," and "income" that reflect the changing economy? How can we restructure our patterns of income distribution to reflect the wealth created by those outside the formal, monetary economy: those who take responsibility for parenting, housekeeping, home gardens, community volunteer work, etc.? How can we restrict the size and concentrated power of corporations without discouraging superior efficiency or technological innovation?

7. **Postpatriarchal Values** How can we replace the cultural ethics of dominance and control with more cooperative ways of interacting? How can we encourage people to care about persons outside their own group? How can we promote the building of respectful, positive, and responsible relationships across the lines of gender and other divisions? How can we encourage a rich, diverse political culture that respects feelings as well as rationalist approaches? How can we proceed with as much respect for the means as the end (the process as much as the products of our efforts)? How can we learn to respect the contemplative, inner part of life as much as the outer activities?

8. **Respect for Diversity** How can we honor cultural, ethnic, racial, sexual, religious, and spiritual diversity within the context of individual responsibility toward all beings? How can we reclaim our country's finest shared ideals: the dignity of the individual, democratic participation, and liberty and justice for all?

9. **Global Responsibility** How can we be of genuine assistance to grassroots groups in the Third World? What can we learn from such groups? How can we help other countries make the transition to self-sufficiency in food and other basic necessities? How can we cut our defense budget while maintaining an adequate defense? How can we promote these ten Green values in the reshaping of global order? How can we reshape world order without creating just another enormous nation-state?

10. **Future Focus** How can we induce people and institutions to think in terms of the long-range future, and not just in terms of their short-range selfish interest? How can we encourage people to develop their own visions of the future and move more effectively toward them? How can we judge whether new technologies are socially useful—and use those judgments to shape our society? How can we induce our government and other institutions to practice fiscal responsibility? How can we make the quality of life, rather than open-ended economic growth, the focus of future thinking?

Charlene Spretnak

from *CARING FOR CREATION*

Max Oelschlaeger

CHURCH AND STATE RECONSIDERED

The orthodox view that church and state are separate spheres is one reason why religion has not effectively addressed environmental crisis. Yet the notion that the church is one thing, concerned with otherworldly, supernatural affairs, and that the state is something else, concerned with this world, our everyday economic and political affairs, cannot be sustained. A closer examination of the role of religion in personal life and in democratic society reveals a different picture. The genius of democracy is not that religion is precluded from influencing public affairs; rather, it is that *no single religion or group of religions is permitted to monopolize the state.* As Garry Wills observes, America was and remains an experiment, since no other Western society has launched itself without theological sanction. The constitutional separation of church and state "gave to religion an initial, if minimal, freedom from crippling forms of cooperation with the state. That, more than anything else, made the United States a new thing on the earth, setting new tasks for religion, offering it new opportunities" (1990, 383). This freedom has been and remains both an opportunity and a danger. Freedom offers religion the chance to find its own essence, to be unencumbered by the demands of politics and economics. Autonomy from the state also poses the threat that the church might become irrelevant in a nation whose legitimating purpose is increasingly economic, that is, the maximization of the GNP regardless of ecological and social consequences.

One thing is clear: from a historical perspective the role of religion in American society has been and remains in flux. The colonists who came to the New World believed in religious establishment, as the history of the Massachusetts Bay Colony certainly shows. Even after the Revolution, establishment continued in some states (the First Amendment precluded establishment at the federal but not the state level). Massachusetts did not give up establishment until 1833. Still, the privatization of religion is one thing. The influence of religion and the church on society is another. Observing the new democracy during the 1830s. Tocqueville concluded that the church, especially by shaping the personality and moral character of individuals, was the primary political institution in the United States. Tocqueville's view, Bellah suggests, is that the political function of religion "was not direct intervention but support of

Reprinted from *Caring for Creation: An Ecumenical Approach to the Environmental Crisis* by Max Oelschlaeger, 1994, Yale University Press. Reprinted by permission of Yale University Press.

the mores that make democracy possible. In particular, it had the role of placing limits on utilitarian individualism, hedging in self-interest with a proper concern for others" (1985, 223).

Clearly, even with the privatization of religion, the church exerts considerable political influence. Many of the faithful recognize that organized religion has an important function to serve in the public realm. Commentators like Wills, Tipton, and Marty argue that the role of the church is at least in part to criticize the state, sometimes even to castigate and break its rules, as in acts of religiously motivated civil disobedience. As discussed earlier, the opposition of church and state has been a characteristic of the biblical tradition since the beginning. Yahwism was a sociocultural revolution anchored in religion, a protest against the hieratic states that surrounded the tribes of Yahweh. And early Christians were united in rebellion against the state, primarily the Roman Empire. Of course, the melding of the church (circa A.D. 400) with the Roman Empire changed the course of history, and for nearly a millennium and a half ecclesiastical and political power were effectively one.[1] More recently, the civil rights movement exemplifies the church's influence on the state. The struggle over abortion is another example, but different in that no religiously inspired and politically effective consensus has emerged.

Increasingly, however, the church *appears to have been marginalized,* excluded from influencing public affairs. This split mirrors the fissure between our private and public lives. It is the consequence of a relatively clear sequence of historical events. Both bourgeois society and science itself initially needed religious warrant, but once the modern turn was made, *organized religion* essentially became a dead letter in public affairs. The modern state, modeled on materialistic atomism, has been founded on the metaphysical belief in the absolute nature of individual (atomic) freedom, be it religious, economic, political, or intellectual.

The individual described by utilitarian individualism is, however, a metaphysical abstraction from the social world in which human beings actually exist. We become caricatures of ourselves when we are conceived in terms of a theory that cannot meaningfully describe social relations. Each of us lives primarily within a social context of sustaining relationships, which can be neither empirically described nor theoretically conceptualized as nothing more than the aggregated interests of autonomous individuals. Given the Enlightenment definition of the individual, the "good society" serves private and primarily economic interests. Any vision of the social matrix as constituted by internal relations among people, especially when these are noneconomic, is inconsistent with the prevailing ideology, since relations between two or more people (for example, mother and child) or between generations violates the premise that the individual is (metaphysically) absolute: an atom, in splendid isolation.[2] Americans, whose experiences of relationships are theorized in terms of the language of external relations—that is, market economics—may have difficulty accepting this premise.[3] But John Cobb and Herman Daly argue that a more accurate (empirically and theoretically) way of describing the individual is as a *person-in-community* (1989, 161).

Max Oelschlaeger

Critics of the prevailing ideology point out that while citizens enjoy freedom from the overt oppression of totalitarian societies (freedom from), they have no freedom to create alternatives to the overriding economic purpose of the corporate state. This lack of positive freedom (freedom to, as distinct from negative freedom, freedom from) is itself a consequence of the narrative that makes the individual a metaphysical abstraction ostensibly enjoying absolute freedom. Society is accordingly conceptualized on the model of utilitarian individualism, where, free from social relations, individuals (either human beings or corporations) pursue their private interests without limit. Society, inevitably, is conceived as nothing more than the aggregate of private interests. Given this Enlightenment narrative, the state can have no other definition than the greatest good for the greatest number of individuals.

The separation of church and state in America exemplifies this liberal-bourgeois theory. Religious believers are guaranteed freedom of worship, that is, the freedom to search for private definitions of the good life. But, on the basis of the liberal tradition itself, the faithful cannot collectively participate in defining social preferences. What this tradition ignores is the fact that on many occasions believers have reached solidarity on the common good (if not so much on specific doctrinal issues). There is nothing to preclude the faithful from coming together in conversation about public issues, such as protection of the biosphere, consistent with the separation of church and state. The word *public* is often misinterpreted as meaning only the enfranchisement of agencies serving the so-called public interest or common good. *But* public *can also mean voluntary associations of people who seek to define and enfranchise common interests.* Political consensus on an environmental agenda is, I have been arguing, something that might be created out of the diversity of faith, but it does not inhere in faith alone. For it is entirely consistent with the principles of our republican tradition.

THE CHURCH AND HABITS OF THE HEART

Granted the power of organizations, we readily see that the corporation and the state move modern society on a relentless trajectory of materialism, of economic growth for its own sake. Religious discourse has been marginalized in public affairs by the gospel of greed. How, the skeptic asks, can the church make a difference? The church is involved, I believe, if for no other reason than the reality that our ethical and political lives are collapsing as the earth is destroyed. As we disrupt the web of life in the unbridled pursuit of a narrowly defined and scientifically tenuous conception of economic success, the fabric of our culture is unraveling. There seems to be no hope as our world plunges toward global ecocatastrophe. The individual, embedded in the institutionalized order of life, can do little to change the course of events. And collectively we are driving nature toward a point where civilization will no longer be sustainable. This is not, I have argued, truly surprising. The modern person has lost sight of the sacredness of creation. Is there any wonder that in becoming Homo oeconomicus we are endangering the Creation? But the real question is: Can the profane person of the modern world again learn to care for creation?

Perhaps.... [T]here is *reason for hope,* a promise of renewal across the spectrum of contemporaneous religious belief. And the importance of finding hope in organized religion should not be underemphasized, since it "rests on something other than its own usefulness" in a time of ecological crisis. Hope, John Cobb argues, is not so much a function of its utility as "a function of what we believe, and in this cosmic and global crisis, it is most clearly a function of what we believe *ultimately and comprehensively*" (1992, 124). It is easy for the overwhelming power of the established order of things to vanquish us psychologically. But for believers, Cobb explains, the experience of the Spirit in themselves calls "forth the realistic hope apart from which there is no hope" (125). The religiously faithful can find, especially in the sustaining community of faith—the local congregation itself—the strength of conviction and the power of hope. With the telling of the sacred story comes the renewal of Spirit. In spite of the diversity of religious belief, there is a common ground for caring for creation that can make organized religion a political turning point. Renewal begins within *the local church*—the immediate faith community to which individuals are committed. The local church is the key place to shaping opinion because (1) the church has had and retains importance as a *mediating institution* between individualism and large institutions and because (2) every church has within its own narrative tradition the power to challenge the language of selfishness and the gospel of greed.

So construed, the church is a fundamental political institution whose function is not to set policy but to support the principles that make democracy possible and to encourage concern for others, including future generations of human beings and the rest of the Creation. Religion does work to shape political attitudes and behavior. President George Bush, for example, invoked religion to justify the righteousness of Operation Desert Storm. Yet it is at this cultural level, as we have seen, that liberals become suspicious and controversy arises over the intrusion of religion into public life. Liberals prefer to think that elected officials and the government more generally stand for the morally right thing, since they enjoy majority support. This is a fallacy, since majority support does not confer morality on governmental power. It is a truism of democratic life that the majority does not necessarily know what the best policy or candidate is. The sorry history of National Socialism and Adolf Hitler, who was installed by a majority of the German electorate acting under the Weimar Constitution, is proof enough. The belief that the majority opinion is intrinsically moral overlooks, according to Abraham Kaplan, the political reality "that consent can be cajoled as well as coerced; virtue is lost to seduction more often than to rape" (1963, 76). Kaplan's remark implies that utilitarian individualism seduces Americans into supporting the economic status quo, the industrial growth paradigm. The irony is that an ecologically sound economy would be good for everyone. Caring for creation entails not economic sui-

Max Oelschlaeger

cide but rather the embracing of economic principles that go beyond merely monetary measures of welfare.[4]

Americans appear to be increasingly skeptical of the results of the electoral process (as distinct from the idea of democracy), politicians, and the policy-making process. The National Commission on the Environment reports that "the percentage of Americans who said they trusted the government 'to do what is right' always or most of the time declined from 76 percent in 1964 ... to 28 percent in 1990. During the same period, the percentage of Americans who thought that the government is 'pretty much run by a few big interests looking out for themselves' went from 31 ... to 75 percent" (1993, 52). Americans are suspicious in part because their votes do not appear to make a difference. Whatever their promises, politicians seldom act in ways that change cultural outcomes: the status quo rules. When politicians drape themselves in flags, stand on podiums framed by the Grand Tetons, and declare themselves "environmental presidents" while their advisers declare that "methane is not a greenhouse gas," something is fundamentally wrong. Skepticism about the political process is not misplaced. The distrust also dramatizes the potential of the church to facilitate the democratic process leading to solidarity on an environmental agenda and, subsequently, to adaptive political responses. More precisely, in serving its role as a mediating institution, the church positions itself at the juncture of politics and ethics. Which is to say that the biblical tradition reinforces the republican tradition—the heritage that seeks the public good and ultimately, through communal discourse, attempts to develop a consensus on the public good.

For most Americans *the local church* is far and away the most likely forum for discussion of moral issues that overlap with politics. The local church is ideally suited to discourse where ecological crisis runs up against the gospel of greed (and where ecology as objective science is reluctant, either incapable or unwilling, to assume a normative stance). The church is a community of memory, tracing its roots back to a covenant relation with God and the celebration of that relationship on the sabbath. The worship retells (better, recreates) the story of the relation between the religious community and God, and the liturgy, ideally, provides a legitimating narrative for the whole of life. Americans have reasons to care for creation. Insofar as these traditions remain viable, they are not confined to a day of worship but shape the believer's character and behavior, spilling out of the church into everyday life.

More fundamentally, the local church starts the body politic moving toward a working version of *the public church*. As Martin Marty (1981) argues, the public church refers not to any actual institution or denomination but to a "communion of communions" that remains consistent with the diversity of faith traditions. The communion of communions flourishes wherever issues of the public good exist—ecocrisis being an obvious example. That the public church exists is beyond doubt. Organizations such as North American Council for Religious Education (NACRE), the North American Conference on Christianity and Ecology (NACCE), and the World Council of Churches (WCC) testify to its reality.

Consider a few examples. NACRE organized a national conference on Caring for Creation, celebrated during May 1990 in Washington, D.C., that was attended by more than 2,500 delegates, including large numbers of clergy as well as representatives from the scientific community. Portions of the proceedings were televised nationally. The WCC has also been very active on issues involving global ecology, attempting to work out ecumenical policy statements for the Protestant community. In February 1991 the WCC held an international conference in Canberra, Australia, with the theme "Come Holy Spirit, Renew Creation." Particularly promising in regard to global ecology is the report to the WCC entitled "Liberating Life: A Report to the World Council of Churches."[5] This report calls for developing a theology for the liberation of life. "Informed by the biblical witness, the insights of science, and our experience of the interdependence of life, this theology needs to address the brokenness of our world and its intricate web of life with a new statement of the healing words of Christian faith" (Birch 1990, 276). The WCC was also present at the Rio Summit (or, more accurately, at the alternative summit held outside the "governmentally sanctioned" activities), where it advocated the theme of "Justice, Peace, and Integrity of Creation."[6]

Beyond the WCC, an organization supported by most Protestant denominations, are denominational statements on ecology and the Creation. As noted, American Catholicism has spoken authoritatively on the issue of ecocrisis; so has American Protestantism. Most American Christians, both Catholics and Protestants, are in churches that have adopted ecological position statements and have active ecological ministries. According to Massey (1991), among the thirty largest Protestant denominations, the only denominations that have no such policy are the National Baptist Convention (fourth largest) and the Church of God in Christ (seventh largest). As noted, the only denomination that has formally stated its opposition to ecology as part of the church's mission is the Church of Jesus Christ of Latter-day Saints. Collectively, however, these position statements indicate a commitment to the public church—to a communion of communions that cares for creation.

In addition to national denominations and international organizations, many regional and local organizations carry on the mission of the public church, including Jewish, Protestant, and Catholic groups. *Shomre Adamah* (Keepers of the earth), for example, provides ecotheological information and books for people of the Jewish faith. Headed by Ellen Bernstein, the organization distributes traditional (selections from the Pentateuch) and nontraditional educational materials. *The Grassroots Coalition for Environmental and Economic Justice,* organized by a former Jesuit priest in 1988, operates in Maryland. Its aim is "to encourage and assist church members to work effectively for environmental justice for our Earth-Community." Members of the grassroots coalition work with local churches (on invitation) to initiate a process of caring for creation within the congregation.

Interestingly, although the ecologically oriented activity of the public church is increasingly evident, the tradition of Judeo-Christians forming organizations that attend to the

Creation dates back to the 1930s. Even as early as the 1940s, according to Rod Nash, some churches were exploring their obligations to the natural world. In the wake of the Dust Bowl, the National Catholic Rural Life Commission brought religion to bear on the issues of soil husbandry. "The observance of Rogation Days, which dates to the Middle Ages and acknowledges human dependence on planting and harvesting, provided a conceptual basis for modern dedications such as Rural Life Sundays and Soil Stewardship Sundays" (1989, 98). And in the 1950s, Nash continues, the National Council of Churches "launched a program called 'A Christian Ministry in the National Parks,' but its emphasis was largely on human appreciation of the beauty in God's world" (98). During the 1960s and 1970s theologians formed a variety of organizations and study groups to ground an environmental ethic in religion. The earlier work of theologians like Joseph Sittler, Charles Hartshorne, and Daniel Day was very influential during this period. During 1963–64 the National Council of Churches formed the Faith-Man-Nature Group, which was dedicated to articulating a Christian environmental ethic, and it held annual meetings from 1965 until 1974 (until financial exigency ended its all-too-brief tenure). The recent activities of both national and local religious organizations, then, are not unprecedented. But what had been largely episodic and fitful from the 1930s through the 1960s and even 1970s is now a steady and growing stream of activity. Put in slightly different terms, the work of the believers who cared for creation during the 1960s and 1970s is bearing fruit. What was for too long nothing more than a few isolated efforts shows signs of becoming a powerful social movement.

NOTES

1. The Marxian critique of religion suggests that, even into the nineteenth century, religion was an opiate that quelled opposition to the state. Yet Marxians specifically, and political theology more generally, have tended to ignore the minority traditions (for example, Gnosticism) within Judeo-Christian culture that were always a thorn in the side of secular power.

2. In economic theory this situation is reflected by the exclusion of nonmonetary income, such as the services of individuals in the household (largely women), public interest groups, and the biosystem from the National Income Accounts. As Ekins et al. point out, "It is arguable that such groups [and biosystem services] do as much for our quality of life as the formal business sector" (1992, 68). The consequence is that very narrow and exclusively monetary measures of wealth are presented to the nation as an index of social welfare.

3. The issue is not the market per se but the attemp to reduce environmental issues to consumer preferences and the question "How much are you willing to pay?" Citizen preferences in, for example, biodiversity, go beyond consumer preferences for inexpensive hamburgers and plywood derived from the short-term exploitation of South American rainforests. See Sagoff 1988 for discussion.

4. Concerning the economic effects of environmentalism, see Meyer 1992, 1993, and Meyer, *Environmentalism and Economic Prosperity* (provisional title, forthcomin g from MIT Press). Meyer argues that environmental policy has in the aggregate no negative economic consequences. "If environmentalism does have negative economic effects they are so marginal and transient that they are completely lost in the noise of much more powerful domestic and internal economic influences" (1993, 10).

5. Reprinted in Birch et al. 1990.

6. See Granberg-Michaelson 1992 for a report on the WCC and the Rio Earth Summit. I am indebted to an anonymous referee for this refernces and other useful information in this section.

REFERENCES

Barbour, Ian G. 1990. *Religion in an Age of Science: The Gifford Lectures, 1989–1991, vol. 1.* San Francisco: Harper & Row.

Birch, Charles, and John B. Cobb, Jr. 1981 *Liberating Life: Contemporary Approaches to Ecotheology.* Maryknoll, N.Y.: Orbis Books.

Cobb, John B., Jr. 1992. *Sustainability: Economics, Ecology, and Justice.* Maryknoll, N.Y.: Orbis Books.

Cobb, John B., Jr., and Herman E. Daly. 1989. *For the Common Good: Redirecting the Economy toward Community, the Environment, and a Sustainable Future.* Boston: Beacon Press.

Kaplan, Abraham. 1963. *American Ethics and Public Policy* New York: Oxford University Press.

McDaniel, Jay. 1986. "Christianity and the Need for New Vision." In Hargrove, ed., *Religion and Environmental Crisis.*

Marty, Martin E. 1981. *The Public Church: Mainline Evangelical Catholic.* New York: Crossroad.

Massey, Marshall. 1991. "Where Are Our Churches Today? A Report on the Environmental Positions of the Thirty Largest Christian Denominations in the United States." *Firmament* 2, 4:4–15.

Nash, Roderick. 1989. *The Rights of Nature: A History of Environmental Ethics.* Madison: University of Wisconsin Press.

National Commission on the Environment. 1993. *Choosing a Sustainable Future: The Report of the National Commission on the Environment.* Washington, D.C.: Island Press.

Wills, Garry. 1990. *Under God: Religion and American Politics.* New York: Simon and Schuster.

"EARTH FIRST!: FROM PRIMAL SPIRITUALITY TO ECOLOGICAL RESISTANCE"

Bron Taylor

FLIGHT IN THE DESERT

The darkness of the high-desert night retreated into the shadows as the FBI's flares launched skyward.[1] The light signaled thirty heavily armed agents to descend on the three ecological saboteurs—and one FBI infiltrator—huddled below the giant electrical towers. Two of the saboteurs were quickly seized. The third disappeared into the shadows. Running with the wild abandon of all prey, pausing to catch her breath, she began to feel herself mystically descend into Earth, sensing it merging with her, surrounding her, protecting her. She had become invisible—ghost-like. When the helicopters passed overhead, she hugged a tree or pressed herself into the ground, invisible. She had become like the ringtail cat, her totem animal. "The ringtail consciousness was in me that night," she recalls. "I ran through cactus gardens without getting stuck. I could feel the ringtail, like it was a part of me, encircling me. I felt its presence." Secure in this sacred mind-space they could never find her. Several hours later, she slipped past her pursuers guarding a road on the edge of town, still imperceptible. Back at work the next day, back in the mundane world, Peg Millett was seized and arrested—but she was not surprised—she had become separated from the Earth's protective intention by the impermeable concrete of the building's foundation.

Mark Davis had been quickly apprehended that night. He was soon charged with several different acts of "ecotage" (a term meaning sabotage defending ecosystems, also known as "monkeywrenching" in movement parlance) including an effort designed to thwart the expansion of a ski resort in Arizona's San Francisco Mountains—an area considered sacred by the Hopi and Navajo tribes. In a letter from a federal penitentiary, he explained this particular action:

> Certainly there was some outrage involved at the blatant disregard of agreements with the Hopi and Navajo tribes, anger at the destruction of hundreds of acres of irreplaceable old growth forest for the new ski runs, and indignation that the Forest Service was subsidizing a

private company with public dollars. But the bottom line is that those mountains are sacred, and that what has occurred there, despite our feeble efforts, is a terrible spiritual mistake.

When arrested in May 1989 in the Arizona desert, both Millett and Davis were involved with Earth First!, the self-described "radical environmental" movement. Also snared in the FBI's net were Earth First! co-founder Dave Foreman, the lead author of *Ecodefense: A Field Guide to Monkeywrenching* (Tucson, Arizona: Ned Ludd, 1987), which described how to destroy logging equipment and otherwise thwart those who would destroy "sacred wilderness ecosystems." The arrest, trial, and eventual conviction of these activists—combined with the 1990 bombing that permanently disabled and nearly killed ancient forest activist Judi Bari—helped catapult Earth First! into the public eye, especially in the western United States. But the sensational headlines that followed rarely mentioned the spiritual perceptions underpinning these tactics, or for that matter, the competing religious perceptions animating their most ardent opponents.

Many Earth First!ers, sympathizers and their opponents, however, recognize the importance of spiritual premises in contemporary environmental conflicts. One extreme example can be found in a letter purportedly from Judi Bari's bomber, who, quoting Genesis 1:26 (the "dominion" creation story), wrote that "this possessed [pagan] demon Judy Bari . . . [told] the multitude that trees were not God's gift to man but that trees were themselves gods and it was a sin to cut them. [So] I felt the Power of the Lord stir within my heart and I knew I had been Chosen to strike down this demon." The letter concludes warning other tree worshipers that they will suffer the same fate, for "I AM THE LORD'S AVENGER." The letter's authenticity is in doubt. Some view it as an authentic, hard-to-fabricate synthesis of Christian fundamentalism and mental illness. Some Earth First!ers believe the letter is an FBI hoax—patterned after similar letters authorities received after abortion clinic bombings—designed to cast suspicion away from law enforcement agencies involved in the assassination attempt. But whether authentic or a ploy designed to divert attention from the actual perpetrator(s), this remarkable letter illustrates dramatically how competing religious values can underlie environmental controversies. Indeed, expressions of distaste and intolerance for the "pagan" spirituality of the radical environmentalists are increasingly expressed by anti-environmentalists and even by some conservationists.[2] Should we fear and suppress, tolerate, or join the radical environmentalists in their spirituality and politics? A fair evaluation depends on accurate description of their spiritual politics.

EARTH FIRST! RELIGION:
A TRADITION EMERGING IN MYTH, SYMBOL AND RITE

Before proceeding, it is helpful to iterate a few preliminary points about religion, especially because many Earth First! militants reject organized religion, some do not view themselves as "religious," and others are uncomfortable with the explicitly religious rituals and songs that have become popular in the movement. With such discomfort in mind, why should we consider Earth First! a religious movement? Because it manifests all the elements that constitute an emerging religious movement.

All religious traditions, whether newer or long established, involve myth, symbol, and ritual. The myths delineate how the world came to be (a cosmogony), what it is like (a cosmology), what people are capable or incapable of achieving (a moral anthropology), and what the future holds (an eschatology). Religious ethics are directly informed by these very mythic elements. Yet religious traditions are plural, they are neither monolithic nor static, they are characterized by ongoing controversies over who owns, interprets and performs the myths, rituals, and rites. Nevertheless, despite great internal plurality, certain core beliefs, behaviors, and values unify and make it possible to speak of a diverse religious movement as a *tradition*. Close observation of Earth First! and of the wider deep ecology movement shows an emerging corpus of myth, symbol, and rite that reveals the emergence of a dynamic, new religious movement.

The theory of evolution provides a primary cosmogony that promotes the *ecocentric ethics* of the movement—namely the notion that all species ought to be able to fulfill their evolutionary destinies, and that ecosystem types should be allowed to flourish. This idea, that all ecosystems and species are intrinsically (or inherently) valuable, apart from their usefulness to human beings, is also the central idea of deep ecology. As Earth First! philosopher Christopher Manes notes in *Green Rage*, if all species evolved through the same process, and none were specially created for any particular purpose, the metaphysical underpinnings of anthropocentrism are displaced, along with the idea that human beings reside at the top of a "Great Chain of Being," ruling over all on Earth. "Taken seriously," he concludes, "evolution means that there is no basis for seeing humans as more advanced [or valuable] than any other species. Homo sapiens is not the goal of evolution, for as near as we can tell evolution has no telos—it simply unfolds, life-form after life-form . . ." The ethical significance of this cosmogony is that since evolution gives life in all its complexity, the evolutionary process itself is of highest value. Consequently, the central moral priority of Earth First! is to protect and restore wilderness because undisturbed wilderness provides the necessary genetic stock for the very continuance of evolution.

This still does not answer the question: Why should we care about evolution, or wild places, in the first place? Manes' argument, where an evolutionary cosmogony displaces human beings as the most valuable creatures, does not explain where *value* actually resides. This is why so much spirituality gets pulled into the Earth First! movement—some form of spirituality is logically needed to provide a basis for valuing the evolutionary process and the resulting life forms—evolutionary theory, as a descriptive cosmogony, cannot provide a reason for valuing the evolutionary process. Manes himself roots Deep Ecology and Earth First! in "the profound spiritual attachment people have to nature." Earth First!ers often speak of the need to "resacralize" our perceptions of nature. Interestingly, Earth First!ers believe that all life is sacred and interconnected, whether or not they consider themselves religious. Even those drawn to an ecocentric ethic based largely on an evolutionary cosmogony eventually rely on metaphors of the sacred to explain their feelings.[3]

Some of the diverse tributaries of the Earth First! movement are *explicitly* religious, tracing their ecocentric sentiments to such diverse religions as Taoism, Buddhism, Hinduism, Christian nature mysticism, witchcraft, and pagan earth-worship. Few Earth First!ers, however, become radical environmentalists due to socialization in or conversion to these traditions. The ecological consciousness uniting Earth First!ers usually begins early in life—in experiences I cannot here typify—long before exposure to these religious traditions. It is usually as young adults or later that many of the activists discover religious traditions sharing affinity with their religious sentiments. Most Earth First!ers are first "generic" nature mystics. Although they appreciate nature-grounded spiritual traditions—few identify exclusively with any particular religious tradition.

With this qualification in mind, we can explore the influences of various nature-sympathetic religious traditions upon the emerging, plural religion of Earth First!. Probably least important is Christian nature mysticism. Two radical environmentalist Christians told me that they no longer directly participate with Earth First! because its members refuse to unequivocally renounce tactics which involve risks to human beings, and because of the anti-theistic attitudes of many members. But I have also found several Earth First!ers who consider themselves Christians. Nevertheless, given the general hostility within Earth First! to Christianity, only once at an Earth First! gathering have I heard anyone argue that Christianity is compatible with deep ecology.

A few Earth First!ers consider themselves Hindu. Yet a much more significant affinity is found in neo-paganism, including wicca or witchcraft. For example, one pagan Earth First!er, speaking at the 1991 Earth First! rendezvous in Vermont, asserted that modern people can no longer experience the world as enchanted because they have paved over wilderness, muting its sacred voices. He proclaimed that Earth First!ers are among the few who can still perceive the sacredness of the Earth, adding that "Gnomes and elves, fauns and faeries, goblins and ogres, trolls and bogies ... [today must infiltrate our world to] effect change from the inside ... [These nature-spirits are] running around in human bodies, ... working in co-ops, ... spiking trees and blowing up tractors, ... starting revolutions, ... [and] making up religions."

Until the early 1990s, the most important spiritual home for Earth First! activists seemed to be in Native American Spirituality, and some activists were appropriating aspects of such spirituality in their own ritual lives, and during wilderness gatherings. By the mid 1990s, however, as a result of increasing alliances between Native American activists and Earth First!ers in defense of areas considered sacred by both groups, the overt expression of such spirituality declined because the appropriation of native American Indian spiritual practices had become controversial.[4]

I have previously referred to the religious perceptions shared by most Earth First!ers as *primal spirituality* and to the movement at large as *pagan environmentalism.*[5] Such labels express the pantheistic and animistic experiences (including shamanistic beliefs and experiences of interspecies communication)[6] that many of these activists share, as well as their common belief that we should emulate the indigenous lifeways of most primal peoples, not just those in North America. Many of these activists call themselves pagans, and believe they are reconstructing nature spiritualities that have been violently suppressed by the world's monotheistic traditions. Others among them express affinity with the holistic religions originating in the Far East, which tend to view the world as metaphysically interconnected and sacred. Generally speaking, these activists consider the natural world to be sacred, especially where it remains wild and undefiled. Through their activism, ritualizing, and efforts at ecological restoration, they venerate wild nature and attempt to re-consecrate it wherever it has been desecrated.

Earth First!ers often call themselves tribalists, and many deep ecologists believe that primal tribes can provide a basis for religion, philosophy, and nature conservation that is applicable to our society. Moreover, Earth First!ers generally agree on the importance of ritual for any tribal "warrior society." At meetings held in or near wilderness, they sometimes engage in ritual war or "tribal unity" dances, sometimes howling like wolves. Indeed, wolves, grizzly bears, and other animals function as totems, symbolizing a mystical kinship between the tribe and other creature-peoples.

Native Americans often conceive of non-human species as kindred "peoples" and through "rituals of inclusion" extend the community of moral concern beyond human beings. Some Earth First!ers have developed their own rituals of *inclusion,* called "Council of All Beings" workshops, which provide a ritual means to connect people spiritually to other creatures and the entire planet. Diverse exercises are employed to help people experience their "ecological self"—namely—the self as embedded within the entire web of life, and therefore not superior to other life forms. During these workshops, rituals are performed where people allow themselves to be imaginatively possessed by the spirits of non-human entities—animals, rocks, soils and rivers, for example—and verbalize their hurt at having been so poorly treated by human beings. As personifications of these non-human forms, participants cry out for fair treatment and harmonious relations among all ecosystem citizens. In the final phase of the Council, the humans seek personal transformation and empowerment, through the gifts of special powers from the non-human entities present in their midst. Ecstatic ritual dance, celebrating inter-species and even inter-planetary oneness, may continue through the night. Such rituals enhance the sense that all is interconnected and sacred. The Council itself has become something of a rite of passage within the movement, or at least a vehicle fostering solidarity among movement participants. Sooner or later most Earth First!ers take part.

THINKING LIKE MOUNTAINS

One of the central myths of the emerging Earth First! tradition has been borrowed from Aldo Leopold's 1949 "Thinking like a Mountain" essay, in *A Sand County Almanac*. He begins with the Pantheistic suggesting that perhaps mountains have knowledge superior to ours. Then he tells of an experience he once had of approaching an old wolf he had shot, just "in time to watch a fierce green fire dying in her eyes. I realized then," Leopold wrote, "and have known ever since, that there was something new to me in those eyes—something known only to her and to the mountain. I was young then . . . I thought that because fewer wolves meant more deer, that no wolves would mean hunters' paradise. But after seeing the green fire die, I sensed that neither the wolf nor the mountain agreed with such a view."

Among Earth First!ers, this story has evolved into a mythic moral fable in which the wolf communicates with human beings, stressing inter-species kinship. (Of course, animal-human communication is a common theme in primal religious myth, and animal-human and human-animal transmogrification and communion are often involved in Shamanism. Many Earth First!ers themselves report shamanistic experiences.) The wolf's "green fire" has become a symbol of life in the wild, incorporated into the ritual of the tradition. Soon after its founding, several Earth First! activists went on "green fire" road shows that were essentially biocentric revival meetings. "Dakota" Sid Clifford, a balladeer in these road shows, referred to them as "ecovangelism." At Earth First! wilderness gatherings, Jesse "Lone Wolf" Hardin, to the sound of pulsating drums and guitars, recounts Leopold's now mythic story, urging participants to dig down deep, discover the wild green fire within them, and use this power to fight the destroyers of life on this planet. In the road shows and wilderness gatherings, the personified wolf of the green fire narrative calls humans to repent from their destructive ways and defend the Earth.

Earth First!ers symbolically express their identification with other creatures through a variety of songs, such as Dana Lyon's sensual affirmation in "I am an animal" (sung to primal chant-rhythms). Sometimes at their wilderness gatherings, innovative and elaborate theatrical performances recount a state of primal innocence when people lived as foragers in harmony with nature, falling from this state with the advent of agriculture and anthropocentric, patriarchal attitudes, eventually experiencing the current period of industrial genocide. The pageant generally ends with a guerilla army of monkeywrench waving children dismantling the industrial machine and resurrecting the remnant animals, including humans, to a new life of natural harmony and ecstasy. At this point, virtually the entire assembly joins in a night of ecstatic dancing, characterized by, as described in the *Earth First!* journal, "pounding drums, naked neanderthals, and wild creatures." Commenting on the scattering of the tribe's warriors after one such gathering in, this article exclaimed, "the green fire is still running wild and free [as] we are once again scattered across the country." The centrality of primal spirituality in the movement can be discerned in such song and ritualized performance, as well as the notion that an authentic human nature is lived wildly and spontaneously in defense of Earth.

Ecotage, of course, is not merely acted out *symbolically* in ritual dance. Ecotage and civil disobedience are real-life ritual actions. Many Earth First!ers have come to recognize this. Dave Foreman, for example, although sometimes claiming to be an atheist, speaks nevertheless of ecotage as ritual worship: monkeywrenching is "a form of worship toward the earth. It's really a very spiritual thing to go out and do." Religious rituals function to transform ordinary time into sacred time, even to alter consciousness itself. Earth First! rituals are no different. A volume edited by Australian Earth First!er John Seed and several others, *Thinking Like a Mountain* (Philadelphia: New Society, 1988), describes how to orchestrate a Council of All Beings. In it, Graham Innes describes "a slow dawning of awareness of a hitherto unknown connection—Earth bonding"—that occurred when he was buried up to his neck while blockading a logging road. The Earth's "pulse became mine," he exclaimed, "and the vessel, my body, became the vehicle for her expression. . . . it was as though nature had overtaken my consciousness to speak on her behalf . . ." Such communion has been reported by more than one Earth First! activist. (For example, several activists, when sitting in trees to prevent logging, have experienced communication with them. One young woman told me that, previous to this experience, she had been a vegetarian. But after sensing that this tree had its own consciousness, she knew that animals were not superior to plants.)

John Davis, an editor of the *Earth First!* journal during much of the 1980s, suggested that tribal rites of passage should be developed that require direct action: "Rites of passage were essential for the health of primal cultures . . . so why not reinstitute initiation rites and other rituals in the form of ecodefense actions? Adolescents could earn their adulthood by successful completion of ritual hunts, as in days of yore, but for a new kind of quarry—bulldozers and their ilk." This is not mere rhetoric. One activist invented a rite of passage to manhood for his son. It included monkeywrenching a bulldozer.

Ecofeminism provides another tributary to Earth First!'s nature-revering spirituality. Many of its ideas have been incorporated into Earth First! liturgy. Songs like *Burning Times* and *Manley Men* satirize macho-hubris and patriarchal domination of nature and women, decry the massacres of witches, and praise various pagan earth-Goddesses.

Ecofeminism and other forms of primal spirituality have a close affinity with yet another tributary to Earth First!—bioregionalism. Bioregionalism is a countercultural movement that envisions self-governing communities living harmoniously and simply within the boundaries of distinct ecosystems. It critiques growth-based industrial societies preferring locally self-sufficient and ecologically sustainable economies and decentralized political structures. Bioregionalists generally share Earth First!'s ecological consciousness regarding the intrinsic value and sacred interconnection of all life. The earth-spirituality of bioregionalists parallels the primal spirituality prominent among Earth First!ers. In some cases their Earth-spirituality is tied to the Gaia hypothesis, a theory which conceives of Earth as a living spirit, a self-regulating organism—named after Gaia, goddess of the Earth.

Before bioregionalism can flourish, however, many Earth First!ers believe that industrial society must first collapse under its own ecologically unsustainable weight. The theory that society is creating an ecological catastrophe containing the seeds of its own destruction introduces another key part of Earth First!'s mythic structure: its apocalyptic eschatology. Earth First! is radical largely due to this apocalyptic worldview: There will be a collapse of industrial society, because this society is ecologically unsustainable. After great suffering, if enough of the genetic stock of the planet survives, evolution will resume its natural course. If human beings also survive, they will have the opportunity to re-establish tribal lifeways compatible with the evolutionary future. The late Edward Abbey, whose novel *The Monkeywrench Gang* helped forge the movement, provides a typical example of Earth First! eschatology:

> Whether [industrial society is] called capitalism or communism makes little difference . . . [both] destroy nature and themselves . . . I predict that the military-industrial state will disappear from the surface of the Earth within fifty years. That belief is the basis of my inherent optimism, the source of my hope for the coming restoration of higher civilization: scattered human populations modest in number that live by fishing, hunting, food-gathering, small-scale farming and ranching, that assemble once a year in the ruins of abandoned cities for great festivals of moral, spiritual, artistic and intellectual renewal—a people for whom the wilderness is not a playground but their natural and native home.

So while bioregionalism focuses on developing models for the future, many Earth First! activists think bioregionalism is impossible without the prior catalyst of an industrial collapse. For this reason, Earth First!ers tend to have a different priority than most bioregionalists, prioritizing ecodefense for now, while awaiting this collapse. Many Earth First!ers believe it is impossible to live sustainably in an industrial society. Thus, Foreman criticizes the priorities of those bioregionalists who become "mired in . . . composting toilets, organic gardens, handcrafts, [and] recycling." Although, "these . . . are important," Foreman concludes, "bioregionalism is [or should be] more than *technique,* it is resacralization [of the Earth] and self-defense."

A good example of Earth First! eschatology and strategy can be seen in Foreman's thoughts about bioregionalism. Bioregionalists should work toward reinhabiting natural preserves.

> That is where the warrior society of Earth First! comes into the bioregional world. In reinhabiting a place, by dwelling in it, we become that place. We are *of* it. Our most fundamental duty is self defense. We are the wilderness defending itself . . . We develop the management plan for our region. We implement it. If the dying industrial empire tries to invade our sacred preserves, we resist its incursions. In most cases we cannot confront it head to head because it is

temporarily much more powerful than we are. But by using our guerrilla wits, we can often use its own massed power against itself. Delay, resist, subvert using all the tools available to us: file appeals and lawsuits, encourage legislation … demonstrate, engage in non-violent civil disobedience, monkeywrench. Defend … Our self-defense is damage control until the machine plows into that brick wall and industrial civilization self-destructs as it must. Then the important work begins [namely, the building of an ecologically sustainable tribal society].

Stopping here would leave a misleading portrait. Certainly ecocentric and evolutionary premises, primal spirituality, Eastern religions, and a panoply of other spiritual tributaries contribute to Earth First!'s worldview. Certainly Earth First!ers often distrust reason, deriving their fundamental premises from intuitions and feelings: their love for wild, sacred places, and their corresponding rage at the ongoing destruction of such places. Certainly the tradition has evolved by appropriating and creating a fascinating variety of myths, symbols, and rituals. But reason is not abandoned: ecological sciences and political analysis is essential to Earth First! praxis. Many within the movement worry about excessive preoccupation with spirituality, with what they musingly call "woo woo." In 1989 John Davis, who was himself responsible for much discussion of spirituality and ritual, cautioned:

> Spiritual approaches to the planet seem to be of growing concern these days. The last issue of the Journal reflects this trend. We ran many articles on sacred sites, rituals, and such, but very few articles pertaining to specific wild lands. (Almost we replaced "No Compromise in Defense of Mother Earth" on the masthead with "All Aboard the Woo Woo Choo Choo.") This is not all to the good. Sacred sites, ritual, and matters of personal growth are important … However, Earth First! may lose effectiveness if it promotes these matters while neglecting the time-worn practices of presenting wilderness proposals … and other such largely left-brain activity.

THREE PILLARS OF EARTH FIRST!'S ETHICS

Thus far we have focused on the essentially religious perceptions that underlie the *moral claim* advanced by Earth First, that all parts of the intrinsically valuable and sacred natural world be allowed to fulfill their evolutionary destinies. This premise constitutes the first pillar of Earth First!'s ethics. But Earth First!'s ethics also depends on two additional claims, this time empirical ones, the first based on the ecological sciences, the second on political analysis.

Based on their reading of the ecological sciences, Earth First!ers add the *ecological claim* that we are in the midst of an unprecedented, anthropogenic extinction crisis, caused most importantly by human overpopulation, greed, and overconsumption; consequently, many ecosystems are presently collapsing. This is the second pillar of Earth First's ethics. Without this claim there is no basis for urgency—no reason for people with deep ecological moral sentiments to risk their freedom or disrupt their private lives. If accurate, such ecological analysis reveals a wide gap between fact and value, between what is and what ought to be: ecosystems that *ought* to be flourishing are being destroyed by human action. This introduces the realm of politics, the necessary arena for strategy over how to bridge gaps between what "is" the relationship between humans and nature, and what such relations "ought" to be like.

POLITICAL ANALYSIS AND THE CALL TO RESISTANCE

Deep ecological moral perceptions combined with ecological urgency do not by themselves enjoin specific political strategies or tactics. The argument for such tactics requires political analysis. The heart of Earth First!'s *political claim* is either: democracy in the U.S. is a sham, thoroughly thwarted by corporate economic power; or, even if not a complete sham, the democratic political system is so distorted by corporate power and regressive human attitudes that it cannot respond quickly enough to avert the escalating extinction catastrophe. Moreover, Earth First!ers would argue that, in light of nature's intrinsic value, governing processes that disregard the interests of non-humans are illegitimate.

Many Earth First!ers add to such critique the ecofeminist contention that androcentrism and patriarchy play important roles in ecological destruction. Many agree that human hierarchy is also a key factor, drawing on Social Ecology or other anarchistic critiques. Few Earth First!ers would suggest, however, that androcentrism or hierarchy alone fully explain environmental degradation. Nevertheless, virtually all of today's Earth First!ers believe patriarchy, hierarchy and anthropocentrism reflect related forms of domination that destroy the natural world. Most Earth First!ers agree that ultimately all such domination must be overcome if humans are to reharmonize their lifeways within nature.

Such political analysis provides the third essential pillar of Earth First!'s radicalism. Without it, in a formally democratic society, it is difficult to argue that illegal tactics are morally permissible. By asserting either that democratic procedures never existed, or that they have broken down, or that they camouflage domination, these activists justify their illegal tactics.

Taken together, these three claims suggest that the current situation—morally, ecologically, and politically—is so grave that tactics usually considered to be wrong are instead obligatory. Such analysis, in turn, leads to a continuum of tactics that parallel these three claims. Some Earth First!ers prioritize efforts to change anthropocentric human attitudes by developing ritual processes that are believed to re-awaken nature-spirituality in humans. Others prioritize the use of scientific knowledge to argue for biological diversity in legal and policy making venues. Still others prioritize even more aggressive political action, using a variety of provocative tactics to directly resist destructive enterprises and to publicize ecological injustices. Still others, especially those most influenced by anarchist ideas, now theorize about "revolutionary ecology," thereby emphasizing their desire to overturn what they consider to be an inherently destructive, capitalist-industrial state.

SCHISMS AND FACTIONALISM

Differences about priorities and tactics, along with related ideological and cultural differences, have contributed to many tensions within the movement. In 1990, such tensions led a number of prominent Earth First!ers to disassociate themselves from the movement. Dave Foreman and John Davis relinquished control of the *Earth First!* journal, and began publishing *Wild Earth* in 1991. They founded, with conservation biologist Reed Noss and several others, The Wildlands Project, which as been designed to promote wilderness conservation in the Americas based on sound ecological science.

Throughout the early 1990s, battles continued among those still conducting their activism under the Earth First! banner. Meanwhile, during the first half of the 1990s, many activists spent less time organizing civil disobedience and ecotage, and more time using "paper monkeywrenching" techniques—namely vigilance and appeals of timber harvesting plans, scientific status reviews of species viability and computer mapping of the habitat requirements for endangered species, combined with appropriate lawsuits, when funds are available. They are doing so because, as one of these activists recognized, "When its time to sit down in front of the bulldozers, we've already lost."

Differences between and among Earth First!ers—both past and present—are likely to continue over the same divisive issues that consumed much of their time over the first fifteen years of Earth First! activism: Is ecological restoration dependent on anarchistic bioregionalism, or must we be more pragmatic, accepting nation-states as givens while resisting their destructive impulses? Is a countercultural and spiritual reformation of all society top priority and our only hope, or rather is preoccupation with, or overt expression of, spirituality counterproductive to movement aims?[7] Is an ecological collapse that precipitates the collapse of industrial society, concomitant with a drastic reduction of human numbers, an unfortunate prerequisite to the restoration of natural evolution? Is ecotage (especially tree-spiking) effective or counterproductive? Should movement activists prioritize building a mass movement through outreach and civil disobedience, or rather work to thwart commercial incursions into biologically sensitive areas through monkeywrenching, and should ecotage be public (more like civil disobedience) or clandestine? Finally, there have been debates over whether violence against humans can ever be a legitimate tactic, and whether this issue should be debated in movement journals.

Despite such factionalism, far more unites than divides these radical environmentalists. They are all animated by a deeply spiritual ecocentrism and they generally share or respect the plural myths, symbols, and rituals of the emerging Deep Ecology worldview. They are cynical about the system's willingness to respond to the ecological catastrophe they see unfolding. They all endorse extra-legal direct action, at least when they judge it to be a reasonable and heartfelt effort to protect biological diversity. Moreover, the majority believe that the struggle for biodiversity must be fought on the three fronts that parallel their ethical pillars: promoting spiritual awakening, ecological education about the biodiversity crisis and the requirements for ecosystem health, and fundamental political change. Despite sometimes profound differences regarding strategic priorities, most past and present Earth First!ers respect the work of those whose priorities differ from their own.

The preceding analysis interprets how Earth First!ers move *from primal spirituality to ecological resistance,* and explains why, in spite of disagreements, it is possible to speak of this diverse movement as a spiritual tradition. Through their activism and spirituality Earth First!ers pose an important challenge to Western civilization, dramatically suggesting that the well being of Earth and her creatures requires a widespread resacralization of human perceptions of nature. They ask us to join them in defending and restoring the natural world to wildness, basing our actions on reverence, love, and sometimes rage.

NOTES

1. This chapter is a revised and updated amalgamation of several articles published previously, including: "Earth First!'s Religious Radicalism" in Christopher Chapple (ed.) *Ecological Prospects: Scientific, Religious, and Aesthetic Perspectives* (Albany, New York: State University of New York Press, 1993), which can also be found in an abbreviated version as "The Religion and Politics of Earth First!" in *The Ecologist,* 21(6):258–266, Nov/Dec 1991.); "Resacralizing Earth: Pagan Environmentalism and the Restoration of Turtle Island" in David Chidester and Edward Linenthal (eds.), *American Sacred Space* (Bloomington: Indiana University Press, 1995); and in chapters two and nineteen in my edited volume, *Ecological Resistance Movements: The Global Emergence of Radical and Popular Environmentalism.* (Albany: State University of New York Press, 1995). "Earth First!'s Religious Radicalism" provides more detail than the present chapter about the rituals of the movement and the 1990 schism. "Resacralizing Earth" argues that "pagan environmentalism" is nothing new in North American history, and provides a contemporary case study religious conflict over a wilderness considered sacred by Earth First!ers and native Americans, at the site of the Mount Graham International Observatory in Southeastern Arizona. The final section of *Ecological Resistance Movements* has the most extensive analysis currently in print of the political impacts of radical environmentalism.

In this chapter, to save space, I have only reproduced citations not recorded in the above mentioned articles. For additional information about the north American deep ecology movement see also my "Evoking the Ecological Self: Art as Resistance to the War on Nature" in *Peace Review: The International Quarterly of World Peace,* 5(2):225–230, June 1993, and my forthcoming book, *Once and Future Primitive: The Spiritual Politics of Deep Ecology* (Boston: Beacon Press, 1996)

This chapter is based on archival research of movement documents, and intensive field-based observations and interviews conducted between August 1990 and November 1994.

2. See especially David Helvarg's *War Against the Greens* (San Francisco: Sierra Club Books, 1994), pps. 142, 279, 281, 224, 414 and 436).

3. On this point, see especially "Resacralizing Earth . . ."

4. For a detailed discussion of this controversy, see "Empirical and Normative Reflections on the Appropriation of Native American Spirituality in the North American Deep Ecology Movement," a paper I presented at the National Meeting of the American Academy of Religion in November 1993.

5. In "Earth First's Religious Radicalism" and "Resacralizing Earth . . .", respectively.

6. Such notions are commonly what most people discussed in this article mean by animism. I use the term non-pejoratively to refer to the belief that the natural world is inspirited, and that communication with nonhuman entities is possible.

7. Since founding *Wild Earth,* Foreman and Davis have paid less attention to spirituality.

"ON SUSTAINABILITY"

B. D. Sharma

Dhorkatta, Bastar, Madhya Pradesh, India—May 1, 1992. Honorable Members of the Earth Summit, Rio, Brazil: We, the residents of this small village republic, deep in the luxuriant subtropical forests of the Indian sub-continent, wish to invite the attention of your august assembly to some vital issues concerning "the future viability and integrity of the Earth as a hospitable home of human and other forms of life," the main theme of your deliberations at Rio. Before we begin, however, we profoundly compliment you on your bold initiative in holding the Earth Summit. At this end of the globe, in our small forest habitats, we too share your fears for Spaceship Earth.

You should know that in our villages we have stopped, totally, the commercial exploitation of our forests. The government of our country, of course, may not appreciate the spirit behind our decision. They have, in fact, taken it to be defiance of the law. For the forests formally belong to the state. We are, accordingly, treated as intruders in our own abodes where we have been living through the ages. Consequently, according to the law, we cannot even dig for roots and tubers, pluck fruits, or even breathe freely the nectar of earth. We cannot pick bamboo to cover our huts, or cut a pole to mend our plough. "That will destroy the forests," they say. And when magnificent tall trees of all varieties are mercilessly felled and carted away, leaving the earth naked and bare, we are told that is scientific management. That such acts are performed in the service of the nation. The little sparrow and owl meanwhile desperately flutter about searching for a place to perch. But even the hollow trunks of dried trees have not been spared!

This perception of national economy which the state today represents is not the perception of the people for whom forest, land, and water together comprise a primary life-support system. The legal fiction of the state's suzerainty over natural resources was created during the colonial era and has been continued and even reinforced after independence, in the name of development. This is not acceptable to us. It is a denial of the very right to life with dignity—the essence of a free democratic society. We are confident that this perception of ours is shared by the people similarly placed across the globe.

We, therefore, respectfully submit that the honorable representatives of governments at the Earth Summit are not competent to speak for the disinherited among us. Your perceptions and therefore your stand will be that of estate managers keen to exploit resources on the lines already set by the North. In the past this has invariably implied deprivation of the mass-

---

Reprinted with permission from *Sanctuary Magazine* and the editor, Bittu Sahgal, Bombay, India.

es to benefit small elite groups. Frankly, we fear that even though the honorable representatives of Non-Government Organizations (NGOs)—notable exceptions apart—may differ in their views with the state, they are, by and large, bound to share such common basic frameworks as are necessary for their acceptance as partners in the negotiating process. It will not surprise us, therefore, if deliberations at the Summit turn out to be partial. In which case the conclusions will almost certainly be one-sided. This fear is amply borne out in the way the agenda has been framed and also by the Prepcon discussions.

The rich countries are justifiably keen that natural tropical forests be preserved. We too feel the same way, but for different reasons. You require "sinks" for the carbon dioxide emitted by your automobiles which are vital for your "civilization on wheels." We hear about a queer proposal for the declaration of our forests as "global commons." Forests as wilderness would be ideal for this purpose, though you would not mind enjoying usufructory rights. But our paddy fields will be out of place, for they produce CO_2 and thus compete with your cars for that sink. So your basic position as far as we can see is identical to that of our governments. In both cases the people themselves are dispensable. In truth, the two are virtually one as the modern sector of our country, for all practical purposes, is a mere extension of the Western economic system. Of late, in fact, even the thin veneer of national identity has been blown away by the gusty winds of globalization. Discussions at the Summit are bound to be in the nature of bouts for booty rather than for responsible handling of a sacred trust of humankind—generation after generation. But this can be avoided. Please give what follows a patient and considered hearing.

Friends, we are surprised at the casual and parochial vein in which grave issues concerning the survival of life itself have been taken up. If you fail, nothing will remain. If nothing remains, what will be there to share and fight about? But this is the way of all estate managers. They must assume they are always right. Our own experience, a very bitter one, bears this out. In the name of preservation of forests, for instance, our ancestors were mercilessly driven out. And what followed in the name of scientific management was catastrophic. Luxuriant natural forests which sustained us were replaced by teak, which does not even provide us shade in summer. Then came eucalyptus under which not even grass can grow! After that, it was the turn of vast plantations of pine, which would burn like a torch in high summer. But each of these decisions was proclaimed as *the* right way. And to question such projects was blasphemous. Tragically for us, the estate-managers never recognized that the true worth of the magnificent sal, *Shorea robusta,* was far, far greater than the cash recovered from a dead log. The sal is *Kalpavriksha,* the tree that fulfills all desires. Once sal vanished from our forests the struggle of forest dwellers became reduced to physical survival—the evening meal. You see the irony. You worry about how your cars and air-conditioners can continue to operate for a hundred, or a thousand years. Our concern is the next meal that has to be procured at any cost. How can these two perceptions ever meet unless *you* see things from our end of the world and set your own perspectives in order. Friends, can you really not see how far such trivial priorities as air-conditioning and aerosol, with all they represent, have pushed the earth? Yet, you continue to talk about business as usual, of development through your lens, fueled by the same ecological system which has pushed us to the brink of an ecological abyss. Worse, you pose poverty as the worst pollutant and dedicate most of your agenda to eradicating this "environmental hazard."

On the face of it your endeavor might well sound laudable, but consider the hackneyed prescriptions you have chosen to tackle poverty—management of capital, technology, and resource flows. There are two reasons why this framework does not sit well with us. Nor, incidentally, can it help you in the long run. Let's first take the economic frame. Be clear that the phenomenon you are talking about has little to do with poverty. The issue is one of deprivation and denial. You seem ignorant of the fact that we have been robbed of not only our resources, but the great wealth of our life-sustaining skills acquired over millennia. Seen from your horizon, ordinary people are ignorant. Even despised.

Why are we despised? Because we live closer to nature, we do not don many clothes, nor do we have much use for your kind of energy options. We are, therefore, "poor" in your book. And since you, with missionary zeal, wish to "eradicate poverty" we must be enabled to acquire more commodities, consume more. Is this not why the czars of your ecological system incessantly bombard us with visuals of the glittering life? Making our simple ways look ridiculous by contrast to your own may well whip up new demands and expand your markets, but can you seriously suggest this to be the way to eradicate poverty? Such approaches have been directly responsible for the phenomenal inequality we see around us today. These are also the very reasons that the ecology of vast portions of the globe has been so terribly fractured. Yet, the estate managers of the world continue to wrangle for inflated entitlements and deflated obligations, indulging in reckless brinkmanship in dealing with the commons.

This, friends, is the law of the market. Little wonder that the focus of the Earth Summit has already shifted from land, water, and air, to the illogical issue of money! This drift, to our minds, is contemptible.

Those who have crossed the Rubicon of consumerism must point out at this stage that the Summit debate seems poised to miss the main point. You are no doubt talking about the quality of life, but *within* the consumerist paradigm of development and bounded inescapably by an economic framework. Other aspects of life have not even been brought up. We do not blame you for this lapse, for as leaders of the "modern" economic world, you have no experience of the "real life." In a bid to make the system produce more, for that is what decides its competitiveness in the market and its ranking in the world, all that is human is squeezed out, bit by tiny bit. Human concerns and relationships are dispensable, or at best market-convertible. Rushing to the faraway home to be by the side of an ailing mother, leaving the working machine unattended, is not rational. "Do not get emotional, you are not a

B. D. Sharma

doctor, send money instead," counsels the manager, worried by the high incidence of absenteeism in his production unit. To us this is the advice of an eccentric. To you it is the cold logic of your economic system. The machine *must* be used round the clock or else you lose your competitive edge. And people? They are but extensions of the machine! For them, even sleeping at night represents lost opportunities! But you have designed ways for the rattled living robot to enjoy "perfect equaniminity." A variety of vintage spirits, or still more modern aids such as heroin, cocaine, and LSD are on hand. At the end of the day, the market determines the cost of life and living.

Look again at your world. The community has already been sacrificed on the altar of productivity. The family now is the last impediment in the way of achieving "perfect rationality" and highest levels of productivity. But even here solutions were at hand. Within the family you dispensed with the burden of dead wood by packing your elders, where necessary, to senior citizen's homes. Now only the nucleus of husband-wife remains, at best. But this too appears to be haunted. Why should a man and a woman remain tied by emotional bonds for life? They too must subjugate themselves to the dictates of the economic system, each one serving the system at points most suited to it. Thus, marriage must break. Living together is good enough for sex. And sex, of course, can be rationally negotiated in a free market. The recent trend towards cynicism about motherhood and about women having eternally to carry the cross of procreation is really the culmination of the challenge of reason against human emotion. Such are the compulsions of perfectly rational beings.

Can you recognize the ugly, twisted logic of your economic system? Perhaps it is too much to ask. For you are clearly dazzled by its benign aura. You have surrounded yourselves and studded your abodes with all sorts of gadgets—surrogates for human concerns, relationships, and emotions. Even your moments of leisure, acquired at heavy financial costs, are determined once again by the market. You are no longer able even to laugh and dream unaided! Having lobotomized the soul from your neighborhoods you now take refuge in the mirage of telecommunications and rapid transport to create the illusion of "one earth."

But let us, for the moment, set aside human concerns and relations. Instead, let us consider the implications of this market-substitution which the economic system is coercing the rest of us to emulate as a lifestyle model. Given the proclamations of your scientists and even some of your world leaders, you obviously admit that we are poised on the brink—even before one in five people (who command four-fifths of the earth's resources) have been able to attain the desired standard of life. How much further must we continue to tread the same lethal path before the final collapse? This is the question the Earth Summit must ponder. Can you really not see the catastrophe you have set into motion? Having "co-opted" your own elite, you state that poverty alleviation is now your objective. This is the mirage we are condemned to chasing in vain, endlessly. Meanwhile you content yourself in tinkering with buttons, watching us follow in your footsteps even as a void engulfs us and our communities and families shatter. The writing is on the wall. The omnipotent, omnipresent market is turning living, breathing men and women into commodities-in-trade.

Honorable members of the Summit: it is in the face of this deluge that we earnestly call upon you to put your agenda, indeed your houses, in order. The development and associated lifestyles you chase are a hallucination. There is nothing sustainable about your ambitions. Your blueprint of sustainability will not even nourish a tiny section of humankind. Ironically, even as the bulk of humanity suffers hitherto unthinkable indignities and hardships, even the few who do manage to monopolize resources will be condemned to a veritable hell, as they stand bereft of the small innocent pleasures of life, the security and the warmth of their community, and the assurance of a family bond.

The basic question then, even before those who represent privileged groups at the Summit, is how long and how far can you afford to ignore and barter away the human face of existence. Such basic human values cannot be taught through lectures and books, nor can they be nurtured in formal systems which at best treat them as naive and irrelevant aspirations. Such values can only be imbibed in human institutions—small face-to-face communities and families where they are assiduously practiced and lovingly cultivated. We must caution you that this great heritage of mankind can be lost to posterity even if one generation trips and thus causes the chain to be broken. Are we prepared for that cataclysm?

Time is of the essence, friends. We, the disinherited of the earth, particularly in India, wish to make our position clear. The tide of "development" which started rising with the industrial revolution and gained huge momentum during the colonial phase of human history, has now run its full course. The allocation of benefits and costs of this development have been oppressively unfair and iniquitous. The more profitable and amenable activities at every stage have been reserved for themselves by the captains of development—the *Brahmins* (the highest caste) of the new order. The drudgery and the sloth was passed over to the *shudras* (outcasts) comprising the rest. Thus, the creation of a Third World was a precondition of your model. And a Fourth World is in the making, now that the Third World countries have accepted your prescription for their economies. This is the cold logic that must sit in the many minds that deliberate ways and means to save the world. The tide, thus, has reached the furthest shore and has begun to turn menacingly inward. The machine must now feed on itself.

We in Dhorkatta, Bastar, Madhya Pradesh, India are a fragment of this newly created Fourth World. As a logical unfolding of your paradigm, the modern economy of our country, a mere extension of the Western system, has misappropriated our resources. On the principle that you cannot make an omelet without cracking an egg, our little world must disintegrate. It cannot be allowed, of course, to stake any claim to the fruit enjoyed by the estate managers. We either get absorbed in the more powerful system, to the extent possible, or get exhumed and expelled. This logic, if accepted, will not remain circumscribed to one area like ours. It will inform all the disinherited of the Third World and also the deprived of the First and the

Second Worlds. The prevailing conditions in the erstwhile Eastern Block and among the non-white minorities in the U.S. and Europe are clear pointers in this direction.

We cannot possibly accept these inevitable consequences of your paradigm as our ordained fate. We do not believe in any iron laws of history, or of economics—free, planned, or mixed in any hue. Man is the maker of history and can chart his own path. Accordingly, after careful consideration, we have rejected outright your paradigm, and its associated lifestyle. It is not only socially unjust, but ecologically unsustainable, besides being devoid of human concerns.

A new paradigm—ecologically viable, socially equitable, and rich in human content—is the historical need of our time. You, at the Summit, have missed the human element totally and considered the social issue only superficially. The outcome of your deliberations will therefore be biased and slanted—perversions which we will have to carefully guard ourselves against. In rejecting your paradigm and raising these issues about the Summit, we are not alone. We echo the deepest feelings of ordinary people across the globe. In doing so, we unwittingly accept a historic role for ourselves, which so far you have refused even to consider. But we are, for all the reasons enumerated above, perhaps better placed in this regard, for we in our system still rank human concerns high. As you can see we have questioned and rejected some of the most fundamental elements of your paradigm. The quality of life cannot be measured by how much we consume or how much energy we utilize. It must, instead, be defined in terms of personal accomplishment of individuals, and the richness of interpersonal relationships within the family and community. A precondition naturally is the fulfillment of basic physical needs for a reasonable living. Accepting this should be the first decisive step towards dismantling the unbearable burden created in the name of so-called development at the cost of earth's fragile ecology. Obviously, human concerns and relationships are non-negotiable. The scope of market, on the other hand, must be circumscribed to the bare minimum. Some areas of life such as enjoyment of leisure must be out of bounds for market, in the interest of a sane society recreating conditions for absorbing dialogue and spontaneous laughter.

Contrary to what the ignorant believe of us, we heartily celebrate advances in science and the expanding horizons of man's universe. But we reject technological regimes built up with an eye on centralization of economic and political power. Technology in such hands has "de-skilled" humans and pushed us from the center to the periphery of the stage. While drudgery can and should be erased through harnessing of technology, it must be remembered that honest physical labor is an essential condition of human life and happiness. In this scheme of things production must be non-centralized in units of human dimension, keeping the master-labor relations to the minimum and slashing heavily on trade, advertisements, and transport. These are the devices of distribution wielded by the haves, whose burden our earth can no longer carry. These are clearly wasteful luxuries created as a sequel to a massive usurpation spree. We reject the production system which has depleted even our non-renewable capital resource-base (subsoil water) for frivolous, temporary gains. By casting this heavy burden on ecology such resources have been rendered out of the reach of ordinary people, forever. Thus, not only do we reject the perceptions and the paradigm, but also the legal framework of the estate-managers which seeks to legitimatize wanton destruction of natural resources and prey even on tomorrow's children of nature.

It should be clear that we are not for the negation of life and progress. What we insist on is that development must have a human face, or else it is tantamount to destruction. Towards this end we wish to announce that a beginning has already been made here in our small corner of the globe. We are clear about our goals, our rights, and our responsibilities. We are establishing village republics (*Nate-na-raj*) in the true spirit of democracy, equity, and fraternity following Gandhian tenets to the extent possible. Our village-republics are not islands in the wilderness, but they encompass even the smallest amongst the ever-expanding circles of the human canvass. We believe that life and vivacity in its totality can be perceived, experienced, and realized only in the microcosms of community and family. It is the community and community alone—not the formal state—which can save the earth for humankind and other forms of life.

So, friends, we have taken upon ourselves a great challenge, with humility yet fully cognizant of the historic role we are playing in one of the most bewildering eras of history. We do not await the advent of a messiah or the conclusion of a revolution—white or red—to move ahead and achieve our goal. The radical structural change associated with the formation of village-republics is a concomitant of the people's struggle. A corollary objective is to assert their will and right of self-governance in the short run and work for a new world order based on equity, fraternity, and democratic values in the long run.

We may, of course, appear momentarily to be moving against the current of history. But that is what it is. We have made a conscious choice that way. But it should be noted, and noted well, that the tide has changed its course. We, therefore, call upon the nations of the world to acknowledge this change, break from the past, and chart out a new path at the Summit for the establishment of a more humane, sustainable, and equitable world.

"PARADISE POLLUTED: RELIGIOUS DIMENSIONS OF THE *VRINDĀVANA* ECOLOGY MOVEMENT"

Bruce M. Sullivan

A brief passage from the *Bhāgavata Purāna*[1] will highlight themes to be encountered throughout this essay.

> The glorious Lord, the son of Devakî, accompanied by
> Balarāma and surrounded by cowherds, went a distance
> from Vrindāvana, grazing the cattle.
>
> Observing that the trees served as parasols by spreading
> their shade in the scorching heat of the sun, Krishna
> addressed his cowherd friends, the residents of Vraja....
>
> "Look at these great blessed souls who live only for the
> welfare of others, suffering stormy winds, heavy rains, heat
> and frost, saving us from these.
>
> The birth of trees is truly the most blessed in the world,
> for it contributes to the well-being of all creatures. Just
> as no one needy returns disappointed from generous persons,
> so also one who approaches trees for shelter.
>
> They meet the needs of others with their leaves, flowers,
> fruits, shade, roots, bark, wood, fragrance, sap, ashes, and coal.
>
> That one should offer life, wealth, intellect and speech to
> benefit others is the height of service of embodied beings
> for fellow creatures."
>
> Praising the trees in this way, the Lord proceeded to the
> Yamunā River, passing between rows of trees whose branches
> were bent low with clusters of sprouts, foliage, bunches of
> fruits, and flowers.

> Having made their cattle drink of the sweet, cool, healthy
> water of the Yamunā, the cowherds themselves drank that
> sweet water to their hearts' content.

So ends a chapter of the *Bhāgavata Purāna* describing the environment around Vrindāvana, Krishna's home.

Vrindāvana is important in the worship of Krishna, and has been for centuries, precisely because Krishna was born there.[2] Bengali (or Gaudîya) Vaisnavism has been very influential in Vrindāvana as well as Bengal for five centuries now. Its distinctive theology was developed after the death in the 16th century of the saint Caitanya. In this variety of Vaisnavism, Krishna is the object of worship and is regarded as the true form of Ultimate Reality. The worshippers of Krishna particularly revere the *Bhāgavata Purāna* for what it reveals about Krishna's human life, especially his youth in and around Vrindāvana. One of the most important ideas in this tradition is its emphasis on the eternal *lîlā* (play, sport) of Krishna in Vrindāvana; its most distinctive practice is the visualization of oneself as a participant in that divine play, so that one is identified with one of the friends, parents, or (best of all) lovers of Krishna—one of the *gopîs* (milkmaids).[3] The afterlife is conceived as a continuation of that *lîlā* in Krishna's paradise, known variously as Vaikuntha ("free from misery") or Goloka ("realm of cows") or Vrindāvana or Vraja.[4] In short, one visualizes oneself in Vrindāvana during this lifetime imitating the paradigmatic actions of devotees of Krishna, attaining liberation from rebirth through pure loving devotion so that one's service and devotion to Krishna may continue eternally. The *Bhāgavata Purāna*, other texts and devotional songs make references to deeds of Krishna in specific places in the vicinity of Vrindāvana: Mount Govardhana, the Yamunā River, etc. Devotees are strongly encouraged go to such places where they can feel a special closeness to Krishna because of his actions there. The texts also refer to the beauty of Vrindāvana and the surrounding land of Vraja, with cattle grazing contentedly among flowering trees and clear waters—a land made perpetually lovely by Krishna. This paradise on earth was the scene of Krishna's *lîlā*, and is regarded as identical with his celestial paradise where the *lîlā* is eternal.

But there is trouble in paradise today, on earth if not in heaven. Vrindāvana in the state of Uttar Pradesh in north-central India is badly deforested, and the area is rapidly turning into desert such as is found just to the west in Rājasthān. Studies are said to indicate that the water table is falling by as much as five feet a year, and the quality of the available water is deteriorating.[5] The Yamunā River is also heavily polluted by industrial runoff from factories upriver and from sewage, some of which comes from Vrindāvana itself. Raw sewage flows over the *parikrama* pilgrimage path in places, and discharges directly into the Yamunā in many places. The problem is very serious—the Government of India has declared the Yamunā unfit for drinking or bathing,[6] which should affect the activities of devotees and pilgrims, though apparently it has not so far. Sadly, ecological damage is not unique to this area. Large areas of

India have been deforested due to the need for farmland and firewood by an increasing population. And sewage is a widespread problem as well; it is estimated that only 10% of India's cities have sewage systems that could be described as "adequate."[7] The deaths by plague in 1994, while not numerous, emphasize the point. But Vrindāvana is unusual, and faces special ecological problems, because it receives some two million pilgrims per year now—modern transportation and the big business of guiding pilgrims to the sacred sites has increased traffic greatly, straining the capacity of municipal services such as water and sewage treatment.

The environment in and around Vrindāvana has also suffered from an influx of people coming to live there; relatively well-to-do Vaisnavas want to retire to the scene of Krishna's earthly activities, there to live out their days in the setting most conducive to worship and the liberation from rebirth that is its reward. Some of Delhi's wealthy devotees maintain second homes here. For them to live in Krishna's land requires the building of houses and flats in large number; the sign of one real estate developer in Vrindāvana read:

> Welcome to this holy land of Lord Krishna. Holy forest plots for sale. Freehold residential complex in very peaceful and tranquility [sic] atmosphere.[8]

Ironically the atmosphere of tranquility and peace that is advertized so persuasively will be destroyed with the bulldozing of the "holy forest" at the site. Sacredness is a marketable commodity. Perceiving this entrepreneurial activity as a problem, the devotees of the International Society for Krishna Consciousness (ISKCON), better known as the Hare Krishnas, have raised money to purchase a forested plot called Ramana Retî, famed as a place where Krishna and Balarāma played in their youth, and the target of real estate developers.[9] Thus one grove has been saved, but in a large region all of which devotees regard as sacred, not all the forests of Krishna are being saved, and many once forested areas are already treeless, or are being covered with buildings and roads.

Deforestation and water pollution in the Vrindāvana region are certainly not caused by the widespread raising of cattle for slaughter, for their meat, as is the case in other parts of the world such as Brazil or the United States. Nonetheless, because of the importance of vegetarianism to the Hare Krishna movement and to devotees of that tradition who are writing ecological works, meat-eating is regarded as a serious ecological problem worldwide due to petroleum usage and polluting waste products that are created. *Manu Smriti* (5.51) is cited as prohibiting the eating of meat, saying that the butcher, vendor, cook and consumer all are murderers and reap bad consequences.[10]

Obviously the degradation of the environment is an ecological problem for the Vrindāvana area, and a problem for the quality of life, but it is also a specifically religious problem for the devotee of Krishna. Pilgrims come to Vrindāvana with the hope of seeing Krishna's land. Devotees want to bathe in the Yamunā to gain merit, but as already noted, to do so could now be dangerous to one's health; observers have commented that parasites and illnesses are often the result of prolonged exposure to the Yamunā, and skin rashes from even brief exposure.[11] Deforestation and desertification are also a religious problem because one is to visualize oneself as a participant in Krishna's *līlā* in the beautiful setting he creates for devotees eternally, but the earthly manifestation of Krishna's *līlā* is not as inspirational or conducive to a sense of wonder as could be desired. The conflict between descriptions in ancient devotional texts and the reality of Vrindāvana today is stark.

The response to the ecocide in Vrindāvana has been led by devotees of Krishna. The general attitude could be described by the following quote, used to generate support: "one who cares for Krishna cares for His land."[12] One well-known devotee instrumental in the effort is Shrîvatsa Goswāmî, who points to Krishna as the paradigm of reverence for nature; not only did he defeat the river-polluting demon Kāliya, but the only two occasions on which Krishna worshiped were when he led the cowherds in worshipping Mount Govardhana and when he worshipped the Sun God to cure his son of leprosy.[13] A major effort to reforest the area began as follows. Ranchor Dāsa, an English member of ISKCON familiar with the situation in Vrindāvana, conceived a plan with Sewak Sharan, longtime resident of the area, to plant trees along the eleven-kilometer *parikrama* path that encircles the town. Travelled by some two million pilgrims per year, the path is no longer the sylvan and pastoral setting for envisioning Krishna's *līlā* which it once apparently was. Now the path is highly urbanized and suffers from the problems of deforestation and pollution already mentioned. Ranchor Dāsa prepared a report to the World Wide Fund for Nature (WWF) in Geneva, an international ecological agency that gives grants for environmental projects. WWF especially wants to highlight the ecological values of the cultures and religious traditions where projects are funded, and this seemed to them an opportunity to do so. Funding was granted for three years, to run from September 1991 through September 1994, some $40,000 per year. ISKCON donated use of 1½ acres beside the pilgrimage path for a nursery to raise some 10,000 trees of local origin to be planted in succeeding months.[14]

Ranchor Dāsa was appointed Director of the Vrindāvana Forest Revival Project. The project was formally initiated on November 21, 1991, the festival day of Vrindādevî, the Goddess regarded as representing the local flora. All present took the following pledge:

> The forest of Vrindāvana is the sacred playground of Rādhā and Krishna. However, we, the people of this region, have cut its trees, polluted its Yamunā River, and spoilt its sacred dust with our rubbish and sewage. I pledge that from now on I will do all within my power to protect Vrindāvana from further destruction and to restore it to its original beauty.[15]

Stage One of the project was to encourage community involvement so that the trees planted would be protected and would survive. Planting began with some 2,000 trees and shrubs along a two-kilometer segment of the path. Stage Two has included further planting along the entire pathway. Assorted eyesores and environmental problems have been dealt with along the way also.

Bruce M. Sullivan

A more serious problem, and even more difficult to solve, is the sewage system of Vrindāvana. Prior to 1970 the traditional latrine method was employed, waste being recycled into fields as fertilizer. At that time work began on a modern system that was designed to treat sewage so that it could be safely dumped into the Yamunā. Some underground pipes were laid and toilets were connected all over town, but the main line was never completed! Blockages and breaks in the lines occurred almost immediately and have never been fixed. Worse still, the treatment plant was never built! Now sewage that does not overflow into the streets and gather in low spots, polluting the groundwater supply, is simply dumped untreated into the river, and most of the municipal water supply is drawn from that same river. Ranchor Dāsa argues that the traditional method worked and should be implemented again, abandoning the inadequate and inappropriate sewage system. In making his case, he cites the *Manu Smriti* (4.56) as follows:

> One should not cause urine, stool, or mucus to enter water. Anything mixed with these unholy substances, or with blood or poison, should never be thrown into water.

Ranchor Dāsa accuses Indians of becoming enamored of new Western technology and of applying the technology inappropriately, in the process forgetting their own ancient and time-tested technology which is appropriate to the situation, and forgetting the injunctions such as those found in *Manu Smriti*. He offers the view that the Western lifestyle is overly materialistic, consumption oriented, not ecological, and therefore must be abandoned both by Indians who have adopted it and by Westerners. He also cites the words of Mahātmā Gāndhi, warning against mechanization and technology and advocating a simple lifestyle.[16] Ranchor Dāsa points to underlying causes of this abandonment of traditional Hindu values and technology, citing centuries of Muslim and British rule as detrimental to traditional Hindu culture and practices.[17] He concludes his discussion of the water pollution problems of the area with reference to the myth of Krishna overcoming the demon Kāliya, who was poisoning the Yamunā, with the result that trees and animals were dying. Finally the cowherds themselves drank the water and fell ill. Krishna wrestled with the demon and subdued it, saving the region from the effects of poisoned water. That myth is regarded as still relevant today, and the paradigm for human action that is desperately needed. The effort to save Vrindāvana from ecocide, from deforestation and polluted water, an undertaking that is essentially religious in inspiration and intent, is based on the hope that people will love the Earth just as they love Krishna.

For devotees of Krishna, the earthly Vrindāvana is identical with Krishna's heavenly paradise. While it may be that for the truly devoted everything is beautiful because it is God's creation, for those who have not yet matured in their devotion the beautification of the environment may be an aid to devotional practice. Certainly it can be regarded as service of Krishna and an appropriate way of caring for Krishna's creation. Yet it must be noted that ascetic and monistic traditions, which are very strong in India, tend to see the natural world as a realm of suffering from which to escape, not as an environment to be cared for in the way theistic traditions do; such a worldview may undercut ecological efforts.[18]

The World Wide Fund for Nature is hopeful that a successful project in Vrindāvana will encourage others throughout India to examine their environment and find ways of improving the situation. This one project is now completed, and it remains to be seen whether it will have an effect throughout India, creating a view of the world as sacred and to be protected from pollution. Even in Vrindāvana not everyone is a devotee of Krishna; some of the trees so recently planted have already been bulldozed for a new road.[19] Clearly it would not be sufficient to clean up the Vrindāvana region by shifting pollution to other regions that are not viewed with the same degree of reverence; the problem is not solved by that approach. Other eco-movements exist: the Chipko movement in the Himālayas, where people are protecting trees from clear-cutting by loggers, and the Trees for Life organization, which has given out over a million saplings for planting all over India. Both movements draw upon traditional Hindu ideas and values for their inspiration. More such movements are needed. Emphasizing the teachings of ecological significance in the religions of the world may be beneficial to programs the World Wide Fund for Nature implements; doing so in India seems an especially effective approach.

NOTES

1. *BhP.* 10.22.; the text is a Sanskrit devotional work composed about the tenth century C.E.

2. S. K. De, *The Early History of the Vaisnava Faith and Movement in Bengal,* 2nd ed. (Calcutta: Firma K. L. Mukhopadhyay, 1961) and E. Dimock's "Doctrine and Practice Among the Vaisnavas of Bengal," *History of Religions* 3, no. 1 (Summer 1963): 106–27 are excellent treatments of the theological aspects of this movement. D. Haberman's *Journey Through the Twelve Forests* (New York: Oxford University Press, 1994) connects the mythology with practices by means of the pilgrimage through the Vraja region. D. Kinsley's *The Divine Player* (Delhi: Motilal Banarsidass, 1979) develops the theme of divine play in the earthly and eternal *līlās* of Krishna.

3. Kinsley (*op. cit.,* p. 113) observes that Krishna's heaven "is nothing else but the idyllic forest town of Vrindāvana unabashedly magnified." ... and "Krishna's heavenly sporting ground is identical with the scene of his earthly life as a youth ...". He also notes that there are three Vrindāvanas: the heavenly paradise, the earthly town of the texts, and the earthly town today. D. Haberman's *Acting as a Way of Salvation* (New York: Oxford University Press, 1988) is a detailed presentation of the devotional practice of "imitation" of Krishna's companions and lovers.

4. De (*op. cit.*), pp. 333–39.

5. Ranchor Dāsa, "Reviving the Forests of Vrindāvana," in *Back to Godhead,* 26, no. 5 (September/October, 1992): 24–39. p. 27.

6. R. Prime, *Hinduism and Ecology* (London: Cassell, 1992), p. 108, citing *The State of India's Environment* (New Delhi: Centre for Science and the Environment, 1982).

7. News broadcast on National Public Radio, October 5, 1994.

8. Ranchor Dāsa (*op. cit.*), p. 27.

9. *Ibid.,* pp. 24–27, including a picture.

10. Ranchor Prime (*op. cit.*), p. 102. See also Cremo & Grant, *Divine Nature* (Alachua, FL: Bhaktivedānta Institute, 1994), especially chapters 2 and 6. It may be noted that verses 27–44 discuss occasions on which eating

meat is acceptable (e.g., when the meat is consecrated for Vedic sacrifice, or when one's life is in danger), but Manu then goes on to discuss (verses 45–56) the karmic benefits of vegetarianism. *Manu Smriti* is a Sanskrit legal text widely cited as authoritative from the early centuries C.E.

11. Ranchor Prime (*op. cit.*), p. 108.

12. Ranchor Dāsa (*op. cit.*), p. 30.

13. Ranchor Prime (*op. cit.*), pp. 54–56.

14. See "Vrindavan Forest Revival Project" flyer from WWF, and Ranchor Prime, pp. 104–118, and Ranchor Dāsa article.

15. Quoted in "Vrindavan Forest Revival Project" flyer.

16. Ranchor Dāsa (*op. cit.*), pp. 109–12; see also Cremo & Grant (*op. cit.*), *passim*. Judah's *Hare Krishna and the Counterculture* (New York: John Wiley & Sons, 1974) reveals a strong tendency among Hare Krishna members to criticize Western materialism and advocate a simple lifestyle based on self-sufficiency. My own M.A. thesis, *The Place of the Spiritual Master: A Study of The International Society for Krishna Consciousness* (Unpublished M.A. thesis, Trinity University, 1975) produced similar findings from interviews of Hare Krishnas in Texas in 1975. Obviously the theme has been a constant for the Hare Krishna movement in the West.

17. Ranchor Prime (*op. cit.*), p. 112.

18. As documented by Lance Nelson in "Seeing the World as Crow Excrement," a paper presented at the American Academy of Religion meeting, November, 1994.

19. Personal communication from David Haberman, November 1994.

BIBLIOGRAPHY

Bhāgavata Purāna. Bombay: Venkateśvara Press, 1910.

Cremo, Michael (Drutakarma Dāsa), & Michael Grant (Mukunda Goswāmî). *Divine Nature: A Spiritual Perspective on the Environmental Crisis*. Alachua, FL: Bhaktivedānta Institute, 1994.

De, Sushil Kumar. *The Early History of the Vaisnava Faith and Movement in Bengal*, 2nd ed. Calcutta: Firma K. L. Mukhopadhyay, 1961.

Dimock, Edward C., Jr. "Doctrine and Practice Among the Vaisnavas of Bengal." *History of Religions* 3, no. 1 (Summer 1963): 106–27. Reprinted in *Krishna: Myths, Rites and Attitudes,* ed. by Milton Singer. Chicago: The University of Chicago Press, 1966. Pp. 41–63.

Haberman, David L. *Acting as a Way of Salvation: A Study of Rāgānugā Bhakti Sādhana*. New York: Oxford University Press, 1988.

———. *Journey Through the Twelve Forests: An Encounter with Krishna*. New York: Oxford University Press, 1994.

Judah, J. Stillson. *Hare Krishna and the Counterculture*. New York: John Wiley & Sons, 1974.

Kinsley, David R. *The Divine Player: A Study of Krishna Līlā*. Delhi: Motilal Banarsidass, 1979.

Nelson, Lance E. "Seeing the World as Crow Excrement: Advaita Vedānta and the Irrelevance of Nature." Unpublished paper presented at the American Academy of Religion meeting, November 1994.

Prime, Ranchor. *Hinduism and Ecology: Seeds of Truth*. London: Cassell, 1992.

Ranchor Dāsa. "Reviving the Forests of Vrindāvana." In *Back to Godhead: The Magazine of the Hare Krishna Movement*. Vol. 26, no. 5 (September/October, 1992): 24–39.

Sullivan, Bruce M. *The Place of the Spiritual Master: A Study of The International Society for Krishna Consciousness*. Unpublished M.A. thesis, Trinity University, 1975.

"AFRICAN INDEPENDENT CHURCHES FACE THE CHALLENGE OF ENVIRONMENTAL ETHICS"

M. L. Daneel

The significant role of African Independent Churches (AICs) in terms of Africanized mission methods, growth rates and development of a contextualized theology, in which the interaction between the gospel witness and African religion and worldviews is paramount, is increasingly recognized. This article will focus on the contribution AICs in Zimbabwe are making in the field of applied environmental ethics.

While the Justice, Peace and Integrity of Creation emphasis of the World Council of Churches is stimulating theological reflection and thought-provoking study on the role of Christ's church in relation to environmental issues, the AICs are making a complementary contribution by tackling environmental problems in the field. They are not in the first place producing environmental literature, but they are proclaiming a widening message of salvation which encompasses all of creation, and in their services of worship they are dancing out a new rhythm which, in its footwork, spells hope for the ravaged earth. They have not worked out a new ethic on paper, but they are "clothing the earth" (*kufukidza nyika*) with new trees to cover its human-induced nakedness. In so doing they have introduced a new ministry of compassion; they live an earthkeeper's ethic.

The "war of the trees" offers an ecumenical platform to unite the churches in a "green army" and to launch environmental reform in terms of the liberation of creation. The "lost lands" which have been politically liberated now need to be recaptured ecologically. In the new struggle ecclesiastical structures are changing, new perceptions of ecological responsibility are emerging and innovative liturgical procedures are being introduced to integrate environmental ethics and church praxis.[1]

AN ENVIRONMENTAL OFFENSIVE FROM AN ECUMENICAL PLATFORM

Since the formation in 1988 of ZIRRCON (Zimbabwean Institute of Religious Research and

Reprinted from *Ecotheology: Voices from North and South* by David G. Hallman, 1994, Orbis Books. Reprinted by permission of Orbis Books and the World Council of Churches, Geneva, Switzerland.

Ecological Conservation), AICs in the country have been challenged on the basis of their Christian faith to engage in tree-planting activities. But the roots of Zimbabwe's ecumenical earthkeepers movement are in the country's liberation struggle and in Fambidzano, the ecumenical movement of Shona Independent Churches, founded in 1972.[2]

The AICs in fact have a rich tradition of enacted liberation theologies.[3] For many years their leaders resisted oppressive rule. Their prophets participated in *chimurenga* (the war of liberation), helped the guerrilla fighters to purge village communities of so-called wizards (counter-revolutionaries), fed and treated wounded fighters and helped to devise—in the name of the Holy Spirit—feasible guerrilla tactics on the war front.

With this background of transcending ecclesial barriers for the sake of a common cause, the climate was conducive for ecumenical ecological mobilization. Some *chimurenga* "war prophets" came to the fore here, including Bishop-prophet Musariri Dhliwayo, whose church headquarters during the war was an operational centre for guerrilla fighters in the Gutu district, who was elected patron of the Christian army of earthkeepers.

For many years churches affiliated to Fambidzano have engaged in united action under the leitmotif of John 17:21, 23, which combines Christian unity and witness.[4] Many agreed that the devastation of the environment constituted sufficient grounds for the formation of a new movement. Early in 1991 the Association of African Earthkeeping Churches (AAEC) was established. It is affiliated to Zirrcon as its think-tank and fund-raiser, and within a year more than a hundred AICs, representing a formidable ecological work force of some 2 million members, had joined the movement.

A new environmental ethic was not formulated in detailed theological statements, but it surfaced in the practical objectives of the AAEC constitution:

- **afforestation**—the production of fuel-wood, the growing of fruit trees for personal and commercial use, exotic trees like blue gums for building operations, indigenous trees to clothe and protect the earth and the slow growing kiaat (*mukurumbira*) and red mahogany (*mukumba*) as a long-term investment for the coming generations;

- **wildlife conservation,** including the establishment of game sanctuaries in the communal lands where hardly any game is left;

- **protection of water resources** through the reclamation of catchment areas to prevent river and dam siltation, the prevention of river-bank cultivation, gully-formation, etc.[5]

AAEC's environmental objectives are seen as being undergirded by a divine mandate. During the founding ceremony I emphasized divine initiative with reference to one of our key texts, Isaiah 43:18–21—"do not remember the former things . . . I am about to do a new thing":

> This association we are creating today is a new thing God is doing in our midst . . . It does not belong to us but to God. Therefore, if we are courageous and persevere, this new movement will perform great deeds.

A brief exposition of the Christological basis for our struggle characterized a focus which would later emerge in a tree-planting eucharist:

> Our mandate derives from our faith that we belong to the body of Christ. As members of that body we are not only commanded to build unity amongst ourselves as Christian churches, but to build new relationships with the entire creation in an attempt to avoid destruction and preserve life for all creatures. I say this because the body of Christ is more than the church . . . In him all things hold together, in him all things are created. That makes him the true guardian of the land (*muridzi venyika*), the great guardian of all creation. Read together with Matthew 28:18, where Jesus claims all authority in heaven and on earth, we take this twofold interpretation of Christ's body to mean that his presence and power pervade all creation . . . The implication is that when we as Christians partake of holy communion we express our unity in the body of Christ, that is the church. At the same time we reaffirm our responsibility for the body of Christ, in the sense of its presence in all creation. The sacrament therefore makes us earthkeepers, stewards of creation . . .

The association's first president, Zionist Bishop Machokoto, emphasized the ecumenical foundation of the envisaged environmental programmes:

> What I ask of God is a true sense of unity amongst us. We have to work together and avoid all forms of confusing conflict. Our unity must rest on convincing works. It is no use coming here to enjoy our tea and meals without engaging in development projects which show convincing progress. The basis of our work, according to God's word, is love, a love which reveals itself in works . . . Let us show our willingness and ability to work. Therefore, each of you, as you leave here, go and prepare yourselves for tree-planting . . . We the churches [of the AAEC] will have to make sacrifices for the causes to which we have pledged ourselves. Therein lies our unity . . .

This call for united action is the key to the kind of ecumenism developed by the AAEC. In a predominantly peasant society with a deforested, overgrazed and over-populated environment, AIC bishops and their churches have not joined forces to realize some abstract ecumenical ideal of church unity as an end in itself. Rather, ecumenicity has taken shape as churches share concretely a newly identified common commitment to healing the earth. In the "battles of the trees," developing nurseries with thousands of seedlings and planting and watering trees in the hot sun, lay the liberation from interchurch conflicts. Not that all the differences and conflicts of the past were suddenly resolved. But they paled into insignificance as the green revolution unfolded during annual conferences and meetings and in the joint labor and celebration of tree-planting ceremonies. A new brotherhood and sisterhood beyond the traditional ecclesial constraints had started to evolve—that between the creator God, earthkeeping humanity and the trees, plants and wildlife. A new myth, arising from the common, holistic subconscious of Africa and blended with Christian perceptions of a realized, observable salvation for all creation in the here and now, had started to emerge.

CHANGING PERCEPTIONS OF THE CHURCH AS HEALING INSTITUTION

The prophetic AICs have always been popularly conceived of as healing and liberating institutions in Zimbabwe, as elsewhere in southern Africa, but there have been historical mutations in this concept as it relates to political and national developments. In the 1930s the Zionists and Apostles emerged as "hospitals," insofar as prophetic healers focused largely on contextualized faith-healing ministries which offered therapeutic solutions to a comprehensive range of human afflictions experienced in terms of African belief systems and worldviews.

Between 1965 and 1980 the AICs, increasingly drawn into *chimurenga,* evolved as sociopolitical healing and liberation institutions. The AIC headquarters still had their faith-healing "hospitals" or healing colonies, but the diagnostic and therapeutic thrust of many prophets had a direct impact on the guerrillas' militant field strategies, as the Holy Spirit was felt to guide positively on behalf of the cause of the oppressed.[6] God's presence translated into the provision of food, supportive prayers, care for wounded and mentally disturbed fighters, blessing of weapons with holy water and numerous related activities enabling harassed bushfighters and suspect members of society to survive and retain some meaning in life in the midst of suffering and deprivation.

As the AICs became increasingly involved in development projects following independence,[7] the image of the church as deliverer from poverty and agent of socio-economic progress began to predominate. Newly built community halls became centers of vocational training and small-scale industries, such as clothing manufacture, sewing and carpentry, augmented in some cases by agricultural projects. Rather than causing fragmentation or secularization, such extension of the church's task in this world implied an expansion and reinterpretation of its healing ministry. The gospel good news, it appears, includes socio-economic healing—healing from poverty, agricultural stagnation and lack of opportunity.

The inception of the AAEC has shifted the focus to the church's healing of a suffering creation. A new perception of the divine-human encounter, emphasizing Christian stewardship in nature, has begun to emerge.

It should be noted that these historically conditioned mutations in the church's ministry have not involved radical ecclesiastical reforms or changes. Rather, the new insights and action programmes have served as modifying extensions and innovative elaborations of existing AIC ecclesiologies.

Tree-planting sermons illuminate how the earth-healing ministry of the AAEC churches is interpreted. These are considered to be environmental "teaching sessions." Consider, for example, the exposition during a tree-planting ceremony by Bishop Kindiam Wapendama, leader of the Sign of the Apostles Church, executive member of the AAEC and ardent advocate of the green revolution:

> Deliverance, Mwari says, lies in the trees. But in the first place the people have to obey. Mwari therefore sends his deliverers to continue here on earth with his own work; that is, all the work Jesus had started here. It is a divine mission. Jesus said: "I leave you, my followers, to complete my work. And that task is the one of healing!"
>
> We are the followers of Jesus and have to continue with his healing ministry. You are the believers who will see his miracles in this afflicted world. So, let us all fight, clothing the earth with trees! Let us follow the example of the deliverers sent by Mwari ... It is our task to strengthen this mission with our numbers of people. You know how numerous we are. At times we count 10,000 people at our church gatherings. If all of us work with enthusiasm we shall clothe the entire land and drive off affliction ... Just look at the dried out and lifeless land around you. I believe that we can change it!

These views are representative. God takes the initiative to restore the ravaged earth, but his divine commission to deliver the earth from its malady lies with the body of Christian believers, the church. The deliverance finds expression in *kufukidza nyika,* that is, "to clothe the land" with trees. This mission is clearly seen as an extension of Christ's healing ministry, which his disciples must fulfill. That this is a communal obligation is highlighted by the bishop's reference to the large church meetings as a potential green labour force. Wapendama's confidence that a mobilization of the AAEC's massive earthkeeping army can overcome the evil of earth-destruction is a significant move away from the fatalism found in peasant society, where little hope is left that environmental restoration is still possible.

True to prophetic perceptions of salvation as human well-being in all sectors of life, achieved through healing in this existence, the earth is to be salvifically restored under the directives of Mwari. But the new order is not one-sidedly ushered in by God; it is also dependent on being "worked out" by human endeavour. The church's mission is thus expanded. The good news extends well beyond soul-salvation and a futuristic eternal life for individual human beings. And the testing ground for the quality of individual conversion and spirituality lies in the ministry of earthkeeping.

CONFESSION OF ECOLOGICAL SINS: A SIGN OF COMMITMENT TO ENVIRONMENTAL REFORM

Confession of sins has always been prominent in the healing and sacramental ceremonies of the prophetic AICs. During faith-healing ceremonies the healer-prophet urges patients to confess their sins. Not only is this a way of placing the afflicted under the care of the Holy Spirit, but the revelation of the dark side in the patient's existence also enlightens the healer-prophet about the cause of affliction and the area in the patient's life which requires therapeutic treatment.[8] The confession of converts prior to baptism symbolically illustrates the neophyte's acceptance of the authority of the church, represented during the ceremony by the prophet's listening to the confessions, as well as the final mystical authority of the Holy Spirit which induces such confessions. Public confession prior to participation in the sacrament of holy communion is in a sense a mass demonstration of right-mindedness and obedience in relation to God.

Some AAEC-related prophets are already applying their newly gained insights about ecological stewardship to their guardianship over the morals of their churches. In the baptismal context they increasingly reveal that the Holy Spirit expects novices to confess not only their moral sins in a society of disturbed human relations but also their ecological sins: tree-felling without replanting, overgrazing, riverbank cultivation and the neglect of contour ridges, thereby causing soil erosion—in other words taking the good earth for granted, exploiting it without nurturing it or showing it reverence.

At "Jordan" it makes sense to the newly converted to confess ecological guilt, where the barren, denuded planes, the erosion gullies, the unprotected river banks and the clouds of wind-eroded dust are clearly in evidence. Crossing the River Jordan in baptism, after such confession, means more than individual incorporation into the body of Christ and the prospect of personal salvation in heaven. It also requires the new convert's commitment to help restore creation as part of God's plan, as a sign of genuine conversion and repentance in recognition of the gift of God's grace.

To many Independents, baptism is also a healing ceremony in which the life-giving water of Jordan, filled by the Holy Spirit, is drunk by baptizands for individual cleansing and curative purposes. Thus the baptismal ceremony offers a unique opportunity for interpreting the Spirit as healer both of the people and of the land. Baptism therefore becomes another feature of an extended ministry of healing—a changing ecclesiology. The drinking of "Jordan"-water symbolizes the shift from personal, individual benefit of the baptizand by the Holy Spirit's healing and saving powers to a ritual statement of solidarity with all creation, an affirmation of a new commitment, through individual conversion, to earth-healing.

Also significant is the combat of AAEC prophets against ecological sins in the context of tree-planting eucharistic ceremonies. During public confessions preceding the bread and wine, "green prophets" from a wide range of Zionist and Apostolic churches are increasingly branding offences that cause firewood shortage, soil erosion, poor crops and the absence of wildlife as a form of wizardry (*uroyi*)—the gravest of all sins, threatening not only human survival but all other forms of life. As the resolve of the earthkeeping churches and the conviction of the prophets that the Holy Spirit rather than human beings motivates and guides the green struggle grow, unrepentant ecological sinners (*varoyi*) in the AICs will increasingly find themselves barred from participation in the eucharist.

M. L. Daneel   577

Discussions with these prophets, who are becoming Christian "guardians of the land," indicate that they generally have a clear idea of who the earth-destroying wizards in their society are: people in resettlement schemes who endanger the common good by indiscriminately felling as many trees as they can for a quick profit from selling firewood; those who refuse to accept the principle that firewood can be used only by those who plant the trees that supply it; those who resist government conservationist measures and tribal elders' prohibition of tree-felling in the traditional holy groves (*marambatemwa*) of the ancestors; and the destroyers of river banks.

The identification of ecological sin with wizardry and the insistence on public confession enable the church in its green struggle to identify the enemy outside and within its own ranks. Identification of wrongdoers enhances and concretizes the church's ethical code and control system. This is reminiscent of the *chimurenga* struggle, during which counter-revolutionaries and collaborators were branded as wizards. Alongside the traditionalist spirit mediums, AIC war prophets elicited confessions from suspects as part of the process of identifying wizard-traitors and singling them out for punitive measures. Unifying the ranks and cleansing the guerrilla cadres from internal subversion in terms of the idiom of wizardry indicated a relentless will to succeed and survive. For *uroyi* is an evil which brooks no compromise.

In the earthkeeping churches the response to wizardry is more nuanced than it was during the war period, when traitors were executed or tortured. Wanton tree-fellers or poachers of wildlife will, upon prophetic detection, either be temporarily barred from the eucharist, or, in the event of repeated transgression of the earthkeepers' code, be excommunicated. The AAEC is only too aware of the common guilt which in a sense makes all of us *varoyi*—earth-destroyers. Still there is a vast difference between admitting earlier guilt and continued deliberate deforestation or related destructive action in the face of a protective environmental code. This selfish environmental exploitation regardless of the will of the community and the destruction caused to nature is branded by the prophets as the evil of *uroyi*, to be stamped out at all costs.

Discussions about ecological *uroyi* and how to combat it stimulate emotive expression of views about the nature of an earthkeeping church. The characteristic attitudes and convictions may be summarized as follows:

•   The earthkeeping function of the church is beyond doubt. As Bishop Darikai Nhongo of the AAEC-affiliated Zion Christian Church says: "The church is the keeper of creation."

•   Part of the church's mission is to develop and apply strict rules against the destruction of the earth.

•   The application of strict environmental laws implies authorization and empowerment of the prophets to expose the ecological wizards during public confessionals.

•   Prophetic exposure is only the first step towards a process of church cleansing, so as to mobilize effectively a Christian "green army," eliminate subversion and realize environmental goals. Paramount is an element of judgment and punishment so that, as in *chimurenga,* the enemy outside and within can be clearly discerned, The church cannot usurp the divine function of final judgment, yet Peter's function as "holder of the keys" justifies expulsion of unrepentant tree-felling *varoyi* to give momentum to the earthkeeping cause.

Some AAEC leaders have proposed working with secular chiefs to act comprehensively against the wizards, not only excommunicating them from church but also having them expelled from their residences—one of the severest penalties imaginable. Not all would favour such radical punitive measures. Some would plead for a ministry of reconciliation, offering exposed ecological *varoyi* the opportunity to mend their ways without undue stigmatization. But it is clear that there is a growing commitment to what is considered a real liberation struggle, for which the church is seen as one of the most important mobilizing vehicles.

ECO-LITURGICAL INNOVATION

The best example of liturgical innovation in the AAEC churches in connection with the emergent environmental ethic is the tree-planting eucharist. This ceremony, which supplements rather than supersedes well-established liturgical procedures for holy communion, is of interest for several reasons. First, the participation of numerous churches in each ceremony and the sharing of ritual officiant roles on an interchurch basis strengthen environmentally focused ecumenism. Second, the integration of eucharist and tree-planting binds environmental stewardship, often treated as peripheral in Christian tradition, into the heart of church life and biblical spirituality. Third, this ceremony highlights characteristic trends of an emergent AIC theology of the environment. And, fourth, the new liturgies are imaginatively contextualized in relation to African religious holism and worldviews. Thus an earthkeeping model is developed which could well challenge AICs elsewhere in Africa to assimilate environmental stewardship through similar liturgical innovation.

In a tree-planting liturgy drafted by AAEC general secretary and Zionist Bishop Rueben Marinda, preparation for the eucharist begins with the digging of holes for tree-planting in the vicinity of an AIC headquarters or local congregation. The lot, sometimes fenced in, is referred to as "the Lord's Acre."

While the communion table, with neatly pressed tablecloth, bread, wine and several seedlings on it, is being prepared, groups of dancers dance around the bulk of the seedlings to be planted, which are stacked nearby. Dance and song bring praise to Mwari the great earthkeeper, encourage the green fighters to be vigilant in the struggle and even implore the young trees to grow well. The service includes several earthkeeping sermons by AAEC bishops and ZIRRCON staff members, as well as speeches by visiting government officials.

The sacrament itself is introduced by the public confession of ecological sins. Participants, including church leaders, line up behind a band of prophesying prophets to confess their guilt and listen to prophetic admonitions. After they file slowly past the prophets, they pick up a seedling and move to the communion table to partake in the sacrament.

The following excerpt is part of the liturgy read out to the congregation in Shona:

Look at the stagnant water
    where all the trees were felled.
Without trees the water-holes mourn,
    without trees the gullies form.
For the tree-roots to hold the soil . . .
    are gone!
These friends of ours
    give us shade.
They draw the rain clouds,
    breathe the moisture of rain.
I, the tree . . . I am your friend.
I know you want wood
    for fire:
    to cook your food,
    to warm yourself against cold.
Use my branches . . .
What I do not need
    you can have.
I, the human being,
    your closest friend,
    have committed a serious offence
    as a *ngozi,* the vengeful spirit.
I destroyed you, our friends.
So, the seedlings brought here today
    are the *mitumbu* [bodies] of restoration,
    a sacrifice to appease
    the vengeful spirit.
We plant these seedlings today
    as an admission of guilt,
    laying the *ngozi* to rest,
strengthening our bonds with you,
    our tree friends of the heart.
Indeed, there were forests,
    abundance of rain.
But in our ignorance and greed

M. L. Daneel

we left the land naked.
Like a person in shame,
    our country is shy
    in its nakedness.
Our planting of trees today
    is a sign of harmony
    between us and creation.
We are reconciled with creation
    through the body and blood of Jesus which brings peace,
he who came to save
    all creation.

At this point the sacramental bread and wine are served. Each participant, holding a seedling in his or her hand while receiving the sacrament, then proceeds to the holes in the new woodlot. Prior to the actual planting the bishop walks through the woodlot, sprinkling holy water on the ground, saying:

This is the water of purification and fertility.
We sprinkle it on this new acre of trees.
It is a prayer to God, a symbol of rain,
so that the trees will grow,
    so that the land will heal
    as the *ngozi* we have caused withdraws.

"Holy soil" which has been prayed over is then scattered in the woodlot with the words:

You, soil . . .,
I bless you in the name of Christ
    for you to make the trees grow
    and to protect them.
Provide the trees with sufficient food
    for proper growth.
Love the trees and keep their roots,
    for they are our friends.

The bishop then leads the green army into the Lord's acre to do battle against the earth's nakedness. The seedlings are addressed one after the other as they are placed in the soil:

You, tree, my brother, my sister,
    today I plant you in this soil.
I shall give water for your growth.
Have good roots
    to keep the soil from eroding.

Have many leaves and branches
>   so that we can
>   breathe fresh air,
>   sit in your shade
>   and find firewood.

To the Western mind this simple liturgy may seem of only relative significance considering the enormous, nearly impossible task of halting deforestation, desertification and soil degradation. As a spontaneous ecological ritual activity in the African cultural and linguistic context, however, it is a powerful statement of Christian commitment to the healing of all creation.

The close identification with water, soil and trees—elevating them ritually to the status of communication with human beings—reflects African religious holism. The holistic intuition of the past is taken to a level at which mutual interdependence is eloquently and meaningfully verbalized. In this overtly declared friendship, following admissions of human guilt for the mindless destruction of nature, mutual responsibility is reaffirmed: the new trees to provide shade and unpolluted air to sustain healthy human life, and the earthkeepers to water and protect their budding friends in the Lord's acre. The liturgy assumes responsible aftercare by the community of believers commissioned to do so, in itself a strong incentive to the wood-lot-keepers not to let the green army and its monitoring agents down. This imaginative stimulation of effective after-care, normally the Achilles' heel of grassroots African tree-planting endeavours, is already proving to provoke sustained, if sometimes monotonous, responsibility in the wake of the more exciting ritual experience of tree-planting.

Impersonating the vengeful *ngozi* spirit in terms of earth-destruction is as potent a way of accepting full responsibility for deforestation as is the confession of ecological wizardry. The *ngozi* is an aggrieved spirit of a murdered person or someone against whom a grave injustice has been perpetrated prior to death.[9] In customary law and traditional religion the *ngozi*, which creates havoc in the offender's family through illness and death, has a legitimate claim to full compensation in the form of up to ten sacrificial beasts, called *mutumbu*, literally "corpse" or "body," as they pay for the corpse of the deceased. In some cases the relatives of the offender also provide the *ngozi* with a young wife, who must sweep and tend to the small hut specifically erected for her disgruntled "spirit-husband." Presenting the trees to be planted as *mutumbu*-compensation for the *ngozi*-spirit provoked by wanton tree-felling is a thoroughly contextualized illustration of appeasement between humans and environment. The ritual, moreover, expresses compassion for the badly abused friends: trees, soil, water and, by implication, all of life in nature.

The *ngozi*-concept has several subtle connotations in the liturgy. It reflects the reckless and distorted spirit of the human "stewards" of the earth who attack nature with a single-minded "vengeance," like that of the *ngozi*, as if they are entitled to cause such havoc. There is also the suggestion that the "murdered" trees themselves exact retribution, like the *ngozi*, and that the seedlings are therefore the legitimate sacrificial replacement of the stricken tree-trunk corpses. Then follows the implicit suggestion in the sprinkling of water over God's acre that it is God who turns *ngozi* to the ecological offenders by retaliation through severe drought. Such an interpretation corresponds with the persistent traditional belief that the creator withholds rain in order to punish transgressions against nature and the guardian ancestors of the land, who are responsible for ecological equilibrium. In the admission of guilt, the ritual plea for the removal of divine discipline and the renewal of human resolve to heed the environment as ordained by God and ancestors, absolution is found. God responds by sending life-giving rain. Transformed as they are in the Christian liturgy, some of these traditional notions are still in evidence. Sprinkling holy water and soil over the barren earth earmarked for repair is a symbolic act of earth-healing. It accords entirely with prophetic faith-healing practice referred to above, thus demonstrating the ecclesiological shift which extends beyond human healing into the realm of healing or liberating all creation.

In the liturgy Christ is presented as the one whose blood works reconciliation between humanity and the rest of nature, the one who brings salvation to all creation. The reference is to Colossians 1:18–20. Although the liturgy here is not explicit on the twofold interpretation of the body of Christ as church and as creation, the central concept behind this Christological feature is that "in Christ all things hold together." The sacramental activity which unfolds around this concept suggests that at the point where believers give expression to their unity in the body of Christ as church through the use of bread and wine, they accept responsibility for the repair of the cosmic body of Christ to which they also belong and which they too have abused. Consequently, they proceed in unity as church to heal the stricken body through tree-planting in partnership with Christ, who as head of the believers is the real *muridzi venyika* (guardian of the land)—in contrast to or fulfilment of the traditional concept of ancestral guardianship.

In the tree-planting eucharist this close identification of Christ's body with the abused and barren soil makes sense. Traditionally, the ancestral guardians of the land belong to the soil. They *are* the soil. Their ecological directives issue from the soil, as expressed in the literal saying *Ivhu yataura* "the soil has spoken." In a sense Christ in this context is both guardian and the soil itself. New perspectives of Christ's lordship and his salvation of all creation can be developed from this essentially African expression of his pervading presence in the cosmos. In African peasant society, at any rate, Christ's reign as *muridzi* (guardian) of the land is an essential part of the gospel, for he is the one who is believed consciously to strike a balance between exploitative agricultural progress and altruistic, sacramental restoration of the land.

Here the AICs give ecological expression to what Moltmann calls the messianic calling of human beings:

> In the messianic light of the gospel, the appointment [of humans] to rule over animals and the earth also appears as the "ruling with Christ" of believers. For it is to Christ, the true and

visible image of the invisible God on earth, that "all authority is given in heaven and on earth" (Matt. 28:18). His liberating and healing rule also embraces the fulfilment of the *dominium terrae*—the promise given to human beings at creation . . . It is to "the Lamb" that rule over the world belongs. It would be wrong to seek the *dominium terrae,* not in the lordship of Christ but in other principalities and powers—in the power of the state or the power of science and technology.[10]

The AICs would agree that their tree-planting eucharist expresses their "ruling with Christ" in his liberating and healing rule as fulfillment of the *dominium terrae.* Inherent in this view is an acute awareness of the incarnate Christ who, despite his lordship, shares the suffering of an endangered creation. The assertion that Christ's body is creation and that he is the fulfillment of all creation underlines the predominant interpretation of the cosmological inference of Colossians 1:15–20: "in Christ all things hold together." Whereas this logos doctrine remained unrelated to Western science and was neglected as a theological basis for referencing nature, according to Carmody,[11] the AAEC depends on it—in its own innovative and rudimentary way—as the cornerstone of its tree-planting eucharist.

In doing so there is no pretence that we, the earthkeepers, are the saviours of creation, for that we can never be. But as believers and disciples of the one who holds all things together, we are erecting not only symbolic but concrete signposts of life-giving hope in a creation suffering while it awaits redemption. For, as Duchrow and Liedke state:

> Spirit-endowed beings do not save creation, but creation looks to us. The way that we cope with its suffering shows how much hope there is for creation. When we increase the suffering of creation its hope sinks. When we sharpen the conflict between human beings and nature, and also the conflict between humans, then creation lapses into resignation. When, instead, in solidarity with nature and our fellow human beings, we reduce suffering, then the hope of creation awakes into new life.[12]

This is precisely what the AAEC hopes to achieve. Through the movement of the earth-keeping Spirit new patterns of solidarity between formerly opposing churches and between a pluriformity of religions in society is being established, thereby giving rise to an ecumenism of hope. This hope takes concrete shape in the form of a healing ministry that attempts to cover and nurture the afflicted land. Serious attempts to expose and discipline those who continue with the rape of the earth embolden the green combatants to intensify the struggle. Replacing the trees in sacramental recognition of the lordship of Christ—the ultimate guardian, who reigns over yet suffers within the stricken earth—brings life and celebration to creation.

NOTES

1. Cf. M.L. Daneel, "The Liberation of Creation: African Traditional Religious and Independent Church Perspectives," *Missionalia,* Pretoria, Unisa, 2d ed., 1991; "Healing the Earth: Traditional and Christian Initiatives in Southern Africa," in R. Koegelenberg, ed., *Church and Development: An Interdisciplinary Approach,* EFSA, 1992; "African Independent Church Pneumatology and the Salvation of All Creation," *International Review of Mission,* LXXXII, no. 326, April 1993, pp. 143–66; "Towards a Sacramental Theology of the Environment," *Zeitschrift für Missionswissenschaft und Religionswissenschaft,* LXXV, no. 1, Jan. 1991, pp. 37ff.; "African Christian Theology and the Challenge of Earthkeeping," *Neue Zeitschrift für Missionswissenschaft,* XLVII, nos 2–3, Apr.–Jul. 1991, pp. 129–42; 225ff.

2. For the history of this movement see M. L. Daneel, *Fambidzano: Ecumenical Movement of Zimbabwean Independent Churches,* Gweru, Mambo Press, 1989.

3. Cf. M. L. Daneel, *Christian Theology of Africa: Study Guide in Missiology,* Pretoria, Unisa, 1989, ch. 3.

4. Daneel, *Fambidzano,* pp. 30f.

5. Cf. Muchakata Daneel, *ZIRRCON: Earthkeeping at the Grassroots in Zimbabwe,* Pretoria, Sigma Press, 1990.

6. Daneel, *Christian Theology of Africa,* pp. 66–72.

7. Daneel, *Fambidzano,* ch. 8.

8. Cf. M. L. Daneel, *Old and New in Southern Shona Independent Churches,* Vol. 2, The Hague, Mouton, 1974, pp. 214f., 292f.

9. *Ibid.,* Vol. 1, 1971, pp. 133–40; M. Gelfand, *Shona Ritual,* Cape Town, Juta, 1959, p. 153.

10. J. Moltmann, *God in Creation,* London, SCM Press, 1985, pp. 227f.

11. J. Carmody, *Ecology and Religion: Toward a New Christian Theology of Nature.* Ramsey, Paulist Press, 1983, p. 91.

12. U. Duchrow and G. Liedke, *Shalom: Biblical Perspectives on Creation, Justice and Peace,* Geneva, WCC, 1989, p. 61.

"INTERVIEW WITH CESAR CHAVEZ"

Catherine Ingram

When Cesar Chavez was thirteen years old, he participated in his first field strike near El Centro, California. His father, Librado, had organized the hundred men who would also participate. They had made their demands to the farm manager clear: they wanted a minimum wage of fifty cents per hour, overtime pay after eight hours of work, no child labor, and separate toilets for men and women. They also wanted free drinking water while picking in the fields, instead of being charged a nickel per ladle. It was dangerous to even approach the farm manager with such demands, and when they did, the manager accused Librado Chavez of being a communist. He also warned the men that the company had ways of dealing with troublemakers.

The grapes hung full on the vines, beckoning to be picked immediately or they would rot. The strikers formed a picket line in front of the vineyard's main gate. On the other side of the entry way, state troopers, labor contractors, and farm supervisors waited forebodingly, periodically glancing down the road.

Suddenly roaring trucks descended on the vineyard amidst clouds of dust. More than a hundred braceros, Mexican peasants, arrived to work the fields. They and the families they had left behind in Mexico were desperately poor and hungry. The braceros were willing to do the lowliest jobs for long hours with little pay. Librado Chavez pleaded with them in Spanish not to cross the picket lines, but although the braceros understood the plight of the grape-pickers, their own needs came first and they sadly crossed the lines.

The following day, it was the striker families' turn to face hunger. Labor contractors refused to hire anyone who had participated in the strike, and the Chavez family was forced to move on—to another field in another town, to another shack that would become home for a picking season.

In that time, there were few precedents for a successful strike by farmworkers. The National Labor Relations Act which Congress had passed in 1935 insured the right to organize of almost every labor group in the country, and it required that industry bargain with organized labor "in good faith." Agriculture was an exception. No protection under the law existed at that time for farm workers; a union was unthinkable. Many years and a "mighty hard road" later, Cesar Chavez would become the first man in the history of the United States to organize a successful union for farmworkers.

Reprinted from *In the Footsteps of Gandhi: Conversations with Spiritual Social Activists* by Catherine Ingram (1990) with permission of Parallax Press, Berkeley, CA.

INTERVIEW WITH CESAR CHAVEZ
APRIL 22, 1989 🐝 KEENE, CALIFORNIA

Catherine Ingram: Do you see any similarities between the civil rights struggle in India and the struggle of the farmworkers? For instance, Gandhi struggled to eliminate the caste system, and, in a way, we experience a modern caste system here with the poor minorities of color.

Cesar Chavez: Oh, there are a lot of similarities. Gandhi was dealing with the powerless and the poor and the ones who were discriminated against, and we have that now—the poor, and the people who are discriminated against. We have classism, racism. Gandhi was also working against a foreign domination, and this is similar to our situation in that agribusiness is really like a foreign domination. They don't live here.

CI: They don't?

CC: The multi-nationals, more and more, are being controlled by foreigners—Japanese, Germans. People don't realize what Japan owns here—they own subsidiaries of subsidiaries, a lot of California. They own a great deal of the wine country.

The other similarity is that people Gandhi dealt with tended to be religious, and the people we deal with tend to be religious as well.

CI: What aspects of Catholicism inspire you in your work, and what aspects have inspired the people you work with? Are there particular teachings that you focus on?

CC: Well, Christ's teachings. The Sermon on the Mount is the most inspiring, and that was one of Gandhi's inspirations also. The message of Christ is all about love, all about loving—not only God, but also one another. I think that's the point.

CI: The teachings of love.

CC: Yes, but what love is, that is to be interpreted. In our work, you know, love is really sacrifice. It's actually not vocal. Although it can be enunciated, it has to be practiced. You need both.

I think part of Gandhi's greatness was that he didn't want to be a servant, he wanted to be of service. It's very easy to be a servant, but very difficult to be of service. When you are of service, you're there whether you like it or not, whether it's Sunday, Monday, or a holiday. You're there whenever you are needed.

CI: I know that a lot of your current work has to do with raising people's awareness about the use of chemicals and pesticides on our food. What is happening to the farm workers who are exposed to these chemicals, and what is happening to the people who are eating the food on which they are sprayed?

CC: Our struggle with pesticides goes back more than thirty years. We raised this issue a long time ago, because we were the victims. In fact, right after the Second World War, I was a victim of pesticide poisoning. I knew very little about it at the time and it took me a few years to learn more. But when most of the people were worried about how thick the eggshells were on the birds, we were talking about human beings—about workers and then about consumers. For many years people would laugh at us, or they would ignore us, or they would just stare at us as if we were crazy. But today, everybody knows about pesticides.

We've been raising this issue a long time. In fact, we were successful in banning the use of DDT about nineteen years ago. We got it banned on grapes, but they came back with other poisons. Those were the ones that Rachel Carson wrote about in *Silent Spring*.

You know, either we ban these poisons and get rid of them, or they will get rid of us. These are deadly, deadly agents. They are organophosphates, nerve gas poisons. That's how they kill the insects; they affect their nervous systems. And so, too, they affect our nervous systems. Pesticides have killed a great number of workers and incapacitated many others; they have wrecked the health of the workers, their families, their children. See, now these pesticides are everywhere—in the water, in the soil, in the atmosphere, every place. And what we've learned is that body weight is a kind of buffer, and the more weight you have the more you can buffer; the less your weight, the more you are at risk. So it is children who are suffering the cancers and the birth defects. The number of miscarriages of women working with grapes is very high. We now see lots of cancer and lots of birth defects—terrible, terrible examples of birth defects—children born without arms or legs.[1] Oh, it's just horrible. We did a video about this, "The Wrath of Grapes."[2] It is just incredible what is happening. We've been campaigning to the point where we now have our workers pretty aware of it, and I think we've played a major role in the awareness of the issue all over the country, all over the world.

CI: I think your fast of last year raised awareness on this issue.[3]

CC: It did a lot. The fast is a great communicator. Like Gandhi, because we don't have the economic or political force, we have to appeal to the moral force, and the boycott is the best instrument. Gandhi said that boycotts were the most near-perfect instrument for social change.

CI: People's pocketbooks often awaken their conscience.

CC: And beyond that, it really is a moral force. Gandhi worked this out for all of us, because it's the moral force that compels, and then it translates into economic pressure. It starts from a moral stance, but it takes time.

CI: When you do these fasts, what gives you inner strength?

CC: That's a good question. I really don't know. Sometimes I fast for only one or two or three days and have a difficult time. In fact, I tried to fast two days ago and I couldn't do it. I'm trying again today, and it's very difficult. Then at other times, it just happens.

Catherine Ingram

CI: Do you think it has to do with the issue you're fasting for or the amount of support you have around you?

CC: I don't know. I've never been able to tell except that, well, Gandhi spoke about the door, or the window, the light. I can't really talk about those things, but sometimes it is *comparatively* easier than at other times. There is . . . there is a force there. I don't quite know what it is.

CI: For a long time your family has had to sacrifice with you for the cause. They've had to watch you go without food, they've seen you be put in prison. There were times when you were so poor you couldn't buy food for them. And when your children were growing up there were many times when you had to leave at crucial moments. I read in your book *La Causa* that even on the day of your daughter's wedding, you had to leave after just one dance with the bride in order to negotiate a contract. This is similar to Gandhi's situation as well. A lot of times his own family had to be relegated to a lesser priority.

CC: Oh, with him it was pretty bad. But I've been very lucky in that I've been able to keep the support of my family. You don't have to be present to spend time with them when you engage in the same struggle, because you are together when you engage in the same project. I think the strength in our family comes because it's always been directed away from ourselves.

When I was growing up, my dad and my mother instilled in us a really strong awareness of doing something for other people. It was preached, and it was practiced by them. We grew up in that way. We thought nothing of doing for other people, and we also saw the great advantages of doing things for others. The great payback comes in feeling good about helping people, and we understood that from the time we were very small. I don't think I have done this as much as my mother did, and I don't think I preached it as much. I think I acted on it quite a bit though, and so my kids—most of them—picked it up, the idea of helping, putting others first. If you do for somebody else, it's really doing for yourself. You can't explain it, but you understand it through doing it and once we experience it, it becomes a lot easier. I think this is what has happened in my home.

Now, with my mother it was planned. For instance, when we were growing up we were very poor, and yet my mother would send my brother and me—we were just small boys—to look for hobos or for people who were hungry and bring them home to eat with us, even though we had barely enough food for our own family. Those are very strong impressions, lasting impressions, to see people willing to do that. I often think that the reason that I discovered and became interested in Gandhi was because of my mother. I was predisposed because of the training at home. Anyway, my kids, most of them, have picked up some of this. Some of them are working with us here, but even those who are not working with us are committed to the ideals of being of service and helping people.

CI: It's been passed down in your family.

CC: Yes, even to the grandchildren. What happens is that they see it in the home. It's like anything else; if they see dope or drink at home, they do that. If they see making money, they do that.

CI: What changes have you seen for the farm workers in all these years?

CC: [Laughing] Our work is like two steps forward, and one and nine-tenths back. We've been able to accomplish quite a bit in terms of increasing society's awareness. We made the plight of the farmworkers a household word throughout North America. We have developed a broad understanding of the problem and a network of support. Some polls show that as much as eighty percent of the public know about the work we do. That's the biggest thing we have accomplished. And as a result of that, a limited number of workers now have traditional union benefits—better wages and so forth—but not a lot of the workers. We still face a day to day battle.

It has taken most unions between thirty and fifty years to get established. We're pioneers in this field, so it's going to be awhile before we really get established. Once we break that barrier, I think it will go very fast. But it's been back and forth and up and down—a long, long struggle.

We've been subjected to so much hardship, legal maneuvering, you name it.

CI: Yes, there's that 1987 lawsuit of $1.7 million, in which a vegetable grower claims that a farmworker strike cost him the loss of a harvest. I don't understand how you can be sued for that. Isn't potential loss the leverage for any strike?

CC: Yes. The claim against us is illegal. That law is unconstitutional. We continually have to challenge the unconstitutionality of such claims. That was the reason for my second major fast back in 1972, a twenty-five day fast, and that was a hard one. I ended it and they took me to the hospital; my vital signs were down. I was in bad shape. Only twenty-five days, but it was hard. We saw even back then that we couldn't get the legislation we needed on this.

Now with the most recent case, it has gone back to the state courts from the Supreme Court to see how they would interpret it. Unlucky for us, it was interpreted with a $5.6 million judgment against us.

Well, the bond itself is $5.6 million to appeal. We don't have $5.6 million. You've got to put up at least the exact amount of money that the judgment is for. So we recently went to court and got a judge in Yuma, Arizona, to set the bond at $250,000, and then the growers appealed too. Oh they drain you. They use the courts.

CI: In other words, even though the growers know that eventually they may lose the case, they can just wipe you out in the meantime with expensive legal tactics.

CC: Yes. Our system is not as democratic as people think. It's not as free as people think. We're quick to make judgments about other countries, but we're pretty bad ourselves. For eight years under Reagan, we were harassed with federal investigations here. It was so bad that we even assigned a room for the investigators. In fact, the last group that was here said, "We've looked at these books three times!" And they left.

See, if they find that I've taken one penny, I can be thrown out of the union. And they've done that to a lot of union leaders. They can't believe that I don't take pay, or that I don't have an expense account. I have to sit here and tell them how I live. If I go somewhere, I don't stay in hotels, I don't buy my food. People give it to me. That's how I do it, so what do I need money for? The investigators at first didn't want to believe that, but finally we convinced them. Well, they laid off of that, but it's always something else. We've been harassed up and down by the authorities.

Our power is with the people. That's where our power is. People—all shapes, all colors, all sizes, all religions. We have people who are very conservative who support what we do, people who are even anti-union. See, everybody interprets our work in a different way. Some people interpret us as a union, some people interpret our work as an ethnic issue, some people interpret our work as peace, some people see it as a religious movement. So we can appeal to broad sectors because of these different interpretations.

CI: How do you organize nonviolently around the issue of pesticides? It's an unseen enemy. I suppose you can say that the effects are seen, but the actual substance is unseen.

CC: It is immediately unseen, though in the long term, it is seen. But it's a lot harder to make people aware, because for the consumer, if you eat this grape, it won't harm you now, but it may harm you ten, fifteen years down the line. But you take the same grapes that may harm you in five, ten, or fifteen years, and you see that they are harming people instantly—you see what the pesticides are doing to the workforce and their children. You carry the message by showing the impact on the people in the front lines.

CI: So the workers are the front lines, and in their exposure and subsequent harm from the pesticides, they represent what is to come for the consumers down the line.

CC: Right, the workers get it instantly, but the consumer is going to be affected later on, because it's cumulative. Now people know this, but for years and years we were just the laughingstock when we spoke of this. Or we would hear things like, "Without pesticides, we'd starve." Well, they didn't have pesticides many years ago, and if people starved, they starved for other reasons. The thing is that about twenty years ago, about twenty percent of the crops of the world were lost to pests and today it's twenty-seven percent with jillions of more pesticides.

CI: The pests get more immune.[4]

CC: Yes. And then they need to use much more poison to kill them. Take, for example, the deadly nerve gas, parathion. Twenty years ago they were using about two pounds per acre. Today they are using up to six pounds per acre.

CI: I have a feeling that we are going to see a lot more immune-deficiency problems in our lives because we're being saturated with these poisons. What must the soil be like after all this spraying?

CC: The soil is becoming like a piece of plastic; you just stick plants there and you grow them artificially.

CI: Who or what would you say is the biggest enemy of the farmworkers?

CC: The biggest enemy is the system. Agriculture has changed from the time that our founding fathers laid out the foundation for our country. But the perception about ownership of land hasn't changed. There is something peculiar the world over about owning land. Land gives you power beyond its wealth, beyond liquid cash. Land has a powerful, powerful influence on people. You're dealing with landowners who literally own where you live, where you walk, and where you breathe. That power is awesome. And power tends to corrupt, and the system gets corrupted.

Agribusiness in California has developed on cheap labor—and not by accident; it's been planned. To maintain cheap labor the growers have worked out a horrible system of surplus labor—a surplus labor pool that they are experts at maintaining. Experts! See, agribusiness controls immigration policy, and it has for years. So much so that not long ago the Immigration and Naturalization Service was part of the Department of Agriculture. They control it.

CI: Do they turn a blind eye and let people get in illegally?

CC: That too. But they also set the immigration policy and control how it will be carried out and how it will be interpreted. They have tremendous influence.

CI: How does that work to benefit the growers?

CC: Let me give you an example. The beginning of agribusiness, the way we know it now, started back in the late 1800s. Curiously enough, unlike most systems, the workers were here before the jobs were. See, all the railroads, like the one running right by here, were built by the Chinese. And after the railroads were built, there were thousands of Chinese without work. So the early entrepreneurs, that's what they were in agriculture, came and saw this tremendous amount of labor, and that's why they developed labor-intensive crops in California, unlike in the Midwest and other places. It was because the labor was here. Other places had the climate and the water, but here they had a tremendous surplus of labor. So that was the beginning. It was in that system the labor contractor system started. And as in all systems, they polished it, they honed it, and now it's . . .

CI: . . . big business. I never realized that California produced so much of our food because of the surplus labor rather than the actual soil, climate, and water.

CC: Oh yes. There are other parts of the world that have the same or an even better climate than we have, although California has about fourteen climatic regions.

Then, too, everything is interwoven with agribusiness, so when you take on the growers you're also taking on the large insurance companies who also happen to be owners of land, and you're taking on the large banks, and the railroads, and the pesticide and fertilizer companies. Talk about a power base against you. That's why legislatively and politically there's no way we can do anything. They've got it clamped.

That's what Gandhi realized and why he went over to the boycott.

CI: I still don't understand exactly what agribusiness does in manipulating immigration policy to create a surplus labor pool.

CC: Well, what agribusiness does is often outside the law. They would recruit in, say China, and then they'd send recruitment teams into Japan (the Japanese didn't last too long, they had different ideas and they came with their families—the only other immigrants who came with families were the Mexicans). Then after that they sent recruits to India, and then they tried the Philippines. After the revolution in Mexico, people came. And then during the Dust Bowl, they went to Mexico and recruited for the Dust Bowl and then there was the Brassario program during World War II.[5] Now they're recruiting in Mexico, Asia, Africa, Honduras, Nicaragua, El Salvador, Guatemala. This is all recruitment for agribusiness, and that's how they do it.

CI: So they bring in all of these foreigners and it's to their advantage that the people remain illegal.

CC: Oh yes, because they exploit them and the illegals can do nothing about it. They cannot make a move. They have to accept whatever they are given. It's terrible.

CI: In your life, in your work, and in all that you have struggled for, is there something you could say about how life is?

CC: Well, not really. Life is so many things. But we're here playing the record every night and finding out every day whether we did what we're supposed to do. The message was clear from Christ, Gandhi, all the good people who said exactly what has to be done. So every night you've got to think, "What did I do today?"

Life is very complicated. But we try to keep it simple. Get the work done. We're essentially activists. We have our precepts and our principles, and then we act.

I was never for writing on nonviolence. What can you add? It's all been written. In the very early days, we gave the impression that nonviolence was sort of saintly, like saints who go around lightly stepping on eggshells. But now over the years we see nonviolence is not that. It is not that.

So we don't write about nonviolence, we don't preach it. We never talk about nonviolence to the workers unless there's a need to talk about nonviolence. In other words, if we're negotiating a contract, I'm not going to talk about nonviolence, but if we're in a picket line I'm going to talk about nonviolence. Because if you talk too much about it, it becomes . . .

CI: . . . less authentic.

CC: Yes, exactly. And we were very worried about that. Now we have legions of people who are nonviolent out there, the workers. But in the early days it was very hard. Now people know how to act, what to do. And not because we have said to do this. We haven't had one hour of teaching; it's all been by example.

We want to be men and women of the world. We want to work. We just want to do things nonviolently.

CI: How did you first come into contact with Gandhi's ideas?

CC: Oh, it was very interesting. As I recall, I was eleven or twelve years old, and I went to a movie. In those days, in between movies they had newsreels, and in one of the newsreels there was a report on Gandhi. It said that this half-naked man without a gun had conquered the might of the British empire, or something to that effect. It really impressed me because I couldn't conceive of how that had happened without guns. Even though I had never heard the name of Gandhi before, the next day I went to my teacher and asked her if she knew anything about him. She said, "No, but I have a friend who knows quite a bit about him." Then she gave me the name of her friend, a construction worker who was studying Gandhi. He gave me a little book on Gandhi. As I grew up, I started learning more, and ever since then, I have made a life project of reading about Gandhi and his message.

CI: What about Gandhi's life and message has most influenced you?

CC: His activism. He was a saint *of the world*. He did things, he accomplished things. Many of us can be so holy, you know, but we don't get very much done except satisfying our own personal needs. But Gandhi did what he did for the whole world. Not only did he talk about nonviolence, he showed how nonviolence works for justice and liberation.

CI: In your own life and work, have you experienced any new thoughts or new ways of seeing how nonviolent strategy works?

CC: No. It was all done by Christ and Gandhi and St. Francis of Assisi and Dr. King. They did it all. We don't have to think about new ideas; we just have to implement what they said, just get the work done. Gandhi offered everything there is in his message.

As I said, what I like about Gandhi is that he was a doer. He did things. He had thoughts *and* actions. Also he did a lot that he is not recognized for but which also has a lot of meaning. You know, he organized quite a few unions—there's nothing much written about this—but even today those unions are active. My biggest disappointment with the movie *Gandhi* was that it mentioned nothing whatsoever about the unions that he built. He organized the clothing workers, as you know, in Ahmedabad. In fact, I had a chance to meet one of the people from that union.

Gandhi was also a fantastic fundraiser. He raised millions of rupees, and he had a huge network of social services. He had probably the largest circulation of any newspaper in the history of the world. Even though there were only one or two thousand copies printed in the original, everybody reprinted it. So the message for me is that of his nonviolence and the fact that he was a doer. He made things happen.

CI: Does the fact that he was successful influence you in your appreciation of him? A lot of people attempt to do similar things, but for whatever reasons—their time in history, or circumstances beyond their control—they're not successful.

CC: No, what influences me is not whether or not they're successful, it's that they don't give up. I lose faith in someone who doesn't continue a project, who starts something and then leaves it. The world is full of us quitters. Even if Gandhi had not liberated India, he stayed with the project all his life. And that is my great attraction. He just didn't give up.

NOTES

1. For example, in the town of McFarland in the California Central Valley which is a crop-growing area regularly sprayed with pesticides, childhood cancers are eight times the normal level. Dr. Marion Moses, a leading medical researcher among farmworkers, cites cancer cases as the "hardest data," and she says that she has "soft data" on stillbirths and miscarriages. However, Dr. Moses suggests caution in concluding culpability and feels that lengthier studies are needed. She also adds that while body fat can more safely harbor chemicals than lean tissue, weight loss or expended energy poses a danger as the chemicals are released.

2. According to the United Farm Workers Union, fifty-four percent of table grapes tested by the government contain pesticide residues, but the government does not test for forty-four percent of the poisons used on grapes.

3. In 1987 Cesar Chavez fasted for thirty-six days on water only to "identify himself with the many farmworker families who suffer from the scourge of pesticide poisonings."

4. According to Professor George Georgehiou of the Department of Entomology, University of California, the number of species of insects resistant to pesticides increased from 224 in 1970 to 447 in 1984.

5. The program was implemented to recruit Mexican farmworkers who, after working the fields, were then sent back to Mexico.

"VALUING THE LAND: ECOLOGICAL THEOLOGY IN THE CONTEXT OF AGRICULTURE"

Judith N. Scoville

Contemporary agriculture is a crucial context for ecological theology and ethics. In today's world, virtually all of our nutrition needs must be met by agricultural production. Agriculture is a primary point of interconnection between humans and the natural world. Unlike other sources of environmental degradation, such as strip-mining, the internal combustion engine, and hazardous waste, agriculture is a genuine necessity. The mode of agricultural production represents not simply the way farmers relate to the earth, but the way in which *all* of us relate to the earth. We are participants in a global agricultural system. Our lives depend upon its production and our future depends upon its sustainability.

Meeting human needs for food and fiber has resulted in massive alteration of natural ecosystems leading to severe and widespread environmental degradation, including the pollution of land and water, soil erosion and loss of fertility, depletion of water resources, desertification and loss of genetic diversity. While agricultural practices have often been destructive throughout history, the industrial model which typifies contemporary American agriculture, a model increasingly adopted throughout the world, has vastly increased both the extent and the severity of the damage. As Dean Freudenberger bluntly puts it: "In our modern world, the way agriculture is done will very much determine the destiny of this planet."[1]

Agriculture poses difficult questions for ecological theology and ethics. Can nonanthropocentric ethics apply to areas of life, like agriculture, where major intervention in natural systems is made solely to achieve human purposes? Does the land itself deserve ethical respect—or is it of only instrumental value? How does the human role in agriculture relate to understandings of the place and role of humans in nature? The relationship of social justice issues and ecological issues in agriculture is also important, but must lie outside the scope of this essay.

I will consider two important recent works in ecological theology, Sallie McFague's *The Body of God* and Jay B. McDaniel's *Of God and Pelicans* and will ask how well they address these issues.[2] I will conclude by suggesting some directions for further development of an ecological ethics more adequate for the issues raised by contemporary agriculture.

THE VALUE CONFLICT IN AGRICULTURE

American agriculture has a profound division of values reflecting radically different conceptions of the natural world and the place of humans. In industrialized agriculture—or agribusiness—agriculture is an *economic* activity whose values are economic values: productivity, efficiency, profit. The social utility of high levels of production and efficiency—large quantities of food at low cost—provides an ethical underpinning for industrialized agriculture.[3] Pointing to the great gains in productivity achieved through technology, industrial agriculture looks to more and better technologies to sustain high levels of food production. The industrialization of agriculture does not take place solely within corporately organized farms, but within family farms themselves. The goals of efficiency and increased production and the "treadmill of technology" create pressures within family farms toward increases in scale, mechanization, and use of capital.[4]

Concern for the environmental and social consequences of industrialized agriculture has produced a growing movement within agriculture that embraces a broader set of values including protection of the land and the welfare of rural communities. The alternative to industrial agriculture has many names, such as agroecology (the term I will use) and sustainable, organic, or regenerative agriculture. It emphasizes the *biological* character of agriculture. At the heart of this view is the recognition that an agricultural field is an ecosystem characterized by the same ecological processes found in all ecosystems.[5] Agroecology seeks to work with and through natural processes and to imitate natural ecosystems in their complexity and diversity. It seeks sustainability by maintaining the productivity of ecosystems and the viability of rural societies.

Industrial agribusiness is based on a mechanistic worldview that legitimates increasing power and control over nature to achieve human material progress. The underlying assumption is that land is inert and productivity the result of human action.[6] Economics treats land "as a mixture of space and expendable, or easily substitutable, capital."[7] The ultimate resource is not nature, but technology—a resource based on the unlimited will and imagination of humans. The obvious limitation of natural resources does not challenge this view, for it rests on the principle of the infinite substitutability of resources.[8]

The ecological vision of agriculture is based on an ecological worldview that reconceptualizes the relationship of parts and wholes, which shape each other and are constitutive of an entity.[9] This understanding of the relationship of parts and wholes breaks down subject-object dualisms, especially those which separate culture and nature. Richard Norgaard states that in the ecological worldview, organisms, including humans, are recognized as evolving within the context of a larger system; people are part of evolving ecosystems. Their social organization, values and knowledge affect the evolution of the ecosystems they inhabit and they, in turn, are shaped by their natural environment.[10] History, which has long been placed in opposition to nature, must now be seen as an interaction of humans with the rest of nature. Nature is active, productive and creative in its own right and responds to our actions through ecological change.[11] Nature is not a stage on which human history is played out, but an active partner in the creation of a shared history. Agroecology is an interaction of nature's economy and the human economy, in which the role of humans changes from an external controller to a participant.[12]

The type of understanding and knowledge required to be such a participant, Wendell Berry asserts, is specific and requires intimate knowledge of one's particular farm. Thus "a healthy farm will not only will have the right proportion of plants and animals; it will also have the right proportion of people."[13] This specific knowledge contrasts with the approach to knowledge of industrial agriculture, which isolates problems from their context and develops generalized solutions.

Agroecological research looks toward two types of models. First, it studies traditional cultures in which the coevolution of social and biological systems has resulted in ecologically stable and sustainable agricultural systems.[14] The agricultural systems of traditional societies have far greater levels of species diversity, genetic diversity within crop species, and natural insect control than do modern agricultural systems and, consequently, require substantially lower levels of human control.[15] Second, agroecology takes nature as a pattern to be followed and seeks to work with and through natural processes by imitating the original biotic community in its complexity and diversity. It makes substantial use of ecology and other biological sciences. Wes Jackson and The Land Institute, for example, are working to develop a system of agriculture based on perennial polycultures which mimic original prairie ecosystems.[16] Intensive rotational grazing, a system promoted by the Land Stewardship Project, imitates the grazing patterns of wild species, thereby preventing the damage often caused by grazing and improving the quality of pastures and grasslands.[17]

Agroecology presents several challenges to theology and ethics. It points to the importance of ecosystems whose patterns and processes must guide our relationship with nature. It shows us that humans must be viewed as living in interaction with nature and that the land-human relationship is a particular one that cannot be generalized. Finally, it shows the necessity of developing theology and ethics within an ecological worldview.

ECO-THEOLOGY: McFAGUE AND McDANIEL

Both McFague and McDaniel seek to overcome the separation between God and the world that typifies much of western theology. Both use organic metaphors for the relationship of God and the world and both work explicitly within an ecological worldview. For McFague, care, stewardship, and partnership with God in solidarity with oppressed and needy nature replaces the view that the earth is but a resource for human use. We need to exercise abstinence, restraint and support rather than control.[18] For McDaniel, an ethic of caring stewardship, rather than arrogance, reflects God's own reverence for life.[19] Empathy for other living creatures has its counterpart in God's empathy for all.[20] For both, sustainability cannot be thought of in solely anthropocentric terms and the natural world cannot be valued solely in terms of its usefulness to humans. But is their development of these important themes adequate to the challenge posed by agriculture?

In the work of both, concern for ecosystems is, at best, a muted theme. McFague states that all are dependent upon life-supporting ecosystems. McDaniel calls for "attending to" and having a "feeling for" the broader matrices, networks and systems on which we and all individual creatures depend.[21] However, emphasis on the intrinsic value of individuals—the value they have in and for themselves—eclipses their discussions of ecosystems and limits the value of ecosystems to their usefulness to intrinsically valuable individuals. The value of the ecosystem is primarily instrumental—as habitat for animals and humans.[22] Certainly, both recognize that organisms have values for each other, but these values are not effectively incorporated into the ethic of either.

One reason they don't find value in ecosystems apart from their benefits to individuals may be that they have surprisingly negative views of natural processes. According to McFague, we participate in the pattern of nature in which "hunger, destruction, sacrifice, waste, death, pain, and suffering are intrinsic . . ." "Nature is red in tooth and claw."[23] For McDaniel, nature is not a harmonious whole, as is most clearly seen in predator-prey relations. "[A]t least from the perspective of sentient prey in the predator-prey relations, it is a disharmonious process, a broken process in which the good of one is evil for another.[24] "We live in a world where life is robbery."[25] If the relationships in nature are understood primarily as ones of destruction and suffering, it is hard to regard the ecosystem as something worthy of moral respect.

McFague makes the important point that we can only be at home on the earth when we "accept our proper place and live in a fitting, appropriate way with all other beings."[26] For her, however, guidance for living in a fitting way comes not from the patterns of nature, but from the Christic paradigm which shows us God's inclusive love for all, with special concern for the poor and needy—a principle that counters "the fang and claw of genetic evolution as well as its two basic movers, chance and law."[27] We are to justly share limited space with others, especially the poor and needy, human and nonhuman. For McDaniel, the practice of a life-centered ethic focuses on rights based on intrinsic value, taking into account differences in value based on varying capacities to experience. Again, the pattern used to determine our fitting response to nature comes not from nature's patterns, but—in this case—from a hierarchy of value based on what we value in ourselves—the capacity to experience.

DIRECTIONS FOR ECOLOGICAL
THEOLOGY AND ETHICS

What kind of an agenda might ecological theology and ethics develop if it were to more adequately meet the challenges presented by agriculture?

First, it is necessary to rethink the concept of value. Intrinsic value is an unecological way to think about value. In an ecological worldview, in which relationships are constitutive of what things are, it is hard to know what it can mean to speak of the value of something simply in and for itself—apart from its relationships. If existence is fundamentally relational and organisms are organisms-in-relationship, valuing must include relationships, be they ones of predation and competition or ones of mutuality. When Aldo Leopold described the land as "a fountain of energy flowing through a circuit of soils, plants, and animals," he was describing land in relational terms.[28]

Second, the most critical single question facing ecological theology and ethics is the goodness of nature. How we view nature shapes the resulting ethic; if natural processes are brutal, it will be hard to value them. "Nature red in tooth and claw" is not an objective, neutral description of nature. It is an interpretation, and like all interpretations it uses evidence selectively to make its point. A more positive view of nature looks at the same facts but puts them in a broader framework that recognizes the positive effects of predation and includes facts about relationships of mutual benefit within and between species which the more pessimistic view overlooks. Richard Cartwright Austin rightly states that environmentally-concerned Christians "must challenge theology to affirm the goodness of God's creation more radically than ever before, so that the natural community may claim value and rights on a par with human culture."[29]

Third, ecological theology and ethics must look to the natural world itself to learn what living in right relationship with nature might be. This does not imply drawing ethical principles from ecology—as Social Darwinism attempted to draw social principles from evolution. Rather, ecology can help us to understand the actions and interrelationships of the land community and better understand what a fitting human response should be. Only by taking the relationships within nature as a guide can our interactions with nature be cooperative with and supportive of the processes that bring forth and sustain all life.

Fourth, the human role needs to be reconceived. Much of environmentalism tends to assume an essentially negative view of the role of humans in the natural world. McFague states, for example, that "humans, as the top of the food chain, 'are consumers *par excellence*' who produce no useful products, use available products, and give back nothing."[30] Agroecology challenges us to develop a positive vision of human relationships with nature. The traditional cultures to which agroecology looks can provide examples of such positive relationships. Gary Paul Nabhan cites the Papago Indians whose fragile soils have not deterio-

Judith N. Scoville

rated during centuries of cultivation.[31] Papago cultivation has benefited wildlife as well, for cultivated areas are graced with many more species of birds than uninhabited areas.[32] Unless we can imagine ourselves able to act positively within ecosystems, we will, in effect, be seeing ourselves as outside of and alien to the natural world.

Fifth, the study of the traditional cultures points toward two related critical themes: place and culture. Farming, by its nature, is rooted in place. Nabhan points out that desert field work requires letting "each distinctive field 'speak' for itself." Such farming must be done in a community. "Just as the wild species must complement and reinforce one another for these field ecosystems to work, farmer's efforts must reinforce one another through time."[33] Donald Worster, in *Dust Bowl*, a study of the Southern Plains in the 1930s, describes how the lack of an indigenous culture adapted to requirements of the land contributed to the ecological catastrophe of the dust bowl. He contrasts this lack with traditional cultures rooted in place.

> When both the identity of self and of community become indistinguishable from that of the land and its fabric of life, adaptation follows almost instinctively, like a pronghorn moving through sagebrush. Houses and fields, tools and traditions, grow out of the earth with all the fitness of grass; they belong in their place as surely as any part of nature does.[34]

In the context of a ecological agriculture, we clearly see that land is not *space* to be distributed, but *place* to be inhabited.

CONCLUSION

What agriculture brings to the fore is the difference between biocentric and ecocentric ethics. McFague and McDaniel have developed essentially biocentric ethics based on the intrinsic value of living entities. The direction I have suggested that ecological ethics should go is essentially an ecocentric one that recognizes the value of ecosystems and the biotic community as a whole.

Two points need to be made about the apparent conflict between ecocentric and biocentric ethics. First, in an ecological worldview in which parts and wholes shape each other, sharp separation of the good of the part and the good of the whole is untenable. Wendell Berry states this well when he discusses health of the land as a criterion of good farming. Health is a comprehensive concept, for the health of individuals, communities, animals, plants and all Creation are inseparable.[35] Second, ecocentric ethics applies to our relationship with nonhuman nature—not with other humans. To respect the distinctiveness and diversity of the nonhuman world, we must respect the ways in which biotic communities are different from human communities and not expect that the same principles of behavior will be appropriate for both.

Without an ecocentric ethic which affirms the value of the land, it is hard to conceive of an agricultural environmental ethic which is not anthropocentric. Farmland is our habitat for all of us, urban and rural, eat off farmland. If the value of ecosystems is their value as habitat, then farmland is primarily of value to us. Without valuing the land itself, nonanthropocentric ethics becomes marginalized, applying mainly to wildlife and their habitats. Such a limited ethic is not the intention of those developing ecological theologies and ethics. McFague states the point well when she writes: "The universal vocation of planetary well-being must coincide with our daily breadwinning activities."[36] What agroecology shows is that we cannot do so without valuing the land.

NOTES

1. C. Dean Freudenberger, *Global Dust Bowl: Can We Stop the Destruction of the Land Before It's Too Late?* (Minneapolis: Augsburg, 1990), 35.

2. Jay B. McDaniel, *Of God and Pelicans: A Theology of Reverence for Life* (Louisville: Westminster/John Knox Press, 1989); Sallie McFague, *The Body of God: An Ecological Theology* (Minneapolis: Fortress Press, 1993).

3. Luther Tweeten, "Food for People and Profit," in *Is There a Moral Obligation to Save the Family Farm?* ed. Gary Comstock (Ames, IA: Iowa State University Press, 1987), 254.

4. Marty Strange, *Family Farming: A New Economic Vision* (Lincoln: University of Nebraska Press, 1988), 40–42.

5. Susanna B. Hecht, "The Evolution of Agroecological Thought," in Miguel A. Altieri, *Agroecology: The Scientific Basis of Alternative Agriculture* (Boulder: Westview Press, 1987), 5.

6. Caroline Merchant, *Ecological Revolutions* (Chapel Hill, N. C.: University of North Carolina Press, 1989), Ch. 6.

7. Herman E. Daly and John B. Cobb, Jr., *For the Common Good: Redirecting the Economy toward Community, the Environment, and a Sustainable Future* (Boston: Beacon Press, 1989), 110–113.

8. Ibid., 107–109; 198–99.

9. J. Baird Callicott, "Agroecology in Context," in *Global Perspectives on Agroecology and Sustainable Agricultural Systems,* ed. Patricia Allen, and Debra Van Dusen (Santa Cruz, CA: University of California, Santa Cruz, 1988).

10. Richard B. Norgaard, "The Epistemological Basis of Agroecology," in Altieri, *Agroecology,* 23–25.

11. Merchant, *Ecological Revolutions,* 7–9.

12. Richard Levins and John H. Vandermeer, "The Agroecosystem Embedded in a Complex Ecological Community," in *Agroecology,* ed. C. Ronald Carroll, and John H. Vandermeer (New York: McGraw-Hill, 1990), 342.

13. Wendell Berry, *The Unsettling of America: Culture and Agriculture* (San Francisco: Sierra Club Books, 1977), 182.

14. Altieri, *Agroecology,* Ch. 6. See also Freudenberger, *Global Dust Bowl* and Stephen R. Gliessman, "An Agroecological Approach to Sustainable Agriculture," in Wes Jackson, Wendell Berry, and Bruce Coleman, ed., *Meeting the Expectations of the Land,* (San Francisco: North Point Press, 1984), 160–171.

15. Altieri, *Agroecology,* 40–41.

16. Wes Jackson, *New Roots for Agriculture* (San Francisco: Friends of the Earth, 1980). See also Judith D. Soule and Jon K. Piper, *Farming in Nature's Image: An Ecological Approach to Agriculture* (Washington, D.C.: Island Press, 1992).

Judith N. Scoville

17. Allan Savory, *Holistic Resource Management,* (Washington, D.C.: Island Press, 1988).

18. McFague, *The Body of God,* 6–7.

19. McDaniel, *Of God and Pelicans,* 60.

20. Ibid., 84.

21. Ibid., 90–92.

22. Ibid., 71. Difficulty in affirming the value of ecosystems can also be seen in the discussion of "biosphere ethics" in Charles Birch and John B. Cobb, Jr., *The Liberation of Life* (Denton, TX: Environmental Ethics Books, 1990), pp. 168–170. While they affirm the value of species and ecosystems, how this is grounded in an ethic based on the capacity to experience is unclear.

23. McFague, *Body of God,* 63.

24. McDaniel, *Of God and Pelicans,* 42.

25. Ibid., 74.

26. McFague, *Body of God,* 112.

27. Ibid., 171.

28. Aldo Leopold, *A Sand County Almanac* (New York: Oxford University Press, 1949), 216.

29. Richard Cartwright Austin, "Review of Jay B. McDaniel: *Of God and Pelicans: A Theology of Reverence for Living* and *Earth, Sky, Gods & Mortals: Developing an Ecological Spirituality,*" *Environmental Ethics* 13 (1991): 364.

30. McFague, *Body of God,* 59.

31. Gary Paul Nabhan, "Replenishing Desert Agriculture with Native Plants and Their Symbionts," in *Meeting the Expectations of the Land,* ed. Jackson, Berry, and Coleman, 172–82.

32. J. Baird Callicott, "Genesis and John Muir," in *Covenant for a New Creation,* ed. Carol S. Robb and Carl Casebolt. (Maryknoll, N.Y.: Orbis Books, 1991), 132–33.

33. Nabhan, "Replenishing the Desert," 182.

34. Donald Worster, *Dust Bowl: The Southern Plains in the 1930s* (New York: Oxford University Press, 1979), 164.

35. Berry, *The Unsettling of America,* 103; 203–204.

36. McFague, *Body of God,* 11.

"NEW STORY/OLD STORY: CITIZENSHIP IN EARTH"

Paul Gorman

I'm told I'm made of stardust but it doesn't feel that way. Getting up in the morning, I don't find myself looking in the mirror, thinking, "Primordial Flaring Forth." That subtitle of Thomas Berry and Brian Swimme's book, *The Universe Story,* inviting us into the Ecozoic Era, more nearly describes some petty outburst of household irritability than the outset of "the universe venture." "There he goes again," sighs my wife after some episode in the kitchen, "Ol' Primordial Flaring Forth." Hey, I'm just another Cenozoic guy, and you know where I live? New York City. We specialize here, you might have heard, in being ontologically undifferentiated cosmos in conscious self-celebration. Come on down.

We have our moments, actually. Last night, I stopped twice to talk to homeless men panhandling. One was a Vietnam vet. He'd look for a job, he told me, but just had no money to buy clothes for an interview. I gave him my "spare change" and said he deserved better. He nodded blamelessly, and actually replied, "Keep hope alive." The other was an older guy, too old for this. I told him I'd been tapped out by a younger brother down the block. As if he knew him, he said, "That's fine, can't feed everybody." There was straighter eye contact with them than most days at the office. I didn't need a New Universe Story to get next to those two guys.

What kept me next to them keeps me next to the Hudson River, or to the faint smell of sea at the arrival of a low front, or, without much effort now, to the rats that scamper in and out of my building. Bare attention, open heart, commitment to communion with whatever is right in front of me. I'm up for entering the Ecozoic Era—but not in some romanticized pastorale, not without the company of those two homeless men. I need to enter in citizenship and solidarity. And these interactions have been no less ruptured than those more "elemental" flows within the biosphere.

All we have been stripping from the natural world we are also stealing from our own public lives. How fares the web of life? Well, how fares the family? Where *is* the family? Where are my neighbors? *Who* are my neighbors? Didn't we all used to have more friends? The natural fabric is being rent, and is it a surprise that we're left feeling lonely?

Citizenship entails consent. But by whose decision, through what collective deliberation are entire species of the planet being killed off . . . how many per week now? Life is disappearing; shouldn't we expect to feel radically disenfranchised?

Citizenship flourishes as a natural expression from within a genuine commonweal. But everything that we unquestionably should share merely by virtue of being here—water, air, soil, fish, fowl, flowers—are these in any way held in common and in trust? How can we expect to share equitably the hard-won wealth of human labor when we cannot even conserve what we were all given for free? The commons are robbed; what else in the wake but loneliness, clinging, and greed.

Do we think our assault on the natural world would leave our civic life untouched?

But if these two worlds are intimately connected, it must follow that the practice of citizenship has something to contribute to healing in Earth. So how to be a citizen in a biocidal age? Here's a question this book might send us all out asking. For me, for the moment, it seems at the very least to require a posture of inquiry into what must be made new again, and recollection of what must not be forgotten, and generally being okay with not being quite sure.

If we are to work in nature's name, we might start out with nature's cues. Embrace diversity. Observe law. Respect process. Care for what is bequeathed. Seek symbiosis. Ally abrasion. Stay in scale. Rest. (And rest a little more.) The challenge, in other words, would be to restore citizenship, not only as action on behalf of ecology, but somehow as the practice of ecology itself. That would mean not only organizing, voting, demonstrating, writing letters—not simply action "out there" about stuff "over yonder." It would invite citizenship from "in here," from within the natural order, drawing where possible on its appropriate images and life-enhancing instructions: cocreate, sow deep, cultivate, fertilize, connect, replenish, vitalize, cleanse, heal, draw forth, give birth, bury, recycle. I take these as civic virtues that can be consciously accorded value as we define and enact nitty-gritty political work.

But citizenship is still a human enterprise, and there is unfinished business in how we view the place of the human itself. Addressing this question—seeking to get the species back in scale—has been the preeminent contribution of such "New Story" thinking as appears in these pages. But I have been having my own little mind-dance with the politics of much "Earth spirituality." Where's *human* suffering in this story? Aghast at anthropocentrism, have many turned to efforts on behalf of nature to avoid facing our failure to heed and heal one another? Is there some new self-hatred at work here? Back to the garden only to rediscover the shame? What we've learned about human citizenship at its best we can't dispose of in our disgust at human behavior at its worst.

That effort isn't any easier when we try to find appropriate political strategies. So much environmental activism has been dry or uninformed by the deepest spiritual impulses of our best new thinking. I'm all for the Environmental Defense Fund weaning McDonald's from Styrofoam, say, but it doesn't quite ease the yearning. And the dualism of more confrontational action seems to violate precepts of communion that ought to be at the heart of planetary healing. But then I find myself flying over New York City on the night of riot in Los Angeles, and the power-plant smokestacks below suddenly turn into great hypodermics shooting smack into the skin of the sky. The culprits and victims of poverty and pollution seem the same. And I'm thinking petrochemical executives are criminal and just plain have to be brought down. "By any means necessary." Yet seconds later, quieter, I find myself asking if we really have no choice but to work with these guys, help them see what they're doing, give them "incentives"—only to realize, to my horror, that these turn out to be incentives to barter "pollution rights." Sigh. I pause, watch a few breaths, resolve to hold on to some essential militancy, dig in on my own work, make peace with ambiguities, and know that there'll be room and time to see more clearly what's called for and what works.

And again in new citizenship's name, I turn to past struggles. I understand what's behind Tom Berry's suggestion that "democracy is a conspiracy against the natural world." I know he's puckish, and enjoys needling us, and I take the point. But there is a noble history of democratic thought and struggle that has moved for centuries toward an increasingly inclusive vision of citizenship. Through it, slavery was abolished, the universal franchise secured, the right to organize unions guaranteed, human rights assured, equal protection of the law, freedom of speech, assembly, the right to freely worship, the right of women (still up for grabs) to make decisions affecting their bodies. No small undertakings. Someone said, "Let's put an end to the divine right of kings." Imagine how it first felt to take on that struggle. Less daunting at the time than seeking to preserve the biosphere now?

People sacrificed and bled and died. And they were people like us—who had dreams and doubts, unsure of what they had to offer and what it would take, had sick friends to care for and got sick themselves, never saw the full fruits of their labor, simply went forth and engaged history, took one step and then another until it became a path.

We are in their debt and in their lineage and that's the Old Story and it's still true. The New Story, of course, is that suddenly there is much more than human well-being for which to struggle now. But then there is so much more with which to feel solidarity. All life.

The effort to newly discover appropriate citizenship, then, can be a vehicle for discovering proper human place. It will be a journey, a climb. But there will be moments, almost certainly unexpected, when we will be given images of hope and promise.

My friend, Drew Christiansen, recounts a visit with a fellow Jesuit to our first national monument, the Pinnacles, where on a winter camping trip, clambering through caves and canyons, awed at the natural history, approaching the top of his last climb, he suddenly came upon what he called the most wonderful sight of the day: a group of handicapped people climbing the mountain, in wheelchairs, on crutches, or held by friends or volunteers, mostly women. There it all is, I thought, when I first heard the story: the wounds and the willingness, the struggle and the celebration, we humans grappling with and grappling within the rest of God's creation.

"That night," he reported, "as I sat under the desert sky, wondering at the plenitude of the heavens and all I had seen that day, Immanuel Kant's dictum came to mind about the two things that inspire awe, 'the starry sky above and the moral law within.'"

"STREET TREES"

Melody Ermachild Chavis

I was drawn to my upstairs bedroom window by shouting in the street. The shouter was a middle-aged black man in shabby pants, and he strode, fast, right down the middle of the street. Storming across the intersection, the man beat the air with his fists and shouted into the sky. "Somalia!" he cried. "Somalia!"

Ours is a neighborhood where poverty and addiction have made misery for years, and this was when airlifts of food to the Horn of Africa were all over the nightly news. "I know what you mean," I thought. "Why there? Why feed them but not you?"

Then he walked up to the newly planted tree under my window, grabbed its skinny trunk with both hands, yanked it over sideways, and cracked it in half on his knee. He threw the tree's leafy top onto the sidewalk and stomped off, cursing. I pressed my palms to the glass as he disappeared up the sidewalk.

The tree was just a baby, one of the donated saplings our neighborhood association planted with help from the children on our block. Men from the public-works department had come and cut squares in the sidewalk for us, reaming out holes with a machine that looked like a big screw. The kids planted the trees, proudly wielding shovels, loving their hands in the dirt.

I had made name tags for each tree, with a poem printed on each one, and we asked the kids to give each tree a name. "Hi, my name's *Greenie,* I'm new and neat, just like the children on our street." If we made the trees seem more like people, I thought, the kids would let them live.

Both trees and people around here are at risk of dying young. After our neighborhood was flooded with crack cocaine and cheap, strong alcohol, things got very rough. In the last five years, 16 people have been murdered in our small police beat. Most of them were young black men, and most of them died on the sidewalks, where the trees witness everything: the children, the squealing tires and gunshots, the blood and sirens.

My neighbors and I did all we could think of to turn things around, including planting the trees.

But the dealers still hovered on the corners and the young trees had a hard time. Idle kids swung on them like playground poles, and peeled off strips of bark with their nervous little fingers.

One of the saplings planted in front of my house had fallen victim to a car, and now the other one had been murdered by a man mad about Somalia.

Reprinted with permission of the author from *Sierra: The Magazine of the Sierra Club* (Vol. 79, No. 4).

Discouraged, I let the holes in the cement choke with crabgrass. In the center of each square, a pathetic stick of dead trunk stuck up.

When things are bad, I stand in my kitchen window and look into my own garden, a paradise completely hidden from the street outside. For 15 years I've labored and rested in my garden, where roses clamber on bamboo trellises. There are red raspberries and rhubarb. Lemon, apricot, apple, and fig trees are sheltered by young redwoods and firs that hide the apartment house next door. I planted the apricot tree 13 years ago when it was a bare stick as tall as myself. Now I mark the seasons with its changes. In early spring the apricot blooms white, tinged with pink, and feeds the bees. When our chimney fell in the earthquake, I used the bricks to build a low circular wall I call my medicine wheel. Inside it I grow sage, lavender, rosemary, and oregano. A stone Buddha sits under fringed Tibetan prayer flags, contemplating a red rock.

Not far from my house is a place I'm convinced is a sacred site. Within one block are a large African-American Christian church, a Black Muslim community center, and a Hindu ashram. Someone put a Buddha in a vacant lot near there, too, and people built a shrine around it. All this is close to the place where the Ohlone people once had a village.

I dream of those who lived here before me—an Ohlone woman, members of the Peralta family whose hacienda this was, and a Japanese-American farmer who had a truck garden here until he lost it when he was interned during World War II.

I often feel I'm gardening with my dear old next-door neighbor Mrs. Wright. An African-American woman from Arkansas, Mrs. Wright came to work in the shipyards during the war. When she bought the house next door this was the only neighborhood in town where black people were allowed to live. She was foster mother to many children, and she was sadly disapproving of the young people who used drugs when that started. Mrs. Wright farmed every inch of her lot, and had it all in food, mainly greens, like collards and kale. She gave most of the food away.

Her life exemplified the adage, "We come from the earth, we return to the earth, and in between we garden." I miss her still, although she died six years ago, in her 70s, after living here nearly 50 years. I was almost glad she didn't live to see the night a young man was shot to death right in front of our houses.

A map of the neighborhood 15 years ago, when my family came, would show community places that are gone now: bank, pharmacy, hardware and small, black-owned corner stores. There are a lot of vacancies now, jobs are gone, and people travel to malls to shop. Many families run out of food the last days of the month.

On my map I can plot some of what killed this community's safety: the too-many liquor outlets—nine within four blocks of my house; the drug dealers who came with crack about

1985. Clustered near the drugs and alcohol are the 16 murder sites: the 15 men, the one woman.

"I want to get away from all this," I think often. But *really* getting away would mean selling our home and leaving, and so far, my husband and I have been unwilling to give up, either on our neighbors or on our hopes for helping make things better.

But we do get away, to the mountains. We've been walking the John Muir Trail in sections the last few summers. I've never liked the way it feels good to go to the mountains and bad to come home. That's like only enjoying the weekends of your whole life.

According to my mail, "Nature" is the wilderness, which I'm supposed to save. And I want to. But right here and now, if I go outside to pick up trash, I might have to fish a used syringe out of my hedge. That's saving nature too. The hard task is loving the earth, all of it.

The notes I stick on my refrigerator door remind me of the unity and sacredness of life. There's a quote from Martin Luther King, Jr. on "the inescapable network of mutuality." I know I can't take a vacation from any part of this world.

Still, the habit of my mind is dual. This I hate: (the littered sidewalk); this I love: (the alpine meadow). I could get into my car and drive to that meadow. But when I drive back, the sidewalk will still be dirty. Or, I could stay here, pick up a broom, and walk out my front door.

The sidewalk yields clues that people have passed this way, like trail markers in the mountains: candy wrappers the kids have dropped on their way back from the store; malt liquor cans and fortified-wine bottles inside brown bags. Sometimes there are clothes, or shoes, or car parts. I tackle it all in thick orange rubber gloves, wielding my broom and dustpan, dragging my garbage can along with me. I recycle what I can. "This is *all* sacred," I tell myself. "All of it."

There are bigger waste problems. But when I think about the ozone hole, I find that it helps me to clean up. Thinking globally without acting locally can spin me down into despair.

Or into anger. I know that other people somewhere else made decisions that turned our neighborhood, once a good place, into a bad one. Like the alcohol-industry executives who decided to aim expensive ad campaigns at African-American teens. I know decisions happen that way to the old-growth forests, too.

I went to a lecture at the Zen Center not far from my house, to hear the head gardener there. She talked about what is to be learned from gingko trees. I've always liked their fan-shaped leaves, bright gold in the fall, but I hadn't known they were ancient, evolved thousands of years ago. They exist nowhere in the wild, she said, but were fostered by monks in gardens in China and Japan. Somehow, gingkos have adapted so that they thrive in cities, in polluted air. They remind me of the kids around here, full of life in spite of everything. I've seen teenage boys from my block, the kind called "at risk," "inner city," sometimes even "thugs," on a field trip to an organic farm, patting seedlings into the earth like tender young fathers putting babies to bed.

The day after the lecture, I went to the nursery, ready to try planting trees again in the holes in the sidewalk. Now in front of my house are two tiny gingkos, each inside a fortified cage of four strong metal posts and thick wire mesh. To weed them, I kneel on the sidewalk and reach in, trying not to scratch my wrist on the wire.

Kneeling there, I accept on faith that this little tree will do its best to grow according to its own plan. I also believe that every person wants a better life.

One evening last summer I lay flat out in a hot spring in the broad valley on the east side of the Sierra. I imagined one of the little street gingkos growing upright from my left palm. Out of my right palm, an ancient bristlecone pine of the White Mountains. This is how the trees live on the earth, as out of one body. They are not separate. The roots of the city tree and the summit tree pass through my heart and tangle.

IMAGINATION, GAIA, AND THE SACREDNESS OF THE EARTH

David Spangler

When the sun rises on the morning of January 1, 2000, it will undoubtedly be a dawn like any other, just another day in the Earth's four-and-a-half-billion-year history. Nowhere is it recorded in the stones of the Earth, the currents of the ocean, or the tempests of the winds that that dawn shall herald some special event. Yet for much of humanity, it will mark the beginning of a new millennium.

This passage into the twenty-first century is a social invention. It is an act of cultural imagination, and as such it provides a catalyst for other similar acts of imagination on which our collective prosperity and health—and even our survival—may rest. It is an invitation to reexamine, reevaluate, and where necessary, change attitudes and habits of culture that increasingly prove dysfunctional on the interconnected planet that we inhabit.

Foremost among these acts of revisioning is a reimagination of our relationship to the world. For nearly three centuries, Western culture has progressively imagined itself as distinct and separate from the natural order, while concomitantly imagining that order as simply a dead, material resource to be used (and used up) according to humanity's will (or more specifically, according to the will of those governments and corporations capable of managing such exploitation). There is now a very real question whether these images can continue or whether they spell disaster for all of us unless changed.

I take the position that we must reimagine the world and ourselves within it in ways that recognize and emphasize the interconnectedness and interdependency that exist within the natural order, an order from which we are not separate. To fail to do so will be to condemn our descendants to lives of increasing misery and danger.

One key area for this reimagination is that of spirituality, theology, and ethics. Given the anthropocentrism of these disciplines in Western traditions, the challenge now is to find images for an ecotheology and a bioethics that extend our context of spirituality to include the nonhuman aspects of the world. We strive to develop a spirituality that embraces Earth as a whole. We seek to reimagine Earth, spirit, and ourselves in ways that synthesize these three into a new wholeness that is healing and empowering. We seek, in the words of Thomas Berry, a "new story," a new myth.

This is vital work, but it is important to remember that the objective of this quest is not simply new images with which to replace those that have grown old and outmoded. What we are after is to change behavior, to embody a new life, and to express a new spirit. Images and myths are powerful tools that can assist this process, but they can also turn in our hands and become obstructions. They can become new beliefs and dogmas that substitute one orthodoxy for another without liberating us into the life of the holistic spirit that is our true goal. So the craft of reimagining Earth and spirit is a delicate one.

To illustrate my point, I want to examine one particular image of the Earth and of our relationship to it that has developed in recent years. This is the image of the world as a living being, an image emerging from a scientific theory known as the Gaia hypothesis. In the decade or so since its appearance, it has become a powerful image that is being widely used or discussed in scientific, philosophical, ecological, and spiritual circles. In some ways the image of Gaia has become a symbol for the ecological and spiritual sensibility that we are trying to understand and cultivate. As such, this image can illustrate both the problems and pitfalls, and the advantages and strengths, involved in reimagining Earth and spirit.

In 1979, James Lovelock, a British atmospheric chemist and inventor, published a book called *Gaia: A New Look at Life on Earth.* In it he presented a theory called the Gaia hypothesis that he had developed in collaboration with American microbiologist, Lynn Margulis. This theory basically stated that the Earth's climate and surface environment are controlled by the planet's biosphere, in effect by all the microorganisms, plants, and animals that live upon and within the world. The core of the theory is that the planet functions as if it were a single living organism. At the suggestion of British novelist William Golding, a neighbor and friend of Lovelock, this planet-sized organism was named *Gaia* after the Greek goddess of the Earth.

Had Lovelock called his theory something more prosaic and scientific, like the Theory of Atmospheric and Environmental Regulation through Biospheric Homeostasis, our story would end here. The idea would have wound its way along a customary path of being published in scientific journals and discussed at scientific conferences. Chances are, though, it would not have emerged from the world of scientific jargon and procedure into public view, nor become a significant idea influencing public debate in political, environmental, philosophical, and religious circles. Cybernetic feedback loops are simply not images capable of firing the imagination and launching revolutions; it is difficult to picture impassioned citizens storming the ramparts of the status quo carrying banners proclaiming "Biospheric Homeostasis or Death!"

Gaia, on the other hand, is exactly such an image. It is the picture of an ancient goddess, arriving on the scene exactly as the feminine movement has been challenging the male, patriarchal view of the world. It resonates with very ancient cosmologies held in nearly every culture of the Earth at one time or another that recognized and affirmed the Earth as a living being possessed of soul. It therefore touches us at a deep level of racial memory and myth.

During a personal visit with James Lovelock in the early eighties, I asked him what the responses had been within the scientific community to his hypothesis. He said that there was interest, but that generally it had been ignored. (This has since changed. In 1988, the American Geophysical Union devoted its entire biannual conference to a discussion and evaluation of the Gaia hypothesis, and since then, the idea has become an accepted theoretical basis for further experimentation and study.) On the other hand, to his surprise, the idea had been taken up enthusiastically by religious and spiritual groups around the world, and that he received hundreds of lecture invitations from such groups. However, in an industrial culture challenged by ecological degradation as well as by a growing feminist sensibility, and therefore looking for new guiding myths, this response is not surprising at all. The idea of Gaia, the living Earth, reunites us with the mythic, feminist, ecological, and spiritual imagination of our ancestors in the currently acceptable form of a scientific image.

Gaia as a mythic idea is definitely alien to the original Gaia hypothesis as developed by James Lovelock and Lynn Margulis. Though it does conceive of the Earth as a living entity, such a being, in the words of Margulis, if conscious at all, has the sentiency "of an amoeba." Hardly the stuff of myth and spiritual invocation. But subjected to the forces of reimagination now going on in our culture, this hypothesis could hardly remain within the more sterile boundaries of "good" science. It is simply too fertile and too powerful an image. So it has exploded to become a one-word hieroglyph suggesting an organizing principle—the central paradigm—of an entire new cultural outlook. In fact, as suggested by such book titles as *Gaia: A New Way of Knowing,* a compilation of essays edited by cultural historian, William Irwin Thompson, Gaia has come to signify a whole epistemology based on a holistic or systems view of the world.

Gaia has also taken on spiritual implications. After all, it was originally the name of a goddess. While in its modern usage it is generally not used to refer to or reinvoke that ancient Grecian deity, it is often used to suggest the existence of a world soul or spirit. I have attended Christian worship services where in a spirit of progressiveness and ecological correctness, the participants call upon the "spirit of Gaia" to heighten their awareness of their connections with the Earth. In such a context, Gaia is not used to refer to deity but, rather, to a kind of oversoul or purposeful planetary spiritual presence, like an archangel presiding over the well-being and wholeness of the world, or perhaps in a more psychological sense, as a collective awareness arising from all the lives, human and nonhuman, that make up our Earth.

So Gaia is used as an image to reimagine the nature of the Earth and of our relationship to it; it is also being used to reimagine the spiritual nature of our planet, since if it is a living being and possesses a soul or spirit of some kind, then we cannot view it simply as "dead matter." If there is a relationship God has to us as living beings, then that relationship also extends to and includes the Earth. If we may participate in sacredness, then so does the Earth, not simply as a valued and cherished environment but as a fellow creature. Furthermore, by virtue of being a *world*, a context that embraces and nourishes trillions of other lives and provides for their embodiment, the spiritual presence of the Earth may have qualities and capabilities exceeding our own. Again, it might be seen as a kind of archangel or guiding spirit implementing and fulfilling God's plan for the Earth.

However we view it, the image of Gaia as a living being is a powerful one filled with unexplored implications for reimagining ourselves, Earth, and spirit. What, though, are some of the pitfalls and potentials involved in using this particular image in this way?

I have already mentioned that the idea of a living Earth and of a world soul is an ancient one, one found in nearly every culture that has existed on Earth except (until now) our own. Gaia reinvokes this sensibility in our modern, materialistic, industrial culture. However, a reinvocation is not the same as a reincarnation. The sense of a living Earth enjoyed and practiced by earlier, nonindustrial cultures grew out of living experience and a closeness to nature that our culture has set aside. It was interwoven into the fabric of life and culture, and it was often part of a matriarchal perspective, or at least one that honored the feminine side of divinity. This is not true for us.

Furthermore, the Judeo-Christian tradition arises from the Semitic spiritual perspective of God and creation being separate and distinct, as well as from patriarchal social structures. In such a context, sacredness has overtones of authority, power, distance, and maleness that would have been alien to the spirituality of, for instance, the ancient Celts or the Native Americans, two cultures that incorporated a sense of the living Earth. This means that when we strive to imagine the sacredness of the Earth, we do so in a very different cultural context than did those who took for granted an immanent, accessible, sacred presence pervading all things.

Can we simply adopt and graft onto our culture their notion of a living, sacred Earth? I don't think so, at least not without distortion. We have to think deeply into and live out this idea in a modern context. Until we do, Gaia, the spirit of the living Earth, is an idea to think about rather than an idea to think with. It is a novelty rather than a tacit assumption, and as a spiritual idea it can be superficial. It lacks the overtones and undertones—the deeper connections with our everyday life and with the mysteries of creation—that is possessed in earlier cultures. As an idea, it becomes a suit to try on, rather than a body to inhabit and live through.

When we talk about the spirit of Gaia, the spirit of a living Earth, or even of the Earth as being alive, just what do we mean in our time? Do we even have the same sense of life—of what being an entity means—as did our ancestors? We are the products of a materialistic, technological, rational, male-oriented culture that over two hundred years ago set aside the medieval notions of the Great Chain of Being in which each and every life had a purpose, a place, and a meaning. The importance of the bottom line has made us forget that there is a

David Spangler

"top line" as well that gives the spiritual value—the holistic value—of a person, a plant, an animal, or a place. If at worst the bottom line represents how entities can be exploited and used for profit, the top line represents how entities can both empower and be empowered for the good of the whole.

It is this sense of the whole and of the individual as an expression of the whole that we do not have. We have a sense of incarnation but not of coincarnation, of the many ways in which the fabric of our identities are interwoven and interdependent in ways extending far beyond just the human milieu. Thus our definitions of life become very reductionist, individualized, and utilitarian. What, then, does it mean to us to speak of the Earth as a living being, not in a biological sense but in a metaphysical sense?

Accepting Gaia simply as a "return of the Goddess" or jumping on the bandwagon of a new planetary animism without thinking through the implications of just what Gaia might mean in our culture can lead to sentimentality rather than spirituality. We think we have made a spiritual breakthrough when in fact we are simply indulging in a kind of romantic fantasy that lacks the power truly to reorganize our lives and our society. To invoke the "spirit of Gaia" is no substitute for hard-edged, practical political, economic, and scientific work to redress the ecological imbalances currently endangering us. If the idea of Gaia is to inform, empower, and sustain our culture to make the hard choices and difficult changes necessary to secure our children's future, then it must be more than just a clever, sweet, or sentimental image.

I believe Gaia is an important spiritual idea for our time, but for it to fulfill its potential, we must remember that a spiritual idea is not something we think about but something that inhabits and shapes us. It is like a strand of DNA, organizing and energizing our lives. A spiritual idea is not just another bit of data to be filed away. It is incarnational rather than descriptive, coming alive only when incorporated (made flesh) in our lives through work, practice, effort, skill, and reflection. It becomes part of the foundation and the architecture of our lives. Being a new icon for worship is not enough. Invoking the spirit of Gaia is insufficient unless we understand just how we shape and participate in that spirit and in turn are shaped by it.

However, a deeper question is do we really need Gaia as a spiritual image? Do we need another spiritual source, another presence to invoke? If there is a true Spirit of the Earth, a Planetary Logos, is it hierarchically superior to humanity? That is, does it stand somewhere between ourselves and God? If so, we run the risk of interposing yet another image between ourselves and divinity. Or if the Earth is seen as sacred, just what does that mean? Why should the Earth be conceived of as sacred simply because it is alive? Do we extend the same privilege to other living things? Is life alone the criterion for sacredness? Or does something become sacred when it is living and powerful, big and capable of doing us either harm or good? Does Gaia become a substitute for God? What would such a substitution mean? Does it bring God closer to us, or does it further muddy the meaning and nature of God, making it yet more difficult to determine clearly just what the sacred is and what our relationship is to it?

These are important questions. There *is* a strong desire to affirm the sacredness of all life and of the Earth as a whole. However, the object of this exercise, it seems to me, is not to come up with new images of divinity but to affect behavior. What we really want is to relate to ourselves, to each other, and to the world as a whole as if we all have ultimate value apart from utilitarian considerations. If something is sacred, it is assumed to have value beyond its form, its usefulness, its duration, and its products. It is valuable and precious in and for itself. It is worthy of respect and honor, love and compassion; it is worth entering into communion with it. Its very being is its only justification; it needs no other.

As things stand, before we can manipulate or exploit something or someone, we must first devalue them, making them lower than ourselves. That which is sacred cannot be devalued, and by naming the Earth and all upon it as sacred, we seek to protect it and ourselves from ourselves. Perhaps, though, this is a form of psychological overkill. Can we not value something just for itself without needing to assign it a special place or condition in the universe? Can we not behave with love and respect for the environment for reasons other than that we come to consider it sacred? The implication is that we would then consider anything that is simply ordinary and not sacred to be fair game for whatever rapacious and manipulative desires we may choose to act upon—which, when you think about it, is a fair description of precisely how much of humanity does act.

By using the image of Gaia to give the Earth special status, we do not really deal with the question of our unwise and uncaring behavior. We are simply setting up a boundary within which we will be good, much as someone will act nicely on Sundays in church and act in a mean-spirited way the rest of the week. Surely, we are being called to a deeper reevaluation and reimagination of human behavior, one that transforms our attitudes and behavior toward each other and the world not because of a label but because it is right to do so.

Turning Gaia into a mythic or spiritual idea may be inappropriate or premature, leading both to misplaced concreteness and misplaced spirituality. On the other hand, Gaia can be an *inspirational* idea. Such an idea, to me, is like an enzyme. It is not important in itself except as it catalyzes a process. An enzyme is a means toward something else, a component of a larger emergence. In this context, Gaia would be an enzyme of consciousness, promoting and aiding a process of expanding our awareness in at least six areas important to our time.

The first of these is the most obvious. The idea of Gaia heightens our awareness of ecological and environmental necessities and responsibilities. It inspires us to translate theory and concern into practical strategies to preserve the environment and to meet ecological crises.

The second area of awareness follows on from this. Gaia shifts our operating paradigm from a mechanical one based on classical physics to an ecological one based on biology. It puts the phenomenon of life itself back into center stage in our culture. It inspires us toward a reformation that produces a culture that is truly life affirming and life centered.

David Spangler

Third, because the phenomenon of life as expressed through organisms and ecologies of organisms manifests more than the sum of its parts, it cannot be understood using solely analytical and reductionist techniques or modes of thought. Thus, Gaia represents an epistemology as well, a way of learning, seeing, and knowing. It inspires us to develop modes of thinking and acting that are holistic, systemic, symbiotic, connective, and participatory. We must learn to see the world in terms of patterns and not just positions and points, in terms of networks and lattices, not just centers and peripheries, in terms of processes, not just objects and things. We are encouraged to develop and practice an "ecology of mindfulness," to paraphrase anthropologist Gregory Bateson, as well as a mindful ecological practice. It inspires us to act toward each other as well as toward the environment in ways that serve and nourish the whole of which we are all participants, and in ways that are compassionate and cocreative, cooperative, and coincarnational.

Fourth, the image of Gaia *does* inspire us to think of the spirituality of the Earth and to explore an "eco-theology." Such a spirituality is important, for beyond ecology and conservation lies a deeper dimension of spiritual interaction and communion with our environment that is mutually important for ourselves and for nature. Within that dimension as well we will find new insights into the meaning of the divine that cannot help but aid us in the emergence of a healthy and whole planetary culture.

Fifth, religion is always defining the sacred in a way that creates boundaries, including some things and excluding others, and then finds itself trapped by its very boundaries. God must laugh at this, but for human beings it can have tragic circumstances, as witness the innumerable religious wars throughout history. A fundamentalist Christian once informed me with frightening sincerity that the only people who had souls, and thus could be considered human beings, were people who had been born again through believing in Jesus Christ. All other people were not human at all but soulless animals who, like all animals and plants and physical matter in general, lay outside God's love and concern and were destined for destruction anyway. So it did not matter what happened to them or what one did to them. They were here simply to be used by true Christians until the coming of the millennium.

Of course, this is an extreme and profoundly non-Christian and unbiblical view that should be rejected by any follower of the Nazarene. However, it is removed only in degree from the more mainstream Christian viewpoint that only humans have souls and that the nonhuman world is therefore of little spiritual consequence and can be used as we wish. In either case, the idea of the sacred is being used as a boundary to exclude some part of creation from having any ultimate value. By calling the Jews nonhuman, the Nazis justified the Holocaust. By regarding the nonhuman, natural world as outside the sacred community defined by a particular religious viewpoint, and therefore outside of moral consideration and subject only to the kind of utilitarian and economic judgments we reserve for objects, we are engaging in another kind of Holocaust. It is the natural world we are feeding into the ovens of overconsumption and technological arrogance. Only this time, because of the interrelatedness of the biosphere, we are all of us—human and nonhuman—becoming the new Jews, heading toward what philosopher and environmentalist Roger Gottlieb calls "Auschwitz Planet."

By expanding our boundaries of the sacred to include all the nonhuman cosmos, we give ourselves a much larger definition of God, a greater community of life in which to dwell, and a larger definition of ourselves as well, since part of how we define ourselves is influenced by how we define the sacred and our relationship to it. Given the comparative size of the human world to the immensity, diversity, and richness of the nonhuman cosmos, it is only the greatest of arrogance that seizes for ourselves the central role in a creation drama, relegating the rest of the universe to playing a supporting role or, at worst, being simply a backdrop for our struggles and adventures. Learning to see the sacredness of the Earth and the cosmos beyond may reintroduce into our culture some needed perspective and some creative humility, a word that itself comes from the same root word as *humus*, meaning "of the soil."

Finally, Gaia provides a mirror in which to see ourselves anew. It inspires us to reflect on our own natures, on the meaning and destiny of humanity. Lovelock paved the way for this in his book *Gaia*. In the last chapter, he suggested that humanity might be the evolving nervous system of the Earth, the means by which Gaia achieves self-awareness. At a time when our society seems motivated by no higher purpose than endless expansion and the making of money, and when humanity seems to have no purpose beyond itself, this image is striking and refreshing. It would seem to suggest a direction, a connection, a role that we can play in a world that is more than just the sum total of human desires.

This image of humanity as nervous system can be a helpful, guiding metaphor if we define the nervous system in a systemic and dynamic way. If by nervous system we mean the wiring that carries the sensations and thoughts of a larger being, then that is not a particularly participatory image, for it reduces humanity to being simply the instrumentality for the transmission and execution of the thoughts of the Earth.

However, if by nervous system we mean the whole system that governs, guides, and controls the organism through reception and integration of sensation and the transmission of thought, then such a nervous system is more than just wiring. As modern medicine and biochemistry increasingly show, the whole body is an integrated sensing and directing organism. Glands, hormones, blood, circulation, physical structure, and interrelationships between organs play as much a role in structuring and transmitting "thought" as does the nervous system itself. Thus, to be the "nervous system" of the Earth really means to be integrated with all the systems of the Earth, from wind and weather to tidal flows and the growth of plants, from the ecology of watersheds to the migration of birds and insects from one bioregion to another, and so on. It means *being* Gaia in a way that transcends and enlarges our humanity. Just what that really involves is what we have to discover, but surely it goes beyond accepting without reflection pat slogans about Gaia and the sacredness of the Earth.

The image of Gaia enlarges our vision of human purpose and activity beyond the personal and the local and puts it into a planetary and cosmic context. At the same time, the actions of Gaia are very local and specific, so that we are made more aware, not less, of our interactions with the particular places we inhabit. This is an important shift in our time.

Gaia *is* an important idea, both as a scientific hypothesis and as a spiritual image. I see it as a transitional idea. It is not so much a revelation in itself as a precursor to revelation or to new insights that can come when that idea is examined and lived with and given a chance to settle into our bones. Its meaning now lies in what it can inspire us to discover about ourselves and the nature of life, in rallying our energies to meet the needs of our environment, and through these processes of discovery and healing, to become a truly planetary species.

Gaia is not the only image we could use to reimagine our relationship to the Earth or to develop a new understanding of the spirituality of the Earth. Yet, however we perform this reimagination and whatever images we may come up with to guide us into the future, for an image truly to live for us so that it weaves into our everyday lives and guides our daily behavior, it cannot be simply imported or remembered. It cannot be grafted on from the outside or from the past. It must emerge from our own personal and cultural experiences of pain and joy in connection with the larger planetary environment. It must emerge from our own contemporary act of embodied imagination. It must emerge as our own act of collective learning that creates a new bond of community between ourselves and the natural order.

We cannot simply take up the mind-sets of our ancestors nor wear their myths as if we have not changed in the interim between their world and time and ours. We cannot *assume* the sacredness nor spiritual livingness of the Earth or accept it as a new ideology or as a sentimentally pleasing idea. We must experience that life and sacredness, if it is there, in relationship to our own and to that ultimate mystery we call God. We must experience it in our lives, in our practice, in the flesh of our cultural creativity. We must allow it to shape us, as great spiritual ideas have always shaped those who invite them in. We must not expect that we can simply use these new images, such as the image of Gaia, to meet emotional, religious, political, or even commercial needs without allowing them to transform us in unexpected and radical ways. The spirituality of the Earth is more than a slogan. It is an invitation to initiation, to the death of what we have been and the birth of something new.

"NOW THAT ANIMALS CAN BE GENETICALLY ENGINEERED: BIOTECHNOLOGY IN THEOLOGICAL-ETHICAL PERSPECTIVE"

Dieter T. Hessel

This essay presents some theological and ethical considerations, grounded in Christian faith, that ought to inform assessments of what is and is not appropriate in applied biotechnics, particularly involving "transgenic" animals. Geneticists and entrepreneurs are now teaming up—often at public expense—to engineer "better" or more "useful" animals. The process of introducing exogenous DNA into the genome of species, a technique already used extensively in plant genetics, has been refined for application higher in the chain of being. This technology involves gene transfers between different kinds of living creatures to make new ones. Experimentation with this startling technology has already become global in scope. A skilled staff with about US$50,000 worth of equipment can engineer transgenic animals by introducing foreign characteristics into the genotype of a creature to produce particular traits that an animal would not otherwise have. Where will it go, or stop? What is a sound ethical and policy framework for animal biotechnics?[1]

I am reflecting on the transgenic alteration of animals to "enhance" food production, to simplify sport fishing or to manufacture new pharmaceutical products. Some examples are super milk-producing cows, physiologically boosted by bovine growth hormone (somatotropin); arthritis-ridden Beltsville pigs engineered by the US Food and Drug Administration with cattle growth-hormone genes to provide leaner and more "cost-effective" pork;[2] and transgenic carp, trout or salmon ("designer fish"), fashioned for economic or recreational purposes. Animals are also being altered with human genes to supply blood plasma and, soon, organs. "Like the recombinant DNA technology that preceded it, uses of transgenic organisms are probably unbounded in potential application."[3]

Animal biotechnology began with mouse-engineering for medical research. Highly publi-

---

Reprinted with permission from *Theology and Public Policy*, Vol V, No. 1, 1993, pages 284–99.

cized examples include Onco-mouse (the first patent-protected, genetically altered mammal, engineered with a human gene to express cancer in its mammary tissue), Alzheimer's mouse and Memory mouse. Such transgenic mice have functioned as models for gene research into debilitating or terminal illnesses. Subsequent genetic interventions with humans, however, are not transgenic in themselves, because a gene from another species is not being put into a human being. Humans may be trying to receive organs from primates, but we are not yet putting animal genes into humans!

More ambitious efforts to create new animals by mixing together the genes of different species are occurring willy-nilly with potentially far-reaching effects discerned only dimly by the initiators. Even the few scholars who discuss the ethics and policies that ought to guide such activity seem unduly influenced by short-term economic calculations. For example, Charles McCarthy of the Kennedy Institute, Georgetown University, writes: "In a utilitarian context, efficiency in food production and ability to compete for world markets stand as high values which must be weighed against our recognized obligation to provide for the interests of the animals."[4] Thus, the larger eco-social good becomes blurred.

TAKING A HOLISTIC VIEW

Molecular biologists, geneticists and scholars in other fields who know about ventures in animal biotechnics differ on philosophical-ethical meanings. Genetic researchers play down the qualitative difference between transgenic manipulation of complex, sentient animals and other gene research, while environmental philosophers and social scientists often emphasize it. But they agree that animal research and production of this kind is likely to intensify and have widening applications in an arena with unclear ecological and social boundaries.[5]

Meanwhile, the world is entering a very different, more crowded future, which demands a different vision and way of life—"eco-just community," I would call it—involving caring and just human relationships, institutional as well as individual, with culturally diverse groups of people and myriad other species. Therefore, the opening sentence of this essay deliberately used the word "appropriate" as a religiously resonant modifier that is both theologically grounded and ethically relevant.

Among twentieth-century Protestant theologians, H. Richard Niebuhr and his prime interpreter James Gustafson have concentrated on fostering an ethic of the "fitting" or "appropriate." In *Ethics from a Theocentric Perspective*, Gustafson gives considerable attention to God's "ordering work" in the created ecological matrix of life. In that frame of reference, Gustafson asks and answers the basic ethical question, What is God enabling and requiring us, as participants in the patterns and processes of interdependent life, to be and do?, and then answers it: We are to relate to all others in a manner appropriate to their relations to

God. When ethics has theocentric grounding, ethical decisions are guided normatively by awareness of God's activity in the world. Particularly as we perceive God to be deeply involved in life's natural and social ecology, enabling right relations therein, our thinking and acting are likely to become more earth-fitting.[6]

Assessing what is "appropriate" or "fitting" is also an important consideration in any ecologically and socially alert ethical critique of modern technological activity. To focus on appropriate activity pushes the conversation towards cultural integrity and public accountability, while expressing realism about the moral ambiguities that continually confront us. In using the term "appropriate activity," I mean to emphasize a moral ecology of values that have environmental and social content similar to the meanings E. F. Schumacher gave to "intermediate" or "appropriate technology." Schumacher's seminal work *Small Is Beautiful* included a somewhat tongue-in-cheek chapter on "Buddhist Economics," to remind us that religious sensibilities matter, along with the sciences, in weighing particular research and development options.[7]

As a Christian theological and social ethicist, I am using the categories of that historic living faith, seeking to discern what it has to offer, in conversation with contemporary modes of thought, as guidance for biotechnical decision-making.

THEOLOGICAL INSIGHTS

Faith affirms spirit, God's loving presence, in nature. Creation—the whole community of being, animated by divine Spirit—is the context of reality. All of the earth community matters, and has intrinsic value, to the one who continues to create, sustain and redeem the whole. God is actively present throughout the creation, generating and sustaining life, reconciling varied forms of being. God has a continuing role as creator-sustainer and expects human creatures to be respectful co-operators.

Ecologically aware "theologizing" about creation challenges modern atomistic individualism, which projects a self-contained God, humanity over nature and a mechanistic view of other being.[8] God is inherently related to the world, indwelling eco-social systems, breathing spirit into all creatures. Theology with this awareness knows that ecosystems—and similarly social systems—are inherently interconnected communities, with reverberations in all entities related therein. "When relations are conceived as inherent . . . justice is a matter of the quality of relationships . . . characterized by freedom, participation and solidarity . . . All entities have a right to be respected appropriate to their degree of intrinsic value and to their importance to the possibility of value in others."[9] This is not radical egalitarianism; different kinds of creatures still have differentiated value.

God is directly related to and cares for other creatures. Otherkind in the first creation saga (Gen. 1) are directly related to God and created to enjoy existence, not simply to function ecologically as a structured community of feeding levels or merely as a resource for

Dieter T. Hessel

humans to harvest, exploit and enjoy on a basis that is deemed to be "sustainable." (It is important to recognize that the word "sustainable" can mean one thing to technologists, quite another to ecologists.) In the second, older biblical creation saga (Gen. 2), the creatures are understood to have both intrinsic and extrinsic or instrumental value. Human earth creatures have community with other species, who are intended to be companions and helpers (Gen. 2:18). At the same time, God grants humans the power to name the creatures and utilize animals for human benefit (Gen. 3:21). "But the resource view, unconstrained by appropriate respect for the full spectrum of animal values, is inadequate for forming a mature Christian environmental ethic."[10]

The society of created being mediates the glory of God to humans and mourns unjust treatment by humanity. Theology with this passionate sensibility discerns that spirited, many-splendored nature bears grace and points to divine power. The diversity of creatures, the grandeur of places and the forces of wind and water deserve human respect and admiration (cf. Job 39–41).

Theology with this sensibility also understands the reign of God, anticipated by the prophets and inaugurated by Jesus, to be "the society for all under God's reign."[11] Thus, biblical "peace pictures" project human harmony with other creatures. We would not be human without them. Without healthy biodiversity, human culture shrivels; without the glories of nature, sacred rituals or vital poems become museum pieces.

God is present in and with a dynamically open, astoundingly biodiverse and coherently indeterminate creation. In process thought as well as biblical theology, it is the divine nature as creative Spirit to love a world with fecund creaturely dignity in organic relation to God. When process thought is linked with biblical memory, it emphasizes God's transcendent immanence as Power of being, creating and sustaining life, Shaper of time in natural and social history and Purpose for good through it all.[12]

Instead of perpetuating a monarchical model of the God-world relation (or a derivative secularism that transfers godlike power to humans), theology informed by process thought features an organic model in which "God not only affects the world but is affected by it . . . The world is understood as organic to God, not as a mere product of God's will. This means also that the world cannot be conceived in narrowly anthropocentric terms, as if it were provided solely for [humanity's] exploitation."[13]

Christology also needs "recycling" in this regard—to clarify what the second person of the Trinity does in and for the non-human creation. In the creeds, Jesus is understood to be the incarnate Word of God, the logos of life and reason from earth's beginning to end. Why should this work of Christ be seen exclusively in terms of human benefit? The prologue of John views the logos as involved in the whole of God's creative activity:

> Nothing has come into being apart from it. [The Word] is found in life, and all creaturely life participates in it . . . A definite difference is asserted between the way that the Word is present

in Jesus and the way it is present in other human beings. The light that enlightens all human beings becomes flesh in Jesus. But despite the difference, there is also continuity. For the light to enlighten all people means that it is somehow present with, to, or in all ... The life is the light. Perhaps the best understanding is to think of the presence of the Word as enlivening all living things and at the same time enlightening all that are capable of being enlightened. In summary, the Word is immanent in the whole of creation with differentiated results.[14]

God covenants with human beings to establish a pattern of right relations within the community of creation. The purpose of this ecumenical and ecological covenant is to secure the well-being of all, "shalom":

> Peace and justice are constitutive elements of the world as created ... Violation of the covenant is an attack upon the created order of the world and is rebellion against God. Faithlessness harms the exploiter as well as the exploited. The symbiotic nature of creation means, therefore, that all action has a boomerang effect, going out towards goals intended but turning back upon the agent originating the action.[15]

Covenant ethics emphasizes human behavior that is faithfully fitting:

> In one sense fittingness underscores the importance of particularity—responding to particular persons, situations and issues. In a larger sense, fittingness requires taking account of the encompassing context of the social and natural environment, so that what is done fits in with everything else that is happening and avoids causing more problems than it solves.[16]

The covenant contains promises and expectations that encompass the land and its creatures. Land is to be rested and needs of otherkind are to be respected in order to enhance regeneration of life. Within this religious-moral view, domesticated animals are not to be abused but to be treated justly by humans who husband and utilize them (Prov. 12:10; Ex. 20:10; Luke 14:5; Deut. 25:4). These animals do have instrumental value, though not that alone. They are to be humanely managed, but not merely for human convenience.

Humans are accountable for the well-being of all. The primary human vocation is to care for creation with love that seeks justice, consistent with the divine purpose. If justice is love distributed, then what is the character and purview of Christian love? When considering biotechnics as a particular eco-social challenge, it is important to emphasize that love expresses other-esteem.[17] "Love does not insist on its own way" (1 Cor. 13:5). It seeks the well-being of other people and otherkind, empathizing to the point that "if one member suffers, all suffer together with it; if one member is honored, all rejoice together with it" (12:26):

> Other-esteem respects the integrity of wild nature—its diversity, relationality, complexity, ambiguity and even prodigality. It is quite content to let the natural world work out its own adaptations and interactions without benefit of human interventions, except insofar as necessary to remedy human harm to nature's integrity and to satisfy vital human interests.[18]

The normative human role is that of earthkeeper or household manager (*oikonomos*), to be exercised with loving intent and appropriate humility. This involves humans in the processes of continuing creation, resisting injustice, overcoming brokenness, restoring health and offering praise for what is good. Such a theological understanding of vocation contrasts sharply with the agenda of modernity which, baldly stated by Francis Bacon, was "to establish and extend the power and dominion of the human race itself over the universe." Bacon viewed the control of nature as the *telos* and test of knowledge; and his 1622 work, *The New Atlantis,* portrayed a biological utopia, organized as a patriarchal, hierarchical society whose priests were scientists. His project assumed the subordination of women along with nature.[19]

Bacon fostered a research paradigm, which is still accepted today, that "there are no unalterable properties of animals or plants."[20] Following Bacon's lead, modern humans have "disenchanted the world," discarding their appropriate vocation in favor of an ambitious project of life-mastery, an historical project based on the arrogant belief that nature exists for us, that we are the artisans of a new world for our benefit and that autonomous human power and purpose will reshape nature, society, psyches and now bodies for the better. Its illusory hope is progress and perfection, not preservation and prevention.[21]

Four centuries later, theological and philosophical ethics converge, with varied sensibilities, to face the environmental consequences of Bacon's paradigm. In this new situation of worldwide eco-injustice, we must reconsider. How do humans who can manipulate the genetic code appropriately express care for the well-being of life on earth? As "limited interventions" occur in ecological systems and in plant or animal life, what is the shape of human responsibility and of healthy culture?

The Genesis themes of dominion and stewardship must be recast. As interpreted by moderns, these doctrines have become part of the problem. Their interpretation in existentialist and utilitarian modes justified risky human activity in technology and politics. "Dare to use this power!" was the moral message. Anyone who questioned the wisdom of plunging ahead had to prove its harm. Today, a continuing emphasis on venturing and remaking is problematic, considering its eco-social effects. Protection and preservation take on more ethical import.

Environmental philosopher J. Baird Callicott has reappropriated themes and images from the sagas of Genesis as a guide for citizenship in the world garden. Callicott urges a re-reading of Genesis in light of John Muir's striking interpretation of "citizenship."[22] Muir's earliest journal, *A Thousand Mile Walk to the Gulf,* "argues for human citizenship in nature squarely on biblical principles", thoroughly discrediting popular anthropocentrism:

> Now it never seems to occur to these far-seeing teachers that Nature's object in making animals and plants might possibly be first of all the happiness of each one of them, not the creation of all for the happiness of one. Why should man value himself as more than a small part of the one great unit of creation? And what creature of all that the Lord has taken the pains to

make is not essential to the completeness of that unit—the cosmos? The universe would be incomplete without man; but it would also be incomplete without the smallest transmicroscopic creature that dwells beyond our conceitful eyes and knowledge.[23]

Callicott observes that Muir seemed to mix his worldviews intentionally, reinterpreting Genesis in light of modern science (and, I would add, social experience). Muir goes into the specifics of the Genesis account to emphasize that other creatures deserve great human respect:

> They, also, are God's children, for [God] hears their cries, cares for them tenderly and provides their daily bread ... How narrow we selfish, conceited creatures are in our sympathies! How blind to the right of all the rest of creation! ... They are part of God's family, unfallen, undepraved and cared for with the same species of tenderness and love as is bestowed on angels in heaven and saints on earth.[24]

Muir emphasizes that we share a common lot—being good citizens—with other creatures, rather than pretending to share God's transcendence over creation. In that light, we should not bifurcate human interests from the interests of the rest of creation. His citizenship ethic connects well with some Christian theological rethinking that is responsive to the environmental challenge. Consider these words by H. Paul Santmire:

> Given the ecological paradigm, the image of God as the one who elicits all things and the vision of nature as communities of beings with their own integrity, it is fitting to think of the human creature no longer as *homo faber* [the "maker"], but as *homo cooperans* [the co-operator] ... The vision of humanity as *homo cooperans* is much more in tune with the biblical vision of shalom than is the popular image of human dominion.[25]

Human activity affects the future of earth community, even though the planet's destiny is God's responsibility. On the one hand, the creation is being threatened with disintegration because of human sin and injustice, which result in oppression of both people and nature. We experience collective consequences that are understood biblically in terms of divine judgment and sorrow. In the language of Lamentations, creation suffers, the creator mourns and the people lament. Or in the words of the Apostle Paul, "creation groans in travail." On the other hand, earth community is dynamic, unfinished, expectant of new creation. One might render Romans 8:20–21: The futility or emptiness to which the created order is now subject is not something intrinsic to it. ... Creation has something better to look forward to—namely, to be freed from its present enslavement to disintegration ... to share in freedom and goodness.

In light of this eschatology, what ought we to expect of human activity in the biosphere as a whole and through biotechnics particularly? Are we to build a wondrous ecological and social future based on biotechnical achievements? Does "gentech" promise another step in evolution where new processes of production can harmonize with, even enhance, natural processes? Or is this an idolatrous stage of "animal slavery,"[26] ecological disruption, social dislocation?

Dieter T. Hessel

There are enthusiastic advocates of this new industry who envision a techno-millennium—a new era of joy, serenity, prosperity, and peace to be brought on through applied biotechnics. Francis Bacon has no shortage of followers in the scientific priesthood that would preside over this new age, filled with the same millennial hope that has fuelled numerous illusory projects in history. Technology, however, presents threat as well as promise. Eco-social dangers must be explored precisely because new things of ambiguous character and effect will be done by innately restless humans applying ingenuity, wisely or not, in this field.

ETHICAL IMPERATIVES

1. Shift to a more appropriate eco-social paradigm.

Christian theology does not provide neat "answers" to the biotechnology question. But sound theology helps to illumine crucial ethical dilemmas by articulating a realistic and hopeful vision, in light of which we perceive the emerging future to be constraining and promising at the same time. Not only do we face sobering, forced options, resulting from deadly patterns of culture and economic life that rapidly deplete common resources and overshoot humanity's appropriate ecological and social limits. We also see better possibilities coming towards us, or an alternative path to the near future. The future invites us to a more appropriate (faithful and fitting) way of being human in the community of creation.

In this regard, it is important to ponder the significance of laws that allow for the parenting of genetically engineered animals, which proved to be a major barrier to a biodiversity treaty at UNCED in June 1992. "The US government has led the commercial drive to exploit the genetic commons," writes Jeremy Rifkin. Beginning in the 1930s Congress allowed the patenting of selected plant varieties. In 1980 the Supreme Court voted 5 to 4 to allow patenting of a microorganism that was genetically engineered by General Electric to eat up oil spills:

> Seven years later, the US Patent Office extended the Supreme Court ruling to the entire living kingdom, arguing that any genetically engineered animal may be patented. For example, under the agency rule, if a human gene is inserted into the genetic code of a pig, both the process and the animal are patentable, the only test of patentability being novel intervention. In one regulatory stroke, the US Patent Office moved to enclose the entire genetic pool, from mice to primates. The Patent Office decision came down with only one disclaimer, excluding genetically engineered human beings from the patent laws because the Thirteenth Amendment to the Constitution forbids human slavery.[27]

2. Anticipate the social impacts of research and development, as well as effects on animals and the environment—all the more so as human power to destroy or reshape nature intensifies, affecting animal, plant and human life together.

Allan S. Miller, an ethicist in conservation and resource studies at the University of California, Berkeley, contends:

> The real issue [posed by recombinant research] is not between Frankenstein and Einstein—between evil science and good science—but between those who hope to use the new science and technology in an appropriate fashion (to actually help those in the world who are most needful of good people-oriented science) and those who will focus on providing high-cost services to the already over-privileged of the world's population in order to maximize market returns. . . If within a decade or two, aspects of the life process continue to become the private property of big business—as happens now when new organisms are patented and become simply additional possessions of great corporations—the ordinary people of the world will inevitably end up as losers.[28]

Miller, like Barry Commoner, locates much of the difficulty in the organization of science, not merely in the attitudes of individual practitioners. He notes that the biotech industry has become a potent lobby for deregulated laboratory research and field testing of genetically altered organisms, and it propagandizes the public with assurances of benign activity that promises positive results.

The "Gene Revolution" is even more threatening to small farmers than was the "Green Revolution," according to Miller. The Green Revolution was based in the public sector with a humanitarian intent. Still, it favoured energy- and capital-intensive agribusiness, leading to export cropping at the expense of small farmers and to less local food sufficiency in poor communities. The gene revolution, while grounded in tax-supported research, is even more tightly tied to private-sector enterprise and may have wider eco-social consequences in pursuing its life-altering agenda.[29]

We are back to the same dialectic of human behaviour that led Reinhold Niebuhr in 1937 to caution against naive and mistaken confidence in science and technology, without taking account of the destructive as well as the creative potential of human power and freedom. He saw the beneficial effects of various technical developments. Yet, "science can sharpen the fangs of ferocity as much as it can alleviate human pain," for "intelligence merely raises all the potencies of life, both good and evil."[30] Scientific and technological power over nature tempts humans to ignore creatureliness and seek the status of ultimacy. That "offends not only against God, who is the center and source of existence, but against other life which has a rightful place in the harmony of the whole . . . [Technological power exerted by humans] to protect themselves against other life, tempts them to destroy and oppress other life."[31]

3. Assess biotechnics qualitatively.

The qualitative character of biotechnics, not only its pace or scale, should be faced directly. While its environmental risks and negative social consequences should not be exaggerated, genetic engineering does raise serious questions about the legitimate uses of human power over plants and animals.

Are nonhuman species just reconstructible "machines" or items of DNA to be reprogrammed? Christian ethicist James A. Nash argues to the contrary that otherkind are in some sense subjects with intrinsic value. So humans intervening in nature in this qualitatively different way must ask:

> What are the limits? What alternatives are available and satisfactory? Should natural species' barriers be honored, so that nonhuman species can propagate their own kind in perpetuity and not some genetically altered kind? Since members of other species cannot be informed or give informed consent, what justifications are necessary for genetic alterations, and who should function as advocates for their interests? These are among the key questions that ecological ethics should direct to the new biological technology.

Nash recognizes that answers depend on worldview and value assumptions. His own position is that the creation of transgenic species is "not the norm but the rare exception on which the burden of proof rests. The genetic reconstruction of some species may be justified for compelling human needs in medicine, agriculture or ecological repairs (e.g., oil-eating microbes), so long as it can be reasonably tested and verified that tolerable alternatives are not available, genetic diversity is not compromised and ecosystemic integrity is not endangered."[32]

4. Establish criteria for eco-just biotechnics.

The preceding paragraphs suggest that something analogous to "just war" criteria are needed to guide biotechnical efforts to manipulate animals. Such ethical criteria would put the burden of proof on those who would intervene drastically in nature to alter species or to proceed in ways that place ecosystems at risk. What is the intention? Are these procedures necessary? Have conventional means that may actually be more appropriate been ignored or exhausted? Are discriminating limits to such intervention articulated and agreed to? Are the means disproportionate to the ends which are being achieved? What are the possible ecological and social dangers and likely effects? How will human and otherkind populations be protected? Who will benefit and who or what will lose (or what is the expected pattern of justice or injustice)? What is likely to be accomplished? How will a particular transgenic biological intervention contribute to a new state of peace, including just distribution of or fair participation in the social power and economic wealth derived from it?

Theological ethics of eco-justice and philosophical environmental ethics flow together in considering criteria of just human intervention in animal life and appropriate developments following from it. This way of thinking can be refined further by exploring the ends being sought, proportional effects of animal use and available alternatives, drawing on experience in discussions of the ethics of animal research. Thus, Strachan Donnelly writes:

Are there experiments, no matter how worthy the theoretical or practical ends, that are simply inadmissible due to the decided violation of our moral sensibilities, not to mention the extreme harm done to animals? Is the use of animal, sentient life, with its attendant harms in suffering and death, necessary to achieve the particular scientific goal? Underlying this question is the possible replacement of a proposed use of animals by other means of research, e.g., computer models and cell cultures . . . [And there are] "alternatives" to animal use, the three R's: *replacement,* substitution of insentient material for conscious living animals; *reduction* in the number of animals used to gain information of a given amount and precision; and *refinement,* decrease in the incidence or severity of inhumane procedures applied to animals still used.[33]

5. Implement a standard of "appropriateness."

These considerations are more than prudential or utilitarian. They involve principles of respect and care for otherkind. What is the value assigned to the integrity of created nature and of species that have evolved over millennia? Keep in mind that human knowledge of speciation is barely a hundred years old and is still quite fragmentary. How much do scientists who are active in the gene revolution really know about the ecological reverberations of their manipulations? The questions involve more than what may be hazardous in the sense of environmentally toxic or ecologically disastrous. Efforts to contain biotechnology by pointing to environmental dangers as such have had little effect on the pursuit of such research and development.[34]

There may be "no straightforward, unambiguous and single ethical guideline for assessing each and every use of animals" in biological science, animal husbandry, agriculture, pharmaceutical development, etc. But there is a "moral ecology," ethical obligations to discern contextually and operationally in research and development. Thus, Krimsky argues that

each judgment should be guided by the same general goal: the promotion of the overall good (human, animal and organic) at the least or ethically tolerable overall cost. The underlying assumption is that the human, animal and organic good ought not to be pursued independently of each other. Finally the human good should exist and flourish only within the wider animal and organic good, since all living beings are inextricably linked together within a single evolutionary and ecological context.[35]

WHAT ECO-SOCIAL FUTURE?

We have now come to the most profound ethical concern raised by nonhuman biotechnology: towards what eco-social future does it move? This question looms large because many of the scientists and corporations now collaborating in industrial biotechnology apparently do not acknowledge the principle of an ecological or organic good that must not be violated, but only a principle of "reasonableness" to be observed in biotechnics—for example: "Attendant on the freedom to undertake research into the exciting and fertile frontiers of the New Biology is a coexistent responsibility to pursue the work in a reasonable, rational manner."[36]

In contrast to this morally empty standard of reasonableness, I recommend a standard of appropriateness, or what is "fitting." It has a religious-philosophical referent, and fosters ecological sensibility, constructive social purpose, appreciation for responsible scientific inquiry and realism about human misuse of power. It is not a rigid standard, recognizing that decisions about biotechnology must be contextual. At the same time, it would not leave decisions to researchers and investors doing as they alone see fit.

The standard of appropriateness underscores the need to institutionalize prospective assessment of all biotechnical innovations, and to monitor this work for ecological safety and its contribution to meeting basic social problems, including malnutrition, disease, environmental degradation, lack of inexpensive and clean energy, expensive health care. Krimsky suggests that a broader system of social guidance is needed. He recommends a system that is able "to reinforce those innovations that meet important social needs and to provide selective negative pressures against unneeded or unwanted innovations."[37] This is consistent with the dialectical view that scientific-technical research demands freedom of enquiry, along with clear understandings of ethical constraints and democratically determined social guidance of its directions and uses.[38]

Otherwise, genetic engineering will continue as a

> growth-oriented technical thrust towards redesigning the gene pool to serve economic criteria ... Natural selection is giving way more and more to economic selection as the directive force of evolution ... Economically directed evolution is biological and ecological central planning! It is a sin against free competition, and an arrogant presumption that we possess knowledge that we do not have ... How far are we justified in rearranging the foundations of creation to better serve our own purposes? That depends on how closely our purposes mirror the creation's purposes.[39]

An adequate social policy with regard to animal biotechnology encompasses ecological integrity and social justice together. It approaches decisions in the larger framework of creation community and fair social participation. The mechanisms of social guidance need to embody a just-intervention ethic with an eco-justice orientation. "Appropriate technology" has a combination of characteristics that move in such a direction—namely, it is relatively simple, locally controlled, environmentally compatible, intermediate in scale, labor-intensive and alert to external and long-term impacts.[40]

Attention to eco-socially appropriate technology does not rule out biotechnics; it asks for deeper ethical reflection, alert to intuitive religious sensibilities about what is good and right, and for more democratic social involvement to limit or channel this qualitatively different human activity for the good of all.

Dieter T. Hessel   631

NOTES

1. For an overview of the origins and cultural significance of the genetics revolution, cf. Sheldon Krimsky, *Biotechnics and Society: The Rise of Industrial Genetics,* New York: Praeger, 1991, ch. 1.

2. *Ibid.,* p.55; cf. George Smith, *The New Biology: Law, Ethics, and Biotechnology,* New York: Plenum Press, 1989, p. 8, who views this event as a pivotal controversy. The Foundation for Economic Trends, together with the Humane Society, took unsuccessful legal action to stop this activity, claiming that "research of this nature not only was cruel and violated animal dignities, but would also have significant social and economic repercussions, in that more expensive animals would in turn cause severe market dislocations in the farm economy."

3. Rivers Singleton, Jr., "Transgenic Organisms, Science, and Society" (draft paper for the Animal Biotechnology Project, Hastings Center).

4. "Toward Development of a Sound Public Policy Concerning Transgenic Animals" (draft paper for Animal Biotechnology Project, Hastings Center), p. 6.

5. For further background, see "The Brave New World of Animal Biotechnology: An Ethical Analysis," special supplement to the *Hastings Center Report,* 1993.

6. James Gustafson, *Ethics from a Theocentric Perspective,* Chicago: Univ. of Chicago Press, 1984, Vol. II, pp. 2, 275, 279. I wish Gustafon had pursued this basic ethical question in a more trinitarian way. Moreover, because of his preoccupation with establishing the positive role of science in mature theological and ethical discourse, he does not offer here a sharp critique of science and technology except in terms of distributive justice.

7. For a useful summary of appropriate technology, see the concluding chapter of Ian G. Barbour, *Technology, Environment, and Human Values,* New York, Praeger, 1980.

8. Jay McDaniel, "Christianity and the Need for New Vision." in *Religion and the Environmental Crisis,* ed. Eugene C. Hargrove, Athens: University of Georgia Press, 1986, pp. 189, 204.

9. Carol Johnston, "Economics, Eco-Justice and the Doctrine of God", in *After Nature's Revolt: Eco-Justice and Theology,* ed. Dieter Hessel, Minneapolis: Fortress Press, 1992, pp.158,161–62.

10. Holmes Rolston III, "Wildlife and Wildlands: A Christian Response," in *ibid.,* p.134.

11. Daniel Day Williams, "Changing Concepts of Nature", in *Earth Might be Fair: Reflections on Ethics, Religion, and Ecology,* ed. Ian G. Barbour, Englewood Cliffs, NJ: Prentice-Hall, 1972.

12. *Ibid.,* pp. 58–61.

13. John Macquarrie, "Creation and Environment", in *Ecology and Religion in History,* eds. David and Eileen Spring, New York: Harper & Row, 1974, pp. 45–46.

14. John B. Cobb, Jr., "On Christ and Animals" (unpublished paper), pp. 4–5.

15. Charles S. McCoy, "Creation and Covenant: A Comprehensive Vision for Environmental Ethics," in *Covenant for a New Creation: Ethics, Religion and Public Policy,* eds. Carol Robb and Carl Casebolt, Maryknoll, NY: Orbis Books, 1991, pp. 215–16.

16. *Ibid.,* p.225.

17. Cf. James A. Nash, *Loving Nature: Ecological Integrity and Christian Responsibility,* Nashville: Abingdon, 1991, p. 153.

18. *Ibid.,* p. 154.

19. Cf. Carolyn Merchant, *The Death of Nature: Women, Ecology and the Scientific Revolution,* San Francisco: Harper & Row, 1980.

20. Krimsky, *op. cit.,* p. 85.

21. For an eloquent critique of the Baconian ideal, see Hans Jonas, *The Imperative of Responsibility: In Search of an Ethics for a Technological Age*, Chicago: Univ. of Chicago Press, 1984, ch. 5.

22. Callicott, "Genesis and John Muir," in Robb and Casebolt, *op. cit.*, pp.107–40.

23. John Muir, *A Thousand Mile Walk to the Gulf*, ed. by Wm. F. Frederick Bade, New York: Houghton Mifflin, 1916, p.139.

24. *Ibid.*, pp. 98–99,139.

25. H. Paul Santmire, "Healing the Protestant Mind," in Hessel, *op. cit.*, pp. 74–75.

26. Cf. Krimsky, *op. cit.*, p.84; Andrew Linzey, "Human and Animal Slavery: A Theological Critique of Genetic Engineering," in *The Bio-Revolution: Cornucopia or Pandora's Box*, London: Pluto Press, 1990, p.182.

27. Jeremy Rifkin, *Biosphere Politics*, New York: Crown Publishers, 1991, p. 70; cf. Krimsky, *op. cit.*, ch. 3.

28. Alan S. Miller, "Science for People or Science for Profit?" in Robb and Casebolt, *op. cit.*, p. 63.

29. *Ibid.*, pp. 69, 74, 76.

30. Reinhold Niebuhr, *Beyond Tragedy*, New York: Scribners, 1937, pp.125–26.

31. *Ibid.*, pp.102–3.

32. James Nash, *op. cit.*, pp. 61–62; cf. p. 211.

33. Strachan Donnelley, "Animals in Science: the Justification Issue," Special Supplement to the *Hastings Center Report*, May–June 1990; cf. W. M. S. Russell and R. L. Burch, *The Principles of Humane Experimental Techniques*, London: Methuen, 1959.

34. See Krimsky, *op. cit.*, ch. 6.

35. *Ibid.*, p.11.

36. George Smith, *op. cit.*, pp. 26–27.

37. Krimsky, *op. cit.*, ch. 11, and pp. 207f.

38. Roger Shinn, *Forced Options: Social Decisions for the 21st Century*, Cleveland: Pilgrim Press, 1991, ch. 9.

39. Herman E. Daly and John B. Cobb, Jr., *For the Common Good: Redirecting the Economy toward Community, the Environment and a Sustainable Future*, Boston: Beacon Press, 1989, pp. 204–6.

40. Barbour, *op. cit.*, pp. 294–99.

"PRINCIPLES OF ENVIRONMENTAL JUSTICE"

The First National People of Color Environmental Leadership Summit

PREAMBLE

We the people of color, gathered together at this multinational People of Color Environmental Leadership Summit, to begin to build a national and international movement of all peoples of color to fight the destruction and taking of our lands and communities, do hereby re-establish our spiritual interdependence to the sacredness of our Mother Earth; to respect and celebrate each of our cultures, languages and beliefs about the natural world and our roles in healing ourselves; to insure environmental justice; to promote economic alternatives which would contribute to the development of environmentally safe livelihoods; and to secure our political, economic and cultural liberation that has been denied for over 500 years of colonization and oppression, resulting in the poisoning of our communities and land and the genocide of our peoples, do affirm and adopt these Principles of Environmental Justice:

1. Environmental justice affirms the sacredness of Mother Earth, ecological unity and the interdependence of all species, and the right to be free from ecological destruction.

2. Environmental justice demands that public policy be based on mutual respect and justice for all peoples, free from any form of discrimination or bias.

3. Environmental justice mandates the right to ethical, balanced and responsible uses of land and renewable resources in the interest of a sustainable planet for humans and other living things.

4. Environmental justice calls for universal protection from nuclear testing, extraction, production and disposal of toxic/hazardous wastes and poisons and nuclear testing that threaten the fundamental right to clean air, land, water, and food.

5. Environmental justice affirms the fundamental right to political, economic, cultural and environmental self-determination of all peoples.

6. Environmental justice demands the cessation of the production of all toxins, hazardous

---

From The First National People of Color Environmental Leadership Summit, June 1991.

wastes, and radioactive materials, and that all past and current producers be held strictly accountable to the people for detoxification and the containment at the point of production.

7. Environmental justice demands the right to participate as equal partners at every level of decision-making including needs assessment, planning, implementation, enforcement and evaluation.

8. Environmental justice affirms the right of all workers to a safe and healthy work environment, without being forced to choose between an unsafe livelihood and unemployment. It also affirms the right of those who work at home to be free from environmental hazards.

9. Environmental justice protects the right of victims of environmental injustice to receive full compensation and reparations for damages as well as quality health care.

10. Environmental justice considers governmental acts of environmental injustice a violation of international law, the Universal Declaration On Human Rights, and the United Nations Convention on Genocide.

11. Environmental justice must recognize a special legal and natural relationship of Native Peoples to the U.S. government through treaties, agreements, compacts, and covenants affirming sovereignty and self-determination.

12. Environmental justice affirms the need for urban and rural ecological policies to clean up and rebuild our cities and rural areas in balance with nature, honoring the cultural integrity of all our communities, and providing fair access for all to the full range of resources.

13. Environmental justice calls for the strict enforcement of principles of informed consent, and a halt to the testing of experimental reproductive and medical procedures and vaccinations on people of color.

14. Environmental justice opposes the destructive operations of multinational corporations.

15. Environmental justice opposes military occupation, repression and exploitation of lands, peoples and cultures, and other life forms.

16. Environmental justice calls for the education of present and future generations which emphasizes social and environmental issues, based on our experience and an appreciation of our diverse cultural perspectives.

17. Environmental justice requires that we, as individuals, make personal and consumer choices to consume as little of Mother Earth's resources and to produce as little waste as possible; and make the conscious decision to challenge and reprioritize our life-styles to insure the health of the natural world for present and future generations.

> —Adopted, 27 October 1991
> The First National People of Color
> Environmental Leadership Summit
> Washington, D.C.

"STATEMENT BY RELIGIOUS LEADERS AT THE SUMMIT ON ENVIRONMENT"

In June 1991, the following statement was issued by the heads of many religious denominations and faithgroups reflecting the growing consensus about the importance of environmental issues in North American religious life. They call upon people of faith to offer their wisdom, courage, creativity, and hope to efforts to preserve and safeguard the Earth.

On a spring evening and the following day in New York City, we representatives of the religious community in the United States of America gathered to deliberate and plan action in response to the crisis of the Earth's environment.

Deep impulses brought us together. Almost daily, we note mounting evidence of environmental destruction and ever-increasing peril to life, whole species, whole ecosystems. Many people, and particularly the young, want to know where we stand and what we intend to do. And, finally, it is what God made and beheld as good that is under assault. The future of this gift so freely given is in our hands, and we must maintain it as we have received it. This is an inescapably religious challenge. We feel a profound and urgent call to respond with all we have, all we are and all we believe.

We chose to meet, these two days, in the company of people from diverse traditions and disciplines. No one perspective alone is equal to the crisis we face—spiritual and moral, economic and cultural, institutional and personal. For our part, we were grateful to strengthen a collaboration with distinguished scientists and to take stock of their testimony on problems besetting planetary ecology. As people of faith, we were also moved by the support for our work from distinguished public policy leaders.

What we heard left us more troubled than ever. Global warming, generated mainly by the burning of fossil fuels and deforestation, is widely predicted to increase temperatures worldwide, changing climate patterns, increasing drought in many areas, threatening agriculture, wildlife, the integrity of natural ecosystems and creating millions of environmental refugees. Depletion of the ozone shield, caused by human-made chemical agents such as chlorofluorocarbons, lets in deadly ultraviolet radiation from the Sun, with predicted consequences that include skin cancer, cataracts, damage to the human immune system, and destruction of the primary photosynthetic producers at the base of the food chain on which other life depends. Our expanding technological civilization is destroying an acre and a half of forest every second. The accelerating loss of species of plants, animals and microorganisms which threatens the irreversible loss of up to a fifth of the total number within the next 30 years, is not only morally reprehensible but is increasingly limiting the prospects for sustainable productivity. No effort, however heroic, to deal with these global conditions and the interrelated issues of social justice can succeed unless we address the increasing population of the Earth—especially the billion poorest people who have every right to expect a decent standard of living. So too, we must find ways to reduce the disproportionate consumption of natural resources by affluent industrial societies like ours.

Much would tempt us to deny or push aside this global environmental crisis and refuse even to consider the fundamental changes of human behavior required to address it. But we religious leaders accept a prophetic responsibility to make known the full dimensions of this challenge, and what is required to address it, to the many millions we reach, teach and counsel.

We intend to be informed participants in discussions of these issues and to contribute our views on the moral and ethical imperative for developing national and international policy responses. But we declare here and now that steps must be taken toward: accelerated phase-out of ozone-depleting chemicals; much more efficient use of fossil fuels and the development of a non-fossil fuel economy; preservation of tropical forests and other measures to protect continued biological diversity; and concerted efforts to slow the dramatic and dangerous growth in world population through empowering both women and men, encouraging economic self-sufficiency, and making family education programs available to all who may consider them on a strictly voluntary basis.

We believe a consensus now exists, at the highest level of leadership across a significant spectrum of religious traditions, that the cause of environmental integrity and justice must occupy a position of utmost priority for people of faith. Response to this issue can and must cross traditional religious and political lines. It has the potential to unify and renew religious life.

We pledge to take the initiative in interpreting and communicating theological foundations for the stewardship of Creation in which we find the principles for environmental actions. Here our seminaries have a critical role to play. So too, there is a call for moral transformation, as we recognize that the roots of environmental destruction lie in human pride, greed and selfishness, as well as the appeal of the short-term over the long-term.

We reaffirm here, in the strongest possible terms, the indivisibility of social justice and ecological integrity. An equitable international economic order is essential for preserving the global environment. Economic equity, racial justice, gender equality and environmental well-being are interconnected and all are essential to peace. To help ensure these, we pledge to mobilize public opinion and to appeal to elected officials and leaders in the private sector. In our congregations and corporate life, we will encourage and seek to exemplify habits of sound and sustainable householding—in land use, investment decisions, energy conservation, purchasing of products and waste disposal.

Commitments to these areas of action we pledged to one another solemnly and in a spirit of mutual accountability. We dare not let our resolve falter. We will continue to work together, add to our numbers, and deepen our collaboration with the worlds of science and government. We also agreed this day to the following initiatives:

1.   We will widely distribute this declaration within the religious community and beyond. We have established a continuing mechanism to coordinate ongoing activities among us, working intimately with existing program and staff resources in the religious world. We will reach out to other leaders across the broadest possible spectrum of religious life. We will help organize other such gatherings as ours within individual faith groups, in interfaith and interdisciplinary formats, and at international, national, and regional levels.

2.   We religious leaders and members of the scientific community will call together a Washington, D.C., convocation and meet with members of the Executive and Congressional branches to express our support for bold steps on behalf of environmental integrity and justice. There too we will consider ways to facilitate legislative testimony by religious leaders and response to local environmental action alerts.

3.   We will witness firsthand and call public attention to the effect of environmental degradation on vulnerable peoples and ecosystems.

4.   We will call a meeting of seminary deans and faculty to review and initiate curriculum development and promote bibliographies emphasizing stewardship of Creation. We will seek ways to establish internships for seminarians in organizations working on the environment and for young scientists in the study of social ethics.

5.   We will prepare educational materials for congregations, provide technical support for religious publishers already producing such materials, and share sermonical and liturgical materials about ecology.

6.   We will establish an instrument to help place stories on environment in faith group and denominational newsletters and help assure coverage of the religious community's environmental activities in the secular press.

7.   We will urge compliance with the Valdez Principles and preach and promote corporate responsibility.

8.   We will encourage establishment of one model environmentally sound and sustainable facility within each faith group and denomination. We will provide materials for environmental audits and facilitate bulk purchasing of environmentally sound products.

It has taken the religious community, as others, much time and reflection to start to comprehend the full scale and nature of this crisis and even to glimpse what it will require of us. We must pray ceaselessly for wisdom, courage, and creativity. Most importantly, we are people of faith and hope. These qualities are what we may most uniquely have to offer to this effort. We pledge to the children of the world and, in the words of the Iroquois, "to the seventh generation," that we will take full measure of what this moment in history requires of us.

In this challenge may lie the opportunity for people of faith to affirm and enact, at a scale such as never before, what it truly means to be religious. And so we have begun, believing there can be no turning back.

June 3, 1991, New York City

BISHOP VINTON R. ANDERSON
PRESIDENT, WORLD COUNCIL OF AMERICA

RABBI MARC. D. ANGEL
PRESIDENT, RABBINICAL COUNCIL OF AMERICA

THE MOST REVEREND EDMOND L. BROWNING
PRESIDING BISHOP AND PRIMATE OF THE EPISCOPAL
CHURCH

REVEREND JOAN BROWN CAMPBELL
GENERAL SECRETARY, NATIONAL COUNCIL OF
CHURCHES OF CHRIST

THE REVEREND HERBERT W. CHILSTROM
BISHOP, EVANGELICAL LUTHERAN CHURCH IN
AMERICA

FATHER DREW CHRISTIANSEN, S.J.
DIRECTOR, OFFICE OF INTERNATIONAL JUSTICE AND
PEACE
UNITED STATES CATHOLIC CONFERENCE

MS. BEVERLY DAVISON
PRESIDENT, AMERICAN BAPTIST CHURCHES

REVEREND DR. MILTON B. EFTHIMIOU
DIRECTOR OF CHURCH AND SOCIETY
GREEK ORTHODOX ARCHDIOCESE OF NORTH AND
SOUTH AMERICA

BISHOP WILLIAM B. FRIEND
CHAIRMAN OF THE COMMITTEE FOR SCIENCE AND
HUMAN VALUES
NATIONAL CONFERENCE OF CATHOLIC BISHOPS

DR. ALFRED GOTTSCHALK
PRESIDENT, HEBREW UNION COLLEGE-JEWISH
INSTITUTE OF RELIGION

DR. ARTHUR GREEN
PRESIDENT, RECONSTRUCTIONIST RABBINICAL
COLLEGE

HIS EMINENCE ARCHBISHOP IAKOVOS
PRIMATE, GREEK ORTHODOX ARCHDIOCESE OF
NORTH AND SOUTH AMERICA

THE VERY REVEREND LEONID KISHKOVSKY
PRESIDENT, NATIONAL COUNCIL OF CHURCHES OF
CHRIST

CHIEF OREN LYONS
CHIEF OF THE TURTLE CLAN OF THE ONONDAGA
NATION

DR. DAVID McKENNA
PRESIDENT, ASBURY THEOLOGICAL SEMINARY

THE VERY REVEREND JAMES PARKS MORTON
DEAN, CATHEDRAL OF ST. JOHN THE DIVINE

DR. W. FRANKLYN RICHARDSON
GENERAL SECRETARY, NATIONAL BAPTIST
CONVENTION

DR. PATRICIA J. RUMER
GENERAL DIRECTOR, CHURCH WOMEN UNITED

DR. JAMES R. SCALES
PRESIDENT EMERITUS, WAKE FOREST UNIVERSITY

DR. ISMAR SCHORSCH
CHANCELLOR, JEWISH THEOLOGICAL SEMINARY

DR. ROBERT SCHULLER
PASTOR, THE CRYSTAL CATHEDRAL

DR. ROBERT SEIPLE
PRESIDENT, WORLD VISION U.S.A.

BISHOP MELVIN TALBERT
SECRETARY OF THE COUNCIL OF BISHOPS
UNITED METHODIST CHURCH

DR. FOY VALENTINE
FORMER EXECUTIVE DIRECTOR
CHRISTIAN LIFE COMMISSION
SOUTHERN BAPTIST CONVENTION

"DECLARATION OF THE 'MISSION TO WASHINGTON'"

Joint Appeal by Religion and Science for the Environment

Despite many philosophical differences, the 150 religious heads and scientists who gathered for the Mission to Washington in May of 1992 reached out to one another across historic antagonisms. Together they issued a declaration dedicating themselves to undertake bold action to cherish and protect the environment and affirmed a deep sense of common purpose.

We are people of faith and of science who, for centuries, often have traveled different roads. In a time of environmental crisis, we find these roads converging. As this meeting symbolizes, our two ancient, sometimes antagonistic, traditions now reach out to one another in a common endeavor to preserve the home we share.

We humans are endowed with self-awareness, intelligence and compassion. At our best, we cherish and seek to protect all life and the treasures of the natural world. But we are now tampering with the climate. We are thinning the ozone layer and creating holes in it. We are poisoning the air, the land and the water. We are destroying the forests, grasslands and other ecosystems. We are causing the extinction of species at a pace not seen since the end of the age of the dinosaurs. As a result, many scientific projections suggest a legacy for our children and grandchildren of compromised immune systems, increased infectious disease and cancer rates, destroyed plants and consequent disruption of the food chain, agriculture damaged from drought and ultraviolet light, accelerated destruction of forests and species and vastly increased numbers of environmental refugees. Many perils may be still undiscovered. The burdens, as usual, will fall most cruelly upon the shoulders of the poorest among us, especially upon children. But no one will be unaffected. At the same time, the human community grows by a quarter of a million people every day, mostly in the poorest nations and communities. That this crisis was brought about in part through inadvertence does not excuse us. Many nations are responsible. The magnitude of this crisis means that it cannot be resolved unless many nations work together. We must now join forces to that end.

Our own country is the leading polluter on Earth, generating more greenhouse gases, especially CO_2, than any other country. Not by word alone but by binding action, our nation has an inescapable moral duty to lead the way to genuinely effective solutions. We signers of this declaration—leaders in religion and science—call upon our government to change national policy so that the United States will begin to ease, not continue to increase, the burdens on our biosphere and their effect upon the planet's people.

We believe that science and religion, working together, have an essential contribution to make toward any significant mitigation and resolution of the world environmental crisis. What good are the most fervent moral imperatives if we do not understand the dangers and how to avoid them? What good is all the data in the world without a steadfast moral compass? Many of the consequences of our present assault on the environment, even if halted today, will take decades and centuries to play themselves out. How will our children and grandchildren judge our stewardship of the Earth? What will they think of us? Do we not have a solemn obligation to leave them a better world and to ensure the integrity of nature itself? Insofar as our peril arises from a neglect of moral values, human pride, arrogance, inattention, greed, improvidence, and a penchant for the short-term over the long, religion has an essential role to play. Insofar as our peril arises from our ignorance of the intricate interconnectedness of nature, science has an essential role to play.

Differences of perspective remain among us. We do not have to agree on how the natural world was made to be willing to work together to preserve it. On that paramount objective we affirm a deep sense of common cause.

Commitment to environmental integrity and justice, across a broad spectrum and at the highest level of leadership, continues to grow in the United States religious community as an issue of utmost priority—significantly as a result of fruitful conversations with the scientific community. We believe that the dimensions of this crisis are still not sufficiently taken to heart by our leaders, institutions and industries. We accept our responsibility to help make known to the millions we serve and teach the nature and consequences of the environmental crisis, and what is required to overcome it. We believe that our current economic behavior and policies emphasize short-term individual material goals at the expense of the common good and of future generations. When we consider the long-term as well as the short-term costs, it seems clear that addressing this problem now rather than later makes economic as well as moral sense. We impoverish our own children and grandchildren by insisting that they deal with dangers that we could have averted at far less cost in resources and human suffering.

We reaffirm here, in the strongest possible terms, the indivisibility of social justice and the preservation of the environment. We also affirm and support the indigenous peoples in the protection and integrity of their cultures and lands. We believe the wealthy nations of the North, which have historically exploited the natural and human resources of the Southern nations, have a moral obligation to make available additional financial resources and appropriate technology to strengthen their capacity for their own development. We believe the poor and vulnerable workers in our own land should not be asked to bear disproportionate burdens. And we must end the dumping of toxic waste materials disproportionately in communities of low income and of people of color. We recognize that there is a vital connection between peacemaking and protecting our environment. Collectively, the nations of the world spend one trillion dollars a year on military programs. If even a modest portion of this money were spent on environmental programs and sustainable economic development, we could take a major step toward environmental security.

We commit ourselves to work together for a United States that will lead the world in the efficient use of fossil fuels, in devising and utilizing renewable sources of energy, in phasing out all significant ozone-depleting chemicals, in halting deforestation and slowing the decline in species diversity, in planting forests and restoring other habitats and in realizing worldwide social justice. We believe there is a need for concerted efforts to stabilize world population by humane, responsible and voluntary means consistent with our differing values. For these, and other reasons, we believe that special attention must be paid to education and to enhancing the roles and the status of women.

Despite the seriousness of this crisis, we are hopeful. We humans, in spite of our faults, can be intelligent, resourceful, compassionate, prudent and imaginative. We have access to great reservoirs of moral and spiritual courage. Deep within us stirs a commitment to the health, safety and future of our children. Understanding that the world does not belong to any one nation or generation, and sharing a spirit of utmost urgency, we dedicate ourselves to undertake bold action to cherish and protect the environment of our planetary home.

Washington, D.C.
May 12, 1992

"CATHOLIC SOCIAL TEACHING AND ENVIRONMENTAL ETHICS"

and

"RECOMMENDATIONS FOR MOVING ENVIRONMENTAL CONCERNS INTO PARISH LIFE"

United States Catholic Conference

"CATHOLIC SOCIAL TEACHING AND ENVIRONMENTAL ETHICS"

The tradition of Catholic social teaching offers a developing and distinctive perspective on environmental issues. We believe that the following themes drawn from this tradition are integral dimensions of ecological responsibility:

•   God-centered and sacramental view of the universe, which grounds human accountability for the fate of the each;

•   consistent respect for human life, which extends to respect for all creation;

•   world view affirming the ethical significance of global interdependence and the common good;

•   an ethics of solidarity promoting cooperation and a just structure of sharing in the world community;

•   an understanding of the universal purpose of created things, which requires equitable use of the each's resources;

•   an option for the poor, which gives passion to the quest for an equitable and sustainable world;

- a conception of authentic development, which offers a direction for progress that respects human dignity and the limits of material growth.

Although Catholic social teaching does not offer a complete environmental ethic, we are confident that this developing tradition can serve as the basis for Catholic engagement and dialogue with science, the environmental movement, and other communities of faith and good will.

A. SACRAMENTAL UNIVERSE

The whole universe is God's dwelling. Earth, a very small, uniquely blessed corner of that universe, gifted with unique natural blessings, is humanity's home, and humans are never so much at home as when God dwells with them. In the beginning, the first man and woman walked with God in the cool of the day. Throughout history, people have continued to meet the Creator on mountaintops, in vast deserts, and alongside waterfalls and gently flowing springs. In storms and earthquakes, they found expressions of divine power. In the cycle of the seasons and the courses of the stars, they have discerned signs of God's fidelity and wisdom. We still share, though dimly, in that sense of God's presence in nature. But as heirs and victims of the industrial revolution, students of science and the beneficiaries of technology, urban-dwellers and jet-commuters, twentieth-century Americans have also grown estranged from the natural scale and rhythms of life on earth.

For many people, the environmental movement has reawakened appreciation of the truth that, through the created gifts of nature, men and women encounter their Creator. The Christian vision of a sacramental universe—a world that discloses the Creator's presence by visible and tangible signs—can contribute to making the earth a home for the human family once again. Pope John Paul II has called for Christians to respect and protect the environment, so that through nature people can "contemplate the mystery of the greatness and love of God."

Reverence for the Creator present and active in nature, moreover, may serve as ground for environmental responsibility. For the very plants and animals, mountains and oceans, which in their loveliness and sublimity lift our minds to God, by their fragility and perishing likewise cry out, "We have not made ourselves." God brings them into being and sustains them in existence. It is to the Creator of the universe, then, that we are accountable for what we do or fail to do to preserve and care for the earth and all its creatures. For "[t]he Lord's are the earth and its fullness; the world and those who dwell in it" (Ps 24:1). Dwelling in the presence of God, we begin to experience ourselves as part of creation, as stewards within it, not separate from it. As faithful stewards, fullness of life comes from living responsibly within God's creation.

Stewardship implies that we must both care for creation according to standards that are not of our own making and at the same time be resourceful in finding ways to make the earth flourish. It is a difficult balance, requiring both a sense of limits and a spirit of experimentation. Even as we rejoice in earth's goodness and in the beauty of nature, stewardship places upon us responsibility for the well-being of all God's creatures.

B. RESPECT FOR LIFE

Respect for nature and respect for human life are inextricably related. "Respect for life, and above all for the dignity of the human person," Pope John Paul II has written, extends also to the rest of creation (*The Ecological Crisis: A Common Responsibility* [=EC], no. 7). Other species, ecosystems, and even distinctive landscapes give glory to God. The covenant given to Noah was a promise to all the each.

> See, I am establishing my covenant with you and your descendants after you and with every living creature that was with you: all the birds, and the various tame and wild animals that were with you and came out of the ark. (Gn 9:9–10)

The diversity of life manifests God's glory. Every creature shares a bit of the divine beauty. Because the divine goodness could not be represented by one creature alone, Aquinas tells us, God "produced many and diverse creatures, so that what was wanting to one in representation of the divine goodness might be supplied by another ... hence the whole universe together participates in the divine goodness more perfectly, and represents it better than any single creature whatever" (*Summa Theological,* Prima Pars, question 48, ad 2). The wonderful variety of the natural world is, therefore, part of the divine plan and, as such, invites our respect. Accordingly, it is appropriate that we treat other creatures and the natural world not just as means to human fulfillment but also as God's creatures, possessing an independent value, worthy of our respect and care.

By preserving natural environments, by protecting endangered species, by laboring to make human environments compatible with local ecology, by employing appropriate technology, and by carefully evaluating technological innovations as we adopt them, we exhibit respect for creation and reverence for the Creator.

C. THE PLANETARY COMMON GOOD

In 1963, Pope John XXIII, in the letter *Pacem in Terris,* emphasized the world's growing interdependence. He saw problems emerging, which the traditional political mechanisms could no longer address, and he extended the traditional principle of the common good from the nation-state to the world community. Ecological concern has now heightened our awareness of just how interdependent our world is. Some of the gravest environmental problems are clearly global. In this shrinking world, everyone is affected and everyone is responsible, although those most responsible are often the least affected. The universal common good can serve as a foundation for a global environmental ethic.

In many of his statements, Pope John Paul II has recognized the need for such an ethic. For example, in *The Ecological Crisis: A Common Responsibility,* his 1990 World Day of Peace Message, he wrote,

> Today the ecological crisis has assumed such proportions as to be the responsibility of everyone. . . . [I]ts various aspects demonstrate the need for concerted efforts aimed at establishing the duties and obligations that belong to individuals, peoples, States and the international community. (no. 15)

Governments have particular responsibility in this area. In *Centesimus Annus,* the pope insists that the state has the task of providing "for the defense and preservation of common good such as the natural and human environments, which cannot be safeguarded simply by market forces" (no. 40).

D. A NEW SOLIDARITY

In the Catholic tradition, the universal common good is specified by the duty of solidarity, "a firm and preserving determination to commit oneself to the common good," a willingness "to 'lose oneself' for the sake of the other[s] instead of exploiting [them]" (Pope John Paul II, *Sollicitudo Rei Socialis* [=SRS], no. 38). In the face of "the structures of sin," moreover, solidarity requires sacrifices of our own self-interest for the good of others and of the each we share. Solidarity places special obligations upon the industrial democracies, including the United States. "The ecological crisis," Pope John Paul II has written, "reveals the urgent moral need for a new solidarity, especially in relations between the developing nations and those that are highly industrialized" (EC, no. 10). Only with equitable and sustainable development can poor nations curb continuing environmental degradation and avoid the destructive effects of the kind of overdevelopment that has used natural resources irresponsibly.

E. UNIVERSAL PURPOSE OF CREATED THINGS

God has given the fruit of the earth to sustain the entire human family "without excluding or favoring anyone." Human work has enhanced the productive capacity of the earth and in our time is as Pope John Paul II has said, "increasingly important as the productive factor both of non-material and of material wealth" (CA, no. 31). But a great many people, in the Third World as well as in our own inner cities and rural areas, are still deprived of the means of livelihood. In moving toward an environmentally sustainable economy, we are obligated to work for a just economic system which equitably shares the bounty of the earth and of human enterprise with all peoples. Created things belong not to the few, but to the entire human family.

F. OPTION FOR THE POOR

The ecological problem is intimately connected to justice for the poor. "The goods of the earth, which in the divine plan should be a common patrimony," Pope John Paul II has reminded us, "often risk becoming the monopoly of a few who often spoil it and, sometimes, destroy it, thereby creating a loss for all humanity" (October 25, 1991 Address at Conference Marking the Presentation of the Second Edition of the St. Francis "Canticle of the Creatures" International Award for the Environment).

The poor of the earth offer a special test of our solidarity. The painful adjustments we have to undertake in our own economies for the sake of the environment must not diminish our sensitivity to the needs of the poor at home and abroad. The option for the poor embedded in the Gospel and the Church's teaching makes us aware that the poor suffer most directly from environmental decline and have the least access to relief from their suffering. Indigenous peoples die with their forests and grasslands. In Bhopal and Chernobyl, it was the urban poor and working people who suffered the most immediate and intense contamination. Nature will truly enjoy its second spring only when humanity has compassion for its own weakest members.

A related and vital concern is the Church's constant commitment to the dignity of work and the rights of workers. Environmental progress cannot come at the expense of workers and their rights. Solutions must be found that do not force us to choose between a decent environment and a decent life for workers.

We recognize the potential conflicts in this area and will work for greater understanding, communication, and common ground between workers and environmentalists. Clearly, workers cannot be asked to make sacrifices to improve the environment without concrete support from the broader community. Where jobs are lost, society must help in the process of economic conversion, so that not only the earth but also workers and their families are protected.

G. AUTHENTIC DEVELOPMENT

Unrestrained economic development is not the answer to improving the lives of the poor. Catholic social teaching has never accepted material growth as a model of development. A "mere accumulation of goods and services, even for the benefit of the majority," as Pope John Paul II has said, "is not enough for the realization of human happiness" (SRS, no. 28). He has also warned that in a desire "to have and to enjoy rather than to be and to grow," humanity "consumes the resources of the earth, subjecting it without restraint . . . as if it did not have its own requisites and God-given purposes.

Authentic development supports moderation and even austerity in the use of material resources. It also encourages a balanced view of human progress consistent with respect for nature. Furthermore, it invites the development of alternative visions of the good society and the use of economic models with richer standards of well-being than material productivity alone. Authentic development also requires affluent nations to seek ways to reduce and restructure their overconsumption of natural resources. Finally, authentic development also entails encouraging the proper use of both agricultural and industrial technologies, so that development does not merely mean technological advancement for its own sake but rather that technology benefits people and enhances the land.

H. CONSUMPTION AND POPULATION

In public discussions, two areas are particularly cited as requiring greater care and judgment on the part of human beings. The first is consumption of resources. The second is growth in world population. Regrettably, advantaged groups often seem more intent on curbing Third World births than on restraining the even more voracious consumerism of the developed world. We believe this compounds injustice and increases disrespect for the life of the weakest among us. For example, it is not so much population growth, but the desperate efforts of debtor countries to pay their foreign debt by exporting products to affluent industrial countries that drives poor peasants off their land and up eroding hillsides, where in the effort to survive, they also destroy the environment.

Consumption in developed nations remains the single greatest source of global environmental destruction. A child born in the United States, for example, puts a far heavier burden on the world's resources than one born in a poor developing country. By one estimate, each American uses twenty-eight times the energy of a person living in an developing country. Advanced societies, and our own in particular, have barely begun to make efforts at reducing their consumption of resources and the enormous waste and pollution that result from it. We in the developed world, therefore, are obligated to address our own wasteful and destructive use of resources as a matter of top priority.

The key factor, though not the only one, in dealing with population problems is sustainable social and economic development. Technological fixes do not really work. Only when an economy distributes resources so as to allow the poor an equitable stake in society and some hope for the future do couples see responsible parenthood as good for their families. In particular, prenatal care; education; good nutrition; and health care for women, children, and families promise to improve family welfare and contribute to stabilizing population. Supporting such equitable social development, moreover, may well be the best contribution affluent societies, like the United States, can make to relieving ecological pressures in less developed nations. At the same time, it must be acknowledged that rapid population growth presents special problems and challenges that must be addressed in order to avoid damage done to the environment and to social development. In the words of Pope Paul VI, "it is not to be denied that accelerated demographic increases too frequently add difficulties to plans for development because the population is increased more rapidly than available resources. . . ." (*Populorum Progressio*, no. 37). In *Sollicitudo Rei Socialis*, Pope John Paul II has likewise noted, "One cannot deny the existence, especially in the southern hemisphere, of a demographic problem which creates difficulties for development" (no. 25). He has gone on to make connections among population size, development, and the environment. There is "a greater realization of the limits of available resources," he commented, "and of the need to respect the integrity and the cycles of nature and to take them into account when planning for development . . ." (no. 26). Even though it is possible to feed a growing population, the ecological costs of doing so ought to be taken into account. To eliminate hunger from the planet, the world community needs to reform the institutional and political structures that restrict the access of people to food.

Thus, the Church addresses population issues in the context of its teaching on human life, of just development, of care for the environment, and of respect for the freedom of married couples to decide voluntarily on the number and spacing of births. In keeping with these values, and out of respect for cultural norms, it continues to oppose coercive methods of population control and programs that bias decisions through incentives or disincentives. Respect for nature ought to encourage policies that promote natural family planning and true responsible parenthood rather than coercive population control programs or incentives for birth control that violate cultural and religious norms and Catholic teaching.

Finally, we are charged with restoring the integrity of all creation. We must care for all God's creatures, especially the most vulnerable. How, then, can we protect endangered species and at the same time be callous to the unborn, the elderly, or disabled persons? Is not abortion also a sin against creation? If we turn our backs on our own unborn children, can we truly expect that nature will receive respectful treatment at our hands? The care of the earth will not be advanced by the destruction of human life at any stage of development. As Pope John Paul II has said, "protecting the environment is first of all the right to live and the protection of life" (October 16, 1991 Homily at Quiaba, Mato Grosso, Brazil).

I. A WEB OF LIFE

These themes drawn from Catholic social teaching are linked to our efforts to share this teaching in other contexts, especially in our pastoral letters on peace and economic justice and in our statements on food and agriculture. Clearly, war represents a serious threat to the environment, as the darkened skies and oil soaked beaches of Kuwait clearly remind us. The pursuit of peace—lasting peace based on justice—ought to be an environmental priority because the earth itself bears the wounds and scars of war. Likewise, our efforts to defend the dignity and rights of the poor and of workers, to use the strength of our market economy to meet basic human needs, and to press for greater national and global economic justice are dearly linked to efforts to preserve and sustain the earth. These are not distinct and separate issues but complementary challenges. We need to help build bridges among the peace, justice, and environmental agendas and constituencies.

"RECOMMENDATIONS FOR MOVING ENVIRONMENTAL CONCERNS INTO PARISH LIFE"

We invite the Catholic community to join with us and others of good will in a continuing effort to understand and act on the moral and ethical dimensions of the environmental crisis.

> *This resource provides some suggestions for initiating a parish environmental justice program. Additional resources and ideas for a more complete program are available from John and Iona Connor, who designed this initial program, and from the USCC Environmental Justice Program. There are also other resources: action steps, parish bulletin recommendations, resource organizations, and a bibliography.*

PRE-MEETING ORGANIZING

Because concern for the environment is a growing phenomenon, many parishioners may respond to an invitation either to become members of a parish environmental justice committee or social concerns committee or to work with committees on special projects. The person who has been designated by the parish leadership to start a program should familiarize themselves with this resource and the USCC Video-Teleconference, *Hope for a Renewed Earth.*

In setting up a first meeting, do not rely only upon putting an announcement in the church bulletin—extend a personal invitation. Ask the pastor for 1–2 minutes at the end of each Mass on a selected weekend to inform the parish about the effort and invite people to participate. Ask anyone interested in the environment/environmental justice to meet very briefly after Mass. Ask those who meet with you to become part of the group that will launch the parish's effort. At a minimum, make sure they are willing to be contacted occasionally for a specific activity. You may find more people are interested in helping the committee on a project-to-project basis rather than being a committee member. Regardless, take the names, addresses, and phone numbers of everyone expressing interest.

Make a point of encouraging teenagers and older church members to come to this brief meeting. Teenagers have energy, enthusiasm, and current knowledge of environmental conditions. Older people have wisdom that should be shared with younger generations. Tell them that you will soon invite them to the first of the meetings at the church. Send them a written invitation within a few days, and phone them before the first meeting as a reminder.

THE FIRST MEETING: GETTING STARTED

Start each meeting with prayer and the first meeting with the eucharist, if possible. Ask someone on the committee to prepare prayer for each subsequent meeting.

Welcome. At this first meeting, welcome everyone and ask each person to give her/his name and to describe for a minute or two what brings her/him to this meeting (i.e., what environmental and social justice problems concern her/him). This sharing is important as it helps committee members get to know each other and makes the committee cohesive and effective. Make sure you get everyone to fill out a sign-up sheet, with name, address, and phone number. If possible, make copies of the sign-up sheet and distribute them during the meeting. If this is not feasible, make copies later and mail them to everyone.

Purpose and Agenda. Explain at the outset the purpose of the first meeting: to initiate the parish's environmental justice effort. Share the agenda for the first meeting as well as the agendas for the subsequent meetings so that they know where the committee's activities are headed and what is expected of them. Try not to let meetings exceed two hours. The agenda for this first meeting could include a viewing of a video and a discussion of how their choices effect and are affected by the environment.

Show the USCC Video-Teleconference and share this parish resource or other materials. This will acquaint the committee with the bishops' program and provide a common starting point. Follow the video showing with a brief discussion of committee reactions.

Most people are understandably more eager to focus on local environmental conditions than global issues. A good opening discussion, then, could focus on community issues in order to bring the issue home and engage the committee's imagination.

A suggested approach might be to examine what committee members are doing now to safeguard the environment. This resource's suggestions regarding lifestyle could be a good place to begin. Since changes to protect the environment and to bring about social justice can be difficult, committee members should be prepared to deal with personal changes as an ongoing effort. Find a committee volunteer willing to undertake a project to place suggestions of environmental changes in the church bulletin on a regular basis. As a follow-up, agree that at the fourth meeting there will be a discussion of how the committee can work further to encourage and assist its members and the other parishioners to make these changes.

To prepare for the next meeting, suggest that the committee read the relevant environment sections of the resource and/or other pertinent materials.

[Special Note: In every session, some time should be devoted to reflecting upon the moral issues involved. Pope John Paul II's 1990 World Day of Peace Message and the U.S. Catholic bishops' statement *Renewing the Earth* are good sources for this discussion. Fundamentally, environmental justice is a moral issue. Helping our communities define environmental justice in this manner is a unique contribution the Church and religious communities can make to this issue.]

THE SECOND MEETING: ENVIRONMENTAL CONDITIONS

The purpose of this meeting is to familiarize the committee and ultimately the parish with the major environmental issues.

This meeting would be a good occasion to invite knowledgeable representatives from local affiliates of environmental groups (see following list) or community groups dealing with environmental issues. They are a good source of information about local conditions and are usually part of a larger local and national network. Materials from these organizations could be displayed on tables, providing additional information.

Ask participants to discuss briefly what they have learned from the presentations and materials. Identify what is happening in your local community. Who is responsible and what are the different organizations doing to address these issues? Discuss whether your parish can help and, if so, how? Always end a meeting with some agreement on how to act upon the items you discussed.

To prepare for the next meeting, have the committee review the environmental justice material in this resource, *Renewing the Face of the Earth,* and the bishops' statement *Renewing the Earth,* which discusses the moral issues and principles from Catholic social teaching that apply.

THE THIRD MEETING: SOCIAL JUSTICE

The objective of this meeting is to bring about an understanding of what is happening to three groups of people as a result of the mistreatment of the environment: minorities, the poor, and indigenous people.

Just as there are representatives of environmental groups in your community, there are also local social justice organizations. Your diocesan Social Action Office or the bishops' national Campaign for Human Development can help you identify some of these organizations in your community. Invite representatives to come to share their story.

What are the major environmental justice issues as they effect your local community? Where are the toxic dumps, landfills located—in rural areas, poor areas, other? What resources do low-income groups need to deal with these issues? How can your parish help?

Ask if anyone is willing to become involved in these organizations and provide the group with information on their activities.

THE FOURTH MEETING: THE FUTURE

The focus of this meeting is on future activities. Remember that the committee is a catalyst to spur parish action. The overall goal is to continue the parish's environmental justice work beyond the initial four-part start-up series.

One mechanism for initiating such efforts is a parish environmental fair. The Grassroots Coalition (see address that follows) has materials that describe how to put on such an event. The fair has two purposes: to inform and to motivate to action.

To meet the information goal, display environmentally appropriate life-style products and activities; nontoxic cleaning substances; composting; organically grown food; precycling and recycling; carpooling; renewable energy resources; water conservation.

Displays of local environmental conditions are of great educational value—local water resources; forests and parks; conditions of local air quality; hazardous waste sites; types of local industries, with an emphasis on those that are or have significant potential for polluting; land planning and use maps; governmental activities to promote environmental protection.

> By age ten, thousands of children living in the Los Angeles area have permanently impaired respiratory systems from breathing smog. ("Long-term Lung Damage Linked to Air Pollution," *Los Angeles Times* [March 29, 1991])

Education should lead to action. Have representatives from the committee available to sign-up volunteers. Representatives from social justice and environmental groups can be on hand to inform parishioners of their activities and to recruit help and or membership where appropriate.

Consult your diocesan Social Action Office or the USCC Environmental Justice Office for local, state, and national public policy information, and set up a booth for display. Encourage voter registration, meetings and discussions on environmental issues with your Congressional and Senatorial representatives (or sponsor candidate nights during election seasons), and participation in legislative networks.

Fairs can be a good opportunity to reach out ecumenically and to build parish spirit.

Preparing for this fair will take several weeks. During this time, a few members of the committee may be interested in working on making the church itself an environmental model and witness for its members. Environmental audits and other suggestions in the life-style section of the resource can aid the committee in helping the parish as an institution in the community.

In addition to the fair, the committee should continue to meet and plan and develop projects. The projects should, as much as possible, involve larger and larger numbers of parishioners. To help keep the committee focused and renewed, consider holding an annual retreat; develop an environmental justice mission statement; hold pot-luck suppers when you meet; develop networks; constantly communicate with other parishioners about your work; work closely with your parish Social Action Committee; and most important, pray and work together.

[Note: For an expanded version of this initial four-step program, write to John and Iona Connor, Grassroots Coalition, Box 1319, Clarksville, MD 21029; Telephone: 410–964–3574.]

SUGGESTIONS FOR FURTHER READING

ADAMS, CAROL, ed. *Ecofeminism and the Sacred.* New York, NY: Crossroads Press, 1993.

ADLER, MARGOT. *Drawing Down the Moon: Witches, Druids, Goddess-Worshippers, and Other Pagans in America Today.* Boston, MA: Beacon Press, 1979.

ALBANESE, CATHERINE L. *Nature Religion in America: From the Algonkian Indians to the New Age.* Chicago, IL: University of Chicago Press, 1990.

ALLEN, PAULA GUNN. *The Sacred Hoop: Recovering the Feminine in the American Indian Tradition.* Boston, MA: Beacon Press, 1986.

ANDERSON, WILLIAM. *Green Man: The Archetype of our Oneness with the Earth.*

ANDREWS, VALERIE. *A Passion for this Earth.* San Francisco, CA: HarperSanFrancisco, 1990.

AUSTIN, RICHARD CARTWRIGHT. *Baptized into Wilderness: A Christian Perspective on John Muir.* Atlanta, GA: J. Knox Press, 1987.

BADINER, ALLAN, ed. *Dharma Gaia: A Harvest of Essays in Buddhism and Ecology.* Berkeley, CA: Parallax Press, 1990.

BARBOUR, IAN G. *Religion in an Age of Science: The Gifford Lectures, 1989–1991, vol. 1.* San Francisco, CA: Harper & Row Publishers, 1990.

BARR, JAMES. "Man and Nature—The Ecological Controversy and the Old Testament." *Bulletin of the John Rylands University Library of Manchester:* 9–32.

BARREIRO, JOSE, ed. "Indian Corn of the Americas: Gift to the World." *Northeastern Indian Quarterly 6,* nos. 1 and 2 (1989).

BASNEY, LIONEL. *An Earth-Careful Way of Life: Christian Stewardship and the Environmental Crisis.* Downers Grove, IL: InterVarsity Press, 1994.

BERGER, PAMELA. *The Goddess Obscured: The Transformation of the Grain Protectress from Goddess to Saint.* Boston, MA: Beacon Press, 1985.

BERMAN, MORRIS. *The Reenchantment of the World.* New York, NY: Bantam, 1984.

BERNSTEIN, ELLEN, and FINK, DAN, *Let the Earth Teach You Torah.* Philadelphia: Shomrei Adamah, 1992.

BERRY, THOMAS. *The Dream of the Earth.* San Francisco, CA: Sierra Club Books, 1988.

BERRY, THOMAS, and SWIMME, BRIAN. *The Universe Story: From the Primordial Flaring Forth to the Ecozoic Era—A Celebration of the Unfolding of the Cosmos.* San Francisco, CA: HarperCollins, 1992.

BIERHORST, JOHN. *The Way of the Earth: Native America and the Environment.* New York: William Morrow, 1994.

BIRCH, CHARLES, and COBB, JOHN B., JR. *The Liberation of Life: From the Cell to the Community.* Cambridge, MA: Cambridge University Press, 1981.

BIRCH, CHARLES; EAKIN, WILLIAM; and McDANIEL, JAY B. *Liberating Life: Contemporary Approaches to Ecological Theology.* Maryknoll, NY: Orbis Books, 1990.

BLACK ELK. *The Sacred Pipe: Black Elk's Account of the Seven Rites of the Oglala Sioux.* Recorded and edited by Joseph Epes Brown. Norman, OK: University of Oklahoma Press, 1953.

BOWMAN, DOUGLAS C. *Beyond the Modern Mind: The Spiritual and Ethical Challenge of the Environmental Crisis.* New York, NY: Pilgrim Press, 1990.

BRADLEY, IAN C. *God is Green: Ecology for Christians.* New York, NY: Doubleday, 1992.

BROWN, JOSEPH EPES. *The Spiritual Legacy of the American Indian.* New York, NY: Crossroads Publishing Co., 1982.

BULLARD, ROBERT D. ed. *Unequal Protection: Environmental Justice and Communities of Color.* San Francisco: Sierra Club Books, 1994.

CALLICOTT, J. BAIRD, and AMES, ROGER T., eds. *Nature in Asian Traditions of Thought: Essays in Environmental Philosophy.* Albany, NY: State University of New York Press, 1989.

CANAN, JANINE, ed. *She Rises Like the Sun: Invocations of the Goddess by Contemporary American Women Poets.* Freedom, CA: Crossing Press, 1989.

CAPRA, FRITJOF. *The Tao of Physics.* Boston, MA: Shambhala, 1975.

CARSON, RACHEL. *Silent Spring.* New York: Houghton Miflin, 1962.

CARPENTER, JAMES A. *Nature and Grace: Toward an Integral Perspective.* New York, NY: Crossroads Press, 1988.

CHRIST, CAROL P., and PLASKOW, JUDITH, eds. *Weaving the Visions: New Patterns in Feminist Spirituality.* San Francisco, CA: Harper & Row Publishers, 1989.

————. *Womanspirit Rising: A Feminist Reader in Religion.* San Francisco, CA: Harper & Row Publishers, 1979.

COBB, JOHN B., Jr., and DALY, HERMAN E. *For the Common Good: Redirecting the Economy toward Community, the Environment, and a Sustainable Future.* Boston, MA: Beacon Press, 1989.

COBB, JOHN B., Jr. *Is It Too Late? A Theology of Ecology.* Beverly Hills, CA: Bruce Publishing, 1972.

DANKELMAN, IRENE, and DAVIDSON, JOHN. *Women and Environment in the Third World.* London, England: Earthscan, 1988.

DEVALL, BILL, and SESSIONS, GEORGE. *Deep Ecology: Living as if Nature Mattered.* Salt Lake City, UT: Peregrine Smith Books, 1985.

DE VOS, PETER, et al. *Earthkeeping in the Nineties: Stewardship of Creation.* Grand Rapids, MI: William B. Eerdmans, 1991.

DE WITT, CALVIN B. *The Environment and the Christian: What Does the New Testament Say About the Environment?* Grand Rapids, MI: Baker Book House, 1991.

DIAMOND, IRENE, and FEMAN ORENSTEIN, GLORIA, eds. *Reweaving the World: The Emergence of Ecofeminism.* San Francisco, CA: Sierra Club Books, 1990.

DOWD, MICHAEL. *Earthspirit: A Handbook for Nurturing Ecological Christianity.* Mystic, CT: Twenty-third Publications, 1991.

DUNN, STEPHEN, and LONERGAN, ANNE, eds. *Befriending the Earth: A Theology of Reconciliation Between Humans and the Earth.* Mystic, CT: Twenty-third Publications, 1991.

EHRENFELD, DAVID. *The Arrogance of Humanism.* New York, NY: Oxford University Press, 1981.

EHRENFELD, DAVID, and BENTLEY, PHILIP J., "Judaism and the Practice of Stewardship," *Judaism* 34 (1985): 301-2.

EISLER, RIANE TENNENHAUS. *The Chalice and the Blade: Our History, Our Future.* San Francisco, CA: Harper & Row, 1987.

ENGEL, J. RONALD, BAKKEN, PETER, and GIBB ENGEL, JOAN. *Ecology, Justice, and Christian Faith: A Guide to the Literature, 1960–1993.* Westport, CA: Greenwood, 1994.

ERDOES, RICHARD, and ORTIZ, ALFONSO. *American Indian Myths and Legends.* New York, NY: Pantheon, 1984.

FERRE, FREDERICK. *Hellfire and Lightning Rods: Liberating Science, Technology, and Religion.* Maryknoll, NY: Orbis Books, 1993.

FOX, MATTHEW. *Breakthrough: Meister Eckhart's Creation Spirituality in New Translation.* New York, NY: Image Books Doubleday, 1980.

―――. *The Coming of the Cosmic Christ: The Healing of Mother Earth and the Birth of a Global Renaissance.* San Francisco, CA: Harper & Row Publishers, 1988.

GADON, ELINOR. *The Once and Future Goddess: A Symbol for Our Time.* San Francisco, CA: Harper & Row Publishers, 1989.

GILKEY, LANGDON BROWN. *Nature, Reality, and the Sacred: the Nexus of Science and Religion.* Minneapolis: Fortress Press, 1993.

GIMBUTAS, MARIJA. *The Gods and Goddesses of Old Europe, 7000 to 3500 B.C.: Myths, Legends, and Cult Images.* Berkeley, CA: University of California Press, 1974.

GLACKEN, CLARENCE. *Traces on the Rhodian Shore: Nature and Culture in Western Thought from Ancient Times to the End of the Eighteenth Century.* Berkeley, CA: University of California Press, 1967.

GOLDSMITH, EDWARD. *The Way: An Ecological World-view.* Boston: Shambhala, 1993.

GOTTLIEB, ROGER S., "Ethics and Trauma: Levinas, Feminism, and Deep Ecology," *Cross Currents,* Summer, 1994.

GOTTLIEB, ROGER S., ed., *A New Creation: America's Contemporary Spiritual Voices,* New York: Crossroad, 1990.

GRANBERG-MICHAELSON, WESLEY. *Redeeming the Creation: the Rio Earth Summit: Challenges for the Churches.* Geneva: WCC Publications, 1992.

GRAY, ELIZABETH DODSON. *Green Paradise Lost.* Wellesley, MA: Roundtable Press, 1979.

GREEN, ARTHUR. "God, World, Person: A Jewish Theology of Creation, Part I." *Melton Journal,* no. 24.

―――. "God, World, Person: A Jewish Theology of Creation, Part II." *Melton Journal,* no. 25.

GRIFFIN, DAVID RAY. *God and Religion in the Postmodern World.* Albany, NY: State University of New York Press, 1989.

GRIFFIN, DAVID RAY, ed. *The Reenchantment of Science: Postmodern Proposals.* Albany, NY: State University of New York Press, 1988.

GRIFFIN, DAVID RAY; BEARDSLEE, WILLIAM A.; and HOLLAND, JOE. *Varieties of Postmodern Theology.* Albany, NY: State University of New York, 1989.

GRIFFIN, SUSAN. *Made from This Earth.* New York, NY: Harper & Row Publishers, 1982.

―――. *Woman and Nature: The Roaring Inside Her.* New York, NY: Harper & Row Publishers, 1978.

GUSTAFSON, JAMES M. *A Sense of the Divine: The Natural Environment From a Theocentric Perspective.* Cleveland, OH: Pilgrim Press, 1994.

HALL, DOUGLAS JOHN. *Imaging God: Dominion as Stewardship.* Grand Rapids, MI: W.B. Eerdmans Publishing Co.,; New York, NY: Friendship Press, 1986.

HARGROVE, EUGENE C., ed. *Religion and Environmental Crisis.* Athens, GA: University of Georgia Press, 1986.

HART, JOHN. *The Spirit of the Earth: A Theology of the Land.* New York, NY: Paulist Press, 1984.

HENDRY, GEORGE S. *Theology of Nature.* Philadelphia, PA: Westminster Press, 1980.

HESSEL, DIETER T. *After Nature's Revolt: Eco-Justice and Theology.* Minneapolis, MN: Fortress Press, 1992.

HUGHES, J. DONALD. *American Indian Ecology.* El Paso, TX: Texas Western Press, 1983.

―――. *Ecology in Ancient Civilizations.* Albuquerque, NM: University of New York Mexico Press, 1975.

HULL, FRITZ, ed. *Earth and Spirit: The Spiritual Dimension of the Environmental Crisis.* New York: Crossroads, 1993.

JACKSON, WES. *New Roots for Agriculture.* Lincoln, NE: University of Nebraska Press, 1985.

JOHNSON, ELIZABETH A. *Women, Earth and Creator Spirit.* New York, NY: Paulist Press, 1993.

JORANSON, PHILIP N., and BUTIGAN, KEN, eds. *Cry of the Environment: Rebuilding the Christian Creation Tradition.* Santa Fe, NM: Bear, 1984.

JUDAISM AND ECOLOGY. New York: Hadassah, 1993.

JUNG, SHANNON. *We are Home: A Spirituality of the Environment.* New York, NY: Paulist Press, 1993.

KAUFMAN, GORDON D. *Theology for a Nuclear Age.* Philadelphia, PA: Westminster Press, 1985.

LA BASTILLE, ANN. *Women and Wilderness.* San Francisco, CA: Sierra Club Books, 1980.

LA CHAPELLE, DOLORES. *Earth Wisdom.* Boulder, CO: Guild of Tutors Press, 1978.

———. *Sacred Land, Sacred Sex, Rapture of the Deep: Concerning Deep Ecology and Celebrating Life.* Silverton, CO: Finn Hill Arts, 1988.

LAMM, NORMAN. "Ecology in Jewish Law and Theology," in *Faith and Doubt.* New York, NY: KTAV, 1971.

LANE, BELDEN C. *Landscapes of the Sacred: Geography and Narrative in American Spirituality.* Mahwah, NJ: Paulist Press, 1988.

LERNER, GERDA. *The Creation of Patriarchy.* New York, NY: Oxford University Press, 1986.

LINZEY, ANDREW, and REGAN, TOM, eds. *Animals and Christianity: A Book of Readings.* New York, NY: Crossroad Publishing Co., 1988.

LOVELOCK, J. E. *Gaia: A New Look at Life on Earth.* New York, NY: Oxford University Press, 1979.

LOVELOCK, JAMES. *The Ages of GAIA: A Biography of Our Living Earth.* New York, NY: Norton, 1988.

MACY, JOANNA. *World as Lover, World as Self.* Berkeley, CA: Parallax Press, 1991.

———. *Despair and Personal Power in the Nuclear Age.* Philadelphia, PA: New Society Publishers, 1983,

McCARTHY, SCOTT. *Creation Liturgy: An Earth-Centered Theology of Worship.* San Jose, CA: Resource Publications, 1987.

———. *Celebrating the Earth: An Earth-Centered Theology of Worship with Blessings, Prayers, and Rituals.* San Jose, CA: Resource Publications, 1991.

MCDANIEL, JAY. *Of God and Pelicans: A Theology of Reverence for Life.* Louisville, KY: Westminster/John Knox Press, 1989.

———. *Earth, Sky, Gods, and Mortals: Developing an Ecological Christianity.* Mystic, CT: Twenty-third Publications, 1990.

McFAGUE, SALLIE. *Models of God: Theology for an Ecological, Nuclear Age.* Philadelphia, PA: Fortress Press, 1987.

McGAA, ED (Eagle Man). *Mother Earth Spirituality: Native American Paths to Healing Ourselves and Our World.* San Francisco, CA: Harper & Row Publishers, 1990.

McKIBBEN, BILL. *The Comforting Whirlwind: God, Job, and the Scale of Creation.* Grand Rapids, MI: W.B. Eerdmans Publishing Co., 1994.

McLUHAN, T. C., *The Way of the Earth: Encounters with Nature in Ancient and Contemporary Thought.* New York: Simon and Schuster, 1994.

MANDER, JERRY. *In the Absence of the Sacred: The Failure of Technology and the Survival of the Indian Nations.* San Francisco, CA: Sierra Club Books, 1991.

MARTIN, CALVIN. *Keepers of the Game: Indian-Animal Relationships and the Fur Trade.* Chicago, IL: University of Chicago Press, 1978.

MERCHANT, CAROLYN. *The Death of Nature: Woman, Ecology, and the Scientific Revolution.* New York, NY: Harper & Row Publishers, 1980.

MOLTMANN, JURGEN. *God in Creation: A New Theology of Creation* New York, NY: Harper and Row Publishers, 1985.

MUIR, JOHN. *A Thousand-Mile Walk to the Gulf.* Boston, MA: Houghton Mifflin, 1916.

———. *The Wilderness World of John Muir,* ed. Edwin Way Teale. Boston, MA: Houghton Mifflin, 1954.

MURPHY, CHARLES M. *At Home on Earth: Foundations for Catholic Ethic of the Environment* New York: Crossroads, 1989.

NASH, JAMES A. *Loving Nature: Ecological Integrity and Christian Responsibility.* Nashville, TN: Abingdon Press, 1991.

NASH, RODERICK. *The Rights of Nature: A History of Environmental Philosophy.* Madison, WI: University of Wisconsin Press, 1989.

———. *Wilderness and the American Mind.* Rev. ed.: New Haven, CT: Yale University Press, 1973.

NASR, SEYYED, HOSSEIN. *Man and Nature: The Spiritual Crisis of Modern Man.* Kuala Lumpur: Foundation for Traditional Studies, 1968. New Ed. New York, NY: HarperCollins, 1991.

NEIHARDT, JOHN G. *Black Elk Speaks: Being the Life Story of a Holy Man of the Oglala Sioux.* New York, NY: Washington Square Press, 1972.

NELSON, RICHARD K. *Make Prayers to the Raven: A Koyukon View of the Northern Forest.* Chicago, IL: University of Chicago Press, 1983.

NIETHAMMER, CAROLYN. *Daughters of the Earth: The Lives and Legends of American Indian Women.* New York, NY: Collier Books, 1977.

NOLLMAN, JIM. *Spiritual Ecology: A Guide to Reconnecting with Nature.* New York, NY: Bantam Books, 1990.

OELSCHLAEGER, MAX, ed. *After Earth Day: Continuing the Conservation Effort.* Denton, TX: University of North Texas Press, 1992.

———. *The Idea of Wilderness: From Prehistory to the Age of Ecology.* New Haven, CT: Yale University Press, 1991.

———. *Caring for Creation: An Ecumenical Approach to the Environmental Crisis.* New Haven, CT: Yale University Press, 1994.

PAEHLKE, ROBERT C. *Environmentalism and the Future of Progressive Politics.* New Haven, CT and London, England: Yale University Press, 1988.

PHILIPPI, DONALD. *Songs of Gods, Songs of Humans.* Princeton, NJ: Princeton University Press, 1979.

PLANT, JUDITH, ed. *Healing the Wounds: The Promise of Ecofeminism.* Philadelphia, PA: New Society, 1989.

PLASKOW, JUDITH, *Standing Again at Sinai: Judaism from a Feminist Perspective.* New York: Harper and Row, 1990.

PONTING, CLIVE. *A Green History of the World: The Environment and the Collapse of Great Civilizations.* New York: St. Martin's Press, 1992.

POPE JOHN PAUL II. *Peace with God the Creator, Peace with All of Creation.* Vatican City, Rome: Libreria Editrice Vaticana, 1990.

ROBB, CAROL S., and CASEBOLT, CARL. *Covenant for a New Creation: Ethics, Religion, and Public Policy.* Maryknoll, NY: Orbis Books, 1991.

ROBERTS, ELIZABETH, and AMIDON, ELIAS. *Earth Prayers from Around the World: 365 Prayers, Poems, and Invocations for Honoring the Earth.* San Francisco, CA: Harper SanFrancisco, 1991.

ROCKEFELLER, STEVEN C., and ELDER, JOHN C. *Spirit and Nature: Why the Environment is a Religious Issue.* Boston: Beacon Press, 1992.

RUETHER, ROSEMARY RADFORD. *Gaia and God: An Ecofeminist Theology of Earth Healing.* San Francisco, CA: HarperSanFrancisco, 1992.

SANTMIRE, H. PAUL. *Brother Earth, Nature, God, and Ecology in Time of Crisis.* Camden, NY: Thomas Nelson, 1970.

———. *The Travail of Nature: The Ambiguous Ecological Promise of Christian Theology.* Philadelphia, PA: Fortress Press, 1985.

SCHARPER, STEPHEN B., and CUNNINGHAM, HILARY. *The Green Bible.* Maryknoll, NY: Orbis Books, 1993.

SCHUMACHER, E. F. *Small is Beautiful.* New York: Harper and Row, 1973.

SHELDON, JOSEPH. *Rediscovery of Creation: A Bibliographical Study of the Church's Response to the Environmental Crisis.* Metuchen, NY: Scarecrow Press, 1992.

SHIVA, VANDANA. *Staying Alive: Women, Ecology and Development.* London, England: Zed Press, 1988.

SJOO, MONICA, and MOR, BARBARA. *The Great Cosmic Mother: Rediscovering the Religion of the Earth.* San Francisco, CA: Harper & Row Publishers, 1987.

SNYDER, GARY. *Good. Wild. Sacred.* N.Y.: Pantheon, 1984.

SORRELL, ROGER. *St. Francis of Assisi and Nature: Tradition and Innovation in Western Christian Attitudes Toward the Environment.* Oxford, England: Oxford University Press, 1988.

SPRETNAK, CHARLENE. ed. *The Politics of Women's Spirituality: Essays on the Rise of Spiritual Power Within the Feminist Movement.* Garden City, NY: Anchor/Doubleday, 1982.

———. *The Spiritual Dimensions of Green Politics.* Santa Fe, NM: Bear, 1986.

———. *States of Grace: The Recovery of Meaning in the Postmodern Age.* San Francisco, CA: HarperSanFrancisco, 1991.

STARHAWK. *Dreaming the Dark.* Boston, MA: Beacon Press, 1982.

———. *The Spiral Dance: A Rebirth of the Ancient Religion of the Great Goddess.* San Francisco, CA: Harper & Row Publishers, 1986.

STOLZENBERG, WILLIAM. "Sacred Peaks, Common Grounds: American Indians and Conservationists Meet at a Cultural Crossroads," *Nature Conservancy* (September/October 1992): 16-23.

STONE, MERLIN. *When God Was a Woman.* New York, NY: Harcourt Brace Jovanovich, 1976.

SUZUKI, DAVID, KNUDTSON, PETER. *Wisdom of the Elders: Honoring Sacred Native Visions of Nature* New York: Bantam Books, 1992.

SWAN, JAMES A. *Sacred Places in Nature.* Santa Fe, NM: Bear, 1990.

TAYLOR, PAUL W. *Respect for Nature: A Theory of Environmental Ethics.* Princeton, NJ: Princeton University Press, 1986.

TOOKER, ELISABETH, ed. *Native North American Spirituality of the Eastern Woodlands.* New York, NY: Paulist Press, 1979.

TUCKER, MARY EVELYN; GRIM, JOHN A., eds. *Worldviews and Ecology: Religion, Philosophy, and the Environment.* Maryknoll, N.Y.: Orbis, 1994.

VECSEY, CHRISTOPHER, and VENABLES, ROBERT W, eds. *American Indian Environments: Ecological Issues in Native American History.* Syracuse, NY: Syracuse University Press, 1980.

WRIGHT, NANCY G.; KILL, DONALD. *Ecological Healing: A Christian Vision.* Maryknoll, NY: Orbis, 1993.

YOUNG, RICHARD A. *Healing the Earth: a Theocentric Perspective on Environmental Problems and their Solutions.* Nashville, TN: Broadman & Holman Publishers, 1994.

SOME ORGANIZATIONS
TO CONTACT

RELIGIOUS ORGANIZATIONS

THE NATIONAL RELIGIOUS PARTNERSHIP FOR THE ENVIRONMENT
1047 Amsterdam Avenue
New York, NY 10025
212/316-7441

ENVIRONMENTAL JUSTICE PROGRAM
US CATHOLIC CONFERENCE
3211 Fourth Avenue NE
Washington, DC 20017
202/541-3160

COALITION ON THE ENVIRONMENT AND JEWISH LIFE
443 Park Avenue South, 11th Flr
New York, NY 10016
212/684-6950

ECONOMIC AND ENVIRONMENTAL JUSTICE AND HUNGER CONCERNS
NATIONAL COUNCIL OF CHURCHES OF CHRIST
475 Riverside Drive
New York, NY 10115

PROGRAM COORDINATOR
EVANGELICAL ENVIRONMENTAL NETWORK
10 East Lancaster Avenue
Wynnewood, PA 19096

AMERICAN BAPTIST CHURCHES, USA
PO Box 851
Valley Forge, PA 19482-0851
Contact: Andy Smith,
215/768-2459 (corporate responsibility) or
Owen Owens,
215/768-2410 (ecology and racism)

BAPTIST JOINT COMMITTEE ON PUBLIC AFFAIRS
200 Maryland Avenue NE
Washington, DC 20002
202/544-4226
Contact: James M. Dunn, Executive Director

B'NAI B'RITH YOUTH ORGANIZATION
1640 Rhode Island Ave. NW
Washington, DC 20036
202/857-6633
Contact: Linda Siegel, Director of Program Services

CHRISTIAN CHURCH (DISCIPLES OF CHRIST)
Department of Homeland Ministries
222 S. Downey Avenue
Indianapolis, IN 46206
317/353-1491
Contact: Dr. Gerald Cunningham, Office of Church and Society

CHURCH OF THE BRETHREN
World Ministries Commission
1451 Dundee Avenue
Elgin, IL 60120
708/742-5100
Contact: Rev. Shantilal Bhagat, Eco-Justice and Rural Crisis

COALITION ON THE ENVIRONMENT AND JEWISH LIFE
443 Park Avenue S.
New York, NY 10016-7322
212/684-6950

CONSULTATION ON THE ENVIRONMENT AND JEWISH LIFE
1047 Amsterdam Avenue
New York, NY 10025
212/678-8996
Contact: Rabbi Steve Shaw

EPISCOPAL CHURCH USA
Episcopal Church Center
815 Second Avenue
New York, NY 10017
212/922-5223
Contact: Ethan Flad, Staff Assistant for Environment and Special Projects

EVANGELICALS FOR SOCIAL ACTION
10 Lancaster Avenue
Wynwood, PA 19096
215/645-9390
Contact: Ron Sider, Executive Director

EVANGELICAL LUTHERAN CHURCH IN AMERICA
Commission for Church in Society
8765 West Higgins Road
Chicago, IL 60641
312/380-2708
Contact: Job Ebenezer, Director of Environmental Stewardship and Hunger Education

INTERFAITH CENTER ON CORPORATE RESPONSIBILITY
475 Riverside Dr., Rm 556
New York, NY 10115
212/870-2623
Contact: Dr. Ariane Van Buren, Director of Environmental Programs

THE JEWISH THEOLOGICAL SEMINARY OF AMERICA (JTS)
3080 Broadway
New York, NY 10027
212/678-8996
Contact: Rabbi Steven Shaw,
Director, Dept. of Community Education

JOINT APPEAL BY RELIGION AND SCIENCE FOR THE ENVIRONMENT
1047 Amsterdam Avenue
New York, NY 10025
212/316-7441
Contact: Paul Gorman, Executive Director or
Amy Elizabeth Fox, Associate Director

LEADERSHIP CONFERENCE OF WOMEN
Religious Global Concerns Committee
8808 Cameron Street
Silver Spring, MD 20910
301/588-4955
Contact: Betty Sundry, CDP

MORNING STAR FOUNDATION
403 Tenth Street SE
Washington, DC 20003
202/547-5531
Contact: Suzan Shown Harjo, President or
Gail E. Chehak, Treasurer

NATIONAL COUNCIL OF CATHOLIC WOMEN
1275 K Street NW
Suite 975
Washington, DC 20005
202/682-0334
Contact: Pat Janik, Program Director

NATIONAL COUNCIL OF THE CHURCHES OF CHRIST IN THE USA
475 Riverside Drive
New York, NY 10115
212/870-2141
Contact: Rev. Joan B. Campbell, General Secretary or
Dr. Jean Sindab, Program Director for Eco-Justice

NATIONAL JEWISH COMMUNITY RELATIONS ADVISORY COUNCIL
443 Park Avenue South
New York, NY 10016
212/684-6950
Contact: Dr. Lawrence Rubin, Executive Director

NATIVE AMERICANS FOR A CLEAN ENVIRONMENT
Box 1671
Tahlequah, OK 74465
918/458-4322
Contact: Lance Hughes

North American Conference on Christianity and Ecology
P.O. Box 14305
San Francisco, CA 94114
415/626-6064
Contact: Frederick W. Krueger, Executive Secretary

North American Coalition on Religion and Ecology
5 Thomas Circle NW
Washington, DC 20005
202/462-2591
Contact: Dr. Donald B. Conroy, President

Presbyterian Church (USA)
Office of Environmental Justice
100 Witherspoon Street
Room 3046
Louisville, KY 40202-1396
502/569-5809
Contact: Rev. William Somplatsky-Jarman, Associate for Environmental Justice

Progressive National Baptist Convention, Inc.
601 50th Street NE
Washington, DC 20019
202/396-0558
Contact: Rev. Archie LeMone, Executive of the Home Mission Board

Rabbinical Council of America (RCA)
275 7th Ave, 15th flr.
New York, NY 10001
212/807-7888

Reformed Church in America
Office of Social Witness
475 Riverside Drive
New York, NY 10115
212/870-2841
Contact: John Paarlberg, Minister for Social Witness

Religious Action Center of Reform Judaism
2027 Massachusetts Avenue NW
Washington, DC 20036
202/387-2800
Contact: Rabbi David Saperstein, Director and Counsel

Roman Catholic Church
U.S. Catholic Conference
3211 4th Street NE
Washington, DC 20017
202/541-3140
Contact: Father Drew Christiansen, International Office Director

Shalom Center
7318 Germantown Avenue
Philadelphia, PA 19119-1790
215/247-9700
Contact: Arthur Waskow, Director
or Rebecca Subar, Field Director

Shomrei Adamah/Keepers of the Earth
50 West 17th Street
New York, NY 10011
212/807-6376
Contact: Ellen Bernstein, Exec. Director

United Church of Christ
Commission for Racial Justice
475 Riverside Drive
Suite 1948
New York, NY 10115
212/870-2077
Contact: Rev. Dr. Benjamin Chavis, Jr., Executive Director

Office of Church in Society
110 Maryland Avenue NE
Washington, DC 20002
202/543-1517
Contact: Patric Conover, Associate for Policy Advocacy or
Charles McCullough, Staff Associate for Church Empowerment

Board for Homeland Ministries
700 Prospect Avenue
Cleveland, OH 44115
216/736-3200

UNITED METHODIST CHURCH
General Board of Church and Society
100 Maryland Avenue NE
Washington, DC 20002
202/488-5650
Contact: Jaydee Hanson,
Assistant General Secretary, Ministry of God's Creation or
Paz Artaza-Regan,
Program Associate for Environmental Justice

General Board of Global Ministries, Women's Division
475 Riverside Drive
Room 1502
New York, NY 10115
212/870-3733
Pamela Sparr,
Executive Secretary of Development Education and Action

ENVIRONMENTAL ORGANIZATIONS

CITIZENS CLEARINGHOUSE FOR HAZARDOUS WASTE
P.O. Box 6806
Falls Church, VA 22040
703/237-2249

CLEAN WATER ACTION
1320 18th St. NW
Washington, DC 20036
202/457-1286

ENVIRONMENTAL DEFENSE FUND
257 Park Avenue South
New York, NY 10010
212/505-2100

Friends of the Earth
218 D. St. SE
Washington, DC 20003
202/544-2600

Greenpeace USA
1436 U St. NW
Washington, DC 20009
202/462-1777

National Audubon Society
700 Broadway
New York, NY 10003-9501
212/979-3000

Natural Resources Defense Council
40 West 20th St.
New York, NY 110011
212/727-2700

Sierra Club
730 Polk St.
San Francisco, CA 94109
415/776-2211

ABOUT THE CONTRIBUTORS

Henry David Thoreau is the author of *Walden* and "On Civil Disobedience."

Barry Lopez wrote *Arctic Dreams,* which won the National Book Award, as well as several other books, including *Of Wolves and Men* and *Crossing Open Ground.*

Rachel Carson was a biologist and naturalist whose study of the effects of pesticides, *Silent Spring,* helped launch the modern environmental movement.

Ralph Waldo Emerson was one of the most important essayists and public intellectuals of nineteenth-century America.

John Muir was a conservationist and writer, who worked to save the Yosemite Valley in California.

Aldo Leopold was a conservationist, forester, writer, and teacher; organizer of the first designated wilderness area in the U.S.; and an intellectual inspiration of modern environmental ethics.

Annie Dillard won the Pulitzer Prize for *A Pilgrim at Tinker's Creek.*

Linda Hogan is a poet and essayist.

Stephanie Kaza teaches environmental studies at the University of Vermont. A long-time student of Zen Buddhism, she has served on the Board of the Buddhist Peace Fellowship.

Fanetorens (Ray Fadden) was a long-time teacher in Native American Schools.

Joseph L. Henderson is an analytical psychologist and member of the C. G. Jung Institute of San Francisco.

Maud Oakes was an anthropologist and artist, author of *The Two Crosses of Todos Santos.*

Robert Pogue Harrison teaches literature at Stanford University and is the author of *The Body of Beatrice.*

Lao Tzu was a Chinese philosopher and spiritual teacher.

Louis Ginzberg was a leading Talmudic scholar of the early 20th century, and the author of the multi-volume *The Legends of the Jews.*

Daniel Swartz is a Rabbi and Director of Congregational Relations for the Religious Action center of Reform Judaism, in Washington, D.C.

David Kinsley is a Professor of Religious Studies at McMaster University.

Michael Kioni Dudley teaches philosophy at Chaminade University in Hawai'i and is a leading scholar of Hawaiian environmental thought.

J. Donald Hughes teaches at the University of Denver is the author of many books, including *Ecology in Ancient Civilizations*.

Chatsumarn Kabilsingh is the chief Thai scholar of the Buddhist Perception of Nature project and teaches at Thammasat University in Bangkok. She has written *Study of Buddhist Nuns: Monastic Rules* and translated the *Lotus Sutra* into Thai.

O. P. Dwivedi is professor of Political Studies at the University of Guelph, Canada, and has served as World Health Organization consultant to the Indian government. He is the co-author of *Hindu Religion and the Environmental Crisis*.

Mawil Y. Izzi Deen (Samarrai) teaches at the King Abdul Aziz university, Jeddah, Saudi Arabia; and co-author of *Islamic Principles of the Conservation of the Natural Environment*.

John S. Mbiti, an Anglican priest from Kenya, taught theology and religion for many years at Makerere University in Uganda. His many writings include *African Religions and Philosophy*.

Lynn White was a medieval historian who taught at Princeton, Stanford, and University of California at Los Angeles.

Roderick Nash teaches history at University of California–Santa Barbara and his written ten books, including *The Idea of Wilderness*.

Pope John Paul II is the leader of the Roman Catholic Church.

John F. Haught is a Catholic scholar who has written *The Cosmic Adventure* and *Minding the Time*.

Sallie McFague is Professor of Theology at Vanderbilt Divinity School. Her books include *Models of God* and *Metaphorical Theology*.

Arthur Waskow is director of the Philadelphia-based Shalom Center, an international network that brings Jewish though and action to bear on protecting and healing the earth. He wrote *Seasons of Our Joy*.

Arthur Green is a Rabbi and has taught at the Reconstructionist Rabbinical College and Brandeis University and is the author of *Tormented Master: A Life of Rabbi Nachman of Bratslav*.

Ken Jones is a student of Zen Buddhism, a founder of the British Buddhist Peace Fellowship and author of *The Social Face of Buddhism*.

Theodore Walker, Jr., teaches Ethics at Perkins School of Theology, Southern Methodist University, and is the author of *Empower the People: Social Ethics for the African-American Church*.

Rosemary Radford Ruether has a been leading voice in feminist religious theory for two decades. Her earlier books include *Sexism and God-Talk* and *Women-Church*.

Anne Primavesi is an independent scholar and theologian. Based Devon, England, she is the co-author of *Our God Has No Favourites*.

Shamara Shantu Riley is a graduate student in political science at the University of Illinois/Urbana.

Susan Griffin is a widely known feminist author. Her books include *Pornography and Silence, Unremembered Country,* and *The Silence of the Stones*.

Paula Gunn Allen teaches Native American Studies at the University of California, Berkeley, is the author of works of poetry and fiction, and is editor of *The Sacred Hoop: Recovering the Feminine in American Indian Traditions*.

Riane Eisler is a scholar, futurist and activist, and is codirector of the Center for Partnership Studies in Pacific Grove, California.

Vandana Shiva, a native of India, is an internationally known environmental activist and theorist. Her books include *Monocultures of the Mind*.

Brooke Medicine Eagle was brought up on the Crow reservation in Montana and combines training in the Northern Plains Indian medicine path and Western ways of healing.

Terry Tempest Williams is the naturalist in residence at the Utah Museum of Natural History. Her books include *Pieces of White Shell* and *Coyote's Canyon*.

Carol Adams is a well-known feminist author. Her books include *The Sexual Politics of Meat*.

Edna St. Vincent Millay was major American poet.

Albert Schweitzer was an internationally respected humanitarian, physician, and musician.

Thomas Berry is a widely read ecotheologian, founder of the Riverdale Center for Earth Studies in New York, author of *The Dream of the Earth* and co-author of *The Universe Story*.

Joanna Macy teaches at the California Institute of Integral Studies and leads workshops worldwide on peace and environmental issues. Her books include *Despair and Personal Power in the Nuclear Age* and *Dharma and Development*.

Brian Walsh is senior member in Worldview Studies at the Institute of Christian Studies in Toronto.

Marianne B. Karsh is a forester working for the Canada Forest Service in St. John's, Newfoundland.

Nik Ansell is a doctoral candidate in philosophical theology at the Institute for Christian Studies in Toronto.

Warwick Fox is a National Research Fellow at the Centre for Environmental Studies at the University of Tasmania.

Thich Nhat Hanh chaired the Vietnamese Buddhist Peace delegation in Paris during the Vietnam War. The author of numerous books, including *Being Peace* and *The Miracle of Mindfulness,* he heads a spiritual community in southern France and has been a leading voice in socially engaged Buddhism.

Ellen Bernstein is the founder and director of *Shomrei Adamah* (Guardians of the Earth), a Philadelphia-based Jewish Environmental organization.

Dan Fink is a Rabbi and leading Jewish environmental educator. He co-authored *Judaism and Ecology*.

Black Elk was a priest of the Oglala Sioux.

Kenneth Kraft is Associate Professor of Asian religions at Lehigh University. His writings include *Eloquent Zen* and the editing of *Inner Peace, World Peace: Essays on Buddhism and Nonviolence*.

John Seed is director of the Rainforest Information Centre, Australia, and has worked to protect rainforests throughout the world.

Pat Fleming has worked as a psychologist, social worker and teacher in the areas of peace, environmental and feminist politics.

Marina Lachecki is an environmental educator living in Wisconsin whose books include *Teaching Kids to Love the Earth* and *More Teaching Kids to Love the Earth*.

Roger S. Gottlieb is the editor of *This Sacred Earth*.

Charlene Spretnak is a leading voice of feminist spirituality, author of *Lost Goddesses of Early Greece* and *States of Grace*.

Max Oelschlaeger is professor of philosophy and religion at the University of North Texas and author of *The Wilderness Condition*.

Bron Taylor teaches religion and social ethics at the University of Wisconsin, Oshkosh; and is the author of *Once and Future Primitive: the Spiritual Politics of Deep Ecology*.

B. D. Sharma is a leading Indian thinker in the area of sustainable development; and an activist in defense of the rights of indigenous peoples.

Bruce M. Sullivan is Associate Professor and Coordinator of Religious Studies at Northern Arizona University, in Flagstaff, Arizona; and author of studies on the Hindu epic *Mahabarata* and Hindu sacred dramas.

M. L. Daneel is professor of missiology at the University of South Africa and founder of the Zimbabwean Institute of Religious Research and Ecological Conservation and the Association of African Earthkeeping Churches.

Catherine Ingram's journalism focuses on mediation and psychology, and their links with social activism, particularly in the areas of human rights and refugees.

Judith N. Scoville is a recent Ph.D from the Union Graduate School. This is her first publication.

Paul Gorman, a long-time political activist and organizer, co-authored *How Can I Help?* and currently directs the National Religious Partnership on the Environment.

Melody Ermachild Chavis is a private investigator working with death-row inmates, and a community volunteer is a youth-and-seniors garden project. She lives in Berkeley, California.

David Spangler is former director of the Findhorn Foundation of Scotland. His other books include *Revelation: The Birth of a New Age* and *Emergence: The Rebirth of the Sacred.*

Dieter T. Hessel, a member of the Princeton Center of Theological Inquiry, has written or edited thirteen books, and currently directs an ecumenical program on ecology, justice and faith supported by the MacArthur Foundation.